"Fr. Thomas Joseph White is a master of theology *sensu eminenti,* and this book is a master course on the Trinity from a Thomistic standpoint. What makes it especially valuable, however, is not just how well it serves as a historical and systematic introduction to Trinitarian theology before Thomas—from the biblical witness to the Cappadocians and Augustine to the Fourth Lateran Council—but that it puts Thomas in direct conversation with modern Trinitarian theology (Bulgakov, Balthasar, Moltmann, and others). The result is an impressive renewal of Thomism and a novel restatement—emphasizing the analogy of divine and human natures in Christ—of Thomas's relevance to contemporary Trinitarian theology."

—JOHN BETZ, UNIVERSITY OF NOTRE DAME

"This book will be very helpful to students and to professors as well. Thomas Joseph White brings together what textbooks too often divide: he offers a study that exposes simultaneously God as One and as Trinity. The patristic and Thomistic parts of the book are very well done (with a solid rooting in the Bible); the critical discussion of contemporary currents of Trinitarian theology is well documented and enlightening. An excellent contribution, in the Dominican tradition, to contemporary theological reflection on the subject."

—GILLES EMERY, OP, UNIVERSITY OF FRIBOURG, SWITZERLAND

"Ask Christians about the Trinity and all too often they respond with 'It's a great mystery' and then change the subject! Thomas Joseph White was never one to evade such a challenge, and here he systematically investigates the central mystery of our faith. Just as people we love are a mystery to us so deep that we can never exhaust who they are as we endlessly discover new depths to them, so Thomas Joseph demonstrates that getting to know the Triune God is endlessly fascinating, meaningful, and life changing. To embrace this mystery is to discover the Absolute is personal, the Totally Other is totally for us. Fr. Thomas Joseph faithfully mines two millennia of human contact with the Trinity in Scripture, in the Fathers, but especially in the greatest theological master, St. Thomas Aquinas. He explains, defends, and creatively extends the master's insights. At the end of this great read you'll know God better and love God more!"

—ANTHONY FISHER, OP, ARCHBISHOP OF SYDNEY

The Trinity

The Trinity

On the Nature and Mystery
of the One God

THOMAS JOSEPH WHITE, OP

The Catholic University of America Press
Washington, D.C.

This book is dedicated to my
confreres in the Dominican Order,
who have been the best of companions
in seeking the truth about God

———————:———————

Nihil Obstat:
Rev. Gilles Emery, O.P.

Imprimi Potest:
Very Rev. Gerard Francisco Timoner III, O.P.
Master of the Order
January 8, 2021

Library of Congress Cataloging-in-Publication Data

Names: White, Thomas Joseph, 1971– author.
Title: The Trinity : on the nature and mystery of the one god /
Thomas Joseph White, OP.
Description: Washington, D.C. :
The Catholic University of America Press, 2022. |
Series: Thomistic ressourcement series ; volume 19 |
Includes bibliographical references and index.
Identifiers: LCCN 2021052913 (print) | ISBN 9780813234830 (paperback) |
Subjects: LCSH: Trinity—History of doctrines. |
Thomas, Aquinas, Saint, 1225?–1274. | Catholic Church—Doctrines.
Classification: LCC BT109 .W55 2022 (print) |
DDC 231/.044—dc23/eng/20211130
LC record available at https://lccn.loc.gov/2021052913

"Poetry is likely to distort the thought of anyone who hears it, unless he has knowledge of what reality is really like, as a drug to counteract it."

"What exactly do you have in mind in saying this?"

"I'll tell you, even though the love and respect I've had for Homer since I was a child make me hesitate to speak, for he seems to have been the first teacher and leader of all these fine tragedians. All the same no one is to be honored or valued more than the truth."

—Plato, *Republic* X, 595b

This then is the Catholic faith: We worship one God in the Trinity and the Trinity in the unity, without confusing the Persons or separating the substance; for indeed the Person of the Father is one, the Person of the Son another, the Person of the Holy Spirit another; but the divinity of the Father, the Son, and the Holy Spirit is one, their glory equal, and their majesty co-eternal.

—The Athanasian Creed, *Quicumque*

"I did not say a creed was everything," answered Reding, "or that a religion could not be false which had a creed; but a religion can't be true which has none."

—John Henry Newman, *Loss and Gain*

Love is the unfamiliar Name
Behind the hands that wove
The intolerable shirt of flame
Which human power cannot remove
We only live, only suspire
Consumed by either fire or fire.

—T.S. Eliot, *Little Gidding*

When you leave a man alone with his Bible and the Holy Ghost inspires him, he's going to be a Catholic one way or another, even though he knows nothing about the visible church. His kind of Christianity may not be socially desirable, but will be real in the sight of God.

—Flannery O'Connor, *The Habit of Being:
Letters of Flannery O'Connor*, Letter to
Sister Mariella Gable, May 4, 1963

Contents

Contents

Tables

Preface

———:———

Of the many people who have assisted in the publication of this book, I would like to thank first David Augustine, who acted at an early stage as an assistant editor. David took a rough draft form of the first three parts of the book, which was developed from courses I have taught, edited them into a unity, and made many suggestions for the final text. Although I reworked and expanded these sections of the book, I retained many of David's editorial suggestions. He was especially influential in the chapter on St. Augustine, which he rightly claimed was necessary, preparing the first draft, most of which I have retained.

I am also deeply indebted to others who have kindly read and commented on portions of the text or discussed ideas with me in conversation: Eleonore Stump, Matthew Levering, Bruce Marshall, Guy Mansini, OSB, Reinhard Huetter, and Mary Christa Nutt, RSM. Many of my Dominican colleagues have contributed as well to my reflections in this book: Bernhard Blankenhorn, OP, Serge-Thomas Bonino, OP, Emmanuel Durand, OP, Simon Gaine, OP, Anthony Giambrone, OP, John Baptist Ku, OP, Dominic Langevin, OP, and Dominic Legge, OP. Most of all I must thank Michael Gorman and Gilles Emery, OP, who each read and commented upon the text and helped me thereby to improve it immensely. Anne Needham from the Catholic University of America Press also has acted as a superb copy editor.

The support and encouragement of the Agape McDonald Foundation, and especially of Peter McDonald, were of great importance to the work I was able to do on this manuscript. I would also like to remember and thank Alonzo and Suzie McDonald in this context, as well as the board of the Foundation. I should also mention Michal Paluch, OP, former rector of the Angelicum, the friars of the university, and especially its students, who have been a great support to the work of research and writing.

Abbreviations of Works of
St. Thomas Aquinas

Credo	*Collationes super Credo in Deum*
De ente	*De ente et essentia*
De malo	*Quaestiones disputatae de malo*
De pot.	*De potentia Dei*
De sub. sep.	*De substatiis separatis*
De rationibus fidei	*De rationibus fidei contra Saracenos, Graecos et Armenos ad cantorem Antiochenum*
De ver.	*De veritate*
Expos. de Trin.	*Expositio super librum Boethii de Trinitate*
In De anima	*In Aristotelis librum De anima commentarium*
In De causis	*In librum de causis expositio*
In div. nom.	*In librum beati Dionysii de divinis nominibus expositio*
In Eph.	*Super Epistolam ad Ephesios*
In Heb.	*Super Epistolam ad Hebraeos*
In Ioan.	*Lectura super Ioannem*
In Matt.	*Lectura super Matthaeum*
In Meta.	*In duodecim libros Metaphysicorum Aristotelis expositio*
In peri Hermeneias	*Expositio libri Peryermenias*
In Phys.	*In octo libros Physicorum Aristotelis expositio*
In Post.	*Expositio libri Posteriorum*

In I Tim.	*Super I Epistolam ad Timotheum*
In Titus	*Super Epistolam ad Titus*
Sent.	*Scriptum super libros Sententiarum magistri Petri Lombardi episcopi Parisiensis*
SCG	*Summa contra Gentiles*
ST	*Summa theologiae*

The Trinity

Introduction

———:———

The human being naturally seeks wisdom. A sign of this is that all human cultures inevitably seek to derive ultimate explanations of reality. These typically function as final principles of explanation, and as references for motivation and moral justification in practical action. A given philosophical or religious tradition aspires to wisdom when it tries to answer questions like, "why do human beings, and the cosmos more generally, exist?" "Can we know the answers to such questions, and should we be concerned with them?" "In light of what is most ultimately real, what can we rightly hope for from life?" Of course there are many forms of wisdom, since the materialist who considers it certain or very likely that human beings are mere products of chance, bundles of matter haphazardly arranged by impersonal cosmic forces, will seek practical ends that differ in noteworthy ways from theists who believe that the universe, in its seemingly contingent existence, vastness, and unfolding order, suggests a Creator who is giving being to all things. Those who maintain a principled agnostic reserve about such questions, treating them as unanswerable, also aspire implicitly to a form of wisdom, since they seek to live by explanations and practical aims that are reserved to the immanent sphere of temporal existence. Do our personal interests in truth and happiness suggest that we have spiritual souls, which have their origin in a transcendent wisdom? Or is our personal life with others reserved solely to a time-bound, bodily frame of reference? Do persons even really exist as a distinct kind of being, and if so, what is the meaning of our personal communion with one another? How should we live in light of our answers to these questions?

When Thomas Aquinas considers such questions, he distinguishes three forms of wisdom, that pertaining to philosophy, to theology, and to the mystical life of union with God. Each of these forms of wisdom is unique and has its own integrity, but they are also arranged hierarchically, as theological knowledge provides more perfect understanding of the ultimate reality than philosophy does, and mystical union provides a more perfect encounter with the ultimate reality of God than theological reflection does. Each form of wisdom is compatible with, and is subject to regulatory influence and inspiration from, the other two. Philosophy, for example, is a form of wisdom insofar as it can attain to a knowledge of the primary cause of all things, who is God, and can identify God as, in some real sense, personal, the author of human persons, and the creator and providential guide behind all created things. The knowledge of God that philosophy provides is indirect, inferential, and imperfect. It does not procure personal friendship with God or any immediate perceptual knowledge of what God is in himself. It does permit us to say, however, by reasonable inference, a great deal about what God is and is not, by comparison of God with his creatures.

The second form of wisdom is that pertaining to theology as a study of divine revelation. God has revealed himself in Jesus Christ as a mystery of the communion of persons: Father, Son, and Holy Spirit. The persons of the Trinity are one in being, and therefore are the one God, such that each person is truly and completely God. How ought we to understand this mystery, and how ought we to understand all other realities in light of this mystery? How is the mystery of the Trinity revealed in the life, death, and resurrection of Jesus Christ? Questions such as these pertain to the "science" of theology as such. Theology here is understood as a form of explanation that begins with the principles of faith revealed by God in Christ and that seeks to provide an objective frame of reference for understanding all of reality in light of these principles.

The third form of wisdom pertains to the mystical grace of wisdom, which the Catholic theological tradition treats as a special gift of the Holy Spirit. The gift of wisdom knits in the souls of its recipients a habit of union with God, one that can be initiated only from God's side but that the human soul consents to receive as a gift. It is an infused grace that elevates the soul into a more experiential, intimate, and illuminative closeness to God. This mystical wisdom is exemplified in the lives of the saints, who are friends of God by grace, and who are conformed in friendship to the mystery of Jesus Christ. In this process they come to know the persons of the Father, Son, and Holy Spirit in an intimate way, in the darkness of faith, by a deep union of love, and by moments of profound spiritual enlightenment. Aquinas characterized this form of wisdom as, above all, affective, meaning that it gives rise to a connatural knowledge born of affective love, as when one friend learns to read the heart and mind of another, by an instinct of loving knowledge. The gift of wisdom teaches us to learn—from the heart of Christ, from the heart of God—who God is, and what he wills.

Each of these forms of wisdom can and should take inspiration from the others, and each has a regulatory function with respect to the other two. The philosopher who aspires to natural knowledge of God can also be open to the possibility of revealed knowledge of God, so long as the latter does not seem in any way to contradict or deny the integral role of philosophy and natural learning in human culture, including the sound acquisitions of the modern sciences. Often theological traditions have provided impetus for new philosophical ideas, and philosophers rightly can gain ideas as philosophers from reading great theologians. So too philosophers can take inspiration from mystics whose lives of contemplation, prayer, and conformity to the passion of Christ suggest a yet higher completion of the search for wisdom, one effectuated by grace alone, as grace transforms our human desire for intimacy with the divine. When philosophical traditions close themselves off a priori to the possibility of revelation or mystical union with God, they self-sterilize by delimiting, in arbitrary and unwarranted ways, the human search for transcendence. In this sense they become themselves unreasonable. Theology and mystical life then stand as a perpetual challenge to those forms of philosophy that refuse the possibility of God, and that seek a wisdom only of this world, without due reference to the human thirst for truth that aims toward transcendent ends.

Theology understood as *sacra doctrina* is the study of the revelation of God confided to the human race by Christ and his apostles, through the medium of the Catholic Church, who preserves the deposit of faith in her teaching tradition. Theological reflection is concerned, then, with an object of knowledge that is revealed, supernatural, and inaccessible to unaided natural reason. Grace, however, does not destroy nature, and faith does not ignore the contributions of natural reason. Those who pursue theological wisdom, therefore, should welcome all the genuine contributions of human philosophical wisdom, and must hold themselves accountable to the legitimate acquisitions of natural reason, be these in the domains of philosophy, natural science, or responsible historical study. If theological reflection on revelation can offer to the philosopher "new information" about God, and about friendship with God, the theologian is nonetheless bound by intellectual responsibility to face scrutiny from philosophical quarters. Is the mystery of God intrinsically intelligible, and are its truth claims compatible with what can otherwise be known by human reason? To the extent that theologians probe the mystery of God and seek understanding of it, they inevitably make some use of philosophy in order to think constructively about the truths of the Christian faith. This assimilation of philosophy is inevitable, because human beings can only think about the God who reveals himself to humanity by, *in part*, making use of the natural knowledge they have of God and of human nature. To speak of Christ as true God and true man, for example, one must have at least some basic natural sense of what God is and what human nature is, even if Christ himself teaches us in a new and more perfect way both what God is in himself and what the human being is and can become. There is no such thing as a pure theology devoid of any philosophical commitments, just as there is no human person who "merely" possesses the grace of faith but does not possess natural reason. All theologians, then, are in fact beholden to various traditions of philosophy, and their work can be measured in part by whether they employ sound philosophical principles and modes of philosophical reasoning. Theologians also can take inspiration from the mystics, who in a sense hold them accountable to the mystery of the living God. The saint, who experiences direct union with God in a higher and more intuitive and loving way, provides an indication to theologians of the more ultimate end toward which all things are directed. In doing so, the mystic is a witness to the transformative power of the friendship with God that occurs in virtue of the crucifixion and resurrection of Christ. Theology is in part a practical science oriented toward union with God by a life of contemplation and love. The mystics illustrate various forms this life can take and, in doing so, serve as reference points to theologians.

Mystical union with God, however exalted, is not a substitute for genuine philosophical or theological understanding. As is well known, those who are genuine mystics have their own profound temptations, one of which is to substitute their own intuitions regarding the mystery of God for the public apostolic teaching of the Church, and for the doctrinal judgements or canonical practices that emerge from ecclesiastical tradition. Without a grounding in sound philosophical and practical reasoning, the aspiration to mystical life can easily fall prey to imprudence, unreasonable claims about human existence, and even religious delusion. Without a grounding in sound doctrinally based theology, the aspiration to mystical life can easily fall prey to misguided charismatic phenomena, theological error, moral deviancy, and possible ecclesial division. If mystical union with God is in a sense what is most ultimate in this life in the order of wisdom, it is also a place of peril. Those who seek union with God by way of friendship with Christ need to be grounded in proven forms of reflection on God, human nature, and the cosmos—perennial teaching that stems from healthy natural and theological wellsprings. Without a grounding in the intellectual life, the culture of Catholic spirituality and devotional practice eventually degrades to shallow emotivism, or individualistic subjectivism, and becomes unsustainable. Ecclesial traditions of theology and Christian philosophy provide trustworthy inroads in this respect, that are meant to dispose human beings to a genuine spiritual life, and that are, in a sense, the attendants to it. Indeed, for Aquinas there is a very close relationship between the study of theology and the search for spiritual union with God. The theologian who studies God because he is motivated by the love of God develops a stable habit of cooperation with the light of faith, directed inwardly by hope and charity toward union with God. This habitual study of God stabilizes the human being in a pattern of living in which it is easier to live in friendship with God in a regular fashion, and this life of habitual reflection on God in study and prayer disposes the human being toward the reception of grace that is unitive. In other words, the study of theology conducted in a stable state of grace does not procure experiential mystical union of its own right, but it does dispose human beings to receive initiatives from the side of God that regularly lift them up, as it were, into the spheres of the divine missions, where they are illumined by the divine Word, and where their hearts are touched and enflamed by the fire of the Holy Spirit. In this sense the search for wisdom in the Christian tradition implies a concurrent distinction of forms—philosophical, theological, and mystical. But this same search also implies an organic and integrative process, in which persons can develop simultaneously as philosophers, theologians, and spiritual friends of God, in ways that are unified and serene, but also dynamic and ever developing.

THOMISTIC TRINITARIAN THEOLOGY

This is a book about Trinitarian theology: the confession of the Church that God is Father, Son, and Holy Spirit, three distinct persons who are one in being and essence. As such this work aspires to be a form of the second wisdom mentioned above, a systematic reflection on the mystery of God revealed to us in Jesus Christ.

It follows from our claims above that if this book is theological, it is not a work about philosophical theism per se, but it does contain a great deal of philosophical argument, employed within a theological context. The presupposition here is that philosophical reflection contributes to our ways of thinking and speaking about God even within theology. Also, this book is representative of the Catholic theological tradition, written against the backdrop of the normative practices, beliefs, and canonized exemplars of the Catholic faith. It is a work that presupposes that figures like Bernard of Clairvaux, Francis of Assisi, Catherine of Siena, and Thérèse of Lisieux have as much to teach us about union with God by their lives and spiritual teaching as anything we can read in books of systematic theology. Their examples and great spiritual writings, nevertheless, are no substitute for genuine theology, which seeks to examine the mystery of God in himself, as he has revealed his mystery to us in Christ. The knowledge of God we gain by looking at his saints is, after all, directed more ultimately to the knowledge of God in himself. Accordingly, this work seeks not so much to be a theology on one's knees, designed to inspire or instigate spiritual prayer, as to be a theology of the mind and heart, aiming to create habitually reflective dispositions to know and love the Trinity, by cooperation with the theological virtues of faith, hope, and charity. Theological understanding allows us to direct our lives toward the mystery of God in stable and enduring ways, not only in prayer but in every facet of life and human culture. In the midst of a complex world, filled with intellectual challenges, tested theological reflection remains of the utmost importance, and, while it can inspire prayer, it has its own internal form of demand, and requires in turn the cultivation of its own habits. The Church is not only a heart that loves God, but also a mind that seeks the truth, and the two go together integrally. Love for the truth leads to greater enlightenment, and knowledge of the truth stimulates greater admiration and love for God.

This is a Thomistic work of Trinitarian theology. As such it takes inspiration from the historical example of Thomas Aquinas, who engaged with the Catholic tradition in its sources and with a wide variety of non-Christian and Christian contemporaries. However, it also seeks to explain, defend, and employ creatively a number of substantive Thomistic theses. We should note briefly what this does and does not imply. Readers should be beware of thinking mistakenly that this book presupposes that Trinitarian theology must be either scholastic generally, or Thomistic specifically. There is a wealth of Trinitarian theological reflection that arises outside of these venues. Indeed, the first part of this book is specifically concerned with the scriptural and patristic "principles" of Trinitarian doctrine, their emergence and historical development, a tradition that precedes the work of any medieval or modern theologian and that remains a normative reference for all those who seek to study and write Trinitarian theology. It is worth noting in this respect that when Aquinas identifies what he takes to be the principles of the faith, as first starting points of the science of *sacra doctrina*, he indicates the basic teachings of the Nicene Creed, which he presumes must be commonly adopted by all who call themselves Catholic theologians. This starting point by definition allows one to include a vast range of theologies under the appellation of Catholic, including many of the famous schools, whether medieval or modern. Though it may appear paradoxical to some, the claim that only Thomists can be true Catholic theologians is itself non-Thomistic and contradicts Aquinas's own criteria. The advantage of a notion of "theological schools" is that it allows one to acknowledge the deeper ground of unity among theologians that emerges from the Church's common confession of faith, while also allowing for constructive debate, disagreement, convergence or consensus, within a shared culture of reflection. Without the unity that underlies the schools, theology becomes insular, sectarian, and narrow. Without the spirit of debate, argument, and engagement, theological culture becomes excessively individualistic, subjectively therapeutic, and intellectually superficial. Consequently, this book does argue in favor of the normative value of many positions that arise from Aquinas himself or from the Thomistic tradition. It does so, however, in a spirit of collegiality and respect for vibrant alternative traditions. My own intellectual preferences for Aquinas's vision of Trinitarian theology, then, presuppose that theologians of different stripes participate in a broader theological culture marked by the shared love of the truth.

A second presupposition that should be noted concerns the logical question as to what one means by "Thomistic" theology. After all, the attentive reader will have noted in the table of contents that this book treats a number of themes that are found in the *Summa theologiae* in the treatise on God as one and as Trinity, in roughly the same order that St. Thomas himself does. Is this book intended, then, to be a historical study of what Aquinas himself believed about the Trinity, or is it a presentation of my own views? And if the latter is the case, how does the extensive treatment of Aquinas relate to the normative claims of the book? The short answer to this question is that the book contains my own claims about the mystery of God and the Trinity, which derive in great part but not exclusively from the analysis offered previously by Aquinas. Where I treat historical authors, like Athanasius, Gregory of Nazianzus, Augustine, or Aquinas, I have endeavored to report accurately or at least interpret plausibly what they themselves actually claimed theologically. However, I have also bothered to present their claims only because I take those claims to be true and believe that they, in some way, build upon one another or converge and can help us engage constructively in contemporary Trinitarian theology. In regard to Aquinas specifically, I presume for the most part that his reflections on the nature of God and the Trinity are true and defensible. I do not consider every important modern objection to them, an aim that would defy the scope of the work.[1] Even less do I seek to interpret him extensively in his historical context. Instead my principle aim in this book is to study Aquinas's reflection on the mystery of God within the context of a work of modern systematic theology. As such, this book aspires to be a work of Thomistic *ressourcement*, a study that contributes to the living Thomistic tradition, through its engagement with contemporary theology, and that contributes to contemporary theology, through its engagement of the Thomistic tradition. In this sense, we can acknowledge that parts 2 and 3 of this book do present the reader with an abridged commentary on the *de Deo ut uno* and *de Deo ut trino* treatises of the *Summa theologiae*, considered together in their unity. As such they do seek to provide readers with a presentation of the analytic cogency of Aquinas's views on the nature and mystery of God. However, this presentation also contains a continual conversation with modern theology, so as to test the viability and perennial value of Thomistic thought constructively and transparently. This book then aspires to be a work of Thomism concerned with the mystery of God itself, and with the Catholic Church's confession of Trinitarian faith.

1. For example, I present below interpretations of Aquinas's five arguments for the existence of God, as found in the *Summa theologiae*, and I think the arguments are reasonable, but I am not able to consider in the context of this work various modern objections that arise in response to these arguments.

STRUCTURE OF THE VOLUME

Each chapter of this book can be read on its own with some utility, as can each of its distinct main parts. Nevertheless, the book as a whole contains a cumulative set of arguments. The book proceeds in four parts, and each part presupposes the prior part, builds on its arguments, and gains in originality with respect to the previous one.

The first part of the book seeks indeed to be rather unoriginal, since it is concerned with the common tradition of the early Church in regard to Trinitarian doctrine. Here the basic presupposition of the whole presentation is that we can identify a coherent form of teaching regarding the Trinity that emerges over time in scripture and tradition. This teaching stems originally from God's revelation of himself in the Old and New Testaments, manifest especially in Christ and the teaching of the apostles, and is subsequently understood adequately in a developmental way by the early Church. In other words, the diverse teachings about God of both the Old and New Testaments can be read as forming a kind of thematic unity, one that indicates that God is Trinity. Jesus himself, by his teaching, action, suffering, and resurrection, reveals the mystery of the Trinity, as does the teaching of Paul and the Gospel of John. This biblical witness in turn serves as a credible basis for the later theological arguments of pre-Nicene Fathers such as Justin and Irenaeus, as well as post-Nicene Fathers such as Athanasius, Gregory of Nazianzus, and Augustine. What the pre-Nicene Fathers say about the Trinity, in the way of a first elaboration, the later Fathers enunciate better and more clearly. A basic aim of this first section, then, is to illustrate a set of common teachings about God as Trinity that emerge from divine revelation itself, and that are received and interpreted in the early Church in conceptually diverse ways over time. I argue that diverse conceptual interpretations of the pre- and post-Nicene Church are not mutually incompatible or heterogeneous, but give rise gradually, through the course of debate, to scripturally well-founded, coherent theological and doctrinal articulations of the mystery of the Trinity.

A second aim of the first part of the book is to identify some of the key themes that emerge from this coherent and mature vision of the early Church, with regard to the inner life and mystery of God. Chief among these are the fundamental claims that God is one in being and essence, and that there are three persons in God. How can the distinction of persons be understood theologically, if they are truly one in being and essence? Pro-Nicene Fathers like Athanasius and Gregory of Nazianzus argued that the persons in God are distinct in virtue of their relations of origin, and that the Son proceeds eternally from the Father by immaterial generation as his Word. Likewise, Augustine characterized the procession of the Spirit from the Father and the Son by way of a likeness to love proceeding from knowledge. In light of this theory of processional distinction of persons, both Eastern and Western thinkers characterized the way we name God in a twofold manner. They noted that there are essential terms that we employ to designate the essence or nature of the one God common to the three persons, and there are personal terms we employ to designate the persons and activities of the Father, Son, and Spirit in their distinctness. As I note in the end of this section, subsequent theologians (especially Dionysius the Areopagite) would elaborate a theory of divine naming that is analogical in nature and that is applicable to both these cases. Theologians can make use of analogical forms of speech to denote *both* the one nature of God common to the three persons, *and* each of the distinct persons themselves according to their proper names.

By setting out this backdrop of common teaching that stems from the patristic era of the Church, I try to set the stage for what will be presented in the subsequent parts of the book as the distinctively Thomistic interpretation of this early tradition. This way of demarcating things aligns with the comments I have made above about "schools" of theology. Aquinas presents us with only one way of interpreting scriptural and patristic principles, and his followers and interpreters may in turn make varied use of his claims and arguments (i.e., we can speak broadly of a Thomistic school or schools of thought, which houses internal debates). However, as I will characterize his thought in this book, Aquinas's theology is something slightly different than simply one account among many. It can function as a kind of Greenwich time in Christian theology. His approach to the mystery of the Trinity has roots in both Eastern and Western Fathers, and contains notable similarities to the thought of both Gregory of Nazianzus and that of Augustine. In this way he is an inheritor of core notions from the patristic tradition. By his distinction of common names for the nature of God, and proper names for each person, and by his account of the persons as distinguished in virtue of their relations of origin, Aquinas articulates fundamental insights of the pro-Nicene authors, and defends the warrant of Nicene and Chalcedonian dogmas in a compelling way. By his balanced use of philosophy in the service of the doctrine of God he provides a profound account of the divine nature, one that respects the mystery and transcendence of God. His Trinitarian theology contains a reasonable use of analogy, so as to measure the distance of divine personhood from human personhood, by which he preserves a sense of the mystery of God the Trinity that avoids anthropomorphism, while also providing readers with genuine insight into the inner life of God. His study of the revelation of God in Christ allows us to understand how the visible missions of the Son and the Spirit reveal the inner life of the Trinity and communicate a participation in that life to human beings by grace. Consequently, while his thought should not be taken to be doctrinally normative for all Christians (as is the case only for the Creed and conciliar definitions that are commonly accepted), it can be taken to reflect an integrally responsible and balanced assimilation of and interpretation of the truths acquired from classical Trinitarian orthodoxy, one that has vibrant potential for the engagement with modern theological questions.

In the second part of the book I consider the ineffable nature of the one God, in a way that brings Trinitarian ideas into the very analysis called *de Deo ut uno*. Evidently in doing so I am taking issue with those who claim or presuppose that any use in Trinitarian theology of a *de Deo ut uno* reflection prior to a *de Deo ut trino* reflection is counterproductive. As my treatment of the Fathers suggests, there is precedent in the tradition for the distinction of divine naming, such that some names are given to the Trinity in virtue of the unity of the divine essence, and others in virtue of the distinction of persons. The Thomistic approach I take, then, claims to build on a patristic precedent that is thoroughly Trinitarian. Nor is the option to begin Trinitarian systematic theology with a consideration of the divine nature one that is inconsequential. The presupposition of any coherent account of Trinitarian monotheism is that the three persons in God are one in being and essence and thus consubstantial (*homoousios*).[2] To speak of the Father's eternal gen-

---

2. In speaking in this way I presume that the words "essence" and "nature" are roughly equivalent and that they signify the specifying characteristics that make a given thing the kind of thing it is. When speaking of the divine essence or nature by analogy, we are speaking of that nature and those characteristics proper to him, in virtue of which God is God. In speaking of God's one being, I am denoting his subsistent reality as one individual who alone is God. In speaking of God's "substance" (*ousia* in Greek; *substantia* in Latin), I am denoting God's singular being, which has a properly divine nature. When speaking of the "divine substance," then, we indicate that in virtue of which the three persons are each the one God, possessing one nature as God. I will return to these terminological definitions in chapters below.

eration of the Son and spiration of the Spirit, as well as the mutual indwelling and communion of the persons, we must have some sense of the principle in virtue of which the three are one, that is to say, the nature of God.[3]
Without a theology of the divine nature, there is no theology of the three
persons, and thus no Trinitarian theology. Nor are modern theologies that
ignore or bid farewell to the classical *de Deo ut uno* treatise as innocent as
they sometimes suggest they are of rendering names to the nature of God.
As I note at times in this second part of the book, modern theologians frequently propose ideas about the divine nature within the context of their
Trinitarian thought even when they renounce any attempt at the formulation of a doctrine of the divine essence. Their implicit conceptions of the
divine nature (often formulated in terms of divine freedom) in turn affect
deeply how they themselves consider the Trinity to be one. This fact suggests that a theology of the divine nature is unavoidable. Trinitarian theologians who opt out of an overt consideration of the divine nature, it seems to
me, ignore key precedents of patristic and Nicene theology. However, they
also often paradoxically allow their creative re-construals of the divine nature to play an inadvertent but prominent role in their understanding of the
distinction of the persons in God, with serious consequences for their conception of Christian faith as a form of monotheism. This is especially the
case in modern theologies of divine suffering, as well as in various kenotic
theologies that posit historical development in the life of the Trinity. I explore some examples of these alternatives and their consequences in parts
3 and 4 of the book, but the developed arguments of those sections have
some of their foundations in part 2.

　　Part 3 of the book is concerned with the immanent life of the Holy Trinity, as understood in the Thomistic tradition. Here I seek to identify the distinctive character of Aquinas's approach to the mystery of Trinitarian persons.

　　First, influenced by Russell Friedman, I note that Aquinas's approach

3. Traditional Western theology speaks of two "processions" in the Trinity, that of the Son,
who is eternally begotten of the Father, and that of the Holy Spirit, who is eternally spirated from
the Father and the Son. I use the word "spiration" here to denote that mode of eternal procession
that is proper to the Spirit, as distinct from that of the Word, who is eternally begotten. As we will
see in part 3 of this book, below, Aquinas distinguishes the two, by analogies, according to knowledge and love, respectively. The Son is eternally begotten as the Word of the Father, analogically
similar to the act of knowing that takes place in us through a conceptual thought, while the Spirit
is eternally spirated (in Latin, *spiratus*, literally "breathed forth") as a mutual impression of Love,
from the Father and the Son.

to the Trinity entails a "relationalist account," in which the distinction of the divine persons is understood principally in virtue of the relations of origin of the persons by way of their eternal processions. The Father, Son, and Holy Spirit are each wholly God, and are each the one God, and thus are distinct only in virtue of the ways that they proceed from one another. This idea is intimately related to Aquinas's notion of the persons as subsistent relations. On this view, each of the persons is wholly relative to the other two in virtue of the processions by relations of mutual opposition, so that the Father is only ever "for" the generation of the Son and the spiration of the Spirit, in all that he is, and likewise the Son is only ever from the Father and for the spiration of the Spirit, and so on. This simple but profound idea has significant entailments and immense consequences, which I seek to underscore in various chapters in part 3.

Second, I defend, in this third part of the book, the centrality and essential importance of the classical use of the psychological analogy, in which the processions of the Word and Spirit are understood by similitude to human immaterial processions of knowledge and love respectively.[4] I argue that this analogy, taken from our inner spiritual life, provides us with a unique resource for right thinking regarding the inner life and mystery of the Trinity. In essence, there is no adequate alternative analogy for immanent spiritual procession available to us from common experience. Consequently, in the absence of this kind of account, one is inevitably obliged to characterize the distinction of persons in God based uniquely on God's activity in the economy (which Aquinas calls "transitive activity"). Such an approach, if it is not informed by the use of the psychological analogy, invariably seeks to distinguish the persons of the Trinity by appealing to the

---

4. The phrase "psychological analogy" is a twentieth-century term of designation derived by historians of dogma for the patristic and medieval notion that immaterial acts of the spiritual soul image or manifest the Trinity. It is sometimes also called the "analogy from acts of the mind" or the "psychological model," based on the root *psyche*, for soul, and thus has little or nothing to do with modern psychology. As a term of designation, it is inevitably somewhat ambiguous, since one can argue that modern historians of dogma oversimplified the history of dogma by the very use of the term. Nevertheless, as I will suggest in this book, there is a common theme that develops in traditional theology in this regard: that immaterial features of human persons as agents of knowledge and love reflect by analogy the two processions of the Son as Word and the Spirit as Love, in God. In using the term "psychological analogy," then, throughout this book, I am not seeking to ally myself with any past historical use of the term as normative. On the contrary, as the reader will discover, I am making creative use of the term to denote something I take to be present throughout the tradition, from the New Testament to the pre- and post-Nicene Fathers, and well into the medieval and modern periods, under different manifestations and with different uses.

persons' various properties or actions that arise from the economy, such as attributing suffering or human obedience to the Son *as God* as a feature by which he is distinguished eternally from the Father. In so doing, it risks confusing the persons in their deity with their created acquisitions or actions, and so undermines an appropriate sense of the unity of nature of the three persons. The identity of the three persons is also then characterized or construed in light of the economy. Understood in this context of debate, the use of the psychological analogy is central to a right understanding of the transcendence of the Holy Trinity with respect to the economy. One fear often voiced by those who see the psychological analogy as disadvantageous is that it makes the inner mystery of God remote with regard to our economic encounter with God in history, specifically in the incarnation of God and the paschal mystery. I argue in this book that God's self-revelation in the incarnation and the paschal mystery are best understood when we understand them to unfold in light of God's inner processional life in its transcendence. It is the eternally transcendent Trinity that is revealed truly in the economy, but we can understand this rightly only if we have a way to think about the immanent life of the Trinity by proper analogy. Christ truly is God made human and crucified. However, this does not mean that the divine nature of God is made human and crucified. The incarnation, crucifixion, and death of God are mysteries in which the transcendent Trinitarian Creator freely self-identifies with us, and suffers and dies in virtue of the human life he shares with us. In doing so, he reveals to us the inner mystery of Trinitarian truth and love, but God's eternal identity as Trinity is not changed or enriched in virtue of his human life, crucifixion, and death. It is the eternal God who enriches us and constitutes us in a new state, by being among us.

Third, I note that Aquinas's understanding of personhood is analogical and as such can be applied in distinct ways to the Trinitarian persons, to angelic persons, and to human persons. The Trinitarian persons are distinct and utterly dissimilar to created persons because they are each the one God, and therefore are able to communicate all that they are to another or to receive all that they are from another, by way of procession. They are likewise immanently present to one another in all that they are, by mutual indwelling. This understanding of the divine persons allows Aquinas to correlate his thinking on persons in God with a theology of subsistent modes of being of the divine nature. The divine nature subsists in three personal modes, based on processional life in God. Therefore, Trinitarian theology is nei-

ther uniquely personalist (pertaining to three distinct persons) nor uniquely modalist (pertaining to three modes of the divine nature), but always
both, in a given order of reflection. Aquinas's analogical conception of divine personhood has significant consequences for his understanding of the
procession of the Holy Spirit from the Father and Son (i.e., his interpretation of the *Filioque*), perichoresis, Trinitarian appropriation, and the divine
missions, as I seek to demonstrate in part 3. It is also important for Christology, since the person of the Son is both God and man, and has a human
natural mode of being that is genuinely filial. That is to say, his human nature
is that of the Son, and so his way of being human always manifests his personal identity as Son, and his relations to the Father and the Spirit. Therefore, Aquinas's conception of divine personhood is intimately related to his
Christology and the ways he understands the human life of Jesus to be revelatory of the inner life of the Holy Trinity.

I note in this section that Aquinas's understanding of the persons of the
Trinity as subsistent relations, allied with his use of the psychological analogy in order to understand immanent immaterial procession, can be depicted
as a conceptual mean between two extremes. On the one side there is the
classical Franciscan tradition, represented by Bonaventure and Scotus, that I
claim is characterized by a tendency toward theologically univocal discourse
in regard to Trinitarian persons. In this tradition the Father can be said to
generate the Word by a natural activity of knowing and to spirate the Spirit
by a natural act of will, in a way that resembles human agents. The person of
the Father is depicted by strong similitude to a human person in his immaterial action of generation and spiration, in which these activities emerge as
properties of the person distinct from the substantial person himself (as in
a human being our free acts are not identical with our substance but emerge
from our being as properties or accidents). For Scotus these actions (generation and spiration) can entail distinct *natural* properties as well, distinct
acts that each pertain to the one nature of God, suggesting the idea of formally distinct natural properties in God that pertain to distinct persons. As
I argue in the book, this conception distantly foreshadows some modern
conceptions of Trinitarian persons, found in thinkers like Moltmann and
Balthasar, in which Trinitarian persons engage in new divine free acts in and
through the economy of salvation, so that their properties and their inner
life of communion are seen to develop in and through the economy. On the
other side there is the nominalist tradition, represented by Ockham. I claim

that this tradition is characterized by a tendency toward equivocal discourse when it speaks of the inner life of the Trinitarian persons. For Ockham, the classical psychological analogy cannot be employed to signify God's immanent life except in a metaphorical sense, or through the medium of a strictly nominal use of semantic definitions. In short, the immanent life of the Trinity can be affirmed, as the mystery of God prior to the economy, but not understood in itself by us according to any proper analogy. This conception foreshadows in its own way modern conceptions of the economic Trinity found in theologians like Barth and Rahner, who eschew the language of personhood for God and argue instead for a conception of distinct modes of subsistence, basing their arguments not on the psychological analogy but on distinctions that emerge in the economy, through God's transitive action in history, a sphere in which we can understand something of God. I suggest in the latter part of part 3 that Aquinas's theology of appropriation and divine missions allows us to offer an alternative to these modern extremes, one that preserves the proper attribution of personhood to the Father, Son, and Spirit in God by making use of a properly analogical conception of immanent processional life in God, and that does so while avoiding any historicizing of the persons, as if their relations or engagements with one another would develop historically or be constituted by the economy itself. Furthermore, I suggest ways that this doctrine of the eternal processions— far from divorcing God from the economy—allows us to understand how the very life of the Trinity is communicated to us in the visible missions of the Son and Spirit. In particular, the visible mission of the Son renders God present to us in an individual human nature, such that Jesus' concrete gestures, words, actions, and sufferings not only reveal his personal identity as Son, and his eternal relations to the Father and the Spirit, but also render them present. The Trinity is not constituted by the mysteries of the incarnation, crucifixion, and resurrection, but is manifest to us in these mysteries in a preeminent way.

     In part 4 I explore this latter idea, the revelation of God in the economy. I begin by noting how the Trinitarian theologies of Barth and Rahner developed in response to the philosophy of Kant, which casts a pall of skepticism over the doctrine of the divine nature and its attributes, the doctrine that is considered in part 2 of this book, and over the doctrine of the analogy of processional life as Word and Spirit taken from human psychological acts of knowledge and love, the doctrine that is considered in part 3. Their thought is also influenced in various ways (positively and negatively) by the ontology of Hegel, which depicts Trinitarian being as spirit in history. As a consequence, Barth and Rahner take up a stance that is not wholly dissimilar to the nominalist tradition as regards the viability of the *de Deo ut uno* treatise and the use of the psychological analogy. This means that they distinguish the persons from one another principally in virtue of their distinct actions in the economy, where God freely discloses himself. In the Father's election of humanity, the Son's incarnation, and the Spirit's activity of sanctification, we discover who God is in himself.

I go on in part 4 of the book to consider how the idea of God in history is explored in different ways in modern theology, and present critical engagements with such perspectives. I consider first the notion of Trinitarian self-revelation as the distinguishing feature of immanent Trinitarian life, as it is understood by Barth and Rahner respectively, and, second, what it means to say that the Trinity is the principle and ground of creation, in the kenotic theologies of Bulgakov and Moltmann. Third, I consider the theology of the incarnation and the theandric action of Christ as it relates to Trinitarian theology. Here I note that thinkers like Pannenberg and Balthasar propose a novel perspective on the human action of Jesus as indicative of the inner life of the distinction of persons, a form of theology I characterize as "inverted monophysitism." The human nature of Jesus, in its action and suffering, is depicted as if it provided a quasi-univocal portrait of the inner life of God and the eternal communion of the persons. As such, the conception that arises is excessively anthropomorphic (so I argue), taking the drama of God's obedient suffering in history and transposing it into God, employing it problematically to engineer differentiations between the Father and the Son. I offer as an alternative proposal a dyothelitist account of Jesus' action as simultaneously divine and human, wherein the human action of Jesus is indicative of the one divine will he possesses with his Father and the Spirit, and therefore is revelatory of the inner life of God. However, on this more markedly dyothelitist account, the distinction of the two natures is maintained consistently. The human nature of Christ is analogically similar to his divine nature, but also irreducibly dissimilar, so that the divine authority and power of Christ as God can be manifest in his human action, but human properties (such as suffering and obedience) cannot rightly be transposed onto the divine life of God. On this account, the Trinity is truly revealed in the human life of Jesus, but is manifest to us precisely in its transcendence.

Jesus reveals in his teaching, action, and suffering, that he is the Son of God and is Lord. It is the Lord and Creator of all things who is human, and his divine nature remains immutably perfect and impassible even as he acts and suffers, dies and rises in his human nature. In the final chapter of part 4, I explore the paschal mystery: how do the death and resurrection of Christ reveal his Sonship, the Fatherhood of God, and the mystery of the Holy Spirit? Here I consider ways that one can speak of divine self-communication in kenotic terms. The Son's intentional self-offering to the Father in obedient love reveals his human awareness that he personally receives all that he has from the Father, as Son. Consequently it denotes Jesus' relational identity as one who is ever from the Father. Likewise, Jesus' life poured out in death by self-giving charity in the crucifixion is a privileged locus for our understanding of the loving desire of Christ as Lord to send the Holy Spirit upon the Church and the world, a sending in time that reflects and expresses the eternal mystery of the procession of the Spirit from the Father and the Son as their Spirit of love. This desire of the Son is confirmed subsequently in the resurrection and at Pentecost. As such, the event of the passion and death of Christ is a place of manifestation of God as a Trinitarian communion of truth and love, and a place in which that communion is opened up to the world through the incarnation of the Word, and the sending of the Spirit. In depicting things in this way, I am suggesting that the Thomistic account of the immanent Trinity studied in part 3 provides us with a viable way to think more deeply about the revelation of the Trinity in the human life, crucifixion, death, and resurrection of Jesus of Nazareth. Far from inhibiting our understanding of the economic manifestation of God among us, this approach to the Trinity, which takes inspiration from the Thomistic tradition, is meant to facilitate a deeper understanding and contemplative inquiry into the mystery of God's crucifixion and his unveiling of his Triune life in the mission of the Son and the sending of the Spirit. My aim is to suggest that the principles of Aquinas, if received and interpreted in balanced ways, can provide us with an enduringly relevant and especially viable form of modern Trinitarian theology.

PART 1

Principles and Disputations

On the Development of
Trinitarian Doctrine

1

The Mystery of God
Religious and Philosophical Origins

Christianity rests upon the conviction that we can come to know the mystery of God. God invites us to encounter him personally by the grace of faith. He has revealed himself in Jesus Christ, as Father, Son and Holy Spirit, the one God and Creator of all that is. In revealing himself, God also communicates to human beings the offer of life with him. "That which was from the beginning, which we have heard, which we have seen with our eyes, which we have looked upon and touched with our hands, concerning the word of life—the life was made manifest, and we saw it, and testify to it, and proclaim to you the eternal life which was with the Father and was made manifest to us" (1 Jn 1:1–2). A dimension of this is intellectual. God's activity of self-manifestation occurs through the prophetic and apostolic teaching of the Old and New Testaments, all of which culminates in the person of Jesus Christ, the Incarnate God.

Nevertheless, this gift of knowledge of God as Trinity and Creator does not present us with the idea of God as something previously wholly alien to our natural understanding. The very idea of a primary truth, an absolute, first origin of all else, has a foundation in human nature, and it is from our nature that the question of God arises in the first place. Accordingly, we will examine in this first chapter what we might call human beings' pre-philosophical dispositions for the mystery of God. Second, we will consider the fact that all human beings exist within a given historical context, that is, within the ambit of the world's existing religious traditions, wherein our individual investigations always take on the character of second-order reflections about the mystery of God. These traditions precede us, whether we participate in them or not, and inevitably constitute the wider horizon and background against which we ask existential and intellectual questions about God. Third, given that this is the case, we will also note the ambiguities and even distortions of the idea of God or the divine that we confront when we consider the human history of religions, and then consider why and how the absolute revelation of God presented to us in Catholic Christianity helps us make sense of these diverse interpretations of human existence. The divine revelation of the Trinity addresses our natural desire to know God. It does not function as a standard by which we can simply reject the world's religious traditions wholesale. On the contrary, divine revelation invites us to value and discern: we can see in the light of Christ that human religious traditions bespeak a powerful desire for intimacy with the absolute, but that such traditions also stand in need, in various ways, of illumination, purification and healing, and higher elevation, which can occur through the grace of Christ.

THE NATURAL QUESTION OF GOD:
PRE-PHILOSOPHICAL DISPOSITIONS

The mystery of God is not simply a question for people of a philosophical turn of mind. It touches upon the intimate meaning of what it is to be human, since it confronts human beings with questions regarding the basic purpose and sense of existence. The question of God is a horizonal point of orientation for a human being: it indicates to us where we are headed or what we are aiming for. And indeed, God, or the mystery of the divine, seems to be at the periphery, if not the center, of every human civilization. Why is this the case? The answer has something to do with our human nature, which is capable of seeking ultimate explanations and that desires the happiness that results from resting in the most ultimate truth.

Thomas Aquinas is known for arguments for the existence of God that are both subtle and complex, but he also mentions ways that ordinary human existence (in both our external and internal experience) confronts us with a sense of the transcendent mystery of God. We can call these *pre-philosophical dispositions* of the human spirit, or intuitions of the mystery of God.

Aquinas names among these pre-philosophical dispositions: first, our *experience of order in the world,* an order that remains within or between beings that change and that are interdependent. In his *Commentary on the Apostles' Creed,* Aquinas says that this experience naturally raises the question of the cause of this ordered-yet-dependent set of realities.[1] Just as if we came into a house and found heat, we would expect there to be a fire somewhere in the house that is the cause of heat, so in this world we encounter an order inscribed in things, that the things themselves are not the origin of, and that leads us to suspect an ordering wisdom that is the cause of the world. It is an undeniable fact that all civilizations seek to accommodate themselves to the basic order of the cosmos, and to make that cosmos inhabitable for human life, which presupposes in turn the question of the origins of cosmic order.

Second, in his commentary on the Prologue of St. John's Gospel, Aquinas mentions the basic human *experience of time, finitude, and contingency,* which confronts us with the fundamental mutability of all things. He notes that this experience naturally raises the question of what remains eternally, or of what lasts, behind or underneath all that changes. Human civilizations are based around various linear and cyclical representations of time, and just as our lives together teach us to measure and live in time, so they also invite us to consider what is truly enduring and eternal. After all, ultimate explanations of change are not located only in particular individual things subject to generation and corruption, but must be found in something perennially true, either transcending or encompassing all things.[2]

Third, Thomas observes that, on a moral and voluntary level, human beings *strive to find happiness* and tend naturally to gravitate toward certain

---

1. See Thomas Aquinas, *The Three Greatest Prayers: Commentaries on the Lord's Prayer, the Hail Mary, and the Apostles' Creed* (Manchester, N.H.: Sophia Institute Press, 1990), 8–10.

2. As Aquinas notes in his *Lectura super Ioannem* [*In Ioan.*], prologue: "[Some in times past] came to a knowledge of God from his eternity. They saw that whatever was in things was changeable, and that the more noble something is in the grades of being, so much the less it has of mutability. For example, the lower bodies are mutable both as to their substance and to place, while the heavenly bodies, which are more noble, are immutable in substance and change only with respect to place. We can clearly conclude from this that the first principle of all things, which is supreme and more noble, is changeless and eternal." Thomas Aquinas, *Commentary on the Gospel of St. John,* trans. J. Weisheipl, vol. 1 (Albany, N.Y.: Magi Press, 1980). [All future translations quoted from this text, unless otherwise noted, will be taken from this edition.] Granted, Aquinas's example presumes a medieval cosmology, in which some physical bodies (stars) are thought to be incorruptible. In a modern cosmological setting, we would now claim that these physical bodies are also themselves ultimately subject to generation and corruption (coming to be and extinguishing). However, this new perspective would not nullify, but instead intensify the relevancy of Aquinas's argument.

goods that they think will procure happiness for them. This raises the natural question of the supreme good, of what is objectively the greatest source of goodness in reality, and of whether there is anything that can really satiate the human desire for happiness. On this point, Aquinas writes in *Summa contra Gentiles* [*SCG*] I, c. 11: "Man naturally knows God in the same way as he naturally desires God. Now, man naturally desires God in so far as he naturally desires beatitude [or happiness], which is a certain likeness of the divine goodness. On this basis, it is not necessary that God considered in Himself be naturally known to man, but only a likeness of God."[3] In other words, human beings may not think or understand that their happiness can be fulfilled perfectly only by the sovereign goodness of God. However, they do inevitably desire happiness and pursue it in all they do. Insofar as they are naturally made for the knowledge and love of God that alone can fully satisfy them, they remain imperfectly oriented toward God just insofar as they seek to be happy. This suggests that where there are human beings, there will be religious striving for the absolute, and, likewise, to eradicate the natural religious desire for God, one would have to eradicate the natural human desire for happiness, which is indeed impossible.

Finally, there is the question for Aquinas *of being and its relation to truth*, or of why things that exist *do* exist, and the question of their true origin: what is the explanation of all that exists, insofar as it exists? What is it that is "necessarily first" or primary in reality, the ground of all the rest? For whatever this is, it must be the "first truth," that which is both most enduring and most explanatory with regard to everything else. The mind is animated by a kind of restless desire for understanding that cannot find rest until it reaches knowledge of this first cause.[4] Indeed, it is not enough even to know that

3. Thomas Aquinas, *Summa contra Gentiles* [*SCG*] I, c. 11. Translation taken from *Summa contra Gentiles* I, trans. A. C. Pegis (Garden City, N.Y.: Doubleday, 1955). [All future translations quoted from this text, unless otherwise noted, will be taken from this edition.]

4. Aquinas puts the argument this way in *SCG* III, c. 25: "There is naturally present in all men the desire to know the causes of whatever things are observed. Hence, because of wondering about things that were seen but whose causes were hidden, men first began to think philosophically; when they found the cause, they were satisfied. But the search did not stop until it reached the first cause, for 'then do we think that we know perfectly, when we know the first cause' [*Metaphysics* 1.3 (983a25)]. Therefore, man naturally desires, as his ultimate end, to know the first cause.... [So] the ultimate end of man is the knowledge of God." And again: "For each effect that he knows, man naturally desires to know the cause. Now the human intellect knows universal being. So, he naturally desires to know its cause, which is God alone. Now, a person has not attained his ultimate end until natural desire comes to rest. Therefore, for human happiness which is the ultimate end it is not enough to have merely any kind of intelligible knowledge; there must be divine knowledge,

such a cause exists, for even when we know that God is, we wish in addition to know God in himself, to see God intellectually face to face. Accordingly, it is unsurprising that we find human civilizations offering us extensive portraits and "revelations" of God, the gods, the divine and the absolute, so as to address the human quest for perfect understanding of God.

In sum, we can see that, as identified by Aquinas, human beings' pre-philosophical dispositions for the mystery of God arise from our experience of order in the world; our experience of time, finitude, and contingency; our striving for happiness and the corresponding goods that will allow us to procure it; and, finally, our quest to know the immutable source of the existents we encounter in this world.

HUMAN RELIGIOSITY IS A SIGN
OF THE MYSTERY OF GOD

Perhaps, then, there is a deep inclination in human nature that disposes us to confront the *question* of God. But this is, in a sense, a second-order reflection, for in most cases, human beings come to reflect on God in cultures where they are already offered *answers* concerning religion, God, or the absolute. That is to say, religious rites and practices, beliefs, theological systems, and cultural symbols often contextualize and deeply condition one's thinking about what is ultimately real. Even secular cultures react to the idea of God by thinking of living religious traditions that they may find strange or familiar. This too seems to be quite natural. One can think of religions as concentrated proposals concerning how we ought to relate to the divine. Taken in this sense, human religious traditions are ubiquitous in virtually every human civilization, and are represented even in the most secular cultures by substantial minority groups of believers and practitioners. Furthermore, it is not easy to eradicate this trait in persons and societies. It seems to spring back up eventually even when it wanes or when a society tries to extirpate and deracinate it in a systematic fashion.

In some sense we should be prepared to think of people being religious as a good thing. Perhaps human religious traditions embody deep and abiding forms of wisdom, and authentically religious people help us discover

---

as an ultimate end, to terminate the natural desire. So, the ultimate end of man is the knowledge of God." Thomas Aquinas, *Summa contra Gentiles* III, vol. 2, trans. V. J. Bourke (Garden City, N.Y., Doubleday, 1956).]

better what it is to be human. If this is the case, then the great figures of religious traditions (saints, mystics) encourage us to find God, and give us indications of who or what God really is.

Let us consider three reasons why this might be the case: first, *the desire for the good*. Religion seems to answer to a reasonable desire not only for understanding but also for loving union with the good. If our true happiness is to be found through some kind of union with God, then it is normal that we should attempt to approach God through religious practices. If this is the case, then religious ethics and practical spiritual knowledge help us embrace the mystery of God. They are something we have to learn by being religious rather than merely by thinking. If so, we will need to consult the religious traditions.

Second, *the unresolved question of providence*. How are our lives governed? Where are they going, if anywhere? For what are we ultimately made, and where might we place our ultimate aspirations and hopes? What happens to us after we die? Is there a final judgment after death? Is there eternal bliss? How can we concretely please (or displease) God in this life by our behavior? Can there be mystical experience of the divine or some kind of higher union with God in this life that prepares us for the next? There are limits to what philosophy can provide. Religion alone, it would seem, can offer a clear answer to these questions, if indeed there are any real answers. The testimony of religious traditions here confronts us anew with the question of revelation. Has God revealed to us how he governs our lives, if he does govern them, and in view of what end? It is reasonable to be open to inquiry in this domain. Clearly, then, we can ask if there is an answer to the question of providence by consulting the existing religious traditions of humanity.

Last, we must consider *the drama of evil, and the question of "theodicy"*: the justice of God in the face of evil. It seems difficult to deny that human existence is marked by evil, whether moral evil or natural evil, and that this is an inescapable dimension of human existence. As such, evil does not offer us salvation or deliverance, but it does raise the question of whether or how we might ultimately overcome evil, or how we might be saved from suffering, moral weakness or wrongdoing, and death. It also raises the question of whether God exists, or—if God does exist—why he permits evil, and how he governs the world with respect to it. Here again, religious traditions offer perspectives, answers, explanations, or practices for coping, or even for transcending the struggle with evil in human existence. The religions also, then, lead us to confront the mystery of God in ways that are not merely reducible to our philosophical or scientific efforts of explanation.

THE MYSTERY OF GOD
IS ALSO A PROBLEM IN THE
RELIGIOUS TRADITIONS

When confronting human religious practices and beliefs, however, we must also draw back and reflect carefully. For what has not yet been mentioned, and what lurks in the background, are the inevitable questions of difficulties raised by the various traditions, regarding the notions of both God and the world, and regarding practices and beliefs. In these areas, ambiguities abound, several of which should be mentioned.

For example, what do we really mean by God, and how should we go about identifying true from false claims, especially given the diversity of claims about God, the gods, ultimate reality, and human existence? Can we even speak about "religion" as a constant phenomenon? Enlightenment-era and modern philosophers often try to get around this problem by beginning with a notional definition of God (derived from a "merely rational" version of Christianity) and then search for rational evidence to suggest that this concept is instantiated or is not substantiated in reality—for instance, rational argumentation that God exists or does not exist. In a sense this Enlightenment project of rational discernment about God and religion is valid and has a basis even in the arguments of the early Church Fathers like Justin, Clement, Lactantius, and Augustine, who argued in engagement with Graeco-Roman religion that Christianity is the "rational religion," because revelation purifies and elevates our philosophical consideration of the divine. But if this kind of philosophical reflection is used to argue against the trustworthiness of any form of revelation, and if in doing so it attempts to abstract entirely from a religious context, it becomes artificial and self-defeating. Anthropologically, we seek God within the existential states mentioned above by Aquinas, where we want to see God and know him personally. This requires something more than "mere" philosophy. It requires revelation, friendship with God by grace, and mystical experience of God. We need to be touched by God directly in some way if we are going to orient our whole lives toward him. Meanwhile, culturally, our religious search is never purely individualistic. No one can live out an absolute religious truth uniquely on his or her own. Realistically speaking, we can find God and give ourselves to the service of others religiously only if we undertake common beliefs and practices of corporate worship, ethical self-governance, and the pursuit of holiness, in a shared life with others. The quest for God, then, needs an objective, external religious structure, but how can we know which one to engage in?

Does this dilemma mean that reason stands helpless before the fact of religious humanity, as something it must submit to blindly? But what should we do, then, with the fact that the explanations of the religious traditions are themselves very diverse, often incompatible, sometimes seemingly plausible, and often evidently impossible or implausible, if not irrational or indicative of psychological pathology? What should we say about religious hypocrisy, moral failure among religious leaders, fanaticism or religious anti-intellectualism? Religion is a philosophical quagmire, and sometimes a dangerous business. Here, above all, we cannot abandon reason.

In addition, the goods we have mentioned—that is, the idea of an ultimate happiness, of a deliverance from evil, of a providential meaning to human existence—are not self-evident realities, and their existence can be disputed. Maybe there is no God, and no religious solution to the puzzle of human existence. Atheism and agnosticism arise, therefore, as a not entirely inappropriate theory or hypothesis for how to think about human existence, and how to approach it, or cope with it, areligiously. There is in each human being a real possibility of refusing the mystery of God, and even people who purport to be religious can often live as if their religions are not true, or are not existentially compelling. Even atheists, however, have to contend with the irreducibility of being, truth, goodness, and beauty present in the created order, traces of God that suggest his hidden presence, and that suggest ever anew the possibility of a real encounter with the living God.

REVELATION, PHILOSOPHY, AND
THE MYSTERY OF GOD

So human beings are in an odd situation. On the one hand, they seem existentially compelled in spirit, both in mind and heart, to ask the question of God, and perhaps even to seek God as the greatest good in their lives. They also have examples and testimonies of religious traditions more or less proximate to them in culture, that suggest to them how they might approach God and what they might expect from him, and these explanations enjoy varying degrees of compelling rationality.

On the other hand, human religiosity seems to be fatally flawed by its ambiguities and by the practical incertitude with which it confronts us. Where might we go to find the words of eternal life? (Jn 6:68) What is the truth concerning God, the human being, fate, evil, death, the afterlife, moral values, and sacrifice? No one seems to be in perfect agreement on these points. We live in a pluralistic world, and therefore an agnostic one, or perhaps agnosticism is the best response to the dilemma. But then, can or should we abandon the search to gain insight into the mystery of God?

Classical Catholic Christianity offers a twofold solution to this dilemma, and it is a twofold solution that will be emphasized and developed within this book. It is the solution of the simultaneous interaction, or synergy, of the agency of divine revelation and the activity of human philosophical reason. Revelation and reason, grace and nature, always go both together, never one apart from the other, each being distinct but inseparable from the other, mutually compatible with one another, and complementary.

Because it is a product of divine grace, Christianity provides a true, reasonable, and ethically noble approach to being religious. Divine revelation does not do away with human religious dispositions and practices, but instead draws them into itself, heals them and elevates them. Beginning in the bible with the call of Abraham (Gn 12:1–3), God communicates personally with human beings and in doing so inaugurates a sacred history. The bible recognizes the antecedent reality of human religion, but approaches it in a critical and nuanced way. It depicts the religion of Israel, and the mystery of the Church, as unique within the history of humanity. In them, divine revelation purifies human religiosity of its many intellectual and practical errors and simultaneously elevates human religious life into the sphere of divine grace.[5] In this process, the gift of faith provides supernatural certitude

---

5. Examples of this approach found in the Torah are the revelation given to Israel that there is only one God, that God is the creator of all things, that God is all good, that all of reality created by God is also good in a limited and finite but real way, that human beings are made in the image of God, and that the precepts of the moral law signified especially in the ten commandments are indicative of true human flourishing. These ideas contrast with erroneous forms of belief that were prevalent in the time of ancient Israel and are prevalent in the wider religious history of humanity: polytheism, dualism, pantheism that identifies, at base, God with the creation, the denial of the goodness of the cosmos and the human body in particular, the claim that human beings are naturally divine rather than human, the attribution of moral evil to God, etc.

regarding the mystery of God and his providence. There, at the juncture where our reason might stand paralyzed before the multiple interpretations of human existence, God speaks and reveals to us his own inner mystery as the Triune God.

Second, this revelation is not received in a purely passive way, but also acts as an invitation to a continued search for God, one grounded in the knowledge of sacred scripture, intimate love of God, the study of theology, and the practice of the sacraments. Christian revelation can never rightfully be interpreted as a pretext to abandon the work of human reason. It must be seen rather as an invitation to deeper understanding of God, as well as to the love of God and neighbor. The friendship with God offered to us by grace, then, is enriched by our attempts at reasonable knowing. St. Anselm's famous dictums are: *fides quaerens intellectum* ("faith seeking understanding"), and *credo ut intelligam* ("I believe, that I might understand"). We might also add *credo ut sperem et diligam*, "I believe, that I might hope and love." Within Christian theology, the search to understand the mystery of God begins in supernatural faith, and makes use of our natural capacity to understand what God is, or is not. The knowledge that comes by way of faith in turn helps us hope robustly in God and pursue union with him in contemplation and charity. This means, among other things, that Christian theology can and should make use of a sound philosophical approach to the mystery of God. Theology can include philosophical knowledge of God within itself, without either violating the integrity of philosophical reason or degrading the quality of theological reasoning. Sound philosophical arguments should contribute to theology and can help purify the practice of Christianity, protecting it at times from various forms of intellectual corruption.

CONCLUSION

To summarize these introductory remarks, in this work we will consider the mystery of the Triune God, revealed in the scriptures of Israel and in the New Testament. But we will also consider God as he may be approached by sound intellectual reasoning, in the Christian theological and philosophical tradition, and particularly, though not exclusively, in the thought of Thomas Aquinas. Without faith, we cannot adequately understand the inner rationality and explanatory power of Christian truth, which casts an ultimate light upon human existence. But by the grace of faith, and in the light of Christ, we not only can know who God is theologically, but also can think speculatively about God philosophically, and can see the deep rationality of the Christian conception of God the Creator. Following Aquinas, we can claim that philosophical monotheism presents us with the uniquely reasonable view of God as the first principle of the creation, even if the mystery of God as we know him in Christian revelation *as Holy Trinity* is a mystery that *simultaneously* utterly transcends the powers of mere human reason. Catholic Christianity is the religion that is simultaneously the most reasonable and the most mystical, that is to say, it is the religion that is the most compelling for human rationality, and that at the same time presents us with a truth about God as Trinity that wholly surpasses the natural powers and acquisitions of human rationality. In these pages, we will seek to explain the truth of both these claims and to show multiple ways that they are interrelated.

2

---:---

The Problem of God in Modernity

Religious belief is prevalent in human history, but is commonly considered strange or unreasonable by many today. Human beings have always been able to reject religious interpretations of the cosmos, or remain indifferent to them, but there are specific causes of secularization in our own age. Before we turn to the revelation of the one God in Israel, it is fitting that we first consider this trend in European culture since the Enlightenment era, which has had global effects. Historically speaking, there are many factors that have contributed to the loss of religious practice in the modern world. I will concentrate briefly on two elements: some of the main philosophical trends that have led to loss of belief in the transcendent God, and the concomitant rise of political secularism. I will then briefly consider modern intellectual responses of the Catholic Church to the emergence of modern secularism. What follows is, of course, only a cursory overview of a very complex cultural phenomenon that is subject to a great deal of historical debate.[1]

1. Genealogies of modernity abound, and often differ from one another in important ways. Among Thomists see Étienne Gilson, *Being and Some Philosophers* (Toronto: PIMS, 1949); Cornelius Fabro, *God in Exile: Modern Atheism* (New York: Newman Press, 1968); Servais Pinckaers, *Sources of Christian Ethics*, trans. M. Noble (Washington, D.C.: The Catholic University of America Press, 1995); Alasdair MacIntyre, *After Virtue* (South Bend, Ind.: Notre Dame University Press, 1981). For a helpful study of the Enlightenment era, see Jonathan Israel, *Radical Enlightenment: Philosophy in the Making of Modernity 1650–1750* (Oxford: Oxford University Press, 2001). Other noteworthy studies include Charles Taylor, *Sources of the Self: The Making of the Modern Identity* (Cambridge, Mass.: Harvard University Press, 1990), and *A Secular Age* (Cambridge, Mass.: Belknap Press, 2007); John Milbank, *Theology and Social Theory: Beyond Secular Reason* (Oxford: Blackwell, 1990); Thomas Pfau, *Minding the Modern: Human Agency, Intellectual Traditions and Responsible Knowledge* (South Bend, Ind.: Notre Dame University Press, 2015); Carlos Eire, *Reformations: The Early Modern World, 1450–1650* (New Haven, Conn.: Yale University Press, 2016).

THE MODERN CRISIS OF

BELIEF IN THE MYSTERY OF GOD

Philosophical Skepticism and the Break

with Classical Ontology

The idea that philosophy should play a role in the critical assessment of re-ligion is very ancient. Early Greek philosophers (Xenophanes, Plato, and Aristotle included) criticized the "gods of the poets" in the name of phil-osophical reason.[2] The early Christian apologists of the first four centuries embraced this idea, and argued that Christianity was "the true philosophy" because it was the "reasonable" religion, freeing human beings from poly-theism and misguided religious practices. They claimed, then, that Chris-tianity is the true inheritor of the spirit of Greek philosophy, in contradis-tinction to the imperfections of Graeco-Roman paganism.[3] Patristic and medieval authors in the Eastern and Western world assimilated a great deal of the ancient patrimony of Hellenistic philosophy, while also critically re-interpreting it. For example, the high medieval theologians centered their ontology around transcendental notions, such as being, unity, truth, good-ness, and beauty, all notions found initially in Plato and Aristotle. However, they wanted to articulate a philosophical conception of reality that pointed toward the mystery of God and that was open to divine revelation.

At the same time, the so-called "Latin Averroists" in the thirteenth cen-tury seem to have insinuated in their writings that a true philosopher has no need of religion, because philosophy is the ultimate and highest form of real knowledge.[4] On this view, divine revelation is neither philosophically interesting nor necessary. In fact, religious appeals to revelation are a veiled

2. Xenophanes, fr. 11 and 14, from *The Presocratic Philosophers*, ed. and trans. G. S. Kirk and J. E. Raven (Cambridge: Cambridge University Press, 1957), 168; Plato, *Apology*, 18c, and *Republic*, 3.398a, from *Plato: Complete Works*, ed. John M. Cooper, trans. G. M. A. Grube (Indianapolis, Ind.: Hackett, 1997); Aristotle, *Metaphysics* 12.8 (1074b1–14), from *The Complete Works of Aristotle*, vol. 2, trans. W. D. Ross, ed. J. Barnes (Princeton, N.J.: Princeton University Press, 1984).

3. Noteworthy examples include Justin Martyr, *Apologia* and *Dialogue with Trypho the Jew*; Ath-enagorus, *A Plea for Christians*; Clement of Alexandria, *Exhortation to the Pagan*; Athanasius, *Against the Gentiles*; and Augustine, *City of God*. An important analysis of this aspect of ancient thought is provided by Joseph Ratzinger in his essay "Truth of Christianity?," in *Truth and Tolerance: Christian Belief and World Religions*, trans. by H. Taylor (San Francisco: Ignatius Press, 2003), 138–209.

4. See Dag Nikolaus Hasse, "Influence of Arabic and Islamic Philosophy on the Latin West," Stanford Encyclopedia of Philosophy, https://plato.stanford.edu/entries/arabic-islamic-influence/; and Hans Thijssen, "Condemnation of 1277," Stanford Encyclopedia of Philosophy, https://plato.stanford.edu/entries/condemnation/

form of philosophy and social control intended for the less educated. (Later this idea would become prevalent in the Enlightenment, as restated in more overt ways.)

The crisis of reason and faith intensified, however, in the following centuries, when theologians downplayed the role of philosophical reasoning in order to augment the place of revelation and divine authority. Nominalism is the fourteenth century movement associated with the English Franciscan, William of Ockham, which gave rise to widespread intellectual skepticism regarding the powers of the mind to know the metaphysical structures of reality.[5] For instance, nominalists would come to argue that we cannot truly identify common natures that are present in multiple individuals, nor grasp the existence of singulars (their being as such), rather than their mere facticity.[6] They also questioned our capacity to understand the existence of *causality* in realities we experience, such that we might affirm that things change or come to be as a result of their intrinsic properties (natural form), through the effects of others (efficient causality), and that they tend toward final ends (teleology or final causality).[7] Here the philosophy of the transcendentals (being, unity, truth, goodness) breaks down, because the notions appear unduly subjective. Nominalism led in turn to increased skepticism regarding our natural capacity to know God or to speak coherently about him, since theological depictions of God in classical scholasticism often appealed to causal dependencies and transcendental features of being in order to identify what we mean when we speak of God and to identify the divine attributes or "names of God," such as goodness, eternity, infinity, and so forth.

This crisis of confidence in natural reason played a complex role in the emergence of modern-day secularism. It was meant initially to underscore the limits of natural knowledge, which in turn invites a greater role for divine authority, the appeal to revelation, and the role of the Church. How-

5. See Armand A. Maurer, *The Philosophy of William of Ockham in the Light of Its Principles* (Toronto: Pontifical Institute of Mediaeval Studies, 1999).

6. It is, in effect, one thing to say, "there are sensible things around us," and another to say, "there are things around us that each *exist*, or that *have being*."

7. On final causality see, for example, William of Ockham, *Quodlibet* 1, q. 16, in *Opera theologica* [hereafter, *OTh.*], vol. 9 (St. Bonaventure, N.Y.: Franciscan Institute Publications, 1980). For Ockham's minimalistic idea of efficient causality as two terms of a relation (a relation between two things), see, likewise *Quodlibet* 1, q. 16. [All quotations of Ockham are taken from the *Opera Theologica*, vols. 1–10 (St. Bonaventure, N.Y.: Franciscan Institute Publications, 1967–86)]. For a sympathetic historical analysis, see Marilyn McCord Adams, *William Ockham*, 2 vols. (Notre Dame, Ind.: University of Notre Dame Press, 1989).

ever, in doing so it gave rise to a general intellectual position (skepticism about classical philosophy) that would influence diverse movements leading in contrary directions. On the one hand, religion became marked by greater authoritarianism in the era of the Reformation, when key questions arose about the authority of scripture, tradition, and the pope. In the face of intellectual incertitude, Luther (who was trained in Augustinian nominalism) posited the essential role of faith in scripture, and grace in the moral life, without a corresponding emphasis on philosophical investigation, or the mediating positions of Church tradition.[8] Some Catholic figures shared Luther's skepticism regarding scholasticism and sought new pathways for modern Catholic thought.[9] During the Reformation era, consensus on the intellectual pathway to God eroded, in the realms of both theology and philosophy. As a result of the deep interrelation in Europe of Christianity and social life, this led to inevitable conflict in the political order. Profound social division and wars of religion became widespread as a result.

Meanwhile, in a second instance, especially in the seventeenth century, the retreat from classical metaphysics began to be coupled with an intensification of development of the observational sciences. Against the backdrop of the past turmoil, there began to emerge a kind of philosophical skepticism that allied itself with the primacy of the scientific method, over against medieval metaphysical ideas, as well as medieval cosmology and natural science. Beginning around the time of Francis Bacon, Galileo, and Descartes, many thinkers began to prefer the methods of modern biology, chemistry, and physics, which were seen as providing a privileged understanding of external reality. In the external world the sciences excel, while in the internal world individual reason and freedom are valued above all.[10] From within this perspective, the physical world is known principally through the senses by means of mathematical-empirical descriptions, and without recourse to classical philosophical analysis. (The most certain and most useful knowledge is empirically observable knowledge.) The modern sciences tend methodologically to focus on the material parts of realities we experience,

8. On nominalist influences in the Reformation, see for example Ulrich G. Leinsle, *Introduction to Scholastic Theology*, trans. M. Miller (Washington, D.C.: The Catholic University of America Press, 2010).

9. Noteworthy Catholic examples include Erasmus, Thomas More, Cornelius Jansen (whose thought would fall under censure but remain influential all the same), Blaise Pascal, and Jacques Bénigne Bossuet.

10. See on this topic, Taylor, *Sources of the Self*, parts 3 and 4.

and the efficient causes that operate among them, without explicit recourse to a concept of essence or purpose. In other words, formal, exemplary, and final causality are typically not considered by the observer, because of the requirements of the modern scientific methods themselves. In thinking of a human being, for example, one studies the organic and cellular composition (including the genetic code), the chemical compounds, and the physical matter and forces that constitute the individual. However, one abstracts from the consideration of what human nature is, as such, and why human beings exist (for example, for the pursuit of truth and happiness, by means of the freely chosen good). If taken in a reductive direction, this form of thought treats as "real" only what is known by such subjects of study.

Modern secularization as such came out of the Enlightenment period, in which key roles were played by figures such as Descartes, Hobbes, Spinoza, Locke, Rousseau, Hume, and Kant. The views of these figures are very diverse, but these thinkers share some common aspirations. The Enlightenment philosophers sought to reset European culture on a common rational footing divorced from confessional theological norms (especially in response to the wars of religion). They also tended to adopt standpoints that emphasized the centrality of observational science, individual free thought, and dissociation of civic society from dependence on the Church. We could say that this movement gave rise to a new metaphysics of the human subject, divorced increasingly from classical notions of nature, causality, teleology, and the transcendentals. In doing so, it severed the philosophical bridge of the mind back to God, which classical culture (both Hellenistic and Christian) had spent time building. Some figures of this movement defended the natural capacity of the intellect to know something of God (Descartes, Locke), while others were atheistic (Hobbes, Hume) and yet others (Kant in particular) sought to demonstrate that the intellect is naturally bound by agnosticism, and cannot know determinatively if God exists. Many Enlightenment figures sought purposefully to break decisively with the Christian patrimony of Europe and appeals to divine revelation (Spinoza, Hobbes, Hume, and Kant), but this was not always the case, as some modern Enlightenment figures (like Leibnitz and Locke) wanted to preserve key elements of Christian tradition.[11] Meanwhile, some major figures who came afterward, like Hegel and Schelling, sought to give a positive philosophical reinterpretation of Christianity, so as to transpose it into what

11. On this division, see Israel, *Radical Enlightenment*, 502–27.

they took to be a rational key. They took the Enlightenment to be the perfection of Christianity rather than its enemy. Philosophy taken in this sense perfects and assimilates Christianity, bringing it into a higher realm. Revelation is philosophy in becoming.[12]

Alternatives to Hegel emerged that posited Christianity not as a precursor to modernity but as a delusion that modern atheism had to overcome. As the notion of God is itself rendered philosophically problematic, and society dissociates from religious practice, modern philosophers also need to generate "secular" theories of why people are religious and how to account for belief in God. In the nineteenth and twentieth centuries, we see emerge the project of atheistic genealogy: of the philosophical and psychological explanation of religion as a pathology. The so-called "masters of suspicion" are most important in this respect: Feuerbach sees God as a projection of human ideals upon reality (God is an idealization of what it means to be human).[13] For Marx, religion is an illusory consolation or "opiate" that anesthetizes the masses to the pains of their economic and social alienation, promising them a future, after this life, that will resolve present injustices. Religion functions, in practice, to maintain social divisions of class, rather than to alleviate them.[14] Nietzsche diagnoses religion as a frustrated expression of the will to power, belief in God being an illusory projection onto reality of a moralistic and resentful deity who will punish those who we (the believers) resent for their nobility, strength, and inner freedom. Religion is used in and by weaker cultures to subjugate the stronger. Christianity is the sign of artificial moralism and existential inauthenticity.[15] Freud, for his part, sees God as the expression of a narcissistic illusion, fueled by the psychological need to perceive the world in personal terms, seeing behind all things a parent figure that provides for us. For Freud, religion results from an immaturity that seeks a misguided sense of security and affection in the face of an impersonal and non-mystical cosmos.[16]

12. See the analysis of Charles Taylor, in *Hegel* (Cambridge: Cambridge University Press, 1975), 408–510.
13. Ludwig Feuerbach, *The Essence of Christianity*, trans. G. Elliot (New York: Prometheus, 1989).
14. Karl Marx, "A Contribution to the Critique of Hegel's Philosophy of Right: Introduction," in *Karl Marx: Early Writings* (New York: Penguin, 1992).
15. Friedrich Nietzsche, *"On the Genealogy of Morals" and Other Writings*, trans. C. Diethe (Cambridge: Cambridge University Press, 2018).
16. Sigmund Freud, *Civilization and Its Discontents*, trans. D. McLintock (London: Penguin, 2002).

Cultural and Political Secularization

Along with the eclipse of classical ontology, the rise of the experimental sciences, and the generation of atheistic philosophies, we see emerge in Western modernity a progressively expanding political secularism, that is to say, a prohibition of reference to divine revelation, or even to religious belief in general, in the public domain. A remote cause may be found in the Protestant Reformation, particularly in Luther's concept of the state as an entity relatively independent from the institutional Church.[17] In addition, the Reformers' attempts to vindicate an interiorization of Christian religion through justification by faith was coupled with a simplification of external religious practices, which included many civic customs of medieval Christendom, such as saints' festivals and public processions. The absolutization of the state's religious authority, begun under Henry VIII in England, foreshadowed the rise of political absolutism and modern nationalism, wherein the modern state takes precedence in practice as well as in theory over the theological requirements of religious civilization.

However, the French Revolution above all was the cultural movement that gave expression to the Enlightenment. It established a purely secular, constitutional state without reference to God, divine revelation, or the Church. The cultural changes that followed suit greatly limited the power of religious activity in public and dramatically reduced state support for any religious activity. Theology was banned from being taught in public universities, and clerics were not permitted to teach in any state university. This divorce intensified in the century to come throughout Europe, not least through the Napoleonic wars, as it produced the social revolutions of the nineteenth century that established modern non-confessional constitutional states throughout Europe.

In the twentieth century, more radical versions of a post-Christian atheist state were undertaken, often in ways that were spectacularly intolerant of religious belief. Both the fascism of the World War II period and the international communist movement that swept over many countries in the twentieth century were examples of totalitarian atheistic regimes that sought to

17. See Eire, *Reformations*, who notes the diverse political arrangements of Luther's movement in Germany, of Calvin's social experiment in Geneva, and in the English-Anglican state after the English Reformation. Brad S. Gregory has promoted a more controversial thesis, that the Reformation led inadvertently to modern secularization, in *The Unintended Reformation: How a Religious Revolution Secularized Society* (Cambridge, Mass.: Harvard Belknap, 2015).

fashion a new humanity, always appealing to modern science and to radical new ontologies of human freedom. After World War II and the fall of communism in Eastern Europe, these ideologies faded, and globalization emerged, animated by a philosophy of democratic liberalism and universal human rights. In this context, religious traditions must be both tolerated but also contained. Side by side with the rise of globalism, many European nations have come to experience a bad conscience concerning their former efforts at colonialism, and this has in turn fueled the emergence of post-modern political philosophies of "difference" or of irreducible pluralism. In this context, one can perceive a deepened tension between the modern secular state and the various religious subgroups that inhabit it, giving rise to the mainstream emergence of a theory of "cultural relativism" or post-modern "pluralism" as the correlate of doctrinaire liberal "tolerance."

Modern liberalism sometimes adopts a politically pragmatic and individualistically therapeutic interpretation of religion. Any given religious tradition is thought to serve the subjective and existential needs of its adherents, perhaps by providing them with unverifiable hopes or benign illusions. This agnostic or skeptical stance accords well with the universal political aspirations of liberalism, which seeks to incorporate a plurality of conceptually discordant religious traditions and practices into a larger overarching secular political ethos. Each religious tradition is granted a right to exist under certain limited conditions, according to non-religious criteria (some of which may be entirely sound, ethically speaking, such as refraining from religiously motivated violence). Religions are seen then perhaps as remnants of pre-modern history, or as customs of non-Christian cultures, which function primarily as working theories of personal meaning. What frequently results from this standpoint in public consciousness is what Pope Pius IX called "indifferentism," the view that all religious viewpoints are unverifiable and arbitrary. The values of religious traditions are to be assessed based on external factors, by non-religious standards of ethical and political utility.

THE CHURCH'S RESPONSE TO MODERN AGNOSTICISM AND ATHEISM

As noted above, the high medieval philosophy of the Catholic Church, developed in the service of theology, was centered around the study of the transcendental dimensions of reality: being, unity, truth, goodness, beauty.[18] While theologians themselves oversaw the deconstruction of this centerpiece of classical Catholic thought, the Church's magisterium eventually reasserted its importance during the early modern Catholic and Renaissance era in the sixteenth and seventeenth centuries. The council of Trent made modern use of the scholastic analysis of the sacraments, and the catechism of the council developed a sophisticated analysis of virtues and vices marked both by Renaissance learning and classical scholasticism, grounded in biblical law.[19] The Tridentine reform of the seminary curriculum of priests enjoined years of study of scholastic philosophy as a propaedeutic to theology, a norm that remains in effect to this day in Catholic canon law. In the early modern Catholic period both before and after Trent, there was a renaissance of scholastic studies in the Catholic religious orders, which trained the missionaries who were sent out to the lands newly discovered by explorers, so that various schools of scholasticism became important rivals and influences in the intellectual life of Europe and in the missions. The modern theory of human rights that developed in relation to European slave trade in South America and Africa came principally from Spanish scholastics who sought to elaborate a universal theory of natural rights in response to the immensely irresponsible colonial practices of some Europeans.[20] Governments in the newly divided Europe had to develop theories of natural ethics that could allow for the universal co-existence of a divided polity, where Catholics and Protestants sought to co-exist.[21] Many Catholic intellectuals assimilated reasonable elements of the Enlightenment project, while also maintaining arguments from revelation and reason for the superiority of the truth of the Catholic faith.[22] In all these matters, the Catholic

18. See the seminal argument of Jan Aertsen in *Medieval Philosophy as Transcendental Thought: From Philip the Chancellor (ca. 1225) to Francisco Suárez* (Leiden: Brill, 2012).

19. On sacramental theology in the post-conciliar period in the Thomistic tradition, in comparison with other schools of the time, see Reginald Lynch, *The Cleansing of the Heart: The Sacraments as Instrumental Causes in the Thomistic Tradition* (Washington, D.C.: The Catholic University of America Press, 2017).

20. See David M. Lantigua, *Infidels and Empires in a New World Order: Early Modern Spanish Contributions to International Legal Thought* (Cambridge: Cambridge University Press, 2020).

21. See Robert Louis Wilken, *Liberty in the Things of God: The Christian Origins of Religious Freedom* (New Haven, Conn.: Yale University Press, 2019). Eire shows, in *Reformations*, 218–47, how the early wars of religion between the Swiss cantons led within a generation to a settlement of religious tolerance accepted by all sides on mutually compelling religious and civic grounds.

22. See Ulrich L. Lehner, *The Catholic Enlightenment: The Forgotten History of a Global Movement* (Oxford: Oxford University Press, 2018).

"both-and" of grace and nature, revelation and reason, theology and philosophy, Church and natural state, were embodied in this response to the challenges of early modernity.

In the post-Enlightenment landscape of the nineteenth century, the Church's most important instance of response to secularization and to the French Revolution came in the form of the First Vatican Council, in its 1870 decree *Dei Filius*. In the decree's second chapter, which treats of revelation, the Council states the following with regard to the rational and supernatural dimensions of Christian faith:

The same holy mother church holds and teaches that God, the source and end of all things, can be known with certainty from the consideration of created things, by the natural power of human reason: "ever since the creation of the world, his invisible nature has been clearly perceived in the things that have been made" [Rom 1:20]. It was, however, pleasing to his wisdom and goodness to reveal himself and the eternal laws of his will to the human race by another, and that a supernatural, way. This is how the Apostle puts it: "In many and various ways God spoken of old to our fathers by the prophets; but in these last days he has spoken to us by a Son" [Heb 1:1–2].

It is indeed thanks to this divine revelation, that those matters concerning God which are not of themselves beyond the scope of human reason, can, even in the present state of the human race, be known by everyone without difficulty, with firm certitude and with no intermingling of error. It is not because of this that one must hold revelation to be absolutely necessary; the reason is that God directed human beings to a supernatural end, that is a sharing in the good things of God that utterly surpasses the understanding of the human mind; "indeed eye has not seen, neither has ear heard, nor has it come into our hearts to conceive what things God has prepared for those who love him" [1 Cor 2:9].

Now this supernatural revelation, according to the belief of the universal church, as declared by the sacred council of Trent, is contained in written books and unwritten traditions, which were received by the apostles from the lips of Christ himself, or came to the apostles by the dictation of the Holy Spirit, and were passed on as it were from hand to hand until they reached us.[23]

23. First Vatican Council, Dogmatic Constitution *Dei Filius* on the Catholic Faith, chap. 2. Unless otherwise indicated, citations and translations of ecumenical councils of the Catholic Church are taken from *Decrees of the Ecumenical Councils*, ed. Norman P. Tanner (London and Washington, D.C.: Georgetown University Press, 1990), based upon the critical edition of G. Alberigo et al., eds., *Conciliorum œcumenicorum generaliumque decreta*, Editio critica, vol. 1, *The Œcumenical Councils: From Nicaea I to Nicaea II (325–787)*, Corpus Christianorum Texts and Studies (CC-TS) (Brepols, Turnhout, 2006); vol. 2-1, *The General Councils of Latin Christendom: From Constantinople IV to Pavia-Siena (869–1424)*, CC-TS (Brepols, Turnhout, 2013); vol. 2-2, *The General Councils of Latin Christendom: From Basel to Lateran V (1431–1517)*, CC-TS (Brepols, Turnhout, 2013); vol. 3, *The Œcumenical Councils of the Roman Catholic Church: From Trent to Vatican II (1545–1965)*, CC-TS

These lines were composed first to respond to atheistic materialism and theoretical agnosticism, so as to emphasize that Catholic belief is in no way unreasonable. Kant, for example, had composed an influential critique of what he took to be all possible arguments for the existence of God, especially in his *Critique of Pure Reason*.[24] He allied this viewpoint with a political treatise arguing that the Church should have no sway on the outward political world of modern democratic societies.[25] In response, the Catholic Church has perpetually asserted that the natural knowledge of God is a key dimension of public reason, not a mere subjective idea. Furthermore, the mystery of God·revealed in Christ has notes of natural rationality associated with it (signs of natural credibility).[26] Second, these lines were also composed in response to various forms of Christian rationalism that would assimilate Christianity to a philosophy, as if the mysteries of the faith are either demonstrable by natural reason, or ultimately symbols of a deeper philosophical dynamic, as may be supposed in Hegel. In response to a rationalism that would posit human reason competent to determine all that can be known of God by its own powers, the Church maintained that supernatural knowledge of God is unique because it is a gift, inaccessible to unaided human reason, but objectively helpful and pleasing to it. The mystery of Christianity has a place in public culture precisely because it is the· true revealed religion, which grants ultimate perspective on reality and facilitates intellectual friendship with God, and because human beings are moved by their in-

---

(Brepols, Turnhout, 2010). When indicated, texts are also sometimes taken from Heinrich Denzinger, *Compendium of Creeds, Definitions, and Declarations on Matters of Faith and Morals*, 43rd ed., ed. Peter Hünermann, ed. for English, Robert Fastiggi and Anne Englund Nash (San Francisco: Ignatius Press, 2012), §§3004–6 [hereafter: Denzinger].

24. Immanuel Kant's highly influential *Critique of Pure Reason* first appeared in 1781 with a revised second edition appearing in 1787. See Kant, *Critique of Pure Reason*, trans. N. K. Smith (New York: St. Martin's, 1965).

25. Immanuel Kant, *Religion within the Boundaries of Mere Reason*, trans. and ed. by A. Wood and G. di Giovanni (Cambridge: Cambridge University Press, 1998).

26. I am referring here to signs such as the perennial existence·of miracles, especially those of Christ and the apostles, but also those of the saints, up to the current age, the early spread of Christianity in the face of persecution, the perennial existence of the Catholic Church and its expansion through time and geographical place, the simultaneous inner consistency of the Church's teaching with its vibrancy of development in new situations, its capacity to make sense of otherwise obscure human enigmas, the Church's preservation of the natural law, which is marked by a demanding moral vision of perfection, the real moral perfection of the saints, and so forth. These signs do not provide knowledge of the mystery of Christ and the Church per se, which is accessible only supernaturally, but they do provide rational warrant for natural reason to treat the mystery as something coming from God, in his omnipotence, who provides to the human race outward signs of credibility that attest to the truth of revelation.

ner nature to seek the truth about God, which in turn affects their capacity
to live in harmony with one another.

The Church, responding to European ideologies of secularization,
would continue to develop this viewpoint, particularly in Leo XIII's great
encyclical on Thomism, *Aeterni Patris* (1879); in Pius X's seminary curriculum; in Pius XII's encyclical *Humani Generis* (1950); in Vatican II's *Gaudium
et Spes* (1965); and in John Paul II's encyclical *Fides et Ratio* (1998). The latter
document stresses that the Church's classical philosophical tradition is mul-
tivalent and not monolithic. It has given rise to forms of modern expression
other than those derived from scholasticism, as we see in influential philosophical figures like Blaise Pascal, John Henry Newman, Edith Stein, or Elis-
abeth Anscombe. However, at the heart of the Church's philosophical tradition (or family of approaches) there is a genuine openness to the study of
being in its fullness. This means that any philosophy genuinely compatible
with Christian revelation (and not therefore inherently secularizing) must
be able to speak about the transcendental dimensions of reality, the enigma
of the origins of being, the transcendent God, the dignity of human personhood, and the concept of human nature.[27] Divine revelation challenges human reason to rise to its highest dimensions, under the influence of grace,
and to reach out toward the absolute.

The Church in the modern era also supplemented her stance on the rationality of belief in God with a deepened diagnostic and counter-genealogy
of the origins of atheism, indifferentism, and secular culture. The intellect
matters, but the will and the formation of desires also play a key role in
persons and cultures. This means that when the will is elevated by grace
to seek the truth about God, one can embrace a religious pathway of seek-

---

27. Pope John Paul II addresses this union of anthropology and metaphysical reflection in the
search for God in his 1998 encyclical on faith and reason, *Fides et Ratio*, as follows: "(Here) I want
only to state that reality and truth do transcend the factual and the empirical, and to vindicate the
human being's capacity to know this transcendent and metaphysical dimension in a way that is
true and certain, albeit imperfect and analogical. In this sense, metaphysics should not be seen
as an alternative to anthropology, since it is metaphysics which makes it possible to ground the
concept of personal dignity in virtue of [the human being's] spiritual nature. In a special way, the
person constitutes a privileged locus for the encounter with being, and hence with metaphysical enquiry." In this connection, the pope speaks about "the need for a philosophy of *genuinely
metaphysical* range ... capable, that is, of transcending empirical data in order to attain something
absolute, ultimate and foundational in its search for truth. This requirement is implicit in sapiential
and analytical knowledge alike; and in particular it is a requirement for knowing the moral good,
which has its ultimate foundation in the Supreme Good, God himself." John Paul II, Encyclical
Letter *Fides et Ratio* (Washington, D.C.: USCCB Publishing, 2008 [reprint]), §83.

ing and self-discipline. When the heart is turned toward merely earthly goods, the speculative mind often follows suit and interprets all of reality in a non-religious way. When this is the case, secular rationality can be tinged with a good measure of irrationality, based on misplaced desires, fear, and hopelessness. Instead of measuring reality in light of God, one measures reality in light of man as the principle being (Feuerbach). Instead of seeking justice with God as the ultimate horizon of history, one places hope in the progress of the sciences and in the political state as the ultimate vehicle to address the human situation (Marx). Instead of a will to the truth and a will to love authentically, one falls into the illusory subjectivism of a will to power and individual creativity, divorced from friendship with others and just responsibility for the common good (Nietzsche). Instead of accepting man's capacity to hope in a transcendent good in the face of evil and death, one recedes into animality, and despair of the transcendent paternity of God (Freud). Instead of encouraging the search for God, and instead of seeing God as the transcendent author and guarantee of human dignity and freedom, one resigns one's self to the culture of public agnosticism, selective tolerance, and therapeutic material comforts (liberal secularism). This latter culture masks a state of collective spiritual acedia.[28]

Behind this form of argument is the *theological* acknowledgment (taken especially from Aquinas) that sin and disordered desire can inhibit the true knowledge of God and the desire for a religious resolution to the mystery of human existence. The aversion to God and to the true practice of religion is a consequence of original sin, and this tendency can be augmented by various "social structures of sin" in a given culture, especially in a cultural setting that is areligious or secularist. For the magisterium's emphasis on how our natural limitations and disordered desires can affect our ability to arrive at natural knowledge of God, of especial significance is Pius XII's encyclical *Humani Generis*, §§2–4, a text in which we can also observe the influence of Thomas Aquinas:

It is not surprising that such discord and error should always have existed outside the fold of Christ. For though, absolutely speaking, human reason by its own natural force and light can arrive at a true and certain knowledge of the one per-

---

28. For gentle versions of this kind of existential apologetics, see Second Vatican Council, *Gaudium et Spes*, §§1–22 (Denzinger 4301–22); Henri de Lubac, *The Drama of Atheist Humanism*, trans. M. Sebanc (San Francisco: Ignatius, 1995); Étienne Gilson, *L'athéisme difficile* (Paris: Vrin, 2014).

sonal God, who by His providence watches over and governs the world, and also of the natural law, which the Creator has written in our hearts, still there are not a few obstacles to prevent reason from making efficient and fruitful use of its natural ability. The truths that have to do with God and the relations between God and men, completely surpass the sensible order and demand self-surrender and self-abnegation in order to be put into practice and to influence practical life. Now the human intellect, in gaining the knowledge of such truths is hampered both by the activity of the senses and the imagination, and by evil passions arising from original sin. Hence men easily persuade themselves in such matters that what they do not wish to believe is false or at least doubtful.

It is for this reason that divine revelation must be considered morally necessary so that those religious and moral truths which are not of their nature beyond the reach of reason in the present condition of the human race, may be known by all men readily with a firm certainty and with freedom from all error.

Furthermore, the human intelligence sometimes experiences difficulties in forming a judgment about the credibility of the Catholic faith, notwithstanding the many wonderful external signs God has given, which are sufficient to prove with certitude by the natural light of reason alone the divine origin of the Christian religion. For man can, whether from prejudice or passion or bad faith, refuse and resist not only the evidence of the external proofs that are available, but also the impulses of actual grace.[29]

To undertake an authentic, rational search to know and understand God, certain cultural conditions are of great assistance. Let us focus on two most especially:

The first condition is the cultural interest in the search for God. Philosophical knowledge of God is best preserved in religious traditions, particularly that of Catholic Christianity, that seek to maintain a living practice of natural reasoning about God, based on the evidences of the created order and the human condition. Of greatest importance here is a living ecclesial culture of grace, of the knowledge of God provided by faith, sacramental worship, and sanctity. Why is a culture of faith so important for the purity and health of human reason? The graces of faith, hope, and charity orient the mind and heart toward God and in doing so provide human beings with an interior impulse to consider God not only theologically, but also philosophically. In this sense grace heals and elevates nature, while in its absence nature tends to curve in on itself. Consequently those who practice philosophy outside of a culture of grace often become locked in immanen-

---

29. Pius XII, Encyclical Letter *Humani Generis*, §§2–4, translated text available from www .vatican.va.

tistic analysis of the material world alone, or of human political problems. In a real sense, it is the saints in the modern world who make the most eloquent case for the intellectual viability of the search for God, as a result of the realism of their way of life, that is to say, the reality with which they acknowledge and manifest the presence of God in their actions, sufferings, and character.[30]

The second condition is the creative preservation of the theological and philosophical heritage of Catholic Christianity, such that the Christian understanding of God is made intelligible and meaningful in academic venues. Here particularly, the pursuit of genuine metaphysical understanding of God is important, as is a contact with the time-tested sources—biblical, patristic, and scholastic—of philosophical and theological belief in God. I have noted above how modern Catholic teaching has emphasized this element.

Finally, the Church has noted within the context of secular democratic societies that the foundations of human political life are rooted in the acknowledgment of human dignity, in the integrity of family life, in the respect of human freedom, in the public search for the truth (in universities and in the arts), and in the recognition of an objective order of justice in view of the common good. These are all realities that can be identified by natural reason as ethical goods, if one acknowledges the human being's capacity for objective understanding of the metaphysical structures of reality.[31] A culture that is deeply affected by traditions of philosophical skepticism cannot identify what is proper to human beings as such (as rational and free creatures, made in the likeness of God the Creator). In such a context, social confidence in both the unity of theoretical learning, and the objective foundations of universal morality, becomes highly contested, as the twentieth century political culture of ideologies and contemporary trends in post-modernism attest. Therefore, it is far from obvious that we can establish a free and tolerant society only if we first reject religious traditions and classical philosophy. In some ways, the twentieth century serves as an instructive illustration of the contrary idea. The ideologies that have arisen in the wake of secularization can be even more destructive than the negative powers unleashed in the wars of religion.[32]

---

30. One may think here of Edith Stein, who converted to Catholicism as a result of reading the autobiography of St. Teresa of Àvila.

31. John Paul II, Encyclical Letter *Veritatis Splendor* (Washington D.C.: USCCB Publishing, 1993), §§98–101.

32. See, for example, John Paul II, Encyclical Letter *Centesimus Annus* (1991), §46: "The

If one acknowledges the nature and dignity of the human being as a rational free creature oriented toward societal communion in the common good, then one is also very likely to perceive the religious origin and destiny of the human person. The human person has irreducible dignity because he or she is a spiritual being possessing an orientation toward truth and love that transcends mere material objects and animal life. If one reduces the human being to mere matter, as a random arrangement of material parts, or even merely to organic animality of a highly evolved kind, then the dignity of human beings and the ethical foundations of political life are rendered obscure. Nor does the realistic acknowledgment of a transcendent and sacred foundation of human dignity require either the aspiration to theocracy or the imposition of intolerant religious obligations on non-religious human persons. On the contrary, precisely because God has created human beings in his image as free and truth seeking, they have a dignity that is inviolable, particularly in regard to their religious conscience, which is the seat of the

---

Church values the democratic system inasmuch as it ensures the participation of citizens in making political choices, guarantees to the governed the possibility both of electing and holding accountable those who govern them, and of replacing them through peaceful means when appropriate. Thus she cannot encourage the formation of narrow ruling groups which usurp the power of the State for individual interests or for ideological ends. Authentic democracy is possible only in a State ruled by law, and on the basis of a correct conception of the human person. It requires that the necessary conditions be present for the advancement both of the individual through education and formation in true ideals, and of the 'subjectivity' of society through the creation of structures of participation and shared responsibility. Nowadays there is a tendency to claim that agnosticism and skeptical relativism are the philosophy and the basic attitude which correspond to democratic forms of political life. Those who are convinced that they know the truth and firmly adhere to it are considered unreliable from a democratic point of view, since they do not accept that truth is determined by the majority, or that it is subject to variation according to different political trends. It must be observed in this regard that if there is no ultimate truth to guide and direct political activity, then ideas and convictions can easily be manipulated for reasons of power. As history demonstrates, a democracy without values easily turns into open or thinly disguised totalitarianism. Nor does the Church close her eyes to the danger of fanaticism or fundamentalism among those who, in the name of an ideology which purports to be scientific or religious, claim the right to impose on others their own concept of what is true and good. *Christian truth* is not of this kind. Since it is not an ideology, the Christian faith does not presume to imprison changing socio-political realities in a rigid schema, and it recognizes that human life is realized in history in conditions that are diverse and imperfect. Furthermore, in constantly reaffirming the transcendent dignity of the person, the Church's method is always that of respect for freedom. But freedom attains its full development only by accepting the truth. In a world without truth, freedom loses its foundation and man is exposed to the violence of passion and to manipulation, both open and hidden. The Christian upholds freedom and serves it, constantly offering to others the truth which he has known (cf. John 8:31–32), in accordance with the missionary nature of his vocation. While paying heed to every fragment of truth which he encounters in the life experience and in the culture of individuals and of nations, he will not fail to affirm in dialogue with others all that his faith and the correct use of reason have enabled him to understand." (Translation from www.vatican.va.)

human being's deepest discernment and elective decision-making.[33] This is the case even or especially when human beings find themselves in religious error, whether innocently or through willful neglect, since the person who is in error is still a free subject, who can seek and embrace the truth only if he or she does so freely. Finally, the recognition that God is the cause of the structures of nature and of the human community, with its political dimension, provides impetus to encourage and respect those structures of nature (including the relative autonomy of deliberative processes, and civic forms of government that make use of public participation, open debate, and free expression). This process can occur in distinction from the Church without separation.[34] Christianity can serve as a healthy influence in society, an influence that strengthens common life by instilling education, virtue, and love. The Church can support the state by underscoring the centrality of the natural law, by promoting the family and education, and by supporting political justice in view of the common good. This process includes the Church's work of ecumenism and interreligious dialogue, which seeks to identify ways that people with partially convergent viewpoints can cooperate in view of common natural ends, despite their differences. The state, meanwhile, can act to protect and even promote the religious freedom, education, and the cultural activity of believers. It should recognize that matters of divine revelation and Christian practice transcend its competence, and work to accommodate the peaceful coexistence of religious and non-religious people. The Christian religious tradition and modern governmental life, then, need not be framed as standing in mutual opposition, but should be understood as mutually complementary phenomena.

CONCLUSION

In sum, significant challenges have arisen in modernity to the perennial Catholic affirmation of the rationality of belief in the mystery of God. These challenges were fueled especially by the rise of anti-metaphysical philosophical traditions that followed in the wake of nominalism and scientism, and were accorded further impetus by the rise of political secularism and the ever-increasing marginalization of the Christian religion from

33. See Second Vatican Council, *Dignitatis Humanae.*
34. See the thematic argument to this effect in the Second Vatican Council document, *Gaudium et Spes.*

the public square. In response to these challenges, the Church has ever
anew stressed human reason's innate capacity for natural knowledge of God
and the rational warrant for belief in positive divine revelation based on
signs of credibility. Coupled with this, she has also come to stress the importance of an existential analysis of human beings, one that acknowledges
the central role of love and of the will in determining how a given person
or culture is open or closed to the sacred. Correspondingly, the Church has
articulated an existential apologetics affirming that the deepest aspirations
of the mind and heart can be fulfilled only by grace and revealed truth. She
has also emphasized that modern democratic cultures, in order to support
the ethical imperatives that animate them, have essential need of the truths
of classical metaphysics. Human dignity has its ultimate foundation in the
spiritual nature of the human person, which in turn points us toward the
hidden mystery of the Creator. The Catholic tradition is in no way opposed
to a healthy political culture. On the contrary, realistic recognition that human beings are *capax Dei*, capable of God, provides one of the deepest motivations for the just respect of persons, solidarity among citizens, care of
the afflicted, and the collective pursuit of the common good.

3

The Revelation of the One God in Israel

Supernatural faith gives us the capacity to perceive the bible as the inspired Word of God and to hear it proclaimed by the tradition of the Church. Through the bible, we are invited into the divine answer to the human question of God, namely: God's revelation of himself to the people of Israel and, through them, to the world. In this chapter, we will approach the revelation of the one God in Israel, first, by considering briefly various kinds of divine names of God in the Old Testament scriptures. In these names we perceive an incipient revelation of the divine attributes. In the second place, we will look at God's revelation of himself to Moses in Exodus 3 as "I AM," and the incipiently metaphysical cast of this revelation, which invites a philosophical reflection on the revelation. In the last place, we will also turn to the question of the Old Testament *vestigia trinitatis*, or traces of the Trinity, that foreshadow its full revelation in the New Testament.

DIVINE NAMES, AND THE THEOLOGY OF DIVINE ATTRIBUTES

Israel's testimony to the unicity of God occurred against the backdrop of a world of religious diversity. Many of the cultures surrounding the ancient Israelites were characterized by polytheistic forms of religious belief. They promoted worship of a multiplicity of deities or pantheons of gods, and their cultures often contained diversified and incompatible religious practices. What is characteristic of the prophetic religion of Israel, of course, is that it promotes a strict form of covenantal monotheism, and the idea of unified cultic worship and legal observance of a collective chosen people. There is one God, who is the unique Creator of heaven and earth. God has revealed himself through prophets to the people of Israel and established a covenant with them in order to bring the truth of salvation to the whole human race. It follows from this perspective that the bible (the Old Testament scripture) is necessarily concerned with the question of what God is, and what God is not. At the center of biblical revelation is the question of the attributes of God.[1]

The Old Testament is a diverse assemblage of writings composed over a vast span of time by authors in diverse historical settings, often edited from preexisting bodies of text or oral traditions.[2] Consequently, one can wonder if it can be read at all in a conceptually unified way so as to speak of the one God of Israel and his attributes. This problem is compounded when scholars posit the hypothesis of a gradual development within ancient Israelite religion of strict monotheism, from the era of the patriarchs to Sinai and the settlement, to the Davidic monarchy, Deuteronomical reform, post-exilic reformation, and the epoch of Second Temple Judaism.[3]

---

1. Various influential modern interpretations of Old Testament theology were developed by Protestant thinkers in the twentieth century, sometimes deeply influenced by or in conversation with the thought of Karl Barth. Barth himself offers a critical re-reading of the divine attributes, in his *Church Dogmatics* [hereafter *CD*], trans. and ed. G. W. Bromiley and T. F. Torrance, 4 vols. (Edinburgh: T&T Clark, 1936–75), 2:1. See especially in this respect Walther Eichrodt, *Theology of the Old Testament*, 2 vols. (Philadelphia: Westminster, 1961); Gerhard von Rad, *Old Testament Theology*, 2 vols. (New York: Harper & Row, 1962); Brevard Childs, *Biblical Theology of the Old and New Testaments: Theological Reflection on the Christian Bible* (Minneapolis, Minn.: Fortress, 1992); Walter Brueggemann, *Theology of the Old Testament: Testimony, Dispute, Advocacy* (Minneapolis, Minn.: Fortress, 2012). It is significant that Catholic biblical scholars have more rarely attempted such projects. This fact may not be accidental, as it suggests that the Catholic tradition recognizes that the Old Testament has to be interpreted within the larger tradition of New Testament, patristic, and scholastic authors, in conversation with acquisitions of the magisterium. This reception process need not require one to ignore the complexities and historical developments within and subsequent to the composition of the biblical text. Of the Protestant theologians mentioned above, the work of Eichrodt and Childs stand out as particularly compatible with Catholic sensibilities, since each in his own way treats the biblical canon as inviting us to a thematically unified vision of the mystery of God, and each defends in his own way the continuity of the biblical text and the classical interpretations of subsequent Christian tradition.

2. For modern historical studies of ancient Israel that promote a moderate conservative presentation of the historical events, see Bernhard W. Anderson, *Understanding the Old Testament*, 5th ed. (New York: Pearson, 2006); Roland de Vaux, *The Early History of Israel*, 2 vols., trans. D. Smith (London: Darton,1978). I am presuming in this presentation a relatively traditional view of the historical unfolding of Israel, though this is a topic subject to great debate. That being said, much of the theological argument of this chapter is unaffected by questions of the precise unfolding of Old Testament events and composition of the text.

3. I take it that some such form of historical development exists. In its broad outlines, we can

see the emergence of the strict monotheism that characterizes Judaism over the course of various broad stages.

The first stage is that of *patriarchal religion*, which we ascribe to the very ancient, first ancestors of the Hebrew people, Abraham, Isaac, and Jacob. The religion of Israel's patriarchs developed in a region where there were local shrines to particular deities. Genesis portrays the emergence of ancient Israelite religion as occurring within this context (of shrines to various deities), but also implies a transformation of that same culture due to the imparting of new, divine revelation. The shrines of the patriarchs are founded to mark the event of their personal encounter with the living God of divine revelation. He who is the God of Israel, and the Creator of the world, also reveals himself to the patriarchs as a God of personal revelation, and, in his historical providence, he associates himself with a particular tribal people.

The next stage consists in the early Mosaic movement and the settlement of Israel as a people. It is witnessed to in the cycle of narratives that extends from Exodus to Joshua. Here, we see the primitive Mosaic religious movement that promotes a strict devotion to the Lord, YHWH, who is the only God and Savior of Israel. Acknowledgment of the Lord has as its context the *mirabilia Dei*—the wonderful works of God's deliverance of the Israelites from Egypt—and the successive covenant with Israel that is given at Mount Sinai. The early settlement of Israel was influenced by this religious movement.

The third stage is that of the pre-monarchic tribal society of Israel, which eventually gave way to the monarchies of Saul, David, and Solomon. Books like Judges, and 1 and 2 Samuel, evoke images of Yahwehistic worship, prophetic activity, and an increasingly centralized governance of the people, undergirded by messianic ideas of kingship.

The fourth stage arises from Israel's struggle with Canaanite religion and the cultic worship of Ashteroth and Baal, which served as the occasion for theological development in ancient Israel. Particularly in the eighth to sixth centuries B.C., the Deuteronomistic reform emphasizes the unique reality of the God of Israel. The real fidelity of the God of the covenant *as the living and true God* is seen in contrast to the gentile gods. It is the Lord YHWH who governs history, and the worship of alien gods constitutes a capital sin of idolatry. Idolatry is understood as a form of spiritual infidelity and represents an injustice toward God.

The fifth stage talks place over the course of the sixth-century B.C. Babylonian exile, during which time there was a development of thinking and prophetic insight regarding monotheism. Paradoxically, it was within the context of an experience of serious political marginalization and near extinction that the Israelites attained new understanding of the unicity of God, the Lord YHWH, as the Creator, and understood the uniqueness of their covenant within the context of God's universal saving activity. The author of Second Isaiah, for example, elaborates a monotheism of creation and universal government. A similar theology of God's universal reign and his particular love of Israel is found in the prophet Ezekiel (who focuses on God's universal governance in view of the reconstruction of God's particular gift to Israel of the Temple in Jerusalem) and anticipates later prophetic works, like that of Daniel (who foresees the messianic vindication of Israel as a way that God will address all the nations).

The sixth stage occurs during the third to first centuries B.C., as Israelite scribes begin to interact with Greek philosophical traditions. Here, we witness the organic integration of two traditions of thought. Biblical monotheism increasingly comes to be articulated through the medium of Hellenistic terms: more distinctly philosophical descriptions are given for the attributes for God. We see this for example in the Septuagint translation of the Hebrew scriptures, in the book of Sirach, and the book of Wisdom. One can note that the integration of these two traditions does not entail capitulation to Greek polytheism, or religious customs. On the contrary: later works like Maccabees, Sirach, and Wisdom all contain acute critiques of pagan religious beliefs and practices.

The final stage comes with the emergence of what we might call New Testament monotheism. The New Testament is decidedly monotheistic, even as it affirms the divinity of the Son and the Spirit. In this respect, there is a profound continuity between the two testaments. The

Thematic Unity of the Canonical Text

Our aim in this chapter is not to enter into questions of historical composition of the books of the Old Testament. However, we can note here three essential points of theological orientation for reading the scriptures as a whole, particularly in regard to the mystery of God. First, *canonicity*: the bible is read in its unity as a canon by the Church, who has received it from the people of Israel, and who considers it inspired by the Holy Spirit. This means that the book is recognized as a unified witness to revelation and a guiding measure of the internal content of revelation, even in the midst of this conceptual plurality and complex history of composition and transmission. Because the book was assembled in a unified way over the course of centuries, its canonical unity is a historical and literary fact, as well as a mystery of faith.[4] Second, *prophetic perspective*: whether the books of the bible were composed and assembled earlier or later in history, the ultimate perspective accorded by inspired authors and editors allows us to see the world supernaturally in light of God.[5] For example, whether the Torah has a deeply ancient origin in the Moses movement, or is largely a product of post-exilic redaction is important from a historical and textual point of view, but, theologically speaking, the divine author (the Holy Spirit) can provide us with an overview of God and his relation to Israel from either vantage point, as sowing seeds in Mosaic revelation that would sprout in the later prophets, or as looking back in light of the exilic prophets to re-read the pre-history of the patriarchs and the exodus in light of the subse-

---

monotheism of the New Testament, one might even claim, is even yet more refined than that of the Old Testament, as it offers an unparalleled and absolutely sublime acknowledgment of the transcendence and majesty of God the Creator and Redeemer.

4. On the theology of canonicity, see the suggestive remarks of Joseph Ratzinger, *Biblical Interpretation in Crisis: On the Question of the Foundations and Approaches of Exegesis Today* (New York: Rockford, 1988), who is inspired in turn by Brevard Childs, *Old Testament Theology in a Canonical Context* (Philadelphia: Fortress Press, 1985). See also R. W. L. Moberly, *Old Testament Theology: Reading the Hebrew Bible as Christian Scripture* (Grand Rapids, Mich.: Baker Academic, 2013); John Goldingay, *Old Testament Theology*, 3 vols. (Downers Grove, Ill.: IVP Academic, 2003–9).

5. See the helpful analysis of inspiration offered by Pierre Benoit in *Aspects of Biblical Inspiration*, trans. J. Murphy-O'Connor and K. Ashe (Chicago: Priory Press, 1965); and Pierre Benoit and P. Synave in *Prophecy and Inspiration: A Commentary on the "Summa Theologica" II-II, Questions 171–178*, trans. A. Dulles and T. Sheridan (New York: Desclée, 1961); Bernhard Blankenhorn, "God Speaks: Divine Authorship of Scripture in Karl Rahner and Pierre Benoit," *Angelicum* 93, no. 3 (2016): 445–62; and the wider background study on tradition by Yves Congar, *Tradition and Traditions: An Historical and a Theological Essay*, trans. M. Naseby and T. Rainborough (London: Burnes & Oates, 1966).

quent illumination. Either way, the history of Israel is a history by which the people came to know the one God, the Creator, as their God, who chose them by grace to live in a distinct covenant with him.[6] Third, *unity of divine naming*: many poetic, ontological, and functional attributes are ascribed to the Lord of Israel in the course of the various scriptural texts. Tensions or seeming contradictions can arise as one considers the various names and designations of God in the Old Testament. However, if there were such tensions present historically, they were ones that ancient editors did not refuse to accept but purposefully retained. This means that they presupposed a deeper thematic unity present amidst the historical and literary diversity, one that could be openly debated and evinced through a dialectical and rational process.[7] The structure of the bible itself, then, invites debate and reflection about the divine attributes. Ancient Jewish and Christian commentators embarked precisely upon this process from earliest times, and it is something basic to Christian theology.

Kinds of Names: Poetic Metaphors,
Proper Analogies, and Personal Names

The divine names given to God in the Old Testament are diverse not only textually and diachronically, based on a complex history of original narrative settings and eventual editing processes; they are diverse also based on genera or kind, since God is named in various modes in the Old Testament. This polyphony of modes is like a music filled with movement and tensions. It should be heard as a harmony, but we first must be able to identify the different notes and discern the unity among them. The names given to God in the bible can be of three general types: some are overtly poetic or metaphorical, some suggest analogies by which we name God's nature literally or in the strict sense, and some are personal titles by which God is addressed in second-person speech.[8] Let us consider each of these in turn.

6. I am presuming that there is a historical foundation for God's election of Israel, from the patriarchal age, to the exodus, to the history of prophets, the monarchy, the temple, etc.

7. See, on this point, the suggestive literary reflections of Northrop Frye, *The Great Code: The Bible and Literature* (London: Routledge & Kegan Paul, 1982).

8. In *ST* I, q. 13, Aquinas treats as various names of God metaphorical expressions (God is not literally a warrior but may be said to be one metaphorically) as well as analogies (said literally or properly of God: God literally is wise and good, but not in precisely the same way as creatures are), and proper titles (personal names: YHWH). I will consider the analogical naming of God in greater detail in this work, but it is worth nothing that, for Aquinas, divine naming is not reducible merely to analogical, literal speech. It also includes metaphorical titles. [All quotations from

Early in the Christian tradition it was noted that God is depicted in the Old Testament under a variety of poetic, metaphorical expressions, while other names can be applied to him in himself, by a kind of proper or literal analogy. For example, Genesis 3:8 depicts God walking in the garden of Eden. Exodus 15:1–18 speaks of God by employing ancient warrior poetry. God exhibits emotional regret in Genesis 6:6 and heated wrath in Exodus 32:10. He is spoken of as a spouse to unfaithful Israel in Hosea 2:1–23, and later in Ezekiel 16; or as a bridegroom in the *Song of Songs*. God is depicted as paternal (a father of Israel) in Isaiah 63:16 and as more compassionate than any mother in Isaiah 66:13. Sometimes God is depicted in quasi-corporeal terms as a man, for example in Exodus 24:11, where he participates in a communion meal with Israel on Mount Sinai, and in Ezekiel 1:26, and Daniel 7:9–14, where he appears in splendor and is seated on a throne. Ancient Christian interpretation perceived in these myriad images metaphorical depictions of God's proper attributes. He expresses his justice and mercy, for example, in his images of paternal education and maternal care, his wrath and compassion. They also perceived in corporeal images of the Lord a foreshadowing of the mystery of the Incarnation: that the God of Israel would take on human nature in Jesus.

Meanwhile, there are other terms ascribed to God that clearly are meant to evoke the truth about who God is in himself, as distinct from his creation. Here we are speaking of names given to God that signify literally what he is in himself, without metaphor. For example, Deuteronomy 6:4 affirms that God is one. "Hear, O Israel: The Lord our God is one Lord." This is said not poetically but "properly," by analogy. The unity that pertains to the God of Israel is distinct from that of any other created thing, and indeed any other "god," for he is unique in nature in a wholly higher and numinous way, proper to him in his transcendence. Likewise, the bible speaks of God as unique in being. God alone gives being to all things as Creator and receives being from no one (Ex 3:14–15; Is 45:5–13; Ps 102:24–25). His existence is unlike ours then, since everything depends upon him and is his gift. Again, God is somehow simpler than the created realities we experience, since he is not a composite physical body and cannot be depicted by images (Ex 20:4; Dt 4:15–16, 5:8). God is omnipresent: he is not spatially located, but he is present to all things (Is 66:1–2). He is from before all time and is eternal

---

the *Summa theologiae* are taken from *Summa Theologica*, trans. English Dominican Province (New York: Benziger, 1947).]

(Dt 32:40; Ps 90:2; Is 57:15). The goodness and beauty of creation derive from him, and therefore we must say that God possesses a hidden goodness and glory that have given rise to creation (Gn 1–2). He is the source of its order and intelligibility, so we ascribe wisdom to him (Jb 12:13; Prv 2:6; 1 Kgs 4:29). He is personal, and can freely disclose his hidden identity. However, we must attribute personal identity to him analogically, since he is not a created person. Rather, we are made in his image (Ezek 1:26; Gn 1:26–28; Wis 2:23). God's actions reveal him as one who is just and merciful, wise and loving (Ex 34:6–7). He is all-powerful or omnipotent (Jer 32:17; Ru 1:20; Jb 24:1). He possesses in himself eternal life, and he wishes to communicate life to human beings (Dt 5:26; Jer 21:8; 31:12; Ps 42:2). He transcends understanding and is incomprehensible, but is himself all-knowing and all-encompassing (Ps 145:3; 147:5; Is 40:12–13). God is radiant in holiness. His holiness is related to his transcendence. Because of his holiness, God is veiled in hiddenness but is also active in his saving designs (Lv 19:2; 21–24; Is 45:15; 1 Kgs 19:11–13).

Finally, we can speak of God's personal names, identity terms by which God is addressed as the personal Lord and friend of Israel. Some of these are nature terms that are used to speak of God personally. For example, God is often called "Elohim": the original word means "deities" or "pantheon." It has a pre-Hebraic linguistic history, and was used by non-Israelite religious traditions to signify the gods. However, ancient Israelites used the term to speak of the one God, much like the Latin Christian word for God, *Deus*, has a pre-history in the Graeco-Roman terminology for *Zeus*. In the bible, *Elohim* can be used, in second person speech, to address God personally or, in third person, to speak of him as an individual person. However, it does this by calling him, in effect, "the deity" much as one addresses God in English also by using a nature term ("O God, come to my assistance"), since, formally speaking, "God" signifies one who has divine nature. Elohim, like "God," then, is a nature term ("the deity") applied in personal way. Meanwhile, the term "Lord," *Adonai*, is a relational term. God is the sovereign Lord over that which he creates, since he is able to govern all things through his power, wisdom, and goodness. To call upon God personally as "Lord," in this sense, is to address him interpersonally as one to whom we are entirely relative. The Lord is he who has the power, wisdom, and goodness to save Israel and the world, and who alone ultimately governs all things. Finally, we should mention the proper name God reveals to Israel as his individual name in Exodus 3:15: YHWH, the tetragrammaton. This is a name that is given to Israel alone to utter, a personal name of friendship by which Israel as an elect people can call upon God. The term is generally veiled in writing and speech by the euphemism "Lord," so as to emphasize the holiness of the name and the privilege of Israel's election that it represents. A gloss on the inner meaning of the name is also offered in Exodus 3:14, which can be read to say of God, "I am He who is." The latter phrase can be read in other ways as well, such as "I will be who I will be." The significations derived from these readings can be multiple. One can take Exodus 3:14 to say something ontological: "I am he who alone has the fullness of being and who gives being to all others," or something ethical and fiduciary: "I am he who always will be and therefore will be faithful to Israel," or something apophatic: "I am the one who cannot be known due to my transcendence." These various significations are not opposed to one another and are in fact compatible. They are ways of thinking about the internal content of the personal name of God, YHWH, which is given to Israel alone. Israel is given to know personally he who alone truly is, the Creator of all things. God will be faithful to Israel in virtue of his abiding perfection, power, and perennial life. God remains hidden and unknown in his transcendence, incomprehensible and impossible to master, even for Israel, who lives in covenant with him.

BIBLICAL ONTOLOGY AS THE INVITATION TO A CHRISTIAN PHILOSOPHY OF GOD

The plurality of the divine names and their various modes of expression are given to us within the context of the Torah, which exemplifies God's covenant with Israel, as well as in prophetic writings, psalms, sacred histories, and other forms of wisdom literature. In other words, the revelation of God in ancient Israel occurs in an existential and soteriological context, in which God is first known by his effects, as one who initiates contact with Israel and inspires her writings about him. This does not mean, however, that God remains merely at the margins of the Old Testament, as if he were to give a law externally and then remain completely hidden from view. Rather, the point of the Law, prophets, and writings is to draw human beings into communion with God. God reveals himself to Israel and the Church in the economy so that we might come to know him personally, even if imperfectly and in the darkness of faith.

It might seem from what has just been said that our knowledge of God derived from the Old Testament must above all be scriptural and theological, in an exclusive sense, and cannot make use of philosophical reflection about God. However, the contrary is the case. In fact, the very diversity of the modes of divine naming mentioned above (poetic metaphors, literal analogies, personal titles) invites distinctly *theological* reflection on what God is in himself. If there is a real distinction between the poetic images of God and the analogies properly stated, then we can discern it only in and through reflection and debate. Is God literally good (said analogically) and does God symbolically walk in a garden (said metaphorically)? To ask such questions is to discern what is said of God literally by analogy and what is said metaphorically, and why the metaphors in turn complement and enrich the significations of the analogies.

In a certain sense, this decision to reflect on God ontologically is inscribed within the logic of biblical revelation itself. It is not only warranted, but intellectually mandated. Why? The issue pertains practically to right worship as distinct from error and idolatry. To speak of the God of Israel personally, as having a distinct identity in and through sacred history in the election of Israel, is to distinguish him realistically from the "gods" of other nations, and therefore to identify the unique knowledge Israel has attained of *who God truly is in his unity and in his divine attributes as Creator.* This is an essential feature of salvation. The biblical claims are intelligible only if in fact Israel's knowledge of the one true God is distinct from and, in a real sense, superior to that of all other nations and religions. But Israel's knowledge is superior precisely because this saving knowledge is knowledge of God (the divine nature). An aspect of Israel's original understanding of reality, then, is located in the bible's depiction of the divine attributes. What is said of God metaphorically, and what is said literally by analogy? If there is no way to distinguish, then God may in fact be the same as the other gods, and, in this sense, the claims of revelation are self-defeating. Nothing unique has occurred in Israel.

It follows from these arguments that there is a theological necessity to think about the divine attributes if one is to think about the identity and exclusive worship of the God of Israel. However, to think about God as one, as the unique Creator, as the source of goodness, order, and intelligibility in the world, and as the governing principle of all things, is *also* to think about God philosophically, since it requires us to reflect intelligently about how all things are derived from God, dependent upon God, and governed by him in view of ends that he designates. To be clear, we are not speaking here of a philosophy of God that replaces biblical revelation nor of a philosophical demonstration of the mystery of God in his election of Israel. Rather, we are speaking of ways that biblical revelation heals, purifies, and makes use of natural human reason. Reflection on the mysteries of faith (the *analogia fidei*) invites a development of reflection on God, as known by way of natural reasoning, of whom we can know something in light of his creation (the *analogia entis*). This biblically enlightened philosophy originally develops already within revelation, and continues afterward in the life of the Church, in the service of theology.

We can see this "philosophical" moment within biblical revelation under at least five thematic developments, all of which are convergent or complementary: wisdom in ancient Israel, the Isaian ontology of the divine name, features of the Septuagint translation, late Hellenistic biblical literature, and Second Temple Judaism eschatology. Let us consider each briefly.

First, we can note that in ancient Israel even before the exile, a form of wisdom literature developed in works like the Psalms and Proverbs, which interpreted Israel's unique vocation and relationship to YHWH in terms of a universal quest for wisdom.[9] The human being seeks wisdom about God and creation, and this wisdom has been given in an abundant way to Israel in light of its privileged relationship to God. The wisdom in question may often be characterized in practical and ethical terms, but the implication is that the general knowledge human beings have of the world and of human conduct can be perfected by the encounter with God and his revelation. This suggests that nature is inherently open (in obediential potency) to the initiatives of grace, and that natural inclinations to knowledge can come under the divine pedagogy of the law and the prophets.

Second, we should mention the Isaian ontology of the divine name. I am referring here to the theology of Deutero-Isaiah, whose author seemingly writes during the time of the Babylonian exile in the sixth century B.C.[10] He appeals to the name of God found in Exodus 3:14–15, which is given to Is-

9. See Gerhard von Rad, *Wisdom in Israel*, trans. J. D. Martin (Nashville, Tenn.: Abingdon Press, 1972); Hans Heinrich Schmid, "Creation, Righteousness, and Salvation: 'Creation Theology' as the Broad Horizon of Biblical Theology," in *Creation in the Old Testament*, ed. B. W. Anderson, 102–17 (Philadelphia: Fortress, 1984); Michael C. Legaspi, *Wisdom in Classical and Biblical Tradition* (Oxford: Oxford University Press, 2018).

10. See the analysis of Brueggemann, *Theology of the Old Testament*, 145–51.

rael alone, but he gives this name a deeply metaphysical interpretation that has a universal significance for all nations. For example, Isaiah 45:14–25 depicts "the Lord" (YHWH), the God of Israel, as the unique Creator of all things, the only true God of all peoples, whom Israel knows in a privileged way. Because he alone exists as the Creator of all else that is, he alone can save the human race. Salvation, therefore, comes through Israel. As interpreted by Isaiah 45:18, the name of God found in Exodus 3:14–15 is now seen to connote an exclusive divine transcendence and existence. "For thus says the Lord, who created the heavens (he is God!), who formed the earth and made it (he established it; he did not create it a chaos, he formed it to be inhabited!): 'I am the Lord, and there is no other.'"

Third, then, the second-century B.C. Greek translation of these passages in the Septuagint highlighted the possibility of a metaphysical interpretation. Thus, the name of God in Exodus 3:14 was rendered: ἐγώ εἰμι ὁ ὤν, which can be translated into English as: "I am He who is," or "I am He who is Being."[11] The Septuagint version of Isaiah 45:18 mirrored this ontological reading of the divine name: ἐγώ εἰμι Κύριος καὶ οὐκ ἔστιν ἔτι, "I AM the Lord—or: I AM He who IS—and there is no other."[12] In the light of the ambient Hellenism of that epoch, this translation conveys a clear conceptual interface with the philosophical inclinations of Greek thought. What the Greeks obliquely seek to discover by the study of being is "He who is," the one who has revealed himself to Israel most perfectly. Therefore, the Greeks seek wisdom in a real but imperfect manner, and worship God as one yet unknown. However, their aspiration toward philosophical knowledge of the deity, even in its frustrations and seeming futility, shows our innate capacity for, or openness to, a higher knowledge of God, one given by God himself to Israel through the law and prophets.

Fourth, this way of thinking is developed in late Hellenistic biblical literature, in books such as Sirach and Wisdom. In these late works that come just before the New Testament period, we see the purposeful engagement

11. See the rendering of Ex 3:14, "ἐγώ εἰμι ὁ Ὤν," in *The Septuagint with Apocrypha: Greek and English*, trans. Sir Lancelot C. L. Brenton (Peabody, Mass.: Hendrickson Publishers, 1992), 73: "I am the Be-ing." On the Hebrew roots of the divine name YHWH as either a *qal* verb meaning "he exists" or as a *hiphil* verb inflection of the root that could mean "He causes to exist," see F. M. Cross, "Yahweh and the God of the Patriarchs," *Harvard Theological Review* 55, no. 4 (1962): 225–59, and my discussion in Thomas Joseph White, *Exodus*, (Grand Rapids, Mich.: Brazos, 2016), 41–43. If either of these interpretations is correct, there is a ground for conceptual continuity between the Hebrew bible and Septuagint renderings of the divine name.

12. For the Greek of the Septuagint, see *The Septuagint with Apocrypha*, 887.

with Greek philosophical ideas, which are sometimes employed in order to express biblical notions. God is depicted in his transcendence as one who has wisdom, through which he creates all things and governs them in view of their various ends. Israel has a distinct place within the order of creation, but all that exists is in some way indicative of the mystery of God, and there is a similitude or analogy between all things and God, insofar as the creatures that are his effects resemble their hidden cause and ground of being. The book of *Wisdom* also speaks of the immateriality and afterlife of the human soul, suggesting that there is a particular analogy of similitude between the human being and God based on the *Imago Dei*, which is immaterial in nature.[13] This idea prefigures the seeming doctrine of personal immortality in Paul's teaching (Phil 1:22–24), and the patristic exploration of the immaterial powers of intellect and will as particular indications of the image of God in the human person.

Finally, we can speak of Second Temple Judaism eschatology and its implicit or explicit appeals to the doctrine of creation. Post-exilic Judaic authors had to confront the question of the fate of the afterlife in a distinctive way. This questioning was provoked by the witness of martyrs first during the times of the exile, and then subsequently in the post-exilic age, when Hellenistic and Roman powers killed practitioners of Judaism for their fidelity to the law. What is the fate of such persons, if they are not vindicated in this life? How will Israel be publicly vindicated in the final age, as an elect people of God, if her monarchy has been dissolved by foreign political powers? Here the eschatological authors appealed to the creative power and righteousness of the God of Israel, his omnipotence and justice. God will vindicate Israel in the end times because he is the universal God of all the nations (Dn 7:1–14). The martyrs and the just are in the hands of God (Wis 3:1–9). God has the power to raise the dead because he has created all things from nothing (2 Mc 7:28). Therefore, protology and eschatology go together. The one who has made all things has the power to remake all things. If he is the original author of all that is intelligible and good, then so too he can refashion all things in accord with his creative power and righteousness.[14]

---

13. Wis 2:23: "... for God created man for incorruption, and made him in the image of his own eternity..." Wis 3:1–4: "But the souls of the righteous are in the hand of God, and no torment will ever touch them. In the eyes of the foolish they seemed to have died, and their departure was thought to be an affliction, and their going from us to be their destruction; but they are at peace. For though in the sight of men they were punished, their hope is full of immortality."

14. In the early twentieth century, the German liberal Protestant theologian and intellectual

TRINITARIAN ADUMBRATIONS:
GOD'S WORD, WISDOM, AND SPIRIT

Before we consider the New Testament revelation of the Trinity, we should inquire whether there are any indications of processions in God in the Old Testament. By this I mean, do we see anywhere in the Old Testament a fore-

historian Adolf von Harnack formalized the idea of a "Hellenization" that occurred in the early Church, especially in the course of the first five centuries, when the Church formulated its principal dogmas regarding the Trinity and the person of Christ. According to von Harnack, early Christianity was progressively corrupted or mixed heterogeneously with Hellenistic philosophy and metaphysics in the course of this process. (For a distillation of the viewpoint, see Adolf von Harnack, *What Is Christianity?*, trans. T. Saunders [Philadelphia: Fortress Press, 1957].) The early Christological councils are therefore an unsound mix of Greek ontology and primitive Christian understanding. They enshroud God and Jesus of Nazareth in artificial dogmas and thus separate us from the "real" historical Jesus, which modern critical study seeks to rediscover. Harnack focuses on Jesus' ethical example as a man, and his spiritual relationship to God as his father. He is depicted primarily as a significant religious genius, a courageous individual who taught the human race the love of God and neighbor, but not as one who is the pre-existent eternal Son of God made man. A further corollary of this idea is that the Hebrew bible is something that we need to see as initially immune to Greek philosophy. The God of the Hebrew bible is decidedly not the God of the philosophers. It was the mistaken attempt of patristic authors to interpret the scriptures metaphysically, using Greek philosophy, that led to the hypostatization of Jesus as being one with God.

Harnack's general hypothesis is difficult to maintain, simply on a factual level, because it is historically inaccurate on several fronts. For one thing, the New Testament repeatedly ascribes ontological terms to Christ that clearly denote belief in his pre-existence and divinity, as well as his historical humanity. Therefore, the ontological claims of the later Church have a clear basis in the teachings of the New Testament itself. (We will return to this topic below.) Likewise, von Harnack's rigid conceptual bifurcation of scripture and Greek metaphysics is untenable and should be rejected merely for reasons of historical accuracy. The reality is much more complex. As noted briefly above, the Old Testament scriptures are already implicitly "ontological" or metaphysical in their way of speaking of God, and this means they have intrinsic points of contact with the Hellenistic philosophy. These connections were explored during the age of Second Temple Judaism, centuries prior to Christ's coming. This led to Judaic reformulations of Greek ontological ideas, not their mere uncritical assimilation, and this process continues in the New Testament itself (which criticizes Graeco-Roman views of God as mistaken). (See, on this point, the landmark work of Martin Hengel, *Judaism and Hellenism: Studies in their Encounter in Palestine During the Early Hellenistic Period* [London: SCM Press, 2012].) This kind of qualified use of Greek philosophy on the part of Christians and Jews in antiquity inspired in turn the missionary works of the early Christian apologists like Justin Martyr, Clement of Alexandria, and Augustine, who communicated biblical ideas to their contemporaries by making use of philosophical notions. Nor is von Harnack's "post-Hellenistic" reading of the bible as pure or "philosophically innocent" as it might seem. In fact, those who appeal to von Harnack tend to create a typological dialectic that is based on a Hegelian interpretation of the bible: the active/reactive God of a modern Hegelian theology is now seen as the true God of the bible, and is contrasted with the God of the patristic and scholastic theologians, thinkers who strongly emphasized the ontological transcendence of God (divine aseity). Under the banner of "dehellenization," a new god of historical immanence is substituted for the Church's traditional understanding of God, derived from the early Church. On Harnack and Hellenization, see also Pope Benedict XVI, "Faith, Reason and the University: Memories and Reflections" (Regensburg Address), September 12, 2006 (the translation can be found online, at www.vatican.va.).

shadowing of the New Testament revelation of the persons of the Trinity, namely, the eternal Word of the Father and the Holy Spirit? The traditional view of Catholic theologians is that there are indeed indications of the Trinity in the Old Testament, but these indications are only implicit and not overt. The higher prophets of the Old Testament era may have foreseen the Incarnation of God in explicit ways, but their writings do not make this mystery completely apparent. Consequently, we can interpret Old Testament language for the Trinitarian processions retrospectively. These are features of the Israelite depiction of God that become clearer or come into focus *only* in light of the revelation of Christ and his Spirit in the New Testament.

These Old Testament adumbrations of the processions of persons revealed in the New can be seen, first of all, in the personification of the Wisdom of God in Proverbs, Sirach, and Wisdom. When the "Wisdom" of God is treated as a person in the literature of the Old Testament, the literary contexts typically suggest that the human author is speaking figuratively. However, the idea that God creates all things in his wisdom is a non-metaphorical claim. After all, God is wise and creates through his wisdom. One can ask, then, whether such passages could also imply a literal generation of wisdom in God, as a personal agent in whom God works. The personification of generated Wisdom as distinct from the Father can at the very least be understood in hindsight, in light of the New Testament, to denote implicitly the person of the Son and eternal Word.[15]

A second adumbration of the mystery of the Trinity is located in the Old Testament notion of God's Word that is active in creation and in the communication of prophecy. The Word of God is the principle of God's action, through which he has created the universe and through which he addresses man in his revelation.[16] This term, Word, is used in the New Testament to denote the eternal pre-existent Son of God, as we shall see.

In the third place, we should also mention the notion of the "Spirit of the Lord." In the Old Testament, the Spirit of the Lord is depicted as coming upon the prophets. The Spirit's task is to inspire or move the human person in accord with God's holiness.[17] The Spirit is a principle of divine action, one by which God communicates to Israel a participation in his wisdom and life.

If we consider these analogies together briefly, we can note that they

---

15. Especially important in this regard are Prv 8:12–14, 9:1; Sir 1:1–4; Wis 8:1–3.

16. Especially pertinent are Gn 1:3, 15:1; Dt 5:4–5; Is 2:3; 55:10–11; Jer 2:1–4; Wis 9:1.

17. See especially Jgs 3:10; 2 Sm 23:2; Is 11:2, 61:1; Ezek 43:5.

suggest three important theological possibilities. First, the analogies for God's inner life given by these terms are immaterial in kind: begotten wisdom, word or thought, spirit. These are terms of immaterial procession. Second, God expresses himself economically to Israel in his Word and Spirit. Consequently, we might say, God utters his Word and sends his Spirit. We see here an Old Testament foundation for the New Testament notion of the divine missions: the sending of the Son and the Spirit into the world. Finally, God has created all things in his Wisdom, so all that is depends upon the Wisdom of God. God gives knowledge of his own inner life through the Spirit of God. Therefore, the Wisdom and the Spirit of God do what only God can do. They are identical with God, in nature.

CONCLUSION

The form of monotheism that emerged within the religion of Israel was distinctive in its historical context and remains so today. Despite the historical complexity and textual variation that stands behind the Old Testament, we can and should read it as a unified inspired text, which allows us to see the world from God's perspective, and to know something of God in himself. While the depiction of God in Israel's scripture is not particularly systematic or philosophically speculative—as it is based more upon the revelation of God to Israel in the historical experience of the covenant made at Sinai—it nevertheless does have a dense and rich intellectual content. The various divine names and distinct modes of divine naming found in the text invite us to theological reflection. Accordingly, even within this revelation itself, we see the progressive acceptance and elaboration of a more "metaphysical" form of reflection upon the identity of God, the divine names and attributes, and the ways we can and cannot speak fittingly about the divine transcendence of God the Creator. In other words, the more "philosophical" approach we will see in the New Testament, and subsequently in the Greek and Latin patristic theologians, as well as the Catholic scholastic tradition, should not be seen as something alien to the divine revelation of the scriptures, but as something developing organically within Jewish and Christian tradition out of a more profound study of scripture itself. Finally, there are adumbrations of the Holy Trinity in the Old Testament and intimations of the Incarnation, which are finally understood perfectly only in light of the New Testament, which presents us with the fullness of revelation.

4

Foundations for Trinitarian Faith in the Life of Jesus Christ

TRINITARIAN DOCTRINE AND HISTORICAL INTERPRETATION OF THE NEW TESTAMENT

The mystery of the Holy Trinity is revealed in the New Testament, and the Church's Trinitarian dogma derives from this scriptural revelation. Simultaneously, the Church's tradition is necessary for an adequate interpretation of scripture. The Church's dogmas are subordinate to scripture, but are also necessary for us if we wish rightly to identify the revealed truth. They indicate the Church's collective discernment of the true mystery of God, acquired through a long history of theological investigation, arguments of schools, refutation of errors, and authoritative resolutions. We should consult the bible, then, to identify the foundation of the Church's teaching about God, even as we make use of the Church's tradition to interpret scripture.

What role does historical-critical consideration of the bible play in this process? From the beginning, the Christian believer reads the New Testament with the epistemological presupposition that Jesus of Nazareth is the pre-existent Son of God, who became human, who atoned for human sins by his death, and who has been resurrected and glorified as man, in his corporeal body and spiritual soul. This is fitting for three reasons. First, such truths cannot be conclusively demonstrated or falsified by mere unaided human reason, even when it makes use of the most sophisticated tools of historical-critical scrutiny of New Testament sources. The knowledge of such mysteries is given by faith, which allows one to perceive intuitively by a supernatural judgment that Jesus exists, is alive in the resurrection, and is one with the Father and the Holy Spirit as Lord. Second, the gift of faith is accorded to persons who first receive the truth from the Church, beginning with the apostles and their disciples, and this primal kerygma is maintained within the preaching and teaching of the Catholic Church. But this teaching itself enunciates the claims mentioned above even within a generation after the death of Christ, in the text of the New Testament. Therefore, one can receive these teachings originally only in their already completed formulation, as proposed by the apostles and their successors as ministers of God, and not by co-determining the content of the Gospel through a historical process of verification, critique, and theological or a-theological (anti-theological) reconstitution. Third, this supernatural standing of the Church's teaching with regard to Jesus of Nazareth provides the Catholic biblical scholar with a theologically informed way of thinking about the history of Jesus as it might have unfolded in time, even when he or she makes warranted use of modern historical-critical methods to construct a narrative life of Jesus in his original context. This fundamental theological commitment does not lessen the historical objectivity of the Catholic biblical scholar, however. On the contrary, if the mystery is real (God became human), then only a person who is so illuminated by faith and sacred tradition can study the historical reality with a sufficient objectivity, so as to be capable of understanding adequately the subject under investigation. Nor is any other alternative method of analysis free of presuppositions, since everyone has implicit philosophical and theological intuitions about what is possible and true in the realms of nature and history, and in regard to divine revelation. No methodologically "innocent" perspective, therefore, exists.

Simultaneously, however, there are also several reasons that historical critical study of the New Testament forms an integral part of Catholic Trinitarian theology. First, by its very affirmation that there is an organic development of doctrine, the Church acknowledges a developmental historicity of understanding that takes place within the deposit of faith, first within the economy of revelation itself, and subsequently in the age of the Church. Historical theology cannot reconstitute a comprehensive portrait of this development, but it can identify and indicate many of its key dimensions. Second, the study of diverse New Testament sources must address the intrinsic challenge of theological pluralism in the New Testament and the ways that the single mystery of God is referred to in various symbolic and conceptual ways by distinct authors in different settings. The unity that is present in the midst of a plurality of scriptural voices must be identified. Third, there is an apologetic value in reflection on the historical life of Jesus and the apostles "before" the New Testament witness. By reconstituting a merely likely or probable account of the historical life of Jesus and his early disciples, one can create a reasonable portrait of who they were that accounts causally for the origins of the early Christian movement, in a way that is compatible with the subsequent testimonies about them given in New Testament revelation. Such depictions do not provide proof of divine revelation as a historical reality but do show that there are reasonable ways for modern historically minded people to think about continuity between the historical life of Jesus and the testimony borne to him one generation later. Finally, thinking about the life of Jesus in his historical context can enrich one's theological understanding of the concrete mode and setting in which the mysteries of the redemption unfolded. The study, for example, of the symbols and terms used by Jesus to indicate the meaning of his own mission within his social context, better helps us understand the high claims Jesus made regarding his identity and the eschatological significance of his activity.

In this chapter I will not attempt anything like a full scale analysis of the Christology of the synoptic gospels. My aim is to identify basic touchstones for Trinitarian doctrine that are found in the synoptic presentation of Jesus of Nazareth. I simply presume that many elements of the presentation found in Mark, Matthew, and Luke do reflect accurately and correspond to the historical Jesus and his self-presentation.[1] I will concentrate below on six ba-

---

1. There are a wide range of influential and potentially helpful books written on the topic of the historical Jesus, frequently containing divergent or partially convergent points of view. Examples that can be dispositive to theological discussion include Ben Witherington III, *The Christology of Jesus* (Minneapolis, Minn.: Fortress, 1990); Raymond E. Brown, *An Introduction to New Testament Christology* (New York: Paulist Press, 1994); Rudolf Schnackenburg, *Jesus in the Gospels: A Biblical Christology*, trans. O. C. Dean (Louisville, Ky.: Westminster John Knox, 1995); N. T. Wright, *Jesus and the Victory of God: Christian Origins and the Question of God*, (Minneapolis: Augsburg Fortress, 1996), and *The Resurrection of the Son of God: Christian Origins and the Question of God*, (Minneapolis: Augsburg Fortress, 2003); Martin Hengel, with A. M. Schwemer, *Jesus und das Judentum, Geschichte des frühen Christentums* (Tübingen: Mohr Siebeck, 2007); John P. Meier, *A Marginal Jew: Rethinking the Historical Jesus*, 5 vols. Anchor Bible Reference Library Series (New Haven, Conn.: Yale University Press, 1991–2016); Dale C. Allison, *Constructing Jesus: Memory, Imagination, and History.* (Ada, Mich.: Baker Academic, 2010), Gerard Lohfink, *Jesus of Nazareth:*

sic themes: the eschatological ultimacy of Jesus' ministry as depicted in the synoptics, the kingdom of God and messianism, language and parables indicating exclusive Sonship identity, pre-existence theology that denotes Jesus as transcendent Lord, the death and resurrection of Jesus as epiphany of his deity accompanied by worship of Christ, and the Spirit of the Father indicated as the Spirit of Jesus.

ESCHATOLOGICAL ULTIMACY

The words and gestures of Jesus as he is represented in the synoptic gospels suggest in many ways that Jesus originally depicted his own life and mission as coinciding with the culmination of the eschaton. There is famous and widespread debate among scholars, both Christian and non-Christian, about the nature and content of Jesus' own eschatological message and the way it relates to the subsequent depiction of him in the New Testament witnesses. Here we can note five distinct but potentially related themes in Jesus' eschatological message as depicted in the synoptic gospels.[2] First, it is apocalyptic in tone, in the sense that Jesus claims that a new order of reality is being inaugurated in his own life and ministry, and that the latter are indicative of the end times of Israel and of the created order.[3] This theme suggests some kind of immanent eschatology in Jesus' message.[4] Second,

---

What He Wanted, Who He Was, trans. L. H. Maloney (Collegeville, Minn.: Michael Glazier, 2012); and in the theological guild, Karl Rahner, *Foundations of Christian Faith: An Introduction to the Idea of Christianity*, trans. W. V. Dych (New York: Seabury, 1978), 228–64; Wolfhart Pannenberg, *Systematic Theology*, vol. 2, trans. G. W. Bromiley (Grand Rapids, Mich.: Eerdmans, 1994); Walter Kasper, *Jesus the Christ*, trans. V. Green (London: Burns & Oates, 1976); Joseph Ratzinger, *Jesus of Nazareth*, 3 vols. (New York: Image, 2007–12).

2. I take it that one can argue for a basis of each of these features in the historical teaching and ministerial intentions of Jesus himself, but that argument lies beyond the scope of this book. I refer to relevant literature in the footnotes.

3. Allison, in *Constructing Jesus*, 78–82, offers a helpful list of passages from the synoptics that suggest, in convergent ways, that Jesus himself invoked images and ideas from various prophetic writings to indicate that his mission was eschatological in nature. See, for example, Mt 10:32–33 // Lk 12:8–9, which depicts the Son of Man confessing or denying those who have confessed or denied Jesus, implying a reference to the eschatological figure of Dn 7. So, also, Mk 8:38. Mk 13:26–27 depicts the Son of Man coming on the clouds in universal judgment of the nations, another image from Dn 7. Mt 19:27–28 // Lk 22:28–30 refers to the followers of Jesus sitting on thrones and judging the twelve tribes of Israel, again seeming reference to Dn 7. I will offer other examples in notes below.

4. The modern claim that Jesus announced some form of immanent apocalypticism originated with figures like Johannes Weiss and Albert Schweitzer. It has recently been rearticulated in a distinct form by Allison, who argues that Jesus made proleptic messianic claims and most likely

Jesus speaks of and symbolically indicates that there is a restoration of Israel coming about in and through his ministry, one that affects the interpretation of the Torah, the sacrifice structure of the Temple, and the relation of Israel to the gentiles.[5] Third, Jesus makes statements that indicate that something eschatologically ultimate will have happened in and through his own suffering and death and resurrection as inaugural events of the eschaton.[6] Fourth, Jesus speaks about the apostles participating in the judgment of the nations, suggesting that the movement he is founding will have a role in the inauguration and unfolding of the eschaton. This idea can be taken as a basis for the institution of the Church, an eschatological society founded intentionally by Jesus.[7] Finally, Jesus speaks about final tribulation, the final

---

accepted his foreseen death as a dimension of the unfolding apocalyptic episode. See *Constructing Jesus*, 244–47, 290–304, 404–5, 428–33.

5. For example, Jesus forgives sins outside the temple sacrifice system, and welcomes public sinners (Mk 2:5–10, 15–17; Mt 21:31), suggesting the fulfillment of prophecies from Jer 31:31–34 and 33:4–11, and from Ezek 36:24–33 and 37:21–23. He overturns the tables used for monetary exchanges in the temple court, symbolizing a cessation of the sacrifice system, and claims the temple will fall (Mk 11:15–17; 13:2). He also institutes a new sacrifice of his body and blood, as the "new covenant" of Jer 31:31–34 (Lk 22:20; 1 Cor 11:25). N. T. Wright argues that Jesus' eschatology is not primarily apocalyptic but restorationist, as bringing about a renewal of Israel in a new mode. Jesus' ministerial aim is to bring about a renewal of God's covenant with humanity, through the forgiveness of sins, the relativization of the temple cult and the establishment of a new order for belonging to the people of God. In doing so, Jesus claims to bring about the immanent judgment of God in Israel, and he does so as one in whom YHWH is present and embodied. See, for example, Wright, *Jesus and the Victory of God*, 208–9; 264–97; 405–39; 612–53. I think it is reasonable to maintain a view of Jesus' teaching that underscores both restorationist and apocalyptic themes.

6. The three synoptic authors depict Christ predicting his death and intimating that it has a universal saving meaning. Mk 8:31: "... the Son of man must suffer many things ... and be killed, and after three days rise again" (see also Mk 9:31 and 10:33–34; Mt 16:21, 17:22, 20:17–18; Lk 9:22, 17:25, 18:31–33). One may also argue that Jesus' denotations of himself as the "Son of man" are eschatological in meaning, and that his several associations of himself with the Suffering Servant of Isaiah 53 are meant to have redemptive connotations. For example, Mk 10:45 "For the Son of man also came not to be served but to serve, and to give his life as a ransom for many." Jesus also speaks of his exaltation, in texts like Lk 18:33 and Mk 14:62: "... you will see the Son of man seated at the right hand of Power, and coming with the clouds of heaven." Wolfhart Pannenberg has argued that the imminent eschatology of Jesus—and all apocalyptic claims on his part—should be interpreted in light of Jesus' claims to kingdom authority, his confrontation with the religious leaders of Israel, and his own foreseen acceptance of his death in this confrontation, as well as the historical fact of his resurrection, which inaugurates the foreseen eschaton (*Jesus: God and Man*, trans. L. L. Wilkins and D. A. Priebe [Philadelphia: Westminster, 1968], 53–73). Stated in more theologically overt terms: the eschaton that Christ came to inaugurate happened principally through his redemptive death and bodily resurrection, which now affects not only Israel and the gentiles, but all of reality.

7. A typical way to articulate this idea is to claim that we really understand Jesus' eschatology only in light of his resurrection, and in the gift of his Spirit that illumines the apostolic Church. Therefore, the writings of the apostolic Church give us a unique vantage point from which to look back on Jesus and understand his true significance in light of the resurrection. The idea is

judgment, and a cosmic re-creation, all elements of an ultimate reordering of creation in an eschatological mode.[8]

Those who attempt to construct hypothetical portraits of the original "Jesus of history" often ascribe only one or two of these eschatological notes to the Jesus of history, while claiming that the others were formulated subsequently by the early Christian movement and projected retrospectively back onto Jesus. However, such forms of reductive minimalism seem methodologically unwarranted and historically artificial. The fact that each of these forms of eschatological discourse was attributed to Jesus by the early Christian community and conscientiously transmitted in oral and written discourse suggests that the followers of Jesus were in fact attempting to preserve diverse elements of his original teaching, not invent new ones. Based on this premise, the evidence found in the sayings traditions of the New Testament suggests that each of these strands derives in some way originally from the teaching of Jesus himself. In saying this we should also acknowledge that Jesus' own original form of teaching may have been slightly different in order and style from the various ways in which it was presented a generation later by his various disciples.[9] Likewise his original mode of communication inevitably differs in various ways from the schematized doctrinal structures of later Catholicism, even if the latter serve to communicate

---

articulated vigorously by Luke Timothy Johnson in *The Real Jesus: The Misguided Quest for the Historical Jesus and the Truth of the Traditional Gospels* (San Francisco: Harper, 1996). See also Lohfink, *Jesus of Nazareth*, esp. 329–47, who argues for a profound form of continuity between the teaching of Jesus concerning his own authority in the nascent kingdom of God and the Church's subsequent confession, in light of the resurrection, of Christ as Lord and pre-existent Son of God.

8. Mk 13:24–27: "But in those days, after that tribulation, the sun will be darkened, and the moon will not give its light, and the stars will be falling from heaven, and the powers in the heavens will be shaken. And then they will see the Son of man coming in clouds with great power and glory. And then he will send out the angels, and gather his elect from the four winds, from the ends of the earth to the ends of heaven." It is not difficult to place this kind of language in the context of Second Temple Judaism. We hear in it echoes of Ezekiel and Daniel, mirrored, of course, in the early eschatology of Paul and in another way in the cosmic, historical and political visions of the book of *Revelation*. On cosmic apocalyptic literature and discourse in the context of Second Temple Judaism, see Richard Bauckham, *The Climax of Prophecy: Studies on the Book of Revelation* (Edinburgh: T&T Clark, 2000).

9. On questions of Jesus' infused science in historical context, see Thomas Joseph White, "The Infused Science of Christ," *Nova et Vetera* (English edition) 16, no. 2 (2018): 617–41. The early Christian movement uniformly witnessed to the fact that the historical Jesus foresaw his death and resurrection, and announced them prophetically during his lifetime. Most Catholic theologians think it is essential to retain this dimension of Jesus' teaching as historically real, and some defend the warrant of such an affirmation by appeal to the convergent indications of New Testament witnesses, so as to employ arguments of natural reason that appeal to historical probability that are complementary to affirmations of supernatural faith.

in ways necessary for subsequent epochs the truth of the original message.

Jesus' eschatological message is accompanied by various signs. His exorcisms are a sign that he is casting down the power of the devil and "binding the strongman," so as to make way for the new regime of the kingdom of God.[10] His many physical healings indicate the fulfillment of Old Testament prophetic tropes, especially those of Isaiah 35:5–6 and 61:1–2, which foretell of sight regained by the blind, hearing by the deaf, and walking of the lame.[11] His prophecies regarding the destruction of Jerusalem and the Temple suggest that some ceremonial practices of the Torah are coming to an end, or are being fulfilled in something greater.[12] Likewise, Jesus indicates at multiple junctures that he has a unique authority with which to determine the meaning of the law of Moses and its ultimate significance.[13] All of these signals form a constellation of eschatological signs that are convergent and mutually reinforcing. There is a decisive indication in the synoptic gospels that Jesus of Nazareth took himself to be God's ultimate eschatological emissary, one who was inaugurating the beginning of the end times in his own life, public mission, death, and exaltation.

KINGDOM OF GOD AND THE
MESSIANISM OF JESUS

The eschatological mission of Jesus is characterized also by his messianic claims. As is well known, the prophets and historical authors of ancient Israel had developed a theology of the coming of the messiah, a descendant of the Davidic monarchy, who would have a public political and eschatological role to play in world history. The textual traditions of Old Testament messianism are diverse and sometimes so symbolic as to seem vague in content. Likewise, messianic expectations at the time of Jesus of Nazareth were extremely diverse. Consequently, we may speak of Judaic messianism at the time as an open and fluid network of prophetic symbols intrinsically capable of a diversity of potential interpretations.

Within this context, Jesus of Nazareth clearly seems to have given this network of symbols an intensive redefinition, purposefully re-concentrated

---

10. Mk 3:27, Mt 12:29, and Lk 11:21–22.
11. Mk 2:1–12; 7:31–37; 8:22–26; cf. Jn 5:1–18 and 9:1–12.
12. Mk 11:15–17; 13:2; Mt 12:42; Lk 11:31.
13. Mk 2:28; 7:19; Mt 5:17–48; 12:8; 15:17; Lk 11:41.

on his own work and identity. Consider, in this respect, various aspects
of Jesus' original, and in a sense radical, "messianism." He repeatedly announces the advent of the "kingdom of God."[14] This term denotes the idea
of God's kingship, but also suggests a messianic emissary, a king of the kingdom, implicitly signifying that Jesus is the Christ who is to come.[15] His public act of seeking baptism in the Jordan seems to symbolize a "reentry" of Israel into the promised land, and thus a re-founding of Israel.[16] The decision
to choose the twelve as his representative followers and apostles suggests a
reformulation of the previously dissolved twelve tribes of Israel, in a new
mode as a new society.[17] Jesus' claim to have the authority to interpret the
law definitively is sometimes cast in messianic terms, and is perhaps related to his repeated claim to authority to heal on the sabbath. His forgiveness
of sins and his table fellowship with sinners signifies the inauguration of a
new practice of forgiveness and reconciliation that takes place outside the
temple system of sacrifices derived from the Mosaic law, an idea that causes
concern and indignation among Israel's scribal authorities. He also applies
Messianic symbolism to himself in the synoptic accounts in ways that suggest a kind of radical reinterpretation of the messianic role. He is the Son of
Man of Daniel 7:14, who will vindicate Israel publicly before the nations, but
he is going to do this as the Suffering Servant of Isaiah 53:11–12, who gives
his life as a ransom for the many: "The Son of Man came not to be served
but to serve...."[18] He is a king who fulfills the promises of the prophets and
who comes to Jerusalem to reign, but he does so in accord with the teach-

14. Often this announcement comes in the form of parables: see, for example, Mk 4:11, 26–34;
Mt 13:24–52; 18:23–36; 20:1–16; 22:2–14; 25:1–30. Sometimes he speaks of it as something immi-
nently forthcoming: see Mk 9:1; 14:25; Mt 8:11; 11:11; Lk 4:43; 7:28; 19:11. It can be something the
disciples are called to enter into: Mk 9:47; 10:15, 23–25; 12:34; Mt 5:3–10, 19–20; Lk 9:60–62. Public
sinners are invited: Mt 21:31. Exorcisms are signs of it: Mt 12:28; The apostles have roles of authority within it: Mt 16:18–19; Lk 8:1; 9:2. Their preaching, healing and exorcisms are signs of it:
Lk 10:9–11; 17:21. It is also associated with the end times: Lk 22:16–18.

15. Mt 13:41–43: "The Son of man will send his angels, and they will gather out of his kingdom
all causes of sin and all evildoers, and throw them into the furnace of fire; there men will weep
and gnash their teeth. Then the righteous will shine like the sun in the kingdom of their Father."
Mt 16:28: "Truly, I say to you, there are some standing here who will not taste death before they
see the Son of man coming in his kingdom." Lk 22:29–30: "... and I assign to you, as my Father
assigned to me, a kingdom, that you may eat and drink at my table in my kingdom, and sit on
thrones judging the twelve tribes of Israel." See Allison's persuasive argument for the idea that,
in the synoptic gospels, Jesus is portrayed unambiguously as the king of the kingdom of God;
Constructing Jesus, 244–47.

16. Mk 1:4–9; Mt 3:11. Cf. Ezek 32:36–28.

17. Mt 10:1–4; 19:28; Lk 8:1; 9:1; 18:31–33; 22:19–20.

18. Mk 10:45.

ing of Zechariah 9:9 as one "humble and riding ... on a colt."[19] Jesus' institution of the Eucharist as the new "blood of the covenant" in the presence
of the twelve, echoes the primal sacrifice of the twelve tribes on Mount Sinai, in Exodus 24:8, where Moses speaks of "the blood of the covenant," at
its inception. However, Jesus' new use of these words suggests that he is
authoritatively opening the covenant beyond the realm of Israel so as now
to include all those who eat and drink with the apostles, in a new form of
sacrifice.[20] He is crucified by the Roman authorities under the ironic title
of "King of the Jews," seemingly reflecting back an aspect of his implicit or
explicit public claims. This public title manifests under a veil of pagan ignorance the paradoxical truth of Jesus' innovative form of "Christ" theology.[21]
In all of these ways, Jesus' eschatology is also "regal" in form. It is the eschatology of a king of Israel, inaugurating a kingdom. But the kingdom is paradoxical. It is the kingdom of an itinerant teacher and miracle worker who
lives by alms, associates with the poor, and forgives sins. He resists physical
violence and political activism, and has no armies other than the "armies of
angels" of his Father.[22] Therefore the message is otherworldly, and marked
by immanent eschatology, as if the other world is now bearing in on our
own. This occurs not only in Jesus' teaching, miracles, and exorcisms, but
above all in his suffering, death, and exaltation.[23] The fluid and open network of messianic symbols derived from past prophets is now reconfigured
by Jesus around this strange new pattern of redemption.

SONSHIP IN AN EXCLUSIVE NOTE

The eschatological and messianic words and signs of Jesus are primarily functional. They indicate his identity as the Son of God only implicitly,
since they are oriented especially toward his soteriological activity and its
effects. In addition to these dimensions of Jesus' teaching, however, there

19. Mk 11:7–10.
20. Mk 14:24: "And he said to them, 'This is my blood of the covenant, which is poured out for
many.'" Lk 22:20: "And likewise the cup after supper, saying, 'This cup which is poured out for you
is the new covenant in my blood.'"
21. Mk 15:2, 9, 12, 18, 26; Mt 27:11, 29, 37; Lk 23:3, 37, 38; cf. Jn 18:33, 39; 19:3, 19.
22. Mt 26:53: "Do you think that I cannot appeal to my Father, and he will at once send me
more than twelve legions of angels?"
23. For pertinent studies on Jesus' distinct form of messianism, see Martin Hengel, *Studies in
Early Christology* (Edinburgh: T&T Clark, 1995), including especially the essay, "Sit at My Right
Hand!," 119–26.

are others concerned more explicitly with his personal identity. The most significant of these in the synoptic traditions is that regarding his Sonship. In the Old Testament, a human being can be denoted as a "son of God" for diverse reasons.[24] The term is sometimes used metaphorically to speak of the messiah or an anointed king.[25] It can refer to the angels, as a pantheon of god-like immortals subordinate to the one God of Israel.[26] In Daniel the term has eschatological connotations, the Son of God is he who walks in fire with Israel's martyrs.[27] In the New Testament one does find language indicating Jesus as "Son of God" that seems primarily messianic or functional in signification. However, the term is more commonly used by Jesus himself or by his followers to signify something unique about him. Only Jesus is "the Son," he alone who truly knows the Father, and who is known by the Father. "All things have been delivered to me by my Father; and no one knows the Son except the Father, and no one knows the Father except the Son and any one to whom the Son chooses to reveal him."[28] Jesus is the Son of God who alone will judge the nations.[29] He is the one whom the Father sent into the world.[30] His status or authority are greater than that of the angels.[31] Jesus is one who calls God his "father," or *abba* in Aramaic, and who teaches his disciples to do so.[32] The early Christian movement clearly retained this practice, using the original Aramaic term as a custom in fidelity to the instructions of their founder.[33]

Jesus' teaching regarding his own Sonship also indicates that God is now

---

24. See the study by Martin Hengel, *The Son of God: The Origin of Christology and the History of Jewish-Hellenistic Religion*, trans. J. Bowden (Philadelphia: Fortress, 1976).

25. Ps 2:7; Ps 72:1.

26. Jb 1:6; 2:1; 38:7.

27. Dn 3:25.

28. Mt 11:27. See likewise Mt 7:21: "Not everyone who says to me, 'Lord, Lord,' shall enter the kingdom of heaven, but he who does the will of my Father who is in heaven." Also Mt 10:32–33: "So everyone who acknowledges me before men, I also will acknowledge before my Father who is in heaven; but whoever denies me before men, I also will deny before my Father who is in heaven"; Mt 18:14: "So it is not the will of my Father who is in heaven that one of these little ones should perish."

29. Mk 8:38: "For whoever is ashamed of me and of my words in this adulterous and sinful generation, of him will the Son of man also be ashamed, when he comes in the glory of his Father with the holy angels." Mt 25:34: "Then the King will say to those at his right hand, 'Come, O blessed of my Father, inherit the kingdom prepared for you from the foundation of the world.'"

30. Mt 10:40: "He who receives you receives me, and he who receives me receives him who sent me."

31. Mt 13:41; 16:27.

32. Mk 14:36; 11:25; Mt 5:45; 6:9.

33. Gal 4:6.

known, through him, as Father. The Father is the one who "sends rain upon the just and on the unjust."[34] Jesus' work and activity manifest the will and activity of his Father.[35] It is the Father whom he calls upon in Gethsemane as the architect of the redemption, and from the Cross, as the principle of forgiveness.[36] Such phrases indicate a relationship to God as his unique Father, and so suggest the notion of a relational identity. The Son is wholly relative to his Father, and the Father is relative to his Son. The Son is the one who has been sent from the Father, and it is the Father, as the God of Israel, who reveals himself in the mission of his Son.[37]

Here I have noted sayings of Jesus that indicate his sense of his own unique filiation. However, the synoptic authors also each relate two epiphanies that occurred in the historical life of Jesus, each of which manifested in a distinct way his filial identity. The baptism of Jesus by John the Baptist, in the Jordan river, is the occasion of an epiphany of the Father, who designates Jesus the Son of God, and of the Spirit, who is seen in visual miracle to descend upon Jesus in the symbolic form of a dove.[38] This event inaugurates the public ministry of Jesus, and suggests that he is the Son sent from the Father, filled with the Spirit as the Christ, one who will descend into the waters of death to redeem the human race. Meanwhile, the event of the transfiguration on Mount Tabor serves as a prelude to the passion of Jesus. In it, the Father denotes to the apostles who are present that Jesus is the Son of God, and Jesus is surrounded by the Spirit who is manifest symbolically in the sign of a cloud.[39] The event is a recapitulation of Sinai, with Moses and Elijah present, in the cloud of holiness and incomprehensibility, indicative of the Spirit of God. Jesus is illumined from within, by the miraculous glorification of his body and soul, so as to indicate proleptically the future

---

34. Mt 5:45.

35. Mt 18:14.

36. Mk 14:36: "And he said, 'Abba, Father, all things are possible to thee; remove this cup from me; yet not what I will, but what thou wilt.'" Lk 23:34: "And Jesus said, 'Father, forgive them; for they know not what they do.'"

37. For a more developed exegetical reflection on the "filial consciousness" of Jesus, see Witherington, *The Christology of Jesus*, 215–33.

38. The image of this descent upon Jesus has a messianic note since it suggests he is one "anointed" in the Spirit, based on Is 11:2–4 and 61:1. Presumably the inspired understanding of the event was given first and foremost to John the Baptizer and experienced by Jesus himself. Aquinas, in *ST* III, q. 39, aa. 6–7, argues that it is fitting to think the dove was not a mere oracular vision but a physical reality, and yet it denoted in outward fashion symbolically an inward plenitude of grace.

39. Mk 9:2–9. For a sound argument in favor of the historicity of the transfiguration event, in response to the skeptical arguments of Loisy, see the commentary on this passage by Marie-Joseph Lagrange in *L'Evangile selon Saint Marc* (Paris: J. Gabalda, 1921).

mystery of the resurrection. Even before his passion, then, Jesus is the Son of God who is one with the Father in an exclusive way, but his true identity will be made manifest fully only in the resurrection, after he has accomplished the redemption.

This filial character of Jesus' mission can be seen to color what we have said above regarding eschatology and messianism. Jesus is the ultimate eschatological emissary of the Father and is sent as this emissary precisely as the Son. So, for example, the parable of the "wicked tenants" in Matthew 21:33–46 // Luke 20:9–19 suggests that Jesus of Nazareth himself characterized his ministry as one that came at the end of time, following all the previous prophets, and that this ministry is unique because it is the ultimate revelation of the Father, made manifest in his Son, who will be put to death, thus inaugurating the judgment of Israel. So too the messianism of Jesus is implicitly filial in tone. The one who inaugurates the kingdom of God, and makes paradoxical symbolic appeal to the messianism of the prophets, is also the Son of God. In his crucifixion, Jesus was not only named "Christ" by the Roman authorities, but was also mockingly called the "Son of God,"[40] a term that seemingly indicates messianic pretensions (Jesus as king), but that also intimates a deeper ontological claim (one who claims to make himself God). He who was executed spoke of himself as the unique Son of his Father, and intimated that he was himself one with the God of Israel. Re-read in a filial light, the end times consist in the perfect knowledge of God, manifest in the Son, and the kingdom of God is in fact the kingdom of the Father, instantiated by the sending of his Son.

PRE-EXISTENCE AND LORDSHIP

In addition to the elements noted above, there are various statements of Jesus reported by the synoptic gospels that suggest the notion of a transcendent personality. Jesus speaks of himself at times as if he is one who had preexisted his historical era and who claims to have come into the world in virtue of a divinely appointed mission.

This is seen first in Jesus' statements that denote transitive entry: "I have come."[41]

40. Mt 27:40–43.
41. On this theme all that I write below is heavily dependent on Simon Gathercole's arguments in *The Pre-existent Son: Recovering the Christologies of Matthew, Mark and Luke* (Grand Rapids, Mich.: Eerdmans, 2006), esp. 148–252.

Mark 1:38 (cf. Luke 4:43): "And he said to them, 'Let us go on to the next towns, that I may preach there also; for that is why I came out.'"

Mark 2:17 (cf. Matthew 9:13; Luke 5:32): "And when Jesus heard it, he said to them, 'Those who are well have no need of a physician, but those who are sick; I came not to call the righteous, but sinners.'"

Matthew 5:17: "'Think not that I have come to abolish the law and the prophets; I have come not to abolish them but to fulfill them."

Luke 12:49: "I came to cast fire upon the earth; and would that it were already kindled!"

Luke 12:51 (cf. Matthew 10:34): "Do you think that I have come to give peace on earth? No, I tell you, but rather division."

Matthew 10:35: "For I have come to set a man against his father, and a daughter against her mother, and a daughter-in-law against her mother-in-law."

Mark 10:45 (cf. Matthew 20:28): "For the Son of man also came not to be served but to serve, and to give his life as a ransom for many."

Luke 19:10: "For the Son of man came to seek and to save the lost."

Such statements characterize Jesus' mission in relation either to Israel or to all of humanity collectively. They denote that his mission has a world-historical and even cosmic significance, a sending that stems from God's pre-existent intention, one that Jesus himself seeks always to act in accord with.

This idea of a transcendent personality entering into a predesignated world-historical role is consistent with some of Jesus' parables in the synoptics, where he intimates that his mission is set against the backdrop of a pre-existent ordination.[42] The parable of Luke 13:6–9 depicts him as one who has come to pick good fruit from the harvest of all Israel. Matthew 18:12–14 depicts him as one who has come to look for lost sheep. Mark 3:27 denotes him as he who has come to bind the strong man (the devil). Mark 4:3–9 shows him sowing the word that will bear a harvest for eternal life. Mark 4:21–23 depicts him as one who brings the coming of the light. In addition, Jesus sometimes speaks of himself in a more overt way as one who has a pre-existent identity. In Mark 12:35–37, he denotes himself as "the Lord" of David, referred to by the Davidic psalter in Ps. 110:1, a seeming reference to himself as the messianic descendant of David who paradoxically existed even before David, as he who is one with the Lord God of Israel. Likewise, in Matthew 23:37–39, Jesus addresses a lament to Jerusalem in which he refers to himself from a transcendent perspective as the divine,

42. Gathercole, The Pre-existent Son, 170–74.

pre-existent protagonist addressing Israel, "O Jerusalem, Jerusalem, killing the prophets and stoning those who are sent to you! How often would I have gathered your children together as a hen gathers her brood under her wings, and you would not!"[43]

We can also indicate language of Jesus in the synoptics that seems to denote implicitly his transcendent Lordship in association with the divine name or with seemingly direct reference to divine authority. In Mark 2:28, for example, after healing on the Sabbath, Jesus resolves his dispute with Pharisees present by declaring that "the Son of man is lord even of the Sabbath." This appeal to the Son of Man image may refer to the eschatological figure of Daniel 7:14, who is messianic, but it also contains a note of transcendent authority, since the "lordship" in question is seemingly greater than that of Moses, through whom God instituted the Sabbath. In fact, the synoptics themselves regularly refer to Jesus as "the Lord," which in turn implies an association with the divine name and a numinous identification of Jesus with the activity and prerogatives of YHWH in the Old Testament.

Occasionally we see this idea manifested by the express use of the divine name employed to designate Jesus. So in the Gospel of Mark, both in 6:50, while walking on the sea of Galilee, and in 14:62, at his trial before the high priest, Jesus uses the saying "I Am" to denote his own identity or presence.[44] The phrase is ambiguous in both instances and may suggest an intimation of the divine identity subtly manifest in Jesus' historical speech acts. In Matthew's resurrection scene, which is no doubt highly schematized theologically, the apostles encounter Christ on a mountain in Galilee, which typologically symbolizes Sinai, and they receive the name of God anew from Jesus, who stands in the place of YHWH: "Go and baptize in the name of the Father, the Son and the Holy Spirit."[45] These various literary portraits of Jesus are clearly highly affected by post-paschal context and Christian confessional awareness. Nevertheless, someone had to have been the first person to designate Jesus as Lord by making use of the divine name, and in fact the gospels are in accord in depicting Jesus of Nazareth himself as this person. Subsequent Christians would speak of Christ as Lord, presumably with

---

43. Gathercole, The Pre-existent Son, 210–21; 236–38.

44. On this point, see the reflections of Larry Hurtado, Lord Jesus Christ: Devotion to Jesus in Earliest Christianity (Grand Rapids, Mich.: Eerdmans, 2003), 285–86, and Joel Marcus, Mark 1–8: A New Translation with Introduction and Commentary, Anchor Bible (New York: Doubleday, 2000), 432.

45. Mt 28:19. See Hurtado, Lord Jesus Christ, 331–32, 338–39.

the implication of the Hebraic euphemism, by which the divine name was denoted in Greek as *Kyrios*.

Finally, we should note that this transcendent identity theology of the synoptics is mirrored in the respective nativity cycles of Luke and Matthew, each of which describes in its own way the mystery of the Lordship of Jesus, as the pre-existent Son who has come into the world. Despite the narrative and theological differences present in the two infancy accounts, they do contain teachings that are significantly similar, in which one can recognize a common tradition that no doubt preceded the compositions of each gospel writer. In each of them, the incarnation of Jesus is first made known to one of his parents by the message of an angelic salutation. His name is given in this vision. He is conceived miraculously in the virginal womb of Mary. He is born in Bethlehem.[46] In addition, the narrative of Luke indicates explicitly that Jesus is the Son of God, and the Lord who visits his people, so that the Virgin Mary is the "Mother of [the] Lord."[47] Matthew denotes Jesus as "God with us," who as a child is worshiped by pagan wise men, a proleptic sign of the conversion of the gentiles to the worship of Jesus as Lord.[48] Clearly, then, their accounts of the conception and birth of Christ contain a pre-existence protology that is meant to mirror the post-resurrection eschatology in which Christ is recognized as Lord, after his exaltation. It is the Lord who has come into this world in his human conception and birth, who has experienced human life and death, and who has been recognized as Lord in light of his resurrection.

RESURRECTION, DIVINE EPIPHANY, AND WORSHIP

Paul describes the bodily resurrection in very concrete historical terms in 1 Corinthians 15:3–8:

For I delivered to you as of first importance what I also received, that Christ died for our sins in accordance with the scriptures, that he was buried, that he was raised on the third day in accordance with the scriptures, and that he appeared to Cephas, then to the twelve. Then he appeared to more than five hundred brethren

---

46. See, on the tradition of the nativity accounts, René Laurentin, *The Truth of Christmas; Beyond the Myths, The Gospels of the Infancy of Christ*, trans. M. J. Wrenn (Petersham, Mass.: St. Bede's Press, 1986), 303–4, and Joseph Ratzinger, *Jesus of Nazareth*, vol. 3, *The Infancy Narratives*, 14–57.

47. Lk 1:32–35, 43, 68.

48. Mt 1:23; 2:11.

at one time, most of whom are still alive, though some have fallen asleep. Then he appeared to James, then to all the apostles. Last of all, as to one untimely born, he appeared also to me.

Here the notion of the resurrection is concrete and bodily. However, in other texts, Paul also characterizes the resurrection as the occasion of the supreme epiphany of Jesus' identity as Lord.[49] Such texts suggest that Jesus is fully recognized as the pre-existent Son and Lord only in light of his resurrection. The resurrection entails, then, not only Jesus' bodily glorification but also his plenary manifestation as both God and man.

This perspective is not absent from the synoptic gospels. In fact they each underscore in their own way that we fully understand who Jesus is only in light of his death and resurrection. The Gospel of Mark provides a paradoxical example of the idea (Mk 15:37–39) when Jesus expires on the cross after crying out with a loud exclamation. The temple veil is then miraculously torn, by the power of God, signifying that the Holy of Holies has been made visible to all the nations in the death of Christ. The Roman centurion in turn exclaims, "Truly this man was the Son of God," a primal confession of the faith of the early Church, of gentiles converted to the God of Israel by the death of Jesus. The original Marcan text probably contains no resurrection scene and instead ends with an empty tomb.[50] Presumably, in Mark's theology, this is because the Lord is now risen, and readers are invited to encounter him not in past history but in the present, in our actual lives, in accord with the instruction of the heavenly messenger, who tells the women at the tomb that Jesus is alive.[51] In light of the crucifixion and the empty tomb, we can recognize that Jesus is the Son of God.

In Matthew, the divinity of Christ is manifest in a hidden way at the Cross, when the Son of God dies and the whole cosmos is affected.[52] The Trinitarian mystery of God is manifest most explicitly in light of the resurrection. As already noted, the risen Jesus encounters the disciples on a mountain in Galilee, a symbolic reference to the original covenant with the Lord on Mount Sinai.[53] They receive an apostolic mandate, learning from

---

49. The idea is thematic, for example, in Phil 2:5–11, to which we will return in the coming chapter. See also Rom 1:3–4, where Paul speaks of "the gospel concerning [the] Son, who was descended from David according to the flesh and designated Son of God in power according to the Spirit of holiness by his resurrection from the dead, Jesus Christ our Lord ..."

50. Mk 16:1–8.

51. Mk 16:6–7.

52. Mt 27:45, 51.

53. Mt 28:17–20.

him the new name of God, which is Trinitarian: "All authority in heaven
and on earth has been given to me. Go therefore and make disciples of all
nations, baptizing them in the name of the Father and of the Son and of the
Holy Spirit, teaching them to observe all that I have commanded you; and
lo, I am with you always, to the close of the age." In addition, the apostles
are depicted worshiping Jesus (v. 17), an action which, within the context of
Second Temple Judaism and its prohibitions on idolatry, designates Jesus as
the God of Israel.

Meanwhile, in Luke's depiction of the crucifixion, Jesus crucified reaf-
firms his filial confidence in the Father, and hands his spirit over to the Father (presumably his human spirit, but possibly the Holy Spirit whom he
breathes forth from the Cross). "Jesus, crying with a loud voice, said, 'Father, into thy hands I commit my spirit!' And having said this he breathed
his last."[54] Subsequently, when the risen Christ appears in bodily form to the
apostles, they recognize him as both "Christ" and "Lord."[55] During the time
of his resurrection apparitions Jesus reasserts that he is the risen Son of his
Father.[56] It is fifty days after his resurrection that the Son sends the Spirit
upon his fledgling Church.[57] The early Christians pray to the risen Jesus (cf.
Acts 7:59) as one who is now recognized as Lord. It is clearly from this assemblage of evidences that the synoptic theology of the resurrection is inextricably connected to the theology of God. In his bodily glorification and
subsequent apparitions, Jesus manifests to us his true identity, as he who is
one in being with his Father, the God of Israel.

SPIRIT OF THE FATHER, SPIRIT OF JESUS

More briefly, so as to fill out our sketch of the revelation of the Trinity in the
life of Christ, I would also like to take stock of a few passages in which the
gospels refer to the Holy Spirit as distinct from the Father and the Son.[58]
The Catholic tradition teaches that Christ is truly God and truly human
and, therefore, acts both as God and as man simultaneously in his earth-

54. Lk 23:46.
55. Lk 24:26, 34, 46.
56. Acts 1:7.
57. Acts 1:5; 2:1–4.
58. For a helpful study of the role of the Spirit in the synoptic gospels, see Simon Gathercole in "The Trinity in the Synoptic Gospels and Acts," in The Oxford Handbook of the Trinity, ed.
G. Emery and M. Levering (Oxford: Oxford University Press, 2011), 55–68.

ly activities, so that his human agency is subordinate to and harmonious with his divine agency (dyothelitism). Insofar as he acts as God, the Son acts with the Father and the Spirit as Lord. Insofar as he acts as man, he acts in subordination to the divine will, as one filled with the grace of the Holy Spirit, who inspires and moves him in his human actions. The synoptic gospels suggest a foundation for this set of theological ideas if we consider the relation of Jesus and the Spirit presented to us in key passages.

The first such passage is Mark 1:8, where John the Baptist proclaims: "I have baptized you with water; but he [i.e., the Christ] will baptize you with the Holy Spirit." The Holy Spirit is depicted in this saying as coming forth from Jesus, and the Holy Spirit here is also clearly the Spirit *of God*. The Spirit is presumably divine, then, but he also comes upon the world through the mission of Jesus the Son. The Son's unity with God and the procession of the Spirit from the Son seem to be implied, or at least suggested.

The second passage immediately follows, in Mark 1:9–12, and consists of the theophany that takes place at Jesus' baptism by John in the Jordan: "In those days Jesus came from Nazareth of Galilee and was baptized by John in the Jordan. And when he came up out of the water, immediately he saw the heavens opened and the Spirit descending upon him like a dove; and a voice came from heaven, 'You are my beloved Son; with you I am well pleased.' The Spirit immediately drove him out into the wilderness...." In this passage the Spirit alights upon the sacred humanity of Christ, and so is the Spirit of the Son, who is from the Father and who rests upon the Son. If we read these two passages in harmony with one another, then we see that the Spirit both comes forth from the Father to rest upon the Son, and that the Son sends the Spirit upon the Church. One might conjecture that the sending of the Spirit from the Father upon the Son is given in view of the second sending of the Spirit from or through the Son upon the Church.

Likewise, in Matthew, we are told that Jesus is conceived of the Holy Spirit.[59] John the Baptist prophesies that Jesus will baptize in the Holy Spirit, again suggesting that the Spirit proceeds in some way from him in his mission, and yet the Spirit also descends upon him at his baptism.[60] Jesus is led by the Spirit into the wilderness to be tempted, and it is he to whom the messianic plenitude of the Spirit is given.[61] However, Jesus also performs

59. Mt 1:18–20.
60. Mt 3:11 and Mt 3:16.
61. Mt 4:1 and Mt 12:18.

exorcisms by the power of the Holy Spirit acting within him,[62] and he can convey to his disciples the Spirit of the Father,[63] indicating that the Spirit is also the Spirit of the Son.

Finally, we can briefly take note of Luke's theological emphasis on the Spirit as the protagonist behind Jesus' mission and human activity. Luke's infancy narrative underscores that the man Jesus is filled with the Holy Spirit from the beginning of his life in the womb of Mary.[64] At Jesus' baptism the Spirit of the Father descends upon him, declaring him publicly as the Son of God.[65] The Spirit leads Jesus into the wilderness to fast and prepare for his public ministry.[66] Jesus claims to fulfill Isaian prophecy regarding the Messiah because the Spirit of the Lord is upon him.[67] If Jesus has received the fullness of the Spirit, it is in view of his acting in the Spirit and communicating it to others. For example, we see in Luke 12:11–12 how Jesus' ministry of proclamation will be furthered by the action of the Spirit after his Ascension: "And when they bring you before the synagogues and the rulers and the authorities, do not be anxious how or what you are to answer ... for the Holy Spirit will teach you in that very hour what you ought to say."

In the synoptic gospels there is already an inchoate theology of the inseparable operation of the three divine persons at work in the salvific deeds of Jesus, the efficacy of which continues on into the life of the Church in an especial way through the sending of the Spirit.

CONCLUSION: THE CHRISTOLOGICAL REEVALUATION OF OLD TESTAMENT MONOTHEISM

The synoptic authors presuppose the truth of God's revelation to Israel, that the Lord God of Israel is one. However, a new revelation of God emerges in the synoptics. The Lord God of Israel is one, but this God is also the Father, who has sent his Son and his Spirit into the world. This new teaching implies at least three mutually related ideas. The first idea is that of Jesus' unity with God the Father and the Holy Spirit: his authority is that of the Lord of Israel. The second is that of his real personal distinction from the Father

---

62. Mt 12:28.
63. Mt 10:20.
64. Lk 1:35.
65. Lk 3:22.
66. Lk 4:1.
67. Lk 4:18; cf. Is 61:1.

and the Spirit. He is "the Son" in an exclusive sense, and his exclusive sonship distinguishes him not only from other human beings (he alone is the
Son of God), but also from the Father and the Spirit (he is personally distinct from the Father and the Spirit even while he is somehow one with
them). Finally, the third idea is that of the mutual relationality of Jesus and
the Father, and of Jesus and the Spirit, and corresponding to this mutual relationality, that of a seeming mutual indwelling. The Son is always identified in relation to the Father and vice versa. "All things have been delivered
to me by my Father; and no one knows the Son except the Father, and no
one knows the Father except the Son."[68] Likewise the Son works in unity with the Spirit in his ministry and visible mission, as they both are sent
forth from the Father. Jesus' actions are depicted as establishing the eschatological reign of God. However, in and through these actions it is the mystery of the inner life of God that emerges in the life and teachings of the
Christ, and that is the true basis for the advent of the kingdom of God. The
kingdom of God at base, then, is the kingdom of the Trinity.

68. Mt 11:27.

5

Pauline Trinitarian Theology

I have argued in the previous chapter that there are clear indications in the synoptic gospels that Jesus partakes of divine authority. Some of the language of Sonship and mission suggests that he has a transcendent identity and a pre-existence with the Father. His eschatological mission and bodily resurrection are meant to reveal his identity as the Son of God. In this chapter I will consider briefly key aspects of St. Paul's Christology and theology of the Holy Spirit, so as to show the foundations in his teaching for the Church's subsequent articulation of the doctrine of the Trinity. In doing so, I will suggest that there are important likenesses between his theology and some of the themes already indicated in the synoptics as originating with Jesus himself. In other words, the presupposition of this chapter is that, just as the synoptics give us something of what the historical Jesus truly taught about himself, so Paul also communicates the teaching of Jesus and the early Christian community in his own mode and style. Here, accordingly, we will turn to the so-called "Christological Monotheism" present in Paul's writings, and, in particular, to the early Christian hymn he has preserved in Philippians 2:5–11. After this, we can consider briefly why Paul's overall doctrine supports a Trinitarian understanding of three persons in one God.

THREE FEATURES OF ISRAELITE MONOTHEISM

In order to understand the theology of Paul, it is helpful to take stock of basic features of Jewish thought about the God of Israel as it had developed in his historical context, in what is conventionally called the epoch of "Second

Temple Judaism." What one typically denotes by this phrase is the complex set of Jewish traditions and religious practices that developed from the end of the Babylonian exile (around 515 B.C.) until the destruction of the Second Temple in 70 A.D. Obviously the early Christian movement emerged, and the New Testament documents were composed, at the close of this period. In recent years, some scholars who focus on notions of God in Second Temple Judaism have argued that there are a number of normative features of doctrinal Jewish monotheism that were present culturally at the time of Jesus and of the composition of the New Testament.[1] If we better understand these normative ideas of Judaism as a backdrop to Paul's theology, we can understand better his distinctive teaching regarding the divinity of Christ.

Such "doctrinal" ideas include the following: first, that there is only one God, who is the Creator of all things, both visible and invisible, including the angelic powers. Therefore, God alone is the sovereign Lord of all things, without equal. Indeed, it is this one and true God who has revealed himself to Israel in the covenant first given at Mount Sinai. Second, only God is to be worshiped and adored, because he alone is the Creator and providential governor of all things. Angels, prophetic human beings, and any other purported mediating creatures, to the extent that they are important to the covenant, depend entirely upon God, and should not be worshiped by Jews. (Gentile worship that fails to understand this basic truth is therefore problematic.) Third, God alone is the eschatological savior of humanity. Precisely because he is the Creator who has power over being, he alone can redeem the human race from sin and death in the resurrection from the dead. Otherwise stated, only he who is from the beginning and has the power to create all things can also re-create all things in the eschaton. Indeed there is a soteriological and eschatological dimension to Israel's existence. God established his covenant with Israel precisely in view of the offer of salvation to the human race, and he has promised to reveal his identity to all the gentile nations. This universalizing aspect of Jewish thought is a basic feature especially of the theology of Deutero-Isaiah that is preserved and further explicated in Paul's epistles.

1. See, for example, N. T. Wright, *The Climax of the Covenant: Christ and the Law in Pauline Theology* (Minneapolis: Fortress, 1993), esp. part 1; Larry Hurtado, *Lord Jesus Christ*, and *How on Earth Did Jesus Become a God? Historical Questions about Earliest Devotion to Jesus* (Grand Rapids, Mich.: Eerdmans, 2005); Richard Bauckham, *Jesus and the God of Israel: God Crucified and Other Studies on the New Testament's Christology of Divine Identity* (Grand Rapids, Mich.: Eerdmans, 2008).

It is interesting to note that these features of doctrinaire Judaic monotheism are all preserved in the earliest Christology, and that they were each
in turn applied to *Jesus Christ* as one whom the early Christians identified
with the God of Israel. We can find telling examples of this identification in
one of the earliest texts of the New Testament, the Christological hymn that
Paul preserves in his *Letter to the Philippians*, 2:5–11.

PHILIPPIANS 2:5–11 AND
"CHRISTOLOGICAL MONOTHEISM"

Paul likely composed his *Letter to the Philippians* between 50 and 55 A.D.
This letter seems to contain a kind of creedal statement of early Christian
belief about Jesus, expressed in the form of a hymn. The text makes implicit
reference to a series of texts from the Hebrew scriptures, mostly from Isaiah, which in their original context refer to God. However, the texts are applied here to Jesus himself, who is in this way identified, by Paul and the
early Christian community, with the God of Israel. And yet, this identity
notwithstanding, Jesus is also portrayed in this text as personally distinct
from the Father. The Father is God, Jesus is Lord, and the Father and Jesus are personally distinct. Consequently, we see here already the seeds of
Trinitarian doctrine, present in the earliest strata of New Testament texts.

In what follows, I will present and offer commentary on the text of the
Christological hymn in Philippians 2:5–11, pointing out, in particular, the
many Old Testament allusions found in the text.[2] Subsequently I will consider parallel texts in Paul and other New Testament passages that confirm the
normativity of this pattern of Christological thinking in early Christianity.

What we have in the text from Philippians 2, in table 5-1, is a clear example of primitive "Christological Monotheism."[3] This is a form of distinctively Jewish monotheism that has the features I mentioned above: God
alone as Creator, who is deserving of worship and is the eschatological savior. However, these features of God's identity are now affirmed in a distinctively Christian way, such that Christ partakes of the features or attributes of

2. Table 5-1 is indebted to the schematic argument of Richard Bauckham, "God Crucified," in
Jesus and the God of Israel, 41–45. See in particular Bauckham's chart on p. 43 that highlights parallels between Phil 2:6–11 and Is 52–53; 45.

3. For further discussion of Paul's Christological rethinking of Jewish monotheism, see Hurtado, *Lord Jesus Christ*, 79–177; N. T. Wright, *Paul and the Faithfulness of God*, bk. 2 (Minneapolis,
Minn.: Fortress Press, 2013), 644–709.

Table 5-1. Christological Monotheism in Phil. 2:6–1

(5) Have this mind among yourselves, which was in Christ Jesus, who,	
(6) though he was in the **form of God**, did not count **equality with God** a thing to be grasped,	Verse 6: According to the interpretation of many scholars, the text intimates here the **pre-existence** of Christ as **God**, before the "Incarnation" in human nature.
(7) but **emptied himself**, taking the form of a **servant [or: slave]**, being born in the likeness of men.	Verse 7: Here the text refers implicitly but quite clearly to Is 53:11–12: "my **servant [slave]** ... [shall] make many to be accounted righteous ... because he **poured out his soul** [i.e., emptied himself]...." Jesus is God become the Suffering Servant.
(8) And being found in human form he humbled himself and became **obedient unto death**, even death on a cross.	Verse 8: Is 53:12 is echoed here as well: ... **to death** ... yet he bore the sin of many, and made intercession for the transgressors."
(9) Therefore **God has highly exalted him**	Verse 9 references Is 52:13: "Behold, **my servant** shall prosper, he **shall be exalted and lifted up**, and shall be very high." (Cf. Psalm 110, Mk 14:62: these are references to the Messiah who is exalted. The Suffering Servant has given his life for the many, then, and has been exalted in the resurrection as the Messiah or Christ.)
and bestowed on him the **name which is above every other name**,	This last part of v. 9 echoes Is 45:22–24: "Turn to me and be saved, all the ends of the earth! For I am God, and there is no other.... To me **every knee shall bow, every tongue shall swear. Only in the Lord [YHWH, *Kyrios*]**, it shall be said of me, are righteousness and strength." The name above every other is the name of the Lord. YHWH in Hebrew; *Kyrios* in OT Greek; cf. Ex 3:14: "I am he who is."
(10) that at the **name of Jesus every knee should bow**, in heaven and on earth and under the earth,	Verses 10 and 11 make clear that Jesus is to be *adored* or *worshiped as YHWH*. He is the God of Israel that all the gentile nations will come to recognize, according to the prophecy of Isaiah 45: How do the gentile nations come to recognize, then, the unique Creator and Savior, the God of Israel? They come to do so through the Incarnation of the Son, who became man, and was the Suffering Servant foretold by Isaiah, who gives his life as a sin offering on behalf of humanity. In his bodily resurrection, Christ is recognized as Messiah and Lord, and is rightly to be worshiped as he who was from the beginning with the Father, but who is also personally distinct from the Father.

the one God of Israel. The person of the Son pre-exists in the "form of God" prior to taking on the form of humanity. (Presumably then he is the one through whom all things are made, a point we will return to below.) Likewise, in his exaltation he is recognized as "He who is," and given the name "Lord," by which one identifies the God of Israel. He is acknowledged by that worship that is exclusively due to YHWH. And he is recognized as Lord precisely because he alone is the one who has offered salvation to humanity through his human obedience, death and eschatological resurrection. Simply put, it is only when the Lord God of Israel is crucified and raised from the dead in his human nature that God is truly recognized among the nations as the Lord, the only true and living God, who has revealed himself to Israel alone and through Israel to all the world. This set of ideas is especially evident from the way in which the "strict" monotheistic text of Isaiah 45:22–24 has been reapplied to the figure of Jesus Christ without there being any indication that Paul or the early Christians saw such attributions as incompatible with their basic affirmation of Jewish monotheism. God the Creator alone is the Lord, and so too Christ himself is the Lord. Only God is to be worshiped, but Christ is also to be worshiped and confessed as the Lord. Only God can save the gentile nations, but all the nations are now coming to recognize God in Christ crucified and resurrected, who alone can save the human race.

There are several other instances of this kind of Christological monotheism in the New Testament, which take the form of a short hymn or creedal-like statement. Especially pertinent here are, from the Pauline corpus, Colossians 1:15–20 and 1 Timothy 3:16. There is also a clear parallel to his theology found in the non-Pauline text of Hebrews 1:1–14. Ben Witherington has referred to these texts, and especially that of Philippians 2, as containing what he calls a V- or U-pattern of reflection.[4] Witherington is referring to the way these hymns follow the career of the Son from his pre-existence to his historical life as man through to his death and exaltation. Accordingly, in these texts, we find the following pattern: (a) Christ's pre-existence as God; (b) Christ's descent into our world through the Incarnation; (c) the suffering of Christ; (d) his subsequent exaltation; and (e) his recognition by humanity in the Church. Not all the texts have all these elements, but all of them have more than one.

---

4. Ben Witherington III, *The Many Faces of the Christ: The Christologies of the New Testament and Beyond* (New York: Crossroad, 1998), 73–90, at 79.

Consider in this respect Colossians 1:15–20:

> He is the image of the invisible God, the first-born of all creation;
> for in him all things were created, in heaven and on earth, visible and
> 　　invisible,
> whether thrones or dominions or principalities or authorities—all things
> 　　were created through him and for him.
> He is before all things, and in him all things hold together.
> He is the head of the body, the church; he is the beginning, the first-born
> 　　from the dead, that in everything he might be pre-eminent.
> For in him all the fullness of God was pleased to dwell,
> and through him to reconcile to himself all things, whether on earth or in
> 　　heaven, making peace by the blood of his cross.

The first verse suggests that Jesus is the pre-existent Son of God ("first born") who derives from the Father as his image. However, he is not a creature, since Judaic language of active creation is ascribed to him in verse 16: it is the Son in whom and from whom all things are created, including the invisible world of angels (thrones, dominions, etc.). Seemingly, then, an exemplary causality is ascribed to the Son: all things are made through him according to the pattern or example of his person, suggesting in turn that he is the pre-existent wisdom of the Father (cf. Col 2:3). Christ is also denoted in his incarnate state as the head of the Church, he in whom the fullness of God was pleased to dwell, suggesting he is both God and human. And his eschatological primacy is affirmed in the order of redemption. He is the first born from the dead, who has reconciled all things to himself, as Lord, through the medium of his crucifixion.

The First Letter to Timothy 3:16 offers us a parallel:

> He was manifested in the flesh,
> vindicated in the Spirit,
> seen by angels,
> preached among the nations,
> believed on in the world,
> taken up in glory.

The idea of a manifestation in the flesh presupposes that he pre-exists being in the flesh and has been sent into the world. His death in the flesh is "vindicated in the Spirit" when he is raised bodily from the dead, made manifest to the nations, and taken up into glory. Here the V-pattern of pre-existence, descent into human nature, death, exaltation and manifestation as Lord, seems to be suggested as well.

Outside the Pauline corpus we see a similar idea in Hebrews 1:1–14. There it is said of the Son that he is "the heir of all things, through whom also he [the Father] created the world. He reflects the glory of God and bears the very stamp of his nature [i.e., the Son has the fullness of the deity in himself], upholding the universe by his word of power. When he had made purification for sins [as man in his descent], he sat down at the right hand of the Majesty on high [as man in his exaltation], having become as much superior to angels as the name he has obtained is more excellent than theirs" (vv. 2–4). The exalted Christ is thus manifest as the one from before all ages, and the author of the letter goes on in verses 5–14 to argue that the Son is both "God" (v. 8) and "Lord" (v. 10), through whom all things have been made, and to whom they are all subject, including all created angelic powers. Clearly this text affirms the pre-existent divinity of Christ in a way that resembles the teaching of Paul.

Consequently, we find the following affirmations present in the primitive Christologies of the New Testament, particularly that of St. Paul: first, that God, the Lord of Israel, was present in Christ. Second, that Israel's God was reconciling the world to himself in Christ through the mystery of his death and resurrection. Third, that Christ is to be adored as the Lord of Israel, in unity with the Father.

It is worth noting that this New Testament pattern of "descent" of God into human flesh, redemptive sacrifice, and exaltation mirrors precisely the later development of the Nicene Creed. For in the Creed we find the following five components with reference to Christ: First, Jesus Christ is God before all time, in unity with the Father. Second, although one with God, Jesus as *Son* is personally distinct from the Father. Third, God the Son descends from heaven to become man, assuming human form. Fourth, Christ dies for us in order to procure our salvation. Finally, subsequent to his salvific death, Christ is exalted in his resurrection and will judge all the "peoples" of the earth. There is continuity of thought, then, between the hymns we find in early Christian literature in the New Testament—particularly in the hymn presented by St. Paul in Philippians 2:5–11—and the development of the Christological dimension of the later creedal statements of the Catholic Church.

THREE PERSONS WHO ACT IN DIVINE WAYS

We can conclude this cursory set of arguments by noting another feature of Paul's theology: his common use of titles for the Father, Son, and Holy Spirit as distinct personal agents, who are denoted as God is denoted, or who act as God acts. This feature complements that already mentioned and further contributes to the development of the doctrine of the Trinity, since it suggests that the one God of Israel who has the name "Lord" is also denoted in a triune fashion, as God the Father, the Lord Jesus Christ, and the Holy Spirit. Indeed, we can speak here of a "Trinitarian" dimension of Paul's language about God, even if some of its doctrinal implications are only suggested. This dimension arises particularly from the fact that he clearly distinguishes the three persons from one another, and yet ascribes to each titles and activities associated with the God of Israel, who is also the God of grace and salvation.

A first facet of Paul's proto-Trinitarian thought emerges from the way he applies divine names for God not only to the Father, but also to the Son and Holy Spirit. Thus, we frequently see in Paul some variant on the expression: "God the Father and our Lord Jesus Christ" (Gal 1:3; see also 1 Cor 1:3; 2 Cor 1:2), in which St. Paul refers to the Father as "God" in distinction from, but doxological association with, Jesus, who is "Lord" (an allusion to the divine name of Ex 3:14–15). Similarly, St. Paul likewise frequently groups the Holy Spirit with the Father and Son in a doxological unity, as in 2 Corinthians 13:14: "The grace of *the Lord* Jesus Christ, and the love of *God* [the Father] and the fellowship *in the Holy Spirit* be with you all."[5]

The second aspect of his thought pertains to the *principality* of the Father. In Paul, the Father is denoted as the origin or source of the life of the Son and the Spirit. This does not necessarily imply an inequality between the persons, but it does denote an order of relational priority within the godhead. The Father alone is unoriginate, and the Son and Spirit are from the Father. Accordingly, Paul stresses the Father's uniquely fontal character in the well-known doxology of 1 Corinthians 8:6: "... yet for us there is one God, the Father, *from whom are all things* and for whom we exist, and one Lord, Jesus Christ, through whom are all things and through whom we exist."[6] The Son is a principle of instrumental and exemplary causality, through

---

5. Emphases added.
6. Emphasis added.

whom all things were made.[7] Consider likewise this statement in Ephesians, from either Paul or one of his disciples: "There is one body and one Spirit, just as you were called to the one hope that belongs to your call, one Lord [i.e., Jesus], one faith, one baptism, one God and *Father of us all, who is above all and through all and in all*."[8] The apostle places emphasis on the Father's principality as the source of all else, as one who fills all things in virtue of his original plenitude. In this text, the Father's fontal character seemingly applies with respect even to the Spirit and the Lord Jesus himself.

Third, Paul frequently affirms the capacity of the Son and the Spirit to act with divine power. This is evidenced by the fact that they can sanctify and deify us as adoptive sons of God the Father. We can see this joint divine action of the Son and Spirit, for example, in 1 Corinthians 12:4–6, in a context in which Paul is discussing the distribution of charismatic gifts in the Church. He writes: "Now there are varieties of gifts, but *the same Spirit*; and there are varieties of service, but *the same Lord* [i.e., Jesus], and there are varieties of working, but it is *the same God* who inspires them all in every one."[9] The Spirit accomplishes the saving work of God, and he does so in concord with the saving activity of the Lord Jesus. God alone can save us, but according to Paul it is the Father who saves us through the activity of his Son and Spirit. Therefore the Son and the Spirit each partake truly of the activity of God. We see again the close connection between God (the Father), the Lord Jesus, and the work of the Spirit in 2 Thessalonians 2:13, where the role of the Spirit in the sanctification of believers is especially emphasized by Paul: "But we are bound to give thanks to God always for you, brethren, beloved by *the Lord* [*Jesus*], because *God* [*the Father*] chose you from the beginning to be saved *through sanctification by the Spirit* and belief in the truth."[10] The Son and the Spirit perform salvific acts proper to God conjointly with the Father.

Fourth, Paul indicates that the Son, too, plays a role in the sending of the Spirit. He does this especially insofar as he maintains that the Spirit the Fa-

---

7. See the discussion of Bauckham, "God Crucified," in *Jesus and the God of Israel*, 26–30. He argues that there is a clear echo in this passage of Dt 6:4: "Hear, O Israel: The Lord our God is one Lord." Paul speaks so as to indicate that there is one God the Father and one Lord Jesus Christ. The Father and Jesus are each the one God of Israel. See also C. Kavin Rowe, "Romans 10:13: What Is the Name of the Lord?," *Horizons in Biblical Theology* 22, no. 1 (2000): 135–73.

8. Emphasis added.

9. Emphases added.

10. Emphases added.

ther sends us is the Spirit *of his Son*. Accordingly, we see the close connection between Christ and the mission of the Spirit in Galatians 4:6: "And because you are sons, God has sent *the Spirit of his Son* into our hearts, crying 'Abba, Father!'" Thus, for St. Paul, the Spirit of God who is sent is the Spirit of both the Father *and* the Son.[11] In Romans 8:9–10, Paul reiterates his emphasis that the Spirit is Christ's own Spirit: "But you are not in the flesh, you are in the Spirit, if the *Spirit of God* really dwells in you. Anyone who does not have *the Spirit of Christ* does not belong to him. *But if Christ is in you*, although your bodies are dead because of sin, your spirits are alive because of righteousness."[12]

Finally, it is worth drawing the reader's attention to St. Paul's well-known reference to Christ as God's wisdom and power, in 1 Corinthians 1:22–24. There, he writes: "For Jews demand signs and Greeks seek wisdom, but we preach Christ crucified, a stumbling block to Jews and folly to Gentiles, but to those who are called, both Jews and Greeks, Christ *the power of God* and *the wisdom of God*."[13] This text will be significant to Trinitarian theology for at least two reasons. First, it attests to Christ's divinity by associating— or even seemingly identifying—him with two prominent divine attributes. Second, however, this seeming identification also raises a problem, namely, how can Christ be God's power and wisdom without dividing up God's substance, as if his attributes can be parceled out? As we will see, Augustine will take up this problem in his *De Trinitate* and thereby contribute to the development of what will come to be called the doctrine of *appropriations*.[14] An appropriation occurs when an individual divine attribute or action is predicated of a single divine person so as to indicate the particular way that person possesses the divine nature, which is held in common by the three persons.

CONCLUSION

In his thinking about God, Paul presupposes truths derived from the regnant monotheism common in Second Temple Judaism. However, he has

---

11. We will return to this motif when we discuss the controverted question of the addition to the Creed, known as the *Filioque* ("and the Son"), below, in chapters 6 and 27.

12. Emphases added.

13. Emphases added.

14. See especially Augustine, *The Trinity*, bks. 6–7, in *The Trinity*, ed. J. E. Rotelle, trans. E. Hill (Hyde Park, N.Y.: New City Press, 1991), to which we will return below.

modified common Judaic convictions in light of Christ in order to acknowledge the revelation of the Son of God and his Spirit. This form of thought is evidenced in a particularly pointed way in the reapplication to Jesus of numerous texts from Isaiah in the early Christian hymn preserved by Paul in Philippians 2:5–11. Moreover, in his letters, Paul doxologically associates the Son and the Spirit with the Father, while simultaneously underscoring the paternal principality. By this pattern of ascriptions, Paul laid the groundwork for the later doctrines of processions and relations with respect to the Father as the unoriginate one. In addition, Paul also stresses how the Son and the Spirit act with divine power, and, moreover, that the Son too has a role in sending the Spirit, such that the Spirit can truly be called the Spirit *of the Son* or *of Christ*. In diverse ways, then, we find in the theology of St. Paul the seeds for subsequent developments of Trinitarian theology in the Catholic Church.

6

Johannine Trinitarian Theology

John's Gospel contains an especially profound depiction of the mystery of the Holy Trinity. The Trinitarian life of God is presented at the beginning, from the Prologue, as the mystery underlying the life, mission, crucifixion, and glorification of Jesus. We should begin our overview of Johannine Trinitarian theology, then, by considering the theology of the Prologue under two vantage points: (a) that which concerns the mystery of the Logos, or Word, and (b) that which concerns the mystery of the only-begotten Son. After this, we can examine John's depiction of Jesus crucified as an ultimate epiphany of God, that is, as "I Am." In the last place, we will turn to John's teaching on the processions of the Son and the Paraclete. As we will see, the Gospel is a rich storehouse for the later development of Trinitarian doctrine.[1]

THE PROLOGUE OF JOHN'S GOSPEL

It is helpful to consider the Prologue of John's Gospel in two parts, the first focusing on Jesus' pre-existence as God's *Logos*, or "Word," and the second on his identity as "Only-Begotten Son." In John's treatment of Jesus'

---

1. The exegetically informed reader should be aware that in this chapter, as in previous ones, I take for granted that John's Gospel and other New Testament writings are subject to multiple possible readings, theologically, including some that are non-Trinitarian. Here I am simply attempting to offer a reading of the Gospel that shows that the bible can be read in a Trinitarian way, without claiming to give definitive exegetical arguments against contrary positions, a program that lies beyond the aims and scope of this book. For a helpful summary of both evidences of Trinitarian dimensions of John's Gospel and contemporary scholarship on this theme, see Harold W. Attridge, "Trinitarian Theology and the Fourth Gospel," in *The Bible and Early Trinitarian Theology*, ed. C. A. Beeley and M. E. Weedman (Washington, D.C.: The Catholic University of America Press, 2018), 71–83.

pre-existence as the Logos of God, we can note four points in particular: first, John's designation of Jesus as the eternal Logos; second, the psychological analogy implicit in this designation; third, John's depiction of creation as accomplished through the Logos; and fourth, his assertion that the Logos was made *sarx*, "flesh."

Jesus as the Eternal Logos

The Logos. To begin, the Prologue clearly affirms the pre-existence of the Logos or Word. The Logos is he who was in the beginning with God, who was God, and through whom all things were made. Here are the opening words of the Gospel itself in the original Greek: "ἐν ἀρχῇ ἦν ὁ λόγος καὶ ὁ λόγος ἦν πρὸς τὸν θεόν καὶ θεὸς ἦν ὁ λόγος. οὗτος ἦν ἐν ἀρχῇ πρὸς τὸν θεόν" (Jn 1:1–2).[2] A literal rendering of this passage into English might read: "In the principle [or in the beginning], there was the Logos, and the Logos was toward God [or with God], and the Logos was God. He who in the beginning [or in the principle] was toward [or with] God."

If we consider these first words, we can see that the book begins from the vantage point of Christ as the *eternal* Word of the Father. This perspective is meant to color our interpretation of the whole of the Fourth Gospel. The figure of Jesus of Nazareth has a pre-existent personal identity as Word that reaches back into the ground of all existent reality, the mystery of God himself.

It is worth noting that the opening words of the Gospel, "*en archē*," hearken back to the Septuagint translation of Genesis 1:1: "ἐν ἀρχῇ ἐποίησεν ὁ θεὸς τὸν οὐρανὸν καὶ τὴν γῆν." "In the beginning God created the heavens and the earth." But the word *archē* can also denote "principle" or "origin," so the Prologue can also be read to mean, "in the principle who is the eternal Father, there was the eternal Logos." In this way, the Father's eternal generation of the Word and the Word's eternal pre-existence are intimated in the Gospel's creative utilization of the opening words of Genesis, with the Word himself now acting as God from within creation's principle, the Father.

Psychological Analogy. Christ is designated by John as the Logos or Word of God. But since *logos* in Greek can signify both the mental concept or the audible spoken word, as well as the human capacity for reason, the term here seems to signify that—prior to the existence of the physical world—

2. All New Testament Greek is taken from *The Greek New Testament: SBL Edition*, ed. Michael W. Holmes (Atlanta, Ga., and Bellingham, Wash.: Society of Biblical Literature and Logos Bible Software, 2010).

the pre-existent Son is *the immaterial wisdom or reason* of God the Father, through whom the Father made all things. The pre-existent Son is, as such, a reflection of God who is eternally with the Father, or in the Father. This is the eternal life of God ("In him was life, and the life was the light of men"; John 1:4).[3] Evidently, this suggests in turn that human reason *in us* reflects something of the pre-existent life of the Father and the Son. We are made in the image of the triune life of God, precisely insofar as we are beings of reason, of logos. Moreover, even if we typically come to discover our own capacity to reason before we encounter the revelation of God as the Word, it nevertheless must be true that logos, or reason, is more said of him, in the order of being, since it is from the transcendent Logos of God that our capacity for reason is derived.

Creation through the Logos. Similarly, by interpreting the Son as the Father's biblical Word, or exemplary discourse, through whom he made all things, the Gospel also interprets *Genesis* in Trinitarian terms. John 1:3 states: "All things were made through him, and without him was not anything made that was made." According to the Judaism of the Second Temple era, only God can create. Here, then, Jewish monotheistic prerogatives are ascribed to the Logos, the Word, through whom the Father created all things. The Logos *is* the One God, the Lord, through whom God made the heavens and the earth in Genesis 1. Accordingly, creation itself has now been reconceptualized so as to center around Jesus Christ in his personal identity as the Word of God.

The Word was made Flesh. After introducing his readers to the figure of God's pre-existent Word, John goes on to make the following astonishing assertion in John 1:14 that articulates the foundational claim of Christianity: "And the Word [*logos*] became flesh [*sarx*] and dwelt among us, full of grace and truth; we have beheld his glory, glory of the only-begotten Son from the Father." In this verse, John makes it quite clear that the Logos has assumed *sarx*, flesh, which is to say, that he has taken on an integral human nature. It is God himself, the Creator and source of eternal life, who has entered human history and has become man in Jesus Christ.

3. We should recall that in Jn 4:24, Jesus claims that "God is spirit," which seemingly denotes that he is not present in a physical place. In Jn 17:24, Jesus speaks of receiving glory from the Father "before the foundation of the world," indicating an eternal distinction of persons and a procession. The Logos is, therefore, a principle of *spiritual* life, distinct from the Father in the eternity of God, whose procession from the Father is depicted by similitude to a human act of the mind.

Jesus as the Only-Begotten Son

In the latter part of the Prologue John characterizes Jesus as the begotten Son of God. We should note three characteristics or implications of this idea: first, the analogical character of the notion of Jesus as the uniquely begotten of the Father; second, what it means for the Son to be in the "bosom" of the Father; and finally, John's claim that it is the Son who reveals the Father.

The Son as Eternally Begotten. As we have just noted above, John 1:14 states, "... and we have beheld his glory, glory as of the only-begotten Son [*monogenous*] from the Father." Then, John 1:18 continues: "No one has ever seen God; *the only-begotten God* [or: *Son*], who is in the *bosom* of the Father, *he has made him known*."[4] The term here for only-begotten Son is μονογενοῦς, which could be rendered: the uniquely begotten. The Son pre-exists the creation as the unique Son *eternally engendered* by the Father, and therefore as proceeding from the Father. The notion of begetting is important here, because it clearly serves as the foundation for the idea that Jesus is not simply the "Son of God" in time, as a man who comes from God, but that his Sonship pre-exists the creation. He is the Son, or the one who is begotten from the Father (and thus proceeds from the Father) prior to the creation, and thus from all eternity.

The Son is in the Father's Bosom. We should also note that John 1:18, as cited above, likewise maintains that the Son or Word is in the κόλπον (*kolpon*, bosom) of the Father. What this means in context is that there is a kind of eternal immanence of the Son in the Father. There is a true distinction of persons (the Father is not the Son) but there is also mutual indwelling. The Son is in the Father and the Father in the Son. This relation of mutual indwelling is what will come to be termed in the later patristic and scholastic theological traditions the περιχώρησις, *perichōrēsis*, or *circumincessio*, circumincession of the divine persons within one another.

The Son Reveals the Father. The above citation of John 1:18 also ends with the statement that: "he [the Son] has made him [the Father] known

---

4. Emphases added. I have modified the RSV here in conformity with the ambiguities of the manuscript tradition of Jn 1:18, which has either *monogenēs theos* or *huios*, "only-begotten God" or "Son". The Greek is "θεὸν οὐδεὶς ἑώρακεν πώποτε; μονογενὴς θεὸς [other authorities read: υἱός, Son], ὁ ὢν εἰς τὸν κόλπον τοῦ πατρὸς ἐκεῖνος ἐξηγήσατο."

[ἐκεῖνος ἐξηγήσατο]." This verb, which in its lexical form is *exēgēomai,* means: "to make known, reveal."[5] It is the word from which we get the English word "exegete." The idea here then is that the Son is the "exegete" or "interpreter" of the Father, who makes known the Father's will. In other words, the Word dwelling among us in the flesh has revealed to us the glory of the Father, who the Father is, the identity of the Father, present in his Son.

THE CROSS AND THE NAME OF GOD: "I AM"

Thus far we have noted the Johannine teaching on Christ as God's eternal Word and Son. However, the author of the Gospel also ascribes to Christ the divine name of God from Exodus 3:14, "I AM," and he interprets this name in light of the Suffering Servant theology of Isaiah 52–53. It is when Jesus is crucified, or "lifted up" and "exalted" on the Cross as the Suffering Servant that he is also revealed to be "He who is," the God of Israel. We will explore these ideas first by turning to John's realized eschatology of the Cross, and second, by looking at how the Cross in turn becomes the place of the manifestation of the divine name.

Realized Eschatology on the Cross and the Exaltation of the Servant. C. H. Dodd, in his influential mid-twentieth-century work *The Interpretation of the Fourth Gospel,*[6] has noted the significance of the Gospel of John's three references to Jesus' crucifixion as an exaltation. As Dodd interprets it, the cumulative effect of these references is to produce a theology of Israel's messiah and his work that Dodd characterizes as "realized eschatology."[7] What this means is that the eschaton, or final state of all things, is realized in advance in the life of Christ, particularly in Christ's redemptive deed, that is, in his crucifixion. Moreover, as we will see below with reference to John 3:14–15, this is also the moment of Christ's definitive revelation of himself as the Suffering Servant of Isaiah.

To explore these ideas further, let us turn briefly to the Gospel of John's

5. See *The Analytical Lexicon to the Greek New Testament,* ed. William D. Mounce (Grand Rapids, Mich.: Zondervan, 1993).

6. C. H. Dodd, *The Interpretation of the Fourth Gospel* (Cambridge: Cambridge University Press, 1968).

7. Dodd discusses the character of the Cross as an exaltation in *The Interpretation of the Fourth Gospel,* 368–79. For Dodd's coining of the term "realized eschatology" to refer to the Kingdom of God as present, see C. H. Dodd, *The Parables of the Kingdom.*

three references to Jesus' crucifixion as an exaltation.[8] The first reference is found in John 3:14–15, in Jesus' appropriation of the Old Testament type of the bronze serpent:[9] "And as Moses lifted up the serpent in the wilderness, so must the Son of man be *lifted up*, that whosoever believes in him may have eternal life."[10] It is worth noting that, in Greek, the italicized portion, "lifted up," is ὑψωθῆναι, *hypsōthēnai*, which can also be translated as "exalted." This word indicates a significant allusion to the Isaian Suffering Servant, since it refers to Isaiah 52:13 in the Septuagint: "Behold, my servant shall prosper, he shall be exalted [ὑψωθήσεται] and lifted up, and shall be very high."[11] The Johannine text presents us with the idea that the crucifixion is an exaltation or glorification of Jesus in which his status as the Suffering Servant of Isaiah is revealed.

The second reference in John's Gospel to Jesus' crucifixion as an exaltation is found in John 12:23, which reads: "And Jesus answered them, 'The hour has come for the Son of man to be glorified [δοξασθῇ] [i.e., on the Cross].'" In this passage—which, when read in context contains a clear reference to the pending "hour" of his passion—Jesus' crucifixion is portrayed as the moment of his glorification. Within the overall perspective of John's Gospel, what this means is that the eternal *doxa*, or glory, that the Son possesses with the Father before the foundation of the world is made manifest on the Cross.

The third reference is found in John 12:32. In this passage, Jesus again refers explicitly to his being fastened to the wood of the Cross as an *exaltation*: "... and I, when I am *lifted up* [ὑψωθῶ] from the earth, will draw all men to myself." In this instance, Christ's elevation or exaltation on the Cross is the occasion for him to reveal himself to others and, ultimately, to draw the human race to salvation.

One can conclude from such passages that Jesus' crucifixion is presented in the Gospel of John as an exaltation that establishes Jesus' status as Suffering Servant, reveals God's glory, and serves as the standard for the salvific ingathering of the human race.

8. I am influenced here by the analysis of Bauckham, "God Crucified," in *Jesus and the God of Israel*, 46–51.

9. See Nm 21:4–9.

10. Emphasis added.

11. The text of Is 52:13 here is RSV, but I have inserted the Greek of the Septuagint. The following verb, rendered "lifted up" in the RSV, is δοξασθήσεται, *doxasthēsetai* in the Septuagint, which could also be rendered "shall be glorified."

The Cross and the Name of God. Secondly, however, we should add that the crucifixion is not only a glorification or exaltation of Jesus; it is also the place of manifestation of his divine identity, of the divine name. This is a point Richard Bauckham underscores in his essay, "God Crucified."[12] Here we take note of three statements of Jesus in John's Gospel, in which he makes use of the divine name.

The first statement is found in John 8:24, where Jesus says: "I told you that you would die in your sins, for you will die in your sins unless you believe that *I am*."[13] The Greek phrase here for "I am" is "ἐγώ εἰμι." This is the interpretation of the divine name we also find in the Septuagint version of Is 45:18: "I am the Lord, and there is no other." Similarly, the usage here references Isaiah 43:10: "'You are my witnesses,' says the Lord, 'and my servant whom I have chosen, that you may know and believe me and understand that *I am He*. Before me no god was formed, nor shall there be any after me.'"[14] These passages from Isaiah not only assert a strict doctrinal monotheism but also denote that the God of Israel (YHWH) is the one true God. Thus, they explicitly echo Exodus 3:14–15, where that personal name YHWH is associated with the notion of God's eternal being: "I Am." Once we identify this set of associations we can understand that John 8:24 refers quite clearly, through the medium of Isaiah 45, to the "I am He who is" of Exodus 3:14. In this statement, Christ identifies himself by the use of the divine name and so identifies himself with the God of Israel.

The second statement in John 8:28 expands on the preceding: "So Jesus said, 'When you have *lifted up* the Son of man, then you will know that *I am*, and that I do nothing on my own authority but speak thus as the Father taught me.'"[15] In this passage the theology of the Servant as the exalted one and the revelation of the name are both present, and complement one another. Christ is accordingly revealed on the Cross not only as the Suffering Servant, but also as Lord, as the God of Israel made flesh. Otherwise stated, Jesus is revealed to humanity as God himself, precisely in the lowliness and salvific service of the Cross, where he effectively redeems humanity.

---

12. Richard Bauckham, "God Crucified," in *Jesus and the God of Israel*, 46–51.

13. Emphasis added. I have slightly altered the RSV rendering of Jn 8:24, modifying the translation of ἐγώ εἰμι from "I am he" to "I am" to better bring out Jesus' identification with the divine name of Ex 3:14.

14. I am grateful to Gilles Emery for pointing out the significance of this verse, in which knowledge and belief are associated with recognition of the true God of Israel, themes that arise in John in regard to Jesus (see Jn 17:3).

15. Emphasis added; RSV slightly modified as above, changing "I am he" to "I am."

The third statement is found in John 8:58 and contains perhaps Jesus' most pronounced use of the divine name: "Jesus said to them, 'Truly, truly, I say to you, before Abraham was, I am.'" Here Jesus clearly ascribes to himself the pre-existence of the godhead, of the Lord of Israel who created all things and who called Abraham into the covenant.

Analogously, Jesus also makes a powerful claim of identity with the God of Israel in John 10:30, when he says: "I and the Father are *one*."[16] In this saying, there is a purposeful echo of the Shema prayer from Deuteronomy 6:4: "Hear, O Israel: The Lord our God is *one* Lord."[17] Jesus is one with the Father as his Word, and yet is personally distinct from the Father. Together with the Father, he is the one God of Israel.

As can be seen from the preceding passages, Jesus identifies himself with I AM, the God of Israel and, in particular, designates the Cross as a special locus of the revelation of his divine identity, which he shares with the Father. What is true eternally of the Son as being one in being with the Father is unveiled on the Cross as the manifestation of the victory of divine love. Clearly, then, we have here the seeds for later Trinitarian theology.

PROCESSIONS OF THE SON AND THE PARACLETE

John's Gospel also makes it clear that there are "processions" in God. These eternal processions are revealed by what later theologians will call temporal missions: the Son and the Spirit are "sent" into the world to reveal the Father. The Son proceeds from the Father both eternally as his Logos and in time by his temporal mission, in becoming man. The Spirit or Paraclete proceeds from the Father and the Son, both eternally and in time, by his temporal mission to reveal the Son and the Father. In what follows, we will accordingly look at the witness of the Gospel of John, first, to the Son's procession from the Father; second, to the Spirit's procession from Father and Son; third, to the nature of the temporal mission and work of the Spirit as Paraclete after Christ's resurrection; and, finally, to the Gospel's identification of the Spirit as the Spirit of truth.

The Son Proceeds from the Father. The strongest statement in John's Gospel that the Son proceeds from the Father is found in John 8:42: "Jesus said

16. Emphasis added.
17. Emphasis added.

to them, 'If God were your Father, you would love me, for I *proceeded and came forth* [ἐξῆλθον καὶ ἥκω] from God; I came not of my own accord, but he sent me.'"[18] In the Greek text of John, the first verb we find here is, in its lexical form, ἐξέρχομαι, *exerchomai*, which literally means, "to come forth." The word "procession," usually used in theology to designate this coming forth, is derived from the Latin of Jerome's Vulgate, where we read: "ego enim ex Deo *processi* et veni."[19] This is not exactly literal, since in Latin the literal rendering would be *Ego exivi*, "I came forth." (A difficulty that historically arose in connection with Jerome's rendering here will be discussed below, when we turn to the question of the Spirit's procession from the Son, in part 3 of this book.)

Likewise, we find the identical Greek verb in John 16:27–30, which I have interspersed throughout with parallels from the Latin of the Vulgate: "'... for the Father himself loves you, because you have loved me and have believed that I *came from* the Father [here Jerome is more literal: *ego a Deo exivi*]. I *came from* the Father [*exivi a Patre*] and have come into the world; again, I am leaving the world and going to the Father.' His disciples said, 'Ah, now you are speaking plainly, not in any figure! Now we know that you know all things, and need none to question you; by this we believe that you *came from* God [*a Deo existi*].'"[20] As we can see, Jesus is presented here in John's Gospel as *coming forth* from God the Father. This coming forth, however, must be held in the first instance to refer to his eternal procession from the Father, which then serves as the intra-divine foundation for his temporal mission. Why must this be the case? Because the one who comes forth in time is eternally from the Father as his Son, as one who is begotten by him from all eternity, and as the Word who proceeds from him.[21] When the Son comes forth in time, then, in our world (by what we can call the temporal mission of the Son), he reveals who he is in his eternal derivation from the Father, the personal procession in which the Father eternally begets the Son as his Word.

The Holy Spirit Proceeds from the Father and the Son. John's Gospel clearly denotes the Holy Spirit as a person distinct from the Father and the Son.

18. Emphases added.
19. All citations from the Vulgate are taken from: *Biblia sacra: Iuxta vulgatam versionem*, 5th ed., ed. B. Fischer, I. Gribomont, et al. (Stuttgart: Deutsche Bibelgesellschaft, 2007).
20. See also Jn 17:8: "I have given them [i.e., the disciples] the words which you gave me, and they have received them and know in truth *that I came from you*." Emphasis added.
21. Jn 1:1–3

He is also said to proceed from them both. In John's Gospel, he is often called the "Paraclete," which means "Counselor." The sense here is legal or forensic. In a court of law, the advocate or legal counsel will do the work of rendering the accused party just before the Judge. The Holy Spirit works inwardly to justify us by faith, giving us the grace of Christ, who has redeemed us.

As to John's presentation of the Spirit's procession from Father and Son, this can be gathered from a sequence of passages. Debate about these passages has played a role historically in the *Filioque* controversy.[22]

The first relevant passage is that of John 14:25–26: "These things I have spoken to you, while I am still with you. But the Counselor [i.e., the Paraclete], the Holy Spirit, whom the Father *will send* [πέμψει] *in my name*, he will teach you all things, and bring to your remembrance all that I have said to you."[23] We should note in this passage that the Holy Spirit is indeed sent into the world by the Father, but only in the Son's name, that is, with reference to the Son.

The second passage is found in John 15:26, which reads: "But when the Counselor comes, whom *I shall send* [πέμψω] to you *from the Father* [παρὰ τοῦ πατρός], even the Spirit of truth, *who proceeds from the Father* [παρὰ τοῦ πατρὸς ἐκπορεύεται], he will bear witness to me."[24] Here, the Spirit is referred to as sent by the Son. In addition, the Spirit is designated as he who proceeds (ἐκπορεύεται) from the Father. What is meant by the Spirit's *procession*? This is a question we will return to below.

The third passage is John 16:7: "Nevertheless I tell you the truth: it is to your advantage that I go away, for if I do not go away, the Counselor will not come to you; but if I go, *I will send* [πέμψω] *him* to you."[25] In this passage, Jesus again designates himself as the one who will send the Spirit to the disciples.

Now, throughout these citations, the Greek verb for "sending" is πέμπω, *pempō*: "to send." Significantly, however, here the Greek word for the Holy

---

22. *Filioque* is the Latin phrase that the Latin Church added to the original Nicene creed, which states that the Spirit proceeds from the Father "and the Son" (*Filioque* in Latin). Eastern theologians have often argued that this is an unwarranted speculation or even falsification of the notion of the Trinity, claiming that both the Spirit and the Son proceed only from the Father, who is the unique fontal source of all Trinitarian life.

23. Emphasis added.

24. Emphases added.

25. Emphasis added.

Spirit's proceeding from the Father is not ἐξέρχομαι, *exerchomai*—as we saw above with reference to the Son's *coming forth* from the Father—but is instead ἐκπορεύομαι, *ekporeuomai*, which literally means, "to go forth from a place, to proceed."[26] Jerome, for his part, translates this (literally) as "procession." Thus we read in the Vulgate rendering of John 15:26: "cum autem venerit paracletus quem *ego mittam vobis a Patre* Spiritum veritatis *qui a Patre procedit* ille testimonium perhibebit de me."

Why should this difference of Greek verbs matter? John's Gospel in Greek speaks of the Son coming forth from the Father, but of the Spirit as proceeding from the Father. In this context, procession refers especially to the economic or temporal mission of the Spirit: the Spirit is sent into the world by the Father. One cannot automatically infer from this what the character is of the eternal procession of the Spirit. As a result, many in the Eastern Orthodox tradition claim, first, that procession as such (*ekporeuomai*) pertains only to the Spirit, while generation pertains only to the Son, who "comes forth" from the Father; and, second, that the Spirit "proceeds" eternally only from the Father, and not from the Son. When the Spirit is said to be sent into the world by the Father and the Son (Jn 15:26), this pertains only to the economic sending (the temporal mission of the Spirit), not to eternal processions. Latin theologians, by contrast, tend to think in terms of two "processions" (following Jerome's language), one of the Son from the Father by generation and the other of the Spirit from the Father and the Son by mutual spiration. This difference is important, because both Eastern and Western theologians traditionally agree on the fact that those relations between the persons that are manifest in the economy (in the temporal sending of the Son and Spirit) truly indicate to us who God is in himself (the processions of the persons, in their eternal relations of origin). We know who God is in himself as Trinity because the Father has sent the Son and the Spirit into the world. Therefore, one may rightly ask: if the Spirit is sent into the world by the Father and the Son, is this because he eternally proceeds from the Father and the Son, or does he eternally proceed uniquely from the Father? The relations of the persons manifest to us in the economy seemingly represent the relations that obtain between the persons eternally. We will have occasion to return to the question of the *Filioque* in subsequent chapters.

---

26. See *The Analytical Lexicon to the Greek New Testament*.

For the time being, let us simply note the following points in potential defense of the *Filioque*. First, the issue cannot be resolved merely by looking at the language. The mode in which the Spirit eternally comes from the Father may indeed be distinct from the mode in which the Son eternally comes from the Father; nevertheless, in both cases there is still a relational origin: each comes forth from the Father from all eternity. For this reason, we do need a common theological term by which to denote this commonality that obtains between them, and "procession" is itself a scriptural term: the Son and the Spirit both relate to the Father as the one from whom they originate, and in that sense they both "proceed" from him eternally.

Second, the Spirit is spoken of in scripture as the Spirit of the Son, or the one whom the Son sends. This means that the two relate to one another in the economy according to an order of relations: the Father sends the Spirit through the Son, or the Son with the Father sends the Spirit upon the Church. We may rightly ask, then, if it is feasible to posit new interpersonal relations that arise between the Son and Spirit only as a result of the temporal economy, personal relations that did not exist from all eternity? As we shall see in subsequent chapters, the persons in God are characterized by relations of origin to one another in all that they are, since each one is truly God and therefore is distinct from the other two not as a result of his divine attributes but as a result of his mode of proceeding. Consequently, were the eternal Spirit and the eternal Son to acquire new personal relations (in virtue of the temporal economy), they would alter their ways of being relative to one another. But since the ways they are relative to one another characterize them in all that they are, such a change would alter their very identity as persons who are God. In this case, God's inner identity would change precisely because of the sending of the persons in time, and so God's identity would come to depend upon his engagement with creation. By the sending of the persons of the Son and Spirit into the world, the persons of the Trinity would be changed and reconstituted, such that God's history with creation would change who God is. But this is impossible if God is truly the Creator of all else that is, who gives being to all else and who does not receive his being from creatures. Consequently, if the Son does send the Spirit in time, within the economy, this can be only because God the Holy Spirit proceeds eternally not only from the Father but also from the Son. (I will return to this argument in subsequent sections of the book.)

Finally, as we shall see, the Spirit is the Spirit of the Father, and has the

Father for his primary origin or principle. This is theologically uncontroversial, and almost all Trinitarian theologians agree on it. And yet this same Father is always the Father of the eternally begotten Son. Consequently, when the Father spirates the Spirit from all eternity, he necessarily does so as Father of the Son and so also in the Son and with the Son. The mutual indwelling of the Father and the Son (their perichoresis) characterizes the Father even when he spirates the Spirit. He spirates the Spirit through the Son, because the Son is always already in him from all eternity, as the one he relates to as Father. Although it might not be immediately evident, arguments of this kind for the *Filioque* can be derived from the principles enunciated in John's Gospel. These are ideas we will explore in subsequent chapters.

The Work of the Paraclete. In John's Gospel, the Spirit is consistently portrayed as continuing the work of the Father and the Son after Christ's glorification. Accordingly, we read in John 16:8–15:

And when he comes, he will convince the world of sin and of righteousness and of judgment: of sin, because they do not believe in me; of righteousness, because I go to the Father, and you will see me no more; of judgment, because the ruler of this world is judged. I have yet many things to say to you, but you cannot bear them now. When the Spirit of truth comes, he will guide you into all the truth; for he will not speak on his own authority, but whatever he hears he will speak, and he will declare to you the things that are to come. He will glorify me, for he will take what is mine and declare it to you. All that the Father has is mine; therefore I said that he will take what is mine and declare it to you.

One of the chief roles of the Spirit in the economy, as presented here, is accordingly to extend Christ's mission in time by guiding his disciples into the fullness of the truth that was present in Christ's person.

The Spirit of Truth. Thus, just as the Son is the interpreter or manifestation of the Father, so the Spirit interprets or allows one to understand the Son and the Father. Christ identifies himself with the truth in John 14:6: "I am the way, the truth, and the life." Accordingly, we find in John 16:13: "When the Spirit of truth comes, he will guide you into all the truth; for he will not speak on his own authority, but whatever he hears he will speak, and he will declare to you the things that are to come." In his *Commentary on the Gospel of John*, Aquinas makes a reasonable inference from the words of Jesus: "He shows the Spirit as related to the Son when he says, 'the Spirit of truth,' for the Son is the Truth: 'I am the way, and the truth, and the life,'

(Jn 14:6).... So to say that the Holy Spirit is 'the Spirit of truth,' is the same as saying the Holy Spirit is the Spirit of the Son."[27] One can infer from this reasoning that John sees the Spirit as one who comes forth from the Son precisely to provide acknowledgment of the Son in the world. The Spirit illumines believers with the grace of faith, which simultaneously convicts them of their sinfulness and justifies them by faith, uniting them to Christ in the process (Jn 16:8–11). The Spirit does not speak in his own name, but instead leads us into the fullness of the revelation given by the Father and Son once for all in Christ's advent.

CONCLUSION

What are the core principles of Trinitarian theology we have identified in John's Gospel? First, the Gospel begins with the affirmation that Jesus is the pre-existent Logos or Word and only-begotten Son of God, who was with the Father, in his bosom, from all eternity, and through whom God created the world. Here we have John's affirmation of the unity and personal distinction of God the Father and his Word. Second, the Word or only-begotten Son is likewise he who reveals the invisible Father to the world. He is the Father's exegete. Third, Jesus' Cross is portrayed by John within the ambit of realized eschatology as an exaltation of Jesus, which reveals God's glory and manifests Jesus' divine identity as "I AM." Fourth, John's Gospel in particular lays the basis for discussion of the processions of the Son from the Father, and of the Spirit from the Father and the Son. The Gospel's language here accordingly points to the intra-Trinitarian basis for the temporal missions of the Son sent forth from the Father, and of the Spirit sent forth by the Father and the Son, in the latter's saving work. Finally, John's discussion of the Spirit's role as Paraclete and Spirit of truth describes the Spirit's work of guiding the disciples into the fullness of truth given in the revelation of Christ. As the Son is the exegete of the Father, so too is the Spirit the exegete of the Father and the Son.

27. Aquinas, *In Ioan.* XV, lec. 5, 2062.

7

Nicene Trinitarian Theology

It took several centuries for the early Catholic Church to develop an official terminology and doctrinal framework for thinking about the Trinity. A key catalyst for this development was the crisis of Arianism in the early fourth century and the emergence of an "orthodox" doctrine of Trinitarian faith, articulated first at the Council of Nicaea in 325 A.D. and subsequently defended and interpreted by fourth- and fifth-century "pro-Nicene" thinkers in the Greek East and the Latin West of the Roman Empire.

The aim of this chapter is not to provide an intricate and nuanced summary of the historical development of Trinitarian reflection of this period.[1] The point rather is to indicate succinctly but clearly that there is a fundamental intellectual and historical continuity between the New Testament revelation of the apostolic age and the subsequent doctrinal definitions of the Catholic Church. The theoretical and contemplative writings of patristic theologians like Athanasius, Gregory of Nazianzus and Augustine were concerned precisely to show that this was the case. Inspired by them, then, we should wish to argue that the story of the early Christian doctrine of

1. See, on this topic, John Henry Newman, *The Arians of the Fourth Century*, 3rd. ed. (London: Longmans, Green and Co., 1908); J. N. D. Kelly, *Early Christian Doctrines*, 5th ed. (London: A&C Black, 1977); Aloys Grillmeier, *Christ in Christian Tradition*, vol. 1, *From the Apostolic Age to Chalcedon (451)*, 2nd ed., trans. J. Bowden (Philadelphia: Westminster, 1988); Frances M. Young, *From Nicaea to Chalcedon: A Guide to the Literature and Its Background* (London: SCM, 1983); Rowan Williams, *Arius: Heresy and Tradition* (London: DLT, 1987); Lewis Ayres, *Nicaea and Its Legacy: An Approach to Fourth-Century Trinitarian Theology* (Oxford: Oxford University Press, 2004); Khaled Anatolios, *Retrieving Nicaea: The Development and Meaning of Trinitarian Doctrine* (Grand Rapids, Mich.: Baker Academic, 2018); Brian Daley, *God Visible: Patristic Christology Reconsidered* (Oxford: Oxford University Press, 2018).

the Trinity is one of a homogeneous and organic development of doctrine. We can do so, however, only if we also acknowledge that this development took place in and through complex and diverse models of thinking over time (from the second to the fifth centuries), and amidst conflictual engagement with problematic ideas that contained partial but one-sided elements of truth, ideas the Church labeled as heresies. Once we see how early Christian thinking about the Trinity crystalized in the mature visions of persons like Gregory of Nazianzus and Augustine, we can in turn perceive the profound continuity between their approaches and that of Thomas Aquinas, to which we will turn in subsequent chapters of this book. Thomism is a form of thinking that develops not adjacent to or over and against patristic understanding of the Trinity, but in profound intellectual continuity with the deepest impulses of pro-Nicene Trinitarian speculation, itself a reflection on the inner meaning of the New Testament.

Any historical analysis of the development of doctrine presupposes a normative view of the doctrine in question. We measure how ideas have developed in history by a standard, which in this case is the eventual dogma that was formulated after centuries of argument and discussion. Since I am presupposing doctrinal formulations that are central to the confession of the Catholic faith, I am also going to use standard terminology from the post-Nicene period, even as it was later formulated by Aquinas, sometimes projecting it back, intentionally, onto authors who did not use it, so as to analyze and evaluate what they achieved or failed to achieve in their historical context according to the measure of subsequent developments.

In this context I will especially make use of a threefold distinction of terms that is a normative part of eventual Catholic doctrine. First, by the terms *person* and *hypostasis* I refer to the three personal subjects of the Father, Son, and Holy Spirit, who are really distinct from one another. Orthodox Trinitarian doctrine holds that there are three eternal persons in God. The word *hypostasis* is of Greek origin and can be translated in this context to mean "singular personal subject." It was used by Church Fathers such as Nazianzus to indicate the Father, Son, and Holy Spirit as distinct persons in God. Second, by the terms *essence* and *nature* I mean to indicate the divine nature that is common to the three persons. Orthodox Trinitarian doctrine holds that there is one nature or essence of God common to the three persons. Third, by *substance*, I mean to indicate one individual being or reality. If we think of three human beings, we are three persons, or hypostatic subjects (Peter, John, and James), who each share a common nature or essence (as human beings), but who do not share a common substance or individual being. They are three individual beings each of whom is human. In the case of the Trinity, however, orthodox doctrine holds that the three persons are not only one in essence (each one is truly divine, as three human beings are truly human), but also that they are each the one God, one in substance or individual being.

The word substance can be used to indicate a singular person, as Aristotle speaks in the *Categories* of primary substance, or it can be used to indicate a given nature or essence, as when he also speaks in the same text of secondary substance.[2] He also uses the term in the *Metaphysics* at times to indicate a singular being of a given kind, that is to say, some one thing, like a human being, a horse, or a tree, each one being a substance or individual being.[3] It is in this latter sense that I am using the term, typically, in accord with the definition given above, to indicate that the Father, Son and Holy Spirit are each the one God.[4]

In addition, we should make mention of two further clarifications to conclude this definitional prolegomenon. The first concerns the individual character of the divine nature. When we speak of any ordinary created thing we normally encounter, such as a human person, a horse or a tree, the nature in question is held in common by many, since there are many such realities. However, in the case of God, the nature is singular: only God is God, only God has a divine nature. Therefore, if the three persons who are God are also one in nature, then they are also one in being or substance. That is to say, they are one individual. How can this be? How can three persons be not only one in nature or essence but also one in individual being? How can three divine persons each possess fully the one individual being of the deity, and the divine nature? As we will see, the Fathers came to the conclusion that the divine persons communicate the divine nature from one to another by way of immaterial processions. The Son and the Spirit proceed eternally

2. See Aristotle, *Categories*, chap. 5 (2a13–17).

3. I take it this is the idea of substance presented in Aristotle, *Metaphysics* 7.17, esp. 1041a34–1041b10.

4. As we will see below, the Nicene definition specifies that the Father and the Son are "one in substance" or *homoousios*, often translated into Latin as *consubstantialis*. I take it that this idea is specifically theological, not "Aristotelian." However it retains some of the significations of the word as it is employed in the pre-Christian philosophical tradition, transposing these into a distinctively theological key to denote a mystery, namely that the Father and the Son are one in individual being and substance as God.

from the Father. These processions are immaterial, so that we can characterize them by analogy to human immaterial activities of knowledge and love.
The Son, who is the eternal Word and Wisdom of the Father, receives the
divine nature immaterially from the Father; and the Spirit, who is the eternal Love of the Father and the Son, receives the divine nature immaterially
from the Father and the Son.

Second, the immaterial processions in God are the basis for what Western theology after Augustine will call temporal missions, which I have referred to in the previous chapter. How should we understand the distinction
between processions and missions? The processions pertain to God eternally. The Son and the Spirit proceed eternally from God the Father, and accordingly God is Trinity before, during, and after his creation of the world.
However, these same processions (the inner life of God) are manifested to
us by the Father's sending of the Son into the world (especially in the Incarnation) and by the Father's and the Son's sending of the Spirit into the world
(especially at Pentecost). This "sending" of the persons in time entails what
we can call a divine mission: the rendering present of the divine persons to
us in the world by grace. A question that arises in patristic theology pertains
to our knowledge of the processions. How do the sending of the Son and
Spirit manifest to us that God is characterized by eternal processions? And
what do these processions consist in?

Our analysis below, in this and subsequent chapters, will consider how
the early Church came to develop a coherent terminology and unified doctrinal form of thinking about the Trinity, largely in keeping with the ideas
just aforementioned. We should keep in mind, however, that this development took place through a series of diverse intellectual movements that
were sometimes unrelated, or logically non-linear, and in which God was
conceived of in various ways or by distinct models, using different terminol-
ogies (especially in Greek versus Latin). The story unfolds then only successively and in a complex sense, as we will note below.

TWO TENDENCIES IN PRE-NICENE
THEOLOGY OF GOD

We can speak helpfully, if somewhat artificially, of two basic conceptual
models that arise in earliest Christian theology as ways to think about the
mystery of God, conceptual models that were based upon the New Testa-

ment.[5] One of these we could call "monological," because it envisages God as the transcendent Creator acting in and through his Logos, as a principle of reason and wisdom. The Logos and the Spirit of God are depicted as truly distinct, eternally pre-existent principles of God's internal identity, manifest in the world by the revelation of Christ. Their distinction arises primarily from their role in God's inner life, not from their role in revelation or the divine economy. We find this model in the early apologists of Christianity, like Justin Martyr, who sought to emphasize the rationality of Christianity in the face of Graeco-Roman religion, as well as the continuity of the New Testament with the Old Testament. The other model is what we can call "economic trinitarianism,"[6] in which the Son and the Spirit are distinguished clearly from the Father as personal agents who are God, but who are also described in their divine agency principally in reference to their economic state. In other words, we know God the Son and Spirit as persons distinct from the Father principally as a result of their activity in the economy, where they are sent by the Father. This tendency of thought, I will argue, is present in Irenaeus (who is nonetheless also a partaker of the first model as well). Once we identify these two models, we can ask ourselves two questions: Is each of them compatible with the New Testament, and, if so, in what form? Are they compatible with each other? The first emphasizes the internal life of God as a life of the Father in his Logos and Spirit, while the second emphasizes the revelation of the persons of the Son and the Spirit in the economy. Third and Fourth century "heresies" arose as modalists, subordinationists, and Arians explored forms of these models that were at base incompatible with the New Testament and that pitted them in various ways against one another. Pro-Nicene theolo-

<hr/>

5. The twofold model I am employing here takes inspiration from both Newman, *The Arians of the Fourth Century*, 156–59, and from Kelly, *Early Christian Doctrines*, 101–8. By "model" I mean only an intellectual schema or collective pattern of thinking. My presupposition is that some comprehensive ideas of the Trinity are better and some worse, based on the ways they are grounded in principles made known either explicitly or implicitly in New Testament revelation and the ways they develop reflection on these principles along internally consistent lines. I am not seeking to introduce the idea of models in a neo-Kantian sense, where one speaks of theological ideas as mental constructs employed to interpret the given phenomena of revelation subjectively, with the latent presupposition that the noumenon itself evades the adequate apprehension by every model, so that at some point one of them is obliged merely by an external imposition of authority. This kind of nominalist and voluntarist theory of paradigm shifts or models of social reasoning is inevitably incompatible with the very notion of theology as *sacra doctrina*.

6. I am not alluding here to Karl Rahner's notion of the "economic Trinity," which I take to be something very different, and to which I will return in the final part of this book.

gians, by contrast, found new ways to articulate the compatibility and mutual coherence of both these models, as each fitting well with scripture and as helpfully indicating the mystery of the Trinity. They did so by coming to a greater understanding of the immaterial procession of the Logos from the Father as the eternal generation of the Son, who is one in being with the Father. This presentation of the historical stages of the "logic" of early Trinitarian thought is no doubt overly schematic (with only two models), but it can help us identify core issues in early Catholic doctrine, so as to understand how that doctrine unfolded over time, and what principles emerged as perennial and enduring.

Justin Martyr and Irenaeus of Lyons

It is helpful in this respect to consider briefly some key ideas of early Trinitarian thought, found in Justin Martyr and Irenaeus, respectively. Justin Martyr (ca. 100–ca. 168 A.D.) clearly affirms that Jesus Christ is the pre-existent Son of God, and he attributes personal agency to the Son, as one really distinct from the eternal Father, in person and not in name only.[7] Justin is not therefore a unitarian theologian, and his thought, when judged by later standards, is unambiguously proto-Trinitarian. Nevertheless, Justin also faced two distinct groups of anti-Christian interlocutors, one stemming from the dominant Graeco-Roman culture that considered Christianity a novel superstition, and the other stemming from members of the Mediterranean Jewish community that considered Christianity a kind of heresy. In his apologetic strategy, then, he argues in a theoretically coherent way with both communities of critics through appeal to his theology of Christ as the pre-existent Logos.[8]

On the one hand, Justin claims that Christ is the eternal reason through whom God has created all things, and the Holy Spirit is the Spirit of God through whom God has inspired the Hebrew prophets and apostles, whose

7. See Justin Martyr, *Second Apology*, chap. 13: "For next to God, we worship and love the Word who is from the unbegotten and ineffable God, since also He became man for our sakes, that becoming a partaker of our sufferings, He might also bring us healing." Justin typically identifies Jesus as the pre-existent Word of the Father. He is clearly a personal subject distinct from the Father whom Christians worship as God. All translations of Justin and Irenaeus are by M. Dods and G. Reith, in *Ante-Nicene Fathers*, vol. 1, *The Apostolic Fathers, with Justin Martyr and Irenaeus*, ed. A. Roberts, J. Donaldson, and A. C. Coxe (Buffalo, N.Y.: Christian Literature Publishing, 1885). See also Justin Martyr, *First Apology*, chap. 63; *Dialogue with Trypho the Jew*, chap. 63.

8. On Justin's theology of Christ as Logos, see Eric Osborn, *Justin Martyr* (Tübingen: Mohr Siebeck, 1973); Brian Daley, *God Visible*, 55–62.

writings contain a superior wisdom to that of the Greek philosophers and poets.[9] This argumentative strategy emphasizes the unity of God over against Graeco-Roman polytheism. It accentuates the idea of an inherent connection between the God of Christianity as the God of "logos" or reason, who has made the world intelligible by his pre-existent wisdom, and the search of Greek philosophy for truth, achieved through the aspirations of right reason. Christianity is the rational religion because it affirms there to be only one God, and provides the needed revelation from the Spirit of God that alone can fulfill the human quest for reasonable truth, initiated in Greek philosophy.[10] Justin's argumentative strategy attempts to drive a wedge between the dominant culture of philosophy in ancient Rome and that of religious cult and liturgy, deemed irrational by the early Christians.[11]

On the other hand, Justin also employs this same Christology of pre-existent Logos and Spirit to respond to the objections of Jews who see the Christian religion as novel. Jesus is the wisdom through whom God has made all things, who appeared in theophany to the patriarchs of Israelite antiquity before taking flesh in more recent times so as to fulfill the prophecies of the Hebrew scriptures.[12] Here the notions found in the Septuagint of God's begotten wisdom, divine Word, and the Spirit of inspiration are seen

9. See, for example, Justin, *First Apology*, chaps. 6 and 13, on God as transcendent Reason, and Christianity as rational worship of the one God. Chap. 5–6: "For not only among the Greeks did reason [Logos] prevail to condemn these things [irrational pagan religious beliefs and practices] through Socrates, but also among the Barbarians were they condemned by Reason [or the Word, the Logos] Himself, who took shape, and became man, and was called Jesus Christ; Hence are we called atheists. And we confess that we are atheists, so far as gods of this sort are concerned, but not with respect to the most true God, the Father of righteousness and temperance and the other virtues, who is free from all impurity. But both Him, and the Son ... and the prophetic Spirit, we worship and adore, knowing them in reason and truth, and declaring without grudging to everyone who wishes to learn, as we have been taught."

10. On Christianity as the "true philosophy," see Justin, *Dialogue with Trypho the Jew*, chaps. 1–9. On the seedlings of the Logos present in pre-Christian philosophers and cultures, see Justin, *Second Apology*, chaps. 8, 10, and 13. Chap. 13: "For each man spoke well in proportion to the share he had of the spermatic word, seeing what was related to it.... Whatever things were rightly said among all men, are the property of us Christians. For next to God, we worship and love the Word who is from the unbegotten and ineffable God, since also He became man for our sakes.... For all the writers were able to see realities darkly through the sowing of the implanted word that was in them. For the seed and imitation impacted according to capacity is one thing, and quite another is the thing itself, of which there is the participation and imitation according to the grace which is from Him."

11. Subsequent examples of such argumentation concerning the superior rationality of Christianity as compared with Graeco-Roman religion are abundant in Clement of Alexandria, Athanasius, Tertullian, Lactantius, and Augustine.

12. See, for example, Justin, *Dialogue with Trypho*, chaps. 56 and 60.

after the fact as indications, however implicit, of a real distinction in the life of God between the Father, the Word, and the Spirit.[13]

What is common to both these ways of articulating the monological model is that they conceive of the eternal Triad in God of Father, Son, and Spirit in largely intellectualist terms, so that God is seen as a rational agent, both in his creation and in his inspiration of the prophets. The distinction of the three as distinct personal subjects is not denied, but it is considered above all in light of a psychological analogy derived from the prologue of John's Gospel, with resonances in Graeco-Roman philosophy, in which one could find the idea that the intelligible universe is reflective of divine logos.[14]

Irenaeus (ca. 130–ca. 202 A.D.) writes with an alternative set of theological concerns. Confronting early forms of Gnosticism, he seeks to address the internal community of the early Church, not its external critics. Against those sectarian, self-appointed "gnostics" who deny the inspiration of the Hebrew prophets and the created goodness of the material world, he sets out to defend the inspiration and unity of both testaments (employing the Septuagint and the New Testament canon) and to provide an articulation of the universal teaching of the Church. His vision centers on the Incarnation: How is it that God has become human, so that human beings—in both body and soul—might be saved and united with God? The Incarnation is the principle of divinization not only for the created spirit of man but also for the material body and the physical world.

In this context we can note three important aspects of Irenaeus's Trinitarian theology that are pertinent for the purposes of our study: First, he affirms unambiguously the real distinction of the Father, Son, and Holy Spirit as personal agents, each of whom is God.[15] The order of the three is conceived of in a monarchical fashion. The Father is the source or origin of the Son and the Spirit, his "two hands" through whom he acts to create the world and to redeem it. The Son, then, is the Incarnate Word of the Father, he through whom God has made all things, while the Spirit is the one sent

---

13. Justin, *Dialogue with Trypho*, chaps. 61, 62, 128, and 129.

14. On the Stoic doctrine of logos and Justin's reinterpretation of this doctrine in light of scripture, see Mark J. Edwards, "Exegesis and Early Christian Doctrine," in Emery and Levering, *The Oxford Handbook of the Trinity*, 80–86.

15. See for example Irenaeus, *Against Heresies* 2.30.9, where he teaches that the Father through his Word and Son creates the physical world. Likewise, Irenaeus, *Against Heresies* 4.20.1 and 3: "... the Word, namely the Son, was always with the Father; and that Wisdom also, which is the Spirit, was present with Him, anterior to all creation."

into the world to sanctify it, to prepare human beings for the Incarnation, and to act in light of the Incarnation to sanctify the Church, including by means of the sacramental life.[16]

Second, then, while Irenaeus clearly believes in the eternal pre-existence of the Son and the Spirit, and their personal distinction from the Father, he explains the relations between the three primarily in light of their activities and functions in the economy of creation and salvation. The Son is understood as he whom the Father sends to redeem the world by his incarnation, life, death, and resurrection.[17] The Spirit is understood as he who is sent from the Father to sanctify the creation, the universal human community, and the Church.[18] To speak in light of later theological distinctions, Irenaeus identifies the eternal processions of the Word and Spirit in light of the missions of the Son and Spirit. That is to say, the functional effects of God accomplished in the economy of the Son and the Spirit are the primary locus or "place" that Irenaeus looks to distinguish the three persons. He affirms their presence in history. While he also affirms a pre-existence of distinction in God of the Father, Son, and Spirit, he does not develop an overt theory of how the relations of the persons exist prior to or in distinction from the activity of God in the economy.[19] Irenaeus's thought implies logi-

16. Irenaeus, *Against Heresies* 5.6.1: "Now God shall be glorified in His handiwork, fitting it so as to be conformable to, and modelled after, His own Son. For by the hands of the Father, that is, by the Son and the Holy Spirit, man, and not [merely] a part of man, was made in the likeness of God. Now the soul and the spirit are certainly a part of the man, but certainly not the man; for the perfect man consists in the commingling and the union of the soul receiving the spirit of the Father, and the admixture of that fleshly nature which was molded after the image of God."

17. Irenaeus, *Against Heresies* 5.16.2: "For in times long past, it was said that man was created after the image of God, but it was not [actually] *shown*; for the Word was as yet invisible, after whose image man was created, Wherefore also he did easily lose the similitude. When, however, the Word of God became flesh, He confirmed both these: for He both showed forth the image truly, since He became Himself what was His image; and He re-established the similitude after a sure manner, by assimilating man to the invisible Father through means of the visible Word."

18. Irenaeus, *Demonstration of the Apostolic Preaching*, 7: "God the Father bestowed on us regeneration through His Son by the Holy Spirit. For as many as carry (in them) the Spirit of God are led to the Word, that is, to the Son; and the Son brings them to the Father; and the Father causes them to possess incorruption. Without the Spirit it is not possible to behold the Word of God, nor without the Son can any draw near to the Father: for the knowledge of the Father is the Son, and the knowledge of the Son of God is through the Holy Spirit; and, according to the good pleasure of the Father, the Son ministers and dispenses the Spirit to whomsoever the Father wills and as He wills" (trans. J. Armitage Robinson [London: SPCK, 1920]).

19. Irenaeus, *Demonstration of the Apostolic Preaching*, 5: "Well also does Paul His apostle say: *One God, the Father, who is over all and through all and in us all.* For *over all* is the Father; and *through all* is the Son, for through Him all things were made by the Father; and *in us all* is the Spirit, who cries *Abba Father,* and fashions man into the likeness of God. Now the Spirit shows forth the

cally that God is eternally trinitarian, since it affirms that the Son and Spirit come from the Father and are truly divine, but Irenaeus does not speculate extensively on how this is the case.

Third, even while this is all said, Irenaeus also clearly maintains elements of the first monological model noted above, in which God creates through his eternal pre-existent Logos and wisdom.[20] The God of Christians is a God of Reason. This is significant, because it suggests the implicit possibility of a logical compatibility between the two models, present already in this earliest strata of the Church's reflection on the New Testament. How is it that God is eternally Father, Word, and Spirit, and how can the two models complement each other? The person of the Word is the eternally begotten Logos or divine reason of the Father, and the divine nature is communicated fully from the Father to the Son. What is only implicit in Irenaeus would subsequently be considered in overt terms by thinkers like Athanasius, Gregory of Nazianzus, and Augustine, but the passage from his thought to theirs is not obvious, and was not evident to all those who came immediately after Irenaeus.

Given the way I have presented these two early models of Trinitarian reflection (sometimes overlapping in a single given author), it is easy to see how imbalances could result by hardening aspects of one model against aspects of the other. The monological model is based on the psychological analogy to human activity as logos-centered. It rightly underscores that the one God of Christianity is personal and that he acts in his Word and Spirit, now manifest in the Incarnation. The tendency here is toward monotheism and the unity of the two testaments of the bible. The risk, of course, is to emphasize these ideas in an exclusive way, so as to render obscure the real distinction of the Trinitarian persons. The model presented by economic Trinitarianism, meanwhile, rightly grasps the real distinction of the persons manifest in the economy, and the functional attributions we make to them of distinct activities. "The Father has created all things in his Word." "The

Word, and therefore the prophets announced the Son of God; and the Word utters the Spirit, and therefore is Himself the announcer of the prophets, and leads and draws man to the Father." See also chap. 47, where Irenaeus speaks of the Father and the Son as each being Lord and God and as sharing in a common substance and power. On this point, see the important study of Michel René Barnes, "Irenaeus' Trinitarian Theology," *Nova et Vetera* (English Edition) 7, no. 1 (2009): 67–106.

20. See Irenaeus, *Against Heresies*, 2.28.4–6; 3.16.2; 4.6.3; see also the study by Khaled Anatolios, "Faith, Reason, and Incarnation in Irenaeus of Lyons," *Nova et Vetera* (English edition) 16, no. 2 (2018): 543–60.

Son has redeemed the human race." "The Spirit inspires the prophets and sanctifies the Church." However, if this model is taken to an extreme, it can lose sight of the truth of Christian monotheism: that the three persons are equally and identically the one God. Instead, an economic subordination-ism can result, in which the Word and Spirit are distinguished from the Father, but with the qualification that they are somehow less than the Father. As we will see, both these reactions did emerge in the third century, and were in turn challenged by the objections of Arius. However, his solution was in fact heretical, and so it in turn catalyzed the response of the great Trinitarian theologians of the Nicene period.

THE THIRD-CENTURY BACKGROUND
TO ARIANISM

In the third century, speculative theology emerged in the likes of Hippoly-tus, Tertullian, and Clement of Alexandria. These authors continued the development of the two models mentioned above. Simultaneously, however-er, there also arose two distinct and, in some ways, opposed errors, which we can term "modalism" and "subordinationism." The former is associated with theologians like Noetus of Smyrna and above all Sabellius (so that it is also sometimes called "Sabellianism").[21] Subordinationism can be associ-ated with the thought of Origen of Alexandria, at least as many commonly interpret him. It is from the dialectical tension between these two poles of thought that Nicene Trinitarian doctrine eventually emerges.

Monarchic Modalism. As I have noted above, there are tendencies in ear-ly Christian thought to depict the Trinity in primarily monological terms, and in primarily economic terms. The former relies heavily on a psycholog-ical analogy in which the Father acts through his Word and Spirit, while the latter focuses especially upon the manifestation of the Son and the Spirit as distinct personal agents in the economy of salvation. One way to har-monize these two notions is to posit that the distinction of persons arises only in virtue of the divine economy and that it does not pertain to God as

21. See the polemical writings against these figures by Hippolytus, *Against Noetus*, trans. J. H. MacMahon, *Ante-Nicene Fathers*, vol. 5, ed. A. Roberts, J. Donaldson, and A. C. Coxe, (Buffalo, N.Y.: Christian Literature Publishing, 1886); and Tertullian, *Against Praxeas*, trans. P. Holmes, in *Ante-Nicene Fathers*, vol. 3, ed. A. Roberts, J. Donaldson, and A. C. Coxe, (Buffalo, N.Y.: Christian Literature Publishing, 1885).

he is in himself eternally. The Father just is the eternal person of God, but he manifests himself under the aspect of the Son in the redemption and as the Spirit in the inspiration and sanctification of creatures.[22] We might say, then, that this classical modalist error arises from the idea that the Father, Son, and Holy Spirit are each divine, but that they are not truly distinct persons. The implicit logic of this line of thinking seems to move along the following lines:

- There is only one God, which entails that God is one in both his nature and ineffable substance.
- The Father is truly God, and the Son and Spirit are truly God.
- However, where there is a real multiplicity of persons, there is a multiplicity of substances, and in God there can be no multiplicity of substances, since God is one.
- Therefore, there can be no multiplicity of persons in God.
- As a consequence, we must stipulate that while the Father, Son, and Spirit are each truly divine, they are not truly distinct persons.
- When we speak of the Son or the Spirit, we are not signifying persons truly distinct from the Father, but rather only various realizations of God's presence in the economy in distinct modes.

Notice that this complex of ideas leads to the conclusion that God reveals himself to be tri-personal in the economy but that we cannot conclude from this that there is a distinction of persons in God himself. Tri-personality pertains to God as he appears to us, in his modes of action in time, but not to God as he is in himself.

Against the modalist conception of God, pre-Nicene theologians responded in a number of ways. First, by noting that the basic error in the argument given above is found in the third claim: where there is a real multiplicity of persons, there is a multiplicity of substances. The presupposition here is that a distinction of persons automatically implies a distinction of substances or beings. It is precisely the contention of Trinitarian orthodoxy that such a distinction does not apply in the case of God, as presented by New Testa-

22. Hippolytus argues against just such a position, for example, in *Against Noetus*, chaps. 5–10, and likewise Tertullian in *Against Praxeas*, chap. 5. Tellingly, both of them employ the same argument, that there is in God eternal Logos or mind, and that this is the person of the Son, therefore the Son is eternally distinct from the Father. In other words, they appeal precisely to the psychological analogy (the monological modal) to defend what they take to be an orthodox interpretation of it and to protect its right use from falling into a form of unitarian modalism.

ment revelation.[23] Second, by pointing out that modalism denies the distinction of persons in the eternal life of God, in the name of divine unity, but this need not follow. In fact, scriptural orthodoxy demands that we uphold *both* the unity of the divine nature and a true distinction of persons.[24]

Third, as Tertullian noted, the logic of modalism leads to a position that is "Patripassianist," namely, it implies that it is the Father who suffers on the Cross. The argument is not based on what the historical modalist theologians actually taught but is a reasonable *reductio ad absurdum* argument derived from their principles. Jesus Christ, who is both God and man, was personally crucified on Calvary. If the Father is the same person as the Son, then it must be God the Father who was personally crucified on Calvary. In keeping with revelation, however, the Church does not confess that the Father was crucified, but only the Son. The claim that the Father was crucified therefore must be rejected. But it follows from this that the Father and the Son are not the same person, even though Jesus is both true God and true man. Therefore, there must be a real distinction of persons in the godhead between Father and Son.[25]

Finally, another critique of modalism concerns the repercussions this doctrine has on our knowledge of God: if the distinction of persons is something that pertains only to the economy of revelation, but not to *God as he is in himself*, then we do not really know God as he is in himself. In essence, God has not revealed himself to us in Christ. God's identity as Father, Son, and Spirit is only an outward show, and is not consistent with who or what God is eternally in his hidden personal identity. Modalism, then, calls into question the very notion of divine revelation and its trustworthiness.

Subordinationism. Patristic scholars debate how to interpret rightly Origen's vast corpus and his historically innovative use of terms to develop a theology of God. Arguably, one should make two basic claims in this re-

---

23. This is why Tertullian insisted on a unity of *substantia* of the three persons, so as to indicate that they are each fully divine and identically God, a position that anticipates in its own way Nicene dogma. See *Against Praxeas*, chaps. 2–3. For an analysis of the Stoic elements in Tertullian's concept of *substantia* see Jean Daniélou, *The Origins of Latin Christianity*, trans. D. Smith and J. A. Baker (Philadelphia: Westminster Press, 1977).

24. It is significant in this respect that already in Tertullian's *Against Praxeas*, we see the emergence in Latin theology of a coherent terminology of God as *trinitas* in which the Father, Son, and Spirit are each distinct *personae* sharing in a common *substantia/natura*. This terminological typology was to have a lasting and doctrinally stabilizing effect upon subsequent theological usage in the Latin world.

25. See Tertullian's argument in *Against Praxeas*, chap. 14.

gard. First, Origen contributed concepts and key Greek terms to the later elaborations of Nicene orthodoxy. This is the case especially with regard to his idea of the generation of the Son as an immaterial, eternal generation of a hypostatic person distinct from the Father. Second, however, his thought also contains clear indications of a subordinationist account of the generation of the Son and the spiration of the Spirit. Origen claims, in effect, that the Son is eternally begotten of the Father, and is a hypostatic subject distinct from the Father.[26] However, he also clearly affirms that the Son and Spirit are less than the Father in comprehension and power.[27] The Son comes forth eternally from the substance of the Father, but is distinct from the Father in degree (or gradation) of substance and subsistence.[28] By its inner logic, this position inevitably leads to the conclusion that there is an eternal subordination in God.[29]

One could present the idea in the following way:

- First let us acknowledge that there is a true distinction of persons (hypostases) between the Father and the Son.
- In addition, Christ is the *eternally begotten* Son of the Father, without beginning or end, through whom all things were created.
- However, where there is a real multiplicity of persons, there is a multi-

---

26. See Origen, *On First Principles*, 1.2.4: "For this is an eternal and everlasting begetting, just as brightness is begotten from light" (trans. and ed. John Behr [Oxford: Oxford University Press, 2017], vol. 1). See also Origen, *On First Principles*, 1.2.6; 4.4.1.

27. In *On First Principles* 1.3.5, Origen clearly delimits the scope of activity and providence of the Holy Spirit in relation to the Father and the Son, and most scholars agree that he suggests, in 4.4.8, a derivation of knowledge from more perfect to less in the Father, Son, and Spirit respectively. See also Origen, *Commentary on the Gospel of John*, 2.2, where he suggests in a similar way that the Son has a more limited scope of providential activity than the Father.

28. Origen, *On First Principles*, 1.3.3: The Son can be said to be created eternally by the Father as his begotten Wisdom; 1.2.6: He is begotten by the will of the Father; 1.2.6: He is the figure of the subsistence or substance of the Father (implying he is not only hypostatically distinct but also substantially distinct); 1.2.11: He derives his subsistence from the Father. Origen, *Commentary on the Gospel of John*, 2.2: He is called God in a lesser sense than the Father. Origen, *Contra Celsus*, 7.57: The Son is to receive less honor than the Father.

29. Origen's ideas regarding the divinity of Christ are distinctly Christian and not philosophical. Nevertheless, they play out against the backdrop of Graeco-Roman Neoplatonic speculations regarding God, in which there are emanations within the godhead. In the *Enneads*, Plotinus, who was a contemporary of Origen in Alexandria, depicts the first principle, God, to be first and foremost the One who is immutable; from the One there then emanates God's *Nous* or mind; and from the *Nous* in turn emanates the life or world soul that informs matter. There is a gradual emanation, then, of the physical world from the mind of God. For the ancients of this period, it is not strange to think of degrees of being in the deity, and to think of the physical world as a lesser and lower manifestation of being emanating forth from the deity.

plicity of substances. Therefore, a real distinction of persons implies a real distinction of substances or hypostatic emanations, with distinct gradations of perfection between them.

- We should not speak, then, of the Father and the Son as being equal in nature or one in being, but rather of there being gradations of being present between them.
- The Father is eternally greater than his Son, while the Son is *eternally subordinate* to the Father. The Son's distinction from the Father is both personal *and* in some real sense substantial, that is to say, the Son is a being eternally distinct from the Father.

As we have noted, Origen does affirm this about the Son in a qualified way, namely that the Son is distinct in being from the Father, and freely produced by the Father from all eternity.[30] Meanwhile, the Holy Spirit, Origen teaches, is a creature subordinate in turn to both the Father and the Son.[31]

On the positive side, for Origen, the Father is eternally Father precisely because he is the eternal Father of the Son. This idea suggests that there are personal relations in God, a motif that will be further developed by the Cappadocians. For Origen, the Father, it seems, is eternally related to the Son, and the Son to the Father, and this relation is constitutive of personal identity. In addition, the Son is understood by Origen to be eternally originate from the Father by *immaterial generation*. Here we find a form of thinking that may be suitable for use so as to transcend merely economic Trinitarianism. The immanent life of God is characterized by processions of generation and spiration.[32] To use the later terminology of Nicaea, the Son is eternally

30. Origen, *On First Principles*, 1.2.6; 4.4.1.

31. Origen, *Commentary on the Gospel of John*, 2.6; "We consider, therefore, that there are three hypostases, the Father and the Son and the Holy Spirit; and at the same time we believe nothing to be uncreated but the Father. We therefore, as the more pious and the truer course, admit that all things were made by the Logos, and that the Holy Spirit is the most excellent and the first in order of all that was made by the Father through Christ. And this, perhaps, is the reason why the Spirit is not said to be God's own Son. The Only-begotten only [alone] is by nature and from the beginning a Son, and the Holy Spirit seems to have need of the Son, to minister to Him ... so as to enable Him not only to exist, but to be wise and reasonable and just, and all that we must think of Him as being." References to the *Commentary on John* and the *Contra Celsus* are taken from *Ante-Nicene Fathers*, vol. 9, ed. and trans. A. Menzies (Buffalo, N.Y.: Christian Literature Publishing, 1896). See likewise Origen, *On First Principles*, 1.3.7; 2.7.3.

32. As I have noted in the introduction, I use the word "spiration" to denote that mode of eternal procession that is proper to the Spirit, as distinct from the eternal procession proper to the Son, who is begotten. Origen does not use this terminology and does not speculate greatly on the property or mode of the Spirit's procession. However, his idea of eternal immaterial begetting of the Son from the Father lays a foundation for the eventual emergence of this idea.

begotten of the Father, as his uncreated offspring. Subsequent theologians will make use of this analogy for immaterial begetting to speak of the eternal personal relation in God of the Father and the Son, separating its usage from Origen's mistaken conception of a subordinate gradation of being.

Against Origen's subordinationism, orthodox Trinitarian thinking, represented initially by Athanasius, would eventually identify two difficulties with Origen's ideas: First, the same basic error is present here as it was in modalism. We see this in the third idea in the sequence above, which is the same as the third point in the previous sequence, namely, the premise that a distinction of persons implies a distinction of substances or beings. This is true for human persons: three distinct individual persons (Peter, James, John) are three distinct substances, or individual beings, but this is not the case with the Trinity, which is wholly dissimilar in this respect, when compared with creatures. Pro-Nicene theologians will underscore that the Father eternally generates the Son as his begotten Word in such a way as to communicate to him the fullness of the divine nature and substance; consequently the Son is equal in nature and one in being with the Father. Second, whereas modalism claimed that the oneness of God required a non-distinction of persons, subordinationism implies that a distinction of persons requires the distinction of beings in God, or at least a gradation of perfections. Consequently, we see emerge in Origen's writings a worrisome ambiguity as to the divinity of the Son and the unity of God. What does it mean for the Son to have a lesser degree of divinity than the Father? How are we to understand his eternal deity, if it is somehow distinct even substantively from the divinity of the Father? On this conception, what then happens to divine unity? Is there truly only one God or is there a gradation of beings in God? The *homoousios* formula of the Council of Nicaea (the affirmation that the Father and the Son are one in being and nature) eventually offers a corrective to Origen's problematic conception.

ARIANISM AS A RESPONSE TO INTELLECTUAL CHALLENGES

As is commonly known, Arius (d. 336) was a priest from Alexandria, Egypt in the early fourth century. Around the year 318, he became involved in a dispute with the Bishop of Alexandria, Alexander, who was the mentor of Athanasius. In this dispute, Arius maintained that the Son and Logos is a created principle, through whom God the Father created the world. Therefore, there was once a time, before he was begotten, that the Logos did not exist.[33] Arius was apparently excommunicated for this teaching in his local church, but the controversy gave rise to debate throughout the eastern Roman Empire. Some bishops came to agree with Arius, or at least with a variant of his thought, understanding the Son as a created principle not identical with but only similar to the Father, through whom the world was created. By the time Constantine came to power as emperor in 324, there was intense debate within the Eastern Church, with various local sees condemning and approving Arius's views.

We only have fragments of Arius's original work, the most important of which is called the *Thalia*, or Banquet. From what scholars can gather, Arius's intelligible theological ideas bear some influence from Origen, but also are posed as reactions against the idea of the Son as an intermediate hypostasis (or person) *within the deity*. According to Arius, the Son is less than the unbegotten Father and is lacking in perfect comprehension of the Father and himself. The Son originates from the will of the Father, coming to be as a creature, and he is not to be prayed to. It is possible, therefore, to interpret Arius above all as a biblical monotheist, who perceives a problem with Origen's subordinationism because it attributes a duality of substance to God, and a gradated hierarchy of perfections to the Father and Son in their co-eternity.[34] In the face of Origen's ambiguous and problematic idea, Arius presumably wanted to underscore that there is only one God, the unbegotten Father and Creator, and that God has one undivided divine nature. The Son therefore is a creature.[35]

However, Arius (unlike Sabellius) also believes that the persons of the Father, Son, and Holy Spirit are truly distinct. He cannot accept the notion of a real distinction of persons within the eternal godhead, presumably be-

---

33. On the unfolding of the Arian crisis and for helpful analysis of Arius's own theology, see Rowan Williams, *Arius, Heresy and Tradition*, and Lewis Ayres, *Nicaea and Its Legacy*, 41–61.

34. See the helpful analysis of various features of Arius's thought by Anatolios, *Retrieving Nicaea*, 36–52.

35. An early manifesto of Arius and other likeminded priests, which was sent to Alexander, states the following: "Before everlasting ages he [God, the unbegotten one] begot his unique Son, through whom he made the ages and all things. He begot him not in appearance, but in truth, constituting him by his own will, unalterable and unchangeable, a perfect creature of God, but not as one of the creatures [among others]—an offspring, but not as one of the things begotten." Athanasius, *De synodis*, 16.3, trans. E. R. Hardy in *The Christology of the Later Fathers*, Library of Christian Classics 3 (Philadelphia: Westminster, 1954), 333. See the analysis of Brian Daley in *God Visible*, 96–100.

cause, in his thinking, this would entail a plurality of substances in God. The logic of this position is clear, since it maintains the unicity of the godhead while still acknowledging the distinction of the persons. To make this distinction, however, one must sharply affirm—and herein lies the whole novelty of Arius's position—that the Son and the Holy Spirit are created beings. As he writes in *Thalia* I-II: "God was not eternally a father. There was [a time] when God was all alone, and was not yet a father; only later did he become a father.... The Son did not always exist. Everything created is out of nothing (*ex ouk ontōn*), all existing creatures, all things that are made; so the Word of God himself came into existence out of nothing. There was [a time] when he did not exist (*ēn pote hote ouk ēn*); before he was brought into being, he did not exist. He too had a beginning to his created existence."[36]

The logic of Arius's idea seems to unfold in the following way:

- There is not and cannot be a hierarchy or plurality in the substance of God, who is one, i.e., there are no interim degrees between Creator and creation. (With this affirmation, Arius establishes a clear distinction between Creator and creature.)
- Moreover, a distinction of persons implies a distinction of substances.
- The Logos is not the unbegotten Father, but is personally distinct from him as one "generated" by the Father.
- Therefore, God "pre-exists" the Son, and is unchangeable and inalienable, while the Son is "produced" or "made" by God the Father as a "creature."

Arius's position is novel in many ways. It breaks with both the models of Trinitarian thinking we examined briefly above, present in the earliest strata of Christian theological reflection. As with both the monological monarchism of Justin, and the modalism of Sabellius, Arius thinks of the unbegotten God above all in unipersonal terms, but in differentiation from both models, he denies the divinity of the Son and, in contrast with Justin, he posits no real distinction in God between the Father and his Word or Son. Instead, the Logos is said to be a creature. As with both the economic Trinitarianism of Irenaeus and Origenist subordinationism, Arius affirms a distinction of personal agents manifest in the economy, Father, Son, and Spirit. In differentiation from Irenaeus, however, he denies the divinity of the Son

---

36. The translation here is that of Rowan Williams in *Arius: Heresy and Tradition*, 100.

and Spirit, and in differentiation from Origen he denies the eternal generation of the Son, whom he sees as a creature.

Presumably Arius's thought was compelling to some of his contemporaries because it looked like a novel solution to a set of outstanding problems. He maintains the scriptural affirmation of the distinction of persons
(Father, Son, and Spirit), and does so while rejecting Origen's emanationist
conception of the deity. Therefore, Arius is neither modalist nor subordinationist. Furthermore his early followers claimed that while the Son is not
true God, he is like the Father and therefore mediates to us a knowledge of
the unbegotten God. Arius's Christology is soteriological, then: Christ the
mediator reveals the Father to us. Significantly, however, Arius shares with
the modalist and subordinationist positions the same contentious premise
that we noted above: a distinction of persons necessarily entails a multiplicity of substances. This is seemingly why he denies the divinity of Christ as
well as that of the Spirit: they are personally distinct from the Father and
therefore they cannot be the same in being as God. As we will see below, it
is precisely this premise that will ultimately be rejected by the Fathers at the
Council of Nicaea—and thereafter by orthodox Trinitarian thought—with
their affirmation of the Son's consubstantiality with the Father.

THE COUNCIL OF NICAEA IN 325 A.D.

The Council of Nicaea was called in 325 A.D. by Emperor Constantine I in
order to respond to the error of Arianism and to the various derivative positions it was giving rise to. While we do not have space here to go into
the Council's historical background or the totality of its proceedings, a few
points should be noted regarding the Council's major creedal affirmations
concerning the Son. In what follows, I will begin by quoting the Nicene
Creed, after which I will then draw out the important doctrinal implications of the Council's affirmations by way of a brief commentary on the
text.

The relevant portion of the orthodox creedal confession of Nicaea affirms:

We believe in one God, the Father all powerful, maker of all things, both seen and
unseen. And in one Lord Jesus Christ, the Son of God, the Only-Begotten, begotten from the Father, that is, from the substance [οὐσίας, *ousias*] of the Father, God
from God, light from light, true God from true God, begotten, not made, consub-

stantial [ὁμοούσιον, *homoousion*] with the Father, through whom all things came to be, both those in heaven and those on earth....[37]

The first thing to note regarding this dogmatic affirmation is the Council's insistence on the real distinction of persons in God, a distinction that does not imply any inequality between the persons. This idea is especially evident in the phrase "the Only-Begotten, begotten [or generated] from the Father, that is, from the substance [or being] of the Father, God from God, light from light, true God from true God...." The Council is affirming here what we might call the doctrine of "derived equality": the Son is eternally derived from the Father as one who is truly God, and so he is personally distinct from but is also equal to the Father.[38] The Father and Son thus partake equally of the unique being and essence of God, which the Son receives eternally from the Father.

With the phrase from the Creed, "begotten, not made," that follows on the words just cited, the Council goes on next to affirm that there is indeed an eternal procession or going forth of the Son from the Father, while also suggesting that this procession takes place *within* the godhead itself and therefore is distinct from the creation. The Son is the eternally begotten one who, though proceeding from the Father, is himself uncreated. Moreover, it is "through [him]" that "all things were made." In this way, the Council interprets scriptural references to the Son's being begotten as references to an eternal intra-divine process wholly distinct from creation.

Finally, with the Council's famous description of the Son's status as *homoousios* or "one in being with the Father"—a term frequently rendered into Latin as *consubstantialis*—we find the famous affirmation of the uniqueness of the divine being (*ousia*). The Son or Word is one in substance, or being, with the Father, as the unique God and Creator of all things. The word *ousia* in this context certainly indicates the individual being of God, but also can indicate the divine nature or essence of God, that deity in virtue of which both the Father and the Son are said to be God.[39] The use of the term *homoousios* signifies that while the Son is personally distinct from the Father,

37. The Nicene Creed has been cited from *Decrees of the Ecumenical Councils*, ed. Tanner, 1:5, which provides an English translation of the Greek text.

38. The notion of derived equality can be found in Eric Mascall, *The Triune God: An Ecumenical Study* (London: Pickwick Publications, 1986), 16.

39. As I have noted above, in common Greek philosophical parlance, the word *ousia* can indicate both an individual being and a common nature, and in this context it seems clearly to indicate both.

he nevertheless is also one in both being and nature with the Father. The Son is truly God.

The Nicaean symbol posits the following, then: first, the distinction of persons in the godhead does not imply any distinction of being or substance. This is the rejection of the faulty premise shared, as we saw, by the arguments advanced by the modalist, subordinationist, and Arian positions respectively. In the case of created persons, a distinction of persons does imply a distinction of substances (i.e., Peter, James, and John are distinct persons and so also distinct individual beings or substances). However, the mystery of the Trinity is different in this regard. The similitude between the Trinity and human persons does not obtain, since in God the distinction of persons does not imply a distinction of beings. The Father and the Son are of the same substance [homoousios], that is to say, they are truly one in both being and nature. They are each truly God and there is only one God. Second, the Council also maintains, then, that there is procession in God without creation: the Son is eternally begotten by the Father, but is in no way made or created. The distinction of persons in God must be understood, then, in light of eternal processions, an idea that will become important in theology immediately after the Council. Third, the Council affirms that the Father and Son are equal in being, even though the Son receives all that he is eternally from the Father. Contrary to the idea of Origen, there are no gradations of perfection in God. This is the case because the Son is of one substance with the Father, and therefore is his equal as God.

This, then, is the faith professed by the Council of Nicaea. It will serve as a normative point of departure for orthodox Trinitarian reflection in subsequent ages.

ATHANASIUS OF ALEXANDRIA

Even if one takes the normative status of the Council of Nicaea for granted, its creedal formulation still raises intellectual difficulties. It was the task of theologians who wrote in the era just after the Council to face various fundamental questions of Trinitarian theology: How can there be eternal procession in God that does not imply creation? How can the Son proceed from the Father, while being one in being with the Father? The first major theologian who grappled with these questions in a constructive way was Athanasius of Alexandria (ca. 293–May 2, 373), the episcopal successor to

Alexander and an ardent defender of Nicene orthodoxy in the course of his long tenure as bishop.

Athanasius's Trinitarian and Christological teachings are set forth in a particularly cogent way in his *Orations against the Arians*.[40] In his arguments, Athanasius develops a number of significant ideas in defense of the divinity of the Son. First, he notes that the distinction of persons in the godhead does not imply a distinction of being or essence. There is only one God, the Holy Trinity, in whom there is a real distinction of persons, Father, Son, and Holy Spirit. This idea is intelligible if we look to the analogies provided by the scriptures themselves, in the writings of John and Paul: the Son proceeds eternally from the Father as his Word and Wisdom, which is to say, by way of immaterial generation. The analogy for eternal generation is taken from intellectual life, not physical generation of one person from another.[41] In material generation, substance is multiplied, but it is not multiplied in the case of immaterial generation, for the logos of a thinker is in the thinker and of the same substance as the one from whom it proceeds. It is in light of this concept of immaterial generation in a subject that Athanasius explores the idea that the Son is eternally begotten of the substance of the Father and therefore is truly God, one in being with the Father. The Father eternally begets his Son as his Logos or immaterial Word. Because the eternal begetting is immaterial, it need not imply any multiplicity of substances or beings as in material begetting. Rather, the Word proceeds from the very substance of the Father and in turn possesses this substance in himself. When the Father knows himself and expresses himself in his Logos, he communicates all he is and has as God to his Logos, as Son. Because the Son is the offspring of the Father, he has the same nature or essence of deity as the Father. The Word therefore possesses in himself all that is proper to the Father.[42] If this

40. All quotations from this work will be taken from Athanasius, "Four Discourses Against the Arians," in *Athanasius: Select Works and Letters*, vol. 4 of *Nicene and Post-Nicene Fathers*, second series, ed. Philip Schaff and Henry Wace (Peabody, Mass.: Hendrickson Publishers, 2004).

41. Athanasius, "Four Discourses Against the Arians," 1.15: "[The Arians] deny that the Son is the proper offspring of the Father's essence, on the ground that this must imply parts and divisions; what is this but to deny that He is very Son, and only in name to call Him Son at all? And is it not a grievous error, to have material thoughts about what is immaterial?"

42. Athanasius, "Four Discourses Against the Arians," 1.9: "For, behold, we take divine Scripture, and thence discourse with freedom of the religious Faith, and set it up as a light upon its candlestick, saying:—Very Son of the Father, natural and genuine, proper to His essence, Wisdom Only-begotten, and Very and Only Word of God is He; not a creature or work, but an offspring proper to the Father's essence. Wherefore He is very God, existing one in essence with the very

is the case, then the Son also has the same will, power, and wisdom as the Father. Consequently, there is a unity of action of the Father and the Son. As God, they share in the same activity. The Father has created, enlightened and redeemed the world by his Word and Wisdom, that is to say, through the eternal Son.[43]

Athanasius makes use of the two models we have noted above from pre-Nicene theology and in effect shows their profound compatibility. We can and should think of God according to the analogy of a monological subject who creates through his Logos, since this analogy is given to us by scripture itself. At the same time, we must affirm in light of the apostolic teaching that there is a real distinction of persons, revealed to us in the works of the economy. The key notion holding these two ideas together is that of the procession of the Word as an immaterial generation according to nature. Because the Logos of the Father is himself God, who eternally proceeds from the Father as a distinct person, he must possess in himself the plenitude of the divine nature, just as a Son receives from a Father the very nature of the Father.

This way of thinking suggests that the economic distinction of the Father, Son, and Spirit (God revealing himself as Father, Son, and Spirit in history) has its basis in the eternal distinction of persons in God. This distinction of persons is understood best in light of the eternal processions in God. God eternally begets his Son, who proceeds from him as his immaterial Logos. The immaterial nature of the begetting of the Son helps us understand how eternal procession can occur within God without introducing inequality among the persons. God the Father can communicate all that he is and has as God to God the Son, by way of immaterial begetting. In making this move, Athanasius avoids both modalism and subordinationism. God is neither unitarian nor divided in substance and nature. God is Trinitarian: three

---

Father." Athanasius develops a more explicit defense of the "*homoousios*" formula of Nicaea in his later work, *On the Nicene Council* (*De decretis*).

43. Athanasius, "Four Discourses Against the Arians," 1.16: "If then, as we have stated and are showing, what is the Offspring of the Father's essence be the Son, we cannot hesitate, rather we must be certain, that the same is the Wisdom and Word of the Father, in and through whom He creates and makes all things; and His Brightness too, in whom He enlightens all things, and is revealed to whom He will; and His Expression and Image also, in whom He is contemplated and known, wherefore 'He and His Father are one (John 10:30),' and whoever looks on Him looks on the Father; and the Christ, in whom all things are redeemed, and the new creation wrought afresh." On the soteriological dimensions of Athanasius's reflection on the divinity of Christ, see Anatolios, *Retrieving Nicaea*, 100–108.

persons who are one in being and nature. Athanasius maintains a biblical theology of the unity of the divine essence and the transcendence of the one God as creator, even while affirming the divinity of the Son and the Spirit, thus refuting the error of Arianism. Most importantly, his theological arguments are scripturally well founded, and therefore provide a biblically warranted basis for orthodoxy.

It also follows from Athanasius's view that the Father does not choose to beget the Son, in contradiction to the claim of Arius, who affirmed the Son to be the product of a free creation on the part of God.[44] Rather, the Father eternally begets the Son *as Father*. As such, begetting is intrinsic to his identity. There was never a "moment" in God when the Father was not Father of the Son. Consequently, the relation between the Father and the Son is constitutive of who each one is. The Father is Father only by and with the Son, and vice versa.[45] This is important, as we will see below, for the Trinitarian theology of the Cappadocians, who develop a relational account of Trinitarian personhood: the persons are always related to one another in all that they are. As we will see, this idea also has consequences for orthodox Christology, because it will mean that everything that the Son does in his person, whether in virtue of his divine nature or his human nature, is expressive of his personal relation to the Father.

As an addendum to our comments above, we should consider in greater detail two ideas that have great import in subsequent Trinitarian theology (both Eastern and Western): first, Athanasius's important interpretation of the psychological analogy as a way of understanding the inner life of the Trinity; and second, his insistence on the unity of the Trinity in all actions outside of God (*ad extra*) of creation and redemption.

Psychological Analogy. For Athanasius, as we have noted, the analogy from human thought is key to understanding the Trinity, because it provides us with a notion of immanent immaterial procession. When he considers the Son's eternal procession from the Father, and its relation to creatures, he has recourse to an analogy from artistic manufacture. One might think of the Word as a mere artifact of God, a creature he has made, but this is mistaken. Instead we should think of the Word as the idea or eternal Reason

44. See Athanasius, "Four Discourses Against the Arians," 1.2–6; 2.1–5.
45. See Athanasius, "Four Discourses Against the Arians," 2.2. Anatolios, *Retrieving Nicaea*, 105, 116, points out that Athanasius makes the very novel argument that if the Son is not God, then God cannot be the Creator, since the Father can create freely only through his eternal Word.

in God through which he has created all things. On this second model, the Word is not derived from God's act of creating, but rather the converse is the case: God creates all things through his Logos, who is uncreated, the eternal offspring of the Father.[46]

How, then, is the Logos always already in God? To understand this we must consider the spiritual activity that occurs within a given human subject, such as the spiritual procession of the inner logos—which is to say, of thought—from the human mind. Conceptual thought proceeds from a human thinker as a qualification of his understanding, while remaining internal to his own mind and being. Our thoughts can emanate forth from within us through our acts of reflection, and yet they remain aspects of our person. Clearly, they are not a distinct subject or substance. While the procession of the Son from the Father in the Trinity is quite different from this, it is nevertheless not entirely dissimilar. Just as the Father is eternally wise, so the Son proceeds forth from him eternally as his Word and Wisdom, as his thought, so to speak, through which he accomplishes all things.[47] In contrast with our human example, however, this intra-divine procession terminates in the production of the Son as a truly a distinct subject, who contains within himself the plenitude of the divine being. In the Trinity, then, the Word is a person truly distinct from the Father, and all that is in the Father as God is in the Son as God.[48]

Moreover, Athanasius utilizes the scriptural references to the Son as the Word and Wisdom of the Father in an exemplary way to purify the notion of divine begetting from its corporeal limitations. He writes:

The divine generation must not be compared to the nature of men, nor the Son considered to be part of God, nor the generation to imply any passion whatever; God is not as man; for men beget passibly, having a transitive nature.... But with God this cannot be; for He is not composed of parts, but being impassible and simple, He is impassibly and indivisibly Father of the Son. This again is strongly evidenced and proved by divine scripture. For the Word of God is His Son, and the Son is the Father's Word and Wisdom; and Word and Wisdom is neither crea-

---

46. Athanasius, "Four Discourses Against the Arians," 2.5: "For if the Son be a creature, by what word then and by what wisdom was He made Himself? For all the works were made through the Word and the Wisdom, as it is written, 'In wisdom have You made them all,' and, 'All things were made by Him, and without Him was not anything made.' But if it be He who is the Word and the Wisdom, by which all things come to be, it follows that He is not in the number of works, nor in short of things originate, but the Offspring of the Father."

47. See Athanasius, "Four Discourses Against the Arians," 2.34; 3.1.

48. Athanasius, "Four Discourses Against the Arians," 1.24–25, 26–29.

ture nor part of Him whose Word He is, nor an offspring passibly begotten. Uniting then the two titles, scripture speaks of "Son," in order to herald the natural and true offspring of His essence; and, on the other hand, that none may think of the Offspring humanly, while signifying His essence, it also calls Him Word, Wisdom, and Radiance; to teach us that the generation was impassible, and eternal, and worthy of God.[49]

We should note that because this begetting is immaterial, it need not imply passibility (i.e., suffering, mutation), change, or temporality in God. By having recourse to an analogy derived from the human mind, a spiritual substance that accordingly has less composition than material bodies, we may arrive at a mental approximation, however imperfect, of the eternal begetting of the Son. Significantly, Athanasius posits that this begetting can occur without prejudice to the simplicity and immutability of the divine essence, an idea we will encounter later with Augustine and Aquinas.

The Unity of Action of Father and Son "Ad Extra." Since the Son is truly one in being (*homoousios*) with the Father, so Athanasius holds, then it must follow that he has the same will and power as the Father. As a result, there is a unity of action of the Father and the Son, insofar as they share the same will and activity. Athanasius puts it this way:

If He [God] has the power of will, and His will is effective, and suffices for the consistency of the things that come to be, and His Word is effective, and a Framer, *that Word must surely be the living Will of the Father, and an essential energy,* and a real Word, in whom all things both consist and are excellently governed. No one can even doubt, that He who disposes is prior to the disposition and the things disposed. And thus, as I said, God's creating is second to His begetting; for Son implies something proper to Him and truly from that blessed and everlasting Essence; *but what is from His will, comes into consistence from without, and is framed through His proper Offspring who is from It.*[50]

The idea Athanasius expresses in this passage is quite significant. It leads to the classical principle in Trinitarian theology that all activity of the Trinity *ad extra*, that is, outside the Trinity, is conducted equally and in one same operation by all three persons. When God acts outwardly, whether in creating or in conferring grace on creatures, God always acts conjointly as Father, Son, and Holy Spirit. Each of them acts equally, and each of them acts

49. Athanasius, "Four Discourses Against the Arians," 1.28.
50. Athanasius, "Four Discourses Against the Arians," 2.2; emphases added, translation slightly altered.

together with the others. They do not merely partake of the work in equal proportions, however, as three human persons might participate in an equal share of work. The three persons in God act *in one and the same operation*, as the one God, in virtue of the same nature, activity, and power that they each possess as God. This common outward activity can and must be distinguished from activity *within* the Holy Trinity. For only the Father eternally begets the Son, and only the Father and the Son eternally spirate the Holy Spirit. It is because the Father alone communicates all that he has and is, as God, to the Son, and the Father and the Son alone communicate all that they have and are, as God, to the Spirit that the three persons can and must all act together as one in all that they do outside of themselves. Consequently, when the persons create or sanctify, they do so in unity, as the one God. It is the Father, Son, and Holy Spirit who create and who communicate grace to human beings. This idea is subject to much more extensive development in medieval theology, and in particular in the thought of Aquinas, as we will see in part 3, below.

CONCLUSION

We can conclude our remarks on Athanasius, then, by observing three key accomplishments of his thought. As we noted above, modalists, subordinationists, and Arians all held in common an erroneous idea: that a distinction of persons (Father, Son, and Spirit) entails a distinction of beings or substances. The Council of Nicaea affirmed the contrary, that the Son is eternally begotten, not created, and that he possesses in himself the plenitude of the divine substance. He is one in being and nature with the Father. Athanasius was pivotal in developing a way to speak about the mystery of internal Trinitarian life in God. He did so by considering the analogy between the procession of the Word and immaterial thought in the human intellect. In light of this analogy, we can think of how the eternal generation of the Son can be immaterial and entail the communication from the Father to the Son of the plenitude of the divine nature, so that the Son is truly God. By positing this kind of immaterial procession according to an analogy from intellect, Athanasius grounded his defense of Nicene dogma in the text of scripture. In doing so he also showed the scriptural foundations for and convergent unity of the models mentioned previously, those that refer to Christ as the Logos of the Father and those that demonstrate the distinction of persons from the action in the economy. Both of these forms of thinking can be employed to contemplate the immanent Trinitarian life of God, and Athanasius correlates the two by employing scriptural analogies of immaterial procession to explain the distinction of persons. Finally, then, this approach permits him to distinguish clearly the eternal mystery of the Trinity in itself from the manifestation of the Trinity in the economy. God reveals himself to us in the economy of the Son and the Spirit, but in doing so allows us to know him as he is in himself, so that we may contemplate his eternal mystery through the medium of scriptural analogies. With Athanasius, we see the first emergence of a fully mature pro-Nicene theology of God, one that resolves many of the theological issues faced by the early Church, and that provides grounding for future Trinitarian thinking in both the East and the West.

8

The Advent of Orthodoxy
Cappadocian Trinitarian Theology

Among the most significant contributions to fourth-century Trinitarian theology was that of a trio of theologians collectively known as the Cappadocian Fathers. Their name is taken from their place of origin, Cappadocia, a region in what is today called Turkey. They are St. Basil, commonly known as the Great (d. 379), Basil's younger brother, Gregory of Nyssa (d. 394), who became a bishop after his wife's death, and Basil's closest friend, St. Gregory of Nazianzus (d. 390), who eventually (briefly) became the Bishop of Constantinople and presided for some time over the Council of Constantinople held in 381. His famous *Five Theological Orations*, preached at Constantinople, are considered a famous statement of theological orthodoxy.

The Cappadocians were, in a sense, the immediate theological successors to St. Athanasius in the Eastern Church, and they wrote important reflections on Trinitarian theology and Christology, in response to the ongoing work of "semi-Arians" and "neo-Arians," churchmen who were influenced in various ways by the original intuitions of Arianism.

Together, the Cappadocian Fathers articulated a sophisticated theology of the Triune God and of the mystery of Christ that places them, together with Athanasius and Cyril of Alexandria, among the most important of the ancient Greek Fathers. In this chapter, I will discuss key themes present in their respective works on Trinitarian theology. Though their various forms of thought are not identical by any means, they do overlap in significant ways on key points.

APOPHATICISM

Early Arianism posited that the Son and Word of God was a creature but one who was like God, who pre-existed all other creation, through whom all other realities were made. Although this position lacked scriptural warrant, it attempted to emphasize a kind of proximity between the Son and the Father. Subsequent to the Council of Nicaea, however, a new form of Arianism arose in the wake of ongoing argument and polemic, represented especially by figures like Eunomius and Aetius. These figures changed the debate because they insisted on the importance of conceptual knowledge of God and the accurate use of divine names. Eunomius, for example, argued that God is rightly defined by the name "unbegotten." When we utter such a name, he claimed, we also come to know God truly in what he really is. To be unbegotten, however, is to be uncaused, and consequently to be begotten is to be caused or created. If God as Father is unbegotten, the Son as the begotten one is a creature. The certitude of this follows from our very definitions of God, which are based in turn on the perfection of our apprehensions of what God is.[1]

Against this form of neo-Arian rationalism ("Eunomianism," "Anomoianism") that emphasizes the aptitude of our definitions of the one God, the Cappadocians—Gregory of Nyssa and Gregory of Nazianzus in particular—developed a thematic account of the apophatic dimension of all our knowledge of the divine essence. Although we have genuine knowledge of God, we do not immediately grasp or comprehend the divine nature. This is due to God's transcendence as the author of existence. We know him only from his effects, which he infinitely transcends as their more perfect cause.

Gregory of Nazianzus states the idea quite clearly: "For our part, not only does God's peace pass all thought and understanding with all the things stored up in promise for the righteous—things unseen by the eye, unheard by the ear, unthought, or at least but glimpsed by the mind—but so does exact knowledge of the creation as well.... Conviction, you see, of a thing's existence is quite different from knowledge of *what* it is."[2] According to

---

1. On the theology and argumentation of Eunomius, see Ayres, *Nicaea and its Legacy*, 144–49; Anatolios, *Retrieving Nicaea*, 158–60.

2. Gregory of Nazianzus, *Oration 28*, no. 5, quoted from St. Gregory of Nazianzus, *On God and Christ: The Five Theological Orations and Two Letter to Cledonius*, trans. F. Williams and L. Wickham (Crestwood, N.Y.: St. Vladimir's Seminary Press, 2002). In what follows, citations of the five *Orations*, 28–31, are drawn from this text, unless otherwise indicated.

Gregory, human reason of itself, even with the assistance of the knowledge granted by faith, can know *that* God is, but it cannot obtain direct perception of his essence. Hence, the human intellect must always keep a reverent distance from any pretension to know too much about God in his hidden nature. This idea is important for Trinitarian theology for obvious reasons. If we cannot know the divine nature directly, then we cannot define that nature simply in terms of its being "unbegotten" (as Eunomius erroneously does). Consequently, we cannot exclude the Trinitarian claim that there is eternal begetting and spiration in God, merely based on our indirect knowledge of the essence of God.

Along these lines, then, against the Anomoian claim that we can define or understand the essence of God, the Cappadocians insist simultaneously on the *simplicity*, as well as the *ineffability*, of the divine essence. The term "simplicity" as applied to God has a primarily negative signification. It points us to the fact that God is not complex or ontologically composite in various ways that all creatures necessarily are. For example, all physical creatures have quantitative bodies with multiple parts, internal organization, and external extension. The divine nature, by contrast, is immaterial. Therefore, God does not develop or change by subjection to physical processes, as all the beings we experience in the world do. The divine nature of God is one, but God does not possess a material unity that is quantitative, which could be subject to physical division. Here is how Gregory of Nazianzus describes divine simplicity under this negative aspect:

What can your conception of the divine be, if you rely on all the methods of deductive argument? To what conclusion will closely-scrutinized argument bring you, you most rational of theologians, who boast over infinity? Is it corporeal? How then can it be boundless, limitless, formless, impalpable, invisible? Can bodies be such? The arrogance of it! This is not the nature of bodies. Or is it corporeal but without these properties? The grossness of it, to say that deity has no properties superior to ours! How could it be worth worship were it bounded? How could it escape elemental composition and disintegration or even total dissolution? For composition is a cause of conflict, conflict of division, division of dissolution. But dissolution is utterly alien to God, the prime nature. So no dissolution means no division; no division means no conflict; no conflict means no composition, and hence no body involving composition. The reasoning stands so, mounting from consequences to first conditions.[3]

---

3. Gregory of Nazianus, *Oration 28*, no. 7.

The divine simplicity points us to the positive truth that God is one. God has a unity of nature that is beyond all matter. It is immaterial and is unchanging.[4]

This nature of God, though one, is utterly incomprehensible to us. Contrary to the rationalism of the Anomoians, the Cappadocians insist upon the ineffability of God, who is enshrouded in darkness. We hope to know God face to face in the life to come. In this life we know God only obliquely and imperfectly.[5] Thus, they insist on what will later be called a merely analogical language for the mystery of God. We cannot denote God in the terms that we use to denote things in creation, at least not in any way that implies a perfect sameness of God and creation. If God truly is "good," he is also "good" in a way that is very different from the goodness of creatures, just as the Creator as the cause of the world utterly transcends the realities that are his effects.

This emphasis on ineffability, while present in Gregory of Nazianzus in a developed way, is more acute with Gregory of Nyssa. Consider this passage from Nyssa's treatise, On "Not Three Gods", where he stresses, in particular, the negative aspect of our discourse about God:

Hence it is clear that by any of the terms we use the Divine nature itself is not signified, but some one of its surroundings is made known. For we say, it may be, that the Deity is incorruptible, or powerful, or whatever else we are accustomed to say of Him. But in each of these terms we find a peculiar sense, fit to be understood or asserted of the Divine nature, yet not expressing that which that nature is in its essence. For the subject, whatever it may be, is incorruptible: but our conception of incorruptibility is this,—that that which is, is not resolved into decay: so, when we say that He is incorruptible, we declare what His nature does not suffer, but we do not express what that is which does not suffer corruption. Thus, again, if we say that He is the Giver of life, though we show by that appellation what He gives, we do not by that word declare what that is which gives it. And by the same reasoning we find that all else which results from the significance involved in the names ex-

4. Gregory of Nazianzus, Oration 28, nos. 6–8.

5. See Gregory of Nyssa, Life of Moses 1, no. 46 (trans. A. Malherbe and E. Ferguson, New York: Paulist Press: 1978), where he speaks of Moses's intimacy with God on Mount Sinai: "Since he was alone, by having been stripped as it were of the people's fear, he boldly approached the very darkness itself and entered the invisible things, where he was no longer seen by those watching. After he entered the inner sanctuary of the divine mystical doctrine, there, while not being seen, he was in company with the Invisible. He teaches, I think, by the things he did that the one who is going to associate intimately with God must go beyond all that is visible and (lifting up his own mind, as to a mountaintop, to the invisible and incomprehensible) believe that the divine is there where the understanding does not reach."

pressing the Divine attributes either forbids us to conceive what we ought not to conceive of the Divine nature, or teaches us that which we ought to conceive of it, but does not include an explanation of the nature itself.[6]

Taken to its extreme, arguments like this one would suggest that we can say nothing positive about the nature of God. We know only that God exists, and can in turn say what God is not. However, there are also kataphatic or positive elements of divine discourse in the Cappadocian Fathers, which they employ precisely to speak about the mystery of the Trinity and the unity of the divine essence common to the three persons.[7]

KATAPHATIC AND APOPHATIC
INTERPLAY IN NAZIANZUS

Gregory of Nazianzus sees the obvious problem that could arise from a one-sided stress on apophatic discourse about God: if our knowledge of God is so obscure, do we really know the persons of the Holy Trinity, even by way of divine revelation? He underscores that we do have true positive (kataphatic) knowledge of God by divine revelation. We know, for example, because of the revelation of the eternal Son, that there is "begetting" within the godhead.[8] But we must also remove from this notion by way of negation a good deal of what we might naturally associate with it. For example, the eternal begetting of the Son is not physical but immaterial.[9] The Son is not generated as one distinct in substance from the Father but as one who has the very godhead of the Father.[10] Ultimately, then, even after being positively revealed, the divine "begetting" for us is still enshrouded in mystery. And yet there has been a true revelation that grants us some genuine insight into the very identity of God.

In his *Third Theological Oration* (Orat. 29), nos. 2–12, Nazianzus stresses, against Eunomius, this interplay of light and darkness, while contesting Eunomius's interpretation of the implication of the claim "God is unbegotten." Even if by this term we mean "uncreated," as Eunomius suggests, we

6. Gregory of Nyssa, *On "Not Three Gods": To Ablabius*, in *Letters and Select Works*, vol. 5 of Nicene and Post-Nicene Fathers, Second Series, ed. Philip Schaff and Henry Wace (Peabody, Mass.: Hendrickson Publishers, 2004).

7. See the helpful study of Nyssa on this issue in Anatolios, *Retrieving Nicaea*, 160–70.

8. Gregory of Nazianzus, *Oration 29*, nos. 2–3.

9. Gregory of Nazianzus, *Oration 29*, no. 4.

10. Gregory of Nazianzus, *Oration 29*, nos. 11–12.

name God with a *negative* term. But it is still also necessary to say what God is *positively*. The argument reinterprets Eunomius's central premise so as to turn it against him. Eunomius claims (1) we must be able to define the divine essence positively; (2) we can do so by calling the divine nature "unbegotten," which is true of it alone, because God alone is the cause of all else; and yet (3) the Son is begotten—therefore, the Son is not God. Nazianzus responds in turn: (1) you wish to identify a positive definition for the divine nature, but "unbegotten" is itself not a positive but a negative term. (2) Adam was unbegotten but was created, so the words "created" and "begotten" cannot have the same significations in ordinary use. (3) All discourse regarding God is imperfect and analogical. If we can speak analogically of a likeness between the created unbegotten (Adam) and the uncreated unbegotten (God the Father), then why can we not also speak analogically of a likeness between created begetting and uncreated begetting (in the case of the Son)?[11]

Theological analogy then, for Nazianzus, is both kataphatic and apophatic. It respects the true character of the mystery of God. What then are the key ways in which we can speak of the Holy Trinity?

---

11. For Gregory's argument, see *Oration 29*, no. 11: "They [the Eunomians] do not hold the view [that God is composite], because these are properties of other beings besides God. The substance of God is what belongs to him particularly and uniquely. The people who allege that 'matter' and 'form' are ingenerate would not agree that ingeneracy is uniquely a property of God…. But suppose it does belong uniquely to God, what was Adam? Was he not alone in being a creation formed by God? *Yes*, you will say. Was he alone in being human as well? *Of course not.* Why? *Because* manhood *is not* formation; *what has parentage is also human.* In the same way, it is not the case that the ingenerate and only the ingenerate is God (though only the Father is ingenerate) but you must allow that the Begotten too is God. The Begotten stems from God, however fond you are of unbegottenness. Next, how are you to talk of the being of God, when what is said about that being is not a positive assertion but a negation? 'Unbegotten' means that he has no parent. It does not state his nature, but simply the fact that he was not begotten. *So what is the being of God?* You must be mad to ask the question, making such a fuss about begottenness! We count it a high thing that we may perhaps learn what it is in the time to come, when we are free of this dense gloom. That is the promise of one who cannot lie. Yes, this is what men, who purify themselves for it, must think of and hope for. As for us, we will confidently affirm that if it is a high thing for the Father to have no starting point, it is no less a thing for the Son to stem from such a Father. He must share in the glory of the uncaused, because he stems from the uncaused. That he has been begotten is a further fact about him, as significant as it is august, for men whose minds are not totally earthbound and materialistic." Much of Gregory's argument here is an echo of arguments previously developed by Basil in his *Against Eunomius*, trans. W. Moore and H. A. Wilson, in Nicene and Post-Nicene Fathers, Second Series [NPNF, 2nd ser.], vol. 8, ed. P. Schaff and H. Wace (Buffalo, N.Y.: Christian Literature Publishing, 1895).

ETERNAL PROCESSIONS, DISTINCTION OF PERSONS,
AND RELATIONS OF ORIGIN

A central concern of the Cappadocian Fathers is to explore ways we can speak rightly about the inner mystery of God as Trinity. Toward this end, they emphasize in particular that there are eternal processions of begetting and spiration within the godhead. This motif comes to the fore in particular when they contest Eunomius's claim that it pertains to God's essence to be unbegotten, and that therefore the Son and the Spirit must be created. To this they respond: it is not of the divine essence itself to be ingenerate or unbegotten. Revelation tells us that both the unbegotten Father and the begotten Son are one in divine essence. Moreover, the Church's Nicene confession of faith affirms that the Son is consubstantial with the Father, receiving the fullness of the deity from the Father. If this is the case, then the terms "unbegotten" and "begotten" refer to the persons of the Father and the Son respectively, but not to the divine essence as such. Nor is this contrary to the affirmation of the existence of only one God. As Nazianzus puts it:

"Father," [the Eunomians] say, *is a designation either of the substance or the activity; is it not?* They intend to impale us on a dilemma, for if we say that it names the substance we shall then be agreeing that the Son is of a different substance, there being a single substance and that one, according to them, preempted by the Father. But if we say that the term designates the activity, we shall clearly be admitting that the Son is a creation not an offspring. If there is an active producer, there must be a production, and they will declare themselves surprised at the idea of an identity between creator and created. I should have felt some awe myself at your dilemma, had it been necessary to accept one of the alternatives and impossible to avoid them by stating a third, and truer possibility. My expert friends, it is this: "Father" designates neither the substance nor the activity, but the relationship, the manner of being, which holds good between the Father and the Son. Just as with us these names indicate kindred and affinity, so here too they designate the sameness of stock, of parent and offspring.[12]

Nazianzus argues that the Son is equal with the Father, and one in being with him, but that the Son possesses this equality of being in a derivative way, as one eternally begotten of the Father.

The Cappadocian Fathers also develop a more precise terminology in order to speak about the real distinction of persons and the unity of being

12. Gregory of Nazianzus, *Oration 29*, no. 16.

and essence in the Trinity.[13] To do so they adopt an important terminological contribution from Origen. He had termed each of the three persons a *hypostasis*: a concrete subsisting subject or person. The Cappadocians employ this language for the three persons while also affirming that each person of the Trinity possesses the plenitude of the divine substance, in keeping with the language of Nicaea. In other words, they wed the language of three hypostases or persons with that of the Nicene *homoousios*, so as to avoid any trace of subordinationism. We noted in the previous chapter that the Council used the term "*homoousios*" to denote the unity of substance of the three persons in God, who are one in being, unlike three individual human persons. However, the term also can denote a common nature or essence. As the Cappadocian Fathers make clear, then, the Holy Trinity is one being in three persons, or three persons who are the one being of God. Likewise, they are three persons who possess the fullness of the divine nature, so that each of them is essentially God. In this way, the Cappadocians make a major contribution to Trinitarian thought by distinguishing clearly the signification and use of the term "hypostasis" in Christian theology from Nicaea's language of *homoousios*. The two terms are employed in distinct and complementary ways to name the persons who are distinguished according to their processions, while stipulating that each possesses the fullness of the deity. The Son is eternally generated of the Father, while the Spirit eternally proceeds from the Father. In the eternal generation and spiration respectively, the Father communicates to the Son and Spirit all that pertains to him as God. Consequently, the Father, Son, and Spirit are three distinct hypostases, three subsistent persons, and are *homoousios*, one in being or substance.

It follows from this that the proper terms of the persons are designated by generation and procession, and therefore, *by relations of origin*. Persons are relational in God. Nazianzus brings this out clearly when he writes:

What then, say they, is there lacking to the Spirit which prevents His being a Son, for if there were not something lacking He would be a Son? We assert that there is nothing lacking—for God has no deficiency. *But the difference of manifestation … or rather of their mutual relations one to another, has caused the difference of their Names.* For indeed it is not some deficiency in the Son which prevents His being Father (for Sonship is not a deficiency), and yet He is not Father. According to this line of argument there must be some deficiency in the Father, in respect of His not

---

13. For the proximate historical background on this development see Ayres, *Nicaea and its Legacy*, 198–211. On the development of the distinction in the thought of Gregory of Nyssa, see Anatolios, *Retrieving Nicaea*, 212–35.

being Son. For the Father is not Son, and yet this is not due to either deficiency or subjection of Essence; but the very fact of being Unbegotten or Begotten, or Proceeding has given the name of Father to the First, of the Son to the Second, and of the Third, Him of Whom we are speaking, of the Holy Ghost, that the distinction of the Three Persons may be preserved in the one nature and dignity of the Godhead. For neither is the Son Father, for the Father is One, but He is what the Father is; nor is the Spirit Son, because He is of God, for the Only-begotten is One, but He is what the Son is. The Three are One in Godhead, and the One Three in properties; so that neither is the Unity a Sabellian one, nor does the Trinity countenance the present evil distinction.[14]

This idea of the Cappadocian Fathers that the persons may be identified from their relational way of being God (in relations of origin to one another) suggests another idea that will emerge more explicitly in later theology. This is the notion that the persons are *subsistent modes* (*tropoi*) of being. In other words, the divine hypostases subsist in the divine nature according to three distinct modes, as Father, Son, and Spirit, related to one another by way of origin.[15] Later, the Western tradition, especially Thomas Aquinas, as we will see, will come to speak of the persons as "subsistent relations." This is a quite different though not altogether unrelated concept.

COMMON TERMS AND PROPER TERMS

If there are three persons in one nature, then it follows that there are *common* terms that designate God's ineffable essence, but also *proper* terms that pertain only to one of the three persons. Consider, first, the following passage from Nazianzus, in which he emphasizes the diverse names that designate the underlying unity of the divine nature (i.e., that which is held in

14. Gregory of Nazianzus, *Oration 31*, no. 9, trans. C. G. Browne and J. E. Swallow, in Nicene and Post-Nicene Fathers, vol. 7, ed. P. Schaff and H. Wace (Buffalo, N.Y.: Christian Literature Publishing, 1894); emphasis added.

15. See especially Gregory of Nyssa's discussion in *On "Not Three Gods"*: "If, however, any one cavils at our argument, on the ground that by not admitting the difference of nature, it leads to a mixture and confusion of the Persons, we shall make to such a charge this answer;—that while we confess the invariable character of the nature, we do not deny the difference in respect of cause [i.e., the Father as begetting the Son], and that which is caused [i.e., the Son by begetting], by which alone we apprehend that one Person is distinguished from another;—by our belief, that is, that one is the Cause, and another is of the Cause; and again in that which is of the Cause we recognize another distinction. For one is directly from the first Cause; so that the attribute of being Only-begotten abides without doubt in the Son, and the interposition of the Son, while it guards His attribute of being Only-begotten, does not shut out the Spirit from His relation by way of nature to the Father."

common by all three persons). In this passage, Gregory underscores the divine nature's unity even while discussing the limitations inherent in all the concepts, drawn from our experience, that we use to describe it:

"Spirit," "fire," and "light," "love," "wisdom" and "righteousness," "mind," and "reason" and so forth, are titles of the prime reality, are they not? Can you think of wind without movement and dispersal? Of fire without matter, with no rising motion, no color and shape of its own? Or light unmixed with atmosphere, detached from what shines to give it birth, so to say? What of mind? Something else contains it, surely; its thoughts, silent or uttered, are movements. How can you think of reason other than as our inner discourse, unspoken or expressed—I shrink from saying "dissolved"? As for wisdom, how can you think of it except as a state involved in investigations human or divine? Justice and love are commended dispositions, surely, the opposites of injustice and hate, now intense, now slack, now present, now absent; in short they make us and change us, as complexions do our bodies. Or must we abstract, using the words to take, if we can, a view of deity in the absolute, making partial images yield some mental picture? Then what scheme will they yield, which is not just themselves? How can the simple, unpicturable reality be all these images and each in its entirety? This way our mind tires of getting past bodily conditions and companying with things sheerly incorporeal, and meanwhile it gazes in impotence at what lies beyond its powers. Because though every thinking being longs for God, the First Cause, it is powerless, for the reasons I have given, to grasp him.[16]

In this passage, Gregory stresses the transcendent character of the divine essence. In so doing, however, he also identifies a number of divine attributes—for example, love, wisdom, and righteousness—while at the same time stressing the hidden divine unity in which they converge.

In order to stress that which is held in common by the three divine persons, the Cappadocians sometimes apply our ordinary use of terms to denote the universal and the particular to Trinitarian discourse. There is in each singular human being (or person) a common nature. We denote the nature in universal terms ("man" or "human being") and denote the individual, that is, the person, by a proper name ("Socrates"). The nature is one, but the persons are many. Likewise, with God, there is the essence or substance of the godhead, which exists in three personal modes, each with its own unique characteristics.

This analogical comparison is legitimate when it is adequately purified of creaturely connotations. It is worth noting, however, that in his work *On*

---

16. Gregory of Nazianzus, *Oration 28*, no. 13.

"Not Three Gods" Gregory of Nyssa employs the comparison in a contestable way. In this work, Nyssa advances the claim that all particular men possess the same nature (presumably in a Platonic sense, as participating in one individual form, as modes of that form). In this case the common nature in humanity would be individual and might be understood univocally in comparison with the unity of nature in God. In each case there is a singular individual nature present in a multiplicity of persons. The problem with this comparison is that it fails to acknowledge the distinction that obtains between the divine and human natures. The nature of God is singular not only in kind or essence (only God has a divine nature) but also in individual being (there is only one God). Human nature, by contrast, is united in kind or essence (all human persons are rational animals) but not in individual being (each human being is substantially distinct from every other one). God is three persons who share in one nature, not only in virtue of their identical kind, but also in virtue of their identical being and singularity. They are each the one God. This is not true of any creature. Human beings are not all one substance or being, even if we do share in a common nature. Due to his way of speaking, Nyssa's comparison could suggest either that all human beings are mysteriously one in being (which is untrue) or that the Trinitarian persons are one in being only in an attenuated sense, in virtue of a shared nature that they communicate to one another, but not necessarily in virtue of a shared individual being. If taken to an extreme, such an analogy could lead to a tri-theistic vision: the Father, Son, and Holy Spirit are three persons who each have divinity, but just in the same way that human beings each have humanity. Nyssa's analogy has value and can be employed to denote something true, but when taken on its own in the terms given, it is imperfect.[17]

Despite this ambiguity, the distinction of nature and persons is a viable distinction to apply, with analogical qualifications, to the transcendent mystery of God. Gregory of Nazianzus articulates the idea more agreeably than Nyssa: in *Oration 29* (*Third Theological Oration*), no. 2, Nazianzus makes it clear that the unity of the three persons in God is not merely notional, but is one of being and substance.[18] Continuing in the same vein, he defines the

17. On this point in Nyssa's treatise, see Ayres, *Nicaea and its Legacy*, 348–51. Anatolios offers a defense of an alternative reading in *Retrieving Nicaea*, 230–34.

18. See Gregory of Nazianzus, *Oration 29*, no. 2: "But Monotheism, with its single governing principle, is what *we* value—not monotheism defined as the sovereignty of a single person.... The result [being] that though there is numerical distinction [of persons], there is no division in

personal characteristics, that is, that which is proper to each of the persons, as follows: *ingenerateness* is proper to the Father; *generateness* is proper to the Son; and, finally, *procession* is proper to the Spirit.[19]

It follows logically ἡ that the Cappadocians maintain that all that God is essentially or substantially is present in each of the three persons. The Father is true and complete God, the Son is true and complete God, the Spirit is true and complete God. There are not three Gods. There are three persons in God, who are each the one God, such that the Father is not the Son and the Son is not the Father, but all that is in the Father is in the Son and all that is in the Son is in the Father. All that is in the Father is in the Spirit and all that is in the Spirit is in the Father.

On this point, Nyssa notes in his *On "Not Three Gods"*: "The Father is God: the Son is God: and yet by the same proclamation God is One, because no difference either of nature or of operation is contemplated in the Godhead. For if ... the nature of the Holy Trinity were diverse, the number would by consequence be extended to a plurality of Gods, being divided according to the diversity of essence in the subjects. But since the Divine, single, and unchanging nature, that it may be one, rejects all diversity in essence, it does not admit in its own case the signification of multitude."[20] Nyssa's point is that there is only one divine essence, only one deity, and it is not multiplied by the real distinction of the persons. Rather, within the life of the Trinity, each of the persons possesses the fullness of the divine essence together with the others, albeit each according to his own mode.

ARGUMENTS FOR THE DIVINITY
OF THE HOLY SPIRIT

The Cappadocians in various writings present theological arguments on behalf of the divinity of the Holy Spirit. These are basically threefold. First, the Holy Spirit must be God, because he works by and in the power of

---

the substance. For this reason, a one eternally changes to a two and stops at three—meaning the Father, the Son, and the Holy Spirit."

19. See Gregory of Nazianzus, *Oration 25*, nos. 15–16: "Uniquely characteristic (ἴδιον) of the Father is unbegottenness (ἡ ἀγεννησία); of the Son begottenness (ἡ γέννησις); and of the Spirit being sent (ἡ ἔκπεμψις)." Quoted in Christopher A. Beeley, *Gregory of Nazianzus on the Trinity and the Knowledge of God: In Your Light We shall see Light* (Oxford: Oxford University Press, 2008), 204.

20. Gregory of Nyssa, *On "Not Three Gods"*.

God, as he is the source of divinization in human beings. No one can sanctify the creation by divinization who is not himself divine. But the Holy
Spirit does indeed divinize us, working as one with the Father and Son in
the economy of salvation.[21]

Second, because he *proceeds* eternally from the Father (see Jn 15:26)—
even as the Son is generated eternally—so the Holy Spirit, like the Son,
must be in personal relation to the Father. Just as the Father exists from all
eternity relationally as Father by the eternal begetting of the Son, so he must
exist from all eternity as the paternal font of the Spirit by spiration. This relational procession of the Spirit distinguishes him from the Son, who is generated. Because the procession is eternal, it is something proper to the godhead. Consequently, the Holy Spirit is truly God.[22]

The third reason is based on the liturgical praxis of Christians. The Holy
Spirit is worshiped, honored, and glorified as God in the New Testament
and in the Church. Christians would not worship him if he were not truly the one God.[23] But the Church's sense of the faith safeguards the faithful from error, and since the Church honors and worships the Holy Spirit,
her spiritual instinct in this matter must be truthful and trustworthy. This is
manifest above all in baptism, where the Church invokes the name of the
Father, Son, and Holy Spirit as indicating the godhead, and in doing so follows the example of Christ in Matthew 28:19. Baptism, as the very foundation of Christian life, indicates that the Spirit is true God.

According to the Cappadocians, then, the Spirit must be considered *homoousios*, consubstantial with the Father and the Son. This teaching was in
fact affirmed at the Council of Constantinople in 381, not without due influence directly from Gregory of Nazianzus, even if the Council did not explic-

21. See Gregory of Nazianzus, *Oration 31*, no. 28: "Were the Spirit not to be worshipped, how
could he deify me through baptism?" See also no. 29 (p. 140): "All that God actively performs, [the
Spirit] performs." See, too, Basil the Great, *The Treatise on the Holy Spirit*, trans. Blomfield Jackson,
in NPNF 2nd Ser., vol. 8, *Basil: Letters and Select Works*, ed. Philip Schaff and Henry Wace (Buffalo,
N.Y.: Christian Literature Publishing, 1895), no. 38: "There is no sanctification without the Spirit."

22. Gregory of Nazianzus, *Oration 31*, nos. 12, 28. For a more extensive discussion of this argument and study of its background in the work of Athanasius, see Ayres, *Nicaea and its Legacy*,
211–18.

23. On this point generally, see Basil's defense of the Church's traditions of prayer, which associate the Spirit with Father and Son in a doxological unity, in *The Treatise on the Holy Spirit*, nos.
66–68. See, in particular, no. 68: "The [scriptural] preposition '*in*' states the truth rather relatively
to ourselves; while '*with*' [used in the Church's doxologies] proclaims the fellowship of the Spirit
with God."

itly apply the term "*homoousios*" to the Spirit.[24] For his part, Nazianzus affirms the Holy Spirit's divinity unambigously in *Oration* 31 (*Fifth Theological Oration*), even going so far as to extend Nicaea's *homoousios* to him: "Is the Spirit God? Certainly. Is He *Consubstantial*? Yes, if He is God."[25]

PROCESSION OF THE SPIRIT FROM THE FATHER IN RELATION TO THE SON?

Do the Cappadocians attest to the idea behind the *Filioque*, that is, the procession of the Spirit from the Father *and* the Son? This is a question that is difficult to resolve. The Cappadocians do not have a "generic" term of "*processio*" to apply both to the Son and Spirit. They do not articulate a very developed theory as to how the two relate to one another eternally. Basil does famously write, however, of the Spirit's relationship to the Father *through* the Son. In his *Treatise on the Holy Spirit*, he writes: "One, moreover, is the Holy Spirit ... conjoined as He is to the one Father *through the one Son*."[26] And he continues shortly thereafter: "the inherent Holiness and the royal Dignity [i.e., of the divinity] extend from the Father *through the Only-begotten* to the Spirit."[27] Beyond language of this kind, the Cappadocians also sometimes speak of the Father *causing* the Son and *causing* the Holy Spirit *through* the Son.

Later, in the Western Church, Augustine, as we will see in the next chapter, develops the notion of the Holy Spirit as the procession from the Father of spirated love, and Augustine argues that this spiration is also from the Son. The Son receives from the Father all that the Father has, including the Father's power to spirate the Spirit, so that just as the Father is the relative principle of the Spirit, so too is the Son. Likewise, the Son spirates the Spirit, who proceeds from the Son as his love, the love that he eternally shares with the Father. The Spirit, then, is the mutual indwelling love of the Father and the Son. This Augustinian idea is not found in the Cappadocians, but it is in some respects compatible with what they say.

---

24. On the Council's terminological choices, see Beeley, *Gregory of Nazianzus*, 53.

25. Gregory of Nazianzus, *Oration* 31, no. 10, quoted in *On God and Christ*, 123, emphasis modified. For Gregory's account of the gradual revelation of the Spirit's divinity in the life of the Church, see *Oration* 31, no. 31.

26. Basil, *Treatise on the Holy Spirit*, no. 45.

27. Basil, *Treatise on the Holy Spirit*, no. 47.

In all actions of God with respect to creatures the three persons act by the same will and power, as the one God. The Cappadocians reiterate this notion, which, as we saw above, was identified by Athanasius.[28] However, they also rightly insist that the persons of the Holy Trinity *even when they act as one* always act personally in accord with their relations of origin. As such, the singular actions of God proceed *from* the Father, *through* the Son, who is his Wisdom and Word, and *in* the Holy Spirit, the Spirit of holiness and love.

In the following passage from *On "Not Three Gods"*, Nyssa closely follows the argument made by Athanasius in his *First Epistle to Serapion:*[29]

But in the case of the Divine nature we do not similarly learn that the Father does anything by Himself in which the Son does not work conjointly, or again that the Son has any special operation apart from the Holy Spirit; but every operation which extends from God to the Creation, and is named according to our variable conceptions of it, has its origin from the Father, and proceeds through the Son, and is perfected in the Holy Spirit. For this reason the name derived from the operation is not divided with regard to the number of those who fulfill it, because the action of each concerning anything is not separate and peculiar, but whatever comes to pass ... comes to pass by the action of the Three.[30]

For Nyssa, then, the Father, Son, and Holy Spirit have one common action *ad extra*. This action, however, is always exercised by each person in a manner consonant with his relation of origin and the mode in which he possesses the divine nature. The Father acts in creation as the paternal font of his Word and Spirit. He acts through his Word and in his Spirit. The Word acts as the Word of the Father, as he through whom all things are made, as they are fashioned in the Wisdom of God. The Spirit acts as the one who proceeds from the Father and is the Father's Spirit of holiness, sent upon the world to communicate eternal life to the world.

28. See the helpful study of this idea in the Cappadocians by Ayres, *Nicaea and its Legacy*, 244–51.

29. See Athanasius, *First Epistle to Serapion*, no. 28 and 30ff.

30. Gregory of Nyssa, *On "Not Three Gods"*.

CONCLUSION

The Cappadocians make a major contribution to the speculative development of Nicene doctrine in a number of ways. First, against the neo-Arian Eunomius, who maintained that he had definitional knowledge of the divine essence (as "unbegotten"), the Cappadocians stress the apophatic or negative character of all our knowledge of the divine nature. Second, however, Gregory of Nazianzus in particular stresses the necessary interplay between positive and negative language in all our discourse about God. In doing so he initiates increasingly sophisticated discussions in patristic theology concerning the nature of analogical discourse about God. Likewise, the Cappadocians stress, again countering Eunomius, that not only is it not the essence of God to be unbegotten per se, but there is, according to scripture, eternal begetting *within* the life of God. Thus, the Son is eternally begotten of the Father. They also wed Origen's designation of the three persons as hypostases to the Nicene *homoousios* formula, thereby making a major conceptual and terminological contribution to subsequent Trinitarian discourse.

In addition, the Cappadocians employ the distinction between nature and hypostasis (or person) in a helpful and clear way to designate what is common and what is proper to each person in God, even if Gregory of Nyssa utilizes this distinction incautiously. They also stress that the hypostases (or persons) are delineated in their particularity within the Trinity by relations of origin, precisely so as to distinguish the persons while still granting that the fullness of the deity is present in each person. They develop the logic of the Council of Nicaea organically by stressing that the Spirit is likewise *homoousios* with the Father and Son and, thus, is God. With Athanasius, they stress the unity of all the hypostases in God's action *ad extra*, while noting, however, that each of the divine persons acts according to the mode in which he possesses the divine nature. Finally, the Cappadocian Fathers also affirm that the Spirit processes from the Father *through* the Son, suggesting that there is an eternal relation that obtains between the Son and the Spirit, even if all the implications of such a position are not immediately clear.

9

Augustine's Trinitarian Theology

The contributions of St. Augustine of Hippo (354–430) to Western, Latin Trinitarian theology are almost too numerous to mention, just as the extent of his influence on this tradition is difficult to overstate. Given the magnitude of Augustine's influence—and the highly nuanced character of his thought—our considerations of his Trinitarian thought must necessarily be selective.[1] In this chapter, I will accordingly draw on Augustine's mature Trinitarian insights as found in his great speculative work, De Trinitate, a work that also had an extensive influence on Aquinas's own Trinitarian theology in the Summa theologiae (to be developed in part 3 of this book). De Trinitate is a fervently anti-Arian and anti-modalist work, yet it also represents a sincere quest on Augustine's part to draw nearer to the mystery of God, through a contemplative exercise undertaken for its own sake.[2] Though the book was written as a defense of the Nicene tradition, it is also a highly innovative work of theological reasoning. Its now-traditional place in the Western canon can tend to leave today's readers somewhat inoculated as to the extent of its speculative audacity.

I will proceed in this chapter by highlighting six areas in particular where Augustine has made especially lasting and influential contributions to West-

1. On Augustine's Trinitarian theology see Lewis Ayres, *Augustine and the Trinity* (Cambridge: Cambridge University Press, 2010); Michel René Barnes, "De Régnon Reconsidered," *Augustinian Studies* 26, no. 2 (1995): 51–79; Anatolios, *Retrieving Nicaea*, 241–80; Basil Studer, *Augustins "De Trinitate". Eine Einführung* (Paderborn: Schöningh, 2005).

2. See Edmund Hill's introduction to Augustine's *The Trinity*, 20: "[De Trinitate] is not really a polemical work, though at times [Augustine] puts himself into a kind of conventional polemic stance,.,. De Trinitate seems to be, so to say, a gratuitous work, undertaken to express the interest that lay nearest the author's heart. That interest was the quest for God."

ern Trinitarian thought. These are, first, his careful distinction between the divine persons' temporal missions and eternal processions, distinctions that close the door to every form of Arianism and economic subordinationism; second, his clear and repeated affirmation of the claim that the Spirit eternally proceeds from the Father *and* the Son; third, his concomitant designation of the Spirit as Gift and Love; fourth, his characterization of relation as a distinct category of predication for God, as distinct from substantial predication; fifth, his development of the doctrine of appropriations; and finally, his speculative deployment of various psychological models—drawn from human acts of intellection and volition—that, through inspection of the created image of God, tell us something about the procession and circumincession of the divine persons.

FROM TEMPORAL MISSIONS TO
ETERNAL PROCESSIONS

Augustine's aim in books 1–4 of *De Trinitate* is to distinguish the eternal basis in God for the temporal missions of the Son and Spirit in the economy of salvation by identifying the eternal processions as such and by distinguishing these from the temporal missions themselves. Augustine undertakes this argument in order to address the economic subordination of the pre-Nicene era. In effect, there was an ambiguity present in some of the early Christian authors, since they often described the Father, Son, and Spirit theologically as they appear in the temporal economy, where the Son and Spirit are sent from the Father into the world and where the Son in particular is subordinate to the Father in virtue of his human life of development, obedience, death, and resurrection. By this same measure pre-Nicene authors could intimate that Christ was God or say so explicitly, but they also failed to think through fully what consequences this might have for our understanding of the eternal identity of God as Father, Word, and Spirit. As a result of this ambiguity, some contested the eternal and pre-existent nature of the Son and Spirit as God, and instead came to view the Son and Spirit as generated *ad hoc* for their economic functions as God's self-revelation in creation. As we noted above, this was the case in differing ways for the Sabellian and Arian and neo-Arian theological positions. Other authors who appear clearly to be "orthodox" by later Nicene standards still articulated the mystery of the Trinity almost exclusively in "economic" terms. They depicted the Son as a subject distinct from the Father primarily by referring to the Son's temporal mission as redeemer, wherein he is sent by the Father and is subordinate to him in virtue of his human nature.[3]

Augustine responds to this lack of clarity in preceding Christian authors by positing an intra-divine differentiation that is the basis for the economic processions or missions. Thus, for Augustine, the economy is not productive of but revelatory of the Trinity of persons in God.[4]

Augustine begins his case in *De Trinitate*, book 1, by arguing for the equality of the divine persons. That is to say, he underscores that the Father, Son, and Holy Spirit are all equally God and possess in themselves the divine essence. The passages in scripture that seem to speak of an inferiority on the part of the Incarnate Son, he maintains, are to be referred to the form of a servant assumed by the Son for our salvation (Phil 2:7). Precisely because he has become human, the Son of God is subordinate to the Father in certain respects.[5] There are, of course, other passages, as Augustine notes in book 2, that refer to the Son's being *from* the Father, but these passages refer, not to his incarnation, but to his relational distinction from the Father, whose Son he is from all eternity. In other words, some passages that denote the Son as being subordinate to or inferior to the Father refer principally to the Son's being human and to his obedience as man. Other passages that speak of the Son being entirely relative to the Father denote his eternal generation and relation of origin as one who receives all that he is from the Father eternally. This relational *from*-ness, Augustine will argue later, is the intra-divine basis for the Son's being able to be sent at all. It is only because he is eternally the Son of the Father that the Son can be the one sent from the Father into the world.[6]

In order to distinguish adequately the missions of the Son and Spirit from their basis in God, Augustine needs to begin by formulating an adequate definition of what a mission is, and how the divine missions relate to the eternal processions. This is why Augustine spends the bulk of *De Trin-*

---

3. See Hill's introduction in *The Trinity*, 37–45, where he begins by discussing the theologies of the pre-incarnate Logos of Justin, Irenaeus, and Tertullian.

4. For a thematic consideration of Augustine's notion of divine sending, see Ayres, *Augustine and the Trinity*, 181–87, 233–50.

5. See Augustine, *The Trinity*, 1.3.14: "So the Son of God is God the Father's equal by nature, by condition his inferior. In the form of a servant which he took he is the Father's inferior; in the form of God in which he existed even before he took this other he is the Father's equal."

6. See, for example, Augustine, *The Trinity*, 4.19.25–26.

itate books 2 and 3 sifting through the various Old Testament theophanies and examining the intermediary work of angels therein—he is trying to determine what it is that is novel in the New Testament theophanies of Son and Spirit as opposed to God's self-revelation in the Old Testament. To this end, he will argue that, since the Trinity was not yet clearly revealed in the Old Testament, none of these theophanies are, in fact, missions of the divine persons, properly speaking, even if, after the fact, we can discern that this or that divine person was revealed implicitly through the various theophanies of angels acting as God's creaturely messengers.[7]

What, then, is distinctive about the New Testament theophanies of Son and Spirit that make them *missions* properly speaking? Augustine's answer to this question is that the theophanies in question are truly *missions* when they reveal the eternal processions, the relational basis in God that allows the proceeding persons *qua proceeding* to be sent. He writes: "Just as being born means for the Son his being from the Father, so his being sent means his being known to be from him. And just as for the Holy Spirit his being the gift of God means his proceeding from the Father, so his being sent means his being known to proceed from him."[8] This, then, is why "the Father alone [i.e., among the divine persons] is nowhere said to have been sent"[9]—in God he proceeds from no other and so can only send but never be sent.

Augustine uses this same logic to explain why the theophanies of the divine persons in the Old Testament are not, properly speaking, divine missions—the Son and Spirit are not revealed as proceeding from the Father in them. The preparatory revelation of the Old Testament must await its explicit revelation in the New Testament with the sending of the Son in the Incarnation, and the sending of the Holy Spirit in the form of a dove at Jesus' baptism, and in a rushing wind and tongues of fire on Pentecost. It is only in the light of the Incarnation and Pentecost that the proceeding persons are revealed by temporal effects as proceeding from the Father from all eternity.

Augustine's identification of an eternal intra-divine basis for the pro-

---

7. See Augustine, *The Trinity*, 3.4.26–27: "Acting in and through these angels, of course, were the Father and the Son and the Holy Spirit. Sometimes it was the Father who was represented by them, sometimes the Son, sometimes the Holy Spirit, sometimes just God without distinction of persons.... whenever God was said to appear to our ancestors before our savior's incarnation, the voices heard and the physical manifestation seen were the work of angels."

8. Augustine, *The Trinity*, 4.5.29.

9. Augustine, *The Trinity*, 2.2.8.

ceeding persons' economic manifestation represents a significant insight into scripture and a milestone for Catholic theology. By articulating the distinction between processions and missions, and the connection between them, Augustine fends off the different forms of subordinationism that see the Son in particular as the, put crudely, visibility of the invisible Father, or even as a created effect *ad extra*. Augustine's theology of the divine missions acts as a theological corrective to the subordinationist tendency contained within the pre-Nicene tradition, which reaches its logical dead end in Arianism. The Son's appearance in time is a revelation of the fact that he is Son from all eternity and so is *from* the Father, even as the Spirit's economic sending by the Son is a revelation of the fact that he eternally proceeds from both. We should note that there is a significant soteriological corollary to this viewpoint. The Incarnation saves the human race fundamentally because it unites God to us and us to God, and in so doing reveals to us who God truly is in himself. This can be the case, however, only if Jesus is true God and man, and not merely a creature. The corollary, then, is that Jesus as the Son is our savior only if the Son is God and if the relation of the Father and the Son revealed in the temporal mission is itself an eternal relation, one based on the eternal procession of the Son from the Father. Thus it is truly God whom we come to know through Jesus' temporal mission among us, and it is this knowledge of the Trinitarian God, and our union with him by the grace of the Incarnation, that alone can truly save us.

THE PROCESSION OF THE
SPIRIT FROM THE FATHER
AND THE SON

Augustine emphasizes repeatedly that the Spirit proceeds from both the Father *and the Son*, not only in time, but also in eternity. "Nor ... can we say that the Holy Spirit does not proceed from the Son as well [i.e., in addition to proceeding from the Father]; it is not without point that the same Spirit is called the Spirit of the Father and of the Son."[10] Augustine expresses the same idea elsewhere when meditating on why the third person in the Trinity is called "Holy Spirit," when the terms "holy" and "spirit," taken individually, are clearly also common to the other two persons: "He is not alone

10. Augustine, *The Trinity*, 4.5.29.

in the triad in being either holy or spirit, because the Father too is holy and
the Son too is holy, and the Father too is spirit and the Son too is spirit, a
truth about which piety can have no hesitations; and yet he is distinctively called the Holy Spirit, and with good reason. Because he is common to
them both, he is called distinctively what they are called in common."[11]

For Augustine, the very fact that the Holy Spirit's name is common to
the other two persons tells us something proper about the Spirit, namely,
that he proceeds from both and so his personal characteristics arise, too,
from this fact. Or, as Augustine puts it in one passage, with reference to the
Holy Spirit's name "Gift" (more on this in a moment)—"the Holy Spirit is a
kind of inexpressible communion or fellowship of Father and Son."[12]

What is at stake with regard to this idea of the procession of the Spirit from both the Father and the Son, as one principle, or "the *Filioque*"? A
key concern for Augustine is to consider the power of the New Testament
to reveal God's interior life. If the Spirit proceeds proximately from the Son
in the economy (and he unquestionably does, according to the New Testament),[13] then this points back to an eternal intra-Trinitarian relation: the
procession of the Spirit from the Father and Son, which is now revealed in
time in the Spirit's temporal mission. We will explore this topic further in
subsequent chapters but for now the idea can be stated this way: If the temporal missions (the sending of the Son and Spirit) truly reveal the eternal
processions, then the missions must "contain" the processions, so that the
relationships revealed in the missions are truly those relationships that obtain eternally in the very life of God. Thus, if the Son is sent from the Father
into the world to take on a human nature, this "being sent" presupposes that
the Son is eternally from the Father as his begotten Son and Word. This is
why the Father cannot be sent by the Son or the Spirit, and they can only
be sent by him: because he is the one who is unoriginated from all eternity.
The Holy Spirit, however, is not sent forth in time uniquely from the Father,
but also from the Son. As Jesus says in John 16:7: "Nevertheless I tell you
the truth: it is to your advantage that I go away, for if I do not go away, the
Counselor will not come to you; but if I go, I will send him to you." Consequently, the temporal sending of the Spirit from the Son tells us some-

---

11. Augustine, *The Trinity*, 15.5.37.
12. Augustine, *The Trinity*, 5.3.12.
13. See John 15:26: "But when the Counselor [i.e., the Spirit] comes, whom I shall send to you
from the Father...."

thing about their eternal relation: the Spirit proceeds from both the Father and the Son. It is this procession that makes the visible mission of the Spirit possible in the first place. The Spirit can come forth from the Father and the Son in time only because he is from them eternally. The visible mission of the Spirit thus reveals the inner life of the Trinity, wherein the Father and Son are one principle from whom the Spirit proceeds. This relation of the Spirit's coming forth from the Father and the Son as their mutual love is the eternal basis for Jesus Christ's sending of the Spirit upon the Church. The Spirit we receive is the Spirit who is eternal love.

THE SPIRIT AS GIFT AND LOVE

Augustine's doctrine of the Spirit's procession from both Father and Son is closely connected with his teaching that the Holy Spirit's proper names in the Trinity are "Gift" and "Love."[14] The reason these names are connected with the doctrine of the *Filioque*, or procession of the Spirit from Father and Son, is that the names Gift and Love have a "mutuality" about them that suggest a reciprocal give and take. Augustine searchingly describes it this way:

And yet the Holy Spirit, whom we understand as being not the triad but in the triad [i.e., the Third Person], insofar as he is properly or peculiarly called the Holy Spirit, is so called relationship-wise, being referred to both Father and Son, since the Holy Spirit is the Spirit of the Father and of the Son. This relationship ... is not apparent in this particular name, but it is apparent when he is called *the gift of God* (Acts 8:20; Jn 4:10). He is the gift of the Father and of the Son, because on the one hand he *proceeds from the Father* (Jn 15:26), as the Lord says; and on the other the apostle's words, *Whoever does not have the Spirit of Christ is not one of his* (Rom 8:9), are spoken of the Holy Spirit. So when we say "the gift of the giver" and "the giver of the gift," we say each with reference to the other. So the Holy Spirit is a kind of inexpressible communion or fellowship of Father and Son.[15]

We should note that the idea Augustine is formulating is that the Holy Spirit is first an "uncreated" gift of love shared by the Father and Son, in their reciprocity from all eternity, "before" he is a gift given to the Church. "The

14. For a contemporary defense of Augustine's teaching that the Spirit's names are "Love" and "Gift," see Matthew Levering, *Engaging the Doctrine of the Holy Spirit: Love and Gift in the Trinity and the Church* (Grand Rapids, Mich.: Baker Academic, 2016), 51–70.

15. Augustine, *The Trinity*, 5.3.12.

Spirit ... is everlastingly gift...."[16] Likewise we can also say that what is given to the Church in time is the eternal Spirit of love, who is himself the uncreated gift of the Father and of the Son.

Moreover, if the Second Person as Son and Word is eternally begotten, this is not true of the Spirit, who proceeds in a different fashion altogether, by way of being "given." Accordingly, Augustine writes: "He comes forth, you see, not as being born but as being given, and so he is not called son, because he was not born like the only begotten Son, nor made and born adoptively by grace like us."[17] For Augustine, the Holy Spirit's character as gift is closely intertwined with his other name, also discerned from scripture, Love. "So the love which is from God and is God is distinctively the Holy Spirit; through him the charity of God is poured out in our hearts [cf. Rom 5:5], and through it the whole triad dwells in us. This is the reason why it is most apposite that the Holy Spirit, while being God, should also be called the gift of God."[18]

This idea of the Spirit as the mutual love of the Father and the Son has a significant importance for thinking about the Church's response to Arianism. We noted above that the early "economic Trinitarianism" of the second and third centuries could be subject to misconstrual. The idea could and did arise that the Son and the Spirit are eternally subordinate to the Father. Augustine's vision of the Spirit as the mutual love of the Father and the Son gives us another way to think about the processional order of the persons of the Trinity, in God from all eternity, "prior to" the sending of the Son and the Spirit in the economy. The Trinity is an eternal communion of interpersonal love, which precedes all creation and is the ground of all being.

That being said, Augustine also thinks that this procession of the Spirit from the Father and the Son as their mutual gift also tells us something about the economy of salvation. The charity that is poured into our hearts by grace is indicative of God's uncreated charity or eternal love, since he

16. Augustine, The Trinity, 5.4.17.
17. Augustine, The Trinity, 5.3.15.
18. Augustine, The Trinity, 15.5.32. In fact, as Gilles Emery has pointed out to me, Augustine argues in book 5 from the created gift of the Spirit in the economy to the foundation in the life of God of the Spirit as an uncreated gift that the Father gives eternally to the Son and the Son to the Father. This idea of the Spirit as gift implies a relation of origin, and thus a proper name: the Spirit is the one who originates from the Father and Son as their mutual gift and as the expression of ineffable communion they share with one another. In book 15, however, Augustine goes on to argue that the Spirit is called "gift" in virtue of his being Love. It is in virtue of his being the Love of the Father and the Son, whom they spirate, that he is their mutual gift and bond of communion.

gives us the grace of charity out of his eternal love. When we speak of divine love in God, however, we can attribute it to the Holy Spirit not only by appropriation (as something common to all three persons, attributed to the Spirit in a distinct way) but also properly, because the Spirit is himself the uncreated Love of the Father and the Son.[19] "So the Holy Spirit is something common to Father and Son, whatever it is, or is their very commonness or communion, consubstantial and coeternal. Call this friendship, if it helps, but a better word is charity. And this too is substance because God is substance, and *God is charity* (1 Jn 4:8, 16)."[20] As love unites, so the Holy Spirit is the eternal love that unites Father and Son, and is the basis for God's give-ability in love *ad extra*, which unites us to God: the Holy Spirit "is supreme charity conjoining Father and Son to each other and subjoining us to them."[21] "According to the holy scriptures this Holy Spirit is not just the Father's alone nor the Son's alone, but the Spirit of them both, and thus he suggests to us the common charity by which the Father and the Son love each other."[22] The grace of charity we receive in the economy of salvation, then, has its ultimate basis in the mystery of the Trinity, in which the Spirit is the mutual love of the Father and the Son.

Here we begin to see how the Holy Spirit's characteristic name of Love is closely bound up with his procession from both Father and Son as their mutual love. The Son proceeds from the Father as his generated Word or Logos (*Verbum* in Augustine's Latin). The similitude for this procession is intellectual: the Son proceeds as one who springs from the Father's eternal knowledge of himself. The Spirit, by distinction, proceeds from the Father and the Word as Love. The similitude for the Spirit's procession is grounded in the will. As a human being comes to know a reality and then to love that reality known, so the Father, in knowing, from all eternity generates the Word, and, in loving, from all eternity breathes forth the Spirit as an eternal expression of his love. We will return to this analogy of Augus-

---

19. "Appropriations" are attributes common to all three persons (like power, wisdom, or goodness) that can be appropriately ascribed to one person in some indicative way even though they are also attributable to all three persons. I will return to this topic shortly. Proper names pertain to one person alone, as only the Father is called Father, not the Son. Thus the Spirit is called Love in this latter proper sense, as the mutually spirated Love of the Father and Son. However, he also possesses divine love in the former sense, as having that love that pertains to the nature of God, which is common to all three persons.

20. Augustine, *The Trinity*, 6.1.7.

21. Augustine, *The Trinity*, 7.2.6.

22. Augustine, *The Trinity*, 15.5.27.

tine's below, after we have first considered his notions of predication and appropriation.

In *De Trinitate* book 5, Augustine sets forth his doctrine on relation as a distinct category of predication for God, in addition to substantial predication. The starting point of Augustine's contention here is a premise that the orthodox Nicene believers shared with the Arians regarding divine simplicity. God is perfect in his being and therefore cannot undergo accessions of progressive perfection. It follows from this that nothing is predicated of God accidentally or with reference to potential modifications he might undergo, but only substantially. Thus, instead of saying that God possesses wisdom as a feature or quality, as one who can evolve or grow in wisdom, we should say instead in virtue of God's perfection and simplicity that God just is his own wisdom, goodness, etc.

Where this gave rise to a problem for neo-Arianism, as we saw in the previous chapter, is that some wanted to claim that attributes like being "unbegotten" are also predicated of the substance of God and that, likewise, being "begotten" is predicated of the substance of the Son. It would follow from this, however, that God and Christ are substantially distinct, and that the Son is ontologically inferior to the Father.[23]

It is at this juncture that Augustine intervenes. He notes that, indeed, attributes of being unbegotten and begotten are certainly not said of God as denoting merely accidental properties or qualities of the godhead. In this way he upholds the idea of the simplicity and perfection of God's incomprehensible essence. However, he also rejects the Arian notion that terms pertaining to the processions of generation or spiration must be attributed to the substance of God as such. In fact, the use of such terms in Trinitarian formulas must form an exception to the rule that all predication of God is substantial. "Nothing therefore is said of him [God] modification-wise because nothing modifies him, but this does not mean that everything said of him is said substance-wise."[24]

23. See the Arian argument presented in Augustine, *The Trinity*, 5.1.4.
24. Augustine, *The Trinity*, 5.1.6.

Instead, Augustine begins to explore the idea that terms like unbegotten and begotten, just as terms like Father and Son, are said *relationally* of God.

"If on the other hand what is called Father were called so with reference to it-self and not to the Son, and what is called Son were called so with reference to itself and not to the Father, the one would be called Father and the other Son substance-wise. But since the Father is only called so because he has a Son, and the Son is only called so because he has a Father, these things are not said substance-wise, as neither is said with reference to itself but only with reference to the other. Nor are they said modification-wise [i.e., as denoting accidents like qualities], because what is signified by calling them Father and Son belongs to them eternally and unchangeably. Therefore, although being Father is different from being Son, there is no difference of substance, because they are not called these things substance-wise but relationship-wise; and yet this relationship is not a modification, because it is not changeable."[25]

Augustine employs relation terms, then, to denote the very persons of the Father, Son, and Spirit. He justifies this by noting that the divine persons as persons are wholly relative to one another. The Father is only ever the eternal Father because he is relative to the Son in all that he is, and recipro-cally. At the same time, as Augustine notes, the use of relation terms here does not merely refer us to properties or accidents of the essence of God, because the persons each possess the divine essence in its fullness, and are each the one God. In other words, each person is truly God and each per-son is entirely relative to the others in all that he is. At the same time, Au-gustine upholds that there is no accidental predication of God. When we ascribe properties to the nature of God, these should be taken to indicate God's very essence (i.e., we must not only say that God is good, but also that God is his goodness). Relations between the persons, however, are dis-tinct in this respect. Trinitarian relations are neither properties of the di-vine essence nor simply convertible with the essence. Instead they denote the persons in their relational distinction from one another. We might say that each of the persons is wholly related to the other two in all that he is, and as such, the Trinity is constituted by personal interrelationality. It fol-lows that when we designate personal relations in God we cannot do so by employing the categories of substances and accidents in ways we typically do when we encounter created substances that are related to one another.

25. Augustine, *The Trinity*, 5.1.6.

Augustine employs relation terms in a highly original way, for theological purposes, to speak of the mystery of God.[26]

THE DOCTRINE OF APPROPRIATIONS

In *De Trinitate* books 6 and 7 Augustine developed what eventually would come to be known in the High Middle Ages as the doctrine of appropriations. The doctrine of appropriations has to do with biblical language that applies this or that divine attribute to one of the divine persons seemingly exclusively, the simplicity of the divine nature notwithstanding, or applies this or that divine action to one of the persons as if it were proper to him, despite the unity of God's action *ad extra*. For example, we might speak in a seemingly exclusive way of "the power of the Father" or "the wisdom of the Son" or "the goodness of the Spirit." Each of the persons is powerful, wise, and good, but a given term might be associated typically with only one of them. Expressions of this kind are commonplace in writings of many prominent Fathers of the Church.

Augustine begins by noting that the three persons of God do indeed each possess the fullness of the deity, which is itself simple and perfect. Consequently, they cannot possess different degrees or kinds of perfection. Furthermore, they all act *ad extra* as one, so that they cannot distribute gifts in the order of creation or of grace that spring from radically distinct or diverse qualities in the three persons: "I will say ... with absolute confidence that Father and Son and Holy Spirit, God the creator, of one and the same substance, the almighty three, act inseparably."[27]

What leads to Augustine's discussion of appropriations in books 6 and 7, however, among others, are difficulties posed by the biblical verse, 1 Corinthians 1:24: "Christ the power of God and the wisdom of God." One in-

26. On the question of whether Augustine's doctrine of Trinitarian relations prefigures Aquinas's theology of "subsistent relations," see Ayres, *Augustine and the Trinity*, 268–72. As Ayres points out, Aquinas's account of the processions of the Son and Spirit is more detailed and highly qualified by a later scholastic context. It seems best to say that Augustine's theory does present points of continuity with that of Aquinas, especially because of the former's insistence on the simplicity of the divine essence, the co-eternal equality of the three persons, and the distinction between them that derives from relations of origin. However, other "Augustinian" Trinitarian theologies emerged in the medieval period that made use of his principles but interpreted them otherwise, without embracing the notion of Trinitarian persons as subsistent relations. In this respect, Aquinas is one of the great Augustinians, but he is also an Augustinian among others.

27. Augustine, *The Trinity*, 4.5.30.

terpretation of this verse would be that the Son of God is the Father's power and wisdom, in such a way that the Father is wise and powerful only by the Son. If taken seriously, this would involve splitting up divine attributes and assigning them to different persons. The Father is not powerful and wise in himself, and can only be said to be so in virtue of the Son, or vice versa. Such an idea is clearly problematic. But there are dangers on the other extreme as well: we might say that when the Father, Son, and Spirit act together, they only do so as one principle in virtue of their common essence. Consequently, we really can only speak of all three persons acting, and never of a distinct person acting as such. This is clearly erroneous. The basic question is whether we can predicate attributes and actions to each of the persons in a distinctive way, without claiming that the attribute or action in question is something exclusively proper to him.[28]

Augustine's answer to this question is grounded in his idea of persons as relations. Yes, it is true that each of the persons possesses all of the properties and actions of God equally and identically. But it is also true that each of them possesses such properties and actions in a particular personal mode, as Father, Son, or Holy Spirit. We might take the example of wisdom. On the one hand, wisdom must be understood as pertaining to the very substance and nature of God. Understood in this way, both the Father and Son are perfectly wise, since they are both God.[29] And yet on the other hand, the Father and the Son each possesses wisdom in his own mode, in the way he possesses the divine nature in a peculiar mode resulting from the relations. "So Father and Son are together one wisdom because they are one being, and one by one they are wisdom from wisdom as they are being from being."[30] The Father has wisdom from all eternity in an unoriginated mode, as he who communicates divine being to the Son and the Spirit. The Son has wisdom from all eternity in an originated mode, as he who is the generated Word of the Father, and as one who breathes forth the Spirit eternally as the shared Love of the Father and the Word.

Thus, wisdom is common, and yet in scripture it is almost always predicated of the Son. Why? Here, using the divine attribute wisdom as a case study, Augustine draws out the logic of appropriations. Wisdom is almost always predicated of the Son because it tells us something about the way

28. This is how Augustine ultimately frames the question in *The Trinity*, 7.1.1.
29. See Augustine, *The Trinity*, 7.1.3.
30. Augustine, *The Trinity*, 7.1.3.

he possesses the divine nature, and for this reason too, also reveals to us his function in the economy. The Son has his plenitude of wisdom from the Father, as his eternally begotten Word, and the Father does all that he does in the economy through his Word. So wisdom is appropriated to the Son in particular (in distinction to the Father and the Spirit) because "it is through the Son that the Father makes his revelation, that is through his Word."[31] The Father communicates to us a participation in his uncreated wisdom through the medium of his divine Word, as a principle by which the Father makes us wise.

Analogous things can be said regarding "power" as attributed to the Father. The Son and Spirit possess the very power of God, for they have in themselves the divine essence and life received eternally from the Father, and it is through the Word and in the Spirit that all things have been made. And yet power is rightly attributed to the Father (as when we speak of the "all-powerful Father") because power subsists in him as one who is eternally unoriginated, from whom all comes forth in the Holy Trinity, including the all-powerful life of the Son and the Spirit, who proceed from the Father.

PSYCHOLOGICAL MODELS OF THE TRINITY

In book 8 of the *De Trinitate*, Augustine begins to develop a number of psychological models for the Trinity. By considering vestiges of the Trinity in the created image of God, he hopes to gain some insight into its transcendent archetype. Augustine's tentative and exploratory proposals in this regard throughout the second half of *De Trinitate* were to have a lasting influence on Western Trinitarian thought.

Augustine employs a number of similitudes in his work that are satisfactory to a greater or lesser degree.[32] One of these is that of a lover, his beloved, and the love itself: "Now love means someone loving and something loved with love. There you are with three, the lover, what is being loved, and

---

31. Augustine, *The Trinity*, 7.2.4.

32. On the historical context and searching way in which Augustine explores his models of Trinitarian interiority, see Anatolios, *Retrieving Nicaea*, 258–74; Ayres, *Augustine and the Trinity*, 275–318. See, likewise, Gilles Emery, "Trinitarian Theology as Spiritual Exercise in Augustine and Aquinas," in *Trinity, Church, and the Human Person* (Naples, Fla.: Sapientia Press, 2007), which discusses Augustine's purpose and method on pp. 34–39, and his use of the similitude of the image on pp. 39–49.

love."[33] These correspond to the Father, Son, and Holy Spirit, respectively.

More penetratingly, Augustine next constructs a trinity based on the mind, its self-knowledge, and corresponding love of self. Augustine's psychological model here is based on, but also in turn reinforces, his understanding of the two Trinitarian processions as analogous to acts of intellect and will. Viewed in this way, scripture's designation of the Son as Logos, or *Verbum*, becomes the governing motif that explains the Son's generation as an intellectual conception, as too the Spirit's procession from both the Father and the Word as a movement of will.[34] While the Father knows himself and expresses this knowledge in his begotten Word, he also loves himself and his Word, and expresses this love in his spirated Spirit. The human image of God in us, expressed especially through our knowledge and love, becomes most perfect when we begin to know and love the Holy Trinity.[35] And yet even the perfected image, in the souls of the saints who see the very essence of God, is very unlike God.[36]

Augustine also depicts a further mental trinity from the three mental acts of memory, understanding, and will. "These three then, memory, understanding, and will, are not three lives but one life, nor three minds, but one mind. So it follows of course that they are not three substances but one substance."[37]

Of course, all of these models imperfectly reflect the Trinitarian life of God. The first, based on mutual love, runs the risk of overlooking the essential unity of the three persons, and can obscure the intellectual dimension of the Son as Word. The second, based on self-reflexivity, represents the Father knowing and loving himself in such a way as to give expression to himself in his Word and Holy Spirit respectively. But this model does not communi-

---

33. Augustine, *The Trinity*, 8.5.14.

34. We see this self-reflexive Trinity, for example, in the following passage: "But with these three, when mind knows and loves itself the trinity remains of mind, love, knowledge. Nor are they jumbled up together in any kind of mixture, though they are each one in itself and each whole in their total, whether each in the other two or the other two in each, in any case all in all." Augustine, *The Trinity*, 9.1.8.

35. "This trinity of the mind is not really the image of God because the mind remembers and understands and loves itself, but because it is also able to remember and understand and love him by whom it was made.... let [the mind] worship the uncreated God, by whom it was created with a capacity for him and able to share in him. In this way it will be wise not with its own light but by sharing in that supreme light." Augustine, *The Trinity*, 14.4.15. "For only when it comes to the perfect vision of God will this image bear God's perfect likeness." Augustine, *The Trinity*, 14.5.23.

36. See Augustine, *The Trinity*, 15.4.2, and what follows.

37. Augustine, *The Trinity*, 10.4.18.

cate as clearly how the Son and Spirit are each truly persons who possess in themselves the plenitude of the divine life, and are not mere emanations of the Father. The final model raises interesting questions about spiritual memory and whether it really constitutes a faculty distinct from understanding. It also renders somewhat opaque the real distinction of the persons in their interrelational mode.

CONCLUSION

St. Augustine made many key contributions to Western Trinitarian thought, as we have noted in this chapter. First, and arguably most importantly, he closed the door on Arianism and every form of economic subordination by carefully distinguishing the temporal missions from the eternal processions. To this end, Augustine defined temporal mission as the revelation of the eternal processions, something that happens clearly only in the New Testament. This means that the economy of salvation is revelatory of, but not productive of, the immanent Trinity. For Augustine, God in his transcendent simplicity and immutability is never entangled in the world process. Second, we saw how Augustine expressly affirms what later will come to be called the *Filioque*, the doctrine that the Spirit proceeds conjointly from the Father and Son in the immanent Trinity. Third, in connection with this doctrine, Augustine discerns in the New Testament that the names that best characterize the Spirit's person are Gift and Love. The *Filioque* is implicated in these designations insofar as gift and love here are taken to imply mutuality, that is, the Holy Spirit is a person who is the uncreated love of Father and Son and their gift to one another.

Fourth, even though Augustine affirms that all accidental predications are substantial when it comes to God, he nevertheless also affirms an exception when it comes to the relational designations of the persons. This is similar to the Cappadocians' rejection of Eunomius's definition of the divine substance as unbegotten. As we saw, Eunomius was proceeding on the basis of a category error. Augustine argues that unbegotten and other relation terms indicate the persons in God, not the divine essence that is common to all three. But relations are not accidents in God either: the Trinitarian persons are somehow constituted by the relations that characterize them. Fifth, Augustine affirms the scriptural practice of appropriating various divine attributes to this or that divine person and provides a rationale for this practice: against the backdrop of the divine unity and simplicity, the appropriations highlight the characteristic way that the persons possess the divine nature, and so also, in the case of the proceeding persons, their function in the economy (i.e., the Father sends, the Word reveals, the Spirit bestows charity and unites diverse created persons by the bond of love). Finally, Augustine employs a number of psychological models for the Trinity that focus, in particular, on human acts of knowing and loving, and which, for that reason, seek to understand the divine spiritual processions and productions as acts of knowledge and love. Later, as we will see, Aquinas will employ this similitude drawn from human intellectual and volitional acts to argue that there are only two processions in God, for the simple reason that there are only two processions in his created spiritual image: those of knowledge and love, which correspond to the processions of the Word and Spirit, respectively.

10

Trinitarian Analogy

Dionysius the Areopagite and the
Fourth Lateran Council

The purpose of this chapter is to provide a short bridge of transition from our study of the patristic era to the consideration of Thomas Aquinas in the high Scholastic period. To do so we will consider briefly the development of two forms of analogical thinking regarding the Trinity, first, in the apophatic theology of Dionysius the Areopagite, and second, in the conciliar determinations of the Fourth Lateran Council directed against Joachim of Fiore.

We noted above that in both the Cappadocian Fathers and in Augustine a self-conscious concern emerged to make a distinction between "common names," pertaining to the nature of God, in virtue of which the three persons are one, and "proper names," pertaining to the persons in their distinction. What we should consider in this chapter are key locations within the tradition where each of these kinds of names is understood in analogical ways, as indicating both a similitude and yet also a greater dissimilitude of God to creatures. The work of Dionysius especially underscores the apophatic character of all our names for the divine nature, and it influences greatly both Albert the Great and Thomas Aquinas. The declaration of the Fourth Lateran Council meanwhile underscores the analogical character of all our conceptions of the divine persons, and this idea also is pivotal when we come to the consideration of the mystery of the distinct persons in the thought of Thomas Aquinas.

THE APOPHATICISM OF DIONYSIUS THE AREOPAGITE

Dionysius the Areopagite is the pseudonym of an anonymous theologian and mystical philosopher, who probably wrote in the late fifth or early sixth century. His corpus of writings purports symbolically to derive from the ancient Greek convert of St. Paul in Athens, the Dionysius of Acts 17:34. He most likely adopted this name not to incite undue credence in his own ideas, but rather as form of self-effacement. This New Testament reference is no doubt meant to allude to the conscription of Greek learning in the service of the gospel and the mystery of Christ. What survive of his writings are *The Divine Names*, *The Mystical Theology*, *The Celestial Hierarchy*, *The Ecclesiastical Hierarchy*, and various epistles. Albert the Great and Thomas Aquinas were both greatly influenced by this author and wrote some of the first major commentaries on his works in the Western medieval Church. Dionysius's corpus introduced important elements of Eastern apophatic theology into Western Trinitarian thought.[1]

Here we should note one idea in particular that builds in its own way on the thinking of the Cappadocians and which is quite central to the thinking of Aquinas as well. This is the issue of the analogical character of our language for God, or of the similitudes between creatures and God that our language can seek rightly to acknowledge in a qualified way.

Let us begin by considering an extended text of Dionysius's, the opening paragraphs of his brief work *The Mystical Theology*, where he stresses the limitations of our language before the ineffable divine essence. He writes:

> Trinity!! Higher than any being, any divinity, any goodness!
> Guide of Christians in the wisdom of heaven!
> Lead us up beyond unknowing and light,
> up to the farthest, highest peak of mystic scripture,
> where the mysteries of God's Word
> lie simple, absolute and unchangeable
> in the brilliant darkness of a hidden silence.

---

1. On Dionysius and his subsequent influence, see Eric D. Perl, *Theophany: The Neoplatonic Philosophy of Dionysius the Areopagite* (New York: SUNY Press, 2012); Filip Ivanovic, *Desiring the Beautiful: The Erotic-Aesthetic Dimension of Deification in Dionysius the Areopagite and Maximus the Confessor* (Washington, D.C.: The Catholic University of America Press, 2016); Fran O'Rourke, *Pseudo-Dionysius and the Metaphysics of Aquinas* (Notre Dame, Ind.: University of Notre Dame Press, 2015), and the study by Bernhard Blankenhorn, *The Mystery of Union with God: Dionysian Mysticism in Albert the Great and Thomas Aquinas* (Washington, D.C.: The Catholic University of America Press, 2015).

Amid the deepest shadow
they pour overwhelming light on what is most manifest.
Amid the wholly unsensed and unseen
they completely fill our sightless minds
with treasures beyond all beauty.

For this I pray; and, Timothy, my friend, my advice to you as you look for a sight of the mysterious things, is to leave behind you everything perceived and understood, everything perceptible and understandable, all that is not and all that is, and, with your understanding laid aside, to strive upward as much as you can toward union with him who is beyond all being and knowledge. By an undivided and absolute abandonment of yourself and everything, shedding all and freed from all, you will be uplifted to the ray of the divine shadow which is above everything that is.

But see to it that none of this comes to the hearing of the uninformed, that is to say, to those caught up with the things of the world, who imagine that there is nothing beyond instances of individual being and who think that by their own intellectual resources they can have a direct knowledge of him who has made the shadows his hiding place. And if initiation into the divine is beyond such people, what is to be said of those others, still more uninformed, who describe the transcendent Cause of all things in terms derived from the lowest orders of being, and who claim that it is in no way superior to the godless, multiformed shapes they themselves have made? What has actually to be said about the Cause of everything is this. Since it is the Cause of all beings, we should posit and ascribe to it all the affirmations we make in regard to beings, and, more appropriately, we should negate all these affirmations, since it surpasses all being. Now we should not conclude that the negations are simply the opposites of the affirmations, but rather that the cause of all is considerably prior to this, beyond privations, beyond every denial, beyond every assertion.[2]

In light of this passage, we can simply note some characteristic features of Dionysius's thought on the limitations of our language about God. First of all, for Dionysius, God is the author of all hierarchy within creation, but he also utterly transcends all hierarchy. That is to say, God is the author of all things but is not contained somehow within the extension of the scale of perfections as another finite being within the scale. Consequently, the vast plurality and hierarchical stratification of creatures bear witness to what God is in his transcendent nature, each and all together. And yet, our notion of God cannot be reduced to that of any one being, however perfect, that we find within the realm of created perfections.

Likewise, since God transcends creation, he is both ineffable and un-

---

2. Dionysius, *The Mystical Theology*, nos. 1–2, quoted from *Pseudo-Dionysius: The Complete Works*, trans. Colm Luibheid and P. Rorem (Mahwah, N.J.: Paulist Press, 1987).

knowable from the perspective of his creatures. Any philosophical terms we use to speak of God (such as unity or being) must be rethought and in a sense denied, when we apply them to God. God is "above" or "outside" our concepts of being or unity, and so is truly not being or unity as we experience them in creation. This emphasis on apophatic discourse paradoxically leads to a materialistic feature of Dionysius's thought: *because* of the divine ineffability, God can be "imaged" in material symbols metaphorically, precisely because these latter do not merely disclose God, but also conceal God. Material symbols of the bible and the liturgy depict God as hidden and at the same time as numinously present and manifest in physical creation. That said, the metaphysical terms we use for God based on analogy ("being," "unity," etc.) give us a greater sense of the divine transcendence, because of their semantic precision. However, they function in tandem with metaphorical or symbolic discourse that has its origins in biblical symbols.

In light of the limitations on our language outlined above, one of Dionysius's most significant contributions to theology is his elaboration of the *triplex via*, or threefold way of denoting God based on the perfections of creatures. The three forms of denotation are to be understood in a kind of logical succession, each one qualifying or perfecting that which precedes it. The first form is that of the *via causalitatis*, or causal way: God has in himself the perfections of all creatures, of which he is the cause. As such, we can denote God by way of the perfections that are his effects. For example, God is good, because what he produces is good.

The second form is the *via negationis*, or way of negation: what God is in himself utterly transcends all creaturely perfections, as well as the grasp of the human mind. Divine darkness accordingly ensues for the human intellect in its attempt to reach out to God. We cannot call God "good," for example, in any way that we ascribe that word to creatures, because his goodness utterly transcends theirs and is ultimately unknowable by us.

This leads to the third form, the *via eminentiae*, or way of eminence: God in his "super-essential" perfection transcends all the perfections of created, finite realities in a plenitude of perfection that is incomprehensible for us. God then is "good" not as creatures are, but in a superabundant way that is as unspeakable as it is mysterious. Moreover, God's hiddenness to us results not from an ontological deficit on his part, but from his ontological superabundance. God is unknowable to us not because he is unintelligible, but because he is supra-intelligible.

Dionysius stresses the limitations of all our terms for God, whether material or immaterial, in the following passage from *The Celestial Hierarchy*, where he emphasizes the importance of the *via negationis*:

Now these sacred shapes [i.e., spiritual names for God based on causality, such as "being" and "goodness"] certainly show more reverence and seem vastly superior to the making of images drawn from the world. Yet they are actually no less defective than this latter, for the Deity is far beyond every manifestation of being and of life; no reference to light can characterize it; every reason or intelligence falls short of similarity to it.

Then there is the scriptural device of praising the deity by presenting it in utterly dissimilar revelations. He is described as invisible, infinite, ungraspable, and other things which show *not what he is but what in fact he is not*. This second way of talking about him seems to me much more appropriate, for ... *God is in no way like the things that have being and we have no knowledge at all of his incomprehensible and ineffable transcendence and invisibility.*

Since the way of negation appears to be more suitable to the realm of the divine and since positive affirmations are always unfitting to the hiddenness of the inexpressible, a manifestation through dissimilar shapes is more correctly to be applied to the invisible.[3]

In this passage, Dionysius accordingly stresses the necessity of the way of negation for purifying all our concepts, whether they refer originally to material things or spiritual perfections. He does this in order to invite the intellect to move beyond all created reality, setting the mind out on the way to God so that it can take the "plunge into that darkness which is beyond intellect."[4]

Dionysius's affirmation of the value of the way of eminence can, in turn, be seen in a complementary passage, taken this time from *The Divine Names*. There, he writes:

We must interpret the things of God in a way that befits God, and when we talk of God as being without mind and without perception, *this is to be taken in the sense of what he has in superabundance and not as a defect.* Hence we attribute absence of reason to him *because he is above reason*, we attribute lack of perfection to him *because he is above and before perfection*, and we posit intangible and invisible darkness of that Light which is unapproachable *because it so far exceeds the visible light.*[5]

3. Dionysius, *The Celestial Hierarchy*, chap. 2, no. 3, in *The Complete Works*, emphases added.
4. Pseudo-Dionysius, *The Mystical Theology*, no. 3.
5. Pseudo-Dionysius, *The Divine Names*, chap. 7, no. 2, in *The Complete Works*, emphases added.

In this passage Dionysius seems to be saying that the *via negationis* does not have the last word. We negate our affirmations of God so as to make another affirmation: the mystery of God exceeds all created realities, which defectively image him as their infinitely superior cause. Creaturely perfections, as such, are found in God in a superabundant fashion.

Dionysius's contributions to high Scholastic theology are numerous, but for our present purposes it suffices to note how Dionysius develops the Cappadocians' stress on the interplay of light and darkness in regard to discourse about God. Dionysius is the author associated most with the so-called *triplex via* or threefold way of (1) affirmation of creaturely perfections, (2) negation, and (3) eminence or superabundant predication. Through the *triplex via*, Dionysius paves the way for medieval refinement of analogical discourse about God, as we will see especially in part 2, when we turn to St. Thomas Aquinas's discussion of how we name God analogically.

FOURTH LATERAN COUNCIL (1215)

As just noted, Dionysius the Areopagite helped in his own way to develop a notion of theological, analogical discourse regarding the divine nature, a notion found inchoately in the Cappadocians. This idea was presented differently and given explicit and authoritative articulation by the Fourth Lateran Council, held in 1215. There the notion of analogical naming is applied more formally to the mystery of the Trinitarian persons. Let us leap ahead and turn to the formulations of this Council, which can serve then as a proximate preparation for our discussion of the Trinitarian theology of St. Thomas Aquinas.

The context for the text of Lateran IV that is significant for our purposes concerns the condemnation of the Trinitarian theology of the Cistercian abbot Joachim of Fiore (d. 1202).[6] Theologians at that time typically commented upon the *Sentences* of Peter Lombard, which was itself a collection of theological opinions of the Fathers gathered together into a large work. The *Sentences* functioned as a kind of compendium of sound theological tradition, which left open a number of issues or questions, which commentators then discussed. Where this becomes relevant to the condemnation of Joa-

---

6. For theological analysis of Joachim Fiore in his historical context see Gilles Emery, *The Trinitarian Theology of St. Thomas Aquinas*, trans. F. Murphy (Oxford: Oxford University Press, 2010), 145–48.

chim's Trinitarian theology is as follows. Lombard, in the *Sentences*, had discussed the unity of the divine essence and had claimed that each of the three persons possesses the divine essence or substance equally. Consequently he insisted that the Father begets and that the Son is begotten, but that the divine essence does not beget and is not begotten. Joachim opposed Lombard on this point, because he thought that it implied the essence as something existing alongside the three persons, calling this a quaternity. Seemingly Joachim took Lombard to be an inadvertent Sabellian, who held that the divine essence merely presents itself in three modes. He wished to say in response that the relational processions of the Trinity just are the essence of God. The essence of God is a process of eternal begetting and spiration, so we can speak of the essence of God itself as begetting and begotten, spirating and spirated. However, by virtually equating essence with processional relations Joachim failed to safeguard an adequate way of speaking of the divine essence as that in virtue of which the persons are one, for example, in virtue of their common goodness, wisdom, and so on. Instead he conceived of the essence itself in relational terms. In effect, then, he mistakenly attributed actions proper to the three persons to the essence as such, so as to speak not only of the Father as begetting and the Son as begotten, but also of the divine essence as itself begetting, and as begotten. What results from this is an idea of three persons differentiated by different essential properties (the essence insofar as it begets is proper to the Father, while the essence insofar as it is begotten is proper only to the Son), or of an essence that itself changes so that it comes to exist in three distinct forms (God is essentially Father while begetting and essentially Son while being begotten). In either case, this theory provides us with no way to maintain adequately the unity of the Trinity. As an effect of the theory, Joachim's opponents took him to be construing the *unity* of the persons not as a unity of nature or essence, but as a *communal* unity resulting from their collective action. The Father and Son are not essentially one in being but distinct in virtue of their "essentially" distinct properties of begetting and being begotten. In this case the unity of the three persons would be construed merely as a moral union resulting from the concerted activity of three distinct agents, not unlike a communion of human persons joined by grace. What was eclipsed in this theology is the mysterious unity of the Father, Son, and Spirit, who are truly one in virtue of their unique substance (their individual being and essence as God), and whose unity is not due merely to a collaborative moral union.

Against the theories of abbot Joachim, Lateran IV responded with a great restatement of Trinitarian monotheism, insisting strongly on divine simplicity and the consubstantiality of the three persons. According to Lateran IV, there is only one individual divine essence, such that the Father, Son, and Holy Spirit are personally distinct, yet each possesses in himself the complete and unique essence of God. The persons are each the same reality. Each is wholly and entirely the one God. All that God is is found in the Father, in the Son, and in the Holy Spirit, respectively.

Lateran IV affirms the unity of essence in the three persons against Joachim in the following words:

He [Joachim] professes ... that such a [divine] unity is not true and proper but rather collective and analogous [*similitudinariam*], in the way that many persons are said to be one people and many faithful one church.... We, however, with the approval of this sacred and universal council, believe and confess with Peter Lombard that there exists a certain supreme reality, incomprehensible and ineffable, which truly is the Father and the Son and the Holy Spirit, the three persons together and each one of them distinctly. Therefore in God there is only a Trinity, not a quaternity, since each of the three persons is that reality—that is to say substance, essence or divine nature—which alone is the principle of all things, besides which no other principle can be found.[7]

The Council underscores that the three persons are one in being, essence, and nature, and that this plenitude of the divine essence is integral to each of the persons, not extrinsic to him. For this reason, there is no quaternity—that is, the persons plus the essence as a "fourth thing"—but each of the three persons simply is the one God. The Father is God as one who is unoriginated. The Son is God as one who is eternally begotten. The Spirit is God as one who is eternally spirated.

Lateran IV likewise goes on to stress, against Joachim, that it is the persons and not the nature that are the principle of the processions. It is the Father who begets the Son, not the essence of the Father. There is no procession of essence begotten from essence begetting, nor is there a division of essence. This points toward what Western medieval theologians called the distinction of "notional acts" (the Father begetting) versus "essential acts" (the divine wisdom, goodness, etc., creating). The Council states:

---

7. Fourth Lateran Council, chap. 2, from *Decrees*, ed. Tanner, 1:232 [translation slightly modified].

This reality [the divine essence] neither begets nor is begotten nor proceeds; the Father begets, the Son is begotten and the Holy Spirit proceeds. Thus there is a distinction of persons but a unity of nature. Although therefore the Father is one person, the Son another person and the Holy Spirit another person, they are not different realities [*non tamen aliud*], but rather that which is the Father is the Son and the Holy Spirit, altogether the same; thus according to the orthodox and catholic faith they are believed to be consubstantial. *For the Father, in begetting the Son from eternity, gave him his substance.... It cannot be said that the Father gave him part of his substance and kept part for himself since the Father's substance is indivisible, inasmuch as it is altogether simple.* Nor can it be said that the Father transferred his substance to the Son, in the act of begetting, as if he gave it to the Son in such a way that he did not retain it for himself; for otherwise he would have ceased to be substance. *It is therefore clear that in being begotten the Son received the Father's substance without it being diminished in any way, and thus the Father and the Son have the same substance. Thus the Father and the Son and also the Holy Spirit proceeding from both are the same reality.*[8]

According to the Council, it is the Father *in his person* who generates the Son and not the divine substance generating. The Father does not give a part of himself, as if his supremely simple substance were capable of division. Rather, he communicates the totality of his divine life to the Son and Holy Spirit so that the three together form one and the same *res*, reality: three persons in only one God.

The Council's response to Joachim, however, also becomes the occasion for a conciliar affirmation of the principle of analogy, governing how we apply created concepts and terms to God. The Council's affirmation on this point comes in response to Joachim's likening of the unity of persons in God to the unity of the Church on the basis of Jesus' prayer in Jn 17:22: "that they [i.e., Jesus' disciples] may be one in us just as we [i.e., Father and Son] are one."[9] The Council contends, against Joachim, that the scriptural use of "one" here is analogical and so governed by the dissimilarity that exists between God and creatures. The divine unity (a unity of essence shared identically by three distinct persons) is utterly different from any unity we experience in the created order. We may think of it theologically, then, only by a similitude or analogy. Here is the key text from Lateran IV on this point:

When, therefore, the Truth prays to the Father for those faithful to him, saying I wish that "they may be one in us just as we are one," [Jn 17:22] this word "one"

---

8. Fourth Lateran Council, chap. 2, quoted in *Decrees*, ed. Tanner, 1:232, emphases added.
9. See Fourth Lateran Council, chap. 2, for the Council's statement of Joachim's position.

means for the faithful a union of love in grace, and for the divine persons a unity of identity in nature, as the Truth says elsewhere, "You must be perfect as your heavenly Father is perfect" [Mt 5:48], as if he were to say more plainly "you must be perfect" in the perfection of grace, just as "your Father is perfect" in the perfection that is his by nature, each in his own way. *For between creator and creature there can be noted no similarity so great that a greater dissimilarity cannot be seen between them.*[10]

Commentators commonly note the strongly apophatic character of this text. Every similitude between creatures and God implies a "greater dissimilitude." Apophaticism can serve, then, as a guard against rationalism in matters of theological mystery. We do not know the simplicity and unity of the godhead in itself. The unity of the Trinity can be indicated only by comparisons that are analogical, in the service of a respectful contemplation of a mystery of faith.

It is important to realize that the concept of analogy employed by the Fourth Lateran Council does pertain to the divine nature as such, and in that sense the doctrine of the Council develops in implicit organic continuity with the previous teaching of the Cappadocians, Augustine, and Dionysius, among others. However, the teaching of the Council also has inevitable implications for the way we think about the Trinitarian persons and their distinction. Where Joachim's theology had led people to the idea that God could be conceived of by a kind of anthropomorphism, a likeness of three agents in moral cooperation, the Council wanted to underscore that Trinitarian *persons* are not to be thought of simply after the likeness of created human persons. Precisely because the persons of the Trinity are distinguished by relations of origin but are consubstantial, so too they cannot be understood in comparison with human persons except by way of dissimilitude. Here the process of divine naming is applied not only to the common nature but also to the persons as such. What is emerging is an exploration of the analogy of personhood between the Trinity and human beings. This process of theological investigation will be further developed by Thomas Aquinas, who reflects not only on the analogical notion of divine persons, but also on the analogical use of proper names for the Father, Word, and Spirit respectively.

---

10. Fourth Lateran Council, chap. 2, *Decrees*, ed. Tanner, 1:232, emphasis added.

CONCLUSION

We can draw the following conclusions from Lateran IV's normative clarifications of Trinitarian theology, articulated in response to the errors of Joachim of Fiore. First, Trinitarian theology must speak of the divine essence or nature, which is common to the three persons. This essence is not some "fourth thing" forming a quaternity with the three persons. Instead, it is the ground of unity of the three persons who are each the one God. The Father communicates the divine essence to the Son by generation and the Father and the Son communicate it to the Holy Spirit by spiration. Second, we must speak of this nature both by employing similitudes drawn from creatures ("unity," "goodness," "being"), which we can speak of as "divine names," and by qualifying them negatively, by way of an apophatic theology. There is always a greater dissimilitude between creatures and God than there is a similitude. Third, it should be noted that this analogical character of language for God applies to the divine persons, also, as well as to their notional acts. That is to say, we speak analogically not only of God's oneness or goodness, but also of the Father or the Son, and of the notional acts of begetting or spiration. Trinitarian theology, therefore, must make use of an analogical discourse for speaking of God, who is both one in essence and three persons, and who is both known and unknown. As we will see shortly, this manner of proceeding is also typical of the approach of St. Thomas Aquinas.

In the first part of this book we have been concerned primarily with the scriptural and patristic foundations for the Church's Trinitarian faith. We began with an overview of the origins of man's search for God, which can be found in man's pre-philosophical dispositions or intuitions that there is a God. We then discussed the ambiguities of the question of God found in the formulations of the world's ancient religious traditions. In this connection, we also looked at the contemporary crisis of belief in God in the modern world and the Church's response to this existential crisis of ambivalence and religious disorientation.

From this starting point, we then turned to the revelation of the one God in Israel, and the progressive emergence of a strict monotheism within the historic milieu of ancient Israel, as attested to by a diachronic reading of Israel's scriptures. In the next place, we directed our attention to the New

Testament scriptures and considered the attestation of an inchoate Trinitarian faith found in the revelation of Father, Son, and Holy Spirit, in the person and work of Jesus Christ.

Last, we turned to an overview of the developments of Trinitarian thought in the Church's theological and dogmatic traditions. This articulation of the Church's Trinitarian faith occurred gradually over time, mostly in response to ancient errors or heresies, but also, more broadly, in light of the searching activity of human reason seeking ever greater understanding of the mystery of faith—this is Anselm's so-called *intellectus fidei*, human inquiry into the meaning and interrelationship of the articles of faith.

On the basis of this foundation laid in part 1, then, our task going forward will be to consider the developed Trinitarian faith of the Church through a sustained study of one of its foremost exponents: St. Thomas Aquinas. We will do this in two parts. In part 2 of this work, we will study Aquinas's teaching on the unity of the Trinity, that is, his teaching on the one God and his attributes (the "divine names"). After this, in part 3, we will study Aquinas's explicit articulation of Christian belief in the Trinity of persons. In light of our consideration of Thomistic Trinitarian theology in parts 2 and 3, we will turn in part 4 to a Thomistic consideration of contemporary Trinitarian theology.

PART 2

On the Mystery
of the Divine Nature

St. Thomas Aquinas's
De Deo Uno Treatise

11

Analogia Entis within *Analogia Fidei*
Arguments for God's Existence

In the second part of this book we turn to knowledge of God in the thought of Thomas Aquinas, with a particular focus on the mystery of the divine nature. What does it mean to say that God is one? What can we say about the essence of God? As is well known, Aquinas makes concerted use of philosophical arguments when reflecting on the divine nature, and he ascribes names or attributes to the one God, such as simplicity, perfection, goodness, infinity, and so forth. He develops a treatment of these attributes of the divine nature in questions 1–26 of the *Summa theologiae*, before going on to treat the mystery of the Trinitarian persons in questions 27–43. Some critics of Aquinas claim that this first part of his treatise on God as one in nature (*de Deo ut uno*) can be separated out from the treatise on the Trinity, and that this implies that the Trinitarian theology of Aquinas is an addendum of secondary importance, a postscript to a unitarian monotheism of the philosophers. This reading is erroneous and stems from a serious misunderstanding of the structure of Aquinas's *Summa theologiae*. In fact, Aquinas undertakes an order of inquiry that he thinks will facilitate the greatest insight into the Christian mystery of God. He studies the mystery of the one nature or essence of God in view of an analysis of the three persons in their distinction and their unity. After all, they are intelligible as distinct persons who are each God only if they are also intelligible as persons possessing the divine nature. The study of God as one, in the first part of Aquinas's treatise, is geared toward the study of the distinction and communion of the three persons, which succeeds it. These two sections of

Aquinas's treatise on God are organically related.[1] Consequently, his Trinitarian thinking resembles that of both Gregory of Nazianzus and Augustine, each of whom is concerned to speak of both the unity of nature and
the distinction of persons in the one God, as a way of casting light on the
mystery of God as Tri-une. It is helpful to read these great Doctors of the
Church in relative continuity with one another so as best to understand
their own intentions. They saw themselves as contributing collectively to a
common project of ecclesial wisdom and were seeking to promote a common patrimony. This is a far less artificial way of interpreting them than
one finds in those who juxtapose Aquinas and the Fathers in opposition-
al fashion, a standpoint that fails to acknowledge how deeply the scholastic
thinkers of the thirteenth century were influenced by patristic authorities,
especially in their interpretation of scripture and assimilation of doctrinal
principles.

This all being said, it is also true that Aquinas does make use of philosophy to speak about the divine nature, the one God of the Old and New Testaments. Indeed, he begins his study of the divine nature with his famous
quinque viae or five arguments for God's existence. Consequently, we too
will begin with this aspect of Aquinas's teaching.

People commonly make one of two errors when they study Aquinas's
arguments in the *Summa theologiae* for the existence of God. Some presuppose that Aquinas is attempting to present his distinctly philosophical arguments in separation from his theological study, so that the arguments function merely as preludes to theology, or perhaps even as rational justifications
for why one ought to take Christian belief seriously. Others think, to the
contrary, that the arguments are uniquely theological reflections meant to
explain how one might speak about the God of Christian revelation, but
that they are not meant to have a distinctly philosophical, rationally demonstrative content as such. On the first view, Aquinas is either seeking to provide rational demonstrations of God so as to lead one to the truth of Christian revelation (as if belief in God would lead one to belief in the Trinity),
or he is seeking to remove obstacles to faith (much as he does seek to do in
his arguments in the *Summa contra Gentiles*). On the second view, Christian
revelation of the Trinity does away with the need for or possibility of philosophical argumentation regarding God. Whatever pre-Christian philoso-

1. For a more developed analysis of Aquinas's treatise on this point, see Emery, *The Trinitarian
Theology of St. Thomas Aquinas*, 44–50.

phy may have said about God can be assimilated into a distinctively theo-logical project. Both views are problematic. We will, accordingly, begin this chapter by considering how to situate Aquinas's philosophical inquiry into the existence of the one God within his total theological project. After this, we should consider the metaphysical presuppositions underlying Aquinas's arguments for God's existence. We can then look at why Thomas advances what he calls *quia* arguments for God's existence rather than *propter quid* ar-guments. Finally, we will analyze briefly Aquinas's five proofs for God's ex-istence in the *Summa theologiae*.

THE THEOLOGICAL CONTEXT OF THE FIVE WAYS

Aquinas's arguments in the *Summa theologiae* for the existence of God are intended to function as demonstrations of natural reason, precise-ly because they are said to derive from philosophical premises, not from truths of divine revelation. Does this mean we can rightly interpret them by prescinding from any consideration of their theological context? Here we must make a distinction. In one sense the answer is clearly positive. In the famous "Five Ways" of *ST* I, q. 2, Aquinas makes philosophical argu-ments for the existence of God. Some of these are spelled out in more de-veloped ways in other of his writings that are unambiguously philosophical in form. Much of what he will eventually derive from these arguments, in his treatment of divine attributes in *ST* I, qq. 2–26, is philosophically de-fensible and has roots in his philosophical argumentation from the start. In another sense, however, the answer to our question is negative. His use of philosophical argumentation throughout the *Summa theologiae* takes place within a distinctively theological context. The mystery of the Trinity that Aquinas is examining is not subject to discovery by natural reason alone, even if one can reflect on God philosophically within the context of Trini-tarian theology.

In fact, even when making distinctively philosophical arguments for the existence of God in *ST* I, q. 2, Aquinas is conducting what he takes to be an exercise in Catholic theological *sacra doctrina*. That is to say, he is seek-ing to understand the mystery of God that has been revealed in scripture and tradition, and that is confessed by the Church in the Nicene Creed. The nature of theology as *sacra doctrina* is the subject of discussion in *ST* I, q. 1, where Aquinas treats theology as a science of revelation: an organized body of knowledge that is concerned with a unified object, God, who is revealing himself to humanity.[2] His analysis there leads logically to qq. 2–3, where Aquinas treats the question of our natural, philosophical capacity for knowledge of God. The order of the questions is not accidental: it signals a passage from grace to nature. Aquinas makes it clear already in *ST* I, q. 1, a. 5, that *sacra doctrina* can and should make use of philosophical argumentation, but that it does so within the context of the more ultimate explanatory science of theology. Nature blossoms within grace, and philosophical reason within the sphere of revelation. The revelation of God as Trinity casts an ultimate light upon reality, but it does not suppress our natural understanding of God. Indeed, the grace of faith in divine revelation revives, stimulates, and makes use of our natural capacity for thinking about God.[3] In *sacra doctrina*, then, one undertakes an examination of the mystery of the one true God, revealed first to Israel and finally to the world in Christ. Therefore, it is the Holy Trinity that is under consideration. The Trinity, however, is the one God and Creator, and we can think about the one God even by means of our natural reason. God is approachable intellectually "from below" through human rational intuition and reflection, even as he addresses us from above. Before the symphony of reasoning theologically about the Trinity is conducted, then, Aquinas is assembling his instruments. Philosophical reflection about God is appropriate in this context, since it pertains

2. On *sacra doctrina*, see James Weisheipl, "The Meaning of Sacra Doctrina in *Summa theologiae* I, q. 1," *The Thomist* 38, no. 1 (1974): 49–80.

3. I am suggesting here that grace can act upon human nature to initiate its inner healing, so that persons (and cultures) that receive the grace of Christian faith can be inwardly disposed and motivated by that grace to seek philosophical understanding of God. However, I am not suggesting that this same activity of grace in the human person substitutes for or evacuates the "formal" content of philosophical, natural reason pertaining to God in human beings or culture. The philosophical vocation and "rational essence" of man remain even after Christianity. In fact the scope of this vocation is augmented, as Christianity creates the space in human culture for integral philosophical reflection on God. Nor am I suggesting here that natural knowledge of God is impossible for fallen human beings without the aid of grace, or for that matter, in non-Christian cultures. Human beings have some natural capacity to think about the first principle of reality, God, his deity, and his providence, even without the internal help of grace, or the assistance of an intellectual culture directly informed by divine revelation. In concrete history this typically occurs through the medium of diverse religious traditions and schools of metaphysical thought (ancient or modern), in which one often finds remarkable human reflection on God, even if such reflection is often also admixed with error, confusion, and ambiguous or problematic views of the divine. Against the backdrop of this complex cultural patrimony of humanity, divine revelation provides both internal grace and a developed tradition of external cultural influences that help focus, sharpen, purify, and dispose natural reasoning regarding God as Creator, in his distinctness, transcendence, incomprehensibility, and immanent presence to all of created reality.

to us as rational creatures, even as it is being employed instrumentally in the service of faith.

What should we conclude thus far, then? If Aquinas is studying God as one, it is because he also wishes to study the mystery of God as three. Consequently, when Aquinas does consider the unity of the divine nature, he does so not only theologically, by way of a reflection on scripture, but also philosophically, placing metaphysical reasoning in the service of the mystery of faith. However, we can now tack in the other direction. Philosophical reasoning has its own integrity even when employed in the service of theology and indeed should aspire to be all the more rigorous in this context, so that we can distinguish clearly what is known with certitude by faith and what is attained by reason. As a consequence, we should also seek to avoid the second extreme mentioned above, which would treat the philosophical elements in Aquinas merely as an internal exploration of the grammar of theology. This view is found among postmodern, anti-foundationalist theologians who presume that Aquinas's project, precisely because it is holistically theological, must not admit a sharp distinction between philosophical knowledge and theological reflection on revelation. In their view, the so-called philosophy in Aquinas is always already a kind of extension of theology, by which he speaks about the God of scripture in the terminology of the contemporary humanities of his time, making use of Aristotelian and Neoplatonic terms to characterize the God of the bible.[4] On this reading, *sacra doctrina* alone would seem to provide Aquinas with the normative science of being, so that all metaphysical forms of reflection are mere adumbrations of theology. The formal objects of the philosophical disciplines are resolved into the study of *sacra doctrina*, and all pre-Christian terminology for the divine is at best an anticipation of the scriptural-linguistic depiction of reality.

Is such an idea historically defensible? Of course Aquinas does affirm

---

4. This interpretation has been developed especially by contemporary post-liberal theologians influenced by a combination of Barth, Balthasar, and Wittgenstein. See, for example, Victor Preller, *Divine Science and the Science of God: A Reformulation of Thomas Aquinas* (Princeton, N.J.: Princeton University Press, 1967); David B. Burrell, *Aquinas: God and Action* (London: Routledge & Kegan Paul, 1979); George Lindbeck, *The Nature of Doctrine: Religion and Theology in a Post-liberal Age*, 2nd ed. (Philadelphia: Westminster, 2009); Eugene F. Rogers, *Thomas Aquinas and Karl Barth: Sacred Doctrine and the Natural Knowledge of God* (South Bend, Ind.: Notre Dame University Press, 1999); D. Stephen Long, *Speaking of God: Theology, Language and Truth* (Grand Rapids, Mich.: Eerdmans, 2009); Frederick Christian Bauerschmidt, *Thomas Aquinas: Faith, Reasoning, and Following Christ* (Oxford: Oxford University Press, 2015).

the unity of all knowledge (philosophical and theological truths are harmonious with one another), but he does not hold that the formal objects of philosophy and theology are identical in kind.[5] On the contrary, he clearly distinguishes the study of God as first cause in metaphysics from the knowledge of God derived from divine revelation. He does make use of pre-Christian thought in the service of a philosophy that is thoroughly Christianized, but he is also unambiguous in affirming that philosophy is a form of *scientia* (demonstrative knowledge derived from naturally known principles) and even *sapientia* (contemplative understanding of reality in light of God) distinct from theology.[6] Indeed he clearly affirms that it is possible for the human being to demonstrate the existence of God by natural, philosophical argumentation.[7] While Aquinas distinguishes grace and nature, revelation and natural reason, theology and philosophy, he is also careful never to oppose or separate the two. They are meant to operate organically in synergy with one another, in the concrete lives of Christian persons, who are rational animals progressively redeemed and healed by grace.

Here, then, we may note that there are two opposed errors that Catholic theology traditionally seeks to avoid. Aquinas is aware of each of them and navigates between them very deftly. One consists in positing a kind of epistemological extrinsicism between divine revelation and philosophical thinking about God (often labeled "natural theology"). Such extrinsicism would claim that divine revelation is something entirely alien to all human attempts to know God naturally. God does not address the human being by grace so as to elicit the use of that dimension of us that is capable of know-

---

5. There is widespread textual evidence that Aquinas affirms a distinction of philosophical objects and sciences (bodies of knowledge) based on demonstrative reasoning from first principles. See, among others, the clear indications of his commentary on Boethius's *De Trinitate, Expositio super librum Boethii de Trinitate* (*Expos. de Trin.*), which attempts to treat the very question under consideration in a systematic way. For translations, see Thomas Aquinas, *Faith, Reason and Theology*, trans. A. Maurer (Toronto: PIMS, 1987); *The Division and Methods of the Sciences: Questions V and VI of his Commentary on the De Trinitate of Boethius*, trans. A. Maurer (Toronto: PIMS, 1986). See likewise Gilles Emery, "Thomas Aquinas, Postliberal? George Lindbeck's Reading of St. Thomas," in *Trinity, Church, and the Human Person*, 263–90; Anna Bonta Moreland, *Known by Nature: Thomas Aquinas on Natural Knowledge of God* (New York: Crossroad, 2010).

6. Here again the textual evidence is widespread, but see, for example, *SCG* II, c. 4; *ST* I, q. 1, a. 6, ad 2; *In octo libros Physicorum Aristotelis expositio*, II (*In II Phys.*), lec. 6, 196; *In duodecim libros Metaphysicorum Aristotelis expositio*, IV (*In IV Meta.*), lec. 1, 1149–51; *In XI Meta*, lec. 1, 2151. For discussions of "Christian philosophy," see my *Wisdom in the Face of Modernity: A Thomistic Study in Natural Theology*, 2nd ed. (Naples, Fla.: Sapientia, 2016), esp. Appendix C.

7. See the dossier of evidence and analysis offered by Lawrence Dewan, "The Existence of God: Can It Be *Demonstrated*?," *Nova et Vetera* (English edition) 10, no. 3 (2012): 731–56.

ing God naturally. Rather, divinely inspired faith offers the unique means by
which we can know God effectively, by grace, and not by human works of
reasoning or reflection. In differing ways, this is arguably the view of Martin
Luther, for example in the *Heidelberg Disputation*,[8] and most certainly that
of Karl Barth, in his famous *Church Dogmatics*.[9]

The contrary extreme posits a kind of identification between natural
and supernatural knowledge, and terminates in a form of nature-grace immanentism. One version of this view stems from major contributors to the
Enlightenment tradition. It claims that when we come to know anything
true about God by appeal to "divine revelation," such knowledge, if genuine, is in fact merely natural and properly philosophical in origin. The presupposition behind this view seems to be rationalistic: any appeal to divine
revelation in the strict sense would necessarily imply some kind of affront
to human reason. Philosophy, then, must proclaim its absolute sovereignty or omni-competence with regard to any and every affirmation or negation concerning the question of God. If we were to try to retain some truth
from the Christian religion, then, we would need to demythologize the symbols of purported revelation to identify their inner philosophical or rational
core. In short: we must rationalize Christianity, denude it of its mysterious,
symbolic, or miraculous content, and explain it philosophically. This is the
view that Immanuel Kant develops systematically in his work *Religion within the Boundaries of Mere Reason*,[10] and it is arguably the underlying stance
of G. W. F. Hegel in his influential oeuvre.[11]

Another way to hold this immanentist view—an inverted contrary in
the same genus—is to reduce all philosophical knowledge of God to a kind
of implicit theological knowledge. In other words, all natural knowledge, insofar as it tends toward true knowledge of God, is always already implicitly
a grace, a gift of participation in the divine knowledge of God that comes by
revelation. Consequently whatever we come to know of God by reason is always already supernaturally oriented, an implicit invitation to the fullness of
the knowledge of God in Christ. This immanentistic viewpoint is integralist
rather than rationalist, because grace is conceived of as being in a sense integral to nature. Nature is always already on the way to grace, and reason is

---

8. See Martin Luther, *Heidelberg Disputation*, trans. Aaron T. Fenker (Holt, Mo.: Higher
Things, 2018).

9. See especially Karl Barth, *CD* 1:1 and 2:1. The topic is treated thematically in both volumes.

10. See Immanuel Kant, *Religion within the Boundaries of Mere Reason*.

11. See the argument to this effect by Charles Taylor in *Hegel*, 480–509.

always already on the way to theological ontology. Such a view seeks to attenuate or dissolve the strict distinction of grace and nature, so as to resolve
any possible tension between the two. Arguably one finds a prime example of this tendency in the contemporary theology of John Milbank.[12] We
should note that the integralist view and the philosophically naturalist or
rationalist view are mirror images of one another and readily nourish opposition to one another. In the face of a secularized modern rationality that is
dismissive of revelation and its cultural relevance, Christian theologians can
respond that in fact there is no genuine rationality present apart from theology, so that all thought is in some sense dependent upon its attentiveness to
revelation. On a deeper level, however, both these positions actually share a
common stance, since they both reject the premise of two distinct orders of
knowledge—one stemming from supernatural objects of faith and one from
objects of natural reason. The two orders are thus collapsed or fused into
one another, with one being all encompassing of the other.[13] The tendency
of Aquinas's thought works against this basic premise, as does the dogmatic teaching of the First Vatican Council, which has been recently restated by the magisterium of the Catholic Church.[14] Accordingly in our arguments below we will approach the matter in both a non-extrinsicist and
non-integralist fashion, in keeping with the acquisitions of the Catholic tradition.

Let us return, then, to the Thomist approach. On this view, revelation
provides a pathway to knowledge of God and intimacy with God that is
not procured merely by natural philosophical reason, but the grace of revelation also appeals to our natural reason and stimulates our efforts to try
to come to terms with the truth of God's existence. Who or what is the one
God, who has created all things? What does it mean to say that God exists?
Here we can see the justification even within theology to undertake a dis-

12. See, for example, the systematic argument of John Milbank, *The Suspended Middle: Henri de Lubac and the Debate concerning the Supernatural* (Grand Rapids, Mich.: Eerdmans, 2005);
and the helpful presentation of James K. A. Smith, *Introducing Radical Orthodoxy: Mapping a
Post-secular Theology* (Grand Rapids, Mich.: Baker Academic, 2004).

13. On the extremes that derive logically from this type of nature-grace integralism, see the
dialectic Matthias Joseph Scheeben presents in the opening pages of his *Nature and Grace*, trans.
C. Vollert (Eugene, Ore.: Wipf & Stock, 2009), 1–16.

14. In his 1998 encyclical *Fides et Ratio*, John Paul II appropriated the analysis of Vatican I's
Dei Filius so as to underscore the distinction of formal objects in philosophy and theology and
the relative autonomy of specification that is proper to philosophical investigation even when it is
conducted on Christian soil: see §§45, 48, 67, 77.

tinctly metaphysical form of reflection directly influenced by philosophy, even if this approach need not and should not function in total autonomy from faith (i.e., in absolute separation from the influences of grace and revelation). Such metaphysical reasoning can in fact be placed at the service of faith, and provide us with resources for thinking clearly and deeply about the mystery of the Holy Trinity.

Aquinas's *de Deo ut uno* treatise (*ST* I, qq. 2–26), then, is indeed concerned with what can be known of the nature of the one God by means of natural reason operating at its summit. However, it is also a treatise of Christian theology, one that makes use of natural knowledge of God in the context of a study of the one essence and three persons of the Trinity. Given this methodological viewpoint, it is not strange that Aquinas will insist repeatedly that *revelation itself* teaches that man is naturally capable of authentic *natural* knowledge of God. He frequently cites in this regard Romans 1:19–20: "For what can be known about God is plain to them [i.e., the gentiles], because God has shown it to them. Ever since the creation of the world his invisible nature, namely, his eternal power, and deity, has been clearly perceived in the things that have been made. So they are without excuse," that is, for failing to acknowledge the truth about God in their lives.[15] Interestingly, then, Aquinas appeals to scripture even as the deepest starting point epistemologically for a twofold acknowledgment. Without grace, even human natural knowledge of God often fails to come to perfect fruition; and within grace, scripture itself by divine authority invokes natural reason to accept its own philosophical inclination toward God as a means of cooperation with the revelation of God.

This pattern of reasoning (divine revelation at the start and conclusion of ontological reflection) will unfold systemically in the *De Deo Uno* treatise as Aquinas considers each "divine name" or attribute of God's nature. He consistently appeals first to scripture or the Fathers in the *auctoritas* of his various articles in the treatise, to show that he is beginning from scripture and tradition (i.e., divine revelation) and is then offering a developed reflection on fundamental biblical truths by employing metaphysical reasoning as a subordinate science (in the body of the articles). The notion of the lesser human *scientia* of philosophy as subordinate to theology is explained in *ST* I, q. 1, a. 5: the study of philosophy retains all of its integrity as a form of de-

<hr/>

15. See for example in this regard, *ST* I, q. 2, a. 2, s.c. Another relevant scriptural passage is Eph 4:17–19, which Aquinas notes in his commentary in *Super Epistolam ad Ephesios* (*In Eph.*) IV, lec. 6.

194 The Divine Nature

monstrative reasoning even within theology. Philosophical argument functions demonstratively on the basis of its own natural premises and logical conclusions. However, distinctly philosophical arguments can be employed reasonably within theology at the service of the greater understanding of theological mysteries. For instance, if divine revelation teaches us that there is one God, the Creator of all other realities, we can make use of warranted philosophical analysis to clarify what it means and does not mean to call God "one" and "Creator."

Thus, in making demonstrative philosophical arguments for the existence of God in *ST* I, q. 2, a. 3, Aquinas is being entirely consistent with the principles of his whole theological enterprise. Metaphysical reasoning is employed in the service of faith. Are these philosophical proofs *within* a theological context? Yes: they are a Christian theologian's search for a philosophical account of what we mean when we say "God." In other words, they are indeed genuine philosophical arguments.

We might next ask, then, does the word "God," as employed in *ST* I, q. 2, aa. 2 and 3, have an exclusively Christian significance, or also a natural, philosophical significance? The answer is that it has both significations insofar as they overlap in semantic content. The Christian notion of God (including the biblical notion of God in the Old Testament) presupposes some minimal natural capacity on our part to employ the word "God" with positive signification. Were this not the case, the revelation of God in biblical semantics would remain wholly alien to our world of grammatical syntax, so as to be linguistically unintelligible. However, biblical and Christian theological words about God are not simply meaningless or inaccessible to ordinary human reason. The word "God" has a presumed natural significance, meaning something like "transcendent universal providence." God is the transcendent unoriginated source of the world, and he governs it in view of ends foreordained by himself. Indeed, our graced knowledge of the triune God made possible by scripture presupposes this more fundamental notion of the one God and builds upon it, even as it also purifies, elevates, and enriches it.[16]

16. It follows from this line of reasoning that the revelation of God's oneness in scripture also functions as a form of natural enlightenment to human cultures that have adopted polytheistic traditions of thinking, precisely because the human mind is capable of understanding eventually that God must truly be one.

AQUINAS'S EPISTEMOLOGICAL PRESUPPOSITIONS

Classical arguments for the existence of God originating from the pre-modern Christian tradition are sometimes dismissed in the modern academy not primarily because they are unreasonable (though of course many modern philosophers do claim this), but because they begin from basic presuppositions that are commonly questioned by post-Enlightenment philosophers. A key presupposition, arguably the one that is most contested, concerns the affirmation that we can know that there exist in the world we experience distinct concrete beings (substances), having a variety of properties (or, in the scholastic terminology, "accidents"), and that these beings around us are genuine causes of change in one another. Not least due to the widespread cultural influence of figures like David Hume and Immanuel Kant, it has become customary in some sectors of modern philosophy to call into question the presupposition of this basic, seemingly realistic, affirmation: that we can know directly in themselves distinct existent realities characterized by different natures (having a given essence, which implies formal causality); that these realities act upon each other (by way of efficient causality); and that these realities tend toward certain ends or intrinsic states of relative perfection (teleology or final causality).[17]

Consider, for example, what Thomists sometimes call the "principle of identity." This is the notion that there exist around us real substances of diverse natural kinds, with inherent ontological properties such as qualities, quantities, and relations.[18] Or the principle of causality, the notion that

17. For more on this subject, see my arguments in *Wisdom in the Face of Modernity*. In diverse ways Hume and Kant each question whether our causal explanations about extra-mental realities are attributed with warrant to the ontological structures of the realities themselves, or derive primarily from our way of repeatedly perceiving phenomena and constructing notions of such realities through our imagination or reason. I am drawing attention to their views in particular because of their widespread influence in modern theology, as well as in philosophy. However, today in Analytic philosophy there is a renewed interest in metaphysics that takes issue with some of their key presuppositions. See, on this development, the helpful introduction of Robert C. Koons and Timothy H. Pickavance, *Metaphysics: The Fundamentals* (Oxford: Wiley Blackwell, 2015).

18. The Aristotelian roots of this principle are found in the idea that the human being encounters and begins to understand (prior to reasoning) the fundamental categorial modes of being in things. We simply apprehend the existence of substances, their quantities, qualities, relations, actions, passions, habits, time, place, and position, even if we initially understand these "folds" of reality imperfectly. See Aristotle, *Metaphysics* 4.2 (1003b23–35), and Aquinas's commentary in *In IV Meta.*, lec. 2, para. 561. In *De veritate* (*De ver.*) q. 1, a. 1, Aquinas speaks of *res* and *aliquid* as transcendental notions, that follow closely upon *ens* and *unum*. In other words, where there is a being, it has some kind of unity, but also some kind of intelligible content (*res*), and a kind of actuality by

nothing that we experience is the cause of itself, but that each individual thing is caused (in various ways) by others. Or the principle of finality: everything we experience tends by its natural properties toward certain ends, or produces predictable outcomes of a given kind. Hume, Kant, and philosophers influenced by them claim that these notions are at worst delusions of human subjectivity, and at best a kind of human construct fabricated by the mind in order to impose stable forms of intelligibility upon the phenomena of sense experience. For these thinkers, the notions of formal, efficient, and final "causes" do indeed help us order our thinking about the data of the senses, but they ultimately do not necessarily tell us anything about the intrinsic natures of the realities we experience, or of what is happening in the realities themselves, or between these realities. Human patterns of thought and language readily become unmoored from their point of contact with the realities of sense experience.[19]

This view is in fact excessively idealistic, even when it claims to be rigorously empiricist, because it understands human knowledge of the very causes of things to stem from mere constructions of reason or to originate merely from elements of imagination.[20] If, by contrast, we start from the investigation of ontological structures in the realties we encounter around us

which it is differentiated as "something" (*aliquid*) distinct from other things. See the helpful study on this subject by David S. Oderberg, *Real Essentialism* (London: Routledge, 2007).

19. Hume famously argues that our notions of causality arise from experience rather than reason, and are connections we draw from one thing to another based on custom and repeated occurrences in nature. However, it follows from this position that we cannot attain causal understanding of essences, powers, innate dispositions, teleological inclinations, or of the proportionate reason why one thing acts by nature in such a way upon another. Nor can we obtain any genuine "causal" knowledge of any purported non-empirical reality, be it the soul, God, or divine providence. The idea of causality when ascribed in any of these domains suggests a kind of idealism unmoored from empirical evidences. See Hume, *Enquiries concerning Human Understanding and concerning the Principles of Morals*, 3rd ed. (Oxford: Oxford University Press, 1975), nos. 23–33; 39–45; 49–57; 78–81; 102–15. Kant, in the *Critique of Pure Reason*, posits that basic notions of causality pertaining to substance, efficient causation, and finality are derived not from experience but from a priori forms of reasoning that the subject employs to organize experience constructively. Our notion of God is an aprioristic idea that allows for an organization of all forms of knowledge in light of the idea of a total primary cause, though the reality itself of a God is an unverifiable hypothesis. See, for example, a2 / b4–b6 and a9 / b13 on the aprioristic origination of our notion of causes, and their inevitable necessity and use in experience (against Hume); a204–211 / b249–256, on the a priori origination of the notion of substance, not strictly derivative from experience as such; a414–419 / b441–446 on the a priori notion of a first cause; a578 / b606 on the a priori idea of God as a transcendental ideal of reason.

20. On Hume and causal skepticism, see the analysis of Lawrence Dewan in "The Seeds of Being," and "St. Thomas and the Principle of Causality," in *Form and Being: Studies in Thomistic Metaphysics* (Washington, D.C.: The Catholic University of America Press, 2014).

through sense experience, with a confidence in their causal determinations, then the traditional arguments for the existence of God can be seen to have a firm foundation in our basic human experience. In this sense, Thomistic argumentation for the existence of God is eminently realistic in its roots.

PROPTER QUID VS. QUIA DEMONSTRATIONS
OF GOD'S EXISTENCE

Aristotle notes in his *Posterior Analytics* that all forms of explanatory demonstration proceed from two questions: *does a given thing exist* and, if so, *what is it?* Priority is given to the real existence of a given reality that in turn shapes our inquiry, as we seek to discover its causes.[21] This too is where St. Thomas begins his *De Deo Uno* treatise. In *ST* I, q. 2, he accordingly asks whether God exists. It is in q. 3 then, on divine simplicity, that he turns to the question of what God is (and, as we will see in this case, what God is not).

In light of what we have mentioned above regarding the theological context, why would Aquinas ask whether God exists? In one sense his question is genuinely philosophical. What intelligibility is there to the human use of the word "God," and what might we really mean when we use that word? Does it signify the transcendent source of created reality, and if so how is this the case? On another level, Aquinas is simultaneously exploring the natural capacities or dispositions of the human mind to receive and cooperate with divine revelation. If we are to think about the mystery of the Holy Trinity, how can we, even within faith, employ our natural human language so as to refer to God? How is our human nature, particularly the intellect, even capable of being placed in the service of grace?

When he treats the philosophical question of whether God exists, Aquinas distinguishes two ways that philosophers typically approach a theoretical demonstration of this kind. The first way is what he terms *propter quid*

---

21. Aristotle, *Post. Analytics* 2.7 (92b5–12): "Again, how will you prove what a thing is? For it is necessary for anyone who knows what a man is or anything else is to know too *that* it is (for of that which is not, no one knows what it is—you may know what the account or the name signifies when I say goat-stag, but it is impossible to know what a goat-stag is). But if you are to prove what it is and that it is, how will you prove them by the same argument? *For both the definition and the demonstration make one thing clear; but what a man is and that a man is are different*. Next, we say it is necessary that everything that a thing is should be proved through demonstration, unless it is its substance. But existence is not the substance of anything, for being is not in any genus" (translation slightly modified, emphasis added). See the commentary of Aquinas in *Expositio libri Posteriorum* (*In Post.*) II, lec. 6.

demonstration, which proceeds from established knowledge of an essence or cause to the demonstration of its effects or properties. The other he terms a *quia* demonstration, which proceeds not from knowledge of a cause to its effects but from prior knowledge of effects to the demonstration of a cause.[22]

In *propter quid* reasoning, knowledge of the essence of a thing as cause serves as the middle term of the demonstrative argument. "All men are capable of laughter (by virtue of reason)." "Socrates is a man." "Therefore Socrates is capable of laughter (by virtue of reason)." The middle term is provided by the notion of humanity. We can engage in this form of reasoning because we have genuine knowledge of the essence of the human being, understood as a rational animal capable of intelligence and sensation, and therefore susceptible to laughter. (Animals cannot perceive the ironies of reason and angels cannot smile physically; consequently, only the rational animal is capable of laughter.) The obstacle to using this kind of reasoning to argue for God's existence is that we lack any prior innate knowledge of what God is in himself. Nor do we experience God's nature immediately in sense experience. His being or essence transcends the realm of our immediate experience and exceeds the limitations of the finite human intellect. According to St. Thomas, then, we cannot simply begin from a pre-established definition of God and prove from such a definition itself that God exists, or reason deductively from this definition to statements about God's attributes.

It is for a related reason that Aquinas rejects the validity of St. Anselm's well-known ontological argument from *The Proslogion*.[23] Anselm affirmed in this argument that the notion of God includes the notion of a most perfect being.[24] But it is most perfect for a being to be real rather than merely an idea. Therefore, the reality of a most perfect being would follow from the notion of God, since that notion includes something that is most perfect. Aquinas counters by saying that such notional definitions only provide us with the idea of a most perfect being that exists necessarily, but do not yet constitute a demonstration or proof that such a being actually exists. Anselm shows that our notion of God is a notion of something that exists, which is not the same as showing that the thing we have a notion of exists.

22. Aquinas sets forth this distinction in *ST* I, q. 2, a. 2.

23. In *ST* I, q. 2, a. 1.

24. For Anselm's so-called ontological argument, see Anselm of Canterbury, *The Proslogion*, in *Anselm of Canterbury: The Major Works*, ed. Brian Davies and G. R. Evans (Oxford: Oxford University Press), 87–88, where he argues that a "that-than-which-a-greater-cannot-be-thought cannot exist in the mind alone," but must also exist "in reality."

In other words, Anselm has not been able to justify the leap from the concept of God to extramental reality.[25] We cannot demonstrate the existence of God simply by spelling out the internal content of a nominal definition of his essence.

Aquinas's demonstrations for God's existence, on the other hand, are *quia* demonstrations, which proceed from a known effect to its unknown cause. Here the process passes from the created order, which is perceived precisely as dependent or in some way caused, to the source of that order and effect. The goal with this procedure is not to apprehend immediately *what* God is, but first only to establish *that* something we typically name "God" exists. We can then begin to understand positively and negatively what the reality is in itself by comparison with its effects, without immediate perception of it. Put differently, the goal is to demonstrate the undergirding rational intelligibility for our use of the word "God," in reference to an ultimate explanation for the fact that the world exists in the way that it does. In effect, we are asking: what is the indirect but real evidence indicated in the world around us that there exists a primary causal origin of all that we experience? From there we can begin to understand what God is and is not, based on a comparison of God with creatures.

In such *quia* reasoning, knowledge of the essence of a thing is not given, but the existence of that reality can be known indirectly from its effects. The notion of a reality as a cause of an effect plays the role of a middle term, instead of an essential definition of that cause. "There is smoke rising from the trees of the forest." "Because smoke does not self-originate and must be the effect of another reality, its presence alerts us to the presence of that reality acting as a cause. But the trees are not themselves the cause of smoke." Therefore, "there must exist a cause of the smoke other than the trees." At this point, we still do not know what the cause of the smoke is. But we do know with certitude that it exists, and that it is something other than the trees in the forest. The middle term of this *quia* argument is provided by the indirect perception of a cause whose directly perceived effect (smoke) cannot be caused by the realities we already know directly (trees).

Based on this type of approach, we need not have any recourse to innate

---

25. See *ST* I, q. 2, a. 1, ad 2: "Yet, granted that everyone understands that by this word *God* is signified something than which nothing greater can be thought, nevertheless, it does not therefore follow that he understands that what the word signifies exists actually [*in rerum natura*], but only that it exists mentally [*in apprehensione intellectus*]."

knowledge of God or so-called a priori definitions. We may have nominal definitions of God drawn from "pre-philosophical" basic intuitions, such as the idea drawn from the order in the world of a possible first source of order and so forth. Likewise, we may have, from religious traditions or divine revelation, a complex narrative-based ontological notion of God as Creator or as the source of divine providence. Philosophically speaking, however, we should acknowledge that our notional definition of what we mean by God is determined by beginning first with realities we know immediately and analyze as caused effects. From this analysis we can raise the *question* of the necessary existence of a cause that we do not know immediately, but only mediately and indirectly, which is different from those caused realities. By "God" we mean that which is "the cause of X," where "X" stands for some ontological characteristic found in creatures that implies causal dependence, and that points us in turn toward a transcendent cause of their existence. Thus, God is philosophically accessible insofar as he is the ultimate cause of movement and change, or of the very being of things, or of non-necessary, contingent beings, or of the hierarchy of perfections, or of the intelligible order-towards-an-end in things.

This way of reasoning gives rise to a search for a principle of ultimate explanation. What if all the realities we experience are caused? And what if they cannot explain themselves as existing? It will be seen to follow from this that they all have a cause that is as yet unknown, but that must exist, precisely so as to explain their existence. This primary reality cannot be a being like them, that is, it must be a cause or origin that is not ontologically dependent upon others. Attempts to reduce the first cause to the conditions of those beings that are themselves dependent and require explanation by reference to another foil our attempts at comprehensive explanation, which are not only intellectually warranted but are obligatory if we wish to understand the world around us in a rationally adequate way.

In each of Thomas's *quia* demonstrations in *ST* I, q. 2, a. 3, there is accordingly a basic logical structure that is similar in kind:

1. There exists some property of each of the realities we experience directly that signifies that these realities cannot account for their own existence, but are derived or caused by another, or others.

2. However, it does no good to posit an infinite series of such interdependent causes, since this will not provide an adequate explanation of why there exists a series of caused, dependent realties in the first place.

3. Therefore, there must exist a cause that is the origin of such dependent realities and which cannot itself be subject to the same characteristics of dependence and derivation that they are. This is the primary cause and giver of being. We can know that it exists, but cannot know by immediate experience what it is. We can know, however, that it is not like the realities we do experience around us, in that it does not have their imperfections. Accordingly, we can say something about it positively, in virtue of the perfections that it must have as the primary cause of all that is.

Notice, again, that the middle term is the cause: it must exist and it cannot be like the realities we experience in the world around us. Therefore, this cause is something primary that is utterly different from these other, dependent realities.[26]

However dry this line of reasoning may appear initially, it is not only logical and rational, but also apophatic and mystical. We simultaneously affirm the necessity of God's existence, but also his transcendence and incomprehensibility. To follow the path of reason in considering the transcendent origins of the world is to be led right into the heart of a philosophical "mystery." There is a mystery at the periphery of ordinary reality—or in the depths of this reality—that calls out to our reason and reveals to us that reason itself terminates in mystery.

With this in mind, let us turn, in the remainder of this chapter, to an overview of Aquinas's five arguments from *ST* I, q. 2, a. 3.[27] In this way, we

26. We note that this use of causality as a middle term is meant to be sufficiently weak and sufficiently strong, under different aspects. It is "weak" because it does not entail the effort to define the essence of God by prior knowledge and so avoids some of the dangers of rationalism or idealism associated with onto-theology or with Anselm's ontological argument. It is meant to be sufficiently "strong" as to permit genuine demonstrative knowledge, by employing analogical conceptions of causality and of being, able to denote God by way of similitude. This feature allows the Thomistic form of argument to present valid syllogistic arguments for the existence of God that are immune to the criticisms of Scotists or nominalists who claim (in different ways) that only a univocal knowledge of God's attributes will permit demonstrative reasoning about God.

27. On the Five Ways see John Wippel, *The Metaphysical Thought of Thomas Aquinas* (Washington, D.C.: The Catholic University of America Press, 2000), 442–500; Rudi te Velde, *Aquinas on God: The 'Divine Science' of the "Summa Theologiae"* (Aldershot: Ashgate, 2006), 37–64; Edward Feser, *Aquinas* (Oxford: Oneworld, 2009); Pasquale Porro, *Thomas Aquinas: A Historical and Philosophical Profile*, trans. J. Trabbic and R. Nutt (Washington, D.C.: The Catholic University of America Press, 2016), 222–28; Serge-Thomas Bonino, *Dieu, "Celui Qui Est"; De Deo ut Uno* (Paris: Parole et Silence, 2016), 159–219; Thomas Joseph White, *Wisdom in the Face of Modernity*; on the longer arguments from the *Summa contra Gentiles*, see in particular Wippel, *The Metaphysical Thought of Thomas Aquinas*, 413–40; also relatedly, Norman Kretzmann, *The Metaphysics of Theism: Aquinas's Natural Theology in "Summa Contra Gentiles" I* (Oxford: Oxford University Press, 1997).

will be able to see how his *quia* demonstrations for God's existence work in practice.[28]

THE ARGUMENT FROM MOVEMENT

OR ONTOLOGICAL CHANGE

The "first way" or demonstration found in *ST* I, q. 2, a. 3, is based on the existence of change in all the realities we experience. Its starting point is the principle that whatever is changed or moved is moved by another.

Thomas begins his argument with the observation that some things we observe around us are in motion, that is, they are being changed by something else. Aquinas's notion of movement here is properly philosophical and multifaceted. It is Aristotelian not Newtonian. He is speaking about physical change as a form of ontological alteration in a given reality, which he characterizes as a change from potency to act. Now, change here can be "local" (meaning change of place or position), quantitative (change of size or shape), qualitative (change of qualities), or substantial (the generation or corruption of one being by the activity of another). Ontological change of this kind can occur only because the reality in question is in potency toward further transformation. To be heated, the cold water must be potentially hot, that is to say, capable of being heated by fire (in a way, for example, that the sun would not be). Likewise, things can *cause* change in others only because they possess some actual characteristic that can initiate the process of change or motion in another. To heat, fire must be actually hot, that is, it must possess in act that quality which effects change in another. Thus, fire, being hot, is able to impart its heat to cold water or to a length of iron. Now, a thing in the process of changing cannot be both in act and in potency under the same aspect or characteristic at the same time. (For example, a given container of water cannot actually be 212°F and not 212°F under the same aspect at the same time.)

It follows from this that if a thing is subject to passive change of some kind, it undergoes this through the causal action of another. For example, a physical reality cannot both be heated by another and be heating another under the same aspect at the same time. The boiling water that cooks the boiled egg is heated by the fire on the stove, while the stove is fueled by electricity, and so forth. Therefore, Aquinas concludes, everything undergoing a process of change is changed from potency to act by another, or others. But

28. See also Aquinas's similar and more extensive arguments in *SCG* I, c. 13.

every physical being is subject to such processes. Therefore, every physical reality in the universe is subject to changes of place, quantity, quality, or generation or corruption that are due to the actual activity of others.

In many places in his work, St. Thomas distinguishes between two kinds of ordered causal series. One is *per se* and the other *per accidens*.[29] A *per se* causal series is one in which each of the causes, in its very exercise of causality, depends upon an anterior cause, in such a way that the first cause is the cause of the others in their actual exercise of causality. As the pot of boiling water is boiling the egg, and the stove is heating the pot, simultaneously the turning earth is moving the place of the stove, and the earth itself is being moved by gravitational forces, and so on. Everything in the causal series depends concurrently on something else, which in turn also depends on something further. A *per accidens* causal series, by contrast, concerns one in which the activity of one thing is indeed presupposed antecedently in time as the cause of another (especially in a historical series of causes), but the former is no longer the actual cause of the second. Parents, for example, cause their children to come into being by substantial generation, but the child once it is begotten no longer depends actually on the parents for its very being. Likewise, physical realities in the cosmos currently may well have arisen historically from those past processes denominated under the rubric of "Big Bang cosmology" but physical realities in the world today are not actually causally dependent upon any historically remote processes that have already ceased to exist. In light of this distinction we can understand that a *per se* causal series pertains to a series of actually dependent realities, where one is caused to be by another (under some aspect), and the next one by yet another, and so on. There is a simultaneity of actuality in the causal chain. By contrast, a *per accidens* series is one that does not entail actual causal dependency between members of the series. The sun heating the earth is a per se cause of all living beings on earth, constantly altering them qualitatively in actual time, while remote ancestors are only a *per accidens* cause of any living thing's current existence.

It is in the former respect (*per se* causality) that Aquinas is considering physical realities subject to change, that is to say, as they actually exist, and not as they came to be historically. Seen in this way, each substantial thing in the world currently subject to movement is affected ontologically by something that is itself currently subject to movement by another, and that next

29. On this distinction, see Aquinas, *In VI Meta.*, lec. 3, 1202–22, and the discussion of Kretzmann, *The Metaphysics of Theism*, 106–12.

thing in turn, and so on, such that everything in the series is subject to causal dependence on others. Every actually moved reality is dependent in this
respect upon another or other realities for its manner of being. Consequently no such reality "explains itself" sufficiently or accounts for its own being
without pointing us to yet another reality upon which it depends, if the reality in question is a physical being subject to change. How then do we explain the actually ordered series of finite causes we see around us, series in
which physical realities are all caused by other realities, themselves in turn
also actually dependent upon other such causes?

We cannot attain an adequate explanation by multiplying the series of
moved movers infinitely, since such a hypothesis simply extends indefinitely
the chain of yet-to-be-explained effects, which themselves point toward a superior cause. We will remain haunted by the potency and causal dependence
found in all material things crying out for an ultimate explanation. After all,
it was precisely these kinds of dependent realities that started this whole line
of inquiry to begin with. A series of indefinite, "infinite" extensions simply
keeps posing the question why the first in the series is moved by yet another
before it. If there were not a first mover that is unmoved (transcendent of the
material potencies specified above), there would be no adequate explanation
of other realities subject to change. Yet there is a world of changing realities
that requires explanation. Since changing dependent realities would not be
explained realistically unless there were ultimately a first mover who is unmoved, we can conclude demonstratively that a primary cause exists who is
beyond change from potency to act, and who is, for that reason, not a dependent, caused being.

It should be noted that Aquinas is not arguing in the first way from cosmic history, appealing to a chronologically primal event. Bonaventure embraced this form of argumentation, and some contemporary analytic philosophers do so also by applying the *kalam* argument to the consideration
of modern Big Bang cosmology.[30] To argue for a first beginning for the his-

---

30. The argument for the existence of God from the supposed necessity of a temporal beginning of the universe has its origins especially in the work of Al-Gazali (1058–1111) in his *The Incoherence of the Philosophers*. Bonaventure does not think it is inherently contradictory to claim that
a perpetually existing reality should be caused, but he does think it is self-contradictory to posit
that an eternally existent universe is created out of nothing, since he takes *ex nihilo* causation (as
proposed in Christian doctrine) to include creation *in time* by definition. See Bonaventure, *Comm.
II Sent.*, 1.1.1.2; *Comm. IV Sent.*, 2.1.1.1.3, in *Commentaria in quatuor libros Sententiarum*, 4 vols.
(Quaracchi: Ex Typographia Collegii S. Bonaventurae, 1882–89). For a contemporary analytic defense of the *kalam* argument that attempts to appeal to modern cosmology for sufficient evidences,

tory of the universe is to argue from *per accidens* causes that no longer exist in act. Our biological parents were the generative causes of our coming into existence, but they no longer are causes of our existing (even if they are still alive), so long as we are not dependent upon them for our existence. By way of contrast, the heat of the sun is an actual cause of our existence, without which we would not exist. The first way does not appeal to what may or may not have happened in the distant and non-observable past. The first historical beginnings of the cosmos cannot be experienced directly, however probable our inferential knowledge about its unfolding may be. In fact, Aquinas thinks that the teaching that the universe has a discrete beginning in time is a matter of Christian doctrine, that is, it is something revealed by scripture and maintained in Catholic teaching, but it is not something philosophical argumentation as such can demonstrate or disprove. As is well known, he even argued in contrast to Bonaventure that, seen merely from the point of view of philosophical consideration, it would be possible for the world to have existed everlastingly, provided, of course, that it was always and everlastingly dependent upon God for its movement and change.[31] This everlasting world would still be a created world in which we could demonstrate that God exists as the unchanged cause of all that changes, but it would not be a world that had a demonstrable beginning in time.

Consequently, Aquinas is arguing in the first way not chronologically but metaphysically, from causal dependencies that are actually existent. We cannot adequately explain what is changing or moving in the world actually simply by having recourse to an interminable series of dependent causes. A universe in which everything is subject to constant movement or change cannot be explained by itself and indicates by its very existence the necessary existence of God as the primary source of beings subject to physical change.[32]

see William Lane Craig, *The Kalām Cosmological Argument* (Eugene, Ore.: Wipf and Stock, 2000). Thomists generally remain reserved about the warrant for these forms of argument, despite their logical sophistication and historical pedigree.

31. See Aquinas, *On the Eternity of the World*, in *Thomas Aquinas: Selected Writings*, trans. by R. McInerny (London: Penguin Books, 1998), where he argues that the notion of God's giving the totality of being to the creation (which he treats as the essential content of the confession of creation *ex nihilo*) is logically compatible with an everlasting creation that has always existed.

32. It is true that we do not experience the whole cosmos, but only some small part of it. However, we do see realities in the world around us actually submitted to the ontological conditions analyzed above. From these we can conclude to the necessity of *something* that is purely actual, that is not subject to the same kind of conditions that the things we experience (including ourselves) are. Aquinas will argue only later in the *ST* (in q. 3) that this implies in turn that the reality in question is immaterial and has existence by nature and so forth, considerations we will return to below.

There must then exist a first, unmoved, unchanged source of movement, who is pure actuality, and this is what we call "God."[33] As pure actuality, God is not inert, static, or passive and reactive, but perfectly active. Consequently his reality completely transcends our experience and our comprehension. As we will see in due course, the affirmation that God is an unmoved mover does not imply that God is indifferent, or morally removed from creation; in fact, in many respects, it even proves the contrary. Because God is pure actuality, there exists in him a plenitude of perfection in the order of being, wisdom, and love, one that is not subject to diminishment from any created thing, and one that gives being and life to creatures not from any need, but by pure gift.

THE ARGUMENT FROM THE
DERIVATION OF BEING

Aquinas's second way is also known as the argument from efficient causality. It is concerned with causal explanation for the very existence of things. In this sense, it bears a resemblance to Aquinas's arguments in the *De ente et essentia*, which he wrote at an early stage in his career. There he argues that there is a real distinction of essence and existence in all things we experience, which shows that they must derive their existence from one who possesses existence by nature. It is God alone who gives created existence to all things.[34] In the second way, Aquinas approaches the argument slightly differently.

---

33. As Aquinas notes, in ad 2 of *ST* q. 2, a. 3, if God were not in pure actuality, his potency for alteration would make him in turn subject to change by another through relational engagement with others, so he too would require explanation by recourse to yet another who is purely actual.

34. For St. Thomas's argument that essence is really distinct from existence in everything but God, see especially St. Thomas Aquinas, *De ente et essentia* (*De ente*), chap. 4, where Aquinas affirms that existence is really distinct from essence in all created substances. Only in God are essence and existence said to be identical. We know this to be true because existence in all the realities we experience is never reducible to any one natural kind or genus of being. Physical realities, plants, animals, and human beings all exist and *have* being, but none of them is *identical* with existence as such. Furthermore, no natural reality we experience is the cause of its own existence. Its nature does not cause it to be but instead is caused by others. It comes into being and eventually goes out of being, and thus has a derivative existence received from others, but does not have being by nature. However, we cannot adequately explain the existence of such derivative beings, which receive their existence from others, simply by appealing to an infinite series of such caused realities. Rather, there must be something that communicates being to all things, and that has existence by nature, in whom essence and existence are mysteriously identical.

In the world of sense we find there is an order of efficient causes.... There is no case known ... in which a thing is found to be the efficient cause of itself; for so it would be prior to itself, which is impossible.... In all efficient causes following in order, the first is the cause of the intermediate cause, and the intermediate is the cause of the ultimate cause, whether the intermediate cause be several, or only one.... But if in efficient causes it is possible to go on to infinity, there will be no first efficient cause, neither will there be an ultimate effect, nor any intermediate efficient causes; all of which is plainly false. Therefore it is necessary to admit a first efficient cause, to which everyone gives the name of God.[35]

The argument is simple and vertical in orientation. Each being we experience comes to be or is given existence only as a result of the activity of another or others. For example, a human person typically comes into being because she is conceived by parents and gestates in the womb of her mother. The parents, in turn, also depend for their existence upon others. And so it is similarly for all the realities in the universe that we come to know. All that exists depends upon another for its existence. Here again, however, we encounter the problem of the infinite regress: this process cannot continue on infinitely, for then everything would receive existence, but nothing would possess it of itself.[36] Therefore, there must exist some being for whom existence is necessary, whose nature it is to exist. This being does not receive its existence from others, but gives existence to all others. If God exists by nature, as one who has existence in virtue of what he is, then we can also say that it is of God's essence to exist. God is truly "He who is." To be in a way that can know no diminishment or alteration—characterizes the essence of God.

THE ARGUMENT FROM CONTINGENT POSSIBILITY AND NECESSITY

The third way begins from the experience of contingent realities in the world around us. The argument is based on an appeal to modality: the re-

---

35. *ST* I, q. 2, a. 3.

36. In the second way, I do not think it matters particularly whether one refers only to *per se* actual causal series or also to *per accidens* causal series (as it did in the first way), since we are not speaking here of one being causing another under an aspect (the actuation of a potency for material change), but of each thing being caused with respect to its whole existence. Each reality that is caused to be depends upon another. One cannot explain why things exist merely by appeal to an infinite series of such realities. This is true whether we consider those realities that existed in the past and no longer exist, or those that exist actually.

lation of possible beings to necessary being. It begins with the observation that all the things we experience in this world are materially corruptible and therefore merely contingent. In is in this sense that they are said to be merely possible beings, not necessary beings. It is worth bearing in mind in this context that Aquinas does not think the property of contingency to be co-extensive with the property of being caused to be. In fact he presumes there are created realities like angels, and the subsistent spiritual souls of human beings that are "necessary" in a special sense. They can exist or not exist (and in that sense are not strictly necessary ontologically) but they are not subject to material corruption and therefore are not "contingent" in the sense of the term Aquinas adopts in this argument. The vast world of material beings we experience, however, is composed of "contingent beings," meaning beings that are subject to generation and corruption.

In the third way Aquinas is asking whether one can rationally affirm that all beings are contingent material beings, such that nothing exists which is ontologically necessary. The logical structure of his argument, while initially confusing, is actually quite sensible. Let us suppose that there are only material contingent beings and that they have always existed (since if they did not always exist they would need a cause of their existence that is not contingent but necessary). Furthermore, let us presume that all of them are truly contingent, in which case there is no necessity that they exist. Everything that can fail to be (in virtue of its being merely possible) will indeed fail at some point, so every contingent being must cease to be. Over an infinite time, what is true for each contingent being would be applicable to all of them collectively. At some point everything would cease to be. However, non-being cannot give rise to being. Nothing cannot give rise something. Therefore, if all things had ceased to exist at some time in the past because of the possibility of the radical corruption of the whole, the world of generation and corruption we live in now would not exist. But it does exist. Consequently, there cannot be merely contingent being, but there must be something necessary and non-contingent. If this being that is necessary is itself caused (as in the case of angels or spiritual souls, which are not corruptible but are caused), then it can be caused ultimately only by something that is itself necessary and uncaused. There cannot be an infinite series of dependent realities that exists on its own, so there must be a necessary reality that exists eternally and that causes the universe of contingent things to be. This is the reality we call God.

The typical concern that arises with this argument has to do with the claim that if everything that exists is contingent and therefore a possible being, then at some point everything must cease to exist. Why can there not simply be a world of successive contingent beings, one after another, that have always existed and that will continue to be forever? If there are only possible contingent realities in the world that can be or not be, then over an infinite time stretching back into the past, either they could have ceased to be collectively or they could not have. If they were able to, the argument made above obtains, because over an infinite time what is ontologically possible would have come into effect. But if they were not *able* to cease to exist collectively, this can only be because something in the universe exists necessarily, and cannot fail to be. That this necessity is present follows precisely from the logic of the objection: "But what if it is truly possible for corruptible things to go on existing forever?" This "possibility" entails precisely that there is something "in" the universe that cannot fail to be, that is enduringly necessary. We have seen, however, that all material realities we experience are contingent and possible beings, therefore if there is something truly necessary in a universe of contingent things, it can only be a non-material reality.[37]

In a way the argument is very simple, then. Either the existence of contingent things is explained by recourse to God as the primary necessary being, who is himself non-contingent, or we must posit a world in which there exist only contingent things, subject to material generation and corruption.

---

37. Porro, *Thomas Aquinas: A Historical and Philosophical Profile*, 227: "It might be objected that perhaps it is not inevitable that all possible things not exist at the same time. We could think of a kind of continual succession of possible things. One would permit another to come into being and then go out of being, etc. However, even in this case we would have to come to a first possible thing that would have had to come into being from nothing. If it had always existed, it would not be possible but necessary and would go on existing always, which is precisely what Thomas intends to demonstrate." It should be noted that Porro is not interpreting Aquinas to be stating some version of the *kalam* argument in the third way. Aquinas presupposes that if there is a transcendent first cause and Creator, then an eternal creation is possible in principle, and therefore one cannot argue philosophically for the existence of God from an appeal to creation's first beginning in time. However, Aquinas does hold that if there are only contingent things, then there can be no eternal world of contingent things. Therefore, there must be something necessary to sustain them in being. The two claims are not contradictory. On the contrary, they are coherent with one another. The first way does not argue from linear causes through time but hierarchically from per se, essentially ordered causes that occur actually rather than historically. There could be an eternal creation but it would depend actually upon an immaterial first mover, or non-actuated actualizer. The third way argues from the possibility in all contingent things to be or not be to the existence of something that is not contingent and that exists necessarily. Only if there is such a necessary reality could there be an eternal creation.

In the latter case, however, there is no adequate explanation for why such realities exist. If we try to argue that they simply perpetuate one another over time, in unending succession forever, then we posit the idea (or hypothesis) that they cannot cease to exist. But this would entail that they exist necessarily. However, no contingent thing does exist necessarily, and adding an infinite series of such things together will not provide necessity to the series as a whole. Therefore to explain why contingent things exist, we must have recourse to something that must always exist. This reality cannot be a material, contingent being. Therefore something immaterial exists necessarily that is the cause of contingent possible beings.

THE ARGUMENT FROM DEGREES
OF PERFECTION

The fourth way takes its point of departure from the existence of degrees of perfection found in things.

The fourth way is taken from the gradation to be found in things. Among beings there are some more and some less good, true, noble and the like. But "more" and "less" are predicated of different things, according as they resemble in their different ways something which is the maximum, as a thing is said to be hotter according as it more nearly resembles that which is hottest; so that there is something which is truest, something best, something noblest and, consequently, something which is uttermost being; for those things that are greatest in truth are greatest in being, as it is written in *Metaphysics* II. Now the maximum in any genus is the cause of all in that genus; as fire, which is the maximum heat, is the cause of all hot things. Therefore there must also be something which is to all beings the cause of their being, goodness, and every other perfection; and this we call God.[38]

Most commentators on this text take Aquinas to be referring to perfections that are transcendental in kind. That is to say, they are not predicated of only one genus of being, but are found in all beings (transcending all genera), and are predicated analogously rather than univocally (more about this in coming chapters). These are perfection terms that imply no inherent limitation, and therefore can be ascribed analogically to God. Such transcendental terms include the notions of being, essence (*res*), unity, truth, goodness, and beauty.[39] Everything that exists, insofar as it exists, is charac-

---

38. *ST* I, q. 2, a. 3.
39. Aquinas analyzes the transcendentals especially in *De ver.*, q. 1, a. 1, where he lists them as being, *res* (which I take to denote identity or intelligibility of kind), unity, *aliquid* (distinction in

terized in some way by these transcendental characteristics, which are present in every genus and species of being. However, we also can note that degrees or scales of perfection exist in things, considered precisely along these lines. For example, some things exist in more perfect ways than others (either in the order of causality or longevity or in virtue of their form of excellence). Some beings have natures or essences of greater nobility than others, as in the case of human beings compared with animals, or animals compared with non-sensate living things, or living things compared with non-living things. Some beings or collections of beings evince more perfect unity than others, or are "truer" than others if they explain the reason for the others. Some beings are greater in goodness either due to their nature or their activities, as when we say that a human child is of more objective worth than an insect, or that one human person is a more virtuous person or a better artist than another. Some realities are more beautiful or perfect than others in the order of their species, as when we speak of a horse, a tree, or a mountain that is more perfect or more beautiful than another.

This point of departure is more difficult for modern people to grasp since we are commonly tempted to try to explain these various modes of perfection by appeal only to material and efficient causes, and have difficulty acknowledging formal and exemplary causality. However, once we acknowledge that these characteristics pertain to the very natures of things in themselves, and that they invite us to make objective comparative judgments of scale according to degrees of perfection, we see that there is an ontological scale of gradations present within the world. The things themselves are more or less good, more or less perfectly existent, more or less perfect in nature, and so forth. It follows from this that there is a commonality of characteristics present in all of them that exists according to degrees of perfection. How can we account for this hierarchical scale or degree of perfections in the things themselves, which invites us to compare and measure them? On the one hand, nothing we experience can be the cause of the hierarchy, because each thing is itself a formal participant in the scale of perfections, and not the source or origin of the hierarchy within which it is embedded. This must be the case precisely because we measure each thing by comparison

---

virtue of actuality), truth and goodness. Whether beauty is a transcendental is a famous question of debate among interpreters of Aquinas. Based on Aquinas's comments in *In librum beati Dionysii de divinis nominibus expositio* (*In div. nom.*) cap. 4, lec. 5, para. 348–49, I have argued that it is, in "Beauty, Transcendence and the Inclusive Hierarchy of Creation," *Nova et Vetera* (English edition) 16, no. 4 (2018): 1215–26.

with others insofar as it falls somewhere within a range of perfection, under this or that note or property. On the other hand, the hierarchy of perfections is not self-originating, because it is instantiated only in and through all the individual realities in question. Being, unity, truth, goodness, and beauty are not platonic forms separated from the concrete world around us, but are notes or properties in the concrete existent world that characterize its diverse entities, and that are present in differentiated modes in all the individuals that exist. All realities we experience "participate" in being, unity, truth, goodness, and beauty. They each possess such perfections but are not the ultimate measure and source of them.

We cannot simply posit an infinite series of beings that possess perfections in a limited way, each of which refers us in turn to a yet greater reality. Since none of the individual things we experience possesses the transcendental perfections perfectly, none of them explains sufficiently why there is a scale of perfection in being, which they themselves participate in. Consequently, we must look to a transcendent exemplary cause that possesses these perfections most intensively and that effectively causes them in others. As Aquinas notes, any measure of greater and lesser perfections makes sense only in reference to something that is greatest. "'More' and 'less' are predicated of different things, according as they resemble in their different ways something which is the maximum.... so that there is something which is truest, something best, something noblest and, consequently, something which is uttermost being." Consequently we must posit something we call God, who contains in himself to a maximum degree those perfections found in all other things, and who communicates those perfections to all others. The fourth way suggests from the outset that God is infinite in perfection, an argument we will return to in ensuing chapters. At the same time, the very terms of the proof make clear that God, precisely because he is the cause of hierarchy, must be outside of every hierarchy or measure of perfection. He is the one who gives being, unity, truth, goodness, and beauty to all things, but he is not measured alongside them within a continuum or by a common measure. God remains hidden from us, even in the final conclusion of the fourth way, since he is not comprehended by our conceptual appeal to the transcendental characteristics of created existence.

THE ARGUMENT FROM TELEOLOGICAL ORDER

Aquinas's fifth way is an argument from the teleological order we find in things in the world. This is distinct from William Paley's well-known argument from design. The two should not be confused.[40]

Aquinas's argument begins with the observation that things of all kinds in the world possess intrinsic tendencies, or natural inclinations, toward certain final goods or states that characterize those realities. For instance, human beings naturally desire to know the truth, and seek happiness. That this is naturally inevitable is seen from the fact that human beings do not like to be deceived, and that they act through reasoned deliberations in view of what they take to be genuine goods, and seek to avoid what they take to be evil or harmful (even if they may be confused about the content of the true and the false, the good and the harmful). Animals and plants are naturally inclined to nourish themselves, grow, struggle to repair after injury, reproduce, and flourish as a species. Inanimate realities tend to maintain and preserve stable forms. They have characteristic qualities or internal organizational patterns that characterize what they are and that produce predictable actions and effects.[41] From these various inclinations in things we gain insight into their respective natures. Each thing is characterized by natural capabilities and activities, of which we can make sense by appealing to prin-

---

40. William Paley's eighteenth-century "argument from design," begins from premises fundamentally different from those of the fifth way. He lays out his famous argument from design in *Natural Theology: Or, Evidences of the Existence and Attributes of the Deity Collected from the Appearances of Nature* (Boston: Gould and Lincoln, 1869 [originally published in 1802]). The argument begins on p. 5 with his famous analogy that the world is like a watch someone happened to find. The watch evidences purposeful design, and so cannot be a product of chance. So too the world evidences purposeful design, and therefore cannot be a product of chance any more than the watch can. The watch example suggests that the divine mind has imposed an order from the outside upon pre-existing natural materials. The image of nature Paley provides is mechanistic. The divine mind imposes order extrinsically upon a material world that cannot provide such order from its own principles. Aquinas's argument, by way of contrast, does not proceed from the appearance of artistic design, but from the teleological inclinations that emerge within natural entities themselves. On this view, all natural beings are characterized by various inclinations proper to them, by which they tend toward distinctive operations and ends. As a consequence, they are naturally intelligible in virtue of their own principles. This formally intelligible nature does not need its order imposed from without by a divine artist. However, the natural order still cannot account for why it is intelligibly ordered, from the perspective of efficient causality. Why is there a world of natural intelligibility?

41. The forms of teleology found among inanimate realities are more modest or humble than those found in living things and human beings, but the former still contain something in common with the ontological inclinations of the latter, despite the limits of the analogy.

ciples of potency and act. A seed has the potential to become a tree, a child has the potential to become an adult human being, a violist has the capacity to become a virtuoso. Moreover, each of these realities can potentially attain its end or purpose but is capable also of being impeded in its movement toward its end and so may not achieve it.

The tendencies in question give rise to natural order, and this order in turn provides us with a stable ontological framework in which to study the intelligibility of things. We expect birds to fly and human beings to solve math problems, not the inverse. As things develop and either undergo change passively or exert their agency upon others, we see their natural potencies unfold. The order of nature emerges.

Where does this intelligible order of nature come from? Aquinas argues that order is the sign of intelligence. Natural order cannot be explained merely by appeal to the material elements in things. These elements are already contained within and organized by overarching substantial natural forms. Furthermore, material elements themselves are characterized by intelligible order and diversified natural inclinations at a more microscopic level, so they in turn raise the same question in this respect. The observable world of plants, animals, and human beings is clearly not the source of order and teleological inclination, since these beings exist within the world of order and are themselves characterized by such inclinations in all they are. Consequently, the intelligence behind the teleological order found in all things we experience is not explained by any of the aforementioned things themselves. They are not the primary efficient source of the order that is present in them in virtue of their natures and properties.

It is not possible, however, to posit simply an infinite series of dependent realities, for whom the tendency toward a given end is received from others, and in whom there is a composition of potency and act (i.e., a potential for perfection that may or may not come to pass, and which depends for its realization on external conditions and the activity of others). If we were to posit such an infinite series, this would ultimately explain nothing in a sufficient manner, since each member of the series is somehow dependent upon and caused by another. As such, each member—or the whole set together—points us necessarily toward something more ultimate. For this reason, we must posit a primary intelligence that we call God. His wisdom is the ultimate transcendent source of the intelligible order we find present in natural realities. He is the source of their intrinsic teleological inclinations.

CONCLUSION

It seems reasonable to conclude that Aquinas's Five Ways unfold in a natural order of progression. The first way considers the various forms of ontological change that characterize physical bodies—changes due to the material cause. The second way considers the efficient causality of being in all things that come into being. The third way is concerned with formal causality insofar as it considers substances that are contingent in nature and therefore ontologically possible. The fourth way begins from degrees of perfection and in so doing considers exemplary causality. The fifth way appeals to the final cause and to the order that is manifest in nature based on the teleological inclinations in things. What can we conclude cumulatively from the Five Ways? They alert us to the existence of a transcendent cause of the physical cosmos, a cause that is immaterial and not subject to physical alteration, whom we call God. God gives existence to all things that come into being or cease to be. He exists of necessity and accounts for those realities that are possible and contingent. God is a hidden exemplar who must be the transcendent cause of all creatures that fall within a spectrum of formal perfections. He is the primary source of the teleological inclinations and intelligible order we find in creatures, and is therefore wise and provident.

In this chapter we sought to identify the theological context of Aquinas's arguments for the existence of God, and to explain how these arguments are situated within his larger theological project of *sacra doctrina*, holy teaching. We concluded that the arguments presented in *ST* I, q. 2, a. 3, are indeed intended as philosophical demonstrations—that is, they do not depend on any revealed premises—and yet they operate here within a properly theological context. Aquinas seeks to employ genuine metaphysical arguments to illustrate how the human mind already enlightened by faith can move by its natural powers *within* faith toward the creedal profession of the "one God." From here it can make use of philosophical reasoning in the service of theology so as to study the divine nature, and the mystery of the Trinitarian persons.

It is significant that Aquinas answers the question of ST I, q. 3, a. 3, "whether God exists?" by citing Exodus 3:14: "I am Who is." The revelation of God the Creator in his transcendence, as it is provided by the prophets, invites Christians to philosophical reflection, while arguments like those indicated in the Five Ways provide diverse philosophical pathways to God the Creator, who is naturally discernible insofar as he gives being to all things. The first way concludes with one who is an unmoved mover or unactuated actualizer, free from quantitative dependence and limitation, whose being does not depend upon physical bodies, and who is perfectly in act. The second way concludes with one who is by nature, whose essence it is to exist, and who gives being to all other things. The third way concludes with one who is absolutely necessary, from whom all possible beings receive their being. The fourth way concludes with one who is perfect in truth, goodness, and beauty, the source of all created perfections. The fifth way concludes with a transcendent source of order in nature, one who is intelligent and provident. Through such pathways, theologians even "after grace" and within faith are able to undertake a form of intellectual cooperation with the biblical revelation of God, to speak about the divine nature. The Five Ways initiate this process, which is carried forward in various ways in the ensuing sections of the *Summa theologiae*, which are concerned with the divine attributes.

Having now set forth Aquinas's metaphysical arguments that answer, in the affirmative, the question "whether God is," we must now turn to the next step in our discussion and ask the question of "what God is." How can we even discuss the mysterious nature of God, conceptually and linguistically, if God is so utterly transcendent of his creation? To address this question, we must now turn to Aquinas's treatment of analogy.

12

Naming God Analogically

We have noted in previous chapters that the mature pro-Nicene theologians of the fourth and fifth centuries distinguished terms that are ascribed to the distinct persons of God and those that are ascribed to the divine nature common to the three persons. We also saw that Dionysius proposed an apophatic way of speaking of the divine essence common to the three persons, thereby providing initial grounds for a theory of analogical predication. The Fourth Lateran Council, meanwhile, indicated that a language of likeness and dissimilitude must be employed when speaking about the three persons of God, in order to avoid anthropomorphism or tri-theism.

Aquinas brings these various elements together when he considers divine names for the divine nature that is common to the three persons, and the proper names of each person, as Father, Word, and Spirit. The study of the divine names in the first part of Aquinas's treatise on God, in the *Summa theologiae*, is a distinctively theological study of the mystery of the divine nature: it is conducted in view of a consideration of the persons of the Trinity, who are mysteriously one in nature. This study makes use of philosophical argument in order to reflect on the God of the Old and New Testaments, who is the transcendent Creator of all things, present to all things, one who is closer to us than we are to ourselves, and yet who remains numinous and hidden. This is the case even after he has become human and revealed himself to us in his threefold personal mystery.

St. Thomas's Five Ways were meant to navigate us through a difficult first beginning. What do we mean when we say "God" in the first place, since we do not see the divine nature face to face, and know of God only indirectly?

We said earlier that Aquinas follows Aristotle in posing two basic explanatory questions in a particular order: "does a given thing really exist?" and, if so, "what is it?" God is a unique subject of study, because he alone is the cause of all else that exists, and, as we have noted, there is knowledge of his existence *only from his effects.* Those effects are universal, and consequently he is "studied" as the universal cause of all that exists. It was, accordingly, through an examination of his effects that we then came to the affirmation that God exists, that is, as the cause of this world and as the universal providence that governs all things. But now the question naturally follows: "*What is God?*" And here again we are going to have to answer the question in a particular way, for the simple reason that we do not have any direct access to the essence of God.

In the prologue to *ST* I, q. 3, Aquinas creatively adapts the Aristotelian form of reflection on the questions whether a thing is and what it is, as it here applies to God:

When the existence of a thing has been ascertained there remains the further question of the manner of its existence, in order that we may know its essence. Now, because we cannot know what God is, but rather what He is not, we have no means for considering how God is, but rather how He is not. Therefore, we must consider: (1) How He is not; (2) How He is known by us; (3) How He is named.

Now it can be shown how God is not, by denying Him whatever is opposed to the idea of Him, viz. composition, motion, and the like. Therefore (1) we must discuss His simplicity, whereby we deny composition in Him; and because whatever is simple in material things is imperfect and a part of something else, we shall discuss (2) His perfection; (3) His infinity; (4) His immutability; (5) His unity.

The third consideration Aquinas mentions in this passage is the question of how God is named. In *ST* I, Aquinas reflects upon this structure of divine naming in q. 13, *after* he has analyzed the mystery of the one God in qq. 3–11 (in q. 12 he reflects upon how God is known by us). Here, however, we will consider q. 13 first, in order to treat analogical naming of God, or knowledge of God by analogy as a basis for our discussion of the divine names. We will reflect on this first, since Aquinas's mode of analysis of the divine names has a common structure, one that colors his treatment of all of them.[1]

---

1. The literature on the topic of analogy in Aquinas is immense. See, among other resources, Bernard Montagnes, *La doctrine de l'analogie de l'être d'après saint Thomas d'Aquin* (Louvain: Éditions Peeters, 1963), Gregory Rocca, *Speaking the Incomprehensible God: Thomas Aquinas on the Interplay of Positive and Negative Theology* (Washington, D.C.: The Catholic University of America

TRANSCENDENCE, IMMANENCE, AND THE TRIPLEX
VIA "TOWARD" THE DIVINE NAMES

The problem with which we are confronted is how to think rightly about God, who so utterly transcends this world that we have no clear concept of him, but who is yet so immanently present to this world, as the actual origin of all that is, that the creatures to which he communicates being must in some way resemble him. Because we cannot clearly define God, or grasp what God is essentially, we have to begin by thinking about his nature by ontological similitude, that is to say, by comparison with the world we experience, attempting to say in the process what God is not, what he must be as the transcendent source of all that is, and how his perfection remains utterly beyond our understanding.

We have noted above that St. Thomas refused to grant human beings any *propter quid* demonstrative knowledge of God, such as that which is obtained when we begin our deductive reasoning from knowledge of the essence of a thing. When speaking of God we begin instead from a mere nominal definition of the divine nature, which we enrich through forms of *quia* argumentation like those examined in the last chapter. In this way, Aquinas substitutes for any a priori knowledge of the essence of God a thematic appeal to Dionysius the Areopagite's *triplex via* taken from his work *On the Divine Names*, as discussed in chapter 10.[2] We come to know "what" God is through this process. In his presentation of Dionysius's proposal, Aquinas typically reinterprets the three forms of reflection in the following order, to end on a kataphatic note:

1. *Via Causalitatis.* God is known first *per viam causalitatis*, that is, by way of causality, as the transcendent cause of creatures. Because creatures must in some way resemble their cause, therefore, certain attributes of creatures may be ascribed properly to God (albeit, of course, in a transcendent way, signified analogically).

2. *Via Negationis.* However, because of God's utterly ineffable and tran-

---

Press, 2004), Thierry-Dominique Humbrecht, *Théologie négative et noms divins chez Saint Thomas d'Aquin* (Paris: J. Vrin, 2005); Rudi te Velde, *Aquinas on God*; Joshua P. Hochschild, *The Semantics of Analogy: Rereading Cajetan's "De Nominum Analogia"* (Notre Dame, Ind.: University of Notre Dame Press, 2010); Thomas Joseph White, *Wisdom in the Face of Modernity*; Steven A. Long, *Analogia Entis: On the Analogy of Being, Metaphysics, and the Act of Faith* (Notre Dame, Ind.: University of Notre Dame Press, 2011); Bonino, *Dieu, "Celui Qui Est"*, 483–548.

2. The basic text of Dionysius on the divine names is found in *The Divine Names*, chap. 7, no. 3.

scendent manner of existing, these attributes must be "thought" *per viam negationis*, or *remotionis*, that is to say, by negating or removing from them all that necessarily pertains to creaturely imperfection.

3. *Via Eminentiae.* Finally, *per viam eminentiae*, that is, by way of eminence, these analogical ascriptions given to God may again be thought to exist in him, but now in an all-surpassing, preeminent way, stripped of the imperfections found in any creaturely form.

St. Thomas presents the rationale for his interpretation of the *triplex via* in *ST* I, q. 12, a. 12:

From the knowledge of sensible things the whole power of God cannot be known; nor therefore can His essence be seen. But because they are His effects and depend on their cause, we can be led from them so far as to know of God *whether He exists*, and to know of Him *what must necessarily belong to Him, as the first cause of all things, exceeding all things caused by Him.* Hence we know of His relationship with creatures in so far as He is *the cause* of them all; also that creatures *differ from Him,* inasmuch as He is not in any way part of what is caused by Him; and that creatures are not removed from Him *by reason of any defect on His part, but because He superexceeds them all.*[3]

Aquinas goes on in *ST* I, q. 13, a. 1, to use this procedure to explain precisely how we can "name" God by the use of our words taken from creatures. He writes: "we can give a name to anything in as far as we can understand it. Now ... in this life we cannot see the essence of God; but we know God from creatures as their principle, and also by way of excellence and remotion. In this way therefore He can be named by us from creatures, yet not so that the name which signifies Him expresses the divine essence in itself." Clearly, the appeal to this *triplex via* of causality, remotion, and excellence is at the center of Aquinas's method in divine naming. Let us proceed now to a more detailed explication of Thomas's doctrine of analogy by first looking at the interrelationship he sees between negative and positive affirmations in our discourse about God.

---

3. *ST* I, q. 12, a. 12, emphases added. Note that just after this text Aquinas proceeds to clarify (in q. 13) the analogical character of the knowledge this way of thinking permits. For similar texts, employing the *triplex via*, see *SCG* I, c. 30; *In div. nom.*, c. 7, lec. 4; *De potentia Dei (De pot.)*, q. 7, a. 5, ad 2.

NEGATIVE AND POSITIVE PERFECTIONS AND
THE INTERPLAY BETWEEN THEM

The foundational, epistemic priority of positive to negative knowledge is first of all a general truth for Aquinas. Following Aristotle, he insists that every negation is in fact a mental act or intention predicated upon the prior admission of something existent.[4] Even a negation is, for this reason, epistemically positive and affirmative. If one says, "there is no large bird in this room," this negation presumes more fundamentally that one knows what a bird is, and more basically still, that such beings as birds exist. Even if one says "the phoenix does not exist," the negation still presupposes knowledge of the real existence of other things to which one can compare the legendary entity (the phoenix being like a bird with added features taken from other entities, like fire and ash). We may negate the existence of something or characteristics of a certain kind only because we already have some prior, positive knowledge of beings, upon which we base our understanding of what is and is not the case. Thus every negation implies some kind of prior positive knowledge of reality.

Building off of Aristotle, St. Thomas applies this general noetic principle to the specific problem of negative knowledge of God: whatever is negated of God presupposes some positive knowledge, including positive knowledge of God's existence. Writing against Maimonides, Aquinas states:

The understanding of negation is always based on an affirmation. And this is clear because an affirmative proposition proves every negative proposition [*omnis negativa per affirmativam probatur*], and so, unless the human intellect were to know something affirmatively about God, it could not deny anything about God. But it would not know anything if nothing said about God were to be affirmatively verified about him. And so, according to the opinion of Dionysius [*Divine Names*, c. 12], we should say that such terms signify the divine substance, although defectively and imperfectly.[5]

The logical presupposition for *any* negative or apophatic theological reflection concerning God is the prior knowledge of three things: (a) the knowl-

---

4. See Thomas Aquinas, *Aristotle: On Interpretation; Commentary by St. Thomas and Cajetan*, trans. J. T. Oesterle (Milwaukee, Wisc.: Marquette University Press, 1962), I.8, where Aquinas comments upon Aristotle's *De interpretatione*, chap. 5 (17a8–9): "First affirmation, then negation, is enunciative speech that is one."

5. Thomas Aquinas, *De pot.*, q. 7, a. 5, in *The Power of God*, trans. R. J. Regan (Oxford: Oxford University Press, 2012). See the analysis of this text by te Velde, *Aquinas on God*, 74.

edge of existence in creatures, (b) the knowledge of the existence of God, which knowledge is derived from creatures (i.e., God is known indirectly as their *cause*), and (c) the knowledge of the necessity of the ascription of some perfection-names of creatures to God (in an analogical fashion) as the primary cause. Simply put, the similitude between God established by the *via causalitatis* precedes, contextualizes, and gives warrant to the *via negationis*, and these two in turn allow for the *via eminentiae*. This means, for instance, that we can begin from the affirmation that creatures are good and subsequently call God good by analogy, since he is the cause of their goodness. His nature is not good in the same way as that of creatures, however. Rather, it is "good" in an incomprehensible and super-eminent way proper to God alone. In this qualified sense, then, we can attribute definitional names to God.

THE MODE OF SIGNIFICATION VERSUS
THE THING SIGNIFIED

What are the linguistic procedures for this model of divine naming? In *ST* I, q. 13, a. 3, Aquinas distinguishes between the *modus significandi* and the *res ipsa significata*, the mode of signification and the thing signified. The distinction plays a key role in his theory of theistic language. We can consider the example of divine goodness. One might begin from a common definition of goodness as found in creatures: it is a characteristic of their being ascribed to them insofar as they attain a given kind of intrinsic perfection and in doing so are able to effectuate a perfection in others. As we will see shortly, goodness for Aquinas is not a generic term proper to one kind of thing, but a transcendental term coextensive in an analogical way with all that exists. It can apply, then, to artifacts, non-living natural realities, living beings, and human beings. It can apply to them either substantially, in all they are, or in virtue of a property (usually a quality) of being. One might say, for example, "this is a *good* coat, because it keeps one warm and protects the body in winter," or "that is a good species of rose plant, since it is healthy and produces an abundance of flowers," or "she is a good person, because she is affable, charitable, and seeks the good of other people." In an even broader and more general way, we can also say the creation as a whole is good, since there is a sense in which each thing is good just insofar as it exists, and all natures immanently possess a certain degree of ontological perfection. When we speak of the thing signified in all these examples, we refer to the onto-logical goodness present in these diverse realities, realized in diverse ways. However, precisely because the ontological goodness in question is not ge-nerically identical in each case, it can be signified only analogically, and the diverse modes of signification follow from this way of speaking. The good-ness we are seeking to identify in things has complex ontological realiza-tions that are not generically identical with one another. Consequently, our diverse modes of signification of what is "good" arise from the various sematic qualifications we must make when using the word across a spec-trum of contexts so as to indicate the various modes of realization of good-ness found in the world.

What does it mean, then, to call the divine nature "good" in comparison with creatures? We will discuss this more fully as we proceed in our discus-sion of St. Thomas's *De Deo Uno* treatise. For the moment, let us simply note that even when human beings speak of God's goodness, they initially devel-op their language about goodness based on the prior experience they have of created goods. And as just noted, the term "goodness" is complex even when speaking of created goodness, characterized by a range of "modes of signification" proper to created entities. Consequently, when speaking about God, human beings inevitably employ terms like "goodness" according to modes of signification originally derived from the experience of creatures, and adapt this language in order to signify God in himself. To do so, they must refine and qualify their speech about God, so that what they say about the divine nature is genuinely truthful, that is, it is based on sound reason-ing about God, so as to indicate something of what God is in himself, albeit indirectly and very imperfectly. This means that, when we speak about God, the *res ipsa significata*, or reality signified, is God himself, even if the "mode of signification" of our language for God is originally derived from creatures. We can begin from modes of signifying goodness, for example, that are ap-propriate to creatures and adapt our language analogically in order to speak truly, albeit imperfectly, of the goodness of God.

This theory is advantageous because it allows us to avoid two unhelp-ful extremes. We could characterize one extreme as a form of linguistic de-spair, in which it is said that our ordinary language is incapable of denoting God in himself, as a result of our epistemological limitations and his tran-scendence. We could characterize the other extreme as a form of linguistic presumption, in which our speech is thought to be capable of denoting God in just the same way that it is capable of denoting created realities. The first tendency leads to semantic agnosticism, while the second leads to semantic idolatry. Aquinas's use of theological semantics walks down the reasonable middle path between these two extremes. We can truly speak of God in himself, with our human names for God, even if these names are imperfect since they are drawn from our limited human way of thinking about and signifying created reality. Furthermore, even if our names, like "goodness," are drawn from beings of limited goodness and then applied to the divine nature, they also signify God as something more than a cause of goodness in creatures: they denote God as being preeminently good *in himself*. Aquinas emphasizes this point in *ST* I, q. 13, a. 3, when he writes: "So when we say, *God is good*, the meaning is not, *God is the cause of goodness*, or *God is not evil*; but the meaning is, *Whatever good we attribute to creatures, pre-exists in God*, and in a more excellent and higher way." It follows from this that we not only say in proposition, but also know with certitude, that God is preeminently good in himself. At the same time, we recognize that the reality signified in such propositions remains beyond the possession of our plenary comprehension or experience. We speak rightly of God only as one who is unlike every created thing we know, and thus, we speak of God apophatically, as if in darkness.[6]

To this presentation of divine naming, one might object that our terms for God come not from creatures primarily but from scripture, in which it is revealed to us that God is good. "O how abundant is thy goodness, which thou hast laid up for those who fear thee, and wrought for those who take refuge in thee, in the sight of the sons of men!" (Ps 31:19). "God is light and in him is no darkness at all" (1 Jn 1:5). It is true that scripture reveals the

---

6. In this connection, we should note that the generation of divine names by humans is always something complex. We employ a multiplicity of terms, whose significations are refined through the medium of ornate arguments, to speak eventually of the nature of God, using terms like simplicity, goodness, omnipotence, and so on. This is true even though there is no complexity in God, who is simple, having a reality more actual and incomprehensibly profound than any of our very imperfect significations can convey. Our various names for the divine name rejoin something that is mysteriously one in God himself. God's simplicity is his wisdom, which is his goodness, etc. As Aquinas states in *ST* I, q. 13, a. 4: "our intellect, since it knows God from creatures, in order to understand God, forms conceptions proportional to the perfections flowing from God to creatures, which perfections pre-exist in God *unitedly and simply*, whereas in creatures they are received and divided and multiplied." As such, what is diverse for us in creatures is one in its divine source, similarly to the way the spectrum of colors unites indivisibly in white light. In this sense, it is inevitable that we should have a complex discourse pertaining to a simple God, since we approach God only as rational animals, in our own distinctly human way.

mysterious goodness of God, especially through the revelation given to the prophets and apostles. However, in doing so it makes use of terms drawn from ordinary human language and employs them in distinctly supernatural ways to signify the mystery of God.[7] We should note the twofold aspect of this truth. First, the inspired scriptures themselves help human civilization recover a natural grammar for God, by inaugurating a process of divine naming even within the life of grace. The bible invites its readers to employ human language to speak of the divine mystery in myriad ways, including both the poetic and philosophical, in keeping with human rational capacities. We can infer from this fact that divine revelation makes use of the prophets' natural capacity to speak about God, even when it simultaneously conveys truths about God that transcend all natural understanding; and in doing so it incites in us the rediscovery of our native linguistic capacity for God. Second, however, this use of even natural terms for God (like "wise," "good," or "one") is always already employed in scripture to denote a mystery of God as the Lord, who reveals himself to Israel in covenant and who has become human in Jesus Christ. It is language about the mystery of the Father, Son, and Holy Spirit, the one God, who is revealed to the world in Jesus Christ.

It is precisely in this context that the apophatic character of our knowledge of God is significant, as the Cappadocian Fathers underscored in their refutation of Eunomius. When we "name" the divine nature, employing scriptural terms like "goodness" and "unity," we also acknowledge in the heart of this very process that our understanding of the divine nature is obscure and indirect. This kind of epistemic humility is entirely reasonable and warranted, but also complementary to our simultaneous acknowledgment in faith of the gratuity and fittingness of God's unveiling of the Trinity. Just as we know God in a limited way in his natural unity, so too we are able to be receptive to the gift of the knowledge of God's inner life as Trinity, which is given to us from "above and beyond" all our natural capacities. This is a truth acknowledged not only outside or before Christian theology but also from within, in our very way of studying the mystery of the Holy Trinity.

---

7. The formal object denoted by scripture is supernatural even as the terminology employed is natural in origin. See, on this point, Aquinas, *ST* II-II, q. 1.

226 The Divine Nature

THE ANALOGICAL KNOWLEDGE OF GOD

Aquinas presents us with his mature doctrine of analogical predication of terms to God in *ST* I, q. 13, a. 5, where he seeks to navigate between what he takes to be two unworkable extremes.[8] On the one side, he wishes to avoid Avicenna's theory of "univocal" predication of divine names (a position later famously reformulated by the Franciscan John Duns Scotus). On the other side, he is opposed to an "equivocal" theory of predication, such as that advocated by the twelfth-century Jewish thinker Moses Maimonides. We will discuss these in turn, after a presentation of Aquinas's theory.

Analogical Predication for Creatures and for God

Aristotle had originally defined univocal predication as the ascription of a term to two different subjects in essentially or generically the same sense.[9] He takes as his typical example the predication of a common species or common genus to two or more objects. Paul and John are both human beings (having the same form or natural species). Human beings and birds are both animals (sensate living beings, having the same natural genus). Much of our human speech is univocal in this sense. However, Aristotle famously argued against Plato that we cannot employ univocal terminology when speaking of certain subjects, even pertaining to ordinary realities around us. Goodness is a case in point. It does not fall into any one genus or species of being. For example, there is no "form of the good," because goodness is not present in any particular nature or form, but in every kind of being.[10] Indeed when we speak of being, unity, truth, or goodness, we are considering properties or notes found in everything, which cannot be relegated to only one category or genus of being. The medievals, following Aristotle, called these "transcendental" notions precisely because they transcend any one genus of being.

Aristotle notes that properties like being and goodness can be denoted only analogically, not univocally. If univocal predication specifies that two things possess the same trait in the same way, analogical predication signifies that they possess the same property in ways that are not generically or

---

8. See also *SCG* I, c. 30–36; *De pot.*, q. 7, esp. aa. 5–7.
9. See Aristotle, *Categories*, chap. 1 (1a1–15).
10. Aristotle, *Nicomachean Ethics* 1.6 (1096a12–29); *Metaphysics* 12.5 (1071a18–24); *Metaphysics* 4.2 (1003a35–1003b8).

specifically identical. The being of a substance (a horse) is formally distinct from the being of a quality that inheres within it (the power to run, which can develop over time), but both the substance truly and the quality truly have being in common, and the latter depends upon the former. The subsistent goodness of a man (which he possesses simply in virtue of his being) is formally distinct from his moral excellence (his charity or courage), but he is truly good in both senses. Being and goodness are thus predicated analogously to beings around us in accord with their complex ontological determinations.

We can make this idea clearer by listing Aristotle's categories and then thinking about how certain "dimensions" of being transcend any one category and apply to them all. Aristotle's divisions of categories are as follows.[11]

The first division refers to those terms that are predicated among creatures *univocally*. These are:

Substance:
    1. Essence (e.g., human nature)
    2. Concrete individual (e.g., Peter, Socrates)

Accident:
    1. Quantity
    2. Quality
    3. Relation
    4. Action
    5. Passion
    6. Habit
    7. Time
    8. Place
    9. Position

We can denote reality univocally (in precisely the same sense) using these terms. If we say these two realities before us are both "human beings," we mean they both possess exactly the same essence (the first category or genus above). If we say that they are both intelligent or courageous, we might say that these *qualities* admit of degrees, but they are denoted univocally as qualities (the second accident listed).

11. See Aristotle, *Categories*, chaps. 1–15 (1a1–15b32).

The second division refers to those terms that are ascribed *analogically* to all the categories of being, whether substance or accident, listed above. These predicates are commonly called the transcendentals, because they apply to all the categories listed above, and so transcend them.

This is the list of "transcendentals" provided by Aquinas in *De veritate*, q. 1, a. 1.[12]

1. Being/Existence (*ens/esse*)
2. Reality (*res*)
3. Unity
4. To be something distinct (*aliquid*)
5. Truth
6. Goodness

The idea is that terms like "being," "unity," and "goodness" are said of a given subject (such as this particular human being, Paul), and similarly are said of a given nature (like being human), or of a quality (like the capacity to play the violin), or of a quantity (like height and shape). The goodness of being Paul is not generically or formally identical with the goodness of being human, which is in turn not identical with the goodness of being able to play the violin, or Paul's being a good height for violin playing. However there is, by ontological similitude, something common to all these realizations of being, insofar as they really exist, and are good. "What" the existence or goodness is is signified by analogical discourse, which allows us to disclose simultaneously these various ontological similitudes and dissimilitudes and the ground of unity that is found within them. When we speak of being, unity, goodness, and so forth, these terms indicate common features of existence that occur across a range or spectrum of realizations that is trans-generic, that is to say not proper to any one genus or species of being, but wherein there is a real unity of content, one that can be identified

---

12. The basic text on the transcendentals in Aquinas is *De ver.*, q. 1, a. 1, where he justifies the above-named fivefold distinction of terms coextensive with *ens* and *esse* through a series of "modes of differentiation." Being can be considered (1) either per se or with respect to another. If per se, then (2) either positively (as *res*, or "a determinate reality") or negatively (as *unum*: that which is indivisible); and if with respect to another, then either (3) in distinction from it (as *aliquid* or "something other") or as fitted to it (*convenientia*). If the latter is the case, this can be with respect to intellect (*verum*, all that is, is somehow true) or with respect to appetite (*bonum*, all that is, is somehow good). See the English translation in Aquinas, *Truth*, 3 vols., trans. by J. V. McGlenn, R. W. Mulligan and R. W. Schmidt (Indianapolis: Hackett Publishing, 1994). I take it that beauty is a transcendental implicitly contained in truth and goodness, as a co-emergent dimension of each.

only analogically. We should note that on Aquinas's account, the analogical application of the transcendentals is something that already, necessarily, takes place in the sphere of inner-worldly, created realities, even before we come to the question of discourse about God. To deny an "analogy of being," then, is to deny something properly basic to the way we all necessarily think and speak about ordinary reality all the time whenever we use terms that denote existence, reality, unity, goodness, truth, and so on.[13]

According to Aquinas, God does not enter into the study of metaphysics as an object of that science *per se*, nor should God be considered as a member of "common being." We cannot derive an adequate concept of God merely from the consideration of the transcendental notions, as if he were a particular realization of being, unity, truth, and goodness, like one created being among all the others. Instead, God is approached within the science of metaphysics not as its subject of consideration, but as *the cause* of the subject of consideration. The subject of metaphysics is every categorical mode of created being (substances, with their various qualities, quantities, etc.) as well as the transcendental characteristics of created beings (their existence, goodness, unity, truth, etc.). God is not one of these subjects but the cause of all of them as Creator. We may ascribe categorical names and transcendental names to God in virtue of this causality, then, but only analogically. This means we cannot speak of God univocally or "essentially," as we do the beings in the world (like substances of various kinds having specific properties). Nor can we speak of God analogically merely as we do in the case of the transcendental notions, as if he were something common to all that exists (like existence, unity, goodness, and other transcendental features of all that exists). Instead, we can speak of God only analogically, as one who is the transcendent cause of all creatures, of both substances with their various properties and those transcendental features of being in which they all participate (like existence and goodness).[14] All of these categorical modes

---

13. There are problems with Karl Barth on this front. Barth famously rejects the use of the *analogia entis* as a mode of speaking about God in philosophical theology. In CD 3:3, 102–4, he argues that this form of thinking reduces God and creatures to a common genus of being. The irony is that one of the main purposes of Aristotle's theory of analogy is to avoid reducing being to a given genus, an error he thinks would follow from Plato's theory of forms. Barth manifests little or no comprehension of this fact, even though it is a common theme in classical philosophy, and on the basis of his oversight, he fails to consider whether we can speak *even of created natural realities* without recourse to the analogy of being. Aquinas shows why one cannot, since these features of reality are not generic or formal but are proper to every genus or nature. See Aquinas, *In V Meta.*, lec. 9, 889–90.

14. See, on this famous point, Aquinas, *In Meta.*, prologue, and III, lec. 8, 433.

of being, together with their transcendental properties, *resemble God in some way* and *all of them fail to resemble him in some way*, because of his incomprehensible perfection and transcendence of all created realities.

The purpose of analogy theory, accordingly, is to try to speak rightly of how creatures are like God so that we may truly name him, while at the same time calling our attention to how God is utterly unlike creatures, so that he remains beyond our comprehending grasp.

This is why Aquinas rejects a notion of analogy that would put God in a common group with creatures as one being among others, and instead conceives of God by analogy *ad alterum* (in *ST* I, q. 13, a. 5). His point is that God is known only analogically or conceived only by comparison with creatures *as their cause* and as a cause that remains unknown definitionally in himself.

Univocity Theory and Equivocity Theory

Like Aquinas, the medieval proponents of the univocal theory of divine names also adopted Aristotle's original schema of univocal and transcendental terms. However, they sought to interpret it in an alternative way. They claimed that for the purposes of clear definition and valid syllogistic argument, our language must always employ terms in a formally identical sense, and in a quasi-generic way. Otherwise our capacity to make valid syllogisms breaks down, since "merely" analogical predication does not provide enough specific content to allow for demonstrative reasoning. This concern applies whether we speak about the transcendentals in created beings, or about God himself, and indeed it must apply in both cases, otherwise we will be unable to speak clearly about these most important topics. If we say, "the whiteness of the cat exists," "Aidan exists," and "God exists," we denote univocally in each case something that contains a formally identical core. Existence is common to each realization of being in a quasi-generic sense, no matter how diverse the realizations are.[15] Despite its Aristotelian pedigree, this idea clearly has Platonic overtones. The form of being is in all things.

Aquinas's analysis of analogy presumes that there are various problems with this univocal theory of predication. First, as we have noted, terms like being, unity, and goodness are applicable to irreducibly diverse categorial

---

15. See, on these issues, Richard Cross, *Duns Scotus* (Oxford: Oxford University Press, 1999), 16–41, 139n35; *Duns Scotus on God* (Aldershot: Ashgate, 2005), 36–37, 258.

and generic modes of realization. A good *quality* of drinking water is generically distinct from a good *quantity* of drinking water. Quality and quantity
cannot be assimilated to one another formally, yet both are good. Being a
human being is distinct from being a given color, like white or black, as nature is distinct from quality, even though common natures and skin colors
both exist. Consequently, we cannot employ terms like being or goodness
except as intrinsically analogical terms applicable to a diversity of natures, or
else we would relegate existence and goodness to one nature alone or some
limited subset of natures.

Second, serious problems would arise if we were to try to ascribe being,
goodness, or other such notions to only one particular genus of being. Can
one reasonably say that only stars exist or that only human beings are good?
If one genus of reality has a monopoly on being, the others cannot properly be said to exist, or have unity, or be intelligible and good, and so forth.
However, it is evident that every distinct nature and every genus of being
we observe in the world truly does exist, and none of them is co-extensive
with existence, unity, truth, or goodness. So the claim that their existence
can fall into a distinct genus is absurd, but this is what would be required for
univocal predication in the strict sense of transcendental features of reality.
So analogical attribution is inherent to any properly universal form of thinking and proposition-making about the genuine range of existent realities.[16]

Third, our use of analogical attribution to make ontological distinctions
between beings need not impede the validity of our semantic logic. In fact, if
there are any logical demonstrations that pertain per se to common features
of being such as existence, unity, or goodness, then a right understanding of
analogical predication is necessary as a presupposition of such demonstrations, precisely so as to identify what is under discussion. One cannot accurately make use of transcendental notions as middle terms in syllogisms
unless one has a sense of that which is common to the terms under consideration, and what the terms signify. Analogical predication, on this view,
serves as a key condition for nuanced and accurate syllogistic reasoning,
rather than as a hindrance to it.

Finally, if we place God alongside creatures as a possessor of a common
formal property of being (as univocity theory does), it follows that our con-

16. Aquinas makes this argument in many places, but a good example is found in *SCG* I, c. 25.
For more on the intrinsically analogical nature of being, see Long, *Analogia Entis*, esp. ch. 1, "First
Principles and the Challenge of Parmenidean Monism," 13–37.

The Divine Nature

cept of being applies equally to both God and creatures under a term common to both. We can think about being in distinct modes as either infinite
or finite, uncreated or created. However, in this case both God and creatures
enter into the science of metaphysics as considered under the same formal
object (considered across the spectrum of finite and infinite modes).[17] All
that exists becomes subject to a common concept of being, one that is adequate to both God and creatures and which encompasses both noetically.
Aquinas was concerned that this epistemological approach to God fails to
respect the divine transcendence and wholly-other incomprehensibility of
God. We do not possess this kind of mastery of the concept of God.[18] It is
precisely for this reason that he posits the idea that God enters the subject
of the study of metaphysics not as its formal object, but only as the transcendent Creator of the object, creaturely being.

Equivocity theory stands at the opposite extreme from univocity theory. Maimonides, like Aquinas, develops only *quia* arguments for the existence of God. He is wary of any direct ideational intuitions of the divine
and seeks instead to derive knowledge of the necessary existence of God as
the Creator of the world, who exists without ontological change or limitation of power, from the transient and finite entities of the world we perceive,
considered as effects.[19] Nevertheless, for Maimonides such argumentation
does not terminate in any form of positive consideration of the attributes of
God, but only in what we might term an equivocal form of discourse: God

17. See, for example, Scotus, *Ordinatio* (hereafter, *Ord.*), I, d. 3, q. 1, nos. 25–26, on the univocal concept of being, an idea he took in part from Avicenna. See, likewise, Avicenna, *Liber de Philoso-phia Prima* I, c. 2, nos. 12 and 14, in *Liber de Philosophia Prima sive Scientia Divina*, ed. S. Van Riet (Leiden: Brill, 1977), vol. 1, pp. 11, 14. For Scotus, this idea is related theoretically to the inclusion of the notion of God as infinite being within the "subject" of the study of metaphysics. References to Scotus, unless otherwise indicated, are taken from *Opera omnia*, ed. C. Balić and others (Rome: Typis Polyglottis Vaticanis, 1950–2013). See also the study of this topic in medieval thought by Albert Zimmermann, *Ontologie oder Metaphysik?* (Louvain: Peeters, 1998).

18. Aquinas, *In librum de causis expositio* (*In De causis*), prop. 6: "For what the intellect first grasps is being [*ens*]. The intellect cannot apprehend that in which the character of being is not found.... But, according to the truth of the matter, the first cause is above being [*supra ens*] inas-much as it is itself infinite *esse*. 'Being,' however, is called that which finitely participates in *esse*, and it is this which is proportioned to our intellect, whose object is the quiddity or 'that which is' [*quod quid est*].... Hence our intellect can grasp only that which has a quiddity participating in *esse*. But the quiddity of God is itself *esse*. Thus it is above intellect." *Commentary on the Book of Causes*, trans. V. Guagliardo, C. Hess, and R. Taylor (Washington, D.C.: The Catholic University of America Press, 1996). (Translation slightly modified).

19. See Maimonides, *The Guide of the Perplexed*, trans. S. Pines (Chicago: University of Chi-cago Press, 1963), 2, c. 1.

can be named only negatively.[20] Famously, Maimonides claims that divine names can be taken in two ways. First they can signify not what God is in himself, but only likenesses of effects derived from God with effects produced by creatures. To say, for instance, that God is wise is to say that God is the cause of beings that are themselves wise, and that he acts through his effects as does one who is wise. However, we cannot properly attribute wisdom to God in and of himself. Second, to attribute to God a name is to affirm only that the negation of that name cannot be ascribed to God. To say that God is living, for example, is only to say that we cannot ascribe to God the mode of being proper to non-living things.

Aquinas offers a number of responses to Maimonides's arguments. His simplest and strongest is the following: if all our language concerning God were simply utterly equivocal, we would be incapable of saying anything about God at all, whether positive or negative, even by way of demonstration. All the demonstrations concerning God advanced by the philosophers would be sophistical. For example, if it were said that whatever is in potency depends upon the prior causality of a being in act, and from this it were concluded that God, as the cause of all that comes into being, is being in pure actuality, there would be a fallacy of equivocation, since we cannot say truly that God is pure act.[21]

Likewise, if God is spoken of from his effects only by comparison with the effects of creatures and not in himself, then we may say God is water in that he cleanses us like water cleanses physically, or that he is wise because he creates order, just as wise persons are the source of order in human affairs. This criterion is so minimal, however, that it permits us to attribute terms such as water and wisdom to God with equal and undifferentiated validity. If Maimonides is correct, there is no differentiation possible between properly analogical names, such as divine simplicity, goodness, wisdom, and so forth, and metaphorical terms, such as water, lion, or sunlight.[22]

Finally, if there were no difference between affirming that God is alive and saying that God is not a non-living thing then there would be no discernable difference between God and, for instance, a lion. For a lion is also not a non-living thing. The differentiations between God and creatures must be identified not only through the elaboration of purely negative differenc-

20. Maimonides, *The Guide of the Perplexed*, 1, cc. 52–59.
21. *De pot.*, q. 7, a. 7
22. *De pot.*, q. 7, a. 5.

es, but also through the articulation of positive differentiations within creatures and between creatures and God.[23]

MODERN ANALOGUES AND

TRINITARIAN CONSEQUENCES

Modern analogues exist with respect to the two aforementioned positions. Richard Swinburne, for example, appeals to the univocal predication theory of Scotus in order to articulate aspects of his own understanding of religious language.[24] Based on this theory he ascribes to God such properties as beliefs, real relations to creatures, existence in time, and being a substance, in a common genus with created substances.[25] These are all ascriptions that Thomists find anthropomorphic. For others, meanwhile, Aquinas's theory of analogical naming is too ambitious and fails to acknowledge the limitations of all our attempts to ascribe attributes to God, even when an analogical distance is acknowledged. The equivocal nature of our terms for God recalls to us the truth of his unspeakable and incomprehensible transcendence: the divine darkness. This view originates with Martin Heidegger, who builds upon the Kantian prohibition of classical arguments for the existence of God and who characterizes scholastic thinking about God as a form of "onto-theology," an unwarranted mental construct having no adequate foundation in experience.[26] Today this view is most eloquently represented by Jean-Luc Marion, who appeals to Dionysius the Areopagite's apophaticism in order to develop a phenomenological ontology of divine love. We can derive no natural, metaphysical knowledge of God from the world we experience, and any pretension to do so gives rise to a form of "conceptual idolatry."[27] We can, however, learn to see the world we experi-

23. *De pot.*, q. 7, a. 5.
24. See especially Richard Swinburne, *The Coherence of Theism*, rev. ed. (Oxford: Clarendon Press, 2010), chap. 5. There are further qualifications and applications of the doctrine in Swinburne, *Revelation* (Oxford: Clarendon Press, 1992), chap. 3, and *The Christian God* (Oxford: Clarendon Press, 1994), chap. 7.
25. See, for example, Swinburne, *The Coherence of Theism*, chaps. 10 and 12.
26. See in particular Martin Heidegger, "The Onto-theo-logical Constitution of Metaphysics," in *Identity and Difference*, trans. J. Staumbaugh (New York: Harper and Row, 1969), 42–74. The notion of ontotheology in the work of Immanuel Kant appears most importantly in *Critique of Pure Reason*, II, III, 7.
27. On this idea, Jean-Luc Marion, "De 'la mort de Dieu' au noms divines: L'itinéraire théologique de la métaphysique," in *L'Être et Dieu*, ed. D. Bourg (Paris: Cerf, 1986), 113. In his early work, Marion suggests this ascription could be given even to the work of Aquinas himself. In

ence as an enigma of givenness or gift.[28] This philosophical stance prepares us to interpret the world in light of divine revelation, which alone provides us with genuine knowledge of God.[29]

As often noted, these opposite positions reassert medieval ideas in creative modern ways, and in doing so renew classic debates. What is less often noticed is that they also introduce new Christological and Trinitarian ideas into modern theology, that move in competing and opposed senses. Swinburne, for example, follows through on his program of qualified univocal predication coherently not only when considering the divine nature, but also when speaking of the three persons of God, who precisely because they are persons after the essentially univocal fashion that this term suggests when drawn from creatures, must be three individual substances. To mitigate against the conclusion that the Trinity is composed of three distinct beings or gods, having a common nature (much like three human persons would), Swinburne argues that the persons of the Trinity share in a superior moral union of their three minds and wills. Because each of the three persons possesses a most perfect nature, which implies an optimal extension of mental knowledge and moral probity, they will always come to agree with one another in common actions, even though they each possess a substantial autonomy and real distinctiveness of mind and will.[30] This formulation contrasts in marked ways with the Nicene formulations considered in the first part of this book, in which the tradition of the early Church posited that there is one being and essence (and thus one wisdom and will) common to all three persons.

Marion's ideas are not less radical. Having distanced himself from the transcendental illusions (in the Kantian sense) of classical "divine attributes" and any possible ontological discourse concerning the divine nature,

God without Being, trans. T. A. Carlson (Chicago and London: University of Chicago Press, 1991), 29–32, 73–83, Marion underscores both difficulties and promising possibilities in Aquinas's analogical approach to metaphysical thinking about God. Aquinas is not seen to escape entirely from the dangers of onto-theology. Subsequently, however, he argues that Aquinas's thought does not represent a species of onto-theological thinking. See Jean-Luc Marion, "Saint Thomas d'Aquin et l'onto-théo-logie," *Revue Thomiste* 95, no. 1 (1995): 31–66.

28. See, for example, Jean-Luc Marion, *The Idol and the Distance*, trans. T. A. Carlson (New York: Fordham University Press, 2001); *God without Being*; *Being Given: Toward a Phenomenology of Givenness*, trans. J. L. Kosky (Stanford, Calif.: Stanford University Press, 2002).

29. See Jean-Luc Marion, *Givenness & Revelation*, trans. S. E. Lewis (Oxford: Oxford University Press, 2016).

30. See the forthright proposals of Swinburne in this regard in *The Christian God*, chaps. 6 and 8.

he is obliged to locate all genuine knowledge of God in the mystery of Jesus Christ, and specifically in the human life, actions, and sufferings of Jesus. The transcendence of God is literally unthinkable (if we accept the consequences of a thorough-going apophaticism). Consequently, the humanity of God now becomes the unique cipher or prism through which any access to God is made possible. However, precisely because we can no longer speak of the transcendent divine nature of God ontologically, even in respect to God made human, we must now conceive of the distinction of persons in God only on the basis of Jesus' human historical actions and operations, including his passivity and suffering. The Son as man obeys the Father unto death, and in doing so discloses his relation to him. His relation to the Father has a grounding in God himself, a Trinitarian relation that remains opaquely hidden from view behind the dead Son. The persons of the Trinity can be distinguished by us, then, only insofar as they are agents of mutual historical engagement and temporal self-disclosure.[31] If this is the case, it seems we can speak of God only in his economic mode of being among us. No possibility remains to think theologically about the transcendent Trinitarian life of God in itself, even by analogy.

What we see from these two brief examples is that analogical predication is never "just about" the divine nature, let alone philosophical knowledge of God. It is also always about the theological language one uses to signify the persons of the Trinity, their distinction and their unity, and the mysterious mode in which their communion of persons is both like and unlike the relations that arise among human persons. The embrace of either univocity theory or equivocity theory has Trinitarian consequences, and each leads in its own way, as I have suggested above, to a form of anthro-

---

31. On these matters, see Marion, *Givenness & Revelation*, chaps. 3 and 4. Marion's position is very close to that of Barth, but the two differ in key ways. Both deny any appeal to a classical ontological philosophical tradition as a mode for speaking about God, and both claim that the Trinity is revealed in Christocentric fashion in the humanity of Jesus. Barth, however, claims in *CD* 2:1 and 4:1 that a doctrine of divine attributes pertaining to the essence of God can and must be articulated on the basis of scripture and Christological revelation. Marion's project, by contrast, seems to impede all access to such a venture. Despite his Trinitarian aspirations, Marion's thought brings us much closer to the theological world of a Schleiermacher, Harnack, or Wobbermin than anticipated, since it is Christ's moral perfection in his human form of life and death (i.e., a sentiment of absolute dependence on God as Father, in self-offering obedience) that manifests God to the world, in a way that corresponds to the descriptive religious anthropology provided by Marion's philosophy. It is difficult to avoid the conclusion that we have returned to the early modern, post-Kantian theology of German liberal Protestantism, from which, ironically, Barth's very criticisms of the *analogia entis* in *CD* 1:1 were intended to deliver us.

pomorphism. On one side, we are moved by an overly kataphatic presumption of sameness to predicate human modes of substantial autonomy to the distinct Trinitarian persons so as to conceive of the persons anthropomorphically and obscure the mysterious unity of the persons. On the other side, we are moved by apophatic excess and fear of human projection to predicate human modes of behavior to the eternal inner life of the Son, so as to conceive of the Trinitarian relations in God anthropomorphically. Ironically this latter practice itself constitutes a projection of all too human ideas onto God, and diminishes a genuine sense of the transcendence of the divine nature, in virtue of which the three persons are eternally one in being. To avoid both these extremes, not only in thinking about the mystery of the divine nature, but also the distinction of the persons in the Trinity, it is crucial to note the objective merits of the Fathers' and Aquinas's analogical form of discourse regarding God, which provides us with a well-balanced approach to the mystery.

CONCLUSION

Our purpose in this chapter was to show how Aquinas appropriates Dionysius's *triplex via*—the *via causalitatis, via negationis,* and *via eminentiae*—to develop his theory of analogical discourse about God. In his theory of analogy, Aquinas stresses, first of all, the epistemic priority of affirmative over negative discourse. We can make negations only as a way of qualifying or reacting to prior affirmations. In discourse about God, this means that there is a certain dependence of apophatic discourse on kataphatic, or positive, discourse. Aquinas does not espouse a purely negative theology in which we know nothing of God's attributes. Rather, St. Thomas's *via negativa* is contextualized by the *via causalitatis,* and in turn gives rise to further affirmations about God (the *via eminentiae*). We noted Aquinas's distinction between the *modus significandi* and the *res ipsa significata,* the mode of signification and thing signified. Aquinas employs this distinction to explain how we can apply to God terms that originate with creatures, while at the same time recognizing that they apply to God differently than they apply to creatures. This distinction permits us to identify the modest ambitions of a properly analogical discourse about God. We saw how Aquinas situates analogical discourse about God as a mean between the opposed extremes of univocity and equivocity. In this connection, we noted that, even among creatures, transcendental predicates are applied analogously to all other categories of being, whether substantial or accidental. When it comes to God, however, terms are predicated by a kind of *super-analogy*, since God is himself the cause of all substances and accidents, together with their transcendental properties (being, goodness, etc.).

Equipped now with St. Thomas's theory of analogical discourse, it is time we turn our attention to his attempt to answer the question of what God is and what God is not. We will accordingly begin with Aquinas's treatment of divine simplicity in *ST* I, q. 3.

13

Divine Simplicity

The idea that God's nature is simple is one of the most misunderstood attributions of traditional Christianity. The basic idea is that God is not composed in ways that some or all creatures necessarily are. Despite its reasonableness, typical objections to this teaching are twofold and related. The first is that the notion is not of biblical provenance nor essential to the integral confession of traditional Trinitarian faith. Rather, it is an alien Hellenistic philosophical idea imported into Christianity, and quite possibly an outmoded one at that. The second objection is that traditional notions of divine simplicity impede a genuine understanding of God since they depict God as one who is unable to relate to his creation, interact with it, undergo suffering or personal change.

I will return to the second objection in the final part of this chapter. Here at the start we can consider briefly why the first objection is problematic. Rightly understood, the traditional notion of divine simplicity is clearly of biblical provenance, since it negates the presence in God of the various complex ontological compositions found in creatures, which characterize them precisely as derived and dependent entities. In the Old Testament, the idea of God's transcendence of creatures is key to Israel's conception of God. This transcendence implies non-composition or simplicity. The Decalogue, for example, underscores that God cannot be represented in an image, an ancient indication of the idea that God is not an embodied being. This prefigures the developed teaching in Second Temple Judaism that the divine nature is incorporeal and non-representational.[1] Israel's crit-

1. Ex 20:3–6; Lv 26:1; Nm 33:52; Dt 4:16; 5:8. See the study of Sven Petry, *Die Entgrenzung*

ical claims of idolatry in other religious traditions depend in great part upon such an idea. Second, the Israelite prophets and scribes clearly developed a mature notion over centuries of YHWH as the exclusive Creator and only God who truly exists. In doing so they effectively moved beyond any idea of their God as one god among others (a merely local or national deity), and developed the idea of God as the only "individual" who possesses deity. YHWH alone is God.[2] This corresponds to the non-distinction in God of individual and nature, to which we will return below. Third, clearly by the final age of the Second Temple, Judaism achieved a clear notion of God as Creator, the unilateral giver of being, upon whom all things depend, who gives existence to all things and who does not receive his existence from any creature.[3] God does not have a derived existence, and therefore his nature and existence are unlike that of all creatures, who receive all they are from him. This suggests, as we shall see, that there is no composition of essence and existence in God. Finally, authors in the period of Second Temple Judaism did not teach that God evolves historically alongside creation in relation to it, as if he would become more perfect eventually than he is currently or was in the past, but understood instead that God is eternally himself, ever perfect, possessing for all eternity a plenitude of divine wisdom and goodness.[4] This idea corresponds, in Aquinas's terms, to the non-distinction of potency and act in God's life, and therefore also the non-distinction of substance and accidental property. Creatures progressively improve or evolve in virtue of their properties, which gradually actuate and come to fruition. This is not the case for God, since God does not improve upon himself ontologically through his engagement with creation.

In Christian Trinitarian theology as such, the notion of simplicity is also of ancient pedigree and critical importance. Already in the second century, Irenaeus, in *Against Heresies* II, against Valentinus, appeals to the affirma-

---

JHWHs: Monolatrie, Bilderverbot und Monotheismus im Deuteronomium, in Deuterojesaja und im Ezechielbuch (Tübingen: Mohr Siebeck, 2007). Petry proposes judgments about date and composition of legal and prophetic texts that are disputable in various regards, but his work shows the integral relation of ideas in the legal and prophetic writings between the Judaic emergence of monotheism and the idea of that God cannot be represented, i.e., is not corporeal.

2. Dt 4:32–39; Dt 6:4; Is 46:9–11; Ps 18:31–50. See the argument from a systematic theological perspective by Steven J. Duby, *Divine Simplicity: A Dogmatic Account* (Edinburgh: T&T Clark, 2015).

3. See the study by Marcus Bockmuehl, "*Creatio ex nihilo* in Palestinian Judaism and Early Christianity," *Scottish Journal of Theology* 65, no. 3 (2012): 253–70.

4. Sir 16:26–30; Wis 7:22–30.

tion of God's simplicity to underscore that there is no pleroma of composite sub-deities in God. The Father is immaterial, as is his Word and Spirit, and consequently we should see the divine nature as simple, not composite.[5] The Cappadocian Fathers, as we noted above, underscored the simplicity of the divine nature precisely as an essential aspect of Trinitarian orthodoxy. The three divine persons are not one as three human persons are one. Three human beings are merely one in nature but remain distinct in individual substance. The Trinitarian persons are not only one in nature but also one in being or substance. Each person is truly the one God, having in himself the plenitude of the divine nature, either from another or for another. The Trinity is therefore simple in a way three human persons are not, since there are three divine persons but not three gods. Furthermore, the divine nature is not a composition of parts and we cannot say that each person possesses only some part of it, as if some divine names pertained only to one person, not to another. The very attribution of "common names" to all three persons implies some form of the doctrine of divine simplicity, since God's power, wisdom, and goodness are present in a co-extensive way. Augustine likewise saw that the distinction of persons by relations of origin allows us to affirm the unity of nature and equality of being in the three persons. Each of the persons has all that he has as relational and each is also truly God. If this is the case, then the divine essence is wholly present in each of the persons, which entails some version of the doctrine of divine simplicity. We can understand the transcendent otherness of the divine unity of the Trinitarian persons only when we see that they are one in being and essence (*homoousios*), and each possesses in himself all that is God. Similar views are found in Maximus the Confessor, John Damascene, Albert the Great, and Bonaventure.[6]

5. See Irenaeus, *Against Heresies*, 2.13.8, and the analysis of Barnes, "Irenaeus' Trinitarian Theology," 81–85.

6. For a few instances, see Augustine, *The Trinity*, 15.22: "What is God's knowledge is also his wisdom, and what is his wisdom is also his being or substance, because in the wonderful simplicity of that nature it is not one thing to be wise, another to be, but being wise is the same as being"; for the Cappadocians, see our early discussion of Gregory of Nazianzus, especially citations from *Oration 28*, no. 7; for Maximus, see *Chapters on Knowledge*, 2.3, in *Maximus Confessor: Selected Writings*, trans. George C. Berthold (Mahwah, N.J.: Paulist Press, 1985), 148: "God is altogether simple"; for John Damascene, see *An Exposition of the Orthodox Faith*, 1, c. 10, in Nicene and Post-Nicene Fathers, second series, vol. 9, ed. P. Schaff and H. Wace, trans. E. W. Watson and L. Pullan (Buffalo, N.Y.: Christian Literature Publishing, 1899); for Bonaventure, see *Commentary on the Sentences: Philosophy of God*, trans. R. E. Houser and T. B. Noone (St. Bonaventure, N.Y.: Franciscan Institute Publications, 2013), 138–48.

Most noteworthy in this respect are also the conciliar definitions formulated by the Fourth Lateran Council (against the theological ideas of Joachim of Fiore),[7] as well as the First Vatican Council, in *Dei Filius*, ch. 1, "On God, Creator of all things," which states:

The holy, catholic, apostolic and Roman church believes and acknowledges that there is one true and living God, creator and lord of heaven and earth, almighty, eternal, immeasurable, incomprehensible, infinite in will, understanding and every perfection. Since he is one, singular, completely simple [*simplex omnino*] and unchangeable spiritual substance, he must be declared to be in reality and essence, distinct from the world, supremely happy in himself and from himself, and inexpressibly loftier than anything besides himself which either exists or can be imagined. [8]

In this context, the doctrine of divine simplicity is meant to underscore the transcendence and alterity of God. It places us before the divine darkness that surrounds and permeates all creation. God is not a composite creature who receives his being from another. He is utterly unlike all creatures in this respect. As suggested above, the idea of divine simplicity also has an important Trinitarian consequence: it allows us to underscore the unity of the divine essence and therefore the monotheistic character of Trinitarian faith, that is to say, God as a Tri-*Unity*. If the divine nature or essence of God is absolutely simple, and if the Father begets the Son from all eternity in such a way that the Son possesses in himself the plenitude of the divine essence, then it follows that all that is in the Father (in virtue of the divine essence) is in the Son, and likewise all that is in the Father and the Son is communicated to the Spirit by spiration. There is only one God, who is absolutely simple, and the relations of the Trinitarian persons must be understood in such a way as to respect the absolute simplicity of God. (We will return to this point in part 3 of this book.)

AQUINAS ON DIVINE SIMPLICITY:
FROM COMPOSITION AND MULTIPLICITY TO
SIMPLICITY AND UNITY

Aquinas's account of divine simplicity is only one of many in the Catholic tradition, but it has a particular cogency and depth that are unique.[9] The

---

7. See Fourth Lateran Council, chap. 2, in *Decrees*, ed. Tanner, 1:232: "since the Father's substance is indivisible, inasmuch as it is altogether simple [*simplex omnino*]...."

8. First Vatican Council, *Dei Filius*, chap. 1, in *Decrees*, ed. Tanner, 2.805, emphasis added.

9. See, on this topic, Norman Kretzmann, *The Metaphysics of Theism*, 113–38; Eleonore Stump,

most frequent error in interpretation of his teaching is found in those who
claim that he basically negates any distinction whatsoever as pertaining to
God. This is clearly false, since he thinks there is a real distinction of persons in God. In fact, Aquinas's doctrine of "non-compositions" is restricted
to a very limited set of ontological topics: form and matter, individual and
essence, existence and essence, and substance and accidents, each of which
we will examine briefly.

It is important to see that when he negates that these compositions characterize God, he is employing the threefold Dionysian *via* in order to name
God by analogical similitude. By the *via causalitatis*, we can say that God is
known as the uniquely non-dependent cause of all created realities, which
depend upon him for their actual existence. But ontological complexity and
composition as we encounter them in each created reality (on a variety of
levels) are signs of that thing's dependence. (I will return to this claim below.) Therefore, if God is not dependent on another or others, as his creatures are, then he also is not ontologically complex or composite in the way
they are. This realization invites the application of the *via remotionis* or *via
negationis*. Divine simplicity is a primarily apophatic name, since it originates from a series of negations. Each article begins with compositions we
encounter in created realities and will negate these forms of composition
when speaking of God, in order to stress *what God is not*, thereby emphasizing the transcendence and incomprehensibility of the divine nature. This
leads us to the *via eminentiae*. In speaking of God's simplicity, we also speak
truly of what God is, of something pertaining to God's very identity, even if
his nature remains beyond our full understanding. Considered in this light,
when say that God is absolutely simple, we are making a true ontological
statement that is affirmative. God is pre-eminently simple in a way that no
creature is or ever could be. In our ordinary experience, simplicity often signals a lack of perfection and development, or an absence of higher qualities.
Something that is "simple" does not have enough complexity or richness to
attain to a greater perfection. God's simplicity, however, is completely different. It is a simplicity of fullness, associated with God's perfect plenitude

---

Aquinas (London: Routledge, 2006), 92–130; Rudi te Velde, *Aquinas on God*, 72–94; Juan José
Herrara, *La simplicidad divina según santo Tomás de Aquino* (Salta, Argentina: Ediciones de la Universidad del Norte Santo Tomás de Aquino, 2011); Bonino, *Dieu, "Celui Qui Est"*, 229–96; Thomas
Joseph White, "Divine Simplicity and the Holy Trinity," *International Journal of Systematic Theology*
18, no. 1 (2016): 66–93, and "Nicene Orthodoxy and Trinitarian Simplicity," *American Catholic Philosophical Quarterly* 90, no. 4 (2016): 727–50.

of being. All creatures that derive from God are, even in their most active perfections, imperfect, finite expressions of the richness of God's being in its simplicity; and our ontological complexity and multiplicity are signs of our poverty or utter imperfection when compared with his fullness and pure actuality. In fact, this is why God creates a multiplicity of finite creatures: their diverse, intrinsically complex perfections reflect, in their very diversity, something of the plenitude that resides in God in an eminently higher way that is simple and indiminishable.

The compositions in created realities, which Aquinas begins from, are identified by means of a philosophical analysis of those realities. They are not something immediately accessible merely to our senses (like a visual figure or image) or something measurable or imaginable, such as the atomic or chemical complexity we might measure or represent in modern science. These forms of complexity derive from deeper structures within reality, compositions of a distinctively metaphysical kind. This does not mean, however, that Aquinas's views defy common sense. On the contrary, they are intuitively accessible and quite reasonable.

Is God a Body? Is There Corporeal Potentiality in God?
The first form of negation stems from the affirmation that God is immaterial in nature, and as such is not a physical body among other bodies. In *ST* I, q. 3, a. 1, Aquinas gives three arguments for why the divine nature cannot be material, arguments that follow directly from the first, second, and fourth ways of *ST* I, q. 2, a. 3.

First, material bodies are put in motion by being moved. Even when they are movers of other bodies, they are moved movers. God, however, is not moved or determined in his being by another reality, but is an unmoved mover, and an unchanged changer. Therefore, the divine nature is immaterial. More generally we should note that a physical body is a reality subject to motion and determination by another, and God transcends this kind of ontological dependency entirely.

Second, God is not a body, "because the first being must of necessity be in act, and in no way in potentiality" (*ST* I, q. 3, a. 1). Here we should think of potentiality as a source of imperfection, whether it pertains to the substance of a thing or its properties. A material being, for example, is in potency to substantial change by way of corruption, and is therefore subject to a limitation of perfection in the order of existence. Likewise, in the realm of accidents, the inactivity of a bodily thing can be altered, such as when water is made to boil. Any such actuation of a thing's potency implies a transformation from one state to another, by a kind of progression or alteration, through the actual causality of another. God, however, is the source of existence in all others, and is not therefore in potentiality to undergo actuation from any creature. He is pure actuality. It follows from this that he is not a material body.

One might think analogously of the actuation of the potency of life in a new living thing, a plant or an animal that can progressively grow to perfection, or the potentiality of the human mind and heart that can grow in understanding and virtue. There is no such potentiality in God, because God is not subject to transformation by another. He will not grow to a perfection-in-life that he does not yet possess, through his engagement with others. He is not learning or growing in virtue, but is pure actuality. God is, in his simplicity, a plenitude of perfection that is beyond all changing physical things, beyond all developing living things, and beyond all finite wisdom and love in created persons, but who is the source of all these. It is he who actuates them, from within the inmost of their own being and history, allowing them to move from potency to act (and not the inverse: as if creatures were to perfect God, who the cause of their being). His actuality is the ground and foundation of all that is and that undergoes change and development.

Third, based on the fourth way, we can say that God is the most noble reality, but the soul and intellect in creatures are more noble than the body, and God is more noble than any created spirit. Therefore, God is not a body.[10]

We should note the foundational conceptual iconoclasm inherent in St. Thomas's position. If God is not a body, then we cannot imagine God or form any sensible comparison of him. Although he is the producer of all physical, sensible beings, his nature is utterly beyond all sensate representation. Aquinas is thinking here simultaneously in both a deeply biblical way and in a deeply philosophical way, and he is indebted in part to the metaphysical iconoclasm of Moses Maimonides. In effect, Aquinas's teaching in this article enjoins us to "make no graven images" of the divine essence.

10. Thomas's fourth way in *ST* I, q. 2, a. 3, argues from the gradations in perfection in realities we experience to a transcendent source that is the cause of this scale of perfections. The presupposition here seems to be that immaterial reality has more inherent natural dignity and greater causal extension and efficacy than material substance does, so God cannot be a material substance, because of his transcendence of all finite created perfections.

Is God Composed of Form and Matter?

The answer to this question, posed in *ST* I, q. 3, a. 2, follows naturally from the answer to the previous one. If God does not have a body, then there is no matter in God. In this case, his nature contains no ontological composition of form and matter, a distinction found only in physical creatures.

The idea that each physical reality is composed of form and matter comes from Aristotle, of course, and not from divine revelation.[11] However, it accords with common sense realism and is concordant with scripture. Each physical being we observe is a specific kind of thing (having a formal nature), and is composed of material parts, subject to potential transformation and corruption. The world we live in is a world of human beings, aardvarks, orange trees, stars, and so forth. "Form" here denotes a wholistic metaphysical determination in each individual of a given kind that accounts for that being's substantial unity and natural integrity. The form is what provides organization from within to the compositional parts, giving them order within a larger whole. It perdures through time in the midst of changes. The substantial form of a human child when it is one month old is exactly the same twenty years later when the person is mature, because the reality is still "formally" human, and is in fact the very same concrete individual substance.[12] Such beings are also composed of matter, since they have material parts and possess an underlying potency that renders them physically alterable, divisible, and corruptible. Consequently it is realistic to affirm that every physical being is a composite of form and matter.

Why is there no such composition in God? Simply stated, God is pure actuality, so his divine nature has no material potency. He does not have a body that participates in the perfection of his natural form as our body participates in the perfection of our soul and spiritual operations. Instead, he is sovereignly perfect in all he is, as unparticipated goodness and being. God's nature does not realize its actions through embodied activities, as in the case of plants, animals, or humans. The perfection of his action stems from the perfection of his form or nature, which is immaterial. Epistemologically, this means we must think about God very differently than we do about any material being. We know the forms of material beings by abstracting their na-

11. See Aristotle, *Physics* 2.1–2 (192b9–194b15).
12. In a human being, the "form" that gives us our fundamental determination and human nature is our spiritual soul. For the soul as *forma corporis*, or form of the body, in Aquinas, see *ST* I, q. 76, a. 1.

tures from the consideration of multiple individuals. We grasp in a universal concept that there is a common nature proper to each person, aardvark, orange tree, or star. But God is not a material individual of a given kind existing alongside other such individuals. Based on the limits of our immediate experience, we cannot grasp his form in any way. Our concepts for his nature, then, cannot be abstracted univocally from sensate experience, but must be formulated analogically to speak of him in his unique transcendence.

Is There a Distinction of Individual and Essence, or Nature, in God?

Aquinas denies any composition in God of individuality and essence, or nature, in *ST* I, q. 3, a. 3. Why does this distinction not pertain in God's case?

In every created being we can identify a real distinction between the principle of nature and the principle of individuality. The principle of nature is what is common to all. Each human being, for example, is a rational animal. He or she possesses the same essential determination of being. Yet none of us could say that some individual human provides the very definition of what it is to be human (i.e., "Socrates is humanity"). If that were the case, when Socrates died or ceased to exist, the whole human race would cease to exist. In addition to our human nature, then, there is the principle of individuality. This is the irreducible individuality of substance that is proper and unique to us as persons, and which, as such, is not shared by the rest of the human race. We are born and we die individually. We can explain this individuation by appeal to our material singularity (there is designate matter proper to each person). Individuation also follows from our natural form itself, since each of us is an individual realization of what it is to be human (a singular human nature realized in a distinctive mode).[13] This is why on the one hand none of us is co-extensive with what it is to be human, and, on the other hand, there is something in each of us that is distinguishable from our common humanity. The real distinction of essence and individual is proper to every created nature.[14]

13. I am suggesting here that individuation in material substances follows not only from the designate matter of there material body but also from the ontological singularity of the form of each substance. In the case of the human being, for example, the matter of the body individuates, but the ontological singularity of the soul does as well. To be this individual person here, and not that one, is to be a unique ontological realization of human nature, one human being who is unique in both body and soul.

14. In his later work Aquinas holds that the distinction of individuation and essence applies

God is the cause of every individual created being and every natural kind. We can speak by analogy, then, of God having a divine nature, and of God being unique or individual. Nevertheless, he is not characterized by the distinction of nature and individual we find in creatures. This is true first of all because he is immaterial, without composition of matter and form, so he has no designate matter. He is not one God among others, like one orange tree among others or one human being among others. He alone is God. Likewise, the divine nature is incommunicable to all who are not God. This follows from our consideration of the second way, noted above. He whom we call God is alone the cause of all other things, the creatures that emanate forth from God, and the power to communicate being to created realities is proper to the divine nature alone. It follows from this that this nature is incommunicable and cannot itself be given to creatures. (They themselves would then be necessary being, and thus uncaused, which is contradictory to their being created.) Consequently we must say that God alone possesses his divine nature, and the composition of individual and essence that we find in creatures does not obtain in him. Rather, we must say that God is individuated by his nature. As scripture attests, he is not one God among others, nor are there multiple gods. His individuality and unique singularity are proper to his essence and nature.

This singularity of the divine nature is unimaginable for us, but that "unimaginability" is part of the point. What God "is" is utterly beyond the physical beings we normally experience. He does not fall within a larger set, as one individual creature who shares in a common lot with others. Only God is God. He alone possesses the divine nature.

---

not only to form-matter composites but also to angelic beings, albeit in a distinctive way. He famously holds that each angel is its own species of purely spiritual creature, so that in contrast to human beings each angel has a unique natural form. The form of each angel individuates it. Therefore, it would seem that no distinction of nature (or essence) and individual obtains in any separated substance. However, in *quodlibetal question* II, q. 2, a. 2, Aquinas argues that each angel has existence as something distinct from its essence, and therefore its individual existence has to be distinguished from its essence as such. The angel does not exist simply in virtue of its nature but participates in existence. Likewise, Aquinas notes that angelic properties are not ascribed to the angel's essence, but to the individual angel as such. Consequently, there is in each angel a real ontological distinction of essence and individuated mode of being. This type of distinction cannot obtain in the divine nature because of the latter's pure actuality and perfection of being. See *Thomas Aquinas's Quodlibetal Questions*, trans. T. Nevitt and B. Davies (Oxford: Oxford University Press, 2020).

*Is There a Composition of Essence and
Existence* (Essentia et Esse) *in God?*

The central article in Aquinas's treatment of divine simplicity is *ST* I, q. 3, a. 4. It addresses what he takes to be the most fundamental type of composition in created beings, more profound and universal than the form-matter distinction. This composition pertains to the distinction, found in *all* created beings, between their essence and their existence. He takes it to apply not only to all physical beings—ourselves included—but also to angels, that is, to separated substances who are created by God.[15]

The so-called real distinction between *esse* and *essentia* (existence and essence) is an important facet of Aquinas's thought, central to his metaphysics, and is also one of his more original philosophical contributions to the history of human thought. He develops this idea particularly in order to be able to think about what it means to say that all creatures receive their being—their existence—from God, and so "participate" in being or receive a share in being from another, while God himself is eternally subsistent by nature. God necessarily subsists of his own nature and essence as *Ipsum esse subsistens,* "Subsistent existence itself."

The first point that Aquinas makes in this famous article is that whatever a thing has besides its essence must be caused either by its essential principles or by an extrinsic agent. The argument proceeds as follows:

First, whatever a thing has besides its essence must be caused either by the constituent principles of that essence (like a property that necessarily accompanies the species—as the faculty of laughing is proper to a man—and is caused by the constituent principles of the species), or by some exterior agent—as heat is caused in water by fire. Therefore, if the existence of a thing differs from its essence, this existence must be caused either by some exterior agent or by its essential principles. Now it is impossible for a thing's existence to be caused by its essential constituent principles, for nothing can be the sufficient cause of its own existence, if its existence is caused. Therefore that thing, whose existence differs from its essence, must have its existence caused by another.

Aquinas here presupposes that existence, in all things we experience around us, is not identical with essence. There are several reasons to affirm this. First, as we noted in the previous chapter on analogy, existence is ascribed to every categorial mode of being (individuals, natures, quantities, qualities, etc.)

and is not found in only one kind of thing or one natural form. Therefore, existence is not identical with essence as such in anything we experience. Second, as noted in the second way, everything we experience has a cause of its being. It does not exist by essence or nature. Therefore there is a distinction of essence and existence in all things that come to be and that can be or not be. Likewise, existence cannot be a mere accident of the substance or a property derived from its essence, since existence is not reducible to accidents but is proper to every substance or individual itself. We do not merely say that the properties of Paul exist or that they receive their being from his substance, but that the individual substance Paul exists, and that he receives his existence as one who is caused to be in all that he is.

Let us presume, then, that existence is distinct from essence in all the realities we encounter, and that whatever a thing has besides its essence must be caused either by the essence itself or by an extrinsic agent. Clearly existence cannot be caused in a thing simply in virtue of its essence, so it must have an extrinsic cause. To illustrate Aquinas's point, we can take the example of a human being. The intrinsic principles of his or her essence are the body and the soul. The material body of a given person is certainly not the efficient cause of the existence of that person. We each receive existence or come into being as a living body, and we each go out of existence as a living body. Our bodies therefore are not the origin of our being. Nor is the formal principle the efficient cause of our being, that is, our souls do not cause us to come into being. Rather, our souls, like our bodies, are given existence. Each human being is a reality that receives existence in both soul and body from another or from others. It follows from this that there is a real distinction between what each of us is—our essence as a form-matter composite, as a human in both soul and body—and our existence, which is the act of being of our essence.

God, however, must be distinct from creatures in this respect. Creatures are characterized by a real distinction of essence and existence because they receive their existence from another. But God is the first efficient cause of being, the transcendent source of all existence. Therefore he cannot be one who receives being from another and cannot be characterized by a real distinction of essence and existence.

Aquinas's second argument, in *ST* I, q. 3, a. 4, appeals to the distinction of potency and act as applied to the distinction of essence and existence. Each created reality can exist in actuality or not exist in actuality. Its essence may be thought of, then, as a principle of potentiality, corresponding to its existence (*esse*), as a principle of actuality. Aquinas here understands *esse* as the *actus essendi* of the created reality, its act of being. Any given nature may be or not be, and if it does actually exist, this actual being occurs in virtue of the *esse* of the thing. For example, a given human being prior to his or her conception and creation, had the potential to exist in a given nature. When the person is conceived and created, however, the person receives existence, *esse*, so that his nature now exists in act. This deepest actuation of his person reaches down into the very roots of his concrete being, to all that he is. In speaking of the created *esse* of the person, then, we are indicating that he is given existence, so to speak, all the way down, in all that he is. Likewise, we can speak of his or her existence in act to denote that this existence is gratuitous. It is a kind of metaphysical gift that did not have to be. We have each received being as a gift from a higher source. But what is it that is given existence in each of us? What exists? It is a human being, a rational animal composed of body and soul. We see in each concrete human existent (*ens*) the human essence (*essentia*) of such and such person which exists in act (*esse*). The concrete existent is thus a composite entity, composed ontologically of both essence and existence.

As Aquinas notes in his second argument, however, God is pure actuality, the one who gives existence to all others, and who is not in potentiality to receive existence from another or others. As the primary source of all that is, he must possess the fullness of existence in pure actuality, in virtue of his divine nature. Consequently there is no possibility for him to be or not to be, and no real distinction of essence and existence that characterizes his nature. While creatures receive their being from God and therefore have an essence in potency to exist or not exist, God exists by nature as pure actuality in all that he is. In this respect, the divine nature is transcendent and simple when compared with creatures.

Aquinas's third argument is based on participated being. All realities that receive their being from another participate in existence. They do not have being by nature but partake of being. Yet, as we have seen, it cannot be the case that simply all realities receive their existence from another who gives them being. There must be something first that gives being to all the rest. In this case, however, not all realities simply participate in existence. There must be something first and transcendent that possesses being essentially or by nature. The one who gives being to others does not participate in being but is unparticipated being.

As we have seen above, then, Aquinas argues in this article that there can be no real distinction of existence and essence in God. First, he argues this precisely because God cannot receive existence from another but is the first efficient cause of existence, who actively sustains all created things in being actually, even now and indeed forever, so long as there are creatures. God is the sovereign giver of being, from whom and by whom all that is receives its being, and who infinitely transcends all limited being.

Second, existence gives actuality to an essence, so that the distinction of essence and existence in material and immaterial beings denotes a composition. In every created reality, the being in question receives its existence, so that it might or might not exist. But God is pure actuality and cannot cease to be or in any way be diminished. He possesses no potentiality, especially potentiality of this deepest kind. God, because he is pure actuality, cannot not exist.

Third, God does not participate in existence received from another, but is he in whom all else that exists participates. He must therefore be existence in his very essence. We can say that it is of God's nature to exist. This is both a deeply mysterious and an entirely rational truth.

With the treatment of the composition found in creatures between essence and existence, and its negation in God's case, we have hit upon the deepest dimension of divine simplicity. God's essence is identical with his existence. He is not in potentiality to exist but is pure actuality. His divine nature is not caused or received. It exists necessarily. God simply is, and he gives being to all others. He is, in the words of Exodus 3:14, "He who is."

Is There a Composition of Genus and Difference in God?

In ST I, q. 3, a. 5, Aquinas argues that there is no composition of genus and specific difference in God. Genus and difference are logical terms used for arranging our concepts; they are not terms that pertain to ontological distinctions, strictly speaking. The genera of being are denoted by the various categories of Aristotle, which we have noted above. Substances, natures, qualities, quantities: each of these categories can be said logically to denote a given genus of being. There are, in addition, sub-genera within genera. For example, within the genus of substances in general, there is the genus "animal" and the species "man." Or within the genus of "qualities," we could speak of the sub-genus "color" and the species "blue." "Difference" is under-

stood in this context as that which differentiates one kind of thing from another within the genus, creating logical subsets. The difference "rational," for
example, is a specific difference that marks the human race out as a species
within the larger genus of animals.

Obviously this set of categories, though conceptual, is based on and reflects distinctions that can be found in reality itself. Logical categories therefore reveal something ontological, even if we should not say that there is in
each human being a real distinction of genus and species. In the context of
the theology of God, Aquinas is asking how we designate or name God *logically*.

Aquinas, in this article, presumes the transcendental character of existence itself, which, like truth and goodness, is common to every category of
being, to every genus, to each individual thing that exists. All participate in
being, and so we can speak of *ens commune* or common being, as a transcendental, as something common to all finite beings. He notes first that every
composition of genus and species presupposes a composition of potency
and act. A given genus of being (living beings) is one potential realization of
being distinct from others (non-living), and so characterized by distinction
and limitation. Specific differences realize distinctions within the various
genera, as act to potency (e.g., animals are specifically different from other
living things because they have actual sensate knowledge). God, however,
is purely actual in existence, so there can be no generic potency in him, as
there is in any particular genus of being. God's nature is not contained in a
genus. Likewise, God's essence is his existence, so if he were contained in a
genus, then existence as such would be contained in a genus, which is clearly false. Or if he were contained in a genus, his existence would have to lack
something found in another genus, in which case there would have to obtain in him a real distinction of essence and existence. None of these options
are possible.

The conclusion Aquinas is pointing us toward in this article is decidedly apophatic. God is not denoted logically as having any distinctive genus or species of being. He cannot be indicated semantically in any collection alongside others, such as "giraffe," "tree," "blue," "musical" or "rational."
Rather, God is the author of all that is, of all the genera and species of being.
Consequently, he stands outside all the normal categories of things. It also
follows from Aquinas's line of reasoning that God is not "common being."
He is not the existence that is present in all things, even across the various

genera of being. For example, God is not some kind of created cosmic sub-stratum, a murky "existence" common to all physical and spiritual things, an immanent principle holding all things together. Rather, God is the source of common being, the unknown God who gives existence to all that is. For this reason, he remains transcendent of things that are given being and distinct from them, even as he is utterly immanent to them in a hidden way. God is a mystery that eludes our logic, not because he is illogical, but because he is the founder of all logic, beyond all comprehension.

Is There a Composition of Substance and Accidents in God?

Aquinas in his final negation teaches that there is no composition in God of substance and accidents.[16] God does not have any properties in himself that are other than his essence, accidental features of his person that can come or go, or develop, or which can be distinct from what he is essentially and eternally.[17] Why must this be the case? The main reason follows from our previous argument. God's essence is identical with his existence, and he possesses in himself the plenitude of being. If God could progressively develop accidentally by properties, then his essence would be subject to qualification by new forms of existence and consequently would not be identical with his perfection of existence. He would actuate a potency, and in doing so cause something secondary to come to be within himself, as a *causa sui*. However, God is pure actuality and underived being. God, then, does not contain any real distinction of substance and accidental proper-ties. This does not mean that God is merely static or inert. Qualities like stasis and inertness pertain to things in potency not to what is pure actu-ality. Nor does God's perfect actuality impede him from producing new ef-fects or undertaking new initiatives in creation, that are wise, virtuous, or loving. God can and does do novel things in his creation, and so can be said to act dynamically. However, when God produces new effects in his cre-ation in ways that reflect his wisdom, benevolence, and love, he does so be-cause of what God is essentially in himself, not because of any new acciden-tal perfections or gradual actuations that he acquires in the process. If we

16. See *ST* I, q. 3, a. 6.
17. See, too, Augustine's affirmation, discussed in part 1, that there are only substantial and relative predications for God. The predications for God that would represent modifications and so be accidental for creatures are in God's case substantial predications: Augustine, *The Trinity*, 5.

speak, then, of God as wise, benevolent, or loving, we are inevitably speaking not of properties that in some way qualify what God was previously or apart from these attributes. Rather we are speaking only of God's very essence. It is of the essence of God to be wise, and to be love. He is wisdom and love substantially.

God Is Altogether Simple.

By a recapitulation of previous arguments, *ST* I, q. 3, a. 7, makes the point that God is *omnino simplex*, altogether simple. In the incomprehensible actuality and richness of his being he is without those forms of ontological composition, complexity, and dependence that we have seen are characteristic of creatures. All lesser realities imitate him only very imperfectly, as finite beings participating in something utterly beyond them that has given them a partial share in its own plenitude of being and life.

At the term of our investigation we see that the divine nature is mysterious because of its alterity. When learning to speak of God we also undertake a structured form of unlearning. He is not a material reality, a species among others, an individual of a common kind, a being among beings, or an agent who lives and develops by relating to us. In saying that God is simple we say something true, then, referring to God as he is himself. However, the reality denoted transcends our ordinary human experience and eludes all our typical modes of denoting all creatures. God's essence in virtue of its simplicity defies our facile conceptual grasp.

Does God Enter into Composition with Created Things?

In *ST* I, q. 3, a. 8, St. Thomas reminds us that God is utterly distinct from the created order and cannot be conceived of as the sum total of created beings. Consequently, the affirmation of God as Trinity excludes various forms of pantheism. We will examine in the final part of this book the post-Hegelian theologies of divine kenosis, in which God subjects himself freely to a historical process of diremptive movement between contraries, and develops by means of historical evolution, in virtue of his human nature.[18] At this juncture we can simply note that the hominization of God in

---

18. Cf. Georg W. F. Hegel, *The Phenomenology of Spirit* (*The Phenomenology of Mind*), trans. J. B. Baillie (Overland Park, Kans.: Diigreads.com Publishing, 2009), 18: "The Truth is the whole. The whole, however, is merely the essential nature reaching its completeness through the process

the incarnation does not entail a change in his transcendent divine nature. The eternal Son assumes a human nature personally, but he retains two natures. His divine nature is not confused with or identical to his human nature. The divine simplicity likewise excludes certain conclusions of process metaphysics—as one finds in the philosophy of Albert North Whitehead, or in the theories of Open Theism—in which God is undergoing continual change in relation with and reaction to the world, in an inward historical time within God's own nature, like a kind of duration of consciousness.[19] Such theories, for all their conceptual sophistication and historical interestingness, render obscure a profound understanding of the mysterious transcendence of God in his simplicity and perfection, and also fail to understand adequately God's identification with us in his incarnation as human.

CAN GOD KNOW AND LOVE US
IF HIS NATURE IS SIMPLE?

We noted above that some analytic philosophers object to the doctrine of divine simplicity because, they claim, it impedes genuine understanding of the God of the bible.[20] The God of the bible knows contingent truths

---

of its own development. Of the Absolute it must be said that it is essentially a result, that only at the end is it what it is in very truth." See the thematic treatment in the later work, "The Consummate Religion," vol 3 of *Lectures on the Philosophy of Religion, The Lectures of 1827*, ed. P. C. Hodgson, trans. by R. F. Brown, P. C. Hodgson, J. M. Stewart (Berkeley: University of California Press, 2006), 452–69. Hegel inverts, as it were, the perspective of the Tübingen school regarding the communication of idioms to Christ (the predication of divine and human terms). Whereas they speculated on how or in what way the attributes of the deity might be communicated to the humanity (omnipresence, omnipotence), Hegel speculates on how the attributes of the humanity might be communicated to the divinity. The condition for this to occur is the capacity of the deity as spirit to self-identify with its ontological contrary by way of free, self-exploratory diremption. The most famous case is that pertaining to the human death of Christ, which Hegel posits as an ontological reality pertaining to the very being of God as spirit, who is subject to "death" in the divine nature. This occurs internal to a process of dialectical reconciliation in the very life of God, which is accomplished in the resurrection, wherein God as spirit is revealed to be and reaches self-actualization as love. I will return to this thesis in part 4 of this book.

19. See Albert North Whitehead, *Process and Reality: An Essay in Cosmology*, ed. D. R. Griffin and D. W. Sherburne (New York: The Free Press, 1978).

20. For broader critical engagements with the doctrine of divine simplicity, see for example, Alvin Plantinga, *Does God Have a Nature?* (Milwaukee, Wisc.: Marquette University Press, 1980); Christopher Hughes, *On a Complex Theory of a Simple God: An Investigation in Aquinas' Philosophical Theology* (Ithaca: Cornell University Press, 1987); Richard Swinburne, *The Christian God*; William Hasker, *Metaphysics and the Tri-Personal God* (Oxford: Oxford University Press, 2013). These thinkers make a number of criticisms of the doctrine of divine simplicity, including (1) Plantinga's influential objection that Aquinas's theory has as a consequence that it makes God into an abstract

and performs actions that he is not necessitated by his nature to perform. He is personally responsive to human beings and loves them, which entails God's making himself really relative to creatures. Neither of these activities of God would be possible if the divine nature were simple.

I will respond to these objections briefly by articulating three contrary perspectives. First, one should note that there is no incompatibility between the affirmation that the divine nature is simple and the affirmation that God (as he is depicted in scripture) knows the world, that he performs actions not necessitated by his nature, and that he acts in novel and dynamic ways out of love for human beings. Without anticipating later arguments that are developed below, we can state at this juncture that not only is it the case that God as Creator can know and love all things perfectly in a way no other can, but that we understand best how God does so only if we also understand the simplicity of his nature. The reason is evident from the arguments given above. If the divine nature is not composed of essence and existence, then God is his own existence essentially and, by that very measure, is plenary being, pure actuality. If this is the case, all created being derives from him, from his own knowledge and love of himself. Far from sequestering him in a compartmental isolation from creation, this perfection of simple knowledge and love is omni-comprehensive and all-inclusive. God can know all

object, (2) the objection that distinct properties cannot be identical, (3) the objection that God cannot be his existence, (4) the objection that God cannot be free if his nature is simple. For helpful responses to Plantinga and others on these topics, see Lawrence Dewan, "Saint Thomas, Alvin Plantinga, and the Divine Simplicity," *Modern Schoolman* 66, no. 2 (1989): 141–51; Jeffrey Brower, "Making Sense of Divine Simplicity," *Faith and Philosophy* 25, no. 1 (2008): 3–30; Brian Davies, "Simplicity," in *The Cambridge Companion to Christian Philosophical Theology*, ed. C. Taliaferro and C. Meister (Cambridge: Cambridge University Press, 2010), 31–45; Eleonore Stump, "Simplicity and Aquinas's Quantum Metaphysics" in *Die Metaphysik des Aristoteles im Mittelalter: Rezeption und Transformation, ed.* Gerhard Krieger (Berlin: De Gruyter, 2016), 191–210. It should be recalled that every attribute we ascribe to God is taken from "merely" human abstraction and has to be applied to God with that qualification and is filtered by Aquinas through a special theory of analogical predication which is designed, among other things, to make it clear that God has no Platonic formal properties. (I will return to this point in the next chapter). In addition, there are non-trivial ascriptions of properties to God in substantive ways that seem to fall into the same or similar difficulties on Plantinga's account, namely from 1 John 4:16: "God is Love." The apostle here appears wantonly pre-analytic. It is true that for Aquinas, God is not only *ipsum esse subsistens*, but also an *ens*, i.e., a denoted concretely personal being, but it matters just as much that we say that God is *ipsum esse subsistens*, to make clear a differentiation. All created beings have their existence from another, while God is wholly different, because he has in himself the plenitude of being and can alone give and diffuse being to others. Without this qualification, there are not inconsiderable risks of depicting God merely as an *ens* among other beings, a highly qualified knowledgeable and powerful individual, who thinks propositionally, has beliefs, self-actuates by contingent actions, and develops his life through time—forms of anthropomorphism abundant in analytic literature.

that is and love all that is precisely as the cause of its very existence and out of the perfection of his own goodness. This entails that God alone in his simplicity is utterly present to all that is in the most intimate of its existence (because he causes it to be) and that he is present to it precisely in his perfection of infinite wisdom and goodness, in virtue of what he is essentially. Consequently, God's essence is never at any remove from creatures. This set of ideas, which we will explore further below, is indeed reflective of biblical realism, which affirms the unique transcendence, perfection, and presence of the Creator.

Second, the theory of divine relativity that some analytic theists develop as an alternative to the traditional doctrine of simplicity has repercussions for their understanding of the divine nature that are problematic. Some posit, for example, a divine nature that, precisely because it is ontologically relative to and qualified by creation, is also temporal and developmental. God exists in time because he undergoes durational states of consciousness as he learns from creation, interacts with it, and wills new things for it. It follows logically that God evolves from lesser to greater in knowledge and love, and is enriched by his engagement with creation. In this case, it would seem that God receives at least some non-trivial characteristics of his being (such as being fully knowledgeable or truly loving) from engagement with the creation, and therefore depends upon it for his perfection. In his case he not uniquely a communicator of being, but also the receiver of being. Since he cannot be both under the same aspect at the same time, it must be the case that God and the world exist within a larger ontic system, in which both are mutually perfective of one another. This position seems to make God virtually a part of the cosmos, akin to a world-soul. Such a vision is philosophically anthropomorphic and theologically un-biblical, no matter how well intentioned. It obscures true knowledge of the transcendent Creator.

Finally, this view has non-trivial consequences for Trinitarian theology. If the nature of God is determined in new and ongoing ways by his relation to his creation, how are we to understand the unity of nature present in the three persons, and their distinction according to eternal relations of origin? Let us posit that there are truly distinct persons in God, each of whom is a genuine subject of divine knowledge and love, *and* that the persons are distinguished by their relations of origin such that each possesses the same divine essence as God, *and* that the essence of God is altered accidentally by its relations to creatures. In this case we must also affirm one of two things.

First, we might say that the new properties that God acquires naturally over time in relation to creatures differentiate the persons of the Trinity (because the perennial intra-Trinitarian relations of origin are determined by particular historical relations of God to creatures). In this case the Trinity comes into being or depends for its identity upon the historical economy of creation, an idea we will take issue with in the final part of this book. Or, second, we might say that the three persons are not fully constituted in their eternal unity prior to their engagement with history, because they also share equally and identically in all the accidental attributes of the divine nature that are acquired down through history, in God's development of becoming in relation to creatures. In this second case, then, a central principle of unity, by virtue of which the three persons are one (various divine qualities that each person possesses in common), is subject to historical development as God engages with creatures. Consequently, the *unity* of the Trinity *at least in part* cannot be constituted prior to the creation and *cannot even ever be fully constituted*, so long as God continually relates to his creation in ontological dependency. It is unclear in what way traditional theism (which posits God as the Creator of all else that is) is truly maintained if it is understood in this sense. It would seem rather that the godhead that is shared in equally by the three persons depends for its ongoing developmental identity upon created things.

In addition, however, we should consider that it is the divine nature that is communicated from the Father to the Son (from all eternity) as a prerequisite for any minimal affirmation of divine unity of the Father and the Son. But if the divine nature is subject to gradual ontological enrichment in virtue of its development in relation to creation, then how can the divine nature that the Father transmits to the Son as the principle of their unity not depend upon historical relations to creation for its constitution (at least in part) even "when" the Father generates the Son and spirates the Spirit? If this is the case, then we revert to something like a Hegelian conception of God: God is not constituted as Trinity "from all eternity" but only through God's historical relationship to creatures. Again in this case, God is really a historical process that is still developing in ongoing relation to the creation. This is an unappealing viewpoint for those who wish to preserve any coherent version of classical monotheism, based on the revelation of the Old and New Testaments.

CONCLUSION

Having discussed the divine simplicity so as to establish by way of a series of negations what God is super-eminently, we can follow St. Thomas by turning to the next two divine names, divine perfection and divine goodness. It is especially important to examine the divine perfection after the divine simplicity, since, with creatures, simplicity often signifies less perfection than complexity does, whereas, with God, precisely the reverse is the case.

14
——— : ———

Divine Perfection and Goodness

In most of the realities we experience, perfection requires a certain complexity rather than simplicity. Horses or dolphins are more complex living things than protozoa, or single-cell bacteria. And they are also, for that reason, more perfect living things. Developmental perfection brings with it greater complexity. This is not the case with God, however. Accordingly, so as to deepen our understanding of the reasons for this difference between God and ourselves, we next turn to the mystery of divine perfection. Aquinas's treatment, in the *ST*, of the perfection of God is succinct but incisive. It contains some of his most important and beautiful reflections on God. After the consideration of divine perfection, we will then turn to the Thomistic topic of goodness in general and divine goodness, as depicted in *ST* I, qq. 5–6. As we will see, goodness highlights the aspect of desirability inherent in the perfection of God's being.

Whether God Is Perfect?

In *ST* I, q. 4, a. 1, Aquinas begins his analysis by arguing that matter in physical realities is a source of potentiality and indetermination. The material reality, because it is material, is capable of being transformed into another state. This capacity is indicative of limitation and ontological imperfection. In effect, wherever there is a form-matter composite, the reality in question exists in actuality and is the source of dynamic activity in virtue of its formal nature, while it is characterized by not-yet-realized potency and static non-activity in virtue of its matter. Consequently, the perfection of a material reality is realized most fundamentally in virtue of its natural form, while its material constitution necessarily implies finite realization and ontological limitation. Given that this is the case, the natural form of a given reality must actuate its internal perfection in matter over time and through the gradual diversification of its material potency. We might say that the more perfect the form, the more unified and noble its self-expression, in and through a variety of material parts. If this is the case, then a material reality is perfected by its ornateness: the complexity of the ways the matter is structured or unfolded to embody a deeper and richer, more perfect form. For material beings, then, it follows that a greater perfection requires a greater complexity. As matter is actuated in more complex ways by form, material bodies acquire more intensive perfections.[1]

What, then, is perfection, ontologically speaking, and how can we identify a definition of it that is sufficiently adaptable as to apply not only to material beings, but also to immaterial realities, and eventually, by analogy, to God? Commenting on this article, Thomas de Vio Cajetan interprets the universal ontology of perfection in two ways: on the one hand, as a quality, and, on the other, as a mode or state of being of a thing, which manifests its qualities to a greater degree.[2] For example, a living animal reaches the perfection of biological maturity as an animal when it can engender one of its own kind. Biologically perfect horses can engender in turn another horse, and thereby perpetuate the species. This capacity to reproduce is a quality of living animals, but it is not static. Rather, perfection is a modal quality that can and does often emerge through a progression of gradual states. The horse does not reproduce when it is newly born, nor in its infancy and youth, but only when it has reached an animal maturity. The perfection of the horse is manifest gradually in and through successive states.

We could just as well speak analogously about the gradual development of the human eye, or the gradual formation of muscles and the capacity to run, the formation of flowers and fruits on various trees, or, in the human

---

1. This perfecting actuation can be more quantitative or more qualitative. If quantitative, it can be more intense (the more intense heat of a star), or more extensive (the more quantitatively complex physical body of a more perfectly powerful animal). If qualitative, the perfection of the matter can be diverse in its properties, in view of a coordinated activity, like the organic complexity of the human brain and nervous system, in sensing, or that of the organ of the human eye, in the act of seeing.

2. See the commentary on *ST* I, q. 4, a. 1, in *Summa theologiae*, vols. 4–12 of *Sancti Thomae Aquinatis opera omnia* (Rome: Leonine Edition, 1888–1906).

spiritual world, the gradual emergence of qualities that allow one to think mathematically, or to act with prudence, or to pray habitually in virtue of a genuine interior life of prayer, or to think about God philosophically, all of which can develop over time. These are gradually emergent perfections. But they also imply, in each case, the actuation of a potentiality in things: material potentiality in the water that is boiled to reach the perfect temperature, living potentiality in the horse that learns to gallop and eventually produces a like kind, spiritual potentiality in the person studying mereology, or developing a habit of spiritual prayer. In all of these movements, there is a transition from potency to act.

In what sense, then, can we say by analogy that God is perfect? Aquinas again underscores the radical otherness of God with respect to creatures. He argues that there is no principle of progressive development in God, who is the first cause of all actuality: "Now God is the first principle, not material, but in the order of efficient cause, which must be most perfect. For just as matter, as such, is merely potential, an agent, as such, is in the state of actuality. Hence, the first active principle must needs be most actual, and therefore most perfect; for a thing is perfect in proportion to its state of actuality, because we call that perfect which lacks nothing of the mode of its perfection" (*ST* I, q. 4, a. 1). The *triplex via* is at work in the argumentation. As the primary cause, God is (1) the *cause* of all perfections in creatures. (2) *Negatively*, God lacks any of the imperfections encountered in creatures that originate from their wellspring of potency, whether material or spiritual. (3) Therefore, God is *eminently perfect*. His nature is perfectly actual and transcendent of the limitations that characterize creatures. He is the incomprehensible first origin of actuality behind every created actuality.[3]

Are the Perfections of All Things in God?

In *ST* I, q. 4, a. 2, Aquinas highlights two distinctions that help illustrate how the perfections of all things are in God. The first distinction is that between univocal and equivocal efficient causality. The second is that between pure perfections and mixed perfections. Let us consider each distinction briefly.

---

3. See likewise Aquinas, *De ver.*, q. 2, a. 3, ad 13: "Perfection ... is used more negatively of God than positively. Hence, He is said to be perfect because nothing at all is lacking to Him, not because there is something in Him which was in potency to perfection and is perfected by something else which is its act. Consequently, there is no passive potency in God."

When Aquinas discusses efficient causality he sometimes distinguishes between univocal and equivocal causality. This is the case in q. 4, a. 2. Univocal causality denotes causality by a being that produces an effect of identical kind or species. So, for example, a horse engenders another horse of the same species, or a plant gives rise to another plant of the same kind. This is a univocal cause because we call the effect by the same name as the cause, because of a unity of essence or nature.[4]

Equivocal causality, meanwhile, implies a likeness between the cause and the effect, where the cause is not of the same species or kind as the effect. In this case, the cause transmits a property to the effect even though the two do not partake of the same nature. For example, the sun is not a living being and does not transmit its own life to others, but it does impart an effect to living things as an equivocal cause, transmitting heat and light to plants and animals, providing them with a life-sustaining environment. The sun is, then, a cause of the perfection of living creatures due to its superior perfection in a given order (its perfection in the order of heat and light), which are necessary for the sustaining of life.[5]

Obviously Aquinas does not hold that God is a univocal cause of creatures, since he does not communicate to them his being as God or his divine nature. Rather, God is their equivocal cause, in the sense that he is the transcendent efficient cause who gives perfections to creatures, but who does not share a common specific nature with any of them. In fact, as Aquinas will make clear in the next article (ST I, q. 4, a. 3), God does not share even a common genus with creatures (as, for instance, we might say that the sun and living things are both physical bodies). Nor does God even share a common trans-generic perfection, such as being, with them, as when we say that the sun and plants are both beings. In a certain sense, for Aquinas, God does not exist, in the sense that God does not participate in existence alongside creatures, nor is God the being common to plants and the sun, as if he were

4. It is true that according to modern evolutionary theory, and its accompanying genetic evidence, various natural kinds of beings can give rise to other natural kinds, and Aquinas is not aware of this aspect of natural history, but we can simply suggest here that without some notion of univocal causality in the generation of living beings one cannot depict sufficiently the kind of natural "sameness" over time required to arrange a given biological species in the same taxonomy either prior to or subsequent to a genetic and evolutionary change of natural kinds. In other words, something like Aquinas's notion of univocal causality of living beings is not only compatible with but in a sense presupposed by any intelligible modern evolutionary account of the natural history of living beings.

5. Aquinas does not hold, as Aristotle did, that the stars are alive.

the being of the universe. Rather, God is the equivocal cause of the existence of creatures, that is, the hidden and unknown origin of their being. He is the cause of all that participates in existence, whether this being pertains to the sun, to living things, or, indeed, to any created thing whatsoever.

Ultimately, this is why we can attribute perfections to him only in a very particular, analogical manner. God, as the transcendent cause of all things, does not share in the being of any of his creatures, even as all his creatures participate, albeit in diverse ways, in his perfections, in a manner only remotely similar to how life on earth is nourished by the life-giving rays of the sun.

The next distinction St. Thomas takes up in this article is that of mixed versus pure perfections. Mixed perfections are those that are in some way bound up in their very manner of being with the material world and with the potentiality of finite, created existence. An example of a perfection of this kind would be the perfection of reason in a physical being, like the perfection of the detective who solves murders (Holmes, Brown, etc.), or that of the doctor who cures the patient. The kind of intellectual perfection in question reaches its perfection only within the context of a complex set of material conditions. Other examples drawn from lower levels in the hierarchy of being would include the horse capable of running and jumping in the steeple chase, or the plant capable of flowering and producing fruits.

Such mixed perfections cannot be properly attributed to God without qualification, as if God were literally and properly speaking a genius detective or an able doctor, a noble animal, or a flowering tree. The reason is that such perfections are *essentially* related to material existence, and so their attribution to God, who is not a physical body, is necessarily merely metaphorical. A metaphor denotes God by a likeness of effects, without indicating an analogical perfection term proper to the divine nature. We can speak of human nature as essentially good and of the divine nature as essentially good, by proper analogy. We can speak of Holmes as inductive or the doctor as medical, univocally, but we cannot speak of the divine nature as inductive or medical in the proper sense. Nevertheless, metaphors can function as significant images of God that indirectly make sense of features of God's nature and activity. We might speak meaningfully, for example, of God as a divine physician in order to indicate metaphorically the good effects of his healing power. The metaphorical likeness is made by an analogy of effects, rather than an analogy of essence. The effects of a doctor's healing are like the effects of God's healing, but God is not literally or essentially a physician. The ontological basis for the metaphorical attribution is causal. God in his wisdom and power has created all the realities we might use metaphorically to denote him (detectives, physicians, horses, plants and so on). He is the source, therefore, of all mixed perfections of form-matter composites, that is, of embodied beings. Such materially realized perfections, even in their limited way, indirectly indicate various of God's intrinsic perfections, such as his wisdom and power.

Pure perfections, meanwhile, are perfections of being and of the spiritual life found in creatures, that of themselves need not imply any intrinsic limitation or imperfection. For this reason, they are perfections that can be attributed to God in his perfect actuality, without a trace of potentiality or limitation. Perfections of this kind include being, unity, truth, goodness, knowledge, love, justice, and mercy. Such perfections can be attributed analogically to God in himself without any metaphorical content. God in his perfection truly is *Ipsum esse subsistens*. He is in himself perfectly wise, perfectly just and merciful, and so on.

It should be noted that none of the perfections of creatures, whether pure or mixed, can be said to add ontologically to the perfection of God. Rather, the absolute perfection of God is the origin and ground of all limited perfections in creatures, which proceed from God and which participate in his perfection. The diverse finite perfections in creatures imperfectly manifest the unique divine perfection, as the colors of the spectrum refract out from pure white light when they pass through a prism. The prism adds nothing to the light—in any event, it is only passively dependent upon the activity of the light—but it gives, as it were, an outward, participated expression to different aspects of the light's otherwise simple and undivided perfection.

Can Any Creature Be Like God?

In *ST* I, q. 4, a. 3, St. Thomas appeals to the distinction between univocal causes and equivocal causes in order to speak about the similitude, or likeness, between creatures and God. In what way can creatures be said to be like God? In the first place, creatures obviously cannot be said to be like God univocally, e.g., as one human being resembles another in natural kind. Creatures are not of the same species as God. They do not partake of the nature of God.

In the second place, if creatures resemble God as an effect resembles its *equivocal* cause, then they do so even here only in a very extraordinary way. For, ultimately, creatures do not partake of a generic likeness with God either. Thus, when the sun generates heat in a living being, this implies the participation of the living being in a generic property of the sun. Both are, generically speaking, physical bodies in the cosmos. And so too, both partake, generically speaking, of the same quality of heat, albeit in differing degrees, the net result being that living things are warm, but less warm than the sun. But creatures cannot resemble the perfection of God in this way, since they do not partake of a common genus with God. God is not another substance or kind of being among us, no matter how general the category of likeness. Rather, God is the unknown cause of the existence of every genus of being, of all kinds of things that are, insofar as he gives to each its existence and its perfection.

For this reason, Aquinas's conclusion is that, although creatures in their multifarious perfections *do resemble* God, they nevertheless do so neither in essence and nature, nor in genus. Rather, they resemble God "only according to some sort of analogy; as existence is common to all. In this way all created things, so far as they are beings, are like God as the first and universal principle of all being."[6] God does not partake of the transcendental features of all things that exist, but he is the origin of their being, goodness, and truth, and, therefore, they resemble him as the universal cause of being. Thus, we can ascribe the perfection names (like being and goodness) to God supremely, as denoting perfections that must exist in God, but we understand these perfections only imperfectly, and we do not know them as they exist in God per se. All this is to say that the perfect essence of God eludes our comprehension and complete understanding.

DIVINE GOODNESS

God's perfection is closely related to his goodness, because, to the extent that a thing attains perfection, it achieves a kind of goodness and is called good. This leads to the question, what is goodness in general, and what does it mean to speak of the goodness of God? Aquinas treats the first question in *ST* I, q. 5, and the second in *ST* I, q. 6.

6. *ST* I, q. 4, a. 3.

In its basic structure, q. 5, aa. 1–4, functions as a synoptic treatise on the good, considered metaphysically. It asks the question: What is goodness? Q. 5, aa. 5–6 then serves to interpret previous traditional Christian teaching concerning goodness. Q. 5, a. 5 addresses Augustine's speculation that goodness consists in the "mode, species and order" of a thing. Aquinas interprets this in light of his own understanding of goodness. In a. 6, he then goes on to discuss a traditional distinction of the good (taken from St. Ambrose) into (a) the good as virtuous or noble, (b) the good as useful, and (c) the good as pleasant. After this, St. Thomas turns, in q. 6, a. 1, to the goodness of God in himself, that is, the divine goodness. Q. 6, aa. 2–4 then goes on to treat of the goodness of God both in its relation to the goodness of creatures, and as distinct from them.

In what follows, we will concern ourselves especially with q. 5, aa. 1 and 4, and thereafter with the whole of q. 6.

Does Goodness Differ from Being?

In *ST* I, q. 5, a. 1, Aquinas argues that we should interpret goodness in reference to being. A thing is metaphysically good because it has existence, and because of the existence in it of certain properties and perfections. In interpreting goodness in terms of being, Aquinas is appropriating and reinterpreting in his own way the Aristotelian understanding of goodness, which depicts the good in terms of being and actuality, as well as in terms of perfection and teleology.[7] This account differs notably from that of Plato in the *Republic* and serves as an alternative to theories of various Neoplatonists, especially Plotinus, who see the one or the good as something beyond being, superior to being, and, in general, above all existence as supra-existent.[8]

On Aquinas's understanding, goodness adds the note of desirability to being.[9] Goodness can be said to be related to desire in two senses. The first sense is intrinsic in designation: it pertains to a tendency in the thing itself, a desire of its being. Aquinas claims that all that exists, even non-rational liv-

---

7. See Aristotle's *Nicomachean Ethics*, 1.6; *Metaphysics*, 9.8–9; 12.4–5.

8. See Plato's discussion about the sun of the good in relation to the intelligible forms, in the *Republic*, bk. 6, 508a–509c, and on the "form" of the good, 505a2–507b10; also Plotinus, *The Enneads*, trans. S. MacKenna (Burdett, N.Y.: Larson Publications, 1992), 5.5.13: "Thus is revealed to us The Primarily existent, the Good, above all that has being, good unalloyed, containing nothing in itself, utterly unmingling, all-transcending, cause of all."

9. See *ST* I, q. 5, a. 1: "It is clear that goodness and being are the same really. But goodness presents the aspect of desirableness, which being does not present."

ing things and physical non-living things, are characterized by natural inclinations or teleological orientations that are proper to their very natures. Of
course, he does not think that non-sensate physical realities have sensate appetites or rational volition. (He explicitly denies this.) Rather, he thinks that
beings act in various ways to achieve stable forms of perfection over time.
The tree "desires" to thrive and bear fruit. It tends toward the accomplishment of its nature. Fire tends to emit heat and light, and so it can heat or il-
luminate water or other physical bodies with which it comes into contact.
Even chemical compounds and atoms have stable and predictable properties, outcomes of their natures that allow us to categorize them under various taxonomies. This is the intrinsic account of goodness as "desire": all realities have certain tendencies inscribed into their very natures by which they
tend to their own perfection.

The second sense in which goodness is related to desire has to do with
the communicability of the good to others. When a thing attains a kind of
perfection, it can perfect others by communicating to them some effect of its
goodness. This is where the Aristotelian maxim "the good is that at which all
things aim" can be read as "the good is that which all things desire."[10] Realities that come to perfection alter the realities around them. The more a reality is perfect (in any given genus) the more it communicates its perfection, fa-
cilitating in turn the desire or tendency toward the good in those that receive
the communication. For example, perfect sunlight provides the right conditions for the growth of organic life. Analogously, a very good teacher is like
a light who has the capacity to communicate the truth to others, and facilitates in them the love of the truth. Or a preacher of *sacra doctrina* may communicate truth about God and incite in others knowledge and love of God.
A virtuous, affable person who exhibits interpersonal love for another calls
forth love of friendship from the other, and in turn invites the other to be
friendly and virtuous. When animals achieve mature perfection they attract
other animals of like kind who are drawn to them to seek to reproduce with
them. Good specimens of plants produce viable offspring that in turn thrive
and communicate life to others. They also act as a good biological source of
nourishment to animals, as plants and animals are a good resource for human
beings. Even merely physical, natural things—when they emit or embody a
stable order according to their properties and natures in and through pro-

10. See Aristotle, *Nic. Ethics*, 1.1 (1094a1–3).

cesses of change—provide a good environment for living things, and manifest a kind of intelligibility that the human mind admires and finds good in some way. We can love the goodness and beauty of the cosmos and the world of nature, based on properties we admire in the things themselves.

Aquinas, in *ST* I, q. 5, a. 1, ad 1, also interprets the ontology of goodness by appeal to notions of actuality and potentiality. For Aristotle and for Aquinas, there are different modes of being in act and being in potentiality in a given substance or being.[11] First, there is the being in act of *a substance as such*, which can be in act or merely in potentiality. This is sometimes called a substance's *primary act.*[12]

Then, there is the actuality and potentiality of the *operations* of a substance. These are sometimes called *secondary acts*. These acts are accidental properties that can exist or not exist *in a being*. They are not substantial, but in some way qualify a being, giving it properties that perfect it to the extent that they exist or not. A human person exists in act whether he is reasonably just or not, but if he becomes reasonably just, he begins to exist in act in a particular way. His being is qualified by a particular kind of goodness in act. If he does not become virtuous, he is deprived of this quality, and is not good in a distinctive and important way.[13]

There is also the being in act and being in potency of the *matter* of a material substance. There is a partial actuation of matter in each material substrate, for instance in the human body, which is informed in some way by the form that determines it. But there is also indetermination or potency that makes the body subject to further transformation, such as growth, or to corruption, such as sickness.

---

11. See Aristotle, *Metaphysics* 9.3 (1047a30–b2); 6 (1048a25–b9); Aquinas, *In IX Meta.*, lec. 3, 1805, and lec. 5, 1824–31. *In IX Meta.*, lec. 5, 1826–29: Aquinas follows Aristotle in distinguishing between the actuality of substance and the actuality of operations. He defends Aristotle's "proportional and analogical" induction of actuality in *Metaphysics* 9.6 (1048a35–b9). Because being in act exists only in these intrinsically diverse modes, it can be known only through analogical comparisons, and, consequently, "actuality is one of those first simple notions. Therefore it cannot be defined [i.e., by recourse to a more fundamental notion]."

12. Aquinas, *In IX Meta.*, lec. 5, 1828.; lec. 9, 1870; *De ver.*, q. 21, a. 5.

13. *ST* I, q. 77, a. 1: "For the soul by its very essence is an act. Therefore if the very essence of the soul were the immediate principle of operation, whatever has a soul would always have actual vital actions, as that which has a soul is always an actually living thing.... So the soul itself is called first act, with a further relation to the second act. Now we observe that what has a soul is not always actual with respect to its vital operations ... the potentiality of which, however, does not exclude the soul. Therefore it follows that the essence of the soul is not its power. For nothing is in potentiality by reason of an act, as act."

Once we consider goodness in terms of the relationship of potentiality and actuality, the conclusion we should draw from the diverse modes of being in act and being in potency (pertaining to substance, operation, and material movement respectively) is that goodness in creatures—especially in material creatures—is always complex. That said, it is also always related to actuality. Let us consider these different modes of being in act and being in potentiality in their relation to goodness as they apply in the case of the human person. In terms of the goodness of simply existing in act, a human being, by its very substance's being in act, is good. It has a kind of substantial perfection in act. Then, there is the goodness of the qualities and operations of the human person that will perfect him or her spiritually to the degree that these are actuated. They are actuated through intellectual, moral, and artistic habits of reason that are expressed through the medium of our embodied animality. These are habits that are learned and that, over time, come to qualify and perfect a person. In the third place, there is the goodness of the human body that takes on a perfection to the extent that the matter of the body is moved and actuated by the soul as the animating principle within it, which then organizes and guides the development of the matter of the body, so that the body expresses the goodness and activity of the form.

In sum, Aquinas, in *ST* I, q. 5, a. 1, interprets goodness in terms of being. Goodness presents being under its aspect as desirable. Moreover, goodness is related to desire in two ways: first, as referring to the tendencies inscribed in things so that they strive for the perfection of their own natures, and second, insofar as a perfected nature can become a good for others. On Aquinas's understanding, insofar as goodness is a dimension of being, it is also always related to actuality.

Does Goodness Have the Aspect
of a Final Cause?

In *ST* I, q. 5, a. 4, Aquinas takes up the question of goodness's aspect as a final cause. Already in *ST* I, q. 5, a. 2, ad 1, he says that "goodness, since it has the aspect of the desirable, implies the idea of a final cause, the causality of which is first among causes, since an agent does not act except for some end." As noted, the final cause for Aquinas denotes that which a thing tends toward in virtue of its very being and nature. Human animals desire by nature to know and to love. Perfection and goodness come from attaining one's true end. A person begins to reach intellectual maturity when he or she comes to know significant truths, seeks to deepen knowledge of the truth, and can communicate truth to others. A person comes to ethical maturity when he or she acquires the capacity to pursue friendship with God and neighbor, by means of charitable love, affability, justice, temperance, and other virtues.

Notwithstanding the good's aspect as a final cause, Aquinas will also say here, in *ST* I, q. 5, a. 4, that goodness implies efficient and formal causes as well. The good is that which gives of itself. And since it gives of itself, it gives of its own form, from the deep determinations of its own nature. So, the good comes from what a thing is, from its natural capacity to communicate its own goodness, from its desire to attain to a perfection of operation. To give an example: the horse reproduces because (1) it is a horse (formally) (2) that is capable of generation (efficient causality), (3) and that tends toward the communication of its own species (final causality). Aristotle says, in *De anima*, bk. 2, chap. 4, that a thing is most perfect when it can reproduce its like.[14] The philosopher is perfect when he or she can transmit genuine wisdom to students, and the saint is perfect when he or she can communicate a charism, a stable rule of life, to those seeking a tested pathway to holiness. Goodness, then, has the aspect of a final cause, since it is desirable. However, inasmuch as the good gives of itself, it implies efficient and formal causes as well.

The Goodness of God

Aquinas first treats of the goodness of God in *ST* I, q. 6, a. 1. The argument here comes in two stages. In the first stage, Aquinas argues from the general principle that things tend toward a certain perfection, and things that pursue their own perfection do so under the influence of agents on whom they depend for their pursuit of the good. Now, if a being who pursues the good depends upon another agent to become good, and every agent makes its like, then the agent that causes goodness in turn has a goodness that is communicated to its initial subject.

We can illustrate St. Thomas's idea here with an example: A class of students learning symbolic logic pursue knowledge of symbolic logic, which is a genuine perfection of its own kind. Moreover, they do so under the agency of the symbolic logic teacher, who has a formal knowledge of the subject,

---

14. Aristotle, *De anima*, 2.4 (415b 1–3).

a perfection which he or she is trying to impart to them. So, there is in the symbolic logic teacher a greater goodness or perfection as regards knowledge of the subject than there is in the students, and the students are trying to assimilate or become increasingly familiar with the form of knowing that exists in greater perfection in the mind of the teacher.

In the second stage of the argument, Aquinas applies the above line of reasoning to the mystery of God. All creatures tend toward various forms of perfection, from the physical beings of the cosmos that tend toward the expression of properties and laws, in a collective set of relationships; to the living world of plants and animals that tend toward growth and reproduction of their own diverse species; to human beings, who tend to perfection especially in their diverse expressions of knowledge and love, and, above all, in their return to God through knowledge and love of God, the First Cause.

However, all these things are made by God, the first author of the perfections found in all things. So, God, as the first efficient cause of all things, is the primary source of the goodness and the tendency toward perfection that is found in all creatures whatsoever. And this means, in turn, that God must be that which all lesser realities imitate when they strive for perfection, inasmuch as their tending toward goodness is itself derived from him. For this reason, God must possess in himself the plenitude of goodness that surpasses all the finite expressions of the good found in his creatures. In this sense, one can say that God is the exemplary good that every creature imitates and desires, albeit each in its own way.

Aquinas explicitly makes this last point in *ST* I, q. 6, a. 1, ad 2, where he claims that all creatures not only derive from the goodness of God as their first cause, but also strive to return toward God in some way as their final end, imitating his goodness by tending to the full actuation of perfection for which he made them, which is an expression of his own wisdom. If we acknowledge that all creatures have their natures from the divine nature, then this claim clearly makes sense. All of the good they have in themselves substantively or operationally in virtue of their natures derives from the uncreated goodness of the divine nature, and so their perfections must in some way be indicative or reflective of something that exists in a higher and superlative way in God.

Notice too that it would seem to follow from this set of claims that there can exist in God no moral imperfections or vices. God is the author of perfect virtue and is more perfect still than any created virtue. In his pure actuality he can suffer no deficit of potentiality or imperfection, but evil is always a privation or imperfect actualization of the good. Therefore, God is perfectly good, and cannot be evil in any way. On the strength of this argument, moral evil as well as natural evil (i.e., ontological defect) are incompatible with the goodness of God.[15]

God's Goodness in Relation to Creatures

Having treated of God's goodness in itself in *ST* I, q. 6, a. 1, Aquinas now turns to its relation to creatures in aa. 2–4.

He begins, in a. 2, by considering God's character as the supreme good. In his treatment of God as supreme good, Aquinas returns to a number of themes we have seen before: God is not in any species or genus of the created good but is the author of all that is good in creation. He can be called good, therefore, only analogically, as pertaining to him in an utterly transcendent way, distinct from the goodness of all creatures. When we say that God is "the supreme good" we do not mean that he is one good reality among others, nor that he is the goodness contained in all things, nor

---

15. The reasoning is compounded if we have an account of evil as a privation of goodness, which Aquinas has, following Augustine. Precisely because any privation implies potency or non-actuation, God, who is purely actual in his perfection, cannot be subject to any privation of evil. It does not fall within the scope of our considerations here to wrestle with the objections to the existence of God based upon the appeal to evils in the world. Suffice it to say that for Aquinas the following claims are all simultaneously true and mutually logically compatible as well as either philosophically or theologically compelling:

1. God is mysteriously, sovereignly good, and is infinitely so, without any capacity whatsoever of moral or natural diminution of goodness.

2. God, who is infinitely good, has indeed created a world of finite goodness, in which both moral and natural evils are permitted. God's permissions of evil do not compel us to assert that God is morally negligent or lacking in goodness or power. It is possible to claim that human beings are culpable for their morally evil actions without claiming that God is morally culpable for these same acts.

3. God creates the world of angels and human beings in view of the communication of beatitude to them, eternal life (or union with God by knowledge and by love) given to them by grace. Even after human beings sin and forsake the grace of God, God retains this intended eschatological end for human beings.

4. Without being a cause of evil, God can use all the forms and occasions of evil that he merely permits in view of the ultimate good of human beings, so as to "draw good out of evil," i.e., to accomplish, as a response to evil, greater good than has previously existed in the world.

5. God has made himself subject to the human experience of evil by his Incarnation, life, crucifixion, and human death so as to demonstrate his proximity to those who suffer, his desire for union with human persons, and his capacity as God to overcome the power of evil. This is accomplished in this world principally by the gift of the grace of Christ, and in the eschatological state by beatification of human souls, and the eventual resurrection of the dead, inaugurated in Christ's resurrection from the dead.

even that his goodness can be contained or denoted from within the transcendental science of all good realities. Rather, he is the incomprehensible author of all good realities. Moreover, as St. Thomas notes, in *ST* I, q. 6, a. 2, ad 1, the addition of "supreme" to "good" does not imply a real relation of God to creatures, but the inverse: the goodness of all created things derives from God and is therefore actually dependent upon, indicative of, and wholly relative to his uncreated goodness.[16] Thus, the attribution of supreme goodness does not signify any composition in God, but rather the deficiency of creatures in relation to him.

In a. 3, Aquinas asks whether it belongs to God alone to be good essentially. His purpose here is to clarify how the goodness of God is utterly distinct from that of any created reality. To explain this distinction, let us consider an analogy drawn from the goodness of human friendship. The goodness of a person in human friendship implies: (1) the existence of the person, who is not the cause of his or her own existence, but who is given existence; (2) the qualities that are accidents (or properties) in the person, operations of virtue by which he or she is good (intelligent, generous, affable, temperate, etc.); and (3) the other reality (other persons or a person) to whom the friend expresses this goodness. On the human level, there is an ontological complexity inextricably built into the goodness of human friendship.

God, however, has none of these aforementioned complexities: (1) God does not receive his goodness from another, but is essentially good of himself; (2) his goodness is not an accidental quality added to his being and essence, but is his very essence—God is his goodness; (3) God does not become good by loving another reality, but instead possesses the plenitude of goodness in himself and is the originative source of goodness in all others. In other words, God's goodness does not depend on creatures. On the contrary, they exist, become good, and are sustained in goodness actually, because he first loves them.[17] Ultimately, there is no potency in God to become good, but he is eternally good, in his pure actuality and simplicity.

Finally, in *ST* I, q. 6, a. 4, Aquinas asks if it is by the divine goodness that all things are good. The core question here is: What is the relationship be-

---

16. For Aquinas on the question of real relations of God to creatures, see esp. *ST* I, q. 13, a. 7.

17. This is sometimes called the principle of predilection, as it stresses the primacy of God's loving initiative over creaturely goodness. See *ST* I, q. 20, a. 3: "For since God's love is the cause of goodness in things ... no one thing would be better than another, if God did not will greater good for one than for another."

tween the divine goodness and the goodness of creation? Aquinas lays out his basic stance in the *sed contra*: "All things are good, inasmuch as they have being. But they are not called beings through the divine being, but through their own being; therefore all things are good not by the divine goodness, but by their own goodness." St. Thomas's point is that things are not *formally* good by the goodness of God, but by and through their own goodness. God is not himself the intrinsic goodness of creation. This means, for example, that angelic natures are intrinsically good, human nature is intrinsically good, plant natures are intrinsically good, and so on, not because these realities are God, but in virtue of what they are formally in themselves. As the being of created things is not the divine being, so too just for this reason their goodness is not the divine goodness. However, God has truly given them their being good in and of themselves. Just as they can be true causes, even as they depend ontologically upon the first cause for their actual being, so too they are truly good in and of themselves, even as they depend ontologically upon God's hidden and unparticipated goodness, who communicates all existence to them.

In the first paragraph of the corpus, Aquinas discusses Plato's doctrine of separate ideas or forms. Plato seems to have considered these ideas to be the truest expression of singular realities, such that what Socrates and Alexander are in essence is the idea of man, a separate or distinct form in which each participates. Aristotle roundly criticized this idea. On his conception, with which St. Thomas agrees, Socrates is formally a man in virtue of the intrinsic form, his individualized nature, which is that of a human being.[18] It is by virtue of this intrinsic form that he is a man and exists. In the same way, he also has an intrinsic goodness. His individual human nature is good. There are no separate, subsisting forms. What is true, however, in Plato's theory is that there is indeed a separate, self-subsisting existence and goodness that is the first exemplary, efficient, and final cause of all created goodness, and Christian theology recognizes that this is God the Creator. God is himself essential existence and goodness, and all secondary, created beings participate in the existence and goodness of God. God, who is himself essentially good, is the transcendent cause and exemplar of all created goodness. Nev-

---

18. See, in this respect, Aquinas's discussion in *De substatiis separatis* (*De sub. sep.*), cc. 3, 4, and 9, where he emphasizes that the notion of participation should be interpreted in light of the Aristotelian distinction of actuality and potentiality, with criticism of Plato's theory of forms.

etheless, each thing is good formally by its own goodness. As St. Thomas puts it in the third paragraph of the corpus: "everything is called good by reason of the similitude of the divine goodness belonging to it, which is formally its own goodness, whereby it is denominated good."

CONCLUSION

Some critics of Aquinas's theology claim that he has a concept of God as a set of abstract properties, in which terms like perfection or goodness are attributed to God as pre-existent abstract objects. The arguments of this chapter suggest, however, that Aquinas rejects the notion that we can attribute properties to God as abstract entities. His criticism of the Platonic notion of the good is telling in just this respect. Goodness, for Aquinas, is not a "form," that is, a universal property found in all things that can be apprehended in a generic way, which would indicate a pre-existing abstract object in which all things are said to participate. There are no such separated properties or abstract forms for Aquinas.

Instead, as we have seen, talk of God's perfection and supreme goodness originates from the consideration of God's causality of creatures. Perfection and goodness do not possess natures (abstract or concrete forms). They are understood analogically in terms of being and teleology. Every kind of nature that exists has a certain goodness and perfection, in virtue of the fact that it exists and possesses natural integrity of a given kind. Goodness and perfection are especially manifest in creatures in their progressive teleological actuation, as a result of operational activity. God can be known to be perfect and supreme goodness not as one who possesses an essence or property in common with creatures, but because he is the source of the existence and teleological operations found in all creatures. Therefore, he must be perfect and good in some other and higher way, which we approach by considering how God is not like creatures.

In creatures, perfection follows upon complexity. With God, perfection follows from simplicity. His is a perfection without any static limitation, or gradual development, and without any movement from potency to act. Moreover, God's perfection is the archetypal and efficient source of all creaturely perfections: the perfections of all creatures pre-exist in him, albeit in a more eminent manner. As such, he is the equivocal cause of creaturely perfections in the sense that he is their transcendent efficient cause. Accordingly, creaturely perfections resemble God, but only on the basis of a certain analogy, and not by any generic or specific likeness.

Goodness is understood for Aquinas in terms of being. Good signifies the aspect of desirability inherent in being; as such, it is always related to actuality. It also has the aspect of a final cause, even as it implies efficient and formal causes. The good is that which communicates some kind of perfection to others through its effects. When it comes to the divine goodness, St. Thomas stresses that God is the source of the goodness in all things. Moreover, he is that which all things imitate and desire, each in its own way according to the diversity of natures. God possesses goodness essentially and is the transcendent cause and exemplar of the goodness of all creatures. However, for this very reason, creatures also are formally good in themselves, in virtue of the intrinsic goodness that God has imparted to them by creation.

15

Divine Infinity and Omnipresence

St. Thomas Aquinas treats of the attributes of God's infinity and omnipresence in *ST* I, qq. 7 and 8, respectively. Both denominations have clear biblical foundations. For example, God's infinity is attested to in Psalm 145:3 "Great is the Lord, and greatly to be praised, and his greatness is unsearchable [the Vulgate renders this last phrase: *non est finis*, is without end]."[1] Likewise, God's omnipresence, his presence in and to all things, is attested to in an especially clear way by the Psalmist in Psalm 139:7–10, where he writes: "Where shall I go from your Spirit? Or where shall I flee from your presence? If I ascend to heaven, you are there! If I make my bed in Sheol, you are there! If I take the wings of the morning and dwell in the uttermost parts of the sea, even there your hand shall lead me, and your right hand shall hold me."[2] In treating these divine attributes, Aquinas is attempting to provide a metaphysical grammar for what scripture affirms, in keeping with his overall program of *sacra doctrina*. His approach to these topics, however, can be counterintuitive, because it precedes historically an alternative and today influential way of treating divine infinity, derivative from Scotus and Descartes. After considering this alternative view first, we will turn to Aquinas's treatment of the divine infinity. After this, we will then turn to a survey of Aquinas's treatment of the divine omnipresence.

---

1. For additional biblical references to the divine infinity, see Ps 147:5; Sir 1:2; Ps 90:2.
2. Further biblical references to the divine omnipresence can be found in 1 Kgs 8:27; Jer 23:24; Ps 145:18; Jb 11:7–9; Acts 17:26–28.

THE MODERN PRIMACY OF THE INFINITE

Following the example of René Descartes, some modern philosophers and theologians identify the infinite as first in the foreground among the divine attributes. A famous example of Descartes's view is found in the *Meditations on First Philosophy*, III, 45, where he writes: "By the word 'God' I understand a substance that is *infinite*, [eternal, immutable,] independent, supremely intelligent, supremely powerful, and which created both myself and everything else (if anything else there be) that exists."[3] In this case, infinity has become definitional to philosophical theology. It is the attribute par excellence that provides us with a way of identifying what is essential to God as distinct from all other beings. As a result, the concept of God is virtually identified with the concept of infinite being, and the very question of the existence of God takes its origin from the question of the infinite.

A further characteristic feature of this conception is that the infinite is now regarded as a positive feature rather than an apophatic attribute of God. The infinite needs to have this positive function if it is to serve in a privileged and primary way to help us define God. The seeming advantage of this point of departure for thinking about God is that it permits one to give a very clear and distinct content to the definition of God. If we consider first an attribute such as being, goodness, or power, creatures must be said to possess it in a finite way, while God possesses it in an infinite way. God can be readily defined then, a priori, as infinite being, goodness, knowledge and so forth.[4] A language of univocity develops around this way of speaking, where God and creatures both possess or inhabit the same characteristics, the only difference being that one possesses them in an infinite way, while the others possess them in an infinite way.

A telling example of this kind of univocal predication is found in Descartes's *Meditations on First Philosophy*, IV, 57:

---

3. René Descartes, *Meditations on First Philosophy: With Selections from the Objections and Replies*, ed. and trans. John Cottingham (Cambridge: Cambridge University Press, 2013), III, 45, emphasis added.

4. In the case of Descartes, the idea of God as infinite being is apprehended by the mind a priori, in seeming independence of our external experience of the sensible world, and as a condition for the evaluation of all certitudes regarding knowledge of sensible realities. It permits us to identify that God must exist necessarily, through the medium of the ontological argument, and from this certitude, one can maintain a confidence in human knowledge of the world derived from external experiences.

For although God's will is incomparably greater than mine, both in virtue of the knowledge and power that accompany it and make it more firm and efficacious, and also in virtue of its object, in that it ranges over a greater number of items, *nevertheless it does not seem any greater than mine when considered as will in the essential and strict sense. This is because the will simply consists in our ability to do or not do something* (that is, to affirm or deny, to pursue or avoid); or rather, it consists simply in the fact that when the intellect puts something forward, we are moved to affirm or deny or to pursue or avoid it in such a way that we do not feel ourselves to be determined by any external force.[5]

In this passage, Descartes is saying that divine freedom and human freedom are formally or essentially exactly the same in species, and that they differ only by degree of magnitude, as one is infinite and the other is finite.

This univocal line of thinking is derived historically from Duns Scotus. As Thomas Williams notes: "Remember one of Scotus's arguments for univocity. If we are to follow Anselm in ascribing to God every pure perfection, we have to affirm that we are ascribing to God *the very same thing* that we ascribe to creatures: God has it infinitely, creatures in a limited way. One could hardly ask for a more harmonious cooperation between ontology (what God is) and semantics (how we can think and talk about him)."[6] Matters are very different, however, when we come to Aquinas, who treats the subject of the divine infinity rather sparsely. For Aquinas, God is indeed infinite, but this is not the primary truth to consider when thinking of God.

In order to correctly understand Aquinas's view of the divine infinity, it is important to make two points straight away. First, Aquinas understands this divine attribute or name primarily as a *negative* name. God is not-finite. Second, this notion of the "negative infinity" of God is integrally related to God's simplicity and perfection, the two more basic "name generators" of Aquinas's theology. Because God does not receive his being from another but is the giver of all existence in created beings, God is simple and perfect, having in himself the perfection prior to and superior to all creatures. God

---

5. Descartes, *Meditations on First Philosophy*, IV, 57, emphasis added.

6. See Thomas Williams, "John Duns Scotus," *The Stanford Encyclopedia of Philosophy* (2019), online: http://plato.stanford.edu/entries/duns-scotus/#DivInfDocUni. Williams argues that infinity is the primary "divine attribute generator" in Scotus's thought. Scotus does not affirm the absence of the distinction of essence and existence in God (Aquinas's doctrine of God as *ipsum esse subsistens*), and consequently must have another way to identify what is proper to God as distinct from all creatures. The infinite plays that role, since it allows us to identify ways that any univocally denoted attribute that God "shares" with creatures conceptually exists in a unique and distinctive way in God.

is pure actuality. He is not limited in being. But just so, he also is not limited in perfection or act, and thus he is not finite, that is, he is infinite.

This negative approach to talking about the infinity of God is more in keeping with the Cappadocian Fathers, who directly address the question of God's infinity in response to Eunomius. As we saw in chapter 8, Eunomius's theology had strongly rationalistic characteristics. He seems to have maintained that the human mind could have definitional knowledge of God's essence as one and unoriginated, from which one could conclude philosophically, as it were, that God could not be trinitarian. In stating that the essence of God is infinite, the Cappadocians wished to emphasize, by way of contrast, that our theology of God is largely apophatic and so proceeds by way of negation. We simply do not know what God is: his being and life are not finite and therefore stand beyond the pretensions of human rationalism or the grasp of our knowing.

When seen in this historical light it is ironic, then, that, in prominent strands of modern philosophy, this very attribute of infinity has been used, not as an apophatic bulwark against rationalism, but as a positive definitional attribute that gives God's existence the maximum intelligibility and comprehension. By transforming this formerly negative attribute into a positive one, philosophers have embedded discourse about God within a univocal framework that places God's being in a line with creaturely being.

NEGATIVE CHARACTER OF GOD'S INFINITY

In ancient authors, prior to Aquinas, the infinite was sometimes characterized in negative terms, that is, as a negation of limitation. The infinite is that which is not in any way limited. However, the term was used in a wide variety of senses. Aristotle, for example, employed the notion almost exclusively in order to think about the quantitative extension and mutability of physical beings.[7] Meanwhile, Platonists like Plotinus (204–270 A.D.) and Proclus (412–485 A.D.) speculated on the idea that the first principle was unlimited in being and power, a view adopted in turn by Church Fathers like the Cappadocians and Dionysius.[8] Defined as such, however, the infinite was understood in two distinct ways, which Aquinas would charac-

7. Aristotle, *Physics* 3.4–8 (202b30–208a20); 6.1–10 (231a18–241b20).
8. Plotinus, *Enneads*, 4.3.8; 5.5.4 11; 6.7.17; Proclus, *Elements of Theology*, trans. E. R. Dodds (Oxford: Clarendon, 1963), chaps. 1 and 86.

terize as the "privative infinite" and the "negative infinite." Let us consider in turn these two distinct notions of infinity.

The first kind of infinity, which is the older notion historically speaking, has nothing to do with God, but rather with this world. More particularly, it was developed as a way of speaking about the pure potentiality of matter. This is the concept of the infinite we find in Aristotle: there is in every material subject, in every material substrate of every material body, a quasi-infinite potential for further transformation.[9] How far can we go, for example, in splitting an atom into smaller and smaller particles? Will we ever reach a limit beyond which no further division is possible? Or in how many different ways can we alter something by uniting it materially with something else? The fact is that, no matter how much a material thing undergoes change, it can still change further, due to the pure potentiality of matter. This divisibility is the foundation for discussions of the numeric or quantitative infinite. For instance, no matter how much one might divide a physical thing, to make two or four or eight things from what was formerly one, it can be divided without end, in principle, because of the divisibility of matter.

This kind of infinity is what Thomists call the *privative infinite*. We should make two observations in its regard.

First, this kind of infinity is a manifest imperfection. The infinite possibilities of transformation and change in material things result from a lack of determination or definition in them, and from their static potency. In other words, they result from a lack of natural form. For this reason, it should be evident that this kind of infinity, which results from the plasticity and imperfection of fluctuating, changing things, is not found in God, who is all perfect.

Second, this privative infinite is an infinitude only ever in potency, never in actuation. There never is nor can be an actually infinite set of material beings in the world, and thus the world is inherently finite. This truth follows from the very nature of matter itself. Material bodies can always be further divided, to make more things, to make a greater number or magnitude. Every material being forever remains subject to further alteration. Consequently, material things insofar as they are material—and therefore are sub-

---

9. See Aristotle, *Physics*, trans. R. Waterfield (Oxford: Oxford University Press, 2008), 3.6 (206a15–18): "no actual magnitude can be infinite, but it can still be infinitely divisible ... and so we are left with things being infinite potentially."

ject to further *potential* change on account of their matter—are *necessarily finite*. It follows that the material universe is necessarily finite, and we never can actually encounter a quantitative infinite, either in the real universe or in number (since both matter and number always remain capable of further division). An actually infinite extension or actually infinite number of distinct things exists only as an abstract idea, which has its basis in the divisibility of matter. The only thing that can faintly approximate the infinite in the material world is temporal duration: there is a basis in reality for the unending, that is, of infinite continuation, change that goes on from one thing to another to another. However, at any given point in time, in actuality—for example right now in this given moment—there can be no infinite number of material things.

The second kind of infinity referred to above is the Neoplatonic conception of the infinite. This form of thinking was developed by thinkers like Plotinus and Proclus, and exists in the Christian world particularly in the work the Cappadocian Fathers. Proclus attributes infinity to God as the first principle in a way that is very different from the older, privative infinitive discussed above. Here the term represents not infinite potential divisibility, but instead, an absence of imperfection. The term can be thought about as a double negative in its formulation. That is to say, what is not perfect in creatures is *not* attributed to God. The result of this formulation is that it enshrouds God's nature in mystery, as he infinitely transcends our grasp of merely created reality. As mentioned above, the Cappadocians utilized this kind of reflection on the infinity of God's perfection as incomprehensible mystery as a firewall to check the rationalist pretensions of the Eunomians, who claimed to know God's essence.

This second kind of infinity is what scholastics call the *negative infinite*. The negative infinite pertains to God's simplicity and perfection, and thus the infinite refers back in the first instance to the primary "name-generating" attributes of Aquinas's theology. The infinite on this conception refers, then, to God in his nature as pure form: (a) without the limitation of matter; and (b) without a participated *esse*, or an existence received into a finite essence, as is the case in all creatures. Rather, in God *esse* is identical with essence: God is his existence, and as such is perfect in being without limitation. While all creatures who receive their being from another are necessarily finite, God receives his being from no one. His nature is infinite in being (non-finite, not received), having in itself a plenitude of perfection.

We can see the apophatic character of this argument in *ST* I, q. 7, a. 2, where St. Thomas, in discussing God's properly essential infinity, strips away every form of composition from God, up to and including the essence-existence distinction, to show how only God is truly infinite, that is, unbounded as regards his incomprehensible nature.[10]

Some important conclusions follow from this kind of reasoning about the infinite. First, in thinking about the infinity of God, we are thinking not about numbers or a quantitative magnitude, as if God were the greatest physical body. Second, with this kind of infinity, we are thinking primarily negatively about the absence of imperfection or limitation in God, yet without knowing what God is in himself. We are saying more about what he is not than what he is. Third, spiritually speaking, we learn from St. Thomas's approach that we ought to avoid a kind of metaphysical vertigo in thinking about God's infinity in an exclusive or one-sided way. It is not rare in the Christian tradition, for example, to find sermons that seek to produce angst or terror by referring thematically to the infinite justice of God. Whatever the spiritual productivity of such exercises, it bears keeping in mind that the names we attribute to God denote something that is mysteriously one in him. The infinity of God qualifies his goodness: God is infinitely just and powerful, but also infinitely good and merciful, and we know from divine revelation and from the faith that he uses his power in the service of goodness and mercy, even going so far as to render us "justified" in the mystery of the Cross.[11] Christian reflection on the infinity of God, in light of faith in the providence of God in Christ, can and should inspire in us a confidence in God, who can accomplish all things.

---

10. *ST* I, q. 7, a. 2: "Things other than God can be relatively infinite, but not absolutely infinite.... [If] we speak of the infinite in reference to form, it is manifest that those things, the forms of which are in matter, are absolutely finite, and in no way infinite. If, however, any created forms are not received into matter, but are self-subsisting, as some think is the case with angels, these will be relatively infinite, inasmuch as such kinds of forms are not terminated, nor contracted by any matter. But because a created form thus subsisting has being, and yet is not its own being, it follows that its being is received and contracted to a determinate nature. Hence it cannot be absolutely infinite."

11. See Rom 5:6–10: "While we were yet helpless, at the right time Christ died for the ungodly. Why, one will hardly die for a righteous man—though perhaps for a good man one will dare even to die. But God shows his love for us in that while we were yet sinners Christ died for us. Since, therefore, we are now justified by his blood, much more shall we be saved by him from the wrath of God."

Consideration of divine omnipresence follows logically from a consideration of his infinity. As stated in the prologue to *ST* I, q. 7: "After considering the divine perfection we must consider divine infinity, and God's existence in things, for God is everywhere, and in all things, inasmuch as He is boundless and infinite." Aquinas accordingly treats the divine omnipresence in *ST* I, q. 8, immediately after the divine infinity. We will see in the course of the considerations below why it follows from God's infinite perfection that he is present everywhere, to everything that exists.

Is God in All Things?

In treating divine omnipresence, Aquinas returns to the topic of being, as he does in the consideration of each divine name. God is in all things in a unique way, proper to God alone, because he is the author of all that has created existence. He is most immanent to all that is precisely as the total cause of all that is. What emerges is a creation mysticism, in which God is understood to be intimately present at the heart of all reality, a hidden presence as Creator that remains in and through all things, and which is presupposed to all that God does in the order of redemption.

Aquinas's argument, in *ST* I, q. 8, a. 1, for God's being in all things has three basic entailments. First and most fundamentally, God the Creator is in all things insofar as he is the cause of all things. It should be noted that the causality in question here is not one that operates primarily on the level of the properties or accidents of a thing, and even less does it have to do with a mere sensory relationship of one thing acting on another. Rather, the causality St. Thomas has in mind operates on a most profound and fundamental level: the level of the very being or existence of the things themselves. In other words, the kind of causality that renders God present in all things is the total causality that allows the creature "to be." God alone is capable of this kind of causality and therefore he alone is omnipresent. This is an incommunicable feature of his divine nature.

Second, as a direct result of God's conferral of being on the creature, God is most intimately present to each created thing. For this reason, there is nothing that exists to which God is not intimately present, and God is in fact present to each thing more intimately than it is to itself, at the very heart, or in the very depths of its existence.[12] The world is not "exterior" to God, we might say, but rather, in some real sense, the world is "within" God.[13] We must simultaneously affirm the most absolute transcendence of God as infinite and, as following directly from this, the most absolute immanence of God to creatures as omnipresent.

Third, what we denote by the term "God" is not something synonymous with beings of the created order. Even if God is present to all things in virtue of their very being, their created existence, he is the giver of that existence, and not the being of creatures themselves. God cannot be identified with the being of creatures, and therefore is utterly distinct from all things, not only in the way they are distinct from one another, but in an entirely unique way, proper to God alone.[14]

God Is Everywhere: Presence by Essence, Wisdom, and Power
In *ST* I, q. 8, a. 2, Aquinas goes on to argue that, as a result of God's conferral of being, power, and operation on creatures, God does indeed fill every place, albeit not spatially. Or, in St. Thomas's words: "by the very fact that He gives being to the things that fill every place, He Himself fills every place."

How, then, is God present to all that exists? In *ST* I, q. 8, a. 3, Aquinas argues that God is present everywhere by his "essence, presence, and power." There are two forms of God's presence mentioned in this article. The first form is that by which God is present *in all things* created. He is said to be so by his "essence" and "power" because he is immediately present to all he creates in virtue of his power to give them being, which in turn pertains to what he is essentially, his very nature. Meanwhile, "presence" here denotes (a) a kind of personal care or attentiveness, which derives from divine knowledge

12. See Augustine, *The Confessions*, trans. M. Boulding, (New York: Vintage Spiritual Classics, 1998), 3.6.11: "You [God] were more intimately present to me than my innermost being, and higher than the highest peak of my spirit."

13. This is in keeping with Paul's citation of Epimenides in Acts 17:28: "In him we live and move and have our being."

14. All of which is to say: to believe that God is omnipresent as the Creator and giver of all existence and life is also to believe that God can in no way be identified with his creation. Every form of pantheism—i.e., the human confusion of God with the cosmos or the history of the world—is therefore philosophically and theologically unwarranted, as the First Vatican Council maintained. See *Dei Filius*, chap. 1: "[God] must be declared to be in reality and essence, distinct from the world, supremely happy in himself and from himself, and inexpressibly loftier than anything besides himself which either exists of can be imagined." *Decrees*, ed. Tanner, 2:805.

and love. God is present to his creatures by knowledge and love. However, this divine presence also denotes (b) an actual contact, or proximity. In this case, the proximity is established in virtue of divine causality: God is present to all things that exist as one who is personally causing them to be, in virtue of his power as Creator, as well as his knowledge and love.

The second way in which God is present is proper to rational creatures (angels and human beings). God is present to them, not only by his essence and power, but also as the object toward which they tend, or with whom they are united spiritually, by grace. This is a higher form of presence than his common mode of presence to creatures.[15]

The first, then, is the "omnipresence" that characterizes God as Creator. God is present to all that he sustains in being, including physical realities and non-rational living things. There is a spiritual beauty to this teaching. In light of the divine omnipresence we can learn to see the world of nature as a kind of vast iconostasis of God the Creator, which manifests God indirectly by its intelligibility, goodness, and beauty, but which conceals God due to its mere finitude. There is also a spiritual sobriety that stems from this teaching. We see in its light that God's presence is inescapable, but that this fact alone does not provide for human salvation. On the contrary, this form of presence is extended even to those in a state of sin, and includes the souls of the damned, and the fallen angels.[16] No creature, no matter how disinterested in the sacred, or hostile to it, can truly escape God in its ontological roots, since God sustains all things in being, as the Creator of their existence.

The second form of "being in," by way of contrast, is that which pertains to the activity of grace in the souls of human beings and in the spiritual life of angels. Grace is the gift of divine life in which spiritual creatures are called to participate. When human beings begin to know God by grace, they are illumined intellectually by faith and are moved freely toward union with God by hope and love in the will. As a consequence, they begin to possess God

15. Aquinas discusses this special mode of presence in *ST* I, q. 43, a. 3, when discussing the missions of the divine persons: "For God is in all things by His essence, power and presence, according to His one common mode, as the cause existing in the effects which participate in His goodness. Above and beyond this common mode, however, there is one special mode belonging to the rational nature wherein God is said to be present as the object known is in the knower, and the beloved in the lover. And since the rational creature by its operation of knowledge and love attains to God Himself, according to this special mode God is said not only to exist in the rational creature but also to dwell therein as in His own temple. So no other effect can be put down as the reason why the divine person is in the rational creature in a new mode, except sanctifying grace."

16. On God's mode of presence in the fallen angels, see *ST* I, q. 8, a. 1, ad 4.

mystically, even if inchoately, and this process can culminate in the beatific vision, in which the human person is given to see God by immediate intellectual vision and so also to possess God by a love that can never fail or be diminished.

A great number of forms of metaphysical mysticism confound these two levels. There are Eastern mystics in Hindu Vedantism or Western mystics in the Christian tradition (arguably Meister Eckhart) for whom the first form of presence, the omnipresence of God the Creator, seems to be the basis for affirming a kind of non-distinction between God and creatures, and so a mysticism of divine-human union.[17] As Aquinas points out, however, while there is a mysticism of being—since we come from God and depend upon him and his activity at the center of our lives and persons—this numinous presence of God as Creator ought not to be identified with a mysticism of *union* with God. Divinizing union occurs only by an elevating gift of grace, not in virtue of our created nature or its innate powers.

That being said, one should also avoid an alternative extreme, the claim that the affirmation of the presence of God the Creator by his essence, power, and presence serves to rival the flourishing or the freedom of the creature. On this view, we ourselves could truly exist and be genuinely free only to the extent that God would retire from the universe. Deism presents us with a kind of opposite error to pseudo-mystical pantheism. Even as God's essence cannot be identified with the creatures he makes and to whom he is present, it also ought not be placed in competition with them. Rather, it

---

17. An Eastern example can be found in the thought of Shankara and his interpretation of Advaita Vedantic tradition. See the analysis of Natalia Isayeva, *Shankara and Indian Philosophy* (Albany, N.Y.: SUNY Press, 1993). On the controversial character of Eckhart's mysticism, see discussion in Bernard McGinn, *The Harvest of Mysticism in Medieval Germany (1300–1500)*, vol. 4 of *The Presence of God: A History of Western Christian Mysticism* (New York: Crossroad, 2005), 83–194. See, in particular, the discussion of the ambiguities of the *grunt/abgrunt* (ground, abyss) language found in Eckhart and others: "The creation of *grunt/abgrunt* language was not a solitary effort, despite Eckhart's central role, but a response to a widespread yearning to give expression to a new view of how God becomes one with the human person: no longer through mystical uniting, that is, an intentional union between God and human emphasizing the continuing distinction between the two entities, but in a mystical identity in which God and human become truly indistinct, at least on some level" (87–88). See too the discussion of "the ground as fused identity" in Eckhart's mysticism, on 118–24. For John XXII's 1329 Bull *In agro dominico*, which condemns a number of propositions drawn from Eckhart, see Heinrich Denzinger, *Compendium of Creeds, Definitions, and Declarations on Matters of Faith and Morals*, 43rd ed., ed. P. Hünermann, R. Fastiggi, and A. E. Nash (San Francisco: Ignatius Press, 2012), nos. 950–80 [hereafter cited as Denzinger]. All this being noted, there are also ways of reading Eckhart's work that seek to preserve the distinction of Creator and creature and to acknowledge thematically the gift of election and the elevating work of grace.

is precisely by being present as Creator that God gives creatures their very goodness, radiance, and natural glory. Human persons flourish in their autonomous activities of knowing and loving precisely because they are given existence and sustained in being by God. The more God is present, we might say, the more a personal agent flourishes, acts according to its nature, and becomes free, rather than vice versa.

The spiritual consequences of this kind of monotheistic vision are important: It provides us with a sense of the providence of God, which is present and active at all times and places without fail, and of the power of his grace, which can be present to our souls and bodies no matter what may come. In effect, it is a matter of fundamental realism to acknowledge that our spiritual soul is truly in the hands of God in life and in death. God is omnipresent, and therefore is utterly, intimately present to all that we are, if we wish to acknowledge his presence as Creator, and to cooperate with his presence by grace as our Redeemer. Nothing can thwart the work of God in our lives, except our refusal to acknowledge his dominion and universal providence over us as Creator and Redeemer.

In addition to these two forms of presence, we should also mention a third: the presence of God to the universe in virtue of the Incarnation. In the Incarnation God is made present in his creation in a yet more perfect way than by the communication of sanctifying grace to angels and human beings.[18] This presence is effectuated by means of the hypostatic union, wherein God the Son becomes human and makes himself personally known in a human nature and by means of his human life, death, and bodily resurrection. His presence in the world is also mysteriously prolonged in the sacraments. He is substantially present in the Eucharist, in a sacramental mode, so that any human being who is in the presence of the Eucharist is objectively and really in the presence of the glorified Christ, albeit in a mysterious way. Beyond this, in the other six sacraments, Christ is also present not substantially but operatively, since he communicates distinctive forms of grace actively, in and through the celebration of these diverse sacraments.

From a consideration of the mysterious omnipresence of God in all things, we can begin to recognize that the creature exists only within a dynamic tension. It both manifests and conceals one who is inescapably present and utterly transcendent. By the gift of natural existence founded in

18. For Aquinas's treatment of the singular mode of union proper to the Incarnate Word, see ST III, q. 2.

God's creative act, the creature itself invites us by a kind of natural mystery to acknowledge the hidden presence and power of God the Creator. This knowledge, however, is indirect and, for that reason, imperfect. This very imperfection, in turn, seems to invite the rational creature to go still further. This "going further" can transpire only by grace, in which the mind and heart are led to participate in the mystery of God's own life, that is, in the mystery of the Holy Trinity, by a higher form of presence and a higher form of union.

CONCLUSION

In this chapter, we have looked at St. Thomas's treatment of God's infinity (ST I, q. 7) and omnipresence (ST I, q. 8). As regards the divine infinity, we saw how a prominent strand of modern philosophy (exemplified by Descartes) places infinity in the foreground of the divine attributes. In so doing, it proceeds with a positive conception of divine infinity, and is often allied with a univocal cast of mind with respect to philosophical discourse about God that, on our view, fails to adequately recognize divine transcendence. By way of contrast, Aquinas, like the Cappadocians, conceives of the divine infinity negatively. He understands it as a non-limitation of form that removes every kind of composition from the divine nature, up to and including the most fundamental form of composition, the essence-existence distinction. This is why, for Aquinas, God's infinity is closely related to his simplicity and perfection.

For St. Thomas, God's omnipresence, his presence to all things, is grounded in his creative causality. For the simple reason that God continuously confers being on creatures, God is more intimately present to the creature in its very depths than it is to itself. Similarly, for this very same reason, God is present in every place, not spatially, but because he confers being on things in every place. Moreover, beyond the common mode by which he gives being to all things, he is present also to rational creatures by grace as an object of knowledge and love.

We will now turn to the next divine attribute St. Thomas discusses, namely, God's immutability, which we will treat together with its necessary entailment, divine impassibility, that is, God's inability to suffer.

16

: ─────

Divine Immutability and Impassibility

St. Thomas's discussion of divine immutability, in *ST* I, q. 9, is terse, comprising a mere two articles. The reason for this is likely to be found in the fact that divine immutability follows so surely from Aquinas's earlier conclusions regarding the divine simplicity, perfection, and infinity that hardly any further discussion seems required to establish the fact. And yet, in a great deal of modern philosophy and theology of the last century, the traditional teaching on divine immutability and impassibility has been challenged on a number of fronts. Given this breakdown of the traditional consensus, we will accordingly spend the greater part of this chapter bringing the traditional teaching, as represented by Aquinas, into dialogue with a number of the modern objections to it in order to show not only this position's traditional roots but also its explanatory seriousness, especially in light of soteriological considerations.

SOME OBJECTIONS TO DIVINE IMMUTABILITY IN CONTEMPORARY THEOLOGY

In the past century, multiple objections have arisen to the classical idea that the nature of God is immutable or unchanging. The objections themselves arise from a variety of historical conditions.[1] Principal among these is a loss of confidence in the eighteenth-century Enlightenment tradition

---

1. For more on this, see the essay "Divine Impassibility in Contemporary Theology," by James F. Keating and Thomas Joseph White in *Divine Impassibility and the Mystery of Human Suffering*, ed. J. F. Keating and T. J. White (Grand Rapids, Mich.: Eerdmans, 2009), 1–26.

of "rational theism," especially in the wake of the criticisms of such theism that were developed by Hume, Kant, Nietzsche, and Heidegger, as well as Karl Barth's critique of "natural theology." What depictions of God might scripture provide in a post-Enlightenment context characterized by skepticism? Perhaps the widespread demise of confidence in Enlightenment theism presents theologians with an opportunity to recover anew the biblical idea of a God who is subject to change and suffering.[2] Second, there is the influence of the creative modern ontologies of Hegel and Schelling, who understand God as a Trinitarian process of historical unfolding, emphasizing in various turns that God undergoes being with humanity by way of reason-in-history or freedom-in-history.[3] Third, there are a set of theodicy questions that arise after the moral devastation of the Second World War and the intentional genocide of the Holocaust in particular. Where is God in the suffering of human persons, and how can God truly redeem us from suffering unless he too is subject to it in his very being? Is it not precisely in virtue of his solidarity with us in our condition of suffering that we can truly come to know God as a God of love? The logic of this position reaches its apotheosis in the mystery of the crucifixion, where the very deity of God is subject to the human experience of death.

The idea that God is subject to change and suffering—and so possible— in his very essence, has immediate consequences for Trinitarian theology. This is the case for at least two reasons. First, if the three persons of God are indeed one in nature and that nature is subject to ongoing alteration, then we must also consider whether and how this process affects the relations of the divine persons, and therefore the very identity of the Trinity. Second, as it is clear that one of the Trinity suffered by way of human crucifixion and death, should we understand the suffering of the Son as indicative of a change that occurs in God, in his very deity? If so, how is it the suffering of

2. This challenge is a key theme in Eberhard Jüngel, *God as the Mystery of the World: On the Foundation of the Theology of the Crucified One in the Dispute between Theism and Atheism*, trans. D. L. Gouder (Grand Rapids, Mich.: Eerdmans, 1983); and Jürgen Moltmann, *The Crucified God: The Cross of Christ as the Foundation and Criticism of Christian Theology*, trans. R. A. Wilson (San Francisco: Harper and Row, 1974).

3. See the helpful analysis of Schelling in this respect by Walter Kasper, *The Absolute in History: The Philosophy and Theology of History in Schelling's Late Philosophy*, trans. K. Wolff (New York: Paulist Press, 2018). On the "dipolar" kenoticism that arises in modern theologies of divine mutability, such as in Balthasar, Bulgakov and Moltmann, see Gilles Emery, "The Immutability of the God of Love and the Problem of Language Concerning the 'Suffering of God,'" in Keating and White, *Divine Impassibility and the Mystery of Human Suffering*, 27–76.

only one person in the Trinity and not of all three? There are two basic strategies that frequently arise in this regard, concerning the two questions. The first common strategy consists in positing that precisely because God does change through time, the Trinitarian mystery is affected in itself, and the three persons are in some real sense constituted even in their personal relations by their ongoing engagement with history. If the divine nature changes, then the three persons are also changing naturally as God, and this process "reaches up" into their mutual relationships, as constitutive of all they are. The second common strategy that responds to the second question admits that the Son's suffering does affect his divinity (God suffers naturally in his crucifixion and death) but differentiates the natural modes of suffering proper to the three persons. The divine nature therefore exists in distinct ways or under distinct aspects in the three persons, unfolding in a dipolar or dialectical and historical way. The Father possesses the deity in a way distinct from the way the Son does, having distinct divine attributes, while the Son, in his way of being God, accepts to be emptied of some divine prerogatives out of love, for the sake of crucifixion.

For an example of the first strategy (Trinitarian becoming through history) consider the following passage from Robert Jenson.

The Lord's resolve to meet and overcome death and the constitution of his self-identity in dramatic coherence are but one truth about him. For if death-and-resurrection occurs, this is the infinite dramatic crisis and resolution, and so God's own. Since the Lord's self-identity is constituted in dramatic coherence, it is established not from the beginning but from the end, not at birth but at death, not in *persistence* but in *anticipation*. The biblical God is not eternally himself in that he persistently instantiates a beginning in which he already is all he ever will be; he is eternally himself in that he unrestrictedly anticipates an end in which he will be all he ever could be.[4]

Jenson continues this line of thought by stressing how the event character of God's very being is manifested in Jesus' death on the Cross, thus touching upon the second strategy. He continues: "Death is time's ultimate act. Normal gods transcend death by immunity to it or by being identical with it. The triune God ... transcends death by triumphing over it, by the Son's dying and the Father's raising him again.... The one God is an *event*; history occurs not only in him but as his being.... God is the event of the world's

---

4. Robert Jenson, *Systematic Theology*, vol. 1, *The Triune God* (Oxford: Oxford University Press, 2001), 66.

transformation by Jesus' love, the same love to which the world owes its ex-istence."[5] This "event ontology" pertains to the divine nature and the divine being, in Jenson's theology of God, but it also differentiates the persons by way of distinct natural attributions. The Father is able to raise the dead, while the Son is able to evacuate himself of divine prerogatives. That is to say, God is by nature a process of historical development, and various natu-ral differentiations in God are embodied in or give rise to distinct persons.

We find a similar idea in the theology of Moltmann. For Moltmann, the crucifixion of Jesus reveals a God who suffers in history as one of us, in his very being:

> When the crucified Jesus is called the "image of the invisible God," the meaning is that *this* is God, and God is like *this*. . . . The nucleus of everything that Christian theology says about "God" is to be found in this Christ event. The Christ event on the cross is a God event. . . . So the new christology which tries to think of the "death of Jesus as the death of God," must take up the elements of truth which are to be found in *kenoticism*. . . . It cannot seek to maintain only a dialectical relation-ship between the divine being and human being, leaving each of these unaffect-ed. . . . That means that it must understand the event of the cross in God's being in both Trinitarian and personal terms. In contrast to the traditional doctrine of the two natures in the person of Christ, it must begin from the totality of the person of Christ and understand the relationship of the death of the Son to the Father and the Spirit. . . . From the life of these three, which has within it the death of Je-sus, there then emerges who God is and what his Godhead means. Most previous statements about the specifically Christian understanding of talk about "the death of God" have lacked a dimension, the Trinitarian dimension.[6]

Moltmann sees the human death of Jesus as an event affecting the very be-ing of God. Death and time enter into the very life and character of the Son as God. This also means that in the resurrection, the life of God overcomes death as part of God's own history. If the Son suffers and dies, the Father grieves, and the Holy Spirit acts to give life again to Christ. Each person is differentiated by distinct natural attributes, sufferings, and engagements with the world. We are very close here, not to a traditional Christian theol-ogy, but to a new form of post-metaphysical mythology that compromises any true realism about the divine nature and the reality of God as the tran-scendent Creator.

Let us ask, then: if these theories are so novel, what is it about them that

5. Jenson, *Systematic Theology*, 1:219, 221.
6. Moltmann, *The Crucified God*, 202–3.

makes them attractive to so many of our theological contemporaries? Part of the answer, at least, is that they are attempts to find an alternative to the classical notion of divine immutability, a doctrine which frequently gives rise to various objections. By taking a moment to survey these objections, we will perhaps be better able to see what it is in these alternative positions that arouses the sympathies of so many important modern theologians.

The first objection is based upon the following claims: the conviction that love implies solidarity with suffering people. If God truly loves human beings, then God accepts suffering empathetically in who God is, in God's very being. In the now well-known words of Moltmann: "were God incapable of suffering in any respect, and therefore in an absolute sense, then he would also be incapable of love."[7] The core of this objection, then, is that an impassible God, qua impassible, would be incapable of love.

The second objection is based on the claim that, in order for God to be personal and present, he must be relational. It follows from this that, if God is not relative to his creatures, he is not personal and present to them. A God who is truly loving must be related to creatures, and therefore subject to being affected or changed by them. For this reason, an impassible God would not be truly personal and present or otherwise related to his creatures in any meaningful way. It should be noted at this juncture—we will return to this point below—that Aquinas expressly denies that there are real relations of dependence of God upon creatures. Only the contrary is the case: the real relation of dependence of creatures upon God.[8] On the terms of this objection, then, God (as portrayed by St. Thomas) is impersonal and unconcerned with the well-being of his creatures.

The third objection starts from the premise that God must take into himself the experience of evil—into his very being, nature, and life—in order to save us from evil.[9] If this claim is true, then it naturally raises the ques-

7. Moltmann, *The Crucified God*, 230.

8. See *ST* I, q. 13, a. 7.

9. See, for example, Hans Urs von Balthasar, *Theo-Drama: Theological Dramatic Theory*, vol. 5, *The Last Act*, trans. Graham Harrison (San Francisco: Ignatius Press, 1998), esp. 265–69. Balthasar claims that the Incarnate Son's potential ability to experience suffering, sin, and hell within himself is rooted ultimately in a feature of the immanent Trinity (the distance between Father and Son), one that is realized economically. On this count, see too Hans Urs von Balthasar, *Theo-Drama: Theological Dramatic Theory*, vol. 4, *The Action*, trans. Graham Harrison (San Francisco: Ignatius, 1994), 362: "the economic Trinity ... always presupposes the immanent. This is because the Son's eternal, holy distance from the Father, in the Spirit, forms the basis on which the unholy distance of the world's sin can be transposed into it, can be transcended and overcome by it."

tion of how we can be saved at all if God does not suffer, let alone if he is incapable of suffering.

How ought we to respond to these objections? We should begin first by considering the topic of divine immutability as it is classically understood. Then, once we have the beginnings of a correct understanding, we can see why these objections, poignant though they may be, are grounded in mischaracterizations or misunderstandings of the classical teaching.

AQUINAS ON DIVINE IMMUTABILITY

Before turning to Aquinas's considered arguments, we should note that the doctrine of divine immutability has not only philosophical foundations, but also clear biblical roots. St. Thomas appeals most frequently in this respect to two passages from scripture. Malachi 3:6: "For I the Lord, do not change," is the text he cites as an authority in the *sed contra* to *ST* I, q. 9, a. 1. He also frequently cites James 1:17, which refers to God as "the Father of lights with whom there is no variation or shadow due to change."[10] Taken in their historical and textual context, both sayings denote first and foremost the moral constancy of God. He is the Lord of the covenant who shows enduring fidelity to Israel, and he is characterized by unchanging goodness, without any possibility of moral corruption or evil. The moral matrix in which these affirmations arise has ontological implications. As Aquinas notes, *agere sequitur esse*: action follows upon being.[11] If God is able to be morally constant and is free in the perfection of his goodness from any possibility of evil, this can only be in virtue of what he is immutably in his mysterious divine nature. To turn the formulation around: if God's actions did not pertain to what is immutable in his identity, then God's actions would not truly reveal to us who God is eternally. However the very premise of Christian theology is that God's nature and very identity are revealed truly to us in his action. Therefore, behind any of our claims regarding the morality of divine agency, there must stand corresponding ontological claims. God can be loving in an enduring way only because he is eternally unchanged in his perfection as one who loves. Indeed this is the truth about God in himself that the New Testament underscores as casting

10. See *ST* III, q. 61, a. 4, obj. 3 and ad 3.
11. *SCG*, I, c. 43.

light on the paschal mystery: "... the Father has sent his Son as the Savior of the world.... So we know ... God is love."[12]

It is easy to see, then, why the immutability of the Triune God is well attested in the Christian tradition as a whole. It follows not only from the truth of the simplicity and eternity of God as Triune, but also from a biblical awareness of the unchanging love of God. The mystery of the Trinity as a communion of persons who are one in essence is a truth that precedes all others and upon which all others are logically dependent. The consensus teaching, then, is that God is who he is from all eternity independently of either the creation or the Incarnation.[13] Creation is not necessary to God— so that God might become more fully himself by a development of his divine nature—nor can his activity as Creator enrich his divine nature. In fact, the contrary is the case: the creation is given being continuously only ever from the abundance or undiminishable plenitude of God's goodness. Nor, then, can the Trinitarian communion of persons be constituted through a progressive history of a shared life with creatures. There is no Trinitarian internal temporal history or progressive enrichment, because God is always already wholly Trinitarian, prior to creation, and prior to the economy of grace he initiates with human beings, as well as prior to the Incarnation and crucifixion of the Son made human. In our own time, the confession of divine immutability has been expressly reaffirmed by the First Vatican Council,[14] and subsequently by the Catechism of the Catholic Church.[15]

Together with its scriptural and traditional bases, divine immutability is also intelligible from a purely rational point of view, that is, metaphysical-

12. 1 John 4:14, 16.

13. For a few representative examples, see St. Augustine, *The Trinity* V, 5: "So there is no modification in God because there is nothing in him that can be changed or lost.... God ... remains absolutely unchangeable." See too, Dionysius, *The Divine Names*, c. 2: "He is one in an unchanging and transcendent way." On the divine impassibility in particular, see John Damascene, *An Exposition of the Orthodox Faith*, 2, c. 26: "The Word of God then itself endured all [suffering] in the flesh, while His divine nature which alone was passionless remained void of passion." Accordingly, the Catholic tradition takes the passages of scripture that attribute change of mentality, passionate reaction, or physical movement to God metaphorically, i.e., as expressive symbols of God's inner life, communicated fittingly, by divine condescension, in a mode adapted to our human way of understanding. See Aquinas, in this regard, in *ST* I, q. 9, a. 1, ad 3, where he discusses metaphorical discourse about God. On the fittingness of the use of metaphors in scripture in general, see *ST* I, q. 1, a. 9.

14. See Vatican I, *Dei Filius*, chap. 1: "Since he [God] is one, singular, completely simple and unchangeable [*incommutabilis*]...." In *Decrees*, ed. Tanner, 2:805, emphasis added.

15. See *Catechism of the Catholic Church*, 2nd ed. (Vatican City: Libreria Editrice Vaticana, 1997), para. 202.

ly. Here again we can note that there is a profound convergence of biblical faith and philosophical reason. Sound conclusions of philosophical reason provide warrant for the Church's affirmation of the unchanging identity of God's divine nature. Since the three persons of the Trinity share in this one nature, our right understanding of God's unchanging *Trinitarian* identity depends in part on a right understanding of the immutability of God's essence. Here again the philosophical arguments do not procure Trinitarian faith, but they are placed in the service of it, within *sacra doctrina*, in key ways.

In *ST* I, q. 9, a. 1, Aquinas gives three arguments in favor of divine immutability. The arguments are simple and stem in a logical way from previous arguments, made above, regarding divine attributes. The first pertains to God's pure actuality and runs as follows: There must be a first being who is pure act and, as such, is not in potentiality. (This follows from the first and second ways that we considered above of arguing for the existence of God.) But everything that is subject to change is in some way in potentiality. Therefore, in virtue of his pure actuality and the perfection it entails, God is not mutable. This argument has a strongly apophatic tone. All creatures in virtue of their potency can become less ontologically perfect or be made more perfect progressively. God is not subject to ontological histories as creatures are. The perfection of his nature transcends the changes to which they are commonly subject.

Aquinas's second argument proceeds from the divine simplicity. Since God is simple, in the respects considered above, he possesses existence in virtue of his own nature, and his properties are identical with his very essence. If follows from this that he cannot undergo the changes to which composite realities are subject. For example, creatures come into being and possess a certain ontological goodness by this very fact, and can then achieve greater degrees of goodness through natural activities and the development of properties. God, however, is his very goodness, and gives goodness to all things (which are said to participate in his goodness). Consequently, he is the recipient of neither substantial being as such nor any qualities of being that he might receive from creatures. He cannot become good in his very being, by coming into being, and he cannot achieve greater goodness by interacting with creatures. More generally, we can speak of no alteration of some property of God distinct from God's essence, since we cannot speak meaningfully of any real distinction in God between properties and essence. As such, we must affirm that God's divine essence is not mutable.

Aquinas's third argument is premised on the divine infinity. Since God is infinite, he cannot change so as to acquire some perfection or addition in the order of being that he did not previously possess. Any such change would presuppose a prior limitation in his being, which is incompatible with his infinity. For this reason, again, God is not mutable. We should note that the infinity of God is depicted here as co-extensive with God's actuality of perfection and life, and as the source of life and movement in all others. God's infinity is in no way something physically static or lifeless.

In *ST* I, q. 9, a. 2, Aquinas proceeds to offer a fourth argument for divine immutability, which runs as follows: God is not conditioned in his existence by another but is the condition for the existence of all others. God cannot undergo non-existence, because it is of the essence of God to exist. Consequently, God is radically and mysteriously distinct from the created world and its history, since everything in the created order and its history is characterized by a coming-into-being and a progressive development of existence. God, then, is the ground of and condition for that history, not a changing subject within the created order. In this respect, God, as the Creator of all that exists, alone is utterly immutable, in a way that only the Creator can be, and that cannot be true of any creature, which receives its being from another, and which is characterized necessarily by ontological composition of various sorts.

To this set of arguments found in *ST* I, q. 9, we can add three addenda that, working by way of negation, will help clarify and crystalize our understanding of divine immutability. The first point that needs to be made is that God is not a body. As such, he does not have physical passions, which characterize the life of sensate animals. In the words of Gilles Emery: "God is not subject to passion *because he is incorporeal*. Passion is not only excluded from God in some particular form that it could take, but passion (*passio*) is excluded in God by reason of its genus, that is to say, because the very notion of a passion pertains to sensible affection, *without which there is no such thing as a passion*. God does not submit to passions, but he is *life* (*vita*) in the highest sense of the word. God is wisdom and love: he exerts by himself not only his operation, free from all external determination from passions, but he *is* this same operation of wisdom and love."[16] It follows from this obser-

16. Gilles Emery, "The Immutability of the God of Love and the Problem of Language Concerning the 'Suffering of God,'" in Keating and White, *Divine Impassibility and the Mystery of Human Suffering*, 66.

vation that God does not have emotions or passions of the sort we find in human beings or other higher animals, with developed internal senses. The passions are proper only to embodied creatures.

The second point has to do with the non-reciprocal relations between God and creatures and the positive soteriological content of this teaching. St. Thomas maintains that God is not really relative to creatures in virtue of any causal dependency, but that creatures are entirely relative to God in all that they are.[17] In other words, God does not derive his being from creatures in any coherent sense of the term, but creatures do derive their existence entirely from God. The relationship in the order of being between Creator and creatures is entirely unilateral in this respect. It follows from this, however, that, God being God, he *alone* can act freely to save his creatures as one motivated uniquely by divine wisdom and love, *without any augmentation of his goodness*. In any spiritual creature, for example, a free act of personal goodness stemming from wisdom and love perfects and augments the goodness of the creature in question. In this case, the act of giving to another is also always ontologically a source of self-amelioration. On God's part, however, this is never the case. He gives being, life, grace, and salvation all as purely gratuitous gifts, that express his plenitude of eternal love, and such gifts are never occasions for his own ontological amelioration in any way.[18] Likewise, God can be present to his creation in his perfect wisdom and love in a way that no creature can, because he is the very source of its being, more interior to creatures than they are to themselves. Indeed, it is only because God is immutably perfect in the order of being that he alone can be present in this way, in the inmost heart of creaturely being. Consequently only a God who is immutable love can be present precisely as perfect love to all that is, that is to say, as the very cause of its being. Finally, God has the power to save his creatures in truth only because he is omnipotent, and so can effectively show love and mercy in a way no other can, as one who can reach down into the very roots of reality and can re-create all things. "Behold I make all things new" (Rv 21:5). But God can act with an omnipotent love and mercy only because of the power he possesses as Cre-

---

17. See *ST* I, q. 13, a. 7.

18. Similarly, we can note that the creature can also suffer in its own nature by undertaking the initiative to help another, which implies a form of ontological self-diminution, at least in some respect (such as when, moved by charity, one incurs harm to the body to help another). The divine nature, however, cannot be subject to diminution as a facet of God's agency in creation and redemption. If God suffers, he does so in virtue of his human nature, a point I will return to below.

ator, and this same perfection of power entails immutability. Consequently, a God who is not immutably perfect in the way the Creator truly is is a God who cannot save his creation effectively by love and mercy.[19] Only if God transcends creation so as to be in no way dependent in his undiminished goodness, can God *as God* communicate his divine life and goodness to us, without being thwarted in this activity. Similarly, we should note that it is only because God has the immutable power to save us, in his transcendent wisdom and love as Creator, that he is also able to become human, to be present among as a human being, in an expression of his solidarity as God with us. A mere creature would not have the power to become human nor the capacity to communicate grace to the world through the medium of the human life, death, and resurrection of Christ, but God the Holy Trinity does have this immutable power.

The third point has to do with the impassibility of the divine nature in Christ. The traditional affirmation regarding the suffering of God in Christ is unambiguous but also entails a distinction. God did assuredly suffer in Christ and indeed one may rightly affirm that God was crucified, died, and was buried. These attributes pertain, however, to God the Son alone, in virtue of his human nature, and therefore do not pertain either to his divine nature considered as such or to the persons of the Father or the Spirit. In other words, it is God the Son (the person of the Word made flesh) who alone suffered, not the Father or the Spirit. Thus the traditional adage states rightly that "one of the Trinity suffered." Yet he did so in virtue of his human nature (i.e., God suffered in his human body and soul, undergoing physical, emotional, and spiritual agony as man). He did not suffer in virtue of his divine nature, in which he is one with the Father and the Holy Spirit. Thus, insofar as he is human, the Son truly suffers personally, but insofar as he is God, one in being with the Father and the Spirit, he also remains impassible in his divine nature. When confusion arises on this point, it typically stems from a failure to distinguish adequately between Christ's divine and human natures, or from a simple refusal of the aptness of the distinction. Some object that if Christ as the Son and Word of God is a divine person, then we must say that God suffers naturally in the Crucifixion. If a divine person suffers

---

19. Perfect love and mercy are not subject to corruption or alteration, but are fully actual, perfect, infinite, and all-powerful. If God's love were qualified by and subject to creation in a developmental relationship, it would become an imperfect love, subject to potential diminishment and inconstancy, limited in power, unable to act on things from within, acted upon, then, instead, from without—in short, a created love.

then the deity itself must suffer. However this does not follow, and the idea incorrectly represents the dogmatic teaching of the Church at the Council of Chalcedon, which is itself based upon apostolic teaching. The Council teaches that it is the person of the Son who suffers, and who is subject to change and death. He does so, however, in a human way, that is to say in his human nature. He does not undergo change, suffering, or death in a divine way, that is to say, in his divine nature.

Correctly understood, then, the Chalcedonian doctrine of the suffering of Christ teaches the following: First, in Christ, it is God who suffers and God who is crucified. Second, this suffering is that of the person of the Son. It is truly God the Son who suffers.[20] Third, the Son suffers in virtue of his human nature, in his human body and soul, in his spiritual and sensate faculties as man. Fourth, the Son does not suffer, but remains impassible, in his divine nature, in which he is one with the Father and the Holy Spirit.

What we can safely conclude from this teaching is that God did not have to suffer as human but chose freely to do so in order to manifest his solidarity with us and to overcome the power of evil in our human history. The teaching also shows us that only God can overcome evil, because, even as he does suffer as man, he also remains as God, all-powerful and immutable in his love, goodness, wisdom, and other divine characteristics. He does not cede the transcendent perfection and infinite goodness he possesses as God in becoming man. He cannot, but even if he could, were he to, this would mean that God would be in the same insoluble difficulties as his creatures, and so he too would need saving, which would amount to an absurdity. It is only because he retains the prerogatives of his divine nature that God-made-man can save us precisely in and through his human life among us.

This brings us to the critical soteriological dimension of the traditional doctrine of divine immutability and impassibility. Simply put, the doctrine safeguards the mystery of our salvation. It is because God in his nature is free from mutability and suffering that he is capable of saving us from suffering and death. We can state this claim in a twofold way. In a first sense, it applies to what God is in himself immanently, as one whose nature transcends and is impervious to all suffering. In a second sense, it applies to God

20. The Church has always rejected every form of Patripassianism (i.e., where the Father is said to suffer on the Cross) as a subspecies of modalism. See, for example, Pope St. Leo I, *Quam laudabiliter*, in Denzinger, no. 284.

in the Incarnation, as one who becomes truly human and is exposed to human suffering in the most intense way, manifesting in this very event his capacity to make use even of evil suffered in order to bring about the divinely willed good.

The first of these soteriological ideas can be grasped by noting that God in his inalienable and impassible nature is the first origin and final end of all of God's soteriological activity. That is to say, if God seeks to actively save human beings from sin, suffering, death, and perpetual damnation, he does so out of his own immutable goodness. He does so also in view of the union of human beings with God, by means of the beatific vision, the immediate knowledge of God's divine essence, which he imparts to redeemed humanity by grace. If, however, we confess that God's divine goodness is intrinsically mutable, so that he is capable of being changed in himself (in his eternal life and identity) by moral or natural evil, then both of these forms of soteriological promise are placed at risk. God cannot forfeit the immutable power and goodness he has as God to redeem us, precisely because these transcendent traits of God are in fact permanent and inalienable. Likewise, if we are united with God eternally and his eternal life is characterized intrinsically by the presence of ontological evil, suffering, death, and moral blight, then eternal union with God is union with one who is partially constituted by evil eternally, even if this occurs by his negative reaction to and ontological endurance of it. However well-intentioned he might be, this God would be uniting us eternally with his own night of suffering, interior separations, and development through submission to death and hell. The soteriological promise of such a "beatitude" is dubious at best.[21]

---

21. David Bentley Hart states the argument this way, in *The Beauty of the Infinite* (Grand Rapids, Mich.: Eerdmans, 2003), 165–66: "The God whose identity subsists in time and is achieved upon history's horizon—who is determined by his reaction to the pathos of history—may be a being, or indeed the totality of all beings gathered in the pure depths of ultimate consciousness, but he is not being as such, he is not life and truth and goodness and love and beauty. God belongs to the system of causes, even if he does so as its total rationality; he is an absolute *causa in fieri*, but not a transcendent *causa in esse*. He may include us in his story, but his story will remain both good and evil, even if it ends in an ultimate triumph over evil. After all, how can we tell the dancer from the dance? ... Only a truly transcendent and "passionless" God can be the fullness of love dwelling within our very being, nearer to us than our inmost parts, but a dialectical Trinity is not transcendent—truly infinite—in this way at all, but only sublime, a metaphysical whole that can comprise us or change us extrinsically, but not transform our very being.... Theology must, to remain faithful to what it knows of God's transcendence, reject any picture of God that so threatens to become at once both thoroughly mythological and thoroughly metaphysical, and insist upon the classical definitions of impassibility, immutability, and nonsuccessive eternity."

The second soteriological idea can be articulated by noting the promise of the unique presence of God with us in the Incarnation, which manifests his solidarity with and love for the human race. St. Paul writes that "in Christ God was reconciling the world *to himself*" (2 Cor 5:19).[22] God in his transcendence is truly present in Christ without ceasing to be divine, precisely so as to manifest himself to us in human flesh, and so as to unite us with himself, even through the medium of the Cross. This requires, however, that the unchanging divine nature be present in Christ precisely in the midst of his suffering and death, so that he may manifest the power and wisdom of God from within the paschal mystery.[23] Nor is God's nature changed by Christ's suffering. Rather, the unchangeable divinity dwelling in Christ is the principle by which all suffering and death are definitively overcome.

Contrary to the objection that divine impassibility renders God insensitive to human suffering or incapable of love, it is therefore precisely the divine impassibility that enables God to victoriously triumph over suffering and death without taking it into himself.[24] In fact, it is only divine impassibility that allows God to truly leave suffering and death definitively behind in the eschaton, as by grace God gives humanity access to a reality—namely, himself—that is free from all suffering. "And God will wipe away every tear from their eyes" (Rv 7:17).

22. Emphasis added. This same idea is expressed in Col 1:19–20: "For in him all the fullness of God was pleased to dwell, and through him to reconcile to himself all things."

23. 1 Cor 1:23–25: "But we preach Christ crucified, a stumbling block to Jews and folly to Gentiles, but to those who are called, both Jews and Greeks, Christ the power of God and the wisdom of God. For the foolishness of God is wiser than men, and the weakness of God is stronger than men."

24. David Bentley Hart, "No Shadow of Turning: On Divine Impassibility," *Pro Ecclesia* 11, no. 2 (2002): 184–206, at 191: "As many of the fathers would have argued, a God who can by nature experience finite affects and so be determined by them is a God whose identity is established through a commerce with evil; if the nature of God's love can be in any sense positively shaped by sin, suffering, and death, then sin, suffering, and death will always be in some sense features of who he is. Among other things, this means that evil must enjoy a certain independent authenticity, a reality with which God must come to grips, and God's love must—if it requires the negative pathos of history to bring it to fruition—be inherently deficient, and in itself a fundamentally reactive reality. Goodness then requires evil to be good; love must be goaded into being by pain."

DOES THE NOTION OF A
PASSIBLE DEITY DETRACT FROM TRUE
UNDERSTANDING OF GOD?

Let us return briefly here to the various objections given earlier against divine immutability and impassibility and offer a contrasting set of reflections as a response.

First, we should be wary of mis-attributing merely created modes of being onto the divine nature. In doing so we may inevitably depict the divine nature in anthropomorphic, intrinsically imperfect, or inaccurate ways. It is not only classical theists who should be warned intermittently of the dangers of "conceptual idolatry." What would be the result for theology if God should be deemed acceptable company only insofar as he conforms to the conditions of our finitude and temporality? What if theologians fixated on contemporaneity and cultural relevance decide to annul all engagements with God due to the moral or intellectual embarrassment he causes them? Theology always runs the risk of refusing to consider God in the terms that rightly denote who God is in his incomprehensible transcendence, as well as in the terms that rightly denote his unique form of omnipresence and immanence as Creator.

Second, there is an added danger in the language of divine passibility of projecting human pathos and suffering back from the economy of creation into the divine nature. In this way of thinking, our evil and suffering come to characterize God in what God is essentially or eternally. This attributive practice not only risks obscuring the true knowledge of God as good and perfect, but also effectively defines God in terms of moral or ontological evil. We are justified in asking if by logical consequence such a God really can save the human race, for the simple reason that he is characterized ontologically by the same quandaries as his creatures, except to a greater degree. Suffering and defect now come to characterize what God is in his very essence. Indeed the eternal life of God is constituted in part by temporal moments of suffering, so that the Trinity is constituted by the Cross. Instead of God saving human beings out of his transcendent goodness, he must instead develop gradually by overcoming evil in a shared history with us. In this case, it is the creation that gives definition and being to the Creator, and not the inverse. As a consequence, it becomes unclear how God can overcome evil and suffering, and indeed it becomes unclear even whether God can overcome evil at all.

Third, the notions of divine suffering and change are frequently associated with a mistaken idea of the Incarnation, which confuses God's humanity, in which God truly suffered, with his divinity, in which the suffering Christ remains impassible and immutable. With one's acceptance of the language of divine passibility, there arises the serious danger of falsifying the Church's traditional confession of faith in the mystery of the Incarnation and passion of Christ as delineated in her conciliar declarations.[25]

CONCLUSION

The foregoing considerations attempt to show why, in spite of contrary headwinds, contemporary theology should retain the traditional teaching on divine immutability and impassibility. The denial of this doctrine is difficult to reconcile with scripture and tradition, and gives rise to acute metaphysical problems. However, the denial of divine immutability also raises significant soteriological concerns. Ironically, insolvable problems arise from the affirmation of divine mutability precisely in that domain where it is supposed to be especially advantageous, with respect to the doctrine of salvation. Simply put, the historicized God that we frequently encounter in contemporary treatments of Trinitarian ontology is consigned to intractable problems of "divine suffering" very similar to those of human beings, and by this very measure, is unable truly to save us.

25. Intellectual progress is sometimes mistaken for heresy, but the inverse is also the case. Disagreeing with or simply ignoring a conciliar dogmatic definition is never a theologically prudent act.

17

Divine Eternity and Unity

Before going on to discuss the divine spiritual operations of knowledge and love, we must first examine two remaining attributes of God's being, namely, his divine eternity and unity. In so doing, we will follow Aquinas's approach in each case by travelling down the *via negativa*, showing how both eternity (absence of mutability and so temporality) and unity (absence of division and thus composition) are in the first instance negative terms. As such, they are pointers that mark out the transcendence of God's being over all creaturely being, which latter intrinsically admits of varying degrees of mutability and division, whereas God does not. We will treat of the divine eternity and unity in succession in what follows.

DIVINE ETERNITY AS A
NEGATIVE ATTRIBUTE DERIVED
FROM IMMUTABILITY

Eternity is a name ascribed to God from the starting point of a negation. It denotes first that God is not mutable or subject to change, and that there is no temporal succession in God. The presupposition here is that time is a measure of change, but since God is perfect in actuality and immutable in his perfect actuation, he is not subject to developmental alteration through time. He is atemporal or eternal.[1]

1. On controversies pertaining to divine eternity, see David Braine, *The Reality of Time and the Existence of God: The Project of Proving God's Existence* (Oxford: Clarendon Press, 1988); William Hasker, *God, Time, and Knowledge* (Ithaca, N.Y.. Cornell University Press, 1989); Brian Leftow, *Time and Eternity* (Ithaca, N.Y.: Cornell University Press, 1991); Eleonore Stump and Norman

Aquinas begins his treatment in *ST* I, q. 10, a. 1, with a preliminary consideration of time. He approaches the definition of eternity through a negation of temporal change in God so as to arrive at a positive conception of eternity as a plenitude of life in God. In article 2 he goes on to draw connections between the immutability of God's perfection and this positive conception of divine eternity. Let us begin, then, by first exploring the nature of temporality so as to more fully understand what is being negated when we affirm God's eternity.

Aquinas follows Aristotle in positing that time is a measure of successive change or movement.[2] In our physical universe, every material reality is subject to progressive alteration (becoming over time), and we are able to study this progressive alteration because we grasp that the changes are happening in a given subject (a human being who is growing) by comparison with other forms of change (the earth revolving once fully around the sun). Changes that are co-simultaneous can be compared in this way, as when we say that a human being has aged one year, based on the date of that person's birth. He or she has developed biologically and has experienced human life for the same duration of time it takes for the earth to travel around the sun. One form of change is used to measure the other or is correlated with the other.

Understood in this way, only the human intellect can measure time. The reason is because the measurement of time presupposes three things that are proper to an intellectual nature. The first is cognitive apprehension of the unified natures and properties of diverse existent realities that are subject to temporal alteration. For example, human beings measure the change of days by a constant presence of the sun and the earth and by an estimation of the ongoing change in relation between them. This procedure, however, requires conceptual knowledge of the earth and the sun as realities, and of their properties of light and darkness. We must be able to identify the sun and the earth essentially and existentially to be capable of this kind of mea-

---

Kretzmann, "Eternity," *The Journal of Philosophy* 78, no. 8 (1981): 429–58; Richard Swinburne, *The Christian God*; Brian J. Shanley, "Eternity and Duration in Aquinas," *The Thomist* 61, no. 4 (1997): 525–48; Thierry-Dominique Humbrecht, *Trinité et création au prisme de la voie négative chez saint Thomas d'Aquin* (Paris: Parole et Silence, 2011); Eleonore Stump, *The God of the Bible and the God of the Philosophers* (Milwaukee, Wisc.: Marquette University Press, 2016); Serge-Thomas Bonino, *Dieu, "Celui Qui Est"*, 393–406.

2. For definitions of time, see *ST* I, q. 10, a. 1: time is "the numbering of movement by before and after." See also Aristotle, *Physics*, 4.11 (219a23–25): "We apprehend time only when we have marked motion, marking it by before and after; and it is only when we have perceived before and after in motion that we say that time has elapsed," and 4.12 (b32), "Time is a measure of motion and of being moved."

surement in the first place. And this, in turn, requires an intellectual nature capable of universal abstraction, a capacity lacking in non-rational animals.[3]

The second presupposition for the measurement of time is the conceptual understanding of the present. To judge that a given event is in the present, past, or possible future, one must be able to judge what is actually present and conceive of it as being so. In other words, the human being who thinks temporally understands the present as something stable against which change is measured. We can measure time as "past" or "future" only against the backdrop of a continual intellectual awareness of what is present. Indeed, only the present exists actually, not the past or the future, but as a result of their sensate and intellectual powers of memory, human beings can grasp by induction that there are stable and predictable forms of change in nature, and make use of these to measure the relative duration of past events, and predict foreseeable outcomes in the future. For example, we can grasp conceptually how long it is actually taking for the earth to revolve around the sun (a year) or rotate on its own axis (a day) and can measure the rate of change in human society by a calendar of years and days.

The third presupposition, then, is implied in the first two, namely, that the intellect itself also transcends time, or, in any event, tends to grasp something above time.[4] That is to say, the intellect by its very nature grasps what remains in things essentially and so exists as present. Not everything is in flux at each moment, and the intellect is able to apprehend in things what genuinely exists in "stillness" and abides in and through various processes of change. For this reason, it is an error to simply say that "everything is change" (the error of Heraclitus, who reduced everything to flux.)[5] Even if every physical reality we sense is changing, it is changing only in certain aspects, while in other aspects it remains the same. So, we can note the reality of change only because we also experience in the present certain stable substances that exist "above" the state of actual change.

3. Animals, of course, live in time and respond to emerging changes based on instinctive reactions and drives toward survival, nutrition, and reproduction; and higher animals possess "prudential" strategies to respond to temporal challenges, learned from sensate memory. But they do not measure time conceptually, or plan or predict outcomes based on their understanding of time, nor fathom divine eternity and seek union with God in his eternal life in an intentional way.

4. Cf. *ST* I-II, q. 53, a. 3, ad 3: "The intellectual part of the soul, considered in itself, is above time [*supra tempus*]."

5. For further discussion of the relationship between human historical analysis, as the study of causes of ongoing change, and the metaphysical awareness of natural essences, see my *The Incarnate Lord: A Thomistic Study in Christology* (Washington, D.C.: The Catholic University of America Press, 2015), 491–93.

All of this is to say that time, as a measure of change, is discerned in the tension that exists between what is stable and what is transitory in the physical realities we experience around us. Discernment of time also, for that reason, is closely linked to mutability of being, since the realities around us evince temporality precisely insofar as they change in one respect while remaining the same in another, thereby allowing us to contrast the present state of things with what was and will be. Moreover, as we will see below, it is precisely because of this close link between mutability and temporality that God, who, as we saw in the last chapter, is immutable, must for that reason also be atemporal.

To approach the divine eternity, then, we can proceed by way of the Dionysian threefold *via*, contrasting what we have gathered thus far about the divine nature with the state of physical beings in which we experience temporal processes of change. These realities, as we have said, develop through time, by successive movements of change, and God is the transcendent cause of their temporal being and becoming. *Per viam causalitatis*, the most coherent resemblance to God in temporal things will be found in those that are alive, because God is alive. Living beings grow and develop organically over time in homogeneous ways in view of teleological ends. (Plants grow and reproduce, animals develop sensate memories and learn as animals about their environment, human beings learn to study, pray, and love.) God is the cause of all living things and therefore can also be said to be alive or have life in an immaterial manner. He is one who lives perfectly and who has teleological ends, like living beings. *Per viam negationis*, however, we must note that God is not subject to gradual development like creatures. This follows from God's pure actuality, simplicity, and perfection. Indeed, God is infinite life in pure actuality, and so he cannot know any diminishment or progressive perfecting through time. We can conclude that there is no temporal succession or development in the life of God, and instead we must affirm that God is eternal life. Positively this leads by a resolution, *per viam eminentiae*, to the claim that eternity implies something more than mere perennial existence. It entails a positive plenitude of life. This is why, according to Boethius's definition, which Aquinas adopts in *ST* I, q. 10, a. 1, eternity is "the simultaneously-whole and perfect possession of unending life."[6]

Note too that the above reference to divine "life" implies the active op-

---

6. Boethius's definition is originally found in *The Consolation of Philosophy*, trans. V. E. Watts, (London: Penguin Books, 1969), bk. 5.

eration of intellect and will. "God is spirit" (Jn 4:24), and so his life is not a physical or sensate life, but a life of contemplation and love. Moreover, this life is perfect eternal life without diminution, that is, it is the life of pure actuality. As such, it is not a life that is qualified or invigorated by creatures but is the source of creatures' coming to exist temporally in the first place.

How, then, can we understand God's eternal life in comparison with the temporal history of his creation? Are the two simply alien to one another? On the one hand, we must be clear that God's life does not evolve or progress against the backdrop of more stable features of being, as if he were a living thing developing within the context of an enduring cosmos, with part of him developing and part of him remaining the same. For this reason, on the Thomistic view, it is an error to consider God's life as a kind of perpetual time, or duration of unending time.[7] He is not living through a time of infinite, unending duration that is composed of successive events. His life transcends any sequence of events that would compose an enduring time. Stated simply, time does not apply to God in his simple, perfect, infinite, and immutable being.

On the other hand, the temporality of creation is not something alien to divine eternity, since God is the cause of all temporal things, and knows them comprehensively, sustaining all things in being by his goodness and love. Consequently, while it is not false to say that God is "outside of time," we might also say more fittingly that God's eternity "encompasses" time. God creates the temporal world as a created expression of his eternity and sustains it in being. Created temporality therefore exists "within" God's divine eternity.[8] This also means that there is no competition between God's

---

7. See Swinburne's arguments for the existence of God in time, in *The Christian God*, 131–42; 248–49.

8. On this topic there are important points of convergence between Aquinas and Barth, identifiable in the latter's extensive treatment of eternity in CD 2:1, 608–77. Barth begins from the classical position (Augustine, Boethius, Anselm, Polanus) that God is not temporal and that this follows from his unchangableness, but also holds that the freedom of God permits God in his perfection to be present to and within all time, encompassing it within himself. Barth claims to be more Boethian than Thomist (CD 2:1, 611), but the rhetorical arguments he presents to contrast his own position and that of Aquinas are not very convincing. God's work includes that of his temporal presence among us in Jesus Christ, so that all that unfolds in time by his Incarnation can be thought about as an expression of what God is eternally. God can be thought of from our perspective as pre-temporal, super-temporal, and post-temporal. God's eternity is identical with his very life. "Like every divine perfection [God's eternity] is the living God Himself" (638). This eternal life is the principle of God's glory (640). The glory of the Lord is the fullness of his deity, by which he manifests himself to human beings luminously and radiantly in Jesus Christ (643).

eternal prerogatives and his temporal initiatives in creation. From all eternity God can understand his creation in any given time. Likewise he can undertake a new initiative in the midst of any temporal event from all eternity, that is, out of the plenitude of his perfect life of knowledge and love. Indeed, it is precisely because he understands the created cosmos comprehensively from all eternity that he can act before, within, and after any temporal event in light of his own eternal designs.[9]

This conception of the divine eternity has significant ramifications for how we understand God's relationship to cosmic history, and his knowledge of the future. The Thomistic tradition argues, in its own characteristic way, that anthropomorphisms should be avoided in this domain. God does not learn from the world through a kind of neutral observation, as if God were to look out into history and perceive the future or estimate its outcomes.[10] Rather, because God is atemporal and eternal, he knows all time just as he knows all creation, namely, as its eternal Author. Nothing in the temporal realm evades the knowledge of God, and nothing in time can exist without his either willing it to be so or permitting it to occur, as in the case of moral evil in creatures (a topic I will return to in the following chapter). God understands the moral evil that angels and human beings do, and knows of these acts in his eternity, but he neither causes nor wills them to occur, either directly or indirectly. This is possible because God can will from all eternity to sustain in being and to assist temporal creatures who are what Aquinas calls true "contingent causes," beings who act by free rational deliberation, and not by mere natural necessity or external compulsion.[11] Aquinas thinks that their freedom comes from God in its very being, but the defective use of it comes from the creature alone, not from the Creator.[12] From all eternity God can merely permit such creatures to do evil, if they negate the truth about themselves and reject some of the developmental inclinations of nature and grace.[13]

9. God can respond to each singular event, person, historical situation, and circumstance from "within" the purview of his all-creating eternal life. For a more developed version of this argument, see Eleonore Stump, *The God of the Bible and the God of the Philosophers.*

10. On Molinism, see Alfred Freddoso, "Introduction to the Problem of Free Will and Divine Causality," presentation at the Aquinas Philosophy Workshop, Mount St. Mary's College, Emmitsburg, Md., 2013, http://www3.nd.edu/~afreddos/papers/freedom%20and%20God.pdf.

11. See *ST* I, q. 19, aa. 8–9.

12. See *ST* I-II, q. 75, aa. 1–3; q. 79, aa. 1–2.

13. For discussion of the so-called antecedent permissive decree whereby God permits evil, see my discussion in Thomas Joseph White, "Catholic Predestination: The Omnipotence

From what we have been saying, one might ask *how* God knows the future, if he knows it "from all eternity"? The answer is that God does not learn from realities outside of himself (as all those with spiritual created intelligences do). Rather, God knows creatures through the medium of his own divine essence (through knowing himself).[14] Creatures learn from the objective determinations of what already exists around them, whereas God in his knowledge gives rise to what exists. He therefore knows creatures as the cause of creatures, as he who wills to create them from and in his own self-knowledge or wisdom. This means, in turn, that God knows the future *as the cause of the future*. It is because God causes all things to be that he knows all that will be in the future, and he knows this temporal reality comprehensively, in that act of knowledge that characterizes his very essence, God's eternal activity of knowing himself.

This is why God *and only God* comprehends perfectly all that will come to pass or has ever come to pass. It is because causal knowledge reaches down into the roots of all that exists and that comes to pass. The fact that this knowledge is from all eternity does not hinder God's freedom to creatively engage with or respond to events that are (from our perspective) in the future, and that do not yet exist. God knows from all eternity that he will undertake certain initiatives in time as relational responses to past or prior states of affairs. He can inaugurate the communication of grace, the Incarnation, and the sacraments, in response to human difficulties of ignorance and sin, just as he can inaugurate the eschaton (resurrection of the dead, final judgment) as a re-creation of the cosmos. It is important not to anthropomorphize this activity "from all eternity" unselfconsciously in latently temporal terms, as if God is acting "before" and reacting "after" to predetermine or to respond to historical events. Rather in each event of history in which God acts, it is the eternal God who acts, whose being mysteriously encompasses all that is subject to change and who can be present to all moments in history in light of his eternal self-possession and mysterious fullness of being. God is not a historical process, but all created historical processes do take place within God.

---

and Innocence of Divine Love," in *Thomism and Predestination: Principles and Disputations*, ed. S. A. Long, R. W. Nutt, and T. J. White (Ave Maria, Fla.: Sapientia Press, 2016), 94–126, esp. 116–18. For further discussion in the same volume, see Serge-Thomas Bonino, "Contemporary Thomism through the Prism of the Theology of Predestination," 29–50, at 45–48.

14. On how God understands things other than himself through the medium of his own essence, see especially St. Thomas's discussion in *SCG* I, c. 49. See also *ST* I, q. 14, a. 5. We will discuss God's knowledge more fully in chapter 18.

Moreover, from what has been said above, we can see why prophecy of future contingent events is rightly taken as an exceptional sign of the miraculous. The reason for this is that only God can know the future of contingent singular events with absolute certitude, rather than prognostication, since he alone causes them to be. This is the case in particular for human free actions, which are not caused directly by any created agent other than the free subject. So only God can know future contingent free actions, just insofar as he is the cause of those actions, who sustains them in being. This is why, if a human person truly possesses miraculous knowledge of future contingent singulars, especially in regard to human action, this can be due only to the gift of God.[15] Vivid examples in the gospel include Christ's three prophecies that he is to be crucified in Jerusalem,[16] and his poignant foretelling to Simon Peter that the latter will deny him three times before the cock crows.[17] Christ knows of these future events as man in virtue of an infused prophetic knowledge, and the fact that he has such knowledge is a manifest sign given to the apostles of the presence of God in his ministry, and in fact of the divine agency abiding within him.

In sum, insofar as time is a measure of change, we can see from a consideration of the divine immutability—as the logical complement to the divine simplicity, perfection, and infinity—that God is eternal. The affirmation of his eternity follows in a straightforward fashion from a consideration of the transcendence of his being with respect to mutable, created being. God exists supra-temporally in an incomprehensible way. As such, his eternity is not to be conceived of merely as an unending succession of events or as some kind of eternally perfected history (this would imply the distinction between potency and act and so put creaturely forms of composition back into God). Categories like succession and history do not apply to him in any proper sense of their signification. Moreover, because of his transcendent relation to creation and its temporality, God likewise knows all times, the future included, insofar as he is their eternal cause.

---

15. Consider the contrasting perspective of Sergius Bulgakov on this point, in *The Bride of the Lamb*, trans. B. Jakim (Grand Rapids, Mich.: Eerdmans, 2002), 242–45, who views God's knowledge of future free actions as non-causal and who therefore deems prophecy as essentially a sophisticated form of prognostication. God kenotically delimits his causal influence on the human agent so as to allow space for the latter to conjecture about the future in prophetical and symbolic ways. These are approximations by which created wisdom seeks to rejoin the divine mystery.

16. See Mt 16:21; 17:22–23; 20:17–19, and parallels.

17. See Mt 26:34 and parallels.

DIVINE UNITY

What does it mean to say that God is one? Aquinas takes up this question in *ST* I, q. 11, when he turns to the topic of the divine unity. We can follow his approach by first examining the kind of unity found in created beings and then applying this concept analogically to God in light of his simplicity and perfection. On this count, several points need to be made.

The first thing to note about unity is that it is a property of being. It is a transcendental notion, like goodness and truth, which means that our terminology for "unity" is in some way co-extensive with our terminology for "being."[18] Whatever exists can be said to be one in some way. This analogical ascription of unity follows the diverse determinations of the categorial modes of being. For example, we ascribe being to substances, their various quantities, qualities, relations, and so forth, by an analogical form of predication. So too we can speak analogically of one substance, one quality, one quantity, one relation, and so forth, for each categorial mode of being. The unity of a substance (such as a human being) is both like and unlike the unity of a quality (such as the capacity to play the violin). What both unities have in common is real ontologically but cannot be specified generically. Unity is not a form or species of being, but is common to every genus of being, as is goodness, which we examined above.

As a transcendental property of being, unity is defined by Aquinas first and foremost negatively, as an absence of division. This is the case because unity implies an *indivisibility*. When we denote something as one, we denote in effect that it is not divided or multiple.[19] Thus, we come to perceive a dimension of being, which is characterized by unity and multiplicity. "This is one, undivided person, Paul, who is ontologically distinct from Peter." Unity implies *separateness*, since what is one in being has a given aseity that sets

18. See *ST* I, q. 11, a. 1: "*one* is the same as *being* [*unum convertitur cum ente*]."
19. See Aquinas, *In IV Meta.*, lec. 2, 553: "It is also evident from the foregoing argument that unity and being are the same numerically but differ conceptually; for if this were not the case they would be wholly synonymous, and then it would be nonsense to say, 'a human being,' and 'one man.' For it must be borne in mind that the term *man* is derived from the quiddity or the nature of man, and the term *thing* from the quiddity only; but the term *being* is derived from the act of being, and the term *one* from order or lack of division; for what is one is an undivided being. Now what has an essence, and a quiddity by reason of that essence, and what is undivided in itself, are the same. Hence these three—thing, being, and one—signify absolutely the same thing but according to different concepts." *Commentary on Aristotle's Metaphysics*, trans. J. P. Rowan (Notre Dame, Ind.: Dumb Ox Books, 1995).

it apart from others. "Peter exists in himself, apart from Paul." When we say that a thing is one or is unified, we are noting its ontological indivisibility and its distinctness in relation to other realities.

This does not mean that unity has a merely relational signification, as if to denote that one thing is not another. Our notion of unity indicates something about the intrinsic nature and existence of those things that we say are "one." Here, however, we must immediately make a key distinction. As Aquinas explains in *ST* I, q. 11, a. 1, ad 1, there is a distinction between *transcendental* unity, which is ontological, and *numerical* unity, which is quantitative. *Transcendental* unity is the unity described above that is convertible with being, which we denote analogically according to a diversity of modes of realization. *Numerical* unity, meanwhile, pertains to the genus of *quantity* alone. So, for example, the unity of substance of a human person is based upon his or her substantial being (unity here is a property of the substance which gives unity to all the parts and in which all the properties inhere). This is related to but distinct from the unity of quantity, which is a quantitative material oneness: for instance, this is one human body, having its own natural dimensions, magnitude, and shape. Clearly God is not "one" in a material sense as a quantity, like one physical magnitude. He is, however, one in the former sense, that is, "one in being," in virtue of the unity of the divine nature. Accordingly, when we speak of divine unity, we are speaking of an ontological unity but not one that is numeric, based on quantitative determinations.[20]

As Aquinas notes in *ST* I, q. 11, a. 1, ad 2, there are degrees of unity, even in things that are one. Why is this? The reason is that an existent can either be simple or compound, insofar as it has a nature that is more or less simple, or more or less complex, that is to say, rooted in a compound. The unity of a complex artifact, like a car, is real, but less perfect than the substantial unity of something organic and living, like a tree or an animal, because in the case of a living thing the soul as the formal principle of life conveys organizational determination to the organic body from within, whereas the artifact receives its "form" extrinsically, through the imposition of a set of relationships upon a preexisting set of natural realities by a given artist or designer. Meanwhile, a human being enjoys the unity of personhood that stems from the spiritual soul as the form of the body, and therefore has a more perfect

---

20. See *ST* I, q. 11, a. 3, ad 2: "One, which is the principle of number, is not predicated of God, but only of material things."

ontological unity than any other animal. An angel is unified in virtue of being a pure spirit, a higher form of unity, because there is no spiritual-material composition in an angelic reality. Obviously, the kind of unity ascribed to God is other than and transcends utterly even the most perfect form of creaturely unity that occurs in angelic beings.

We should note that compound unities can be of two sorts. A compound can be one made up of parts in a whole (like the material parts of a car, or the living organs that are parts of an animal), so that the compound in question is one being instantiated in a complex unity of parts. Or else it can be one of a potency that is capable of some kind of actuation, as when we say that the human mind is in potency to understand, and only progressively understands in act. The mind can acquire a greater perfection in understanding, and this implies that there is a certain underlying complexity within the unity of the mind. Similarly, in this second category, any reality that is characterized by a real distinction of existence and essence must be a compound unity of a certain sort. It is characterized by a composition of act and potency, with regards to existence and essence. Neither of these forms of composition are found in God, however. On account of his absolute simplicity, God's unity is not characterized even by this second type of metaphysical complexity, let alone that of a material compound unity.

It is from complexity that the possibility of divisibility arises in the first place. A plant, for instance, is one thing, but it also has multiple parts that make it complex and divisible. One can cut a rose from a rose tree or prune branches from a living tree. Or a stone is potentially capable of being reshaped to make a statue on account of its material potency. These things are truly one but are one only in qualified ways, because they have a material potency that is the source in principle of their divisibility. Or again, to take another example: while the human mind is one, it is also less simple than the angelic mind, on account of the former's great potency. The human mind learns only a little, bit by bit, through abstraction from many experiences, whereas the angelic intellect is informed immediately upon creation, through intuition into the divine ideas. And yet angels too are complex, not only because of the potency of their knowledge and will, which have to be perfected, but also because they can potentially be or not be, and receive their existence, their actual being, from another. Therefore, there is in them the real composition, or real distinction, of existence and essence. And so even the angels are not absolutely simple and undivided in being, on account of the metaphysical complexity inherent in their relatively simple created being.

We can note, then, that the mysterious simplicity of being that we ascribe to the divine nature implies the absence of composition in any of the senses we have considered above, whether physical or metaphysical. As we will see below, it is especially here that Aquinas's discussion of divine simplicity and ontological unity converge into a coherent whole.

In light of the foregoing considerations on unity in general, what does it mean, then, to say that God is one? Aquinas answers the question in *ST* I, q. 11, a. 3, by showing how the divine unity follows from the divine simplicity, the infinity of his perfection, and the unity of the world.

First, the affirmation of the oneness of God follows logically from the affirmation of his *simplicity*: there is no composition in God of the kind we typically find in creatures, of individual and essence. What makes Socrates a distinct individual is not simply identical with what makes Socrates a man. The latter is communicable to others, while the former is not. By contrast, in God there is no distinction of this kind between individual and essence. God's individual nature is unique, and accordingly there is only one God. God alone possesses a plenitude of existence by nature, and is the author of existence in all others. His nature is therefore incommunicable. He alone is God.

Second, the unity of God follows from his *infinite perfection*. Were there many gods, they would have to differ from one another in some way, and this difference, being either a perfection or privation, would delimit them. Each would contain a perfection that the others did not have. But this is incompatible with God's infinite perfection, and so he must be one. There is no pantheon or pleroma of gods, but only the one true and living God.

Aquinas's third argument is based on the unity of the cosmos. As multiple diverse things in this world harmonize and are ordered to one another, so there must be some one underlying cause of this order, and that again is the one God, who is the intelligent author of that unity.

Finally, in *ST* I, q. 11, a. 4, Aquinas concludes that God is supremely one, that is, he is one in the highest degree conceivable. Why is this the case? St. Thomas's answer again harkens back to the absence of creaturely compositions in God. God is not material, and therefore is not one as a physical being is, subject to potential division, and existing in a material subject. Again, his nature is not characterized by the distinction of substance and properties; that is to say, he has no accidents in himself. Beyond this, he has in him no potentiality for perfection, but is infinitely perfect in his pure actuality. Ultimately, however, God does not have even the paramount and most fundamental form of metaphysical composition: since God does not receive his being from another, there is in him no real distinction of essence and existence. Ultimately, therefore, God's maximal unity is a function of the total simplicity of his being. God is altogether simple, and, as such, supremely one.

CONCLUSION

In this chapter, we have noted that God's eternity implies intemporality and perfect plenitude of life. This understanding follows organically from a consideration of divine immutability. In particular, we also saw how his knowledge of the future derives from his universal causal agency. God does not learn from his creatures in causing them to be. After this, we noted that God's ontological unity follows from his absolute simplicity, and that he lacks various characteristic creaturely forms of composition, whether physical or metaphysical. Having followed Aquinas's discussion of the various divine names in *ST* I, qq. 3–11, we can now proceed to consider God in his spiritual operations of knowledge and love.

18

:

Divine Knowledge and Love

Our procedure thus far has been to consider what the nature of God is and is not, by comparison with creatures. We have especially considered how God is the hidden cause of all perfections in creatures while remaining unlike them in their conditions of being and ontological limitations. In this chapter, we will consider the nature of God in itself, the immanent life and operations of God. Aquinas examines the mystery of the eternal life of God in *ST* I, qq. 14–19, characterizing it in terms of divine knowledge and divine love. For the purposes of this study, I will make selective use of his order of reflection.

Life as we experience it in created things is of three kinds: vegetative life that is present in beings that nourish themselves, grow, and reproduce but have no sensate knowledge or appetites; animal life, present in beings that not only nourish themselves, grow, and reproduce but also have sensate knowledge, appetites, and, in higher animals, imagination and passions; and intellectual and voluntary life, which is found only in human beings.[1] In angels, we also posit a pure intellectual life of knowledge and willing love, one without the material, vegetative, and sensate existence found in animals and human beings.[2]

If we consider the inner life of God, we are of course considering God in his divine nature as immaterial. Jesus Christ affirms in John 4:24 that "God

---

1. For Aquinas's discussion of the diverse powers of the human soul, see esp. *ST* I, qq. 77–78.

2. See *ST* I, qq. 50, 54, 55, 56, 59; and the historical and speculative study by Serge Thomas Bonino, *Angels and Demons: A Catholic Introduction*, trans. M. J. Miller (Washington, D.C.: The Catholic University of America Press, 2016).

is spirit," a teaching that the Christian tradition typically takes to refer to the eternal life of God. This life is one of immaterial knowledge and love. However, it is also a mystery that transcends our ordinary experience and horizon of comprehension. Accordingly, we will need to consider the inner life of God analogically by comparison with the spiritual life and operations of creatures. Moreover, as intellect precedes will in human understanding (because we can love only what we first come to know), we will first consider God's knowledge, and then God's love.

GOD'S PERFECT IMMATERIAL KNOWLEDGE

Why should we think that we can attribute intellectual knowledge to God in the first place, or that God is in some analogical sense "personal" in nature, that is to say, characterized by immaterial operations of knowledge and love? After all, it is one thing to say that God is not a body or that he is good, eternal, omnipresent, and so forth, but it is quite another thing to say that God is characterized immanently by knowledge. And even if we do affirm this, based on divine revelation, how can we avoid projecting onto God an anthropomorphic understanding of God's knowledge that depicts him as another learner among learners, one who has beliefs and thinks in propositions like other human beings, rather than as the mysterious Creator who gives us existence in virtue of the knowledge that he has of himself?

Aquinas engages these questions in ST I, q. 14, a. 1, where he first is concerned to demonstrate that if God is immaterial (if he is not a body), then there must be knowledge in God. Why should this be the case? Similarly, how can we attribute knowledge to God without any form of overt or covert conceptual anthropomorphism?

Aquinas begins by noting that knowledge is related to immateriality, since knowledge allows one to consider a multiplicity of singulars through the "lens," so to speak, of an immaterial form. Here, the notions of knowledge and of immateriality are being used in a very broad sense. On Aquinas's understanding, in plants there is no form of immaterial knowledge, since they do not possess sensation. However, in animals there is immaterial knowledge of a qualified kind precisely insofar as they have sensations and imagination, as well as sensate memory in more sophisticated animals. That is to say, they can assemble images of material realities free from the particular matter of the given things themselves, such as the sensate image a dog has of a tennis ball that is distinct from the material ball itself. This kind of immateriality is imperfect because it functions by an animal's apprehending only the sensate properties of things (their material quantities and qualities). Furthermore, its exercise depends intrinsically upon a physical organ, so that all such apprehensions are rooted within particular material experiences that delimit the scope of universality.[3] Even if the sensate image is rooted in a material operation, it is not rooted in the matter of the realities it originated from, and accordingly it allows the animal to remember and apprehend a multiplicity of objects that correspond to the image, originally derived from such individual material things.

Human beings, meanwhile, possess a higher form of immaterial knowledge through conceptual abstraction that is distinct from sensations and images altogether, as our concept of human nature or of ontological goodness is not an image, nor is it intrinsically dependent for its exercise on any particular organic activity of the body or the senses. The human being learns through the senses and in that respect is dependent upon them, but by abstraction the intellect is able to grasp knowledge of the very natures and forms of things in a universal mode, independently of their individuating material features. This occurs through immaterial conceptual knowledge that is distinct from sense knowledge. For example, we can apprehend "human nature" intellectually as pertaining to a rational animal, and in so doing we form a concept of universal extension that is applicable to all human beings who have ever or will ever be, based on the very nature of what a human being is, independently of age, color, sex, health, geographical location, and so forth.[4] Such immaterial concepts extend well beyond the range of our immediate sensate experiences, and allow us to categorize and so understand by their causes all the realities of a particular kind. Such concepts possess intrinsic universality by nature since they are formulated by abstraction from individual material conditions and attain to the knowledge of the es-

3. In contrast to the immateriality of human conceptual knowledge and free will, sensate knowledge exists in *intrinsic* dependence upon a sensate organ, as the act of that organ (as, for example, the process of seeing is grounded essentially in the eye and the brain and is an act of those organs). Consequently, when the body of the animal is subject to corruption, the activity in question ceases to be.

4. For developed arguments on the immateriality of the human person's intellectual activities, with reference to the degrees of life in the person as a biological living being and animal, see James Madden, *Mind, Matter & Nature: A Thomistic Proposal for the Philosophy of Mind* (Washington, D.C.: The Catholic University of America Press, 2013).

The Divine Nature

sence in every genus and across all genera. They are applicable, for example, to all human beings, or all colors, all music, all acts of justice, all that exists, all that is good, and so forth.

Now, any perfection existing in creatures that is not intrinsically limited can be attributed to God, albeit in a higher and infinitely perfect way. For example, we can rightly attribute to God by proper analogy perfections like existence, unity, truth, and goodness, because in and of themselves such notions imply no intrinsic limitation. As noted previously, this does not mean that we may apply such notions to God in a univocal sense, nor that the "mere idea" of such perfections leads us in an a priori fashion to grasp the notion of God as infinite perfection. However, if there are grounds for the attribution of a given perfection to God due to his causality of this perfection in creatures, and if a perfection is *capable* of being attributed to God properly by analogy, then we may rightly attribute it to God in a highly qualified sense. Following this line of reasoning, we can conclude that, since God is the cause of immaterial knowledge in creatures, and the effects must in some way resemble the cause, and since the notion of immaterial knowledge of itself implies no imperfection, so we can ascribe immaterial knowledge to God by analogy.[5]

Furthermore, as Aquinas notes in *ST* I, q. 14, a. 1, there is an argument for knowledge in God based on God's infinite perfection. As he notes, the divine nature must be immaterial if God is infinite. In effect, any natural form that is material is contracted by matter and limited in being. It is in potency in various respects, due to its corporeality, and therefore is finite. God, however, is pure actuality and is infinite. Therefore the divine nature is not limited by material potency, but must be immaterial. Can we conclude from this that God, who is immaterial, must be endowed with knowledge? As suggested by our analysis above, one is capable of immaterial operation when one is able to assimilate the form or properties of other realities in an immaterial mode, free and distinct from their individual materiality (as when we are able to know that a given thing is essentially a human being without in any way altering or assimilating the physical individuality of the other). In short, immateriality implies some form of knowledge. Likewise, every act of knowledge by which we attain understanding of the essences and properties of other realities around us implies an immaterial form of

5. See the more developed version of this argument by Kretzmann, *The Metaphysics of Theism*, 113–38.

knowing. In effect, one can conceive of an immaterial reality only under the auspices of knowledge. Therefore, if God is infinite, and thus immaterial in nature, and if immateriality implies knowledge, then we must conclude that God possesses immaterial knowledge.

In our analogical application of acts of knowledge to God, however, we need to employ a key distinction, one that Aquinas refers to in the prologue of *ST* I, q. 14. This is the distinction between acts that are transient to the person versus acts that are immanent. In human beings, personal acts of knowledge and deliberate freedom that are transient are those that actively produce an external effect, such as the ongoing act of building a house, playing the violin, or driving a car. The counterpart to these kinds of acts in God will be treated under the heading of the divine omnipotence in the next chapter, when we address the topic of God's activity *ad extra*, that is to say his activity of communicating being to creation.

In addition to external acts, and in logical priority to them, there are also the human person's immanent acts. These are acts that terminate in the subject and include noetic and ethical operations of the person, such as thinking contemplatively about a given truth, willingly loving another in friendship, or praying. Such immanent acts can perfect the subject in his person without immediately producing an external effect. It is this latter type of activity taking place within the personal subject that is the basis for the analogical attribution of knowledge and love to God's nature. In God, the eternal life of knowledge must be an immanent act, and, moreover, must be itself identical with the pure actuality of God. On this account, God is his act of knowledge or contemplation. He is the immaterial act of knowledge in all that he is—perfect knowledge that can know no diminishment or imperfection. How, then, ought we to understand better the mystery of God's knowledge of himself? To answer this question, we need to look at a number of the ways God's knowledge is analogically distinct from our own.

DIVINE KNOWLEDGE AS ANALOGICALLY DISTINCT FROM HUMAN KNOWLEDGE

Aquinas establishes four kinds of comparisons between God's knowledge and that of human beings, so that we can come to clarify, by similitude and dissimilitude, how God in his transcendence is utterly different from us in his act of knowing and what the character is of his perfect knowing. In what follows, then, we can briefly consider these four forms of analogical similitude.

The Object of Divine Knowledge

A first point of contrast stems from the fact that intellectual creatures learn from what exists prior to themselves and seek to conform their thinking to that reality. For example, we may say rightly that a given philosophical claim is true when the claim in question conveys adequately what is the case in extra-mental reality. It is possible for us to speak and think truly only because we have first inquired into the nature of things and informed ourselves intellectually with regard to realities external to ourselves. Ongoing contact with existent reality actuates our intelligence and can become the occasion for us to develop an ever-deeper understanding. As intellectual creatures, human beings form propositions about the world around them, acquire beliefs, and grow in knowledge progressively, based upon an ongoing study of the structure of a reality that pre-exists their own intellectual life. With God, however, such is not the case. God does not learn about creatures through a consideration of them in their pre-existing states. Instead, the unique primary object of his knowledge and understanding is himself. God knows directly the plenitude of his own being, and knows all other things "in himself" in a comprehensive way, not because he learns about them gradually by studying them, but insofar as he is the cause of their very existence. As Aquinas puts it in *ST* I, q. 14, a. 2: "Since therefore God has nothing in Him of potentiality, but is pure act"—meaning: he does not "learn"—"His intellect and its object are altogether the same."

The Medium of Divine Knowledge

Second, God's knowledge also differs from ours according to its medium. Every creaturely knower understands whatever it or he knows through a certain medium. This occurs in diverse ways. The animal knows sensibly through the medium of sense impressions, phantasms, and memories received from the environment. Human beings apprehend and reason through the medium of abstract concepts (concepts like human nature, goodness, etc.). Angels, on Aquinas's account, comprehend through the medium of infused species, a form of knowledge by which they are elevated to peer into the divine ideas, God's exemplary models of creatures.[6] God's

6. *ST* I, q. 54, a. 2.

knowledge contrasts with all these, however. It remains transcendent of all creaturely modes of cognition, since the medium through which he knows is nothing other than his own divine essence.

Since therefore God has nothing in Him of potentiality, but is pure act, His intellect and its object are altogether the same; so that He neither is without the intelligible species, as is the case with our intellect when it understands potentially; nor does the intelligible species differ from the substance of the divine intellect, as it differs in our intellect when it understands actually; but the intelligible species itself is the divine intellect itself, and thus God understands Himself through Himself. [7]

Negatively speaking, this means that God does not have abstract thoughts, nor does he think through the medium of concepts, propositional beliefs, syllogistic chains of reasoning, or processes of logic. These are all modes of thought that characterize human beings alone, who learn by abstract modes of apprehension and reasoning, in reference to their repeated sense experiences of singular existents. On Aquinas's account, neither non-human animals nor angels know in this way, nor does God. Therefore it is problematic to apply to God any form of knowledge that implies discursive syllogisms, logical chains of reflection, propositional knowledge of facts, or developmental beliefs as contingent properties of his person.[8]

Positively speaking, we might say by analogy that God's essence is his own intelligible species. In his eternal activity of knowing he always sees himself, his own infinite divine nature, and in doing so God sees all other realities comprehensively "within" himself or as his effects. God's own essence provides the formal medium by which he knows, and God knows all things (including all created, finite, contingent, and temporal things) through the eternal intuition of his own essence. His eternal contemplation is simple, and allows him to see into all things in one comprehensive vision. This knowledge does not lessen or delimit the reality and autonomy of creatures, but on the contrary is the basis for their very being. In virtue of his self-knowledge, God freely, peacefully, and unceasingly communicates real existence to all that is.

---

7. *ST* I, q. 14, a. 2.
8. For more on the non-discursive character of God's knowledge, see *ST* I, q. 14, a. 7.

Subsistent Intellect

The third point of contrast between creatures and God pertains to the non-distinction between substance, powers, and accidents as it applies to God's knowledge. In human persons, for example, knowledge is never simply synonymous or co-extensive with substantial being. Human beings who exist have an intellectual power (the faculty of understanding), and possess properties of knowledge, but one cannot say that they simply are their intellectual power, or their activity of knowing. Intellectual understanding characterizes human persons and helps us define what they are, but it remains a property of their being. That is to say, the power of knowledge is a proper accident that helps one define human persons in their specific nature as spiritual animals distinct from other kinds of beings in the universe.[9] In God, who is pure actuality and simplicity, however, there is, as we saw earlier, no distinction of substance and accidents. God *is* his intellect. Consequently, God is subsistent wisdom. His wisdom is a property synonymous with his essence and his existence. We can speak about God, then, as "a personal being" in virtue of his wisdom, but we must also qualify this claim. He is not one intellectual person among others, but is the subsistent personal wisdom who has given being to all created personal realities.

An Act of Understanding

Fourth, God's intellect differs from ours according to the nature of its act. In human beings, the power to know passes from potentiality to act. By contrast, God *is* his own act of understanding. Why is this the case? Recall that, as creatures are divided between potency and act, so there is in each of us a passage from the potential of thinking to the act of understanding. There was a time in the life of each human being that he or she could not consider actively, say, the demonstrations of geometry or the notion of di-

9. We can make a series of distinctions here if we wish to be more specific. In virtue of the spiritual soul, which is the form of the body, each human being possesses intellect as an inalienable power of the soul. When this power is actuated, understanding takes place as a "second act" or operation of the soul, in which the power of intellect is perfected (by the active understanding of an object of consideration). Such secondary activity is accidental in a more fluid and impermanent way, even though acts of understanding clearly perfect the human intellectual power. Human beings just are intellectual in nature. They may or may not become active and perfect in knowledge. Meanwhile, intellectual knowledge is expressed in concepts, which form as a result of acts of understanding and are accidents of the soul (qualities) that characterize the human agent. Powers, acts of understanding, and concepts are all *non-substantial* (and thus accidental), but in distinct ways.

vine simplicity, but then progressively the same person acquired (perhaps with difficulty) the capacity to think actively about such topics. God, by contrast, is not composite in this way, nor does he progressively develop in perfection. Rather, as Aquinas notes in *ST* I, q. 14, a. 4, God *is* his act of thinking, and this act is pure actuality, without any diminishment, and is synonymous with the being of God.[10]

Moreover, it is precisely on account of this identity between God's act of understanding and his substance that Aquinas will likewise insist, in *ST* I, q. 14, a. 3, that God's knowledge of his infinite being is *comprehensive*. God is not an enigma to himself. He does not engage in philosophical self-study so as to come to know his own essence more perfectly over time. Rather, he knows all of himself comprehensively by an act of intellectual self-possession, an act which is itself *infinite*. God possesses an infinite knowledge of himself of which no creature is, by definition, capable.[11]

In sum, God's knowledge differs from that of created intellects by the fact that his own essence is not only its object, but also its medium of knowledge or intellectual species. Moreover, since God is pure act, his intellect cannot be an accidental property of his being, but is subsistent. The same is true of his intellect's act, whereby he perfectly comprehends his perfectly simple, intelligible nature: it is identical with his substance. God, therefore, is not only the first truth, from whom all other realities come to be, but is also a mystery of eternal life, characterized by a knowledge and contemplation that are subsistent. It is in light of God's knowledge and contemplation of his own infinite being that all other things come to be.

10. Although we can and should positively ascribe this perfect actuality of knowledge to God, it is something we arrive at thinking about in God only in a very apophatic manner. All human acts of knowledge are measured by the reality of beings that exist and that serve as the measure of our judgments, and when we come to know them in any way we move from potency to act in the process. Therefore, the idea of a non-composite form of self-knowledge is for us impossible to understand experientially. We can conclude that God is a subsistent act of perfect self-understanding and that he actively knows all things in the light of his own perfect act of self-knowledge. Understanding "what" it is for God to be this evades us, precisely because of his perfection and transcendence and because of our creaturely mode of knowing. When we come to know things, we are made more perfect in knowledge passing from potency to act. The inverse is the case with God. All created things come into being out of his perfectly actual self-knowledge.

11. Even by the light of glory, that is to say, the beatific vision of the divine essence, the creature cannot comprehend God. It can see him intuitively by intellectual vision but still cannot grasp him fully. See Aquinas's discussion in *ST* I, q. 12, a. 7: "Since therefore the created light of glory received into any created intellect cannot be infinite, it is clearly impossible for any created intellect to know God in an infinite degree. Hence it is impossible that it should comprehend God."

GOD'S KNOWLEDGE OF CREATED REALITIES

The claim that God's knowledge is identical with his own being has important consequences for how we understand his knowledge of created realities. Some of this we have already alluded to above.

The first important consequence of this identity between God's knowledge and his being is that his knowledge of realities other than himself,
which is to say, of all creatures, can occur only through the medium of his
own self-knowledge. As we have noted above, God does not "learn" from a
prior consideration of the being of creatures. Were one to hold such a view
of God it would imply that the very being of God the Creator would depend
in some way upon the being of creatures, and not the inverse. Furthermore,
it would imply a composite and gradual form of developmental understanding in God, an anthropomorphic conception that ignores the mystery of
God's transcendence and simplicity. Instead we should say that God's own
knowledge of himself—his own act of self-comprehending wisdom—is the
medium through which he knows everything else. As Aquinas puts it in *ST*
I, q. 14, a. 5: "He sees other things not in themselves, but in Himself."[12]

The second consequence, as Aquinas stresses in article 8, is that God's
knowledge is not reactive to but causative of what he knows. God causes
us to be through the knowledge he has of himself. If God's self-knowledge
and self-contemplation are the very source of the being of creatures, then
God comprehends all creatures utterly in all that they are. He knows all other realities comprehensively in the simple act whereby he knows himself.
On this view, creatures are caused by divine wisdom and love, without God
ever having to go "outside" of himself in his divine knowledge, goodness,
and omnipotence. This implies no egoism in God, however, for several reasons. First, in knowing "only" himself, as one who is infinite in perfection,
God has comprehensive knowledge of all that is or that can possibly be in
the created sphere. Far from preventing him from knowing the world as it
"really is," his self-knowledge permits him alone a most perfect and comprehensive knowledge of all created being. Second, in loving his own supreme goodness, God loves what is objectively most good, the highest good
that all created things must stem from, participate in, and imitate, in virtue
of their very being. His love of his own goodness, then, far from alienating

12. On this point, see also *SCG* I, c. 49, in particular.

him from the love of creatures, is the ground of inclusivity by which he can communicate being to all creatures, and understand and love them in their goodness comprehensively, so as to bring them to perfection in conformity with his own eternal goodness. Finally, since God's self-knowledge and self-love in no way rival his knowledge and love of his creation (but are the foundation for the latter), his act of communicating being to creatures is entirely gratuitous, and in no way perfects God. This communication of being is a sheer gift that stems uniquely from the superabundance of God's act of self-possession. It is from the wellspring of his plenitude of perfection and goodness, which God knows infinitely well, that he freely gives being to all creatures as an act of eternal love.

The third consequence of this identity of knowledge and being in God is that God knows all future contingent realities insofar as he is their cause. Why is this the case? As we saw in the last chapter, this is not because God foresees future entities, in the sense that he is learning from them what will or might eventually come to be. For what will come to be does not currently exist. Rather, God knows the future of the creation from all eternity because he will create the future. He foresees all that will come to exist, for, from all eternity, he is the cause of its existence. In other words, God knows future contingents not by any kind of foreknowledge anthropomorphically conceived (as if God were estimating future likelihoods by first observing his creatures), but through the medium of his own eternal knowledge, to which the future (which does not yet exist) is utterly transparent.

This can seem counterintuitive to many, because the human being instinctively wants to attribute to any knower a movement from potency to act: for God to know contingent things truly or for him to will them to be, he "has to" acquire beliefs about them or make choices that newly qualify his being, and in doing so he must develop internally. Therefore, God must be compositional, complex, and developmental, if he truly knows and loves his creation. This kind of objection, however psychologically understandable, is philosophically problematic. It is true that we cannot conceive perfectly nor comprehend what it must be for God to be perfectly knowledgeable and perfectly loving, such that he can create out of the plenitude of his own self-knowledge and self-love, but that is part of the point, for if we could comprehend adequately what it is to be pure actuality, we would ourselves be the Creator. The transcendent alterity of God's perfection evades our comprehensive grasp. We can say, however, based on sound metaphysical reasoning, without contradiction or incoherence, that God in his pure actuality creates not through an acquisition of new knowledge of creatures and love for creatures but from the already existing plenitude of his own divine life of knowledge and love. It is out of the plenitude of the contemplation of his own divine essence and the love of his own divine goodness that God gives being to all things at all times, from all eternity, by a diffusiveness of his own radiant light and goodness. God thus shares being with all creatures out of the delight he has in his own being from all eternity. He is like the artist (Mozart, Bach, Dante, Shakespeare) who creates not to improve himself but out of the plenitude of his own perfected habitus, as a way of being what he is, freely and without compulsion, but also as expressive of his own perfect act of self-possession. Creation is the fugue of God that rages forth from his creative abundance of life.

God's causal knowledge of future contingents, however, does raise a pair of difficult questions. Does his knowledge of the future deprive rational creatures of free will? And, in connection with this, how should we think about the origins of evil? How does evil arise in the creature's will if God has a causal knowledge of the future?

In answer to the first difficulty, we should underscore that, on Aquinas's account, God's causal knowledge does not in any way diminish the reality of free will in creatures, but is instead its true foundation. God wills and foresees the freedom of his spiritual creatures through the medium of his own eternal knowledge, and *therefore is himself the transcendent source* of that freedom. His knowledge of our action is not a rival to our action. Rather it is the transcendent source that gives us *to be*, and to act freely by our own determination and decision. Consequently our contingent, genuine freedom is the product of God's eternal knowledge and love, which cause us to exist as contingent, free creatures in the first place.[13]

13. Our own human freedom is something we understand better and in a more genetically primary way than the mystery of God, according to our natural order of experience and reflection. Our reflections on the mystery of God, then, should not be employed as a means to deny the reality of something we all experience as real (our human moral autonomy). Rather they should permit us to understand that the Creator, in whose image we are made, must be the ultimate foundation and guarantor of our freedom, because he gives us existence. It is because of God's transcendent freedom as Creator and first cause that we who are made in his image and sustained in being by him can ourselves truly be free and autonomous "secondary causes," that is to say, genuinely free causes of our own actions. Freedom is a participative notion, in Thomistic theology, not a binary notion. Created free agents participate in the freedom of the Creator and do not exert their autonomy in opposition to him. The inverse is not the case: we do not depend for our genuine freedom on the delimitation of the Creator's causality. The Thomist can affirm that all

But what about the existence of freely chosen moral evil in creatures?[14] Here Aquinas, following Maximus the Confessor and John Damascene, distinguishes between God's eternal knowledge as causative, and as permissive.[15] Based on previous arguments, we must affirm that God knows of morally evil acts from all eternity.[16] However, while he causes all such acts to exist in one respect, in another respect, he merely permits them. He causes them to exist in at least two senses. First, evil acts take place in an already existent subject, whom God creates and sustains in being as a free agent. For example, God sustains a man in being even as that man tells a deceptive lie or carries out a murder. Second, on Aquinas's account, God also gives positive being to the very act of the person as he or she does something evil.[17] Insofar as the speaker who lies or the agent who murders undertakes a distinctive operation of being, he depends upon God, who gives him to exist

---

this is the case without being obliged to comprehensive knowledge of how it is the case. Multiple non-contradictory propositions can be true simultaneously without our understanding perfectly how they are true. This is frequently the case in the empirical sciences and a host of other domains, and, fittingly, it is even more so the case as the subject matter of consideration is more elevated. *How* is it the case that God himself both knows and causes our human freedom to be without in any way attenuating it? To understand this perfectly one would have to be God. The fact that it is only partially comprehensible to us is not a reason to deny that it is true.

14. For more on this much-discussed topic, see Reginald Garrigou-Lagrange, *Predestination: The Meaning of Predestination in Scripture and the Church*, trans. B. Rose (Charlotte, N.C.: TAN, 1998); Charles Journet, *The Meaning of Evil*, trans. M. Barry (New York: P. J. Kenedy, 1963); Bernard Lonergan, *Grace and Freedom* and *Gratia Operans*, in vol. 1 of *The Collected Works of Bernard Lonergan* (Toronto: University of Toronto Press, 2000); Jean-Hervé Nicolas, *Synthèse dogmatique: Complément, de l'univers à la Trinité* (Fribourg: Éditions Universitaires Fribourg et Éditions Beauchesne, 1993), 361–96; Harm J. M. J. Goris, *Free Creatures of an Eternal God: Thomas Aquinas on God's Infallible Foreknowledge and Irresistible Will* (Utrecht: Peeters, 1996); Michael D. Torre, *Do Not Resist the Spirit's Call: Francisco Marín-Sola on Sufficient Grace* (Washington, D.C.: The Catholic University of America Press, 2013); Bonino, *Dieu, "Celui qui est"*, 676–89.

15. See *ST* I, q. 19, a. 6, on the antecedent will of God and the consequent will of God, which is taken in turn from John Damascene, *An Exposition of the Orthodox Faith*, 2, c. 29. This distinction has its proximate origins in Maximus's doctrine, where it was formulated directly as a response to the problems of Origenist universalism. See Maximus the Confessor, *Ambigua* 7, 1069a11–1102c4, and particularly 1085c9–1089d3. In this latter section of the text Maximus clearly affirms that God truly wills the salvation of all but also truly permits the eternal loss of those who refuse his grace. This loss has its origins in their non-consent to God's design of salvation, and represents a "failure" to cooperate with the economy of salvation, a failure instigated by the creature. See the study of this issue and text by Brian Daley, "Apokatastasis and 'the Honorable Silence' in the Eschatology of Maximus the Confessor," in Maximus Confessor, ed. F. Heinzer and C. Schönborn, 309–39 (Fribourg: Fribourg University Press, 1982), esp. 327–30.

16. The biblical sense of prophecy, which touches in many cases upon future contingent actions of human agents that are morally aberrant, seems to denote just such a sense of God's divine foreknowledge. I have explored this idea, with regard to Augustine's and Aquinas's treatments of God's permission of the hardening of the heart of pharaoh, in White, *Exodus*, 52–70.

17. *ST* I-II, q. 79, a. 2.

in that particular mode and even in this particular actuation of his operative powers. But God, who knows of moral evil from all eternity, does not
ever will or cause the evil in question, either directly or indirectly. Rather,
he merely permits it, mysteriously tolerating the spiritual creature as it culpably falls away from the love of what is genuinely good and right in a giv-
en situation.[18]

There are three corollaries to this view. First, even when a rational creature does evil, it does so in contradiction to its own innate tendencies toward the good, whether in the order of nature or of grace. Otherwise we
could not count the creature in question as culpable or neglectful. Second,
the creature in question must in some significant way know better or have
been capable of knowing better, and the neglect of adverting to the truth in
the matter constitutes a kind of negation (a pure privation of truth) in the
act that makes it ontologically deficient, deprived of right order.[19] Third,
because he had the tendencies to the good and the capacity for right knowledge, which were resisted and ignored respectively, the creature could have
and should have done the good, and he is held responsible, on the part of
God, for not doing so, and can also rightly be held responsible on the part
of human beings, as Aquinas notes.[20] God, then, is not directly or indirectly
responsible for evil. On the contrary, God in his divine providence mysteriously draws good out from evil, despite the creature's misuse of its freedom,
which God merely permits.[21] The creature itself, and not God, is the source
of moral evil through a misuse of its freedom.

That said, God is not ignorant of the morally evil actions of his creatures,
and, indeed, he even knows of all such actions from all eternity prior to their

18. Aquinas does not pretend to explain the metaphysics of evil comprehensively, with a
God's-eye view, but he does hold that God, who is all good, cannot will moral evil in any respect,
even though God in his fidelity to creatures upholds them in being even when they do evil. God
is responsible for holding the creature in being as it "falls away" from the good, but not for the
deprivation as such, which stems from a mysterious defect of love in spiritual creatures, who are
capable of turning away from the good they know, due to disordered love of what is objectively less
perfect or even harmful. In this sense, evil moral action stems from a negation of truth regarding
the good, and thus is deprived of rectitude. See on these matters, among other texts, *ST* I, q. 23, a. 3,
ad 2; *ST* I-II, qq. 75–81, especially q. 79.

19. *ST* I-II, q. 75, aa. 1–2.

20. See *SCG* III, cc. 160–61; *Quaestiones disputatae de malo* (*De malo*), q. 3, a. 1, ad 8; *Scriptum
super libros Sententiarum magistri Petri Lombardi episcopi Parisiensis* II (*In II Sent.*), d. 27, q. 1, a. 4,
ad 4; *De ver.*, q. 24, a. 11, ad 6; *In Ioan.*, XV, lec. 5, no. 2055.

21. For Aquinas's discussion of how Providence brings good out of evil in general, see *ST* I,
q. 22, a. 2, ad 2. See too *ST* I, q. 19, a. 9.

existence in time. In what sense can he be said to know of evil acts? Here
we can consider two analogies, one from practical knowledge and another
from theoretical understanding. By an analogy from practical knowledge,
insofar as God is said to "foreknow" creaturely evil, we can say by analogy
that God knows from all eternity in his prudence or providence, that he will
permit or *allow* a given creature to disobey him, to refuse grace, to sin, and
so forth, and in this way, he knows of moral evil in creatures. We can speak
accordingly of the permissive will of God, and of the mystery of his permissive decrees, which ought not to be identified with God's positive willing
as such.[22] By an analogy from theoretical knowledge, we can say that God
has no divine idea of evil, which is in itself a privation of being, and yet he
understands our evil actions perfectly well. He knows evil in the creature
through the medium of his eternal idea of the goodness of the creature, a
goodness that he knows is diminished by the creature's moral evil. Consequently, God understands moral evil in us as a privation of the good that he
intends for his creatures.[23] This knowledge is most comprehensive because
it entails the understanding not only of what we actually are, in our failures, but also of all that we are capable of being. The divine idea of the good
in spiritual creatures is omni-comprehensive, then, and allows God, who is
wholly innocent, to understand us perfectly even when we defect from the
good, and thus God knows us morally much better than we know ourselves.

The upshot of all this is that God knows created realities, whether present or future, not by some kind of neutral "observation," but through the
medium of his own essence, insofar as he is their cause. Moreover, for this
reason God also knows future free acts of creatures, even as he knows their
evil actions by virtue of the fact that he permits them to occur from all eternity. It is in virtue of the perfection of this same knowledge, however, that
he has the comprehensive understanding of creatures sufficient to intervene
and save human beings, in and through all things, by his providence and

22. As noted in the last chapter, this decision on God's part to tolerate evil is called, in Thomistic discourse, the antecedent permissive decree, i.e., the decree whereby, as part of his governance
of creatures according to their natures, God permits sin to arise in the creature. Human beings
and angels, because of their constituent potency as created spiritual beings, are able to love or
not to love the truth. God's permission of evil is mysterious, but it encompasses his respect for
the freedom of his creatures, who must choose voluntarily to associate themselves with God, his
grace, and saving truth.

23. *ST* I, q. 15, a. 3, ad 1: "Evil is known by God not through its own type, but through the type
of good. Evil, therefore, has no idea in God, neither in so far as an idea is an 'exemplar' nor as a
'type.'"

his designs of grace. It is in virtue of the perfection of his eternal knowledge that we can trust God always and everywhere to save us effectively in Christ. Only he who perfectly knows us, as only the Creator does, can also perfectly save us.

ON DIVINE WILLING

In *ST* I, q. 19, a. 1, Aquinas establishes that there is will in God; this is a necessary corollary to his previous conclusion that there is knowledge in God. The reason for this is that will follows upon intellect. The basic argument here can be stated as follows: First, every being tends teleologically toward perfection. However, intellectual realities tend toward perfection by means of the rational appetite, that is, the elicited desire for the good perceived by the intellectual agent. Therefore, in God, whose life is purely intellectual, there is the elicited appetite for the good, which we call the will. Furthermore, we might add, if God is infinitely and eternally good, and his life is characterized by knowledge of himself, then his knowledge of his own goodness (considered precisely as spiritual appetibility) must contain something analogous to what we call willing.

Having established that there is willing in God, however, Aquinas also must proceed to establish how the divine will differs from will as found in created intellects. Naturally, St. Thomas proceeds here by way of remotion and excess, showing how our understanding of divine simplicity and God's pure actuality must affect our conception of appetite, derived as it is from created realities, as supereminently applied to God.

THE ANALOGICAL CONSIDERATION
OF DIVINE WILLING AS DISTINCT FROM
HUMAN WILLING

Subsistent Willing

Among the dissimilitudes that exist between rational appetite in spiritual creatures and the divine will, we should first note that, just as God is his own intellect, so also he is his own will. As Aquinas notes in *ST* I, q. 19, a. 1, where he proceeds in light of the already established identity of essence and existence in God: "as His intellect is His own existence, so is His will." What we term analogically the intellect and will of God, then, refer to a mystery that is *one* in the eternal life of the divine nature. In human beings the faculties of intellect and will are truly distinct, while in God's essence they denote a unique plenitude of uncreated wisdom and love that produces effects similar to both our intellects and our wills. And as the divine intellect has God's very substance as its object and act, so too does the divine will. That is to say, God wills and loves himself as his own good, and God is his own act of willing and loving himself. For this reason, God is *subsistent love*. He is a pure actuality of love, and so also a pure actuality of spiritual joy or beatitude.[24] Indeed, God is eternal beatitude, a perfect happiness that can never be diminished. He is the author of all our desires, but unlike us he cannot experience insatiated desire, since he utterly comprehends himself in his divine goodness and perfectly possesses this goodness by love in his divine will. This is in some real sense unfathomable for us creatures, who find our end and bliss only ever outside of ourselves, in the love of God and in friendship with others. We best understand what it is for God to love himself not when we love ourselves but when we love God as our highest good.

Divine Gift

The fact that God's love is subsistent, and that he is characterized by an eternal love of his own goodness, means that whatever God loves, he loves because of his own goodness, and in view of his own goodness. When God loves creatures, he loves them not as separate goods, but insofar as he gives them a certain participation in his own goodness. Formally they are good in themselves, but their goodness derives from him. God's love brings all things into existence, sustains them in being, and governs them toward their true end.

As we have noted above, it can appear from this claim that God's activity in creation is self-referential or egocentric, but this characterization rests upon an anthropomorphic misunderstanding. It is precisely the contrary that is the case, as God's love is the most selfless. There are two principal reasons for this.[25] First, the fact that God's love of his own goodness is identical with his very being indicates that God's goodness and love are infinitely perfect and purely actual, independent of creatures. Consequently, his act of creation cannot stem from any project of self-amelioration or from any nat-

---

24. *ST* I, q. 26, aa. 1–2; *SCG* I, cc. 100–102.
25. See *ST* I, q. 20, a. 1, ad 3 and a. 2.

ural need in God's eternal life. Creation is a free gift stemming from God's gratuitous love for creatures, a love that gives all that is. We can consider this idea under two aspects by comparing the creativity of divine love with mere human love. When human beings come to love creatures other than themselves, we do so (1) because other persons are intrinsically good "prior" to being loved by us, and indeed we come to love them based on what and who they are. Their being is a gift to us that precedes us and elicits our love. But (2) for this reason our love for them also qualifies us in some way, improving us, as it were. For example, we become better human beings in the ontological order by being just, fair, affable or charitable to other human beings. In short, we are perfected by our loves when we are led out of ourselves and set in relation to others.

By way of contrast, (1) God can in no way improve himself in loving a creature, since all that is in the creature that is good first exists in God in a higher and more perfect way, who is the giver of being to the creature. The goodness of the creature, then, is a pure gift from God, not something God needs. For this reason also, (2) God alone, unlike any creature, cannot improve himself in any way in loving his creatures, or in creating them out of divine goodness. His activity of creation is sheer giving all the way down. A corollary of this, of course, is that God receives nothing from creatures in the order of goodness, not even glory, if glory be understood to mean some sort of magnification of the divine being affecting God himself. Rather, glory, properly understood, as St. Thomas notes in *ST* I-II, q. 114, a. 1, ad 2, is simply "the manifestation of [divine] goodness," that is, the outward radiance of God's goodness, which indeed perfects creatures, even as God is the living source of their perfection through the diffusion of his own goodness.[26]

The second reason, then, that God's love, unlike our own, is completely gratuitous is that his love is also *productive of being*, and is, as such, the expression of a pure desire to give of one's self. This points again to another profound difference between God's love and that of creatures. In us, the goodness of creatures causes us to love them for what they are, but for God

---

26. Seen in this light, phrases like "*soli Deo gloria*" and "*ad maiorem Dei gloriam*" can be used to denominate the positive value of theocentric human action, but such use should be carefully qualified. Glory in creation is a manifestation of the intrinsic plenitude of the mystery of God that is itself perfectly actual and eternally undiminishable. The great works of the saints add nothing to the glory of God; rather, they participate in it and may manifest that glory in a limited fashion.

it is the converse that is the case: his love for creatures is the source of their existence and goodness. His love gives them the gift of existence and every perfection of being. As Aquinas notes in *ST* I, q. 20, a. 2: "God loves everything that exists. Yet not as we love. Because since our will is not the cause of the goodness of things, but is moved by it as by its object, our love … is not the cause of its goodness; but conversely its goodness … calls forth our love." St. Thomas concludes, "the love of God infuses and creates goodness." Here we see a summit of Aquinas's biblical thinking: God is love, and love is the ground of the world. The goodness of the cosmos stems from the ever-radiant uncreated love of God.

This means, however, that God's gratuitous love for creatures has its origin and root in God's prior love for himself. Our attention must be drawn to this "prior" love and its perfection if we are to safeguard a right understanding of God's elective freedom toward creation and God's so-called sovereignty. This freedom and sovereignty are not indebted to creatures, it is true. They are absolute in this respect, but they are always conditioned by the wisdom and love of God to which they give expression, and therefore cannot be rightly conceived of in a voluntarist or morally neutral way. It is true that God wishes in pure freedom to communicate being and grace to creatures, but he only ever does so out of the "prior" love he has for his own goodness and wisdom, by which he intends creatures to participate in his own goodness and wisdom. Creation exists, then, in virtue of a kind of ordered playfulness on the part of God. He is younger and more alive than all things, just as he is more ancient and perfectly wise, so that the intelligible order, goodness, and beauty of creation are an expression of his eternally playful wisdom and love. This mystery of creative life in God must ultimately be understood in a Trinitarian light, as we will explore in the second half of this book. The deepest and most remote origin of all things is found in the uncreated wisdom and love of the Trinity, and it is out of this Trinitarian life that God wishes to communicate to us a participation in his own divine life, by sanctification and deification. Behind the goodness and wisdom of creation and the Cross, then, there is always an ever more remote horizon of eternal life in God: the mystery of the eternal begetting of the Son from the Father as his Word, and the eternal spiration of the Spirit from the Father and the Son as their shared mutual love.

CONCLUSION

God, who is immaterial, possesses in an analogical sense of the term "personal" immanent operations of intellect and will. Where these differ from our immanent operations, however, the difference has to do, again, with God's absolute simplicity and perfection. As God is his own intelligible object and medium of knowledge, so too he is subsistent contemplation, a perfection of eternal life. Likewise, he possesses a divine will as one who loves his own goodness and is this very act of loving, an eternal life of subsistent love. Moreover, just as God does not learn from his creatures, but his knowledge is causative of their being, so too God's love is not reactive to creatures, but is itself productive of their created goodness. This is also why God's love is the only sheerly gratuitous love: he is not drawn to, and so perfected by, the pre-existent goodness of others. Rather, his self-giving love is the causative source of the goodness of creatures, who receive even the goodness of their very existence from God, who is himself the self-diffusive source of all created goodness.

In this chapter, we have treated of God's immanent operations of knowledge and love, operations that, as immanent, terminate within the acting subject. We must now turn our attention to God's operations *ad extra* under the rubric of "the power of God," which St. Thomas refers to, in the prologue to *ST* I, q. 14, as "the principle of the divine operation as proceeding to the exterior effect," which is to say, in creatures.

19

Divine Omnipotence

God is omnipotent. We find the idea expressed in the Old and New Testaments, in both colloquial idioms and conceptually formal ways. In a narrative context, for example, God comes to Abraham to inform him that his aged and barren wife, Sarah, is to bear a child. Sarah laughs at the announcement, provoking a rhetorical question from God: "Is anything too hard for the Lord?" (Gn 18:14).[1] This same phrase is taken up again in the New Testament in Luke 1:36–37 with the declaration, by the angel Gabriel to the Virgin Mary, that Elizabeth—who, like Sarah, is barren—is to bear a child, the precursor to the promised Messiah.[2] These two narratives of miracles, having to do with human generation, are set against the backdrop of God's act of creation and his historical covenant with Israel, which sometimes entails the presence of miracles and prophecies.[3] The narrative "framing" of these annunciation scenes, then, refers us latently to an undergirding power of God that pervades all things. Jesus accordingly stresses the universal scope of divine power in Matthew 19:26 when he says (in a context concerning the mystery of salvation): "With men this is impossible, but with God all things are possible."

The biblical claim that God is all-powerful, however, is not a teaching reserved to supernatural faith alone. It is also a truth that can be understood

---

1. The same expression is used in Jer 32:27 in the context of a prophecy of the people's return from exile and the establishment of a new covenant: "Behold, I am the Lord, the God of all flesh; is anything too hard for me?"

2. Lk 1:37: "For with God nothing will be impossible."

3. For other examples of such biblical affirmations, see Ps 33:9; 89:8–13; 147:5, Jer 32:17, 27, Is 44:24, Jb 42:2, Dn 4:35, Rom 1:20, Eph 3:20, Heb 1:3; Rv 19:6.

philosophically even from within Catholic theology, in which we retain an explicit reference to revelation. Historically speaking, precisely as a philosophical idea, the affirmation of divine omnipotence developed in large part out of the biblical monotheistic tradition, due in particular to the biblical notion of creation, of God's creating all things *ex nihilo*, that is to say, by his own power, without any instrument and without acting upon a pre-existing substrate.[4] Nevertheless, the notion itself is technically philosophically accessible to human reason and it can be articulated in logical continuity with the "divine attributes" we have explored thus far. As we will see in what follows, Aquinas proceeds along these lines in *ST* I, q. 25, so as to offer a kind of philosophical grammar for the biblical and dogmatic truth of divine omnipotence. We will begin studying God's power by first following St. Thomas in making a key clarification about the kind of power we have in mind here.

DIVINE POWER IS AN ACTIVE NOT A PASSIVE POWER

In his consideration of divine power, in *ST* I, q. 25, a. 1, Aquinas begins, as is typical, by making a distinction. There are two forms of power or potency: active power and passive power. Active potency or power in this context signifies the capacity to act upon another, to do something that is perfect, like the power of the architect to design a safe and functional bridge, or in God's case, the power of creation, that is, the capacity to effect the production in being of a vast and intellectually ordered cosmos, out of nothing. Passive potency, by contrast, signifies the potency that makes one capable of submitting to transformation or change by the actions or effects of another, like a piece of wood, for example, that can be potentially formed into a statue, or the religiously disoriented person who is changed over time in intellect and will, by the inner working of the grace of God. In other words, passive potency is the power to receive the action of another and to be moved—movement being taken here in the broader metaphysical sense of reduction from potency to act.

---

4. For a magisterial definition of creation *ex nihilo*, or from nothing, in response to Albigensian dualism, see Lateran IV, chap. 1, cited in *Decrees*, ed. Tanner, 1:230: God is the "one principle of all things, creator of all things invisible and visible, spiritual and corporeal; who by his almighty power [*omnipotenti virtute*] at the beginning of time created from nothing both spiritual and corporeal creatures...." See the historical and thematic study of Paul Clavier, *Ex nihilo*, 2 vols. (Paris: Hermann, 2011).

It should be obvious by this point that, when we speak of power in God, we can only mean active power and not passive power, since God is pure actuality, and there is no being-in-potency in him whatsoever.[5] As Aquinas states in *ST* I, q. 25, a. 1: "God is pure act, simply and in all ways perfect, nor in Him does any imperfection take place. Whence it most fittingly belongs to Him to be an active principle, and in no way whatsoever to be passive." We can affirm, then, that there is active power in God, to the highest degree, as based upon God's infinite perfection, and his capacity to cause finite existence.

GOD'S INFINITE POWER AND
OMNIPOTENCE

God not only has active power but also has infinite power, as Aquinas affirms in *ST* I, q. 25, a. 2. Why ought we to say that God's power is infinite? In a sense, the infinity of God's power follows very straightforwardly from his essential infinity, which was already discussed above, in chapter 15, in regard to *ST* I, q. 7. The idea here is that the power of an agent corresponds to the degree that it is actual, as the heat generated by a fire corresponds to how hot the fire is. God, however, is infinitely actual. His operational "active power" then, is not limited. Whence follows Aquinas's conclusion in q. 25, a. 2, that "it is [of] necessity that the active power in God should be infinite."

Moreover, Aquinas goes on to affirm, in article 3, that God for this reason is also omnipotent, that is, he has the power to do all things. Again we might ask what precisely does it mean to say that he can do *all* things? In answering this question it is important to realize that God's power does not extend merely to all finite things that actually exist, since God in his power is capable of doing things that he is not currently doing, or has not yet done, or may never do. The power of God extends beyond the horizons of the actual world of finite creation as we know it. However, what is the extent of this power and how ought we to characterize it? To answer this question, it is important to recall that God, as one infinite in his being, has a power

5. After all, as Aquinas notes in *ST* I, q. 25, a. 1, the presence of passive power is not a sign of perfection. The thing possessed of passive power "is deficient and imperfect" in some respect. This is why it must be acted upon by another agent if it is to achieve a new perfection. This power is excluded from God, who is entirely perfect, and its exclusion represents no deficiency in God, but, on the contrary, serves to underscore his divine perfection.

that extends to all that is or that can possibly be in the order of finite being. Therefore anything whatsoever that God should wish to do with respect to existent finite being or merely possible finite being stands within his power.[6]

However, this raises the question of what can have being, that is, what is possible, in the first place. St. Thomas's answer to this question, in article 3—which we will explore further below—is that whatever does not "imply a contradiction in terms" is intrinsically possible and so falls within the scope of divine power. Let us briefly look, then, at the interrelationship Aquinas posits between God's wisdom and divine power, so as to consider the rationale underlying this seeming limitation of God's power to the possible.

LIMITATIONS ON DIVINE OMNIPOTENCE?

Why should God's power operate only in the domain of the possible, that is, only with respect to things in which there is a lack of intrinsic contradiction? An important thing to keep in mind here is that God acts only in accordance with the measure his wisdom provides. St. Thomas specifies the relationship between intellect and will in God especially in his treatment of the justice of God in *ST* I, q. 21. The relationship he posits there between them derives from the way will as intellectual appetite follows intellect in general. As Aquinas states in *ST* I, q. 21, a. 2, ad 2: "Since good as perceived by intellect is the object of the will, it is impossible for God to will anything but what His wisdom approves." This is what he calls God's "law of justice," that is, the justice by which God orders all things in keeping with his wisdom.[7] This tether, so to speak, of divine wisdom on the divine willing and, concomitantly, on the divine power means that we must always avoid the philosophical temptation to think of God's omnipotence in rational abstraction from his wisdom and goodness, or, for that matter, from his justice and mercy. This qualification needs to be kept in mind when one

6. *ST* I, q. 25, a. 3: "The divine existence, however, upon which the nature of power in God is founded, is infinite, and is not limited to any genus of being; but possesses within itself the perfection of all being. Whence, whatsoever has or can have the nature of being, is numbered among the absolutely possible things, in respect of which God is called omnipotent."

7. Described under the language of *debitum*, or debt, this priority of wisdom over will is what St. Thomas will use to secure his metaphysical claims in *ST* I, q. 21, a. 1, ad 3. God acts under a debt of distributive justice to his own wisdom to realize in creatures what his wisdom dictates, so as to appropriately manifest his goodness in creation. In maintaining the structures of nature by his creative activity, God is primordially faithful to himself, eternally loving and freely expressing his own wisdom and goodness.

thinks about what God might do in his omnipotence in comparison with what he is doing and what he has signaled that he will do. In maintaining the natural world in being, with its own stable order, goodness, inclinations, and history, God is faithful to the ordering wisdom he has inscribed in things. By his providence he governs the world and especially spiritual creatures, in view of their true final end, union with God, which is made possible to human beings by grace. In the face of human sinfulness, and consequent suffering in the world, God has initiated the reconciliation of humanity with God and the resurrection of the human race from the dead, through the life, death, and resurrection of Christ. These are all various expressions of God's omnipotence, and they manifest his "yet deeper" wisdom and goodness, justice and mercy.

What is the relationship between God's power and non-being or non-existence? In one sense, God has absolute power "over" non-being, since he is capable of making realities by giving them the entirety of their existence. God can bring to be from what was not. However, nothingness is not a visual void that is somehow real, but is itself merely an absolute absence of being. As such, it cannot be mixed or confused with anything that truly is. It is of key importance to recall this when thinking about the extension of God's power to *possible* being. God's omnipotence, precisely because it extends to all that either exists or might exist, extends to all realities that do not imply a contradiction in terms. Such contradictions imply a literally incoherent conceptual mixture of being and non-being. Thus, to take a trivial example, God cannot make a spherical pyramid. This is not because of a limitation of divine power but because the proposed possible in question entails a blatant contradiction, a thing that both is and is not, under the same aspect at the same time. God cannot make something to be and not to be at the same time and in the same respect, since this would violate the law of non-contradiction. More relevant to properly theological discourse, we should note that, while God's omnipotence does indeed extend to his becoming man in the Incarnation—in which he brings a created human nature into hypostatic union with a divine person—he cannot, inversely, make a creature infinite as such, because this is a plain contradiction in terms. God can become human, without ceasing to be God, but he cannot make a creature into God, or communicate his divine nature to another being so that it is truly God. Creatures, precisely because they receive the gift of existence (and so have their existence limited by their form), are inherently finite. Similarly, God cannot communicate to a creature the power to create, a divine, infinite power. This holds true even for the sacred humanity of Jesus. The eternal Word is a principle of creation in virtue of his divine nature, in which he is one with the Father and the Spirit, and not in virtue of his human nature.

One may object that God is not truly omnipotent precisely because he cannot do something contradictory, like square a circle or make a creature divine. However, such examples are literally non-sense. They are derived from contradictions of human thinking grounded in abstract ideas that have no direct foundation in what is metaphysically real. Consequently they lack intrinsic intelligibility. This is why Aquinas concludes in ST I, q. 25, a. 3, "everything that does not imply a contradiction in terms, is numbered amongst those possible things, in respect of which God is called omnipotent: whereas whatever implies contradiction does not come within the scope of divine omnipotence, because it cannot have the aspect of possibility. Hence it is better to say that such things cannot be done, than that God cannot do them."

We should also note, however, that our affirmation of God's omnipotence does not entail that he is bound to create a perfect world. In fact, if we rightly understand that the world is finite and created, then we also understand it cannot be absolutely perfect.[8] On Aquinas's view, there can never be a best of all possible worlds. Perfection pertains to God alone, while all other realities are necessarily finite in perfection and for this reason could always in some way be greater or more perfect. Nor should we think that God created the world to make a place that is most perfect. God has created the world as an expression of his own goodness and wisdom, and has done so out of the love he has for his own goodness, which he wishes to impart to creatures. This communication takes place, however, in a limited and finite way. Intellectual creatures who long for what is perfect can enjoy the consolation of the perfection of God, especially insofar as they are freely raised above their natures by his deifying grace to come to know God in himself, and to participate in his infinite glory. This assimilation to the perfection of God transpires, however, within their finite created status and in virtue of the relative measure of charity that pertains to each one.

---

8. On this point, see Aquinas's discussion in ST I, q. 25, a. 6: "Absolutely speaking, however, God can make something else better than each thing made by Him."

OMNIPOTENCE AND THE
RATIONAL CHARACTER OF
CHRISTIAN MYSTERY

The Catholic Church holds that natural human reason cannot by its own power arrive at the knowledge of distinctly Christian mysteries of faith, such as those pertaining to the Trinity, the Incarnation, the atonement, or the resurrection. These are genuine realities of the highest explanatory value, but precisely because our knowledge of them depends upon the gift of grace, we acquire access to them uniquely on account of the noetic act we call supernatural faith. It is therefore by grace alone that we may know that God is the most Holy Trinity or that the Incarnation, atonement, and resurrection of Christ are authentic mysteries of salvation. Nevertheless, one can pose the objection, in response to the enunciation of such mysteries, that they are impossible, since they imply states of being, events, or special forms of enlightenment that transcend in some way our common experience of the principles of nature and of natural knowledge. Reason alone, for example, can neither prove nor disprove that there are three persons in God. Is it possible for God to take on a human nature without ceasing to be God? How can the meritorious death of one person have an effect on the whole human race? We have no experience in ordinary life of bodily resurrection. Can God raise the dead? How can we know if any of this is true if we do not have access to it by way of universal natural knowledge?

One important aspect of the teaching on divine omnipotence is that it provides the philosophical foundation for a response to such concerns. Such objections are common in the wake of the Enlightenment (as, for example, in the works of Spinoza, Lessing, or Hume), and are typically framed by appeal to the ordinary laws of nature and their inviolability. In response, one can note that when determining what is rational to believe about the world, we should indeed refer to ordinary processes of nature (their "laws") and to predictable human forms of knowing and behavior (acknowledging that human beings can be subject to superstition, religious delusion, and manipulation). But we always can and should also allude to the ultimate measure of the truth, which is provided not merely by the customary opinions of the human community, nor even by the natural order, but only by God himself, the first truth and cause of existence for all else that exists. It is reasonable to believe in the natural order and stability of the world God has created, and from that order we can learn a good deal not only about the structure of nature but also about God as the Creator. But it is also reasonable to believe that he who is the very source of this natural order can, should he so wish, act in virtue of his transcendent wisdom, love, and omnipotence in a way that transcends the limits and potentialities of nature, precisely so as to reveal himself personally to human beings in an intimate way, and also so as to save and redeem the very order of nature, which he sustains in being, by the power of his grace.

It is true that singular and ontologically contingent events like the Incarnation or the bodily resurrection of Christ are not subject to demonstrative rational proof. We know about them through human witnesses and by the grace of faith. In effect, God offers us the capacity, by grace, to consent to apostolic testimony by faith, and through this consent to gain genuine insight into the very mysteries themselves. None of this is accomplished merely by unaided natural reason. It is, however, reasonable and correct to appeal to divine omnipotence as a kind of intellectual ground-clearing process, to show that the mysteries of Christianity imply no inherent contradiction, and therefore are not impossible as such.[9] Indeed they also can be seen to provide essential perspective on human existence and have a maximally universal explanatory value, but these epistemic properties are discovered principally through the medium of faith, not philosophical demonstration. We find that a claim like this is advanced by the First Vatican Council. In effect, the Council insists that denial of the *possibility of the supernatural* is itself irrational. But if God works supernaturally, he does so in ways that also indicate to us that belief in his revelation is (1) reasonable, given the motives of credibility (i.e., miracles and suchlike that accompany the mystery and act as signs to our reason to confirm the rational plausibility of the revelation);[10]

9. One can point out, for example, that to argue that it is impossible for God to become human, one would have to demonstrate either that God is not omnipotent or that the very idea of the Incarnation entails an inherent contradiction, so that it is literally unthinkable. However, if the world exists and is caused by a Creator, then it follows that the Creator truly is omnipotent. Furthermore, orthodox Christianity teaches that God has become human without ceasing to be God, such that there is a real distinction of natures in Christ, as true God and true man. This idea, when studied closely, implies nothing intrinsically contradictory. Really, then, to exclude the rational possibility of Christianity at the roots, one must argue against the existence of God the Creator, and even seek to demonstrate that God cannot exist. This is a formidable task, since the very existence of the world around us serves as indirect but unambiguous testimony to the existence of God.

10. On this point, see the First Vatican Council, *Dei Filius*, chap. 3, in *Decrees*, ed. Tanner, 2:807: "Nevertheless, in order that the submission of our faith should be in accordance with

and (2) as concerns the mysteries of faith, that they are at least rationally fitting in certain respects, and not impossible.[11]

CONCLUSION

In this chapter, we have considered God's power to act "transitively," that is to say, "outside" of himself or in distinction from himself in his creation. The power of God is infinite and extends to all beings. Furthermore, the omnipotence or "all-powerfulness" of God refers not only to all that exists in creation, but also to all that is merely *possible*. This includes all things that are not inherently contradictory. God does not employ his power arbitrarily, but always in subordination to and as a dimension of his divine wisdom and love. In this respect his power undergirds and safeguards the natural order but also can be at the origin of new initiatives that restore, perfect or re-create the natural order in virtue of God's grace. The appeal to the reality of divine omnipotence can aid in apologetic efforts to show that Christian belief in supernatural mysteries is in no way irrational. At the

reason, it was God's will that there should be linked to the internal assistance of the Holy Spirit outward indications of his revelation, that is to say divine acts, and first and foremost miracles and prophecies, which clearly demonstrating as they do the omnipotence and infinite knowledge of God, are the most certain signs of revelation and are suited to the understanding of all." Reasons of credibility do not provide immediate intellectual contact with the very mysteries of faith, but serve as external proofs or warrants to indicate the reasonableness of Christianity and the rationality of one's consent to the supernatural act of faith.

11. The First Vatican Council maintains a distinction between natural and supernatural truths. The latter can never be positively demonstrated by human reason but can only be accepted in faith. Nevertheless, these truths can be shown to be fitting in the highest degree and internally coherent among themselves. See *Dei Filius*, chap. 4, in *Decrees*, ed. Tanner, 2:808: "The perpetual agreement of the catholic church has maintained and maintains this too: that there is a twofold order of knowledge, distinct not only as regards its source, but also as regards its object. With regard to the source, we know at the one level by natural reason, at the other level by divine faith. With regard to the object, besides those things to which natural reason can attain, there are proposed for our belief mysteries hidden in God which, unless they are divinely revealed, are incapable of being known.... Now reason, if it is enlightened by faith, does indeed when it seeks persistently, piously and soberly, achieve by God's gift some understanding, and that most profitable, of the mysteries, whether by analogy from what it knows naturally, or from the connection of these mysteries with one another and with the final end of humanity; but reason is never rendered capable of penetrating these mysteries in the way in which it penetrates those truths which form its proper object." For a theological overview of the rationale underlying the distinction between these two orders of knowing, one natural and the other supernatural, see especially Matthias Joseph Scheeben, *The Mysteries of Christianity*, trans. Cyril Vollert, SJ (St. Louis, Mo.: Herder, 1954), 3–21. See also Matthias Joseph Scheeben, *Handbook of Catholic Dogmatics*, bk. 1, *Theological Epistemology*, part 1, *The Objective Principles of Theological Knowledge*, trans. Michael J. Miller (Steubenville, Ohio: Emmaus Academic, 2019), para. 26–34.

very least, Christian claims are lacking in inherent contradiction and so are possible for divine power, and if they are real, they are indications of the inner life of God, precisely because only he who is omnipotent could manifest or realize such mysteries. Even so, their inner truth and historical factuality reposes on the testimony of revelation, and the acceptance of their truth by the individual in the act of faith depends upon the inner illumination of the Holy Spirit.

20

Knowledge of the Triune God

We have concluded our study of the oneness of God by considering God's inner life as a mystery of knowledge and love, one that invites us to think about the inner life of the Trinity. After all, it is the Father who, in knowing himself, eternally generates his begotten Word, and who, in loving himself, spirates the person of the Holy Spirit, who is love. It is fitting, then, in light of our consideration of God's inner life, that we begin to pivot toward a consideration of the mystery of the Holy Trinity proper. This mystery will be the subject of the next section of this book. Here, however, as an epilogue to part 2 and as a kind of prolegomenon to part 3, we will consider the *knowledge* we have of the Holy Trinity and how we come by it.

NATURAL KNOWLEDGE OF GOD AND
THE MYSTERY OF GOD IN HIMSELF

At numerous junctures throughout this work, we have stated a common idea: there are things we can know about God both from divine revelation and through the efforts of natural human reason. Included in this category are the attributes of God we have studied in the preceding seven chapters. Let us recall here some basic Thomistic epistemological claims. First, human beings can attain genuine natural knowledge of the existence and attributes of the one God by way of *quia* demonstrations from effect to cause, that argue from creaturely effects to the necessary existence of their transcendent Creator. This knowledge is rationally certain, and does allow us to ascribe attributes to God analogically, so as to designate truly what God is in himself. However, such natural knowledge of God is not immediate, in the sense that it provides no direct perception of the essence or inner life of God. Consequently, it does not permit us to attain personal interaction with God himself, friendship with God, or knowledge of the essence of God that is immediate or intuitively perceptual. In this sense, according to Aquinas, our natural knowledge of God leaves room for a yet higher form of knowledge that may occur in virtue of the grace of faith, whereby we are given a higher form of insight into the mystery of God.[1] It is in virtue of this form of higher knowledge by grace, for example, that we may come to know that God has established a covenant with the people of Israel culminating in the mystery of Christ and the Church, that we are each invited to eternal happiness in the beatific vision of God and the resurrection, and that we may enjoy spiritual friendship with God in this life by grace.[2] Faith, in this sense, implies actual insight into the mystery of who God is, insight that philosophical knowledge of God does not provide. Faith also permits us to obtain not only interpersonal but also propositional understanding of God that we would not have otherwise.[3] After all, it is one thing to know that God must exist and have various personal characteristics, and it is another thing to be introduced to God personally in his Trinitarian life, so as to acquire spiritual friendship with God and know him in himself.

The knowledge we have of God by grace, however, also implies degrees of perfection. For example, God's covenant with Israel, which is established by elective grace, provides us with knowledge of God as one and as Creator, and shows us that God employs his providential governance of the cosmos in view of his covenant with Israel, which is itself established in view of the common good of the whole human race. Of course, we can also align much of our philosophical understanding of God with this revelation, as the previous chapters in this book suggest. Aquinas notes that we can speak rea-

1. See the discussions in *ST* I, q. 12, aa. 4, 12 and 13, and *ST* II-II, qq. 1–2, on the virtue of faith that provides knowledge of the divine essence *in se*, through the veil of faith and so still in an imperfect mode.

2. Aquinas emphasizes, in *ST* II-II, q. 23, a. 1, that there is no natural friendship with God the Creator, but that it becomes possible as a gift of grace. He posits that divine providence is in part knowable by reason but not in the fullness of its designs. See *ST* I, q. 2, a. 2; q. 22, a. 2; *SCG* III, cc. 1–25.

3. See on this point *ST* II-II, q. 1, aa. 1–2: a. 1 underscores that faith is a grace of the intellect that places us in direct personal encounter with God, the First Truth, while a. 2 underscores that faith is enunciated in propositional forms that are veridical. Faith, then, provides the mind with a new personal judgment regarding the very mystery of God unveiled in Christ; it is both interpersonal in nature and veridically propositional in expression.

sonably of the one God as "a person" based on the both the Old Testament revelation of God as YHWH, and our philosophical knowledge of divine perfections.[4] However, the Old Testament revelation contains only adumbrations of the mystery of the Holy Trinity, as we noted in chapter 3. The explicit revelation of the mystery of the Holy Trinity appears only in the Incarnation, in the sending of God the Son, Jesus Christ, into the world, accompanied by the sending of the Holy Spirit. Consequently, the grace of the New Covenant manifests more perfectly who God is in himself, inviting us to know the Father, Son, and Holy Spirit personally, and allowing us to draw true propositional inferences about the immanent life of God as a communion of three persons. This higher knowledge of God as Trinity, meanwhile, while genuine and veridical, is possessed in this life only in faith, which is a form of noetic insight that remains imperfect. Aquinas claims that faith allows us to know God immediately in himself, as Trinity, and in this sense it anticipates the perfect knowledge of God we can have in the life to come.[5] However, it is also a knowledge given to us in darkness or obscurity, since it entails consent of the mind to God's revelation of himself through the medium of the apostolic testimony, without sensory evidence.[6] Faith thus entails both enlightenment of the mind and obscurity. It provides new insights into the mystery of God that are not accessible by mere reason, but the insights are a gift of grace we freely consent to and also can turn away from.[7] The imperfect character of this knowledge invites cooperation through hope and love, by which we consent freely to believe God, and this personal stance of engagement with God in friendship inclines us spiritually in knowledge and love toward a more perfect form of knowledge in the beatific vision, when

4. *ST* I, q. 29, a. 3, corp. and ad 1: "'Person' signifies what is most perfect in all nature—that is, a subsistent individual of a rational nature. Hence, since everything that is perfect must be attributed to God, forasmuch as His essence contains every perfection, this name 'person' is fittingly applied to God; not, however, as it is applied to creatures, but in a more excellent way; as other names also, which, while giving them to creatures, we attribute to God; as we showed above when treating of the names of God.... Although the word 'person' is not found applied to God in scripture, either in the Old or New Testament, nevertheless what the word signifies is found to be affirmed of God in many places of scripture; as that He is the supreme self-subsisting being, and the most perfectly intelligent being." Aquinas is intimating here that it is warranted to speak of God as a "person" in some contexts, even if we as Christians also know God is Trinitarian, insofar as we think of the one God who is Creator as having a perfect life of knowledge and love, abstracting from the consideration of God's inner mystery of the Father, Son, and Spirit as such.
5. *ST* II-II, q. 1, a. 1.
6. *ST* II-II, q. 1, a. 4.
7. *ST* II-II, q. 2, a. 1.

the soul after separation from the body may be inducted into direct union with God by immediate intuition or intellectual apperception.[8] In the beatific vision, the soul sees God "face to face" (Rv 22:4) and possesses God in love by an immediacy of union with the divine by grace.

This complex of ideas still leaves open a major question. Does the philosophical understanding of God by natural reason, which we can attain in this life, also permit us to obtain genuine *natural* or *philosophical* knowledge of God as Trinity? We have seen that Aquinas does posit an "overlap" of knowledge of God as one and Creator, attainable both by Old Testament revelation and by philosophical reflection on the divine nature. Although our reflections in the section of the book above pertain to the divine nature of God *in view of an analysis of the Trinity,* one could in principle abstract the discussion of God as one from the discussion of God as three persons so as to underscore this alignment of Old Testament revelation and philosophical reasoning. This is not what we have undertaken in this book, which is about the Trinity as such, but it is in no way logically impermissible to undertake such a task.

Can we go further, however, and make use of our philosophical knowledge of God's nature as one in order to infer rationally that God is also three persons in communion? Can the mystery of the Trinity be "proven" rationally? A great deal is at stake in the discussion of this question, for several reasons. First, if the multiplicity of persons in God can be demonstrated naturally as a truth of philosophical reason, does it need to be revealed by God? Are the grace of friendship with God and the knowledge of God, attained by way of faith, really unique or necessary, or can we just rely on philosophy? Or, to suggest another possibility, if we cannot rely on philosophy to obtain knowledge of the Trinity as such, why should we, as rational persons, be motivated to believe in it? Can our philosophical knowledge of God itself dispose us to acknowledge the possibility and even the appeal of revelation? Aquinas argues, as we will see below, that the acknowledgement of the *imperfection* of our philosophical knowledge of God disposes us to consider the reasonableness of revelation as a way of knowing God in a yet more perfect fashion. Should arguments for the Trinity from philosophy be a part of that process or could they in fact be misleading?

Second, how does the claim that God is Trinity relate epistemologically

8. *ST* I, q. 12, a. 5.

to the claim that God is one? Here, there is a great deal at stake for the relationship that arises between monotheists who are not Trinitarian and those who are. Can Christians prove to Jews or Muslims, for example, that God is a plurality of persons, if the latter simply concede that God is one and is subsistent understanding and subsistent love? Or is additional revelation required for the latter to come to know the persons of the Father, Son, and Holy Spirit, in virtue of the mystery of Jesus Christ? If there is need for revelation, then how might Christians still find points of profound agreement with Jews or Muslims concerning the divine nature of God, and how might they defend rightly the idea that Trinitarian belief is monotheistic, since all three persons are one in being and nature? How also might they argue both with philosophers and with non-Christian monotheists that the mystery of the Holy Trinity can neither be proven by natural reason nor disproven, since the knowledge of God as Trinity is a gift of grace exceeding the competence of all our natural powers?

The question of the rational knowledge of the Holy Trinity was a matter of dispute in medieval theology. Some influential theologians such as Richard of St. Victor, Bonaventure, and Duns Scotus affirmed (each in different ways) that philosophical argument could establish that there must be a distinction of persons in God, while others argued that the mystery of the Trinity is accessible only in virtue of the grace of faith. As we will note below, Aquinas is in the latter group. He argues that we may indeed know truths about the unity of God by way of natural reason, but that we may know truths about the Trinity as such only by way of divine revelation. It is instructive to contrast his approach with that of Richard, a remarkable twelfth-century Parisian theologian, who first set out what has become the most frequently repeated philosophical argument for the Trinity, based on God's essential attribute of love. As we will see, Aquinas holds that the strictly supernatural character of the knowledge of the Trinity is related to God's essential hiddenness and freedom of self-disclosure. Only God can give us the grace that permits us to obtain intimate knowledge of and friendship with him, as Father, Son, and Holy Spirit. The gift of this contact with God in faith addresses a natural intellectual desire in us to know God in himself, but also elevates us into a range of knowledge that lies beyond our natural capacities. The Trinity is a mystery we know only by the grace of faith, a mystery that utterly transcends the horizon of our merely natural understanding.

RICHARD OF ST. VICTOR

Richard of St. Victor (who died in 1173) is the first great medieval theologian who seeks to provide a systematic argument for the rationality of belief in the Trinity. He does so principally in books 3 and 5 of his work *De Trinitate*.[9] Prior to this, in books 1 and 2, he argues for the existence, eternity, omnipotence, wisdom, and goodness of God, as well as the unity and simplicity of the divine essence.[10] There is only one God, and God is characterized by power, wisdom, and goodness in all that God is.[11] The argument then proceeds in approximately five steps, which we can set out didactically below.

1. By previous argument, God can be understood to be the supreme and most perfect good. "We have learned from our previous discussions that the fullness and perfection of all goodness lies in the supreme and universally perfect good [i.e., God]."[12]

2. However, this goodness in God, Richard notes, implies the presence of personal love, or charity. "Moreover, where the fullness of all goodness is, truth and supreme charity cannot be lacking. Indeed, nothing is better than charity, and nothing is more perfect than charity."[13]

3. In order to be perfect, charity cannot be directed toward one's own person alone but must be directed to another person. If there is perfect love in God, then, it must be directed from one person to another. "No one is properly said to have love on account of a private and exclusive love of one's self. And so it is necessary that *love be directed toward another, so that it can be charity*. Therefore, charity absolutely cannot exist where a plurality of persons is lacking."[14] In other words, if God is truly the highest good and most perfect love, there must be an "other" toward whom God's love is directed, through the medium of a communion of persons.

4. God's love would not be perfect if he did not love one who is su-

---

9. See Richard of St. Victor, *On the Trinity*, trans. C. P. Evans, in *Trinity and Creation*, ed. B. T. Coolman and D. M. Coulter (Turnhout, Belgium: Brepols, 2010).

10. See Richard of St. Victor, *On the Trinity*, 1.9–25; 2.16–19.

11. On the simplicity of God, see Richard of St. Victor, *On the Trinity*, 1.20–23. Richard associates simplicity with the incomprehensible transcendence of the divine essence, an association that is found in Aquinas's theology as well.

12. Richard of St. Victor, *On the Trinity*, 3.2.

13. Richard of St. Victor, *On the Trinity*, 3.2.

14. Richard of St. Victor, *On the Trinity*, 3.2.

premely worthy of divine love. "But a divine person would surely not have someone whom he could love as worthily as himself, if he absolutely were not having a person of equal dignity. However, a person who was not God would not be of equal dignity to a divine person. Therefore, so that the fullness of charity can occur in true divinity, it is necessary for a divine person not to lack the fellowship with a person of equal dignity and, for that reason, a divine person."[15]

5. Perfect love entails the selfless concern for another. For this we need not only two but at least three persons in God. Why should it be so? The fullness of power and wisdom could exist in only one person.[16] The fullness of happiness could exist in a communion of love between two persons alone.[17] However, "the supreme degree of goodness seems to occur when a person bestows supreme love to someone and gains nothing from it toward the fullness of his own happiness."[18] When there are only two persons, however, love risks becoming closed off in itself, and egoistic, rather then genuinely self-giving. Therefore, there must exist a love in God that transcends the mere love of mutual happiness, and this can transpire only if there are three persons in God, where the first two persons share in a self-less love of the third person.[19] Richard seems to imply here that in any love held between only two persons, there must be an imperfect quality of selflessness, due to the closed-off nature of the relationship. This will be the case unless the two persons share a mutual love for a third. If God is perfect in love, then, God must be a shared life of three persons in communion.[20]

15. Richard of St. Victor, *On the Trinity*, 3.2. Richard goes on to state just after this conclusion: "See therefore how easily reason proves that a plurality of persons cannot be lacking in true divinity."

16. Richard of St. Victor, *On the Trinity*, 3.16.

17. Richard of St. Victor, *On the Trinity*, 3.17.

18. Richard of St. Victor, *On the Trinity*, 3.18.

19. Richard of St. Victor, *On the Trinity*, 3.18–19.

20. Richard goes on to argue, in *On the Trinity*, 5.3–9, in rather tenuous fashion, that there can only be three persons in God, not more. The argument, which is complex, passes through the following chain of arguments: We have established that there must be at least three persons in God. However, there also must be procession or order of origin between the distinct persons in God. There must be some person who is absolutely primary, who exists from himself and not from any other. There can be only one such person. It is necessary for there to be a person who proceeds eternally from one person alone (this being the Son). This person proceeds immediately from the first person. There must also be a person who proceeds from two persons (the Spirit). This person proceeds both immediately and mediately (from the Father through the Son). A procession which belongs to a person only mediately cannot exist in the divine nature. Therefore, there can be only two processions and three persons.

Richard's argument is centered around the concept of perfect love. From the idea of God as the highest and most perfect good we can intuit intellectually that God must be love, a love that entails interpersonal communion. If this interpersonal communion is supreme in character, then it must be shared within an uncreated reciprocity of personal love. We know from creatures, however, that mutual reciprocity between only two persons has something about it that is closed in on itself, incompatible with the idea of perfection in self-giving love. Therefore, there must be an uncreated mutual love in God that is fruitful, of two who give rise to a third. A God who is love must be a God who is Triune. From the very idea of love as an essential attribute of God, then, Richard proceeds to discern the necessity of the existence of a second and, ultimately, of a third person, as necessary conditions for God's love to be wholly perfect.

AQUINAS ON RATIONAL KNOWLEDGE

OF THE TRINITY

How might one respond to this argument in favor of Trinitarian ontology, rooted in the confession of God as love? Aquinas considers the argument of Richard of St. Victor, which he knows well, in *ST* I, q. 32, a. 1. He begins by noting that our natural knowledge of God is derived from creatures, which "lead us to the knowledge of God, as effects do to their cause. Accordingly, by natural reason we can know of God that only which of necessity belongs to Him as the principle of things." However, "the creative power of God is common to the whole Trinity; and hence it belongs to the unity of the essence, and not to the distinction of the persons. Therefore, by natural reason we can know what belongs to the unity of the essence, but not what belongs to the distinction of the persons." Aquinas's basic argument pertains to the epistemological limitations of our philosophical knowledge of God, interpreted theologically *in light of* our superior knowledge of God as Trinity, which we have in virtue of faith. We might state the argument this way, noting that it is a theological argument as such but one that seeks to take into account the true scope of our philosophical knowledge of God:

1. When we seek to know God by natural reason, we seek to understand him from his effects of nature, that is, his creation. In so doing we can arrive at a certain knowledge of God understood as the causal principle of all created things.

2. The creation bears indirect but real testimony to the existence of God and his divine attributes of simplicity, perfection, goodness, unity, power, and the rest, which pertain to God's essence.

3. The creative power of God, however, is common to the three persons of the Trinity; hence what we know of God from this power pertains to the unity of the divine essence, and not to the distinction of the persons.

Aquinas here presupposes that creation is a work of the whole Trinity, and therefore equally the work of the Father, Son, and Holy Spirit. Precisely because all three persons possess the plenitude of the divine nature, it is not proper to any one person. Therefore, whenever we attain knowledge only of God's unity of essence, we cannot infer from his natural attributes as God that there is a distinction of persons in God.[21]

In comparing the visions of Richard of St. Victor and Aquinas, one can detect a subtle but important difference of views regarding divine simplicity and the relation of essence to persons. Richard argues for the simplicity of the divine essence, as we have noted. He also claims, however, that the idea of perfect power and wisdom are compatible with the idea of only one divine person, while the notion of perfect happiness requires the idea of two divine persons, and the idea of perfect love requires three persons. Here the diverse divine names for the essence of God (power, wisdom, happiness, love) are not considered to denote in different ways something that is mysteriously one in God, as they are in the thought of Aquinas. Instead they imply formal distinction of some kind in God himself.[22] When Richard speaks of the goodness, happiness, and love of God in his divine essence, he is not

---

21. Therefore, the monotheistic philosopher, when confronted with traditional Christian theological claims about the revelation of the Trinity, should in principle admit that God *could be* in himself a Trinity of persons, but that we are unable either to prove or disprove this truth, from the perspective of natural reason alone. (This is true, incidentally, even if the philosopher in question is a Christian, since the person who has the grace of faith can perceive the limitations of natural knowledge even interior to the act of faith.) It is true that philosophically speaking, for Aquinas, we can say, for example, that God's nature is one, that God is wisdom and love, and that in God essence and existence are somehow identical in virtue of the divine simplicity. However, we cannot from this knowledge infer whether or not there are eternal processions of Word and Spirit in God eternally. To resolve this question, we would need God to reveal himself to us personally.

22. Here, when speaking of formal distinction, I mean to indicate attributes denoted of God's essence that are not considered to be only one in reality but truly multiple and distinct in God, yet without this implying ontological composition of the kind we find in creatures (i.e., real distinctions between individual and nature, existence and essence, substance and attribute, etc.) Of course, Aquinas does not hold such an idea, but Richard's thought seems to me to tend in this direction, however implicitly.

indicating properties that are ultimately merely co-extensive and identical with one another. Furthermore, when one names God's essential happiness or his essential love, one is also bound to indicate, for Richard, something of his personal communion. God's essential attribute of happiness draws out the notion of two persons in a way power and wisdom do not, while love draws out the notion of three persons in a way that happiness does not. Not only are these notions indicative of ontological traits in some way formally distinct in the essence of God, but they also track onto or logically suggest the necessity of distinct personal properties in God: the happiness of the divine essence implies that God is a communion of at least two persons, while the goodness and love of the divine essence implies that God is a communion of at least and no more than three persons.

Aquinas's view of divine simplicity is, of course, very different. For him, the distinct attributes that we assign to the divine essence do each signify in irreducibly distinct ways something genuinely true about God. God is truly powerful, wise, good, and so forth. But there is no real or formal distinction of these attributes in God, so that what we term God's justice or God's mercy are truly one in God, and are in turn identical with his wisdom and goodness, on account of his simplicity. This is the case even if we are obliged to denote God's essence by making use of a spectrum of irreducibly distinct names drawn from our logically prior experience of God's creatures. It follows from this view, of course, that one cannot derive natural demonstrative knowledge of the Trinity from a consideration of the attributes of the divine essence, since each of those attributes denotes something that is simple and one in God, the very nature of God itself, which is common to all three persons. In fact, when one argues that the love of God is something formally distinct in God from his wisdom, and that this formal distinction is a basis for distinguishing the Spirit as love from the Son as wisdom, one also compromises, and in a sense minimalizes, the doctrines of divine simplicity and divine unity. God is simple and is one *up to a point*, but his unity is in fact always already characterized by ontological distinctions, a set of distinctions in his essence that suggests a multiplicity of persons. Richard of St. Victor underscores the unicity of the one God and his simplicity of essence, but his way of maintaining these ideas seems at times to contain internal tensions.

Several related claims follow from Aquinas's perspective; we can add them here as accessory ideas.

1. God's offer of grace to us, by which we are given to know the mystery of the Trinity, is a purely gratuitous gift, not something we can procure for ourselves by our natural powers. Consequently, it is mistaken to think that we can arrive at intimate knowledge of God as he is in himself essentially *as Trinity* merely by the powers of unaided natural reason. All forms of philosophical argument for the Trinity are misleading, then, since they mistakenly give the impression that nature can procure what only grace can provide.[23]

2. Does it follow from this that the graced knowledge of the Trinity is naturally undesirable or rationally unintelligible? St. Thomas argues that it is reasonable to be open to the revelation of the inner mystery of God, if such a revelation exists. Why is this the case? The knowledge of God's essence that we attain by way of philosophical reasoning is indirect and "merely" argumentative and demonstrative, not immediate or intuitively perceptual. Aquinas argues quite reasonably that when we know of a cause inferentially through its effects, we naturally desire to know the cause in itself. Consequently, if we know of God through his effects, we also naturally desire to see God in himself, to know God immediately and directly.[24] We can have this natural desire to see God and acknowledge its philosophical warrant even if we do not possess the capacity to procure this knowledge as such. Christian revelation specifies, however, that we can come to know God personally in his essence in a more perfect way by grace, through faith in this life leading to the vision of God in the life to come. The truth of this claim cannot be verified *philosophically* precisely because the grace in question is a gift that exceeds the capacities of nature, but *if* this grace is real and *if* it provides ultimate knowledge of God, then it is reasonable to desire and embrace what is promised. Philosophically speaking, it is permissible to scan the horizon in search of a possible pathway to perfect knowledge of God. In some respect then, the supernatural gratuity of the grace to see God, which Christianity announces, is a sign precisely of its rationality, in the sense that one may reasonably desire a form of familiarity with God that one knows philosophically one cannot obtain by natural means.

---

23. Aquinas makes this point, in *ST* I, q. 32, a. 1, in response to Richard and others. His concern here is against what one may term a form of "epistemological Pelagianism" that seeks to demonstrate rationally those mysteries that are known by the grace of faith alone.

24. See the argument of *ST* I, q. 12, a. 1. On Aquinas's treatment of the natural desire to see God, see my "Imperfect Happiness and the Final End of Man: Thomas Aquinas and the Paradigm of Nature-Grace Orthodoxy," *The Thomist* 78, no. 2 (2014): 247–89.

3. If Aquinas is correct that all we can know naturally about God by philosophical reason pertains to God in his nature, which is one, but not to the distinction of persons, then there can be no "proof of the Trinity" from consideration of the attributes of the divine essence. But there are also, then, no warranted objections to Trinitarian faith from non-Trinitarian monotheistic traditions if the objections are based on appeals to divine unity or to the attributes of the divine nature. Trinitarian belief is utterly monotheistic precisely because it claims that God is simple and one in essence. Substantive differences between Christians and Jews, and Christians and Muslims, with regard to the mystery of God are based primarily on different understandings of divine revelation, not on the truths that we can know about God by natural reason, nor is Trinitarian monotheism any "less" a form of monotheism than that held by others.

Aquinas continues his line of argument in this article by issuing an epistemological warning. Bad arguments incite skepticism in those who are trying to discern whether Trinitarian faith is reasonable. "For when anyone in the endeavor to prove the faith brings forward reasons which are not cogent, he falls under the ridicule of the unbelievers: since they suppose that we stand upon such reasons, and that we believe on such grounds."[25]

Aquinas argues, against the position of Richard, that knowledge of the mystery of the Holy Trinity cannot be derived from philosophical reasoning, even "after the fact" of divine revelation, by way of rational demonstration. If this is the case, then it must also be true that Richard's argument for the Trinity is problematic in some way. Returning to that argument, then, where are its flaws? The key problems emerge in the third and fifth steps in the argument. In the third, Richard argues that: "No one is properly said to have love on account of a private and exclusive love of oneself. And so it is necessary that *love be directed toward another, so that it can be charity.* Therefore, charity absolutely cannot exist where a plurality of persons is lacking." He goes on to specify that if the lover is perfect, then there must be one who is divinely perfect who receives the love, a second person in the godhead. In the fifth premise, Richard argues that the love between two divine persons would be imperfect if it were not open to the third person, whom they share their love with, so that there must be a third person to whom love is communicated.

25. *ST* I, q. 32, a. 1, corp.

What are the problems with these arguments? First, as Aquinas notes, creation is finite in goodness but does manifest to us that God is infinite goodness. This can be inferred from the finite creation because God's production of being from nothing requires an infinite power, and God's communication of being to the creation stems from his divine goodness. God, then, is both good and infinite. We cannot infer from this, however, that God must produce an *infinite* effect, as if God were to need to communicate his nature to another person in order to be infinitely good. We can only conclude that when God by his divine infinity does communicate being and goodness, each recipient must receive a share in being and goodness according to its own particular mode and capacity.[26] In effect, the "mere fact" of the creation shows us philosophically that the infinite God can communicate himself in finite ways, not that he must communicate himself in infinite ways.

Second, as Richard rightly notes, God is characterized by perfect goodness and love. As Aquinas notes, however, in loving himself, God by nature loves what is supremely good in an infinitely loving way. If this is the case, however, no matter how many persons are in God, they will each possess a perfect love by nature, just insofar as they are each truly God (having the divine essence, which is infinite love). Richard's third and fifth premises attempt in two distinct ways to show that God can be perfect in love only if his love is shared between persons. As Aquinas notes, however, "joyous possession of good requires partnership [only] in the case of one not having perfect goodness."[27] In finite human persons, who are imperfect in nature, love can become more perfect over time through relationships of communion. Indeed, it is true that for a human being to be perfected in nature, according to love, there must be a communion of human persons who share love. God, by contrast, possesses an infinite and perfect love in virtue of his nature. Therefore, whether God is only one person, a communion of only two persons, or three persons, the person/s who is/are God must (each) possess an infinite love in virtue of the unity of the divine nature. We cannot infer, then, just because God is love by nature that God must be a loving communion of multiple persons.

In addition there is a special problem with the fifth premise, since it is not clear based on Richard's logic why we should multiply the divine per-

26. *ST* I, q. 32, a. 1, ad 2.
27. *ST* I, q. 32, a. 1, ad 2.

sons only to three, even if we (problematically) grant that two divine persons might be limited in love or closed in on themselves. For if we grant that
two divine persons can somehow fail to love perfectly, then it must be the
case that divine persons fail to possess infinite love simply due to their nature, and instead can fail to love perfectly unless they have relationships to
other persons. But if we argue that the first two persons thus stand in need
of a third person to love with perfect selflessness, we may go on to use this
argument to argue in turn for yet another necessary person in addition to
this third infinite person. After all, it may be that additional personal properties from a fourth person are required to assure the selflessness of the first
three persons, just as the third person possesses personal qualities that assure the love of the first two persons. (We can ask ourselves, for instance,
how many human persons one must begin to love before one's love is truly
self-less.) There is, then, the possibility of an infinite multiplication of persons in God. In fact, as Aquinas notes, Richard's vision of personal communion is anthropomorphic.[28] Created human persons who are finite cannot
possess a love that is complete if they love only themselves. They accordingly can become perfect in love only if they are open to communion with
others in love. In turn they necessarily depend upon others for their own
growth in the perfection of love. The divine nature by contrast is pure actuality and infinitely perfect, so the love we ascribe to God essentially is not
characterized by potency or defect. God can love perfectly and infinitely in
virtue of God's nature without needing another to love so as to achieve infinite perfection.

IS THERE A TRINITARIAN
APOLOGETICS BASED ON REASON
OR COMMUNION OF LOVE?

Richard of St. Victor's argument produces a paradoxical outcome. It is
meant to illustrate the distinctive rationality of a Christian vision of God
as love, that is to say, as a communion of persons. This form of argumentation could appear particularly relevant in conversation with non-Christian
philosophies, since it underscores that the deepest ground and explanation of reality is a personal communion of love, from which all other

28. *ST* I, q. 32, a. 1, ad 2.

things originate. It also could appear particularly relevant in conversation with non-Christian monotheists or religionists, since it allows one to underscore that the God of Christianity is a God of love, by way of personal communion. At yet at the same time, Richard's argument runs the risk of alienating and further compounding the skepticism of the very people one might wish to persuade. In effect, he depicts in an anthropomorphic way the divine nature as goodness and love, and in doing so misrepresents the infinite perfection of God's essence. If non-Christian monotheists or atheists are given the impression that Christians argue for a communion of persons in God based upon faulty premises—because these in fact depict the persons of the Trinity anthropomorphically—then they are also likely to conclude that traditional New Testament belief in the Trinity is based upon a problematic projection of finite modes of created personhood onto God. In this case, one might conclude that Christianity is a philosophically incoherent mistake or a crude form of conceptual idolatry that projects a multiplicity of imperfect persons onto the one God. Meanwhile, Christians themselves, influenced by dubious theology, will begin to accept an anthropomorphic view of God. In this case we would be wise to heed Aquinas's warning regarding the unintended consequences of bad arguments.

What about the original intention of Richard, however? Does the revelation of the Trinity help us understand the *essential* nature of God as wisdom and as love? And can our presentation of the mystery of the Trinity help illustrate the distinctive depth of a Christian vision of God as love, that is to say as a communion of persons?

These last two questions are posed in such a way as to invert the order of argument we have been considering so far in this chapter. No, it is not the case that mere philosophical knowledge of the nature of God allows us to gain access to the knowledge of the Trinitarian mystery. But can the knowledge of the Trinity given to us in faith suggest to us truths of natural knowledge regarding God that we may have failed to understand by our own natural power? Here Aquinas answers affirmatively. In our concrete existential state, human beings are affected by the individual and corporate effects of original and personal sin, and have great difficulty understanding that God exists, and what God is, even with respect to those truths about God that can be known naturally. Divine revelation of the Trinity is given then *in part* to help us recover a sense of the natural truth about God, which can be underscored by the grace of faith insofar as it suggests implicitly the essential attributes of God. For example, if there truly is in God an eternal procession of the Logos as the begotten Wisdom of the Father, then all things that exist in creation come forth from one who is "reasonable" and understanding, who is the source of order and intelligibility in created things. Likewise, if God truly has created all things in his Spirit of Love, who stems from the eternal communion of the Father and the Son, then there is a communion of persons that is the uncreated ground of all human personal communion. The universe derives from personal communion, and exists for personal communion, and is ultimately grounded in a mystery of love. The revelation of the Trinity can be seen in this respect to invite us to knowledge of God by grace, but also to a renewed natural and philosophical understanding of creation in which reality is "re-read" personalistically, that is, understood to proceed from a transcendent source that is Reason, Love, and communion of persons.

Interestingly, Aquinas seeks to illustrate this idea regarding the Trinity by appeal to the opening pages of Genesis.

[Revelation of the Trinity] was necessary for the right idea of creation. The fact of saying that God made all things by His Word excludes the error of those who say that God produced things by necessity. When we say that in Him there is a procession of love, we show that God produced creatures not because He needed them, nor because of any other extrinsic reason, but on account of the love of His own goodness. So Moses, when he had said, "In the beginning God created heaven and earth," subjoined, "God said, Let there be light," to manifest the divine Word; and then said, "God saw the light that it was good," to show proof of the divine love.[29]

In this context, Aquinas's reading of the Torah is Trinitarian. In light of the New Testament revelation, we see that God has created all things in the Word, who is a person distinct from the Father, but who is also a principle of reason or wisdom. Belief in the Trinity, then, requires and reemphasizes belief in the transcendent rationality and freedom of God, who is the source of all things. This exegetical strategy suggests two things. The first is that belief in the Trinity is a work of faith that "recapitulates" the act of reason, in its acknowledgement of the truth about God as one, and as Creator. Trinitarian belief spurs the believer to acknowledge natural truths about God, and therefore to become more reasonable. Second, the ultimate criterion for the evaluation of the Trinitarian claims that Christians make comes not from philosophical demonstration but from the consideration of the inter-

29. *ST* I, q. 32, a. 1, ad 3.

nal content of divine revelation. If there are in fact adumbrations of Trinitarian revelation in the Torah and the prophets, brought to overt fulfillment in the revelation of the New Testament, then it is here in the unity of the Old and New Testaments read together that we can find the ultimate perspective on who God is.

Constructive debates with non-Christian religionists, especially monotheists, must then proceed always on two fronts. One consists in the examination of philosophical questions, where Christians, Jews, and Muslims, for example, may be able to debate and sometimes to agree on attributes pertaining to the one God, whom we can seek to recognize and name in common ways. The other consists in the examination of our mutual claims about revelation, prophetic history, and the person of Jesus, where there will be points of agreement and disagreement regarding the internal content of divine revelation. It is true that the rejection of the revelation of the Trinity and the mystery of the Incarnation and crucifixion can and will have negative consequences for one's understanding of God as reason and love, as it does for one's understanding of the inner mystery of God. However, Christians rightly should seek to underscore the common confession of those truths about God that they hold in common either with Jews or with Muslims.

With theologically confessional Jews, Christian theologians must rightly insist on the unity of the divine nature, in keeping with the revelation of God as Creator and Savior in his original covenant with Israel. However, they must also underscore the universal orientation of this initial covenant, and the idea that God—who originally has revealed his glory to Israel alone—can also bring this work to perfection by becoming an Israelite and by inviting all the nations to share in the glory of God. The biblical revelation of the transcendence of the one God implies the possibility of Incarnation and Pentecost, that is, that God might speak his Word in our humanity, and send his prophetic Spirit to sanctify the creation. The Church's confession of the unity of the two Testaments requires, then, that she underscore the novelty, truth, and perfection of the revelation of God as Trinity, manifest in Christ, but that she do so without seeking to deny the authenticity and perpetuity of the mystery of Israel and the Old Testament confession of the unicity of God.

With Islam, Christianity must also rightly insist on the unity of the divine nature, so as to counter the crass but widespread misperception that

Trinitarian faith is polytheistic. When rightly understood, the Christian theology of God as Trinity is not only compatible with an affirmation of God's simplicity and unity, but indeed requires just such affirmation. Trinitarian faith is therefore unambiguously monotheistic. However, as Aquinas rightly underscores, from a purely philosophical point of view the human person cannot attain to an immediate knowledge of the essence of God, and therefore cannot procure natural knowledge of the inner mystery and life of God. When considered from within the boundaries of reason alone, then, the mystery of the Trinity can be neither disproven nor demonstrated. By emphasizing this true claim, Christian theology invites the reconsideration of a frequent presumption of intellectual superiority in Islamic theology, the idea that the Koran must be a superior revelation just because it affirms the divine unity of God, and therefore is more reasonable. In fact, both "revelations" assert the divine unity unequivocally and both claim that there is something known about God only in virtue of the revelation that could not be known otherwise. Once this similarity or parity is recognized, it is possible to identify accurately what Christians and Muslims truly agree on, and what they disagree on. The novelty of Christianity can then appear anew, the idea that God has become human and has been crucified, to atone for human sins and to reveal God's mercy and love to the world. By grace God has offered us intimate friendship with God, without compromising his transcendence, so that we might enter into communion with God and aspire to see God face to face. Christians should seek to present these truth claims to Muslims without generating the mistaken view that Christians are not monotheists, or that they hold irrational ideas about God.

Our task in the second part of this book was to study the faith of the Church in the one nature of God as concisely formulated by St. Thomas Aquinas. In this section, accordingly, we first laid out Aquinas's realist epistemological presuppositions and, following on this, his five metaphysical *quia* arguments establishing the existence of the one God as knowable from creation. After this, we looked at his theory of analogical naming of God, which serves as a means between the extremes of purely univocal and equivocal predication. With Dionysius, Aquinas names God following the *triplex via* of causality, remotion, and excellence, thereby preserving both God's exemplary causality with respect to creation, and his infinite and incomprehensible transcendence of it.

After establishing God's existence, we then enumerated various divine attributes or "divine names," beginning with what Aquinas takes as the governing divine attribute, God's simplicity. Simplicity, as we saw, is in the first instance a negative term that refers to a lack of creatively composition in God, whether physical or metaphysical. Following on this, we immediately turned to the divine perfection, since perfection in God, unlike in creatures, follows not from complexity but from the absolute simplicity of his being. We then looked at the divine goodness and saw how God himself is the good that all things desire, albeit each in its own way.

When it comes to the divine infinity, we saw how, in contrast to a prominent strand in modern philosophy, Aquinas takes this as a negative infinity, that is, as a non-limitation of form. God's omnipresence is a non-spatial presence grounded in God's creative causality. Moreover, in contrast to trends that have emerged in the wake of theology after Hegel, Aquinas affirms God's absolute immutability and impassibility. He also affirms his eternity as atemporality, and his unity as an ontological (not numerical) unity that follows from his utter lack of any composition whatsoever.

After looking at what God is and is not in relation to the perfections and imperfections in creatures, we then turned to his immanent spiritual operations of knowledge and love. In particular, we saw how God's knowledge and love, unlike ours, is not reactive to creatures, but is instead causative and productive of their being. Lastly, we looked at God's power to act *ad extra* from the perspective of his infinity and omnipotence, especially insofar as the latter is the power to do all possible (i.e., not inherently contradictory) things.

The preceding reflections represent a Christian theology of the one God of revelation, one that makes extensive use of philosophical reflection in the service of faith. We have noted that the divine attributes of the unity of God the Holy Trinity can be known not only by way of revelation but also by way of natural reason, insofar as God the Holy Trinity is the unitary cause of creation. Likewise, however, we saw that, because of the unity of God's operation *ad extra* in creation, his inner life *as Trinity* cannot be known unless God chooses to reveal himself. However, he has revealed himself to us, in the New Testament, as Father, Son, and Holy Spirit. Accordingly, our aim in part 3 will be to undertake a Thomistic consideration of the eternal processions and the inner life of God, the Most Holy Trinity.

PART 3

The Immanent
Communion of Persons

St. Thomas Aquinas's
De Deo Trino Treatise

21

A Prologue to Thomistic
Trinitarian Theology

We noted above that God is eternal life, but what is this life in itself? Christian revelation tells us that it is the processional life of the Father, Son, and Holy Spirit, the mystery of the immanent Trinity. How can we best understand the Holy Trinity? There are many schools of thought in the Christian tradition, and their accounts of the immanent life of the Trinity sometimes differ in significant ways. As a prelude to our treatment of this topic in the third section of this book, it is helpful to begin by doing three things. First, I will note three prominent schools or traditions of thought about the Trinity that emerged in the Middle Ages (in the thirteenth and fourteenth centuries). For the sake of nomenclature, I will call these the emanationist, relationist, and nominal minimalist intellectual traditions, respectively.[1] The key representatives of these three views are Bonaventure and Scotus for the first, Aquinas for the second, and Ockham for the third. This brief comparative overview can help us identify, then, some of the distinctive features

---

1. Some scholars employ an alternative terminology. I'm greatly indebted in my thinking on these matters to the recent work of Russell L. Friedman, *Medieval Trinitarian Theology from Aquinas to Ockham* (Cambridge: Cambridge University Press, 2013), and *Intellectual Traditions at the Medieval University: The Use of Philosophical Psychology in Trinitarian Theology among the Franciscans and Dominicans, 1250–1350*, 2 vols. (Leiden: Brill, 2012). Friedman speaks of the "emanationist" account of the Trinity that is more typically Franciscan, the "relational" account that is more typically Dominican, and the "praepositinianism" of Ockham and others, which was concerned with the consequences of maintaining a thoroughgoing doctrine of divine simplicity. I have termed the latter approach "nominal minimalist," rather than "nominalist" in part because Ockham's approach to the Trinity influences later thinkers who do not necessarily share his medieval skepticism regarding universals.

in St. Thomas's approach. Second, having noted some of the key aspects of Aquinas's theology of the Trinity, which will be explored in future chapters, I will make a set of claims regarding the advantages of his approach, claims that I will seek to illustrate in greater detail in further chapters. Third, I will consider how some of the common medieval positions mentioned in this chapter are preserved, rejected, or creatively rethought in works of the most influential modern Trinitarian theologians. The fourth part of this book will inquire more deeply into the shape of modern Trinitarian theology and compare and contrast common elements of post-Kantian Trinitarian theology with the Thomistic theological tradition. The presentation in this chapter is a prelude, then, to much that follows in this book. As such, it is meant to be only introductory and to serve as a propaedeutic to points that will be argued for in greater detail below. It serves as a framing device to allow us to see the originality and poise of the Thomistic approach to the mystery of the Trinity, and to suggest why Thomistic principles have not been profitably employed hitherto in the context of modern Trinitarian theological debate, though they can and should be.

THREE MEDIEVAL APPROACHES
TO THE TRINITY

Any brief presentation of three famous Trinitarian intellectual traditions from the medieval period is necessarily schematic and easily risks presenting a caricatured version of the various vibrant thinkers under consideration. Nevertheless, the risk is worth taking in order to see how diverse and interesting medieval Trinitarian thought was, and in order to situate Aquinas better within his context, which in turn allows one to grasp better both his debt to patristic influences and his profound originality in his own historical moment.[2] In this section I will argue that the emanationist approach

---

2. On Aquinas's theology in its historical context see the invaluable studies of Gilles Emery and Russell L. Friedman, already alluded to. Other influential or helpful historical works include Michael Schmaus, *Der liber propugnatorius des Thomas Angelicus und die Lehrunterschiede zwischen Thomas von Aquin und Duns Scotus*, 2 vols. (Munster: Aschendorff, 1930); Luc Matthieu, *La Trinité créatrice d'après Saint Bonaventure* (Paris: Institut Catholique, 1968); Isabel Iribarren, *Durandus of St Pourcain: A Dominican Theologian in the Shadow of Aquinas* (Oxford: Oxford University Press, 2005); Richard Cross, *Duns Scotus on God*; Juan Carlos Flores, *Henry of Ghent: Metaphysics and the Trinity; with a Critical Edition of Question Six of Article Fifty Five of the "Summa Quaestionum Ordinariarum"* (Leuven. Leuven University Press, 2006); Bruce D. Marshall, "*Utrum Essentia Generet*: Semantics and Metaphysics in Later Medieval Trinitarian Theology," in *Trinitarian Theology*

to Trinitarian theology, pioneered by Bonaventure and Scotus, makes use of a more restricted or modest doctrine of divine simplicity and correspondingly presents us with a kataphatic, quasi-univocal way of speaking of processions and persons. The relationalist approach pioneered by Aquinas makes use of a moderate theory of simplicity that allows room for proper analogies for processions and persons in God, understood in terms of subsistent relations. It is moderately apophatic. The nominal minimalist approach pioneered by Ockham presents us with a theory of divine simplicity so exacting that one is led to an equivocal way of speaking about the divine processions; this approach is radically apophatic.

The Emanationist Account: Early Franciscan Theology

We can begin, then, by first noting three key features of the early Franciscan tradition that emerged in the thirteenth and fourteenth centuries, particularly in the thought of Bonaventure (1221–1274) and John Duns Scotus (1266–1308), which were in turn to influence Franciscan theologians such as John Pecham and Peter Auriol, giving rise to what may loosely be termed a school of thought, notwithstanding the significant variations found among these thinkers.

Natural Knowledge of Personal Processions. A first thing to note about the early Franciscan tradition is that Bonaventure and Scotus, each in his own way, follow Richard of St. Victor in arguing from philosophical reason that there must be a real distinction of persons in the godhead. They do so beginning from the consideration of the attributes of the essence of the one God so as to reach the reasoned conclusion that there must be personal distinctions of some kind in the godhead. Richard had done this by appealing to divine love in God, as we saw in the last chapter. Bonaventure generates his own versions of this argument.[3] In addition, he also formulates an original argument based on what many commentators take to be a Dionysian principle: God is most perfect in the order of goodness, and it is proper to the good to be diffusive of self. However, because God is infinite in

---

in the Medieval West, ed. Pekka Kärkkäinen (Helsinki: Luther-Agricola Society, 2008), 88–123; Boyd Taylor Coolman, general introduction to Coolman and Coulter, *Trinity and Creation*, 23–48; J. T. Paasch, *Divine Production in Late Medieval Trinitarian Theology: Henry of Ghent, Duns Scotus, and William of Ockham* (Oxford: Oxford University Press, 2012); Zachary Hayes, "Bonaventure's Trinitarian Theology," in *A Companion to Bonaventure*, ed. J. M. Hammon, J. A. W. Hellmann, J. Goff (Leiden: Brill, 2014), 189–246.

3. Bonaventure, *Comm. I Sent.*, d. 2, a. un., qq. 2–4.

goodness he can diffuse his goodness perfectly only if he communicates his goodness in an infinite way, that is to say, not merely to finite creatures but to another infinite person. There must be in God, then, some kind of personal procession, if God is truly perfectly good.[4]

Scotus does not take up this argument but attempts instead to argue for the distinction of persons based on the knowledge we have that God's essence is characterized by knowledge and love.[5] Scotus thinks that the attributes we ascribe to God's nature (such as knowledge and love, goodness and eternity) are "formally distinct" from one another: they are ontologically distinct in God himself, and not only in our way of thinking.[6] From this one can derive knowledge of the emanation of distinct persons in God. If God knows himself, there must arise in God an ontological distinction between the knower and the act of knowledge (the mental concept or word)

---

4. Bonaventure, *Comm. I Sent.*, d. 2, a. un., qq. 2 and 4; d. 23, a. 2, qq. 1–2. See the arguments of Zachary Hayes, "Bonaventure's Trinitarian Theology," 207–9.

5. Duns Scotus, *Lectura* 1, d. 2, pars 2, q. 4, nos. 165–78, in *Opera omnia*, 14:167–72. See the study of Olivier Boulnois, "Duns Scot et la déduction *a priori* de la Trinité," in *Les Études philosophiques* 2020/2, no. 202: 67–90, and Cross, *Duns Scotus on God*, 127–30.

6. Scotus distinguishes between formal distinctions and real distinctions. Things that are really distinct can be separated from one another, while things that are formally distinct cannot. (See the analysis of Cross, *Duns Scotus on God*, 107–11, 235–40.) Scotus claims that the divine attributes proper to God's nature (such as goodness, eternity, infinity and so on) are formally distinct in God, and thus inseparable. They are not accidents or properties of the divine nature but are identical with the divine nature due to God's simplicity. Nevertheless, they are not identical with one another ontologically. (In this he clearly differs from Aquinas on divine simplicity.) In saying that the divine attributes in God are formally distinct, Scotus wishes to underscore that they each have a really distinct manner of being and essential intelligible content in God himself, and not merely in our way of thinking. Scotus's thinking on this point is integrally connected with his theory of predication of divine attributes, since each attribute we ascribe to God must pertain to something truly in God, something quasi-generically or essentially distinct from all other such attributes, and must be attributed to God in such a way as to preserve some content that pertains to both God and creatures univocally. See Duns Scotus, *Ord.* 1, d. 8, pars 1, q. 4, nos. 192–93 (*Opera omnia*, 4:261–62), translation in Cross, *Duns Scotus on God*, 107–8: "There is therefore a distinction [between essential divine perfections] preceding in every way the intellect, and it is this: that wisdom really exists in reality, but real (*in re*) wisdom is not real goodness. Which is proved, for if infinite wisdom were formally infinite goodness, then wisdom in general would be formally goodness in general. For infinity does not destroy the formal notion of the thing to which it is added, for in whatever degree some perfection is understood to be (which degree is a degree of the perfection), the formal notion of that perfection is not removed by the degree, and thus, if [this perfection] *as in general* does not formally include [that perfection] *as in general* neither [does this perfection] *as in particular* [include that perfection] *as in particular*. I show this, because 'to include formally' is to include something in its essential notion.... Just as, however, the definition of goodness in general does not include wisdom, neither does infinite [goodness include] infinite [wisdom]. There is therefore some formal non-identity between wisdom and goodness, inasmuch as there would be distinct definitions of them if they were definable. But a definition does not only indicate a concept caused by the intellect, but the quiddity of the thing."

that arises as a result of his natural act of knowing.[7] If God loves, then he must love some object voluntarily, which results in a production of love distinct from the lover.[8] However, the distinctions that obtain in God must be proper to one who is perfect, and all that is utterly perfect ontologically is personal in nature.[9] Therefore, there must be personal distinctions that arise in God by processions of knowledge and love. The unoriginated person in God knows and loves. His act of knowing gives rise to a person who is an intellectual production, and his act of loving gives rise to a person who is love. Scotus is not seeking to "demonstrate" the mystery of the Trinity (if by this we mean that philosophy could provide a *propter quid* demonstration of the identity of the persons in God as Father, Son, and Spirit: this must be revealed by grace), but he is seeking to show the antecedent likelihood or fittingness of the revelation of the Trinity, in close coherence with natural reason, since one can argue philosophically for a real distinction of persons in God, and indeed for processions of persons that arise from distinct natural operations of knowledge and love.

Evidently, Scotus's theology of divine simplicity is very different from that of Aquinas. His claim that there obtains in God a real ontological distinction ("formal distinction") of the attributes of the divine nature allows him to generate claims about a real distinction of acts of knowledge and love, by which there must arise a real distinction of persons who emanate in God from an unoriginated source. We see then that Scotus's "attenuated" theology of divine simplicity gives rise to a distinctive theory of the psychological analogy in God. By a qualified form of univocal predication, we can say that there obtains in the divine nature, as in the human nature, a true ontological distinction between the activity of knowing and the activity of loving.[10] This distinction in the nature of God provides us with a way of

---

7. See Duns Scotus, *Ord.* 1, d. 2, pars 2, qq. 1–4, nos. 221–22 (*Opera omnia*, 2:259–61); see Cross, *Duns Scotus on God*, 132–37.

8. See Duns Scotus, *Ord.* 1, d. 2, pars 2, qq. 1–4, no. 226 (*Opera omnia*, 2:263); see Cross, *Duns Scotus on God*, 137–42.

9. See Duns Scotus, *Ord.* 1, d. 2, pars 2, qq. 1–4, nos. 355–56 (*Opera omnia*, 2:336); see Cross, *Duns Scotus on God*, 153–55.

10. It is also interesting to note in passing that Scotus claims that the divine act of knowing is "natural" while the act of love is "voluntary," thus distinguishing what is done naturally from what is done freely. This terminology presupposes that the intellect "naturally" comes to know, while the will acts only freely or deliberately. However, the idea contributes to the western European notion that freedom in personal agents is something that transcends nature or that is distinct from it. See Duns Scotus, *Ord.* 1, d. 13, q. un., nos. 20–21: "Praeterea, istae productiones distinguuntur quia altera est per modum naturae et altera per modum voluntatis..."

thinking about perfect modes of emanation in God, and thus a real distinction of persons in God.

Emanation Theory and the Psychological Analogy. It was customary in the thirteenth century to inquire into the nature of intra-Trinitarian relations, and ask the question whether eternal processions give rise to relations in God or whether the relations give rise to processions. We might ask the question this way: does the Father exist eternally in himself as one unbegotten, and "then" generate the Word eternally, so as to become related to him? Or is the Father "always, already" toward the Son, subsisting in relation, so that he generates the Son eternally precisely because he is the Father? The first concept is emanationist, while the second is relationist. Richard of St. Victor had already suggested that the first option was preferable.[11] There is a life of generation and spiration in God, and *because* of these operations, the relations arise between the persons. Bonaventure follows this line of thinking and considers it a significant matter.[12] On his view, the first person in the Trinity is to be understood by logical priority first and foremost as "innascible" or "unoriginated," and only secondly as "Father." God the Father is the fontal source of all Trinitarian life (since he begets the Son and spirates the Spirit), and it is especially this natural characteristic of the Father (as one who is unoriginated and primary, producing the other two persons) that distinguishes him, rather than his relativity to the Son and the Spirit.[13] We should note that this vision of emanation of all Trinitarian persons from the Father coheres logically with what Bonaventure teaches regarding philosophical knowledge of the Trinity. If God is infinitely good and perfect he must communicate himself to another who is infinite. God the Father's perfection and goodness are manifest especially in his communication of the divine essence to the Son and the Spirit.

It is important to observe what follows from this line of thinking. The Father is understood first and foremost not in relational terms, as being eternally related to the Son and Spirit in all he is (Aquinas's view of the persons as subsistent relations). Instead he is depicted by closer likeness to a

11. Richard of St. Victor, *On the Trinity*, 4.13–15, 5.2–5. See Friedman, *Medieval Trinitarian Theology*, 15–20.

12. Bonaventure, *Comm. I Sent.*, d. 27, pars 1, a. un., q. 2. See the analysis of Friedman, *Medieval Trinitarian Theology*, 24–30.

13. Bonaventure, *Comm. I Sent.*, d. 27, pars 1, a. un, q. 2, ad 3, d. 2, a. un., q. 2. See Hayes, "Bonaventure's Trinitarian Theology," 214–16.

human person, that is to say, as a distinct individual subject who becomes relational only after he acts. Human beings are not subsistent relations but possess relations as properties or accidents of their personhood. The Father, for Bonaventure, is conceived of logically as one pre-constituted, who then acts naturally so as to communicate the divine being to the Son and the Spirit.[14]

Scotus builds on this emanationist idea of the Father by appealing to the notions of formal distinction in God that we have noted in the section just above. If there is a formal distinction in God of knowledge and love, then there must be two distinct natural actions, which in turn produce two distinct persons, that of the Word and the Spirit, respectively. When the Father begets the Son, this occurs in virtue of a distinct operation of the divine nature with regard to intellect. When he spirates the Spirit, this occurs by another distinct operation of the divine nature with regard to the will.[15] We see the coherence of this idea with Scotus's teaching regarding natural knowledge of personal processions in God. As we noted above, he claims that natural "formal distinctions" in God imply personal distinctions. Here he claims that personal distinctions that arise from the processions imply distinct natural operations (the Father in his divine essence as knowing produces the Son, the Father in his divine essence as loving produces the Spirit).[16] In this line of thinking the Father is depicted quasi-univocally by comparison to a human agent as a divine agent in whom relations arise as the result of natural operations. God the Father's inner life is characterized by distinguishable natural acts, and these in turn give rise to processions of

14. Bonaventure does affirm that the Trinitarian persons are to be understood only by relational reference to one another. See *Comm. I Sent.*, d. 26, a. un., q. 3. His position is nuanced. Like Aquinas, he argues that the personal relations are not accidental in the Trinity but are said in two ways, first of the substance of God, since the relational being of the persons is substantial, and second, of the persons, who are really related to one another by way of the processions. The consideration of the Father in a non-relational subsistence "prior" to his giving generation to the Son has to do with a logical order of designation. This does not mean that the differences between Bonaventure and Aquinas are trivial. In the subsequent Franciscan tradition, especially with John Pecham and John Duns Scotus, the persons can be considered in their primacy apart from or independent of the conception of persons as relations, a view made possible in part by Bonaventure's starting point. See Bonaventure, *Comm. I Sent.*, d. 33, a. un., q. 1, and Friedman, *Medieval Trinitarian Theology*, 11–13, 32–41, 109–13, 171–73.

15. See Friedman, *Medieval Trinitarian Theology*, 74–75, 107–12.

16. On the consideration of the persons as constituted logically prior to their relations, see Scotus, *Lectura* 1 on *I Sent.* dist. 26, q. un., nos. 1–78 (*Opera omnia*, 17:317–41). On the distinction of natural properties present in each of the respective processions, see *Ord.* I, d. 13, q. un., nos. 19–23 (*Opera omnia*, 5:73–75).

knowledge and love. In virtue of the Father's diverse natural activities, distinct emanations arise that produce distinct persons.

Personhood in God and Creatures. Medieval Trinitarian theologians were typically concerned to judge between two theories of personhood that were prevalent in the theology of their time, and they tended to privilege one or the other. The older definition was from Boethius, and consisted in the definition of a person as "an individual having a rational nature." The second came from Richard of St. Victor, and consisted in the definition of a person as a subject possessing a nature in an incommunicable way.[17] The key difference between the two has to do with the use of "individual rational nature" as an intrinsic part of the definition of person. Boethius's definition was crafted to speak first and foremost of human persons, who are individuals having a rational nature, and it was employed by some theologians analogically to speak of divine persons. However, divine persons are not merely three individuals having one nature (like three human persons) but are one in individual being and nature, so the Boethian definition cannot signify them in any strong univocal sense. Richard created another definition in part to address this problem, and in doing so he purposefully sought to define the person as something distinct from nature (since the persons in God all possess the same individual nature). In his definition, each person of the Trinity is understood as a distinct subject possessing the divine nature. Personhood is thus defined in terms of an individual subject and not understood, as with Boethius, as the individual realization of a nature. On this account, a divine person possesses the divine nature in an incommunicable way *qua* subject (the Father is not the Son), and a human person possesses human nature in an incommunicable way *qua* subject (Peter is not Paul). Richard thus formulated a definition of personhood that could be applied univocally to both divine and human persons. A divine subject is one who has a divine nature, and a human subject is one who has a human nature. An individual human nature is an individual human person, but the individual divine nature is not an individual divine person. Richard's idea anticipates those modern concepts of personhood in which the personal subject is understood as an individual who has a nature, but whose personhood is not

17. See Richard of St. Victor, *On the Trinity*, 4.22. " . . a divine person is an incommunicable existence of divine nature."

defined per se by reference to nature, and who can deploy his or her natural powers in personal freedom.

Bonaventure and Scotus follow this Victorine path of reflection, and it allows them to forge a concept of personhood that is "indifferent" to divine and human realizations.[18] A person is a subject who has a given nature in an incommunicable fashion (i.e., as one who is distinctive from all other persons of the same nature). This way of thinking of personhood has the evident advantage of being readily adaptable to Trinitarian persons and still ascribable easily to human persons, and is thus more univocal in character.[19] As we will see below, this approach contrasts with that of Aquinas, who begins with a Boethian notion of personhood properly applicable to human beings as such, and then refashions it so as to speak by analogy of divine persons.

Although this presentation of the emanationist approach is admittedly brief and incomplete, we can note here some of its evident strengths and weaknesses. First, this tradition is marked by a confidence in the power of the human mind, as redeemed by grace, to know God as Trinity and to understand the inner life of God. This confidence is due in part to the fact that there is a kind of Trinitarian ontology of processional knowledge and love that is embedded in reality, one that the mind can discern in part even philosophically. The attenuated or "weaker" theory of divine simplicity that is

18. For Bonaventure's appreciation and use of Richard's notion of personhood, see, *Comm. I Sent.* d. 25, a. 1, q. 2; a. 2, q. 1, esp. ad. 4. For Scotus's consideration of personhood in God, which develops a notion of personhood that is derivative of Richard and that is meant to be corrective to that of Boethius, see *Ord.* 1, d. 2, pars 2, q. 4, nos. 359–87 (*Opera omnia*, 2:338–49); and esp. *Ord.* 1, d. 23, q. un, nos. 1–25 (*Opera omnia*, 5:349–63). See, on these matters, Friedman, *Intellectual Traditions at the Medieval University*, 341–75, and Richard Cross, *Duns Scotus on God*, 158–63. I have noted that these Franciscan authors, Bonaventure and Scotus, define personhood in terms of the existent distinctive subject (apart from nature) *and* that they employ formal distinctions from the divine nature to distinguish the persons (as when Scotus thinks of the Word as the distinct product of the natural divine act of knowing). These are not contradictory ideas. On the contrary, just to the extent that one must distinguish the persons in non-relational ways (due to the Victorine concept of personhood), so too one must seek to understand the distinction of persons in God also by reference to formal distinctions in nature. By contrast, Aquinas understands the persons as subsistent relations, in analogical dissimilitude to human persons, and thus distinguishes the divine persons by their modes of subsistence in the divine nature, without distinguishing them by supposed formal distinctions of the divine nature.

19. Bonaventure is clear, for his part, that he wishes to adopt the Victorine notion in view of an analogical use of the term (see *Comm. I Sent.*, d. 25, a. 2, q. 2). However, the definition lends itself to a largely univocal formulation of the notion of person, as Bonaventure himself admits (*Comm. I Sent.*, d. 25, a. 1, q. 2, ad 4).

present in this tradition is related logically to its confidence in the powers of reason to think about the Trinity philosophically, and its ambitions to name God in a quasi-univocal way. Once one has identified distinct attributes in the divine nature that are known by natural reason, one can infer that there must be distinct activities, processions, and persons in God. Correspondingly, there is a kataphatic tendency toward univocity in this tradition that thinks of the eternal processions that arise in the nature of God by strong similitude to psychological processions of knowledge and love in human persons. It also conceives of human persons and divine persons in similar ways.

If there is a weakness to this tradition, it is located precisely in its ambitions. Can the human mind come to know philosophically that there must exist real distinctions of persons in God, or that there are "formal distinctions" of knower and the act of knowing, lover and the act of love, in the divine life itself? Can one infer from this that there are distinct persons in God characterized by distinct natural acts? These kinds of claims seem to compromise or minimize the divine simplicity, since they fail to acknowledge that what is really distinct in us (knowledge and love, or moral goodness and subsistent being), is not really distinct in God but identical. If God has this kind of ontological complexity, is God really one and simple in nature, as the patristic tradition has strongly underscored? Are the Trinitarian persons truly one in being and essence? Likewise, the decision to understand the processional life of God in logically prior terms as emanations, and only secondly as relational, is consequential. As we have seen in part 1 of this book, both Augustine and Gregory of Nazianzus distinguish the persons in God relationally precisely because all three persons are equal. They are identically the one God, having the simplicity of the divine nature in themselves. The persons are therefore distinguished only by their relations of origin. If, however, the Father is constituted "prior" to his generation of the Son and spiration of the Spirit, as Bonaventure posits, then his distinction from the Son and Spirit is based not merely on relations of origin but on something he possesses by nature prior to generation and spiration, which they do not possess (innascibility). The Father thus possesses a natural quality that the Son and Spirit do not possess, one in virtue of which he is distinguishable from each of them. In this case it would seem that the Father is not really equal to the Son and Spirit, and identical in godhead. He seems to be greater than them, since he possesses something by nature that they do not.

The Relationalist Approach in Early Dominican Theology
As noted above, a second theological tradition takes its basic inspiration from the thought of Thomas Aquinas, who was himself inspired by his teacher Albert the Great. His thought, in turn, influenced early Dominican theologians such as Hervaeus Natalis and Jean Capreolus. We can characterize briefly the key Thomistic ideas in comparison with those just mentioned, as they will be the subject of further consideration below.

No Natural Knowledge of Personal Processions. As noted in the previous chapter, Aquinas takes issue with Richard of St. Victor's attempt to demonstrate or argue rationally for the existence of personal distinctions and processions in God. Aquinas's theology differs crucially from that of Richard, Bonaventure, and Scotus, because of the way he understands divine simplicity. Of course, each of these thinkers defends a version of the classical doctrine of divine simplicity, which was reiterated dogmatically at the Fourth Lateran Council, as we have seen. The predominant intellectual tradition of the Franciscans allows, however, for formal distinctions in the nature of God, so that terms like goodness, perfection, knowledge, and love, when ascribed to God, imply some kind of formal, ontological diversity or differentiation, which can then become the basis for a philosophical argument for communion of persons in God. Aquinas, by contrast, affirms, as we have seen above, that the various "names of God" attributed to God in virtue of his divine essence are identical in reality, in God himself. In other words, God truly is good, perfect, intelligent, and loving, and we must employ a mode of signification by which we use these terms distinctly; but in virtue of the divine simplicity, we ascribe these terms to God knowing that they are in some mysterious way one in God. God in his pure actuality is not formally composite or complex, so while we do not know immediately or intuitively "what" God is in himself, we do know that the names we ascribe to the divine essence are somehow co-extensive, united, and indeed identical in the very being of God. Furthermore, the effects of God the Trinity that result from his act of creation are effects of all three persons, who act in virtue of their essential unity, and these effects, insofar as we can understand them by natural reason, do not reflect the inner mystery of the three persons in their distinction. Therefore, we cannot procure knowledge of the Trinity from philosophical argument, but by revelation alone, wherein God freely discloses to us the mystery of his inner life, as a gift of grace and as a gratuitous invitation to friendship with God.

Relation Theory and the Psychological Analogy. As we will consider below in greater detail, Aquinas tackles the same question that Bonaventure did, regarding the logical priority of procession and relation in thinking about God, but answers the question in a different way.[20] When considering the divine persons, Aquinas argues that the notion of relation is of primary importance and must qualify all of our understanding of the two processions of generation and spiration.[21] Here, Aquinas offers his own interpretation of Augustine and Boethius. The category of relation is helpful in Trinitarian theology because it permits one to signify a distinction of persons in God that entails no distinction of essence or substance, and no inequality in properties. In effect, even in our ordinary experience, relations can exist "interior" to a substance without implying inequality or subordination. This idea is helpful by analogy in thinking about the Trinity. In God the divine persons each possess the divine essence in its fullness. Therefore, they are one in being and equal in all that pertains to the divine essence. They can be distinguished, however, according to an order of procession, wherein the Son is eternally begotten of the Father, and the Spirit is eternally spirated from the Father and the Son. In this order of proceeding, each person is distinguished in virtue of his relations of origin, not by diverse natural qualities (such as power, generosity, goodness, knowledge, or love). Relations in God are not mere accidents or properties, however, since God is simple. If the persons are distinguished only in virtue of their relations of origin, then the Father may be characterized as a subsistent relation, that is to say, he is his paternity.[22] He is "always" relative to the Son in all that he is, as he who eternally generates the Son, by the procession of generation. The Son is always relative to the Father as he who, as God, is always eternally derivative of the Father. The Father and the Son are always related subsistently to the Spirit as his eternal principle, while the Spirit is always relative to the Father and the Son as one wholly originate from their common spiration.

---

20. See especially *ST* I, q. 40, aa. 1–4, *De pot.*, q. 10, a. 1, *In I Sent.*, d. 27, q. 1, a. 2. As Emery notes (*The Trinitarian Theology of St. Thomas Aquinas*, 125), Aquinas here is developing the earlier teaching of Albert the Great, in *Commentarii in I Sententiarum*, dist. 27, a. 2, in *Opera omnia* vol. 25 (Paris: Vivès, 1843).

21. See especially *ST* I, q. 40, a. 2.

22. *ST* I, q. 29, a. 4. I will return to this topic below.

This way of thinking preserves the use of the psychological analogy as a proper analogy, not simply a metaphor: the Son is the eternal Word generated by the Father, while the Spirit is the spirated Love common to the Father and the Son, who proceeds from the Father through his Word, just as love comes forth from knowledge in a human person (because we cannot love what we do not first know). However, in differentiation from Scotus, Aquinas's relational account does not ground the use of the psychological analogy in natural distinctions in the godhead, as if the generation of the Word came forth from one distinct natural act of knowing while the spiration of the Spirit came forth from another alternative natural act of loving. The three persons are each the one God, so each person is truly equal in knowledge and love. The Son is not less naturally loving than the Spirit, and the Spirit is not less naturally wise than the Son. Nevertheless, the psychological analogy is applicable to the mystery of the Holy Trinity in truth and not merely metaphorically, because in God there are immaterial processions of the Word and the Spirit, distinguished according to an order of derivation. The persons of the Son and the Spirit are distinguished by their relations of origin alone. Just as there can be no spiritual love in a human person unless there is first knowledge, so the Son is the Word of the Father who proceeds from the Father alone, while the Spirit is the Love of the Father and the Son who proceeds from the Father and the Word. The psychological analogy is employed here in a more modest and apophatic sense than in the Franciscan tradition (truly analogically—not at all univocally), but it still contributes to genuine positive knowledge of the inner life of God.

Personhood in God and Creatures. Unlike Bonaventure, Aquinas does not follow Richard of St. Victor in defining divine persons primarily as subjects who possess the divine nature in an incommunicable fashion. Rather he retains the Boethian definition of personhood, as pertaining to an individual of a rational nature.[23] This decision is consequential, because, as Aquinas realizes quite well, this Boethian definition does not apply readily or univocally to the divine persons and to human persons, since the three persons who are God are one in individual nature (one in being) in a way that three human persons are not.[24] Consequently, Aquinas must "refashion" his notion of personhood analogically so that it can be ascribed to divine persons.

---

23. *ST* I, q. 29, a. 1.

24. See *ST* I, q. 29, a. 3, where Aquinas makes implicit reference to the Dionysian *triplex via* for the ascription of the term to the persons of the Trinity.

This methodological decision suggests that we have no univocal conception of the Trinitarian persons available to us from our ordinary experience of nature. To speak about mysteries of the faith, we must instead make use of our natural concepts in innovative and original ways, by an analogical qualification internal to theology, to speak of the super-intelligible realities that God has revealed to us. In Trinitarian theology, this leads to the notion of a person as a subsistent relation. In human persons, as the Boethian definition suggests, the individual is a substance (a rational animal) who possesses relations as accidental properties in virtue of his various personal actions (such as knowledge or love) or his physical quantity (relative size). God, however, is simple, so in God whatever is, is subsistent. (There are no ontological accidents in God.) If the persons of the Trinity are real relations (being wholly relative to one another in all they are, by generation and spiration) then they are subsistent relations, each one being a relation in all that he is. We will explore the consequences of this idea in greater detail below.

Evidently, when we consider these basic "Dominican" options as compared with those of the early Franciscan school, we can note that this tradition is marked by a more qualified kataphaticism, one tempered by a greater degree of apophaticism. There is a marked sense of confidence in the powers of human reason, to know of the existence of the one God and the attributes of God in his essence, but also a sense of the abyss that lies between our natural knowledge and the gift of supernatural knowledge of the Trinity as such. The use of concepts in Trinitarian theology is highly qualified by analogy, so that the denomination of processions in God is understood to entail real relations that accord with human psychological acts of knowledge and love. However, the ascriptions of such processions to God has an apophatic overtone, since the processional life in God is wholly other than that which we find in spiritual creatures. The persons in God likewise are subsistent relations, not individual substances who acquire accidental relations. We can speak truly, then, of the three persons in God, but only with the accompanying recognition that we signify a reality that escapes our ordinary experience and use of concepts.

Nominal Minimalism

By comparison with both of the approaches considered above, the tradition that emerges from the thought of William of Ockham (1287–1347) is more intellectually modest in aspiration. Indeed, we can denote it by the moniker of "nominal minimalism" for reasons that I will explain below. This approach was to become highly influential in the later medieval period, and may be associated with the work of theologians like Walter Chatton, Robert Holcot, and Gregory of Rimini.[25] Its influence on the thought of Martin Luther is also significant, and, as I will argue below, there are important echoes of this tradition in modern Trinitarian theology.[26]

Minimal Natural Knowledge of God is Possible. As we have seen above, thinkers like Scotus attempt to provide rational arguments for the existence in God of personal processions. Aquinas forgoes such attempts but still seeks to provide philosophical demonstrations for the existence of God and for the determination of divine names or attributes of the divine essence. By comparison with these figures, Ockham takes a more minimalistic pathway. He argues that there is no demonstrative knowledge of the existence of God.[27] One can provide compelling probable arguments for the existence of at least one immaterial reality that maintains contingent material realities in existence.[28] Such argumentation cannot provide proof, however, that there is only one God.[29] Evidently, according to this model, human aspirations of natural reason toward knowledge of God are still acknowledged, but they are thought to be quite modest in scope. Ockham's critical reasoning seeks to delimit the scope of the human pretention to know God by natural powers and, in this way, makes room for the grace of faith. His theology thereby underscores the relative importance of grace, in comparison with natural reasoning, for all our knowledge of God.

---

25. See the extensive study by Friedman in *Intellectual Traditions at the Medieval University*, 597–872.

26. On the speculative Trinitarian minimalism of Luther, who did defend the Athanasian creed, see Samuel M. Powell, *The Trinity in German Thought* (Cambridge: Cambridge University Press, 2001), 12–30. This is by no means to suggest that Luther's minimal commitment to reflection on the immanent life of the Trinity is indicative of Protestant theology more generally, as there exists a tremendous diversity and range of positions in both Lutheran and Reformed thought on this matter.

27. See, for example, Ockham, *Quodlibet* 2, q. 1 (*OTh.* 9) and *Quodlibet* 4, q. 2 (*OTh.* 9), where Ockham argues against the demonstrability of God's existence, as a primary efficient and final cause respectively. See the analysis of Jenny E. Pelletier, *William Ockham on Metaphysics: The Science of Being and God* (Leiden: Brill, 2013), 223–33.

28. See, for example, Ockham, *Ordinatio* d. 2, q. 10 (*OTh.* 9), *Quodlibet* 3, q. 4 (*OTh.* 9), *Ordinatio* d. 2, q. 10 (*OTh.* 2), and the analysis of Pelletier, *William Ockham on Metaphysics*, 227–32.

29. See Ockham, *Quodlibet* 2, q. 1 (*OTh.* 9).

Divine Simplicity and the Psychological Analogy. Ockham inaugurates a tradition of reasoning in medieval theology in which divine simplicity plays an especially normative role, even in the articulation of Trinitarian theology. We have noted above that Scotus correlates the emanation of persons by way of procession with "formal distinctions" in the nature of God. Natural operations of knowledge and voluntary love are formally distinct in God and give rise to distinct persons. The use of the psychological analogy "tracks onto" or corresponds with these formal distinctions in the divine nature, as the natural act of knowledge produces the Word by generation and the natural act of love produces the Spirit by spiration. Aquinas does not make use of such formal distinctions in order to understand the essence of God and therefore understands the production of the persons quite differently. The Father, in knowing himself, generates the Son eternally, communicating to him the plenitude of the divine nature with all that it entails. The Father in knowing and loving himself and the Son eternally spirates the Spirit with the Son, likewise communicating to the Spirit the plenitude of the divine nature, with all that it entails in terms of knowledge and love. The psychological analogy of knowledge and love is retained and can be ascribed to the Son as Word and the Spirit as Love, respectively, due to the relational order of the immaterial processions in God, not due to a formal distinction of acts of the divine nature.

Ockham reacts against both these traditions of thought and breaks with them radically by claiming that there is no sufficient foundation for the use of the psychological analogy in order to understand the inner life of God. In other words, we cannot identify any proper foundation in God for the proper ascription of the notions of Word and Love to the Son and Spirit respectively, even by highly qualified forms of analogy.[30] The reason we cannot use terms derived from immaterial processions of knowledge and love when speaking of the distinct persons has to do with divine simplicity.[31] The divine essence, which the Father, Son, and Spirit share, is identical in every

30. See Ockham, *Ord.* d. 2, q. 1 (*OTh.* 2); d. 1, q. 6 (*OTh.* 1); d. 7, q. 2 (*OTh.* 3); also Friedman, *Medieval Trinitarian Theology*, 125–31; and *Intellectual Traditions at the Medieval University*, 628–51. Durandus of St. Pourçain goes one step further and simply declares that the use of the psychological analogy when applied to the inner life of the Trinity is merely "metaphorical." See Friedman, *Medieval Trinitarian Theology*, 71–73, 113–14, quoting Durandus, *Comm. I Sent.* (C), d. 27, q. 3.

31. Why does Ockham insist so fundamentally on the simplicity of God if he has such a minimal concept of the natural knowledge of God and of the divine essence? The answer has more to do with his theology, his doctrinal commitment to divine unicity in scripture, and his aim for simplicity of explanation, than it has to do with anything that can be demonstrated philosophically.

respect, including with regard to knowledge and love.[32] Consequently, we cannot employ the notion of immaterial processions of Word and Love so as to assure real distinctions in God, including those pertaining to the persons in God. The patristic and Augustinian traditions of using the psychological analogy to denote the inner life of the Trinity are thus are cast radically into doubt.

Persons without an Analogy of Relations: Ascription without Contradiction. How, then, does Ockham wish to denote the distinction of persons in God? He recognizes that the Church's dogmatic tradition posits a distinction of persons in the Trinity and a common language of eternal processions and relations. Unlike Aquinas, however, Ockham can make no use of an analogical language of subsistent relations in God. The reason for this is simple. He does not think that there are real relations in the ordinary things around us, and believes that the very notion of real relations is a mistaken one.[33] If there are no real relations in the world around us, we can hardly transpose the notion onto God by analogy, since the "natural analogate" is simply missing.

Ockham is theologically committed to the affirmation of the Trinitarian faith of the Church and simultaneously holds that Christian belief must accord with natural reason, and thus we cannot say or believe anything about the Trinity that is inherently contradictory. At the same time, because of his commitment to the theology of divine simplicity and his notions of personhood and relation, he faces key challenges, since he lacks any clear analogate from which to derive a notion of relations and immaterial processions in God. Consequently, what Ockham must do is posit that there is something in God, the Holy Trinity, that transcends all our ordinary experience, a distinction of persons who are one in being, and simple in nature, in whom there is an order of processional origins that has no analogate to our ordinary experience. If the Church teaches that there is an eternal procession of the Word in God as a person distinct from the Father, and an eternal procession of the Spirit from the Father and the Son, and that these persons are re-

---

32. In a sense Ockham is simply reacting against Scotus's rendering of the distinction of persons as based on formally distinct natural operations in God. If attentiveness to divine simplicity impedes the attribution of such formal distinctions to the nature of God, then the way in which Ockham's Franciscan confrere had posited a foundation for distinct processions in God must be removed.

33. See, for example, Ockham, *Ord.* 1, d. 30, q. 1 (*OTh.* 4), and the helpful analysis of Adams, *William Ockham*, 1:215–76.

ally distinct and that each is truly and equally God, then we can affirm these various ideas in concord with one another and can believe that they are all true, without understanding how they are each said of God.[34] Ockham retains core doctrinal claims in regard to the Trinity but reduces them to a set of formal semantic propositions held under obedience to divine revelation and the authority of the Church. This is why we can term the position "nominal." Ockham inaugurates a tradition of Trinitarian theology in which one constructs a series of propositions about God as Trinity that are logically compatible, and that allow one at a minimum to affirm the dogmatic teaching of the Church, without the adornments of unreasonable speculative construction.

Ockham's theology is radically apophatic. His view is not contemplative in nature, since there is a firewall erected between God and the human intellect. If the Scotist position on the psychological analogy tends to be univocal in its ascriptions of personal acts to the Trinity, and the Thomist position is clearly analogical, this third position tends toward the equivocal. Our language for the Trinity falls short in this life.

This latter position may seem intolerably minimalist. It does not reflect the mainstream Catholic theological tradition either in the Middle Ages or in the modern period. It does represent, however, an intricate and integral attempt to think out the relations of faith and reason in regard to Christian revelation. Ockham is no mere fideist, even if the tradition he inaugurates does tilt more in this direction. In his own sober and profound way, he attempts to indicate a modern way of harmony between faith and reason, using reason critically to dissolve intellectually what he takes to be theologians' unwarranted arguments regarding God. On this view, many of the famous medieval philosophical arguments for the existence of God, as well as those pertaining to his attributes, are without sufficient foundation. Likewise, much that is said of the Trinity could be understood as unwarranted speculation or even intellectual projection (that is to say, conceptual idolatry). Theological reason should be employed, then, not only in a constructive mode, but also in a destructive mode, to take down problematic theological banalities. What we are left with after this process is over is a very modest proposal for the mere confession of Trinitarian faith. Such an approach heightens the authority of revelation and faith in part by diminish-

---

34. See Ockham, Ord., d. 27, q. 3 (OTh. 3), Ord., d. 7, q. 2 (OTh. 3); also Friedman, Medieval Trinitarian Theology, 128–29.

ing the cooperative role of reason. It also seems to transfer the domain of theological reflection from the more speculative domain to the more practical and ethical. In this life our primary task as theologians is to understand and carry out the commandments of God in faith and love. Knowing "who God is" is something reserved to the life to come. Evidently, this form of thinking places theology on a razor's edge. Such a minimalistic approach can lead easily to speculative agnosticism regarding the existence of God, and an evacuation from theology of the very notions of a divine essence (divine attributes), as well as the notions of divine persons, relations, and processions. If taken to an extreme, this kind of thinking has the capacity to burn down all the bridges of connection between grace and nature, and between Christian theology and modern philosophical reasoning.

SOME CONCEPTUAL ADVANTAGES OF THOMISTIC TRINITARIAN THEOLOGY

Comprehensive consideration of Aquinas's theology in the context of the medieval debates exceeds the scope and aims of this book. However, I will note here some core features of Thomistic theology of the Trinity that are conceptually advantageous for Christian theology more generally. Each is based by argument in scriptural exegesis interpreted through the lens of patristic traditions of the early Church. Aquinas clearly attempts to preserve core elements of the earlier theological tradition of the Church so as to develop them in an organic and logically continuous way. Likewise, I will seek to argue in this third part of the book and the final fourth part that these features of Thomistic Trinitarian thought are of great advantage in a distinctively modern context, and can help theologians make discernments regarding the various strengths and weakness of contemporary Trinitarian proposals.

A first conceptual advantage pertains to Aquinas's relational account of the inner Trinitarian life of God. As we noted in the first part of this book, the Cappadocian Fathers responded to Eunomius and other radical Arians by arguing that the persons of the Trinity are all equal in being and consequently differ not in dignity of nature but according to relations of origin. Augustine, as we also noted, developed his own version of this claim, arguing that the persons of the Trinity are the same in all things that do not pertain to their relational distinctions. Aquinas attempts to think through the implications of this claim.[35] If in the immanent life of God the Trinitarian persons are distinguished principally by their relations of origin, this has two immediate consequences: One is that the persons of the Trinity are utterly equal and are identically the one God, since each of them possesses one and the same divine nature, and differs from the others only in virtue of the relational giving or receiving of all that he is to or from the others.[36] A second is that each person is then characterized as relational in all that he is. The Father is not the Father because he generates. The Father generates because he is the Father, eternally related to the Son.[37] Each of the persons in God is characterized, accordingly, as a subsistent relation. The Thomistic tradition tends to take this idea as a centerpiece for Trinitarian reflection. The idea is eminently Trinitarian since it upholds a real distinction of persons. It is eminently monotheistic since it upholds clearly and coherently a unity and simplicity of essence. There is only one God who subsists in three distinct persons, each wholly related to the others.

A second core feature of this approach, which is closely related, has to do with its positive use of the *psychological analogy*, which as we saw above is derived from scripture (the Johannine prologue especially) and developed in various ways by Athanasius and Augustine in the context of anti-Arian debates. As we shall see in chapters below, Aquinas notes that Arianism posits the procession of the Word and Spirit from the Father as something taking place outside of God, while Sabellianism fails to acknowledge a real distinction of personal processions in God. To respond to these two extreme errors, he makes use of the psychological analogy to designate how there is a procession of persons in God. He affirms a likeness of the generation of human conceptual thought to the procession of the Word and a likeness of human inclinations of love to the procession of Spirit. We might say that this use of the psychological analogy qualifies his relationalist account, and vice

35. Aquinas would have been familiar with the ideas of Gregory of Nazianzus on this point by derivation, through his reading of John Damascene, *An Exposition of the Orthodox Faith*, 1, c. 8, where the Cappadocian idea is transmitted quite clearly.

36. As I have suggested above, there are problems for equality of the three persons that may arise if one defines the Father principally in virtue of his innascibility, as one who is the principle of the two persons, rather than primarily in terms of his paternity, as one who is wholly relative to the Son and Spirit, even while being the fontal origin of all that is in the Trinitarian life.

37. Friedman, *Intellectual Traditions at the Medieval University*, 1:73: "For Aquinas the Father generates because he is the Father, and he is the Father because of the opposition of the *rationes* of the relations paternity and filiation. An order among the concepts attributable to God the Father thus becomes discernible in Aquinas's thought: paternity then Father then generation, relation then person then emanation." See Aquinas on this idea, *ST* I, q. 40, a. 4.

versa. As subsistent relations, the divine persons are distinguished by their relations of origin. However, the relations in question pertain to immaterial processions of generation and spiration. We can formulate proper analogies for the begotten Word and spirated Love based on likenesses to intellectual knowledge and voluntary love. At the same time, these immaterial processions in God are not something accidental, like the intellectual acts of a human person. Nor do they imply formally distinct operations of the nature of God. Rather, they are actions of subsistent persons who are really relative to one another, and who proceed from one another. The divine persons act in virtue of their shared divine nature, which each possesses fully, but they are not products of the divine nature. When the Father knows and loves himself from all eternity, he does so in virtue of his divine nature as God, and in doing so generates the Son as his Word and spirates the Spirit with the Son as their mutual Love. The Son possesses the fullness of the divine nature as knowing and loving, as does the Spirit, but they each possess this plenitude of divine life according to a different relation of origin. This way of conceiving of the immanent life of God provides us with a genuine horizon of contemplation. It allows us to think analogically about the immanent life of the Trinity, in contrast to the minimalism of Ockham, while still respecting the transcendence, mystery, and alterity of God. In this way it resists the temptations of philosophical rationalism, as well as overly ambitious theological depictions of the Trinity cast in univocal terms.

Third, Aquinas's understanding of the distinction of persons according to relations of origin provides us with a way of making distinctions of personal mode regarding the nature of God, based on the order of reception of the nature by the distinct persons. In light of his relational account, Aquinas does not think it is possible to divide the attributes of God between the persons or ascribe activities of the nature of God to only one or two persons, as if to say (with Richard of St. Victor) that one person alone can be called all-powerful, but that it requires two for us to ascribe happiness to God, and three to ascribe love, or as when one says (with Scotus) that the Father acts according to the divine nature in one way when generating the Son and in another in spirating the Spirit. On the contrary, all that pertains to the Father as God (in virtue of his divine nature) is communicated to the Word, who emanates forth from him from all eternity, and all that the Word possesses from and with the Father is communicated to the Spirit. Consequently, the natural attributes and natural actions of God cannot be ascribed

in distinct ways to only some of the persons. This being said, Aquinas does
think that each of the three persons possesses the divine nature in a distinct personal way or mode of being. The Son, for example, is truly omnipotent, but he is only ever omnipotent in a filial mode, as one who receives
all that he has from the Father. This approach contrasts with that of Scotus,
which we considered above, wherein the distinct properties of persons correspond to "formal distinctions" in the nature of God. Aquinas's modal distinctions allow us to emphasize the distinction of the persons without introducing any formal multiplicity into the nature of God. At the same time
they also allow us consider the theological significance of the order of the
persons, even in regard to the divine nature, since the Son, for example, is
all-powerful, but he is so only ever from the Father, just as the Spirit is infinitely wise but only ever from the Father and the Son. Thus one may preserve (against the minimalism of Ockham) the significance that the order of
the processions of persons bears for our theological contemplation of God,
while still evoking a strong set of claims regarding divine simplicity (each
person having the one identical essence of God).

This approach allows one to think simultaneously about both the distinct persons and the modes of God's natural being in a highly aligned way:
concepts of persons and modes go together in Trinitarian theology and are
not separated or opposed. The personal modes of subsistence of the divine
nature reflect the personal order that stems from the processions and relations of origin in God. The Father is infinitely good in a paternal way, the
Son in a filial way (as deriving his goodness from the Father), and the Spirit in a spirated way (as eternally derivative of the Father and the Son). This
idea has significant consequences when one considers the economy of creation and grace. In the economy, the three persons always act as one, *and*
each also acts in a distinctive personal mode. The Father, for example, always gives being to creatures with the Word and the Spirit, but he also does
so in a distinctly paternal way, giving being to the world as the unbegotten
and eternal principle of the Word and the Spirit, and does so in his eternal
Word and in the Spirit. The Word gives being to creatures as the uncreated
Wisdom of the Father, and accordingly is a source of order and intelligibility
in all that is created, but he only ever acts as one who is eternally begotten
of the Father, and who acts with the Father in their common Spirit of spirated love. As we shall see, this pattern of thinking helps us understand the
ultimate foundations of the patristic use of appropriations, wherein a given

attribute of the divine nature (such as omnipotence or wisdom or goodness) is attributed to one person in a distinct but not exclusive way, such as
when we speak of the all-powerful Father, the Son who is eternally wise, or
the Spirit who is good. These nature attributions can be made to any of the
persons, but they are also made in fitting ways to one person in particular.[38]

A final advantage of Aquinas's approach is that it provides us with analogical notions for personhood, relation, and nature that are applicable in
similar and dissimilar ways to divine persons and created persons (both angels and human beings). This is true because Aquinas maintains Boethius's
definition of the person, which includes the notion of an intellectual *nature*
as an intrinsic component. This definition initially applies only to human
persons (i.e., as individuals of a rational nature), but can be stretched analogically so as to designate those who have angelic natures and those who
have the divine nature, that is, the divine persons in their mutual relations.
This practice instantiates, in its own way, the teaching of the Fourth Lateran
Council regarding the "greater dissimilitude" of the Trinitarian persons in
respect to human persons. It respects the apophatic character of our knowledge of the Trinity, even "after" divine revelation and in the light of faith.
However, it also provides enough kataphatic content to allow us to perceive
significant likeness amid the discontinuity between Trinitarian persons and
personal creatures.

Aquinas's approach allows us to interpret or re-read all of creation (with
its various persons, natures, and relations) in light of the Trinity, to see creation as a finite created expression of Trinitarian wisdom and love, without
projecting the created modes onto God. In Christology this set of analogical predications is of especial importance. The Son made man is a divine
person, not a created person, and as God he possesses the plenitude of the
divine nature. However, he also takes on a human nature, in virtue of which
he has many human relations, from conception in the womb of the Virgin,
through his human development in childhood, to his adult apostolic life,
and in his suffering, death, and resurrection. This human nature and these
human relations in turn truly reveal his person, and thus the eternal relations that he has with his Father and with the Spirit. His natural actions as
man also reveal his divine nature and its divine activity, as when he teaches
with divine authority, performs miracles, and so on, in virtue of the divine

---

38. I will return to these themes below.

nature and life that he shares with the Father and the Spirit as Lord. The point of these reflections is simply to underscore that we can come up with a coherent analysis of Jesus Christ as the eternal person of the Son, who is truly God and truly human, only if we have some kind of theological analogy by which to speak of person and nature in the Trinity that safeguards both the transcendence of God and the resemblance of human nature to God. Aquinas's account has the advantage of providing us with this kind of coherent analysis. I will explore these topics further in the fourth part of this book.

MODERN THEOLOGICAL COMPARISONS

In the final part of our prologue, we can note how some medieval positions are reasserted in novel ways by the most influential modern Trinitarian theologians.[39] The argument I am making here will be presented in greater depth in part 4 of this book. However, it is useful at this juncture to consider some of the key claims I will make there so as to anticipate what is at stake when we consider Aquinas's theology of the immanent Trinity, in view of our subsequent discussion of modern Trinitarian theology. The likenesses indicated here between medievals and moderns are partial, to be sure, but they do help us see in advance how the Thomistic account of the immanent life of God—which we will consider in some detail below—can have consequences for one's engagement with modern theological themes.

We should note first that mainstream modern Trinitarian theology has developed against the backdrop of two very influential modern philosophical ideas, one from Immanuel Kant and one from G. W. F. Hegel. The idea from Kant pertains to his so-called Copernican revolution in metaphysics, which he sought to propound systematically especially in the *Critique of Pure Reason*. As is well known, Kant argued there that various metaphysical principles advanced by classical, medieval, and modern philosophers alike pertained not to the structure of reality as such but to the conceptual constructions of the transcendental subject. Ideas such as cause, essence, sub-

---

39. For the sake of my schematic argument I will take the theologies of Karl Barth, Karl Rahner, Hans Urs von Balthasar, and Jürgen Moltmann as representative of the post-Hegelian "Trinitarian revival" within twentieth-century theology. I will engage with these thinkers and other modern Trinitarian theologians in the final part of this book. At this juncture I am only referring to them to indicate themes that will be treated in greater specificity below.

stance, property, spiritual faculty, immaterial soul, and indeed God (as first cause) have no clear foundation or verifiable correspondent in reality, but form part of a mere system of thinking by which human beings seek to regulate their understanding of the world subjectively in an intellectually coherent way. If notions such as the spiritual soul, the universe, and God are necessary for us as heuristic devices for thinking about sensate reality coherently, they are nonetheless unverifiable hypotheses whose real existence can never be verified nor proven unreal.

It follows from this line of thinking that two key elements of classical Trinitarian theology must be denied in principle, if Kant's critique obtains. The first is the pursuit of a treatise *de Deo ut uno* regarding God the Trinity, at least insofar as one might seek to ground upon philosophical argument any claims one might make about God. Second, the use of the psychological analogy is prohibited, since, according to the principles of this philosophy, one can no longer speak about faculties of the mind that are spiritual, their immaterial operations, or the spiritual soul *in human beings*, once the principles of the Kant's critique are adopted. So there is no clear analogate available to theology for the processions of the Word as knowledge and the Spirit as love in the Trinity. The question then arises whether any theologian who adopts such measures comprehensively may even think about God as one or the Trinitarian processions in God in any conceptually coherent way. Kant's philosophy is very different from that of Ockham's, but there are some evident likenesses between the two, even if Kant's critique of all possible theology is much more radical.

The second key idea was developed in reaction to Kant's "a-theology," precisely so as to safeguard the centrality of Trinitarian theology within modern European thought. This is the Hegelian idea of the diremption of divine spirit, which Hegel conceives of by providing radically original notions of revelation, the Trinity, the Incarnation, and the psychological analogy. Although Hegel's thought is notoriously perplexing, it is clear enough that he sees Trinitarian doctrine as a religious representation in symbolic form of a profound philosophical idea. The Trinity is a symbol of the most profound ontological dynamic in human history, which is that of the unfolding of absolute spirit in finite spirit through the medium of human culture. The Incarnation represents the idea that God in his very Logos or Reason has become man, and this for Hegel suggests that the deity itself has become human, the infinite has become finite, and the eternal is developing its own internal identity through history.[40] Here—and this will be discussed at greater length in part 4—Hegel breaks with the traditional understanding of the "communication of idioms," which ascribes the properties of both the divine and human natures of Christ to his one person. ("Jesus is true God and true man.") Instead, he introduces the idea of ascribing the human attributes of Christ to the divine nature. In Christ, the divine nature becomes historical. The concrete individual Jesus is the representation or symbol, however, of a larger world historical process. Once we demythologize the idea of the Incarnation and locate its inner core, we can see that what it really signifies philosophically is that the divine spirit is becoming in all that is human, expressing itself in human freedom, culture, and world history. The future history of human agency, expressed especially in philosophy, politics, and art, is a history of absolute spirit, of the divine manifest in history.

Hegel's quixotic philosophy of culture may not seem like a likely candidate to inspire a renewal of modern Trinitarian theology, and it is true that great figures like Karl Barth and Hans Urs von Balthasar reacted against his ideas in significant ways. Nevertheless, there are intuitions or ideas of Hegelian provenance that entered into the formation of the mainstream "orthodox" modern Trinitarian tradition. With Kant and against Hegel, modern Trinitarian theologians have typically held to the idea that the essence of God transcends human history and cannot be known by our natural powers. The apophaticism of the modern Kantian critique can be adopted in a mitigated or qualified sense, over against the strange philosophical pantheism of the Hegelian system. However, Hegel provides us, in turn, with resources by which to respond to Kant's prohibition on Trinitarian thinking. It may be that after Kant's Copernican revolution we cannot "ascend" by our metaphysical reasoning to any form of coherent thinking about God, his divine attributes or the immanent processions of the persons in God, by analogy with human spiritual operations. However, if God has, in fact, freely identified with us in becoming human, and if he adopts in the Incarnation human characteristics that correspond by analogy to his inner life of Trinitarian love, then we can indeed learn who God is as Trinity by focusing our attention on the human life of Christ. God freely identifies with us kenotically in becoming human, and in doing so he reveals to us in his human life

---

40. See, for example, Hegel, "The Consummate Religion," in *Lectures on the Philosophy of Religion*, 3:452–69.

and relationships the inner nature and mystery of communion that exists in God. We find the Trinity uniquely within the immanence of history, and not as some reality we grasp initially as transcendent to the world. The immanent life of God is now understood primarily in virtue of the "economic Trinity." On the one hand, this theology is radically apophatic, taking inspiration from Kantian prohibitions on metaphysics, a modern echo of medieval equivocity discourse. God in his transcendence is virtually unknown unless he reveals himself in Christ. On the other hand, this theology is radically kataphatic, since what we encounter in Christ's human obedience, suffering, and voluntary love is indicative of the person and nature of the Son from all eternity. This is a modern echo of the medieval univocal discourse. What binds together the idea of God's radical transcendence and his human immanence is a notion of divine freedom that takes inspiration from modern German idealism. God in his very being and nature as God is free to be either transcendent, eternal, impassible, and unknown to us, or immanent to history, temporal, subject to divine suffering, and characterized by human attributes. In his very nature as God he can move in an elliptical fashion around two foci, in virtue of his all encompassing freedom to love. In this schema, the *de Deo ut uno* treatise of classical theology is displaced by a theology of a divine freedom that is able to self-determine for contrary states by a kind of bi-polarity, so that God can be both eternal and temporal, impassible and subject to suffering, omnipotent and subject to creaturely change.

I will explore this idea in greater depth in the final part of this book. Here, however, I would seek simply to note key themes that emerge in modern theology of this kind. Paradoxical as it may initially seem, my claim here is that the modern Trinitarian tradition tends to reproduce various elements of the medieval traditions we examined above, albeit in creative and unexpected ways.

The first striking note of comparison pertains to the use of the psychological analogy in Trinitarian theology, where it is clear that the predominant trend in modern theology is to follow what I have called the nominal minimalist wing of medieval tradition, which claims that this analogy is essentially unworkable or counterproductive when one is seeking to think about the inner life of the Trinitarian God. Karl Barth, for example, in *CD* 1:1, famously relocates the place of identification of personal distinctions in God. We can speak of the Father, Son, and Spirit as distinct from one another not primarily in virtue of eternal relations of origin in the immanent life of God, but in virtue of God's act of self-revelation to human beings in Christ, in which God is self-differentiated as the revealer Father, the revealed Son, and the revealing Spirit.[41] In effect, Barth uses appropriations of divine actions to distinct persons as the privileged, and perhaps exclusive, way to differentiate the persons. This suggests that we must appeal to the economic activity of God in order to distinguish the persons, and not to eternal immanent acts of immaterial generation and spiration. Likewise, Rahner, in his famous treatment of the economic and immanent Trinity, specifies that the psychological analogy can and should be dispensed with and argues instead for a distinction of persons based on the economic relationships of God to the world that obtain in virtue of the Incarnation (a position I will return to in the next section of the book).[42] Balthasar follows suit in an adamant way, as does Moltmann, both of whom treat the psychological analogy as an accretion of medieval theology subject to inflated importance at best and perhaps even as an unwarranted speculation extraneous to the gospel.[43]

A second observation pertains to the attributes of the nature of God, such as simplicity, perfection, and infinity, which we studied in part 2 of this book. While each of the medieval theologians treated these divine names in

41. See especially Barth, "The Root of the Doctrine of the Trinity," in *CD* 1:1, 304–33, where he formulates the notion of the immanent Trinity as an economic Trinity in revelation, a passage that no doubt influenced Rahner. The unambiguous evidence for my interpretation of Barth on this point, however, is found on p. 363, where he is articulates a position—manifestly similar to that of Ockham—concerning the incomprehensibility of any ground for the distinction of relations in God other than the fact that God has revealed it, and then pivots toward a distinguishing of the persons based on the act of revelation itself by which the persons are self-differentiated.

42. See Karl Rahner, *The Trinity*, trans. J. Donceel (London: Continuum, 2001), 19, 46–48, 115–20. I will return to his criticisms of the psychological analogy as "almost Gnostic speculation" in the final part of this book.

43. See Hans Urs von Balthasar, *Theo-Logic: Theological Logical Theory*, vol. 2, *The Truth of God*, trans. A. Walker (San Francisco: Ignatius Press, 2004), 128–34, where Balthasar progressively problematizes traditional notions of the immanent Trinity, suggesting inevitable difficulties that arise from the use of the psychological analogy, traditional notions of the divine essence, Aquinas's concept of the persons as subsistent relations, and the use of appropriations. On p. 132 he bids farewell to the use of the psychological analogy, before embracing a thoroughgoing Barthian conception of the economic Trinity, on pp. 138–41. The radicality of this break with previous Catholic tradition should not be underestimated. Jürgen Moltmann, who is bracingly unrefined, simply characterizes in two pages the centuries-old reflection of the Church on the psychological analogy as an alien projection of a human transcendental subject onto God that eventually gave rise to rejections in modern atheism of an anthropomorphic god, and contributed thereby indirectly to the modern crisis of nihilism. See *The Trinity and the Kingdom: The Doctrine of God*, trans. M. Kohl (San Francisco: Harper & Row, 1981), 14–15. The fact that this view is historically and conceptually crude does not mean that it is not often repeated; quite the contrary.

a distinct way, as a dimension of Trinitarian theology, we can note that, with rare exceptions, post-Hegelian Trinitarian theologians compose no treatises on the divine nature.[44] Consequently, they typically neither seek to distinguish the persons by appeal to the analogy from psychological processions, nor do they underscore the unity of the three persons by appeal to a developed reflection on the mystery of the divine nature. On this point, the radical contrast with figures like Gregory of Nazianzus, Augustine, Bonaventure, and Aquinas should be evident. These figures all made use of an extensive consideration of proper names for the three persons as distinct from common names pertaining to the shared nature. The use of the psychological analogy functioned in different ways for each of them as a way to understand the distinction of personal proper names. In the absence of this traditional motif, the modes of proper identity of the three persons and the nature of their unity as the one God become newly-opened questions in modern theology. In this respect, the approaches of modern authors typically differ radically from those of virtually all of the great patristic and medieval figures.

How, then, are the persons of the Trinity and their uncreated unity typically understood within the context of the modern continental tradition of Trinitarian theology? The distinction of persons is identified primarily by reference to God's economic activity in the creation. We know the distinct persons primarily or exclusively as a result of their historical presence among us. Accordingly, the human activity and suffering of Christ are often taken to be indicative of something present in the eternal life of God that differentiates the Son from the Father. In Barth this is manifest in the Son's divine obedience, lived out in the acceptance of the Cross.[45] In Rahner, it is

44. Barth represents an important exception in this regard, in *CD* 2:1. The late work of the Barthian scholar John Webster sought to underscore the importance of a recovery of the theology of divine attributes, including divine perfection, in conversation with Aquinas. See especially, in this regard, John Webster, *Confessing God: Essays in Christian Dogmatics II* (London: T&T Clark, 2005); *God Without Measure: Working Papers in Christian Theology*, vol. 1, *God and the Works of God* (London: Bloomsbury T&T Clark, 2016).

45. See the thematic treatment of this theme in Barth, *CD* 4:1, section 59, pp. 157–357. There is arguably a great deal of consistency in Barth's thought from *CD* 1:1, on the distinction of the persons as conceived principally in virtue of their activity of revelation, to his treatment of divine election in *CD* 2:2, where the election of God is a Trinitarian act by which God manifests his own distinction of Father, Word, and Spirit in the event of Christ as the elected one on behalf of the human race, to his treatment of the *analogia relationis* in *CD* 3:3, where he claims that God is eternally characterized by his relations to the creation in election, to his treatment of the obedience and dereliction of Christ in *CD* 4:1, where the Son's human relation to the Father is indicative of an eternal

Jesus' human religious consciousness that reveals him as the Word, who is relative to and distinct from the Father.[46] In Balthasar, the Son appears in his eternal differentiation from the Father by his free acceptance of the crucifixion and descent into hell, interpreted as an expression of intra-Trinitarian self-giving love.[47] In Moltmann, the Son is distinguished from the Father by his personal suffering and death, which entails a reconfiguration of the very being of the Trinity, through an intra-divine event of God's loving solidarity with human beings.[48] In short, we see in modern continental Trinitarian theology that God's history of being with us in Christ is crucial to our understanding of the immanent life of God and is in some sense constitutive of God's Trinitarian life in itself. Thomists typically question whether such accounts permit one to maintain in a coherent way that God's incomprehensible nature is truly transcendent of creation, that the three persons are truly one in being, and that Christ's divine nature is truly distinguishable from his human action and suffering.

It may seem at this point that the differences between the medieval and the continental moderns are so important as to make any resemblances trivial. This is not the case however. It is true that the great medieval Doctors

---

divine relationality of the Father toward the Son by which the Father commands the Son and the Son obeys the Father, a seeming precondition for the Son's obedient journey into the far country, that of the incarnation, cross, and resurrection. In all these instances we see both that the persons of the Trinity are distinguished by their relation to creation (in revelation, election, creation, and redemption) and that the relations that are intra-Trinitarian therefore take on their intelligibility principally in light of God's activity manifest to us in the economy.

46. See the Rahner, *Foundations of Christian Faith*, 176–321.

47. Balthasar, *Theo-Logic*, 2:135–49, esp. p. 136: "No one doubts that, as the New Testament tells us, the Father's act of giving up the Son and the Spirit in the economy is pure love, as is the Son's and the Spirit's act of freely letting themselves be given up. But how could this fundamental claim about the economy of salvation have no foundation in any property of the essence of the Triune God?" Balthasar tends to speak of the Trinitarian persons as if they are distinct, pre-constituted personal subjects who chose freely to engage by self-surrender with one another, both in eternity and in the economy. See also *Theo-Logic*, vol. 2, pp. 163–65, where Balthasar appeals precisely to Scotus's notion of the two processions as implying formally distinct natural actions of intellect and will, and to Bonaventure's conception of the Father as pre-constituted, as prelude-concepts that helped medieval theology begin to transcend the limitations of the psychological analogy, providing an initial image of the persons as freely mutually loving in the drama of the economy.

48. See Moltmann, *The Trinity and the Kingdom*, 165, where he affirms the importance of the Bonaventurean and Scotist concept of the Father as constituted by himself, prior to his relationality to the Son. The Son can be understood as the principle of creation and its redemption in light of the Cross (168). The persons of the Trinity are wholly relative to one another, as Augustine affirmed, but their relations include history and are historical, as Hegel held, so that the persons develop relationally through the economy (174).

all differ starkly from the moderns by their primary focus on the psychological analogy and the predications for the divine nature. By contrast, the post-Hegelian moderns focus attention primarily on the economic actions of the Son and the Spirit and the human nature of Jesus as indicative of personal distinctions among himself, the Father, and the Spirit. Precisely for this latter reason, however, the moderns also rejoin, in their own way, the medieval preoccupation with univocal and kataphatic Trinitarian predication. Surprisingly, therefore, we can speak under differing aspects of the simultaneously nominal minimalist and Franciscan-emanationist shape of modern Trinitarian theology. It is minimalist as regards the critical rejection of the use of the psychological analogy and goes further than Ockham in its skepticism regarding natural knowledge of the divine nature (the *de Deo ut uno* treatise). Barth, Rahner, Balthasar, and others resist attempts to rehabilitate these "scholastic" notions within a modern context. The modern trend is "Franciscan," however, in its tendency toward univocal predication of created features of personhood and nature to the inner life of the Trinity, based especially upon the human life of God.

This pairing of two originally opposed medieval tendencies typically occurs in one of two ways in modern theology, based on a division regarding the use of the term "person" when ascribed to God. On the one side, both Barth and Rahner, who appear also on this point to be rather minimalist by our schema, argue that the notion of a divine person is unintelligible in a post-Cartesian context, and consequently should be abandoned when speaking of the intra-Trinitarian life of God. They denote the persons of the Trinity instead as three subsistent modes of being.[49] The three are indicated primarily not as personal agents or subjects of procession, but as three truly distinct modes of being in the life of the one God. However, the distinctions that obtain between them are not understood by the use of the psychological analogy either. Instead of making appeal to the notion of "immanent activity" in God (the eternal procession of generation and spiration), these theologians appeal to what Aquinas calls "transitive activity." That is to say, the three modes of God's being are differentiated primarily by their *distinct natural activities or properties* that accrue to them *in virtue of the divine economy*. The Son is God in his mode of being as incarnate, and his relation to

---

49. See Barth, *CD* 1:1, 363–38, and a nearly identical position in Rahner, *The Trinity*, 103–15, which, indeed, makes overt reference to Barth's text.

creation through self-communication (as the spoken Word) is what differentiates him from the Father. ('This is the view of Rahner.) Or the Son can be distinguished from the Father eternally in virtue of his obedience to the Father manifest in the economy. (This is the view of Barth) The position elaborated by these two thinkers is very like the formal distinction theory of Scotus in regard to generation and spiration, not because it privileges the psychological analogy but because it distinguishes the persons in virtue of natural attributes or distinct operations—in this case, those manifest in the economy. Scotus thinks that the eternal generation of the Word implies a natural act in the essence of God formally distinct from the eternal spiration of the Spirit, which is a natural act of the divine will. Therefore the persons are distinguished in part by reference to distinct aspects of the divine nature. The modern schema retains this kind of formal distinction theory in the nature of God, but sees it happening in the economy dynamically rather than in the eternal processions. When God acts freely in the economy, the Son acts in ways *naturally* distinct from those of the Father and the Spirit. This modern tendency of thought, common to the authors we will study in the final part of this book, thus "exports" the formal distinctions of natural operations of Trinitarian persons from the Franciscan tradition outside to God's action in the economy, in a slight bow of deference to Hegel.

On the other side of the modern debate, both Balthasar and Moltmann criticize Rahner and Barth for their exclusion of the attribute of personhood and instead seek to characterize the distinction in God in terms of persons.[50] However, because the intelligibility of the distinction of persons arises principally from the economy for both Balthasar and Moltmann as well, they each in different ways depict the persons in God in univocal forms in continuity with human persons, that is to say, as distinct agents of freedom, engaged with one another in a shared dramatic history of salvation. For Moltmann, this temporal history takes place in God, as the death and

---

50. See especially Moltmann, *The Trinity and the Kingdom*, 144–48, where he famously accuses Rahner and Barth of advancing a dubious form of modalism. Balthasar, in *Theo-Drama: Theological Dramatic Theory*, vol 3, *The Dramatis Personae: Persons in Christ*, trans. G. Harrison (San Francisco: Ignatius, 1993), 208–20, reacts against a modalistic conception of persons and notes a leaning toward the Scotist theory of the person as pre-constituted prior to relation, which Balthasar prefers to the proposals of the Thomistic school. While I noted above that Thomists hold personalist and modalist accounts together, we see in Rahner and Balthasar that they are pulled apart toward either modalist (apersonalist) or personalist (amodalist) extremes. See also Balthasar, *Theo-Logic*, 2:163.

resurrection of the Son shapes, dissolves, and reconstitutes the very relations of the Trinity, not wholly unlike a history that might unfold between
three human persons subject to changing relations. The Bonaventurian notion of a Trinitarian person as a pre-constituted subject who acquires relations is posited anew here in a novel, evolutive way.[51] For Balthasar, the
unfolding of the drama of the paschal mystery does not reconstitute the
Trinity but has its eternal precondition in the uncreated life of God, so that
in the event of the Cross and dereliction we are able to perceive an eternal, pre-existent separation in God that occurs through freely self-emptying
love, of the Father for the Son and the Son for the Father. This eternal event
of mutual self-giving in God is the precondition for the unfolding of the
Cross-event in time. Here the partial but real likeness to the "Franciscan"
model is evident, something Balthasar comments upon and purposefully
intends.[52] To be free to give himself to the Son, the Father must be depicted by formal likeness with a human person as one pre-constituted in unbegottenness, who then surrenders himself to the Son in freedom, while
the Son similarly is depicted in quasi-univocal fashion by comparison to
a human free agent, as one who freely elects to surrender himself to the
Father.

The sketch I have just given is merely suggestive, and I will return to
many of these themes in greater detail in the final part of this book. What I
am proposing at this juncture, however, is that several core themes in modern Trinitarian theology derive in part from a novel preservation and restatement of elements of the medieval tradition, a restatement marked by a
unique mixture of apophatic minimalist and emanationist-Franciscan influences. The corollary to this claim is just as important, for it would suggest
that within the context of modern theological conversation, the Thomistic
account of the Trinity has not so much been tried and found wanting. Rather, for the most part, it simply has not been tried. The modern continental
theologians mentioned above wish rightly to underscore that the mystery
of the Trinity is truly revealed in the economy and that in an especial way
we can learn something of "what" God is in virtue of the incarnation of the
Son, his life, suffering, death, descent into hell, and resurrection. Barth and
Balthasar do not hesitate to speak about an analogy in this respect between

51. See Moltmann, *The Trinity and the Kingdom*, 165–68.
52. Balthasar, *Theo-Logic*, 2:163–70.

the humanity of the Son and his deity.[53] However, the actual realization of this project is deeply conditioned, on the one hand, by skeptical refusal of classical elements of the tradition (divine names and the psychological analogy) and, on the other hand, by uncritical reception of an all-too-human account of Trinitarian predication (quasi-univocal predication theory for the divine nature and the persons, based on the economy).[54] These two excesses mutually compound one another, because modern skepticism about our capacity to name God in himself or to speak by analogy of the immanent life of the Trinity provides motivation for an economic account of the life of God grounded in univocal forms of predication. What is needed instead is a sense of analogy by which we can speak of the nature of God, the immanent processions of the Trinity, the simultaneous similitude and dissimilitude of the human nature of Christ to his divine nature, and the analogy of God's effects of grace to the divine persons more generally.

We noted above that Aquinas's theological discourse for personhood, nature, and relations is analogical and therefore can be employed to speak of Trinitarian relations, persons, and the divine nature, without confusing the created mode of these features of being with the transcendent mystery of God. This, in turn, also allows him to speak of the incarnation of the per-

---

53. See Barth, CD 2:1, 221–27, where he claims that theology must make systematic use of the notion of analogy (in a distinctively theological, not philosophical, way), and CD 4:2, 97–98, where Barth notes that the two essences of Christ, divine and human, must bear a resemblance to each other. See likewise Balthasar, *Theo-Logic*, 2:81, and *Epilogue*, trans. E. Oakes (San Francisco: Ignatius Press, 2004), pp. 89–98, where Balthasar speaks of Christ as the concrete *analogia entis*.

54. A more complete sketch of the passage from the medievals to the twentieth-century moderns would require attention to at least two other key moments. First, the elaboration of Luther's *theologia crucis*, which weds nominalist-inspired skepticism of our knowledge of the divine nature (*theologia gloriae*, negatively depicted) with a focus on the revelation of God in the crucifixion of Jesus. The crucified humanity of Jesus becomes the cypher of God in a quasi-univocal fashion. Second, the nineteenth-century ontologies of Hegel and Schelling in distinct ways elaborate an event ontology of divine becoming, in which (at least in Hegel's case) the communication of idioms is reinterpreted, so that the human features of Christ are said to pertain to the historical life of God in his deity. This second posture in modern theology is even more significantly univocalist in tendency than the first and opens up the possibility of a kenotic understanding of the very life and essence of God. Against this backdrop, the Trinitarian ontologies of Barth and Balthasar appear as more traditional, since they seek to assert in more pronounced fashion the transcendence of God's life and essence with respect to creation and history. They also, however, seek to integrate elements of nineteenth-century ontologies of divine becoming, diremption, and freedom into their own accounts. Barth's work is of particular importance in this respect, since in CD 2:1, he composed virtually the only modern post-Hegelian work of reflection on the divine attributes pertaining to God's nature and sought therein to integrate elements from both classical and reformed scholasticism with modern ontological motifs inherited from the previous century.

son of the Son in human nature. If this is the case, then it is possible to affirm the following:

1. We can come to know truly, if imperfectly, who God is in himself eternally, in virtue of the consideration of God's creatures, as well as in virtue of God's self-revelation to us in time.

2. Accordingly, we can truly identify, by proper analogy, ways of speaking about the immanent life of God and the eternal processions of the Trinitarian persons. Our statements in this regard are characterized in particular by use of the psychological analogy.

3. This characterization of the immanent life of God allows us in turn to develop an analogical notion of divine persons as subsistent relations, a notion of the divine persons that permits us to understand all human personhood and relationality in light of God, without either excessive kataphatic anthropomorphism or excessive apophatic despair.

4. By use of analogical conceptions of personhood, nature, and relation we can also think about how the incarnation of the Son and the sending of the Spirit in time reveal to us the inner mystery of the life of God.

5. We can consider as well how the revelation of the Trinity occurs in a preeminent way in the suffering, death, and resurrection of Christ, such that the Son, precisely in his human mode of being among us as man, reveals to us his personal identity as Son and Word and his eternal relation to the Father and the Spirit. However, this can be undertaken only while we maintain a sufficiently vibrant sense of the distinction of the divine and human natures in Christ, so as to avoid projecting temporal features of human existence onto God or the intra-Trinitarian relations. Not only will this approach help us maintain a sufficiently profound sense of the mysterious transcendence of the Trinity, who is not identified with the history of his creation, it also will help us maintain a sufficiently profound sense of the presence of the transcendent God in Christ, especially in his passion, human death, and resurrection. The attribution to the Son of all names pertaining to God's nature is not suspended in virtue of the Incarnation, as indeed Jesus Christ has two natures. The one who is eternal dies on a given day. The one who is impassible suffers the greatest of agonies. God is crucified. In the dead body of Christ, who has expired on Golgotha, there resides the power of God to raise the dead. As God, Jesus remains simple, perfect, infinite, and immutable, in eternal union with the Father and the

Spirit, even as he suffers, dies, and is exalted as man. Simultaneously, however, as man he truly suffers, dies, and is exalted in the resurrection not only to redeem the human race, but also precisely to reveal to us the inner life of God as Trinity.

It is to this set of aims that we will turn in the remainder of this book, treating the immanent life of God in part 3, and the economic revelation of the Trinity in part 4.

22

Immanent Processions in God

In the previous chapter I claimed that Aquinas, and the Thomistic school more generally, articulate a relational account of persons in the Trinity. In the chapters to come we will seek to substantiate and explore this claim in clear and succinct ways, mentioning in turn the relevance of this approach to questions that arise in modern theology. Aquinas unfolds his analysis of the Trinitarian persons of God in *ST* I, qq. 27–43, on which we will comment selectively in the nine chapters to follow.[1] A key principle to note first is the question of his point of entry into analysis of the inner life of the Trinity. His first question is not about relations or persons, but is about whether one might even rightly say that there are processions in God. How can we think analogically about the procession of the Word by generation, and the procession of the Spirit by spiration? Aquinas needs first simply to identify a way of thinking about a real distinction of persons in God that does not imply a distinction of substances or an inequality of natures in God. To do so he has recourse to the psychological analogy. This in turn will allow him to identify the relations that exist in God, and therefore to understand the persons and what he calls their "notional acts" of generation and spiration.

It should be noted from the outset that by his appeal to the psychological analogy Aquinas will set the stage for a consideration of the relations in God as *relations of origin*. As we saw in the first part of this book, both

---

1. For a magistral textual study of these questions in their historical context, see Emery, *The Trinitarian Theology of St. Thomas Aquinas*, to which I will make reference frequently in the third part of this book.

the Cappadocian Fathers and St. Augustine underscored the importance of this idea. The persons of the Trinity are truly one in being and essence, and consequently they can be distinguished from one another only in virtue of their relations of origin. Aquinas places this central idea of patristic theology at the heart of his Trinitarian theology. Real relations imply correlative terms that are opposite to one another (as when one causal agent is active upon another that is receptive or passive), and they are "co-simultaneous." Real relations in God are expressed in the origination of one person from another in procession, and thus are instantiated in and through eternal generation and spiration. Consequently, the study of the relations of origin is what gives us the basis for thinking about the persons as subsistent relations. The persons are always already related to one another in all that they are and only ever exist in the opposite relations of generation and spiration. This concept of the persons in turn allows us to understand the personal acts of generation and spiration. In virtue of his paternity, the Father eternally communicates all that he is as God to the Son, and the Father and the Son as a principle of spiration eternally communicate all that they are as God to the Spirit. This notion of relational procession allows us to establish a concept of Trinitarian monotheism. Each of divine persons is wholly relative to the others, truly distinct from the others, and truly God. This is the order of reasoning we will explore in the course of the next few chapters.[2]

Two other comments should be made about this Thomistic treatment of processions as a starting point for analysis. First, we noted in the second part of this book that Aquinas begins his treatment of the mystery of the divine nature by the consideration of divine simplicity, and he completed his consideration with the study of God's immanent life of knowledge and love, in its immanent and transitive activity. He moves then from the consideration of God in his transcendence and alterity to the consideration of God's personal traits, so as to understand God's personal nature in a non-anthropomorphic fashion. The study of the persons of the Trinity contains parallels. Aquinas begins by analyzing the relations that may obtain in God in a way wholly other than they do in us, so as to preserve a sense of the transcendence and alterity of the Trinitarian personal communion, and only subsequently considers the persons in their distinction, their communion or mutual inherence, and finally, their economic missions, at the end

2. On this order of Trinitarian reasoning, see especially Aquinas, *De pot.*, q. 10, a. 3; and *ST* I, q. 40, aa. 1–4.

of his analysis. The order of consideration is not impersonal—quite the contrary: Aquinas wants to underscore that the three-person God who engages with us in the missions of the Son and the Spirit is the one transcendent God whose nature is incomprehensible and whose personal communion is ineffably distinct from that of any human community.

Second, Aquinas's approach will give rise to a structure of nested relations, in which the immanent relationality of the three persons is the prior foundation for all of God's relations to creation. The former relations are eternal and characterize God necessarily, while the latter are not, since creative and redemptive activities emanate from the Trinity freely. In other words, the eternal relations of the Father to his Word and to the Spirit are the inner ground or basis of all that occurs in God when he relates to us in creation and in the order of salvation. The Father creates all things in his Word and in his Spirit, and reveals himself in the Word Incarnate and the sending of the Spirit of his Son into the world. All of this need not have occurred, but insofar as it does, it occurs only ever in and from the eternal processions of the Son and the Spirit, and as extrinsically expressive of them, without the creation or economy of salvation in any way constituting these relations. Indeed, the Trinitarian persons in their relations are immanently present to all creation without God's ever having to go outside himself, for in knowing and loving himself, God can freely create, know, and love all things. God can freely render his Trinitarian life immediately present to the world through the eternal activity of his Word and his Spirit, without in any way self-developing, or evolving in perfection, because that eternal activity is omni-comprehensive of creatures.

ANALOGIES FOR THE ETERNAL DERIVATION OF PERSONS IN GOD

In *ST* I, q. 27, a. 1, Aquinas simply asks "is there procession in God?" We have noted, in chapter 18, that the nature of God is characterized by transcendent knowledge and love, but this truth about the divine life of God in his transcendent oneness does not allow us to conclude that there is a real distinction of persons in God. We noted in chapter 20 that Aquinas thinks knowledge of God's internal mystery as Trinity is accessible to us only in virtue of divine revelation. However, this revelation is intrinsically intelligible, within faith, so the aim of Aquinas's analysis is to consider the mystery itself, so as to understand the claim that there is procession within the godhead.

In this and other texts Aquinas makes use of the twin classical errors of Arianism and Sabellianism to frame his discussion, and he presents them as opposed species within a common genus.[3] He argues that these two landmark heresies are incompatible in one respect but, in another respect, share an erroneous presupposition. In overcoming these heresies, we arrive at a true notion of interior procession in God. On Aquinas's account, Arius made the error of thinking that the Son must be a creature, distinct in essence from the Father, who alone is God. By way of contrast, the Sabellians rightly affirmed the divinity of the Son, claiming that the Son and the Father are essentially identical, both being equally God. In doing so, however, they also seemingly affirmed that the Father and the Son are not really distinct persons within God. They are understood instead as diverse economic manifestations of the one personal God. As Aquinas notes (and as I argued in chapter 7), both of these views share a common erroneous premise, namely, they presume implicitly that *a distinction of persons requires a diversity of essence.*[4] Were this premise true, then there would necessarily result either (1) one essence and one person or (2) a distinction of persons and a diversity of essences. This premise was rejected by the Council of Nicaea in 325 A.D. with its co-simultaneous affirmation of the Son's consubstantiality with the Father and his personal distinction from the Father, and consequently both Arianism and Sabellianism were deemed incompatible with Nicene orthodoxy.

However, Aquinas goes on to note that the common premise these classical errors share is itself based on a problematic presupposition about procession: *they both presume that procession implies exterior action.* As Aquinas states in q. 27, a. 1: "Careful examination shows that both of these opinions [i.e., Arius's and Sabellius's] take procession as meaning an outward act; hence neither of them affirms procession as existing in God Himself." By way of contrast then, precisely if we are to think about the Trinity in the im-

---

3. Aquinas juxtaposes Arianism and Sabellianism not only in *ST* I, q. 27, a. 1, but in several other texts. See *SCG* IV, cc. 5–9; *De pot.*, q. 9, aa. 8 and 9; *De rationibus fidei contra Saracenos, Graecos et Armenos ad cantorem Antiochenum* (*De rationibus fidei*), c. 9, and the analysis of Emery, *The Trinitarian Theology of St. Thomas Aquinas*, 55–57.

4. See *De pot.*, q. 9, a. 8, where Aquinas notes this common erroneous presupposition in the two positions.

manent life of God as ontologically and logically prior to the economy, we must be able to think about procession by way of interior action. But God is immaterial, as we have noted above in our consideration of the divine nature. In effect, then, the similitude we should employ for thinking about the mystery of the Trinity is that of *intellectual* procession. In human beings, operations of the intellect terminate *within* the acting subject, such that the action in question is immanent and not exterior. Furthermore, such human acts are immaterial in kind, since they imply immaterial features that specify the kinds of acts they are. Consequently, such processional activity (immanent intellectual activity) can be attributed to the inner immaterial life of God by proper analogy.

Accordingly, then, Aquinas draws the analogy to procession in God (of the Son from the Father and the Spirit from the Father and the Son) from the immanent spiritual life of intellectual natures, where the "logos" or concept is interior to the mind, and spiritual love is interior to the will. Of course, Aquinas is not pretending to discover this analogy, since it has clear roots in the New Testament and has already been subject to developed consideration in the Fathers before him, as well as in the reflection of other medieval thinkers. He does, however, develop his own interpretation of the tradition, which depends in part on his unique understanding of cognition and volition in human beings, and how these processes may be thought of by similitude to the processions in God.

Aquinas's theory of cognition is based on his original interpretation of Aristotle on abstraction and concept formation.[5] Each human person experiences a plurality of kinds of realities, such as trees, horses, and human beings, and from this multiplicity of singulars draws out a common notion or concept by which each distinct individual of a given kind is understood according to its essence.[6] This abstractive process occurs when the agent

5. Aquinas developed his mature theory of abstraction while thinking through the Trinitarian analogy of the begotten Word, especially in *SCG* IV, the *De potentia Dei*, and *ST* I. On Aquinas's evolution on this point, see Emery, *The Trinitarian Theology of Saint Thomas Aquinas*, 176–218; *Trinity in Aquinas* (Naples, Fla.: Sapientia Press, 2005), 71–120; Harm Goris, "Theology and Theory of the Word in Aquinas," in *Aquinas the Augustinian*, ed. Michael Dauphinais, Barry David, and Matthew Levering (Washington, D.C.: The Catholic University of America Press, 2007), 62–78; L.-B. Geiger, "Les rédactions successives de *Contra Gentiles* I, 53 d'après l'autographe," in *St. Thomas d'Aquin aujourd'hui*, ed. J. Y. Jolif et al. (Paris: Desclée de Brouwer, 1963), 221–40; Henri Paissac, *Théologie du Verbe: St. Augustin et St. Thomas* (Paris: Cerf, 1951). For a depiction of the contrasting views of Henry of Ghent and Duns Scotus, see Friedman, *Medieval Trinitarian Thought*, 75–93.

6. See *In Aristotelis librum De anima commentarium* (*In De anima*) III, c. 5, lec. 10; *SCG* II, c. 48; *ST* I, q. 79, a. 3, and q. 34, a. 1.

intellect present in our sensate experiences selects out the essential features of a given thing so as to apprehend them in a universal immaterial mode, independently of any particular material example.[7] Thus our concept of a human being as a rational animal can apply accurately to all human beings, who have ever, do actually, or will ever exist, both in and beyond our immediate experience, and independently of material features like age, height, weight, color, health, degrees of perfection, and so on. Aquinas thinks that when we grasp the essences of things abstractly we do so by a twofold process in which our intellect (1) is informed passively by an immaterial "intelligible species" that is abstracted from the senses, which the intellect then (2) appropriates actively so as to form from it an immaterial "concept" by which to consider reality anew.[8] While the intelligible species is impressed upon our minds, the concept proceeds from our minds. We go, in effect, from the experience of multiple humans to the passive intellectual reception of the essence of the human in an abstracted mode, to the generation of a concept of the human, by which we make use of that abstract knowledge actively to think about the multiple humans we encounter. The immaterial concept of the human *proceeds forth from our intellect as something immanent to it*, permitting us to grasp intellectually the essences of things around us. Moreover this generation of the concept occurs by way of a *relational procession*.

Aquinas's mature theory of human willing complements that of his understanding of human cognition.[9] If the intellect is assimilative of the essential features of realities around us, the will is inclinational. The will is the rational appetite, by which one is inclined to love the good in the things one first comes to know. Where human knowledge works through abstraction, the will tends toward the concrete good that is first known, and therefore loved.[10] Love, then, can also be thought about in processional terms: it is an immanent activity in us by which we tend to love the goodness of another.

7. See *ST* I, q. 79, aa. 3–4; q. 84, aa. 6–7; q. 85, a. 1; *SCG* II, c. 76.

8. See *ST* I, q. 85, a. 2; *In Ioan.* I, lect. 1, 25–26.

9. In his early works Aquinas treated love as kind of process by which one is informed or transformed by the other, while in the *SCG* IV, c. 19, and in later works such as *ST* I, q. 27, a. 4; q. 37, a. 1; and I-II, q. 26, a. 1, he develops the idea of love as an inclination and affection that the will undergoes in relation to an *impressio* that its beloved effects upon the will. See on this H.-D Simonin, "Autour de la solution thomiste du problème de l'amour," AHDLMA 6 (1931), 174–276; and Emery, *The Trinitarian Theology of St. Thomas Aquinas*, 66–69.

10. *SCG* IV, c. 19: "The beloved is not in the lover by a likeness of species, as the thing understood is present in the one understanding.... The beloved in the will exists as inclining, and somehow inwardly impelling the lover toward the very thing beloved."

This procession is also relational: love in human beings aims toward the good of the beloved.

By appeal to this two-fold psychological analogy, Aquinas will argue that we can discern real distinctions in the spiritual life of a subject without claiming that there are differentiations of substance or being. Once we begin here, the twin errors of Arianism and Sabellianism fall away: in response to each we can maintain that there can be a procession within a subject that is immaterial that does not imply a distinction of being or substance.

IS THERE GENERATION IN GOD?

In *ST* I, q. 27, a. 2, in inquiring whether there is generation in God, Aquinas notes that there are two kinds of physical generation in our world. The first is the physical generation pertaining to all material beings in which one being comes to be out of another. In this kind of generation, what might be potentially comes to be in actuality, as when dry wood is only potentially heated by fire, and subsequently changes gradually so as to actually catch fire and burn. The fire is actually generated by this process.

The second kind of generation is the generation of life. In the order of natural likeness, this entails the reproduction of the species. A living thing reproduces its natural kind, like an oak tree distributing oak seeds, that fall into the earth and that produce more oak trees. Aquinas defines generation in this second sense as follows, in q. 27, a. 2: generation in the domain of living things "signifies the origin of a living being from a conjoined living principle; and this is properly called birth [*nativitas*]. Not everything of that kind, however, is called begotten; but, strictly speaking, only what proceeds by way of similitude [*secundum rationem similitudinis*]."

Of course, living beings in our world also pass from potency to act as physical beings that are generated. Consequently, the passage from potency to act is characteristic of both kinds of generation mentioned above, but only the generation of living beings contains the note of generation unto *similarity* of nature. The oak tree can, after all, produce more oak trees, but it can also be cut down and used as wood for a fire.

In the first section of this chapter we noted that the eternal generation of the Word must be immaterial in kind and be immanent to the very life of God. Now, however, we have just examined two physical analogies, one from non-living things and one from those that are living. Why should these examples be relevant in this context? After all, we began with the psychological analogy precisely because it had to do with immaterial procession, not material generation. The reason is that the two forms of material generation, unlike that of the procession of a concept in the human person's mind, are *substantial* in nature.[11] The wood is altered or changed substantially by fire, and the seedling from the tree gives rise to a completely new substance of the same kind. The generation of the Word from the Father is an immaterial procession, *unlike* both these physical forms of procession. However, it is like the procession of one physical form from another because it implies something substantial: the communication of the very being and nature of God, from the Father to the Son. The Word is not other in being and essence from the Father, but is begotten substantially or essentially, as God from God. Furthermore, the Word is one in nature with the Father, and therefore is analogous to the seedling or living form begotten from another living thing.

How, then, is the Son's generation different from that of either physical non-living or living forms? In thinking about eternal generation in God, we have to keep in mind first and foremost that there is no potentiality in God. God is pure actuality, as we saw in part 2. He does not begin to be, or cease to be, nor does he progressively become more perfect. God is infinitely perfect from all eternity. He is "I am He who is," denoted in Exodus 3:14, which the Christian tradition reads as an indication of God's plenitude of being. Furthermore, God's life is a purely spiritual life, not a physical life, and his spiritual life is his spiritual act of understanding and loving. This means that God is a pure actuality of contemplation of his own divine essence, and love of his own divine goodness. Moreover, this contemplation and love are in no way egoistic, as we have noted, since, as God eternally contemplates the plenitude of his own infinite perfection, he also, with a gratuity that is pos-

11. *ST* I, q. 27, a. 2, ad 2: "The act of human understanding in ourselves is not the substance itself of the intellect; hence the word which proceeds within us by intelligible operation is not of the same nature as the source whence it proceeds; so the idea of generation cannot be properly and fully applied to it. But the divine act of intelligence is the very substance itself of the one who understands [cf. *ST* I, q. 14, a. 4]. The Word proceeding therefore proceeds as subsisting in the same nature; and so is properly called begotten, and Son. Hence scripture employs terms which denote generation of living things in order to signify the procession of the divine Wisdom, namely, conception and birth; as is declared in the person of the divine Wisdom, 'The depths were not as yet, and I was already conceived; before the hills, I was brought forth' [Prv 8:24]. In our way of understanding we use the word 'conception' in order to signify that in the word of our intellect is found the likeness of the thing understood, although there be no identity of nature."

sible only for him, gives being to all other things out of the superabundance of his own infinite goodness and love.

If, then, there is generation in God (by the procession of the Word from the Father), this does not entail any actuation of the divine essence, as if the generation were to make God more perfect or more divine. The Father possesses in himself from all eternity the plenitude of the divine perfection, and it is this actuality of divine perfection that he communicates to the Son. The Father does not become wise because he generates the Son. On the contrary, he generates the Son as the expression of his eternally perfect wisdom. The Father, in his eternal act of self-understanding, generates the Son as the Word that proceeds from himself, and in generating the Son, who is his perfect image, he communicates to him the fullness of the life of God. The Logos, or Word, as the Concept of the Father contains in himself the full plenitude of the godhead, the pure actuality and perfection of the divine nature.[12] Furthermore, since in God his act of understanding and his existence are the same, the Son possesses in himself the plenitude of the existence of God, receiving it eternally from the Father as his begotten Word.

We noted above that in created nature there is a generation of one physical thing from another as the actuation of a potency (flame consuming wood) and of one living thing from another according to species (the tree begetting its like kind). From our initial consideration of the analogy of immaterial begetting in God, we can see that there is generation of the second kind in God insofar as the Father, as a conjoined vital principle, imparts the totality of his simple substance to his Son and Word by way of an intellectual procession unto similarity of nature. It is like the first kind of generation only insofar as it pertains to being and not mere intentionality: it is a substantial generation. However, since God is pure act, there is no potency in the generation of the Son, which is utterly transcendent of any kind of physical begetting whatsoever, since it involves no reduction from potency to act. It follows from this that we must say that whatever is of pure actuality in God the Father is present also in God the Son. All that the Father has in his perfection as God (the divine life and essence) is communicated to the Son, who is one in being with the Father.[13] Aquinas speaks here of an "inti-

12. I will return to consideration of this theological analogy of the Word in God below, in chapter 26.

13. See *In Ioan.* I, lec. 1, 27; *ST* I, q. 34, a. 3; q. 27, a. 1, ad 2; *SCG* IV, c. 11.

mate and uniform procession" of the Son from the Father.[14] In accord with
the Nicene Creed, we can rightly confess that the Son is "God from God,
Light from Light, true God from true God."[15]

IS THERE A PROCESSION OF LOVE IN GOD?

We find, in the Prologue of St. John's Gospel, an identification of the Son
as the Logos or Word of God—and so as the product of an intellectual
procession—and this identification *ipso facto* implies that there is a second procession in God, and moreover, intimates that there is a certain order among the processions in the life of God. For, if the Son as the eternal
Word of the Father proceeds in analogy with the intellectual procession in
the life of the spiritual creature, this logically raises the question whether
there is another procession in the life of God that proceeds in analogy with
the immanent action of will in the intellectual creature. Moreover, as intel-

14. *ST* I, q. 27, a. 1, ad 3: "To proceed from a principle, so as to be something outside and distinct from that principle, is irreconcilable with the idea of a first principle; whereas an intimate and
uniform procession by way of an intelligible act is included in the idea of a first principle. For when
we call the builder the principle of the house, in the idea of such a principle is included that of his
art; and it would be included in the idea of the first principle were the builder the first principle of
the house. God, Who is the first principle of all things, may be compared to things created as the
architect is to things designed."

15. We can already see, even initially, in light of the eternal generation of the Son, how there
are Trinitarian images within the created order, according to begetting, that are perceptible only in
light of our revealed knowledge of the Trinity. The various physical realities that are successively
begotten of another in an almost infinite series of successions and in a complex developmental
history are a sign of the eternal and infinite generation of the Word from the Father, whose wisdom is expressed outwardly in the finite material generativity of the cosmos, with its immensity
and scope as a sort of physical icon of the begotten Wisdom. The world of living forms, with its
teeming vitality, struggle through competition, and progressive evolutionary development, is a
sign of the eternally begotten Word expressed in and through time, in a myriad of living forms,
each seeking to perfect life according to its species, and imitating eternity imperfectly by seeking
to perpetuate its like kind, the transmission of its begotten essence. The human person is a unique
image of God, as having in him- or herself the begotten concept and, by this very fact, the capacity
for the contemplation of the truth, including the first truth of God, so as to be able to "return to
God." But the human being is also able, as a person, to choose freely to communicate human life
with another person and with God, in a covenant of love, and so to contribute to a communion
of begotten persons. Finally and, in a sense, most especially, the human person is able to be an
instrumental communicator of divine grace, by sacramental activity and teaching, and in this way
to participate in the generation of divine life, in subservience to the grace of Christ. In all these diverse and irreducible senses of meaningful begetting we see the "play" of the Trinity that expresses
itself *ad extra* by bountifulness in the communication of its own goodness in analogical, finite, and
created forms.

lect precedes will, so too, if there is a second procession, this also likewise implies, then, an order of operations among the processions.

Aquinas takes precisely this approach, drawn from the analogy of the operations of intellect and will in the intellectual nature, in *ST* I, q. 27, a. 3. His manner of proceeding here is very simple but effective. First in the *sed contra* of the article, he presents evidence from John 15:16 that there is a procession of the Spirit from the Father, and he notes, based on John 14:16, that this procession cannot be identical with that of the Son. Theologically speaking, this first premise is non-controversial. Aquinas is simply establishing that there is an eternal procession of the Spirit in God. He then argues by a reduction of logical possibilities that the only manner in which this procession can be understood by genuine analogy as (1) immanent to God, (2) immaterial, and (3) distinct from a procession of intellectual Logos, is if the distinction can be understood in light of an analogy to spiritual love.

There are two processions in God; the procession of the Word, and another. In evidence whereof we must observe that procession exists in God, only according to an action which does not tend to anything external, but remains in the agent itself. Such an action in an intellectual nature is that of the intellect, and of the will. The procession of the Word is by way of an intelligible operation. The operation of the will within ourselves involves also another procession, that of love, whereby the object loved is in the lover; as, by the conception of the word, the object spoken of or understood is in the intelligent agent. Hence, besides the procession of the Word in God, there exists in Him another procession called the procession of love.[16]

The point of this argument is not to deduce the idea of the Holy Spirit as love from a consideration of the attributes of God (for if we consider the nature of God in abstraction from the mystery of the Trinity, we must say that the knowledge and love of God are mysteriously one in God).[17] Rather, the aim is to show, in light of revelation, that the procession of Spirit is intelligible for us in distinction from that of the Son only if we employ the analogy of love. This is the case because love alone offers us another analogy of immaterial kind, in distinction from intellectual understanding, and it is one that differs in relational origin, since love originates from knowledge. Therefore, the Spirit can be understood, by immaterial analogy to love, as immanent to God, distinct from the Word, and relationally originate from

16. *ST* I, q. 27, a. 3.
17. See, in *De pot.*, q. 9, a. 9, the developed rejection of such an idea.

the Word by way of procession. (We will return to this topic of love and re-lation in subsequent chapters.)

Moreover, he likewise reasons in a. 3, ad 3, that for this same reason there must be an order to these processions. We can love only what we first know, and spiritual love is the appetite of cognitive reason. Accordingly, there is a transcendent correlate in the life of God. The Holy Spirit, who is a per-son distinct from the Father and the Son, proceeds from the Father *and the Word*, just as love in a human being proceeds from knowledge. The Father eternally knows himself and thus generates the Son. The Father eternally loves the Son, and the Son loves the Father, whence proceeds the Holy Spir-it as the spirated love of the Father and the Son. In this way, based on an analogy of the relation of will to intellect in a spiritual creature, we see the first intimations of St. Thomas's teaching, in the *Summa*, on the *Filioque* as the procession of the Spirit from the Father *and* the Son.[18]

In *ST* I, q. 27, a. 4, Aquinas explains on the basis of the psychological analogy why the procession of the Holy Spirit is not also called generation. The intellect, he observes, works by way of assimilation. When we know something rightly, we bring it into ourselves, albeit in a conceptual mode.[19] Love, however, operates not by mode of assimilation (like the intellect), but by mode of inclination. In other words, we do not bring another person whom we love into ourselves when we love him or her. Rather, because we know the person, we begin to love that person, and in loving someone who is genuinely good, we are drawn to him or her. Our love for another person is not assimilative but rationally ecstatic, as it draws us outward toward the other in friendship. The goodness of the other, Aquinas notes, makes an imprint, or *impressio*, upon our wills. The Holy Spirit is not generated (as a concept is generated by the mind, an inward word). Rather, the Spirit is spirated, as love proceeds from the lover to the beloved. Thus, because this procession does not terminate in a kind of (intellectual) conception, it is for that reason also not an act of generation, but an act of love.

18. *SCG* IV, c. 24: "From the very fact of saying that the Holy Spirit proceeds by way of will and the Son by way of intellect, it follows that the Holy Spirit is from the Son. For love proceeds from a word: we are able to love nothing but that which a word of the heart conceives." For Aqui-nas's extended defense and explication of the *Filioque*, see *ST* I, q. 36, aa. 2–4. I will return to this subject below.

19. On the expansive character of the intellect in general, insofar as it is capable of taking into itself the forms of other things, see *ST* I, q. 14, a. 1.

We should note that Aquinas's argument presupposes that the persons in God act in virtue of the divine nature, as we argued in the last chapter. This means that when the Father generates the Son, he does so as the fruit of his eternal self-knowledge and love, and the same is true for the spiration of the Spirit from the Father and the Son. The Father eternally knows and loves himself in the simplicity and perfection of his pure actuality (in virtue of his divine nature as God), and in so doing he eternally generates the Word as the fruit of his self-understanding. So too, the Father and the Son, knowing one another fully (in virtue of the simple perfection of the divine nature), also love one another fully, and in doing so spirate the Holy Spirit. The analogy that is drawn of the two processions of the Son and Spirit, respectively, to immaterial activities of knowledge and love, stems not from distinct natural acts of the divine essence, but from distinct relations of origin. Knowledge proceeds immaterially from a knower, while love proceeds from both a knower and his knowledge.[20] In this way of thinking about the Trinity, the Son and Spirit can "contain" in themselves all that is in God by nature, including the fullness of divine knowledge and love that is in the Father, but they only ever possess this fullness of divine life from another, through immaterial procession. The Son has all that he is as God from the Father, and therefore is intelligible by similitude to a relational procession of knowledge, and the Spirit has all that he is as God from the Father and the Son, and therefore is intelligible by similitude to a relational procession of love.

CONCLUSION: CONDITIONS FOR THE POSSIBILITY OF A THEOLOGY OF THE IMMANENT TRINITY

Our aim in this chapter has been simple: to identify a properly analogical way of thinking about the immanent life of the Holy Trinity by similitude to human cognition and voluntary love. We have noted, in the previous chapter, that the nominal minimalism of the late medievals cast a pall of skepticism over this very idea, and this skepticism has significant consequences in modern theology. St. Thomas, however, offers us a viable model for the genuine theological use of the psychological analogy. At the term of these reasonings, then, we can cast an argument in dialectical terms back

---

20. See Aquinas's analysis of this point in *De pot.*, q. 10, a. 2, corp., ad 7, ad 11, and ad 17.

upon those who refuse the possible use of this analogy, so as to clarify what is at stake theologically.

Let us presuppose that all Trinitarian theologians wish to affirm that we know of the mystery of the Holy Trinity based on God's manifestation of his Trinitarian life to us in the economy, and that based on this manifestation we can come to know truly God's inner life of processions in itself as ontologically prior to and transcendent of the creation.

We can then state the following Thomistic claims:[21] We know what God is in himself only from the economy, and revealed in the economy are distinct personal processions in God. However, the only way we can render the claim that there are processions in God intelligible is to avert to the analogy of immanent activity, rather than transitive activity.

The reason for this is that transitive activity terminates outside a substance, and God is one in nature and substance, mysteriously transcendent of his creation. Consequently, anything produced from him by a transitive act is essentially distinct from him.[22] If we construe our analogies to God's inner life by reference to transitive actions, then, we will define God's inner life in terms of and by necessary reference to creatures. God, however, cannot be defined in himself by reference to creatures, either in virtue of his nature or in virtue of the eternal processions of Trinitarian persons.

If, however, we are bound to think of God by analogy to immanent activity, we can do so only from a similitude to immaterial procession, since God is not material and does not have any potency for development. However, there are only two immaterial activities in human creatures, those of understanding and love.

---

21. See Aquinas's arguments in *ST* I, q. 27, a. 5, and *De pot.*, q. 9, a. 9. As we have seen, Aquinas thinks that there is no positive rational demonstration of the existence of procession in God from the consideration of the nature of God or the divine attributes, as known philosophically. However, he does think that if there is procession in God, it is intelligible only by analogy to immaterial procession, meaning by analogy to intellect and will, and so consequently there cannot be more than two processions in God. Likewise, because God is simple in nature and perfect in act, if there are processions in God, God must communicate all that he is in these processions. Consequently, there can be only one generation of Word and only one spiration of Love in God, if there are such processions, and there cannot be a multiplicity of such.

22. *ST* I, q. 27, a. 1, ad 2: "Whatever proceeds by way of outward procession is necessarily distinct from the source whence it proceeds, whereas, whatever proceeds within by an intelligible procession is not necessarily distinct." This is why if the Son proceeds from the Father by a transitive act, so that the Son is distinct in being from the Father, the Father must in some sense cause the Son to exist. This seems to be the position of Richard Swinburne, in *The Christian God*, 153, 166–77. See the criticisms on this front of Hasker, *Metaphysics and the Tri-Personal God*, 147–54.

Therefore, if there are two truly distinct persons who proceed in God, who are intelligible only in light of the analogy of immanent activity by way of immaterial procession, then they will be intelligible only by similitude to immaterial understanding and love respectively.

The conclusion one can draw from this stark claim is twofold. On the one hand, we do truly have a proper analogy by which to understand the mystery of the immanent Trinitarian life of God. On the other hand, we have no others. This means, in turn, that if one wants to understand the Trinitarian persons in their distinctiveness without doing so by reference to immanent activity of an immaterial kind, one will do so inevitably by appeal to transitive activity. If one does not wish to posit an Arian or subordinationist account of the Son and Spirit, there are two other logical possibilities. One is to understand the constitution of relations within the Trinity in virtue of God's transitive actions in creation and redemption. This means in turn that the Trinitarian processions and relations will inevitably be intelligible in their formal specificity only insofar as they stand in real ontological relation to the history of creation.[23] The other logical possibility is to understand the persons as pre-constituted individuals who have merely transitive relations with one another prior to creation. In this case, there is no theology of procession as such. Instead the persons of the Trinity are depicted as three individual entities who freely entertain moral relations with one another and whose relationships are mere properties or accidents, metaphysically speaking.[24] In this case, however, the relations of the persons that are unveiled to us in the economy are not indicative of an inner life of procession in God.

Consequently, just insofar as the classical use of the psychological anal-

---

23. This is the pathway followed by most modern continental theologians. They certainly wish to avoid the conclusion that the processions of the Trinitarian persons are simply identical with the creation. Consequently, they posit that God exists in transcendence of his creation, freely creates, and freely relates to his creation in the economy. However, it is only in virtue of God's "transitive acts" within the economy that we come to know the eternal relations between the persons. In the absence of any possible immanent analogy, however, this implies that the activities of the distinct persons in the economy must characterize formally those features of the persons by which they are distinguished eternally. Since this is the case, the economic activities in question (a) entail that God acquires real relations to his creation wherein the persons are not only manifest in but also *inwardly determined by* their relation to creation, and (b) real distinctions of natural qualities then unfold between the persons, since the persons must exhibit properties in the economy that are distinct from one another by nature precisely so as to be distinguishable.

24. This is the pathway taken by a certain kind of social Trinitarianism, common among those analytic philosophers who reject a relationalist account of personhood in the Trinity.

ogy is abandoned, God's immanent life will have to be understood as constituted in some sense by and through the economy. Or else the relations of
the Trinitarian persons in the economy will not be understood as expressive of an order of eternal processions between the persons. Either outcome
entails that our first premise will also need to be abandoned: that we can
come to know truly from the economy God's inner life in itself as ontologically prior to and transcendent of the creation and the economy. Without
the psychological analogy, then, Trinitarian theology is compromised in its
essential nature.

We can also state the idea positively, as a way of acknowledging the advantages of the Thomistic approach in a modern context.[25] If we do have a
genuine analogy of procession of the inner life of God, then we can understand how God has truly revealed himself to us in the economy, and how it
is God himself, in his transcendent nature and mystery, who is truly present
in all that he does in creation and redemption. Indeed, it is only because we
do have a genuine psychological analogy for the processional life of the immanent Trinity that we are also able to articulate a genuine theology of the
authentic revelation of God in the divine economy. Far from being opposed
to each other, the appeal to the psychological analogy and the study of the
revelation of God in the economy are mutually implicating features of a genuine Trinitarian theology.

25. To be clear, my argument here is meant to conclude to the necessity of the psychological analogy as a theological analogy for procession as immanent spiritual activity in God, not
to the necessity of a distinctively Thomistic interpretation of the psychological analogy! Broadly
speaking, the analogy is adopted by thinkers as diverse as Justin Martyr, Athanasius, Gregory of
Nazianzus, Augustine, Bonaventure, Aquinas, Scotus, Robert Bellarmine, Philip Melanchthon,
and most reformed scholastics, as well modern theologians as diverse as Jonathan Edwards, John
Henry Newman, Matthias Scheeben, John Meyendorff, Joseph Ratzinger, and many others. The
Thomistic account, therefore, represents only one approach among many in this respect. I am suggesting, however, that it provides a particularly well-construed and balanced account.

23

Trinitarian Relations and Notional Names of Persons

In the previous chapter, we began with the truth of revelation that there are processions in God, and that these spiritual processions are two: the eternal procession of the Word by generation, and the eternal procession of the Holy Spirit by spiration, where the Spirit is a spirated person, who is the love of the Father and the Son.

In this present chapter, we are going to consider how, if there are processions in God, then there truly are relations of origin in God.[1] If the Son eternally proceeds from the Father, and if the Spirit eternally proceeds from the Father and the Son, then, as Aquinas observes in ST I, q. 28, a. 1, there is a real relation, an eternal relativity, of the Father to the Son, and of the Son to the Father, and of the Father and Son to the Holy Spirit, and likewise of the Holy Spirit to the Father and Son.

This also means, however, as Aquinas stresses in article 2, that God simply is this relationality, since there are no accidental properties in God. What differentiate the persons, then, are precisely their relations of origin with respect to one another. Moreover, because the divine essence is wholly in each person, there is nothing in one person that is not in the other, except the relational mode of being, in virtue of which a person or persons communicate the divine life to another or derive it from another.

Our study in this chapter of the divine relations and the related idea of notional names (divine names pertaining only to one person) will provide

1. For historical background and conceptual discussion of real relations in the Trinity in Aquinas, see Emery, *The Trinitarian Theology of St. Thomas Aquinas*, 78–102.

us with a basis for thinking about the mystery of the persons in relational terms, in other words, the divine persons as what Aquinas calls "subsistent relations,"[2] a subject that we will address directly in the next chapter.

Distinct Types of Relations

In order to determine what it means for there to be real relations in God, we must first distinguish real relations from logical relations.[3] Relation signifies reference to another, by which there is established a connection between two or more things.[4] Aquinas notes that relations can be of three kinds. There are relations that are *real* (in which two or more realities are really connected or related in virtue of ontological properties that they possess). There are relations of *mere reason* (which are based on comparisons of things in the human mind alone). And there are so-called pairs of *mixed relations* (in which one thing is really relative to another, but the second reality is not relative to the first except in our way of thinking).[5] Real relations between two entities obtain when there is an ontological connection that emerges between the two that gives rise to a relationship. The man and the woman who are truly in love are really related to one another ontologically in a myriad of ways, having to do with habits of personal exchange, mutual love, emotion, spatial proximity, and common activity. As we will see below, such relations are typically based upon relations of action and passion, or the comparable quantities of diverse entities. The man and the woman love one another. They become parents of a child, whom they conceive, who is related to them, as its parents. The mother truly gives birth to her children. One child is truly taller than another. The relations in question always are properties of substances and inhere in them in virtue of these "prior" properties of action, passion, and quantity, present in substantial entities. Relations are thus secondary and derived properties: the "accidents of accidents," and therefore are the most fragile and derivative of beings.

A logical relation, by way of contrast, is one constructed by the mind

---

2. See *ST* I, q. 29, a. 4, where Aquinas develops the idea of divine person as subsistent relation. This idea will be discussed more fully in the next chapter.

3. In the *ST*, Aquinas develops the distinction between real and logical relations first in *ST* I, q. 13, a. 7, and then again in q. 28, a. 1.

4. See Aristotle, *Meta.* 5.17 (1020b26–1021b11); Aquinas, *In V Meta.*, lec. 17, 1001–32.

5. *ST* I, q. 13, a. 7.

that permits us to think about reality by grouping or pairing together notions of reality. Thus, for example, if I think about a mathematical equation
(such as the proverbial 2 + 2 = 4), this is about a series of relationships that
have to do with quantity, but there is no particular quantitate entity that
the terms refer to in reality (just by the mere fact that I am thinking about
them). The terms refer rather to one another, and are therefore related in
reason alone. Or if I think abstractly of a person being the mother of a child,
this set of mental relations by which I relate the idea of mother to that of
child, is not the same as a real relation, in which one person is in fact really related to her child.[6] Another example of a purely logical relation is the
pairing of the relations of genera and species with animal and man, respectively. Every man really is an animal, not a species distinct from a genus, but
in thinking about the species and genus respectively we can consider the
human being under two aspects, through the medium of a logical relation.[7]
In all of these examples, we are constructing relations of reason through the
comparison of ideas.

Pairs of mixed relations occur when relations are not reciprocal or sym-
metrical, since one of the two terms is really related to the other but this
second reality is not rendered truly ontologically relative to the first. Aquinas gives the example of a person purposefully walking to the side of a Roman pillar, thus really relating to it in action, while the pillar, in turn, does
not relate by an activity to the person in question. Likewise, a person who
is studying human nature philosophically relates really to the subject matter
and has his mind changed by the consideration of it, but the subject matter
itself is not affected by the investigation of the philosopher.[8] More signif-

6. *ST* I, q. 28, a. 1, corp., and ad 4: "Relations which result from the mental operation alone
in the objects understood are logical relations only, inasmuch as reason observes them as existing
between two objects perceived by the mind. Those relations, however, which follow the operation
of the intellect, and which exist between the word intellectually proceeding and the source whence
it proceeds, are not logical relations only, but are real relations; inasmuch as the intellect and the
reason are real things, and are really related to that which proceeds from them intelligibly; as a
corporeal thing is related to that which proceeds from it corporeally." Philosophers who doubt the
existence of real relations are generally hard pressed to explain the nature of efficient causality in
cases of either mixed or real relations, such as how a mother really relates to her child ontologically
in child-bearing or how the mind truly depends upon its subject matter of study in the external
world for the generation of understanding.

7. Aquinas gives this example for logical relations in *ST* I, q. 28, a. 1.

8. *SCG* IV, c. 14: "For the relation of knowledge to the knowable follows on the action of the
knower; not, of course, on the action of the knowable. The knowable maintains itself as it is in
itself, both when it is understood and when it is not understood.... A like situation appears in the
case of right and left. For there is in animals a distinction of the powers from which the relation of

icant examples arise in theology: the creation is wholly relative to God the Creator, since it receives all of its being from him, but God is not ontologically relative to his creation, even if we speak rightly of God freely relating to his creation by acts of knowledge and love.[9] The human nature of the Son of God made man in virtue of the hypostatic union is rendered entirely relative to his person and to his divine nature, so that it is expressive of his person and subordinate to his divine nature, but his divine person and nature are not rendered in any way ontologically relative to or essentially redefined by his human nature.[10]

Intellectual, logical relations, accordingly, are relations fabricated in the mind in order to think about reality. There are, indeed, real relations of ontological dependency between creatures and God, but not the converse, since God is not causally dependent on his creatures, for which reason Aquinas says that there is only a "relation of reason" of God to creatures. However, the relations within the Triune God himself are in point of fact *real relations* (to deny this would be to fall back into Sabellianism). The point here, then, is that the relations in God are not something produced by the human mind but are instead something that obtains in the reality of God himself. Our aim in what follows, then, is to explore theologically the nature of these real, intra-divine relations in more detail.

Real Relations in Aristotle and Aquinas

In order to define more closely what we mean by "relations," let us return to an account of the diverse genera of being, as taken up by Aquinas from Aristotle's *Categories*, which we discussed in chapter 12. The diverse genera of being fall into two overarching categories: substance and accidents. The first grouping, substances, consists of singular subjects (like Agatha, or Lucy) of a given nature (in this case, human beings). The second grouping, accidental being, consists of the properties of substances and includes

right and left arises, on which account such a relation truly and really exists in the animal.... Inanimate things, to be sure, which lack the powers just mentioned, have no relation of this kind really existing in them.... Hence, the same column is called now right, now left, inasmuch as the animal is compared to it in a different situation."

9. The non-reciprocity of the relations between God and creatures was discussed in chapter 16. On the non-reciprocal relativity of God to creatures, see *ST* I, q. 28, a. 1, ad 3; and q. 13, a. 7. We may think of God in relation to creatures mentally, but God is not really dependent upon creatures ontologically.

10. See *ST* III, q. 2, a. 7. I have offered some analysis of the consequences of this teaching for one's understanding of the hypostatic union in my *The Incarnate Lord*, chap. 1.

quantities, qualities, relations, actions, passions, habits, time, place, and position or environment. As already noted, real relations between substances
in our world, as we experience them, always have a basis *only in other categories of being*. Relations between beings are accordingly based upon various
accidental categories. Thus:

1. *Quantities*: These are relationships of quantity, based upon the quantity of extension and number, as well as place, time, or position. For example,
we can compare the relative size of two horses, their shape, extension, and
weight, but we can also talk about their relative position to one another in
place and whether one runs faster than the other. We can also speak here of
degrees of perfection in quantitative terms. Albert was a greater mathemati-
cian than Stephen. It is difficult to say whether Jens is a greater banjo player
than Tony. These are relations based on quality, real relations of similitude
or resemblance, or degrees of difference.

2. *Action and passion (a categorial mode of being derivative of quality)*:
These are relations based on one thing or one faculty acting or producing
some effect. A child is really related to his or her father and mother, because
the child has been given life (i.e., substantially generated), cared for, and
educated by them. There is a real relation between the cricket bat and the
ball when the two make contact, or the car and the person who is driving
it. There is a real relation between the human mind that is actively thinking, and the conceptual thoughts it is producing. Or, again, two persons are
genuine friends because they have real affection for one another, enjoy one
another's company, and for that reason habitually do things together. There
exists in their case, then, a real relation of mutual love.

In all of this, it is important to note right from the outset that real relations
in general always imply (1) two terms really distinct from one another, existent "toward" one another in some way, and (2) terms that are dependent
upon a foundation, and existing in the same order.[11] Accordingly, there is a
reciprocity in being that arises whenever we are speaking about real relations.

If we pass, by analogy, then, into the consideration of the life of God,
among the different forms of relations founded on accidental categories,

---

11. I am summarizing points made by Aquinas in *De pot.*, q. 7, a. 1, ad. 9; *De pot.*, q. 7, a. 11, corp.;
ST I, q. 13, a. 7, corp.

which type of relationality is indicated when one speaks of Trinitarian relations? To answer this question, we need to first recall that the Trinitarian
relations are expressed in the immaterial processions of the persons from
one another. Let us ask, then: what is the foundation of the processions?
Why do we attribute relationality to the persons of God, the Father, Son,
and Holy Spirit?

The first thing to note is that such attribution *cannot be quantitative.*
There is no quantity in God. It is not as if God the Father generated a physical son of such and such a height and corporeal weight. In light of the theology of the divine nature, which we explored in the previous section of this
book, such an idea is absurd, as it stands in contradiction to the mystery of
the divine nature, which is immaterial. This attribution also *cannot be qualitative.* It is true that we may compare the degrees of perfection in created
realities, which we speak of in quantitatively comparative terms of similar,
greater, and lesser. We may recall here, however, that there are no qualities
in any of the divine persons that the others do not possess entirely, with an
identical degree of infinite perfection. The divine goodness, wisdom, omnipotence, and the rest are equally in the Father, Son, and Holy Spirit. So,
we cannot say, for example, that the Father is differentiated in virtue of his
degree of perfection in unbegottenness or power, or that the Son is wiser,
or the Spirit more loving. The three are equal in perfection, power, wisdom,
and love.[12] They are each the one God, each having the full possession of
the unique godhead.

If the basis of the distinction of persons can be neither quantitative nor
conducted on the basis of degrees of qualification, this leaves only *action* as
a possible foundation for this distinction. What kind of action, then, are we
indicating? The answer, of course, is found in the immanent action of the
processions, which we examined in the previous chapter, namely, eternal

---

12. See on this point, Aquinas, *De pot.,* q. 8, a. 1, where he appeals to Dionysius, *Divine Names,*
c. 11, where the latter affirms the perfection of the divine paternity, noting that the Father enjoys a
perfect union with the Son as a result of the perfect communication of divine life from the one to
the other. Likewise, Augustine has considered this problem already in *The Trinity,* bks. 6 and 7, in
connection with 1 Cor 1:24: "Christ the power of God and the wisdom of God." Augustine concludes in 7.3 that all qualitative terms for the divinity are in fact substance terms, and the substance
terms (i.e., those which do not express relation) apply to each of the persons: "So Father and Son
are together one wisdom because they are one being, and one by one they are wisdom from wisdom as they are being from being. And therefore it does not follow that because the Father is not
the Son nor the Son the Father, or one is unbegotten, the other begotten, that therefore they are
not one being; for these names only declare their relationships. But both together are one wisdom
and one being, there where to be is the same as to be wise."

generation and spiration in God. The eternal processions of the Son from the Father and of the Spirit from the Father and the Son establish the real relations of origin that exist between the truly distinct divine persons in God. The Father, then, is in real relation to the Son as the principle of the Son. In virtue of his paternity, he is eternally generating the Son, through the act of his own understanding, as his begotten Word. The Son is in real relation to the Father (and so eternally relative to the Father) because he is eternally generated by the Father. His is the real relation of filiation. The Father and the Son are in real relation to the Holy Spirit as the principle of the Spirit through spiration. Likewise, the Spirit is eternally relative to the Father and the Son, as one really proceeding from the Father and the Son as the mutual spiration of love they share between them.

This affirmation of real relations within the divinity, however, poses a problem. Relation as an accident inheres in a substance as a property of a substance. How can there be real relations in God if relations are accidents (properties) dependent upon substances (and frequently on more than one substance)? Moreover, relations in created beings are the most fragile and imperfect of all accidents. They frequently come and go even while other properties endure. Consequently, we must say that if there are real relations in God, then there is a way that relationality in God is utterly different from relationality in human persons. One person may be related to another person who is currently speaking to him, but if that person ceases speaking to him, the particular relational situation ceases to be and another comes to pass. But in God the real relations of the persons are not only eternal but are in some way constitutive of what the persons are. The Father, Son, and Spirit are eternally relative as such. As we will see, this idea points us toward the mystery of the divine persons as "subsistent relations."

RELATIONS AND ESSENCE ARE
IDENTICAL IN GOD

In *ST* I, q. 28, a. 2, Aquinas takes up the question of the identity of relations and essence in God. To understand this identity, it is important to recall that relations as we experience them in all the ordinary realities around us imply two distinct aspects: (1) two terms really distinct from one another, existent "toward" one another in some way, and (2) those terms' dependence upon a foundation, by which the terms exist in the same order.

The latter aspect, the foundation, is that of a property of a substance, either quantity or action and passion.

In his treatment of relation in God, Aquinas rightly seeks to understand the differences that must obtain in God due to the distinction between the divine nature and creatures, and the distinction of divine relations and persons in comparison with human relations and persons. He is conscious in this context of the previous theological position of the twelfth-century Chancellor of Paris, Gilbert of Poitiers, who sought in good will to understand the relations of origin in the persons of God after the likeness of human relations, and so posited that the relations in God are extrinsic to God's essence. The problem with Gilbert's position is that one might infer from his idea of the relations in God that they are simply unreal, because what does not pertain to God essentially is not God.[13] Bernard of Clairvaux objected to Gilbert's theory based on an Augustinian appeal to the divine simplicity, and Gilbert's position was condemned at the Council of Reims in 1148.[14] Likewise, we have also seen that at the Fourth Lateran Council the language of Joachim of Fiore was eschewed, in which the actions of begetting and spirating were attributed to the essence of God. Although the Council's criticism did not have to do with the language of relations as such, it is clear that Joachim's theory suggests that there are relations that emerge within the nature of God itself, seemingly as accidental properties of the divine essence, by which it is respectively active and passive under distinct aspects in the process of generation and spiration.

In the first of these errors, the relations appear (under the demarcations of Thomistic ontology) as properties wholly extrinsic to the essence of God. In the second, the relations appear as arising between diverse natural states within God. The former position gives us persons who are not characterized essentially by relations of origin, while the second gives us a distinction of persons that arises from distinct natural activities of the divine nature. The latter view implies a complex divine nature, not entirely unlike that of a human nature. Aquinas rightly wants to procure a theory of relation in God

13. See Gilbert of Poitiers, *Expositio in Boecii de Trinitate*, 1.5, nos. 42–42, in *The Commentaries on Boethius by Gilbert of Poitiers*, ed. N. Häring (Toronto: PIMS, 1966), and the analysis of Emery, *The Trinitarian Theology of St. Thomas Aquinas*, 90–91. Aquinas, in *De pot.*, q. 8, a. 2, characterizes the doctrine of Gilbert as leading to the conclusion that there are no real relations in God, whether subsistent or accidental.

14. See G. R. Evans, *Bernard of Clairvaux* (Oxford: Oxford University Press, 2000), 75–77, 123–27.

that avoids either of these pitfalls. In this he will follow Albert the Great, who came up with the notion of subsistent relations, while commenting upon Dionysius the Areopagite.[15] It is significant that the Dominican school crafted an analogical way of thinking about divine relations in God while paying attention to the apophatic and superlative dimensions of Dionysian thought. God is wholly other than us in his relationality but not for that reason unintelligible. In his eminent and hidden perfection, God is especially and incomprehensibly relational and personal.

We have noted already that in creatures, relations imply (1) two terms really distinct from one another, existent "toward" one another in some way, and (2) a foundation in another property of a substance, such as an action or passion. Of these two implications of relation, the first sense of the word "relation" obtains in God fully, namely, that of a being "toward" another. There is real relationality in the persons toward or from one another through the processions of action and passion, and this relationality is eternal. The second sense, however, must be modified when we speak of God. In virtue of the simplicity of the divine nature, there are no accidents in God, and so whatever is in God must be the very substance and essence of God. For this reason, the relations of the persons are not a characteristic or accidental property of God but are identical with God's very essence.[16] In ST I, q. 28, a. 2, Aquinas states this "substantial being-toward-another" in God as follows: "Now whatever has an accidental existence in creatures, when considered as transferred to God, has a substantial existence.... Thus it is manifest that relation really existing in God is really the same as His essence and only differs in its mode of intelligibility; as in relation is meant that regard to its opposite which is not expressed in the name of essence."

Mysteriously, then, we must say that God simply *is* the relational life of the Father, Son, and Holy Spirit. The relations are identical with the essence, and yet the term "relation" draws out the added note of a being-toward-another, which is not expressed by the word "essence." Understood in this sense, the notion of relation in God contains all that is prop-

15. See the studies of F. Ruello, "Une source probable de la théologie trinitaire de St Thomas," *Recherches de science religieuse* 43, no. 1 (1955): 104–28; "Le commentaire inédit de saint Albert le Grand sur les *Noms divins*. Preséntation et aperçus de théologie trinitaire," *Traditio* 12 (1956): 231–314; Gilles Emery, "La relation dans la théologie de saint Albert le Grand," in *Albertus Magnus: zum Gedenken nach 800 Jahren: Neue Zugänge, Aspekte, und Perspektiven*, ed. W. Senner (Berlin: Akademie Verlag, 2001): 455–65.

16. ST I, q. 28, a. 2. See also SCG IV, c. 14; De pot., q. 8, a. 2.

er to the divine persons: they are each relational, and they each contain in themselves the plenitude of the godhead.

If this theory adequately denotes something given to us to know by divine revelation and is non-contradictory (which I take it is the case), then Aquinas has successfully articulated a proper analogy for relational personhood in God that is non-metaphorical. It is based first on a genuine likeness to Trinitarian persons that is found in relations between beings, as we experience them in creatures under the first of two aspects: that of being toward (*via causalitatis*). However, we must deny in God's relations a second aspect of created relations, that of being rooted in a substance and prior property. In Dionysian terms, this constitutes an apophatic qualification (*via negationis*). Our acknowledgment of the transcendent alterity of the relations in God points us, then, toward the absolute novelty and perfection of the Trinitarian relations (*via eminentiae*). The persons in God are wholly relative in all that they are. They are subsistent relations who communicate to one another or receive from one another the plenitude of the divine life. This is a point to which I will return in the next chapter.

NOTIONS FOR THE PERSONS
AND ESSENTIAL TERMS

Essential Terms and Notional Terms

As we have seen, Aquinas follows Fathers of the Church, such as Gregory of Nazianzus, whom we studied in part 1, in distinguishing the persons according to their relations of origin, which are manifest or instantiated in the processions. Indeed, this is the unique way to distinguish the persons. The Son is eternally distinct from the Father because he proceeds from the Father, originating from him as his eternal Word. The Spirit is eternally distinct from the Father and the Son because he proceeds from the Father and the Son as their spirated Love.

From this foundation in relations of origin, medieval theology then developed a distinction between *essential terms* for God and *notional terms* that we can use to name God. Essential terms for God are the "divine names" that we considered in part 2 of this book, terms like simplicity, perfection, goodness, and so on.[17] These pertain to the divine essence and, as such, are

---

17. This would include the whole range of divine attributes that we discussed throughout part 2, originally found in the *De Deo Uno* treatise.

attributed to all three persons: The Father is perfect, good, and wise, the Son likewise is perfect, good, and wise, as is the Holy Spirit.

Notional terms for God, by way of contrast, pertain to the *persons uniquely in their respective distinctness*, and this *according to the relations of origin*. To call the second person the "Son" who is eternally generated from the Father indicates something proper to one of the persons, and so points to the term of one of the relations of origin, in this case, to the Son's filiation from the Father—the counterpart to which is the Father's paternity. In virtue of his filiation, is Son eternally relative to but also distinct from the Father. Notional terms, unlike the essential terms, accordingly point to something *proper* to each of the persons in their distinction from one another.

Aquinas gives perhaps his clearest articulation of notional terms in *ST* I, q. 32, a. 3. There, he defines a notion (*notio*) as "the proper idea whereby we know a divine Person." As the distinction of the persons arises from their origin, and origin includes both the idea of whence and wither, so a divine Person can be known both in terms of his origin (i.e., his relation to his principle), and in terms of what proceeds from him. From this, there result the five notions of medieval theology.[18] As the Father is from no one, so he is known by the notion of (1) *innascibility* or *unbegottenness*, but also (2) *paternity*, insofar as he is Father to the Son, and (3) *common spiration*, insofar as, together with the Son, he spirates the Spirit. Likewise, the Son is known by the notions of both (4) *filiation* and *common spiration*, and the Spirit by (5) *procession*, the notions thereby totaling five.[19]

Essential Acts and Notional Acts

Earlier, we indicated that there is a basic distinction between God's common activity *ad extra*, and his immanent spiritual operations of knowledge and love. This distinction acquires significance again here in a new way by

18. These notions arise especially in the theology of Peter Lombard's *Sentences* so as to become a commonplace in medieval Trinitarian theology.

19. In differentiation from the other four notions, innascibility does not, strictly speaking, denote a relation. Rather, it indicates that the Father uniquely has no term from which he comes, whereas paternity and common spiration point to his role as principle of the Son and Spirit. This is why there are five *notiones* but only four relations. Aquinas calls these relations of opposition, since they are intelligible only in direct reference to one another according to opposite mutual self-definitions. *ST* I, q. 28, a. 3: "The idea of relation, however, necessarily means regard of one to another, according as one is relatively opposed to another. So as in God there is a real relation, there must also be a real opposition. The very nature of relative opposition includes distinction."

contributing to our understanding of the distinction between *essential acts* and *notional acts* in God.

The former kind of acts are acts that are common to the persons. If we call them essential acts this does not mean that they are not personal acts but rather that they are acts of all three persons, which they perform in virtue of their common nature. All of God's actions *ad extra* fall into this category, since they are acts of the Trinity, manifest, for example, by God's actual communication of being to the created world, or his communication of grace to human beings. Because such acts are common to the three persons, they proceed from one principle and so are equally attributable to the Father, Son, and Holy Spirit, even if we might appropriate this or that action to one of the persons so as to indicate something properly personal regarding the way in which he possesses the divine essence within the Trinitarian relations. (I will return to this topic of Trinitarian appropriations in a chapter below.)

Notional acts, however, pertain to the immanent essential activity of God, his interior spiritual operations insofar as they terminate in the production of the divine persons. Earlier, in the *De Deo Uno* treatise, when we considered God's immanent vital operations of knowledge and love, we could not conclude at that juncture that these immanent acts terminated in the production of proprietors of the divine nature. By natural reason, we know only *that* God has and indeed is his own immanent perfect life of knowledge and love. This can be said from the consideration of God's creatures and by analogical comparison with them, and such a statement is consonant with the revelation of the one God and Creator given to us by the Old Testament, where there are only intimations of Trinitarian revelation. However, we cannot say either on the basis of philosophical reason or from Old Testament characterizations of the life of God as "personal" that God's life is Trinitarian. As we have noted, it is a mystery that transcends us and that is made manifest perfectly only in the New Testament revelation.

However, in light of the knowledge of real processions and real relations in God that is proffered to us by the New Testament, we are enabled to move beyond our earlier considerations of God's vital acts of knowledge and love and provide a more ultimate rendering of the immanent life of God. Above, we spoke of the notions that designate the persons, such as paternity and filiation, spiration and procession. However, we can also speak of *notional acts* that characterize the life of God, and therefore qualify how we understand God's life of intellect and will.[20]

So, for example, if we think of the essential activity of God (abstracting from consideration of the Trinity) we can rightly say that God is subsistent wisdom, the operation of contemplation, perfect goodness, and so forth. However, in light of the Trinitarian knowledge of God's mystery, we can also say that God the Father knows and contemplates himself and, from his act of self-understanding, generates his Word, in whom is the fullness of the divine life. The Father loves the Son and the Son loves the Father, and in so doing they spirate the eternal Spirit. We can, in effect, reduplicate the essential acts that pertain to God's immanent life as notional acts.[21] The unknown and transcendent life of knowledge and love that characterizes God is in fact a Trinitarian life. How can we better understand this?

As we saw earlier, God is essentially identical with the medium of his own knowledge. He knows himself through himself. In light of the consideration of the procession of the Word, we can now qualify this initial statement in a Trinitarian fashion. The Father knows himself in virtue of his divine essence, and therefore is, in some real sense, his very act of understanding, a transcendent mystery of subsistent contemplation. However, revelation teaches us that in knowing himself he also eternally generates the Son as his begotten Word, in whom is present the fullness of his divine life and being. Because the Son is eternally generated as the Word who possesses in himself the plenitude of the divine life and being, he also possesses the fullness of God's act of knowledge. All that the Father knows is in the Son, and all that the Son knows is in the Father. The Father knows all that is in the Son and the Son knows all that is in the Father. Consequently, we can also say that the Father creates the world through the subsistent Wisdom who is his Son.

20. On notional action in general, as applicable to both the generation of the Word and the spiration of the Spirit, see *ST* I, q. 41. The persons are distinguished by their relations of origin, therefore wherever we signify divine persons we must signify their notional acts (a. 1). The persons do not proceed in God by an act of the will of the Father (the heresy of Arius) but naturally, by mode of intellect and will (a. 2). The notional acts are rightly said to proceed from the persons, as the Father generates the Son, and they together spirate the Spirit (a. 3). We can say in a qualified sense that persons in God have the power to generate or spirate, so as to mean that the persons are the principles of an act (a. 4). Strictly speaking, however, the ascription of notional power to a person in God denotes the essence of that person, by which the person acts as the principle of another, and does not formally denote the relation as such (a. 5).

21. On Aquinas's reduplication of essential acts of the Trinity *as* notional acts, see for example, *De pot.*, q. 9, a. 9, *SCG* IV, cc. 11, 14, and 19.

Moreover, as we said that God is essentially love, we can now *also* say that there is in God the notional act of the Father and Son, who act eternally as the spirator of the Spirit, who proceeds from them (again, a notional act) as their love. In this eternal act of processional spiration the Father and the Son love one another naturally, and in so doing give the Spirit to have in himself all that is in God in virtue of their deity, the fullness and plenitude of the divine life and being. All that the Father and the Son love in one another is naturally communicated to the Spirit, who contains in himself the plenitude of divine goodness. The Father creates the world through the exemplarity of his Son, the eternal Word and Wisdom who proceeds forth from him, but he also creates the world in and through his Spirit of Love, from which all creation comes forth, so as to manifest the goodness of God. These two conceptual "levels" of reflection (God considered in his essential acts and in his notional acts) do not contradict one another, but they are distinct for our way of thinking, because we must maintain simultaneously the unity of essence of the Trinity and the distinction of persons, by way of their processions and relations of origin.[22]

CONCLUSION: THE EMERGENCE OF TWO CONVERGENT RELATIONAL ANALOGIES

We noted above that Aquinas follows Albert the Great in crafting a theory of relations that allows him to avoid two ambient errors of his own epoch, one that would see relation as an exterior feature of the divine essence and one that would see relations as arising from activities of the divine essence. To do this he has to rethink relations in God in terms of subsistence, so that the persons are themselves understood as relational in all that they are, and as able to communicate or to receive divine life from one another based

22. God's knowledge and love, which God possesses in virtue of his nature, are truly identical, not really distinct, as is also the case for his essential act of knowledge and his essential act of love. By contrast, the notional acts pertain primarily *to persons*, not to the nature of God, even if they implicate the nature of God in some way. Thus, what we have just affirmed about the generation of the Son and spiration of the Spirit does not entail distinct essential activities of the divine nature (distinct essential acts of knowledge and love). Rather, the Father in knowing and loving himself, in virtue of his simple, perfect, divine nature, eternally generates the Word and communicates the fullness of the divine nature to the Word, and also simultaneously eternally spirates the Spirit with the Word, and communicates the fullness of the divine nature to the Spirit. The two notional acts of generation and spriation do not correspond to two distinct essential acts. They are distinguished from one another and compared to knowledge and love—by analogy—on the basis of the relations of origin between the persons, not of real distinctions of activities in the divine nature.

upon these relations. This theological vantage point allows Aquinas to rejoin not only the initial insights of Augustine, but also those of the Cappadocian Fathers, who inaugurated systematic reflection on the Trinitarian
persons in relational terms.

It is worth mentioning in this context that Aquinas's synthetic reflection
on this matter provides the Thomistic tradition with a twofold way of thinking about relations in God, by analogies that are mutually convergent and
mutually compatible. On the one side, Aquinas preserves from Augustine
a robust attentiveness to the use of the psychological analogy, which inevitably considers relations in the Trinity in a qualifiedly unipersonal way, so
as to depict the immaterial processions of the Word and Spirit by analogy
to processions of intellectual and voluntary life in one human person. The
aim of this analogy is, first, to underscore the substantial unity of the Trinitarian persons, who are one in being and nature in a way more analogously
proximate to one human person than to three human persons, and second,
to underscore the immateriality of the processions, as distinct from generative material begetting, as we see in the world of animals and human beings.
On the other side, Aquinas's use of the relation analogy allows him to preserve a comparison of the Trinity to three distinct human persons in a relation of communion, and it has the advantage of underscoring the common
nature of each divine person, who is truly God, just as each human person
truly has a human nature. It also makes clear that we attribute natural acts
of divine knowledge and love to each person and, in fact, to each person in
relation to one another, as each knows and loves the others, in virtue of his
essence as God.

If we make use of the first analogy exclusively, we will fail to grasp adequately that the three persons are each distinct hypostatically and are each
God. Taken to extremes, the danger that arises is akin to that of Joachim in
some ways. The natural acts of generation and spiration will be taken as differentiations pertaining to the nature of God, so that God is understood as
an evolutive natural process or history of self-differentiation. If this is understood in impersonalistic terms, the model projects us toward modalism.
If we make use of the second analogy exclusively, we fail to grasp adequately that the three persons are one in being and essence, and that the eternal
processions in God are immaterial and can be understood properly only by
resemblance to the immaterial life of knowledge and love in human beings.
Taken to extremes, the danger that arises from this model is akin to that of

Gilbert, since relations will appear as something extrinsic to the three persons, or ontologically subsequent to their subsistence. If this model is hardened in the direction of monotheism it simply leads to a denial of distinct
persons in God, while if it is hardened while still holding to the reality of
three distinct persons, it tends toward tri-theism, or towards a form of social Trinitarianism that struggles unsuccessfully to avoid depicting God as
three distinct entities.[23]

Aquinas's correlation of these two analogical modes of thinking about
God has inevitable advantages because he shows us how the two are convergent and mutually corrective. He can do so in large part because of his theory of relations. This is clear first in his treatment of the eternal processions
in God, which pertains to his use of the first analogy from the psychology
of unipersonal acts of knowledge and love. Because the relations in God are
subsistent, the immaterial generation of the Son as Word (by which he is related to the Father) and the spiration of the Spirit (by which he is related to
the Father and the Son) must entail the plenary communication of divine
nature to the Son and Spirit respectively. This is the case because the relational action and passion between the persons in God must pertain to all
that God is substantially. Consequently, the first analogy from psychological
actions is qualified by a substantial account of personal distinction: each of
the persons contains in himself all that is in God, and is truly the one God.
This allows Aquinas to avoid the modalist problem that would evacuate the
distinct persons of their personhood.

23. Where the notion of a unipersonal subsistent generation and spiration (i.e., the psychological analogy) is lost, relations will seem accidental to the three persons, who will risk appearing
as three distinct entities. The normal way to safeguard unity in this case is to insist on the three
persons' perfection of shared knowledge and mutual love that maintains moral unity and that cannot be violated. However, in three autonomous agents with distinct forms of knowledge and love
it must follow as a metaphysical fact that each possesses distinct instantiations of knowledge and
love, which must therefore have limited (finite) modes of realization vis-à-vis one another. Consequently, however perfect their mutual knowledge and shared love, they must in principle be able to
sunder communion of minds and wills precisely because they are autonomously distinct from one
another in intellect and will and, as a result of their mutual limitations vis-à-vis one another, able
to perceive the good differently and pursue it in distinct ways, with assured limitations of power
in regard to one another. The only way to safeguard a genuine sense of divine unity, then, is by
reference back to the first analogy. It is what allows us to articulate how it is that the three persons
are one in substance (being and essence), communicated by generation and spiration, so that they
each are truly one in divine knowledge and divine will. The moral unity of the blessed (angels and
saints) is eternally indissoluble and is shared by finite creatures with distinct spheres of autonomy.
However, this communion is a grace imparted to finite created agents who participate in the life
of God and so do not break communion with one another. It is made possible only by the higher
unity and perfection of God, who imparts a participation in his divine life to creatures by grace.

Meanwhile, Aquinas's account of relation also affects his use of the second analogy, the idea of the persons as three distinct subjects. In human beings relations are accidents and especially ontologically fragile ones, at that. Human beings are meant to become truly related to others by knowledge and by love, but they can fail to do so. Relationality can appear to some, then, as irrelevant to the nature of human persons, each of whom possesses a subsistent autonomy. Certain kinds of relationality perfect human nature but are not identical with it essentially. By casting relation in God in terms of subsistence, then, Aquinas radically qualifies any likeness in the Trinity to three human persons. The Trinitarian persons are each truly personal and are each truly God, but they are also each wholly relational, characterized entirely in all that they are by relations of communication of divine life. This relational mystery of communion in God is best understood by use of the analogy from psychological operations of knowledge and love. Just as the use of relation sends us from the psychological analogy to the interpersonal analogy (by way of the consideration of *subsistent* relation: the communication of the whole of the godhead), the use of relation also sends us from the interpersonal analogy back to the psychological analogy (by way of consideration of subsistent *relation*: each person is wholly relational in all he is).[24] The equilibrium of Aquinas's position is admirable and is of perennial significance for Christian theology in its ongoing effort to receive rightly the patristic heritage of both East and West, in view of its theoretical consideration of the mystery of the Trinitarian relations.

24. See a parallel remark in *SCG* IV, c. 14: "But relations like this are not accidents in God; they are subsistent things; for nothing can happen to God, as was proved above. There are, therefore, many things subsisting if one looks to the relations; there is but one subsistent thing, of course, if one looks to the essence. And on this account we speak of one subsisting God, because He is one subsisting essence; and we speak of a plurality of Persons, because of the distinction of subsisting relations."

24

The Divine Persons

After treating of the divine processions, in *ST* I, q. 27, and the divine relations, in q. 28, Aquinas finally turns to the question of the divine persons themselves, in q. 29. Treating of the divine persons, however, is a metaphysical challenge on several grounds. First, there is the inherent difficulty of defining what a person is even in regard to creatures. Second, there is the issue of a proper analogical transference of the concept of "personhood" to God, while recognizing the transcendence and alterity of God, and finally there is the challenge of speaking of three persons who are each the one God. Inevitable differences of signification arise in the use of the term, because of the consubstantiality of the three persons as one God. This is what leads Aquinas, as we will see below, to define the persons in God as subsistent relations.

WHAT IS A PERSON?

In *ST* I, q. 29, a. 1, Aquinas adopts Boethius's classical definition of person, which he will adapt to his own theological uses. Boethius's definition is a realistic one, derived from our common experience: A "person is an individual substance of a rational nature."[1] How might we understand this definition in regard to created human persons?

---

1. Boethius's definition is cited in *ST* I, q. 29, a. 1, obj. 1. As we noted in chapter 21, this definition was far from noncontroversial in Aquinas's own era. Richard of St. Victor defined a person as "an incommunicable existence of a divine nature," thus defining the concept of personhood in general by primary reference to Trinitarian persons. By beginning from the Boethian definition, Aquinas seeks to work out a perfection term first applicable to human beings, which can be

It is helpful to proceed by breaking down the definition into two component parts. First we can consider the notion of an "individual substance." An individual substance contains within itself, as a concrete existent, all the categories of being that we normally indicate under the headings of substantial and accidental being. Thus, an individual substance is a concrete individual (e.g., Peter or Paul) having a given nature (e.g., a human being) that is the subject of attribution for the various particular accidental characteristics of being (quantity, qualities, relations, action, passion, habit, time, place, etc.).

The second component part is "of a rational nature." Here, the distinctive proper qualities of rational intellect and free will come into play. These are proper accidents, or properties that help one specify what it is to be human, qualifications without which a being is not properly said to be human. This definition does not, of course, mean that a person must exhibit rationality and will *in actuality* in order to be a person. The embryonic human being, the human being who is asleep, or the brain-damaged human being do not exercise such capacities in act. But each of these is, nevertheless, the kind of being who has these properties, even when they are not yet, or no longer, or not currently able to be exercised. Such individuals are still personal beings having a rational nature with its inherent properties, whether they are currently able to exercise the powers proper to their nature or not.

Beyond these two component parts of Boethius's definition, Aquinas proceeds, in article 2, to further define person by elucidating its close connection with the related categories of *subsistence, essence,* and *hypostasis,* respectively. First of all, then, the concept of person is closely bound up with the notion of subsistence. Subsistence is that which "exists in itself and not in another."[2] As subsisting or having subsistence, each person is an ontologically autonomous, distinct being, unlike, for example, an accident, which exists only by inhering in a subsisting reality.

A person is also an individual essence, or a *res naturae.* This means that a person is the concrete realization of a being of a given kind. Thus, Paul or Peter is an individual instance of human nature, consisting of *this* soul and

---

extended to Trinitarian persons in God by analogy. He integrates the notion of dignity into his discussion as a property characteristic of a rational nature, but does not define the person in terms of this property. In this latter respect he differs from Bonaventure. For more on this, see Emery, *The Trinitarian Theology of St. Thomas Aquinas,* 107–11.

2. *ST* I, q. 29, a. 2.

this flesh and *these* bones. Each such individual, then, is a singular instantiation and distinct realization of what it means to be human.[3]

Person is also closely related to the notion of hypostasis. Hypostasis refers to the subject of attribution that underlies all the properties of a given thing: it is that in which properties adhere. Taken literally, it is that which stands under (hypo-stasis) all of a person's accidental properties. Thus, we attribute an accidental property of a given person ("she plays the piano," "she is musically gifted") to a given being as the hypostatic subject ("she" here refers to the named individual, say, Agatha, Lucy, Agnes, or Cecilia).

These terms (subsistence, individual essence, hypostasis) help us enrich our understanding of what it means metaphysically for us to ascribe personhood to an individual. To give a summary example, Paul is a subsistent person, one who exists only in himself and is not another. Paul is a human being, in whom the nature and character of what it is to be human subsists in a particular and unique way. (There is no one who is human in the distinctively individual way that Paul is.) Finally, Paul is the subject to which we attribute all the properties of this being: the qualities, quantity, and relations of Paul, and so on.

Beyond these basic definitions, we are next confronted with the question of what, metaphysically speaking, is the principle of individuation that causes one person to be distinct from another. This is the question of the ultimate basis of the personal uniqueness we find in individual human beings. Put differently, why is one person individually unique when that person has the same human nature as all other persons?

Different answers to this problem have been given. One answer, of course, has to do with the individual matter of the person: Paul has a different material body than Peter or Agnes or Lucy. Nevertheless, the distinctness of persons cannot be explained comprehensively by appeal to individual materiality alone. After all, each human person is distinct on the basis of his or her spiritual soul as well as material body.

Another explanation seeks the locus of distinctiveness in the concrete being (*ens* in Latin) of the reality. Each person is a distinct being or entity (*ens*) consisting of an essence (*essentia*) and a unique act of existence (*esse*). On its own, the act of existence cannot account for individuation, because the individuated being is always a certain *kind* of being (having an essence),

---

3 On this point, see especially *ST* I, q. 29, a. 2, ad 3: "hypostasis and person add the individual principles to the idea of essence."

and essence alone cannot account for individuation, because each thing has a singularity of being only on account of its act of existence. Both *esse* and *essentia* contribute, then, to the individuality of a given *ens*. The two principles interact in a particular order, however. The act of being gives the essence its singular mode of realization. Paul possesses a unique realization of human nature as a result of the singularity of his act of existence (*esse*). Based on this form of thinking, some Thomists identify hypostatic personhood as pertaining to the essence of a being subsisting in a particular mode because of its concrete existence (*esse*).[4] When we say that Paul is a person (or hypostasis or subsistence), we mean that he is a human being (one having a human essence) in a concrete mode. The mode is the particularity of the essence as it is realized in a wholly unique way in virtue of the act of existence. So, in Paul or Peter, Agatha or Lucy, human nature subsists, but each time in a given mode that is hypostatic and unique.

As we begin to refer these considerations to the Trinitarian persons in God by analogy, two observations remain particularly important. The first is that there is no distinction of *esse* in divine persons as there is in human persons, since God's *esse* is identical with his essence. If Trinitarian persons each possess the one essence of God, then they each also possess the one act of existence of God. Secondly, though, this *esse* in God is also *esse ad*: existence toward. The persons in God possess the act of existence only relationally, from and unto one another, and in this sense they can be said to possess the act of being God in distinct personal modes of realization. In his act of being God, the Father is eternally related to the Son and Holy Spirit as a principle of origin, who communicates the plenitude of the divine nature to the Son and the Spirit. What each person is or has as God (the essence

4. See the seminal article of Thomas U. Mullaney, "Created Personality: The Unity of the Thomistic Tradition," *The New Scholasticism* 29, no. 4 (1955): 369–402, which presents a position of the kind I am arguing for, based on the Thomistic arguments of Cajetan and Capreolus. To make use of Aquinas's terms from the *De ente* transposed onto this question of personhood: the *essentia* of a given individual, considered abstractly, is the same as that of all other persons ("human nature"). However, it subsists in this given individual in a unique way or mode, not only as a result of its individual matter (as an individuated nature), but more fundamentally as a result of its unique *esse*. It is not the *esse* that is individual per se, but the nature, and the nature is individual because of the *esse*. In a given person, for example, the body-soul composite (the individual human nature) *exists in act* as a singular entity in virtue of its *esse*. Since the nature in question is personal (characterized by spiritual knowledge and love) the individual mode of realization is that of a unique person. Personhood does not derive, strictly speaking, then, from either the *essentia* principle or the *esse* principle but from the composite of the two, as a modal realization of the essence in a given existent.

of the godhead) is relational in character, because it *is* from or unto another.

Here, quite uniquely, then, the hypostatic singularity or unique subsistence will come from *the relational manner* of being God. Once we acknowledge this dissimilitude of Trinitarian persons to human persons we can begin to see the analogy of personhood. As noted above, the person is the existent mode of realization of the essence. We can say by analogy, then, that in the Trinity there are three ways of existing as God. The Father exists in a unique personal mode *as God* because he is the source of divine life for the Son and Spirit (by generation and spiration). The Son exists in a unique personal mode *as God* because he is eternally begotten of the Father and exists from the Father "toward" the spiration of the Spirit with the Father. The Spirit exists in a unique personal mode *as God* because he is eternally spirated from the Father and the Son, and no one proceeds from him.[5]

The persons each subsist hypostatically as distinct from one another, while each possessing fully the plenitude of divine nature and life (the divine essence). Thus, the divine essence subsists in three distinct modes, and these modes of being are *entirely relational*. The essence of God subsists in the Father in his paternal mode of being, as the divine life of the Father which he communicates to his Son. The essence of God subsists personally in the Son in a filial mode, as the divine life of the Son that he receives from the Father. The divine essence exists in the Spirit in a spirated mode, as the divine life of the Spirit that he receives from the Father and the Son, as their mutual love. Here, then, what makes the three "persons" in God to be a dis-

---

5. Between created human persons there is a shared commonality of essence or nature but an utterly distinct differentiation of *esse* or existence, since one human being is precisely distinct in existence from another (and yet they do both share in the *esse commune* as two really existing beings). Two angels are distinct from each other both in essence and in *esse*, since each is a distinct species (*ST* I, q. 50, aa. 2 and 4). In the mystery of the Holy Trinity, however, the persons of God are one in *esse* and *essentia*, in existence and essence. However, the *esse-essentia* of God (the very being of God) is possessed by each Trinitarian person according to a distinct mode of origin. Consequently, the modal principle of personal distinctness arises not primarily from the uniqueness of *esse* (as in the case of human persons), nor from the uniqueness of *esse* and *essentia* (as in the case of angelic persons), but from the relations of origin, considered as subsistent relations, in which the totality of divine life is truly communicated by generation and spiration from one person to another. Even though the eternal processions are immaterial, there is a "greater likeness" between human beings and God in this respect than there is between angels and God, because in both cases the common essence (of divine persons and human persons, alike) is transmitted substantially by generation, albeit in two wholly different ways. This suggests that material existence allows human persons to better image the mystery of the inner life of the persons of the Trinity, in some respects, and helps us understand why God would create material persons. Angelic persons, however, image the Trinitarian persons more perfectly in the order of immateriality, in virtue of their simpler and higher forms of cognition and love.

tinctly subsisting individuals is the relational mode in which they possess the divine *esse-essentia* with respect to one another.

In *ST* I, q. 29, a. 3, Aquinas discusses how the notion of personhood is attributable to God not only by analogy, but also in such a way as to maintain that personhood is present in God in an ultimate and perfect way that exceeds all we know of personhood in creatures. Significantly, in this context, Aquinas refers back to the distinction he has already articulated, in q. 13, a. 2, between the reality signified and the mode of signification.[6] This distinction helps us understand how personhood is attributed rightly to God in the most perfect of ways, even though our notion of persons first arises from the encounter with created persons we become acquainted with by way of experience.

According to the *res significata*, or reality signified, then, God is more rightly called personal than any creaturely person, just as God is more rightly called wise or good than any creature is. The reason is that "person" signifies what is most perfect in all of nature—a subsistent individual of a rational nature. When perfection terms are attributed to God, even by analogy, they are attributed to him also according to highest excellence, *per viam eminentiae*, on account of his pure actuality. And yet, according to the *modus significandi*, or mode of signification, our grasp of this reality is imperfect. That is to say, God is signified by us as personal through the medium of our ordinary way of denoting personhood, one derived originally from creatures, and adapted for speaking about God on the basis of imperfect knowledge. Considered under this aspect, our designation of God as personal is oblique. The inner life of God's Trinitarian personhood is hidden from us in its transcendence and remains numinous, only imperfectly known, as a mysterious twofold procession of Word and Love. On the one hand, then, the personhood of God is truly signified by our discourse: it is true to say that there are three persons in the Trinity, and that their personhood is purely actual and most perfect. But this is stated according to our analogical mode of discourse, which is bound up with our imperfect and limited knowledge (in this life) of the mystery of God. This disparity between the reality sig-

6. This distinction between the reality signified and the mode of signification was discussed in chapter 12 above.

nified and the mode of signification should bring to our awareness the care with which we must proceed in discussing personhood as it applies to God.

PERSONS AS SUBSISTENT RELATIONS

If God is truly personal, then, and there are "persons" in God, what can this mean? How should we speak about the immanent distinction of persons in the life of God? Clearly, if there is an analogy to the relations that exist among human persons, there are also almost ineffable differences when it comes to speaking about the Trinity. How should we understand the persons of God as truly persons, and yet understand there to be one God?

Aquinas takes up these questions in *ST* I, q. 29, a. 4, taking his lead from the key concept of "relations of origin." He pointedly asks whether personhood in God signifies the relations of origin, or the essence of God, or both? The answer is that it signifies both, but in a given order. Personhood denotes the relation directly. The Son is he who is eternally begotten of the Father, who originates from the Father and is eternally relative to him. But personhood also denotes the substance or essence of God indirectly. The Son is also he who possesses in himself from all eternity the plenitude of the godhead. In other words, we can speak about a divine person only in a twofold way: as related to others in virtue of the processions, and as possessing in himself the fullness of the deity or the divine life. Each person is both "wholly relative" and "wholly God."

Aquinas goes on stipulate that there is no real distinction of substance and accident in God, however. Consequently, if the persons of the Trinity are characterized by their "relationality," then this is also something that characterizes them in all that they are substantially. The Father is "wholly relative" to the Son and Spirit in all he is, by means of his eternal activity of generation and spiration, and so too they are wholly relative to him and to each other in all that they are. The Father is his paternity, the Son is his filiation, and the Spirit is his spiration. For this reason, then, when it comes to God, person signifies a relation as subsisting: it refers to what is distinct in each person in virtue of the relations of origin, and yet these relations are also identical with the divine essence and so are subsisting.[7]

---

7. *ST* I, q. 29, a. 4: "Now distinction in God is only by relation of origin, while relation in God is not as an accident in a subject, but is the divine essence itself; and so it is subsistent, for the divine essence subsists. Therefore, as the godhead is God so the divine paternity is God the

This is why we can speak of each of the persons as a hypostasis, or personal subject of attribution subsisting in the divine nature. That is to say, the Father, who generates the Son and spirates the Spirit with the Son, subsists in the divine nature as truly God and divine. The Son, who is generated by the Father and who spirates the Spirit with the Father, subsists in the divine nature as truly God and divine. The Spirit, who is spirated by the Father and the Son, subsists in the divine nature as truly God and divine. Each of the persons can truly be called "the one God." Moreover, it follows from this that the divine nature simply is this relational subsistence of the Father, Son, and Holy Spirit: God in his eternal life is this relationship of Trinitarian persons.

THE LAW OF REDOUBLING

From what has been said thus far, it follows that each person of the Triune God must be considered under a twofold aspect as: (1) a subsistent relation (and so in relational terms), but then (2) in terms of the divine essence and nature, and so as possessing the fullness of the godhead. This terminological rule can be called the law of redoubling.[8]

We should note that the fullness of the godhead refers to the essential terms for God: those we treated at length, in part 2, in our consideration of the nature of God. These divine names can and must be predicated of each of the persons following upon our affirmation of the processions and how they express the subsistent relations in God. The following chart can help illustrate this point.

As table 24-1 helps show, we can think of a divine person first as a subsistent relation, based on the order of processions between the persons. From this it follows that we can consider each person under a twofold aspect, in relation terms and in essential terms. The Father is he from whom both the

---

Father, Who is a divine person. Therefore, a divine person signifies a relation as subsisting. And this is to signify relation by way of substance, and such a relation is a hypostasis subsisting in the divine nature, although in truth that which subsists in the divine nature is the divine nature itself. Thus it is true to say that the name 'person' signifies relation directly, and the essence indirectly; not, however, the relation as such, but as expressed by way of a hypostasis. So likewise it signifies directly the essence, and indirectly the relation, inasmuch as the essence is the same as the hypostasis: while in God the hypostasis is expressed as distinct by the relation: and thus relation, as such, enters into the notion of the person indirectly."

8. This is my interpretation of a point made by Gilles Emery in his essay "Essentialism or Personalism in the Treatise on God in St. Thomas Aquinas?," *The Thomist* 64, no. 4 (2000): 521–63.

Table 24-1. Reduplication of Trinitarian Persons

Father——[*procession*]——Son——[*procession*]——Holy Spirit		
Subsistent Relation	Subsistent Relation	Subsistent Relation
Paternal	Filial	Spirated
Simplicity	Simplicity	Simplicity
Perfection	Perfection	Perfection
Goodness, etc.	Goodness, etc.	Goodness, etc.

Son and Spirit proceed, but he is also eternally the one God. Therefore we can think of him as a subsistent relation characterized *both* by paternity, *and* by the properties of the divine essence (simplicity, perfection, goodness, and so forth). The Son is he who proceeds from the Father as his Word, but he is also eternally the one God. Therefore he is characterized *both* by filiation *and* by the properties of the divine essence. The Spirit is the spirated Love of the Father and the Son, and he is also the one God. So he is characterized *both* by spiration *and* by properties of the divine essence. In sum, each person of the Trinity must always be considered in reference to this twofold aspect, as an eternally relational subject who possesses in himself the plenitude of the deity.

At the same time, the divine nature is seen in this way to subsist in three personal modes. The Father, for example, is simple, perfect, and good, as is the Son, as is the Spirit. In the Father, however, the divine nature subsists in a paternal mode: his is a paternal simplicity, perfection, and goodness, because these "divine attributes" are predicated of him in a fontal mode of being. In the Son, the divine nature subsists in a filial mode, since the divine simplicity, perfection, and goodness are predicated of him in a begotten mode of being. In the Spirit, the divine nature subsists in a spirated mode, as the simplicity, perfection, and goodness of God are predicated of him as in one proceeding from the Father and the Son as Love. The relational notion of each person, therefore, qualifies the mode of being of the divine nature that is attributed to each. It is false to say, then, that there is no real distinction of persons, and that what we call the persons are in fact merely three modes of being of the nature (the heresy of modalism). But it is also erroneous to say that the three distinct persons possess the divine nature each in precisely the same mode. In a Thomistic conception of the Trinity, the notion of distinct persons in God and the notion of distinct modes of being of the divine nature are neither in competition with one another nor mutually exclusive. Instead, they are mutually reinforcing and interconnected ideas. We can understand how they are connected only once we have grasped the analogical conception of processions in God (the psychological analogy), qualified by an analogical theory of relations in God, which in turn qualifies our interpretation of distinct persons in God, understood as subsistent relations.

We noted in the first chapter of part 3 that the Thomistic school follows Aquinas in presenting a relationalist account of the Trinitarian persons, one that is grounded in an analogical notion of immaterial, immanent processions in God (the use of the psychological analogy), and that makes use of the notion of relation to affirm simultaneously the unity of essence and hypostatic distinction of persons in God. As we just noted, this allows us to think coherently about three subsistent modes of being of the divine nature, each corresponding to one of the persons of the Trinity in their mutual relations. When rightly understood, the notion of three natural modes of being in God and the notion of distinct persons in God are not mutually incompatible notions and, in fact, are logically connected ideas. Nor does this claim pose any threat to the unity of nature in God but, on the contrary, presupposes it. The three persons are each the one God subsisting in three modes, in accord with their relations of origin.

We have already noted, as well, that this Thomistic way of approaching the mystery of the Trinity contrasts in notable ways with the emanationist tradition on the one side, which considers the persons in pre-constituted states logically prior to relation, and in so doing constructs a more univocal notion of persons in God (more closely related to human persons), and with the nominal minimalist tradition on the other side, which denies the possibility of an ascription of the psychological analogy to the inner life of God, or at least claims that the use of this analogy provides us with no intrinsic intelligibility. Such a conception is, obviously, radically apophatic. We have noted that there are parallels to both these forms of thinking in modern Trinitarian theology. On the one side the "personalists," like Balthasar and

Moltmann, overtly appeal to the early Franciscan tradition to argue for a specifically distinct economic theory of Trinitarian persons, where the persons engage one another dynamically and freely interior to an economy of time and history. On the other side, those who incline slightly toward modalism, like Barth and Rahner, deny the utility of an ascription of the notion of persons to God and opt instead to consider the three hypostases as truly distinct modes of being in God. Like Balthasar and Moltmann, however, they claim that we can distinguish these three modes of being in God principally from the activities of God in the economy.

At the term of our study of personhood in the immanent life of the Trinity in Aquinas, we can note several ways that his approach appears to be potentially advantageous within the contexts of both medieval and modern Trinitarian theology.

First, we can note that Aquinas's theory of processions provides us with a genuine analogy for distinctions of notional acts of knowing and loving within the immanent life of God. This distinction in its medieval context allows St. Thomas to avoid the radical apophaticism of the kind that would later emerge in the nominalist tradition. In a modern context, we have argued that this highly qualified use of the psychological analogy provides us with an understanding of the immanent Trinity as "pre-constituted" prior to the economy of revelation. Far from being "anti-economic," this idea conveys the notion that there is a basis in God for the economy. As we will see in the last portion of part 3, this idea comes to term when Aquinas shows how the immanent processions in God are present in and revealed truly by the divine missions of the Son and the Spirit in the world. Such a conception allows us to explain how God is truly revealed in the economy without being constituted by the economy, and this procedure requires a use of the psychological analogy in some form.

Second, we can note that Aquinas's theory of relations, which he uses to qualify his interpretation of the processions, allows him, in the medieval context, to strike an important note of apophaticism, which in turn causes his theory to differ from those emergent in the Franciscan-emanationist tradition. Relation in God is not a property logically adjacent to the person understood as a pre-constituted subject, nor can diverse relations arise from diverse actions of a nature (as they do in us). In God relationality is wholly other, and it constitutes the distinction among the persons. Aquinas's analogical conception of relations in God preserves the notion of a relation as a connection to another by action and passion, while negating the idea of the relation as inhering in a pre-existing substance or accidental property. This notion of relation as subsistent allows him to differentiate the persons in God by way of procession while maintaining that they each possess the plenitude of the divine life and being, as communicating to or as deriving from another. This notion of Trinitarian relations is moderately apophatic, since it allows Aquinas to denote the mystery of God's perfect union adequately, while still respecting the alterity of the persons in God, who differ utterly from three human persons. In a modern context, this form of apophaticism acts as a caution against an anthropomorphic understanding of the Trinitarian relations, wherein those relations are considered to be dynamically actuated within the economy and thus newly constituted only when God the Son enacts his historical mystery of incarnation, passion, and resurrection. Aquinas's conception allows us to argue for a converse perspective: the Incarnation and the human life, death, and resurrection of the Son truly do reveal to us the inner life of the Trinity, precisely because the Son truly does manifest to us in his human life in time his eternal pre-constituted relations to the Father and to the Spirit.

Finally, we can note that Aquinas's conception of personhood has an analogical application, if we interpret it in the Thomistic tradition as a "mode of subsistence of a rational nature." This idea can apply in distinct ways to individual human beings, who are each distinct modal realizations of human nature, to angels, who are each distinct existent species, and to divine persons, who are each distinct modes of realization of the divine nature. In the latter case alone, however, the persons are understood as distinct uniquely in virtue of their relations of origin and thus their processional derivations. This relational conception of personhood allows us to identify something most perfect in God that is transcendent and ineffable: in God alone, the persons who are distinct are also one in individual being and nature. They are each the one God. In this respect, then, their communion of persons is wholly other than and dissimilar to any communion of human persons. At the same time, this communion of Trinitarian persons illumines that of all other, created persons. Communion among created persons, while non-substantial in kind, approximates that of the Holy Trinity and derives its ultimate source of meaning and destiny from this "primal communion" as a transcendent exemplary measure.

Aquinas's notion of persons in God as relational subsistents allows us to understand the unity of God's nature and God's threefold mode of being God, without violating the distinction of persons, and allows us to affirm the distinction of persons without violating the unity of nature. Each person is a mode of subsistence of the divine nature. There are, then, truly three modes of subsistence of the nature of God, but only one God. Within a modern context, this idea allows us to avoid the modalist tendency of Barth and Rahner, which eschews the traditional use of the name "person" for the hypostases of the Father, Son, and Spirit. Viewed relative to a modalist conception, Aquinas's view is kataphatic and personalistic, like that of the Franciscan school, and rejects the temptation to depersonalize the modes of God's being.

At the same time, his view also allows us to understand how the nature of God as it subsists in three modes is not constituted in its modal distinctions (as paternal, filial, and spirated) by the economic activity of God. Modern theologians of the more modalist and personalist stripe alike tend to elaborate a theory of distinction in God based on *natural* properties that the Son has as distinct from the Father in virtue of the economy, as, for example, when the Son obeys, suffers, dies, or is humanly subject to passive resurrection in time: it is precisely these features of his economic life as man that are indicative for them of real distinctions in God. The *human* natural mode of being is thus indicative of a distinct *divine* natural mode of being wherein the Son differs from the Father. (In part 4 of this book I will characterize this idea as what I call "inverted monophysitism," since the human nature here seems to absorb or determine the inner content of a freely kenotic divine nature.) On Aquinas's view, we can avoid the problems associated with both the modern modalist and modern personalist accounts, since the modal distinctions of the nature in God are explained uniquely by appeal to the eternal processions and relations of the persons, as distinct from and prior to God's actions of creation and redemption.

This idea of distinct modes of subsistence will have significant consequences for our understanding of mutual indwelling (perichoresis) and appropriations, to be seen below. Because each person possesses the divine life in plenitude, each in a distinct way, each is also wholly within the other two. God's three eternal modes of being as Father, Son, and Holy Spirit can also be indicated when we attribute essential names to God, by speaking of the Father as powerful, the Son as wise, or the Spirit as good. These expressions are indicated appropriately of one person more than another, even if the essential terms in question are also properly attributed to all of the persons. The reason for this has to do with the personal mode of being of the attribute in question, as we shall see. Far from being external to the economy, these ideas have great consequences for our notion of the economic revelation of the Trinity. The Son alone is human, but in being human he remains truly God. Consequently, all that he does as God he does with the Father and the Spirit who dwell in him (by perichoresis). When he acts as both God and human, he does so only in a filial mode, as one who is from the Father and who sends the Spirit. Therefore, his human gestures, actions, teachings, and sufferings reveal the Trinitarian personal relations and the modes in which each of the persons is God. The Son is powerful, but he is powerful only from the Father, while the Spirit is the Spirit of truth, but only as the Spirit of the Son. Christology, understood in this light, is thoroughly Trinitarian.

25

God the Father

The person of the Father is the unoriginate principle of the other divine persons. In this chapter, we will first look at what it means for the Father to be this eternal fontal principle of the Son and the Spirit in the life of Trinity. We can then identify the precise sense in which "Father" is a personal name attributed to God, and consider diverse ways that creatures that originate from God participate in the Son's filiation toward the Father. After this, we will examine Aquinas's understanding of the Father's characteristic of innascibility as a purely negative one, since it is illustrative of the utterly relative concept of divine personhood that St. Thomas developed. Then, we can draw out the dimension of final causality that is rightly ascribed to the Trinitarian relations, insofar as the persons who proceed from the Father are also relationally "turned toward" or are "unto" the Father. This relationality of the Son and the Spirit toward the Father is, as we will see, the archetype in the Trinity for the economic *reditus* of creatures back to God the Father in the orders of nature and grace. Our consideration of the notion of divine paternity allows us to understand various dissimilitudes that must exist between divine and human persons. Finally, we will consider metaphorical similitudes of human paternity and maternity as they relate to God the Father.

THE FATHER AS PRINCIPLE IN THE TRINITY

In *ST* I, q. 33, a. 1, Aquinas takes up the question of whether the Father is himself the *principium*, eternal font of the intra-divine processions and thus of the relations these processions establish. His argument is simple. Since a principle is that from which something else in some way proceeds, and the other two persons proceed from the Father, the Father then is indeed principle in the Trinity.

Can we also for this reason say that the Father is the *causa*, cause of the Son and the Spirit? This is a more complex question, and its resolution depends on what one means by the word "cause." Such language is in fact traditional in the Greek tradition, since some patristic authors spoke of the Father as the cause (αἰτία) of the Son and the Spirit. By contrast, the Western tradition since the patristic age tended to avoid such language for fear of seeming to denote the Son and Spirit as creatures caused in their being by the Father. This too is why Aquinas prefers the broader notion of "principle": it indicates that the Father is the fontal source of the Son and the Spirit with less danger of the residue of causation of creatures interposing itself and giving rise again to the Arian and Pneumatomachian heresies, which deny the divinity of the Son and Spirit, respectively.[1] Nevertheless, when he considers the question, Aquinas notes, in a spirit of understanding, that the Greek custom of the use of the word "cause" in this context is intended to denote the same mystery of uncreated begetting and spiration that the Western authors signify in speaking of the Father as a principle.[2]

DIVINE PATERNITY AND FILIATION

In *ST* I, q. 33, a. 3, Aquinas takes up the question of whether the name "Father" is applied to God as a personal name. His answer proceeds from the distinction between the full signification of which the term Father is capable, and its various partial, lesser significations. In so doing, he also draws out the various analogical applications which the notion of sonship is capable of signifying in its diverse applications to creatures. If we think of relational procession analogically, we can consider various instances of "filiation" and therefore clarify what we wish to denote when we speak not only of the eternal paternity of the Father in relation to the Son, but also of the

---

1. *ST* I, q. 33, a. 1, ad 1: "This term 'cause' seems to mean diversity of substance, and dependence of one from another; which is not implied in the word 'principle.' For in all kinds of causes there is always to be found between the cause and the effect a distance of perfection or of power: whereas we use the term 'principle' even in things which have no such difference, but have only a certain order to each other; as when we say that a point is the principle of a line."
2. Ibid.

paternity of the Father in relation to creatures. For the Father as Creator gives being to all things through his Son and in his Spirit, and he invites spiritual creatures into filial adoption by grace in the Son and in the Spirit.

The first point to be made here is that Father is a personal name in God. The reason for this is that it is first spoken with reference to the Father in his eternal relation to the Son, in whom, in turn, the plenitude of filiation is expressed in virtue of his generation, as God from God. This relation of the Father to the Son is accordingly the fundamental and entirely sufficient basis for applying to God the personal name of Father, and that relation precedes anything in creation. Otherwise stated, the Father is eternally Father, and would be so even if he had never created any dependent finite reality, simply in virtue of the mystery of the intra-Trinitarian processions. Nor does the creation and economy of divinization of creatures add anything to the infinite dignity and perfection of the Father in his eternal relations to the Son and Spirit. Rather, the Father's temporal effects of creation and filial adoption by grace are expressions, in finite form, of the infinite plenitude of perfection he eternally possesses and expresses in the generation of the Son and in the spiration of the Spirit. The creation does not add to God, then, but is the gratuitous and free expression of God's filial life "externally" in a participated and finite fashion in creatures. We might just as well speak, however, of the Father's giving being to all things "within" his Word and Spirit, as one who is present in his divine eternity to all that is created and that unfolds in time and history.

It is precisely for this reason that God's paternity is capable of a diverse range of analogical applications. Just as the Father begets the Son from all eternity in his own likeness, communicating to him all that he is as God, so too the Father, through the Word, his Son, conceives the creation by similitude to the Son, in a participated likeness. Consequently, all creatures participate in the mystery of Sonship to varying degrees.[3] Creatures produced by God the Father always contain a likeness to the Son, no matter how imperfect and remote this likeness may be in any individual case. We might say that all things that come forth from the Father remain relative to the first person of the Trinity. Their coming to be, their histories, their lives in grace, are all in some way expressive of his divine paternity.

---

3. Thus, Aquinas writes in *ST* I, q. 33, a. 3: "The perfect idea of paternity and filiation is to be found in God the Father, and in God the Son.... But in the creature, filiation is found in relation to God, not in a perfect manner ... but by way of a certain likeness, which is the more perfect the nearer we approach to the true idea of filiation."

In article 3, Aquinas lists the following levels of participation in the relation of sonship on the part of creatures, here given in ascending order: the first is the *vestigia* or vestiges of sonship found in nonrational creatures. These represent the lowest level of filiation and so contain only a trace of likeness to the Son. The second is the much higher similitude or likeness of rational creatures, who possess intellect and will. The rational creature, inasmuch as it bears a greater likeness to the Son than do other creatures, is accordingly placed at the apex of the visible creation in the creation narrative in Genesis 1 and, as such, is designated *imago Dei*, the image of God. The third level of similitude is that of the likeness of grace, which confers on the rational creature a higher assimilation to divine sonship, so much so that the scriptures designate it an "adoptive sonship."[4] The fourth degree of similitude is that of divine glory, in which the rational creature's life of grace is brought to full fruition in an even higher degree of participation in likeness to the divine Son. Finally, there is the Sonship of the eternal Son himself, which is Sonship *par excellence*, that Sonship to which the paternity of the Father is eternally relative, and from which the Father is properly called "Father."

What is common to sonship in all its analogical realizations is the relation to another, who is Father. All that is comes forth from the person of the Father as the fundamental origin, or originator of all things. But there is also an unbridgeable and infinite difference between the eternal Son and all other things. The Son comes forth from the Father personally before the created world, as the expression of the Father's own essence, as God from God and Light from Light. He is the Son, properly speaking, in a way that no creature is or ever could be.

The Son is, accordingly, he through whom "all things were made" (Jn 1:3), such that all other things not only exist by likeness to the Son, but also in dependence upon the Son, who, with the Father and the Holy Spirit, has brought about their existence in freedom. As such, there is a perfection of divine being and life in the Son that is infinitely transcendent of created perfections. As we have noted already, the Father's paternity or personal being as "Father" is relative to *this* transcendent Sonship and so subsists as a relation independent of and without reference to creation. For this very reason, however, creation in turn is patterned after its transcendent archetype in the eternally subsisting Son.

---

4. Cf. Gal 4:5.

THE INNASCIBILITY OF THE FATHER

As we have previously noted, for St. Bonaventure, the contemporary of St. Albert and St. Thomas, the notion of "innascibility" or of being "unengendered" signifies above all *a positive trait* of the Father: that before all else, the Father is the fontal source of the Triune life of the Son and Spirit, prior, as it were, or in distinction from, his acts of generation and spiration.[5] We should note this view in passing, not only because it famously differs from that of St. Thomas, but because it helps us underscore the *relative* character of Aquinas's view of the paternity of the Father. Bonaventure takes the Father to be intelligible as such positively (that is to say, to be denoted by us as a divine hypostasis) in logical distinction from his act of engendering and spirating the Son and Spirit respectively. It is indeed precisely from his plenitude as Source or "Principle without principle," denoted by a positive term, "innascibility," that we can then think of him as communicating the totality of divine life to the Son and the Spirit. For Aquinas, the problem with this view is that it locates the intelligibility of the Father precisely in something that constitutes him as a divine hypostasis *prior to* or *in logical distinction from* the generation of the Son, and indeed as its precondition. While Bonaventure has the laudable desire to designate the Father's fontal plenitude as the first person of the Trinity, his mode of analysis implicitly allows one to think of the Father without considering sufficiently his relativity, his being as relation toward the Son and Spirit, as a constitutive dimension of his personhood and his paternity. In fact, however, as we saw in the analysis of divine persons as subsistent relations, the Father is only ever the Father in being the Father of the Son and the origin of the Spirit.

For St. Thomas, then, in considered contradistinction to St. Bonaventure, this trait of the Father as innascible is denoted in a fashion that is *purely negative*.[6] God the Father is named by us as "innascible" precisely as one who does not proceed from another. Consequently he is the unique source who is *not* "from another" within the Trinitarian life. Why is it of impor-

5. See Bonaventure, *Breviloquium*, trans. D. V. Monti (St. Bonaventure, N.Y.: Franciscan Institute Publications, 2005), 1, c. 3, no. 7: "'Unbegottenness' designates him [the Father] by means of a negation, but this term *also implies an affirmation*, since unbegottenness posits in the Father a fountain-fullness. The 'Principle that proceeds from no other' designates him *by an affirmation followed by a negation*" (emphases added). For a developed consideration of Bonaventure's Trinitarian thought, see Zachary Hayes, "Bonaventure's Trinitarian Theology," 190–245; and Friedman, *Intellectual Traditions at the Medieval University*, 1:64–94.

6. *ST* I, q. 33, a. 4, corpus and ad 1.

tance that this nominative definition be purely negative? The answer is that the Father cannot be positively constituted as Father independently of the act of generation and spiration. The Trinitarian persons in their mystery of mutual communion are rightly understood by us only as wholly relative or as pure relations. The Father is Father only as the one who begets the Son and spirates the Spirit. As such, he is the principle without a principle, the first person from whom the others proceed, and he is therefore *not* engendered, but is innascible. This way of thinking safeguards the "principality" of the Father, who is first and the origin of all else (the idea Bonaventure especially wanted to emphasize), but it also makes clear the absolutely relative identity of the Father, with respect to the Son and the Spirit. God the Father is absolutely first, but he is first only as the Father of the Son and the spirator of the Holy Spirit.

FROM THE FATHER TO THE FATHER

Up until this point, we have for the most part approached the mystery of the persons through relations of origin, and therefore as relative processions from an origin in the Father, for the Son, and from the Father and the Son, for the Holy Spirit. Nevertheless, the analogy from final causality, or perfection of life, is also helpful for our understanding of the Trinitarian relations, the divine persons, and also the *reditus*, or return of creatures to God, from whom they proceeded by way of creation by an analogy with the Son's procession by way of generation.

As we have already established, all Trinitarian life proceeds from the Father: both the Son and the Spirit proceed, albeit in diverse ways (i.e., the one by generation, the other by common spiration), from the innascible Father. And yet the proceeding persons are also always turned "toward" the Father, are "for" him, and in general are oriented to him as their term. The Son, being eternally begotten, eternally knows and loves the Father, such that the Father is, in a certain sense, the Son's own personal term, or finality. Out of this love for the Father, the Son spirates the Spirit with the Father. The Spirit, in turn, is from the Father and the Son as their mutual Love, an eternal term or fruit of their goodness. Yet the Spirit in turn eternally knows and loves both the Father and the Son from whom he proceeds, and in so doing rejoices in them as his term, enjoying the fullness of divine being he receives in eternal happiness. In the perfect life of the Trinity, then, all things come from the Father, but they also in a certain sense return to him, in virtue of the interpersonal communion of the three persons. This is true insofar as the Son and the Spirit know and love the Father from whom they receive all things. When thinking about this eternal communion of persons, then, one can speak in a nuanced sense of both the paternal origin and the paternal term of all Trinitarian life.

Significantly, then, this movement of procession and return—and thus, the *exitus* and *reditus* schema common in medieval theology—also finds an echo in creatures. All things proceed from God by way of creation, and are subsequently called back to God in a return movement expressed in the teleological ordering of their natures to God, each in its own way. This implies that the creation not only comes forth "from" the Father by his Word and in his Spirit of Love, it also returns by grace toward the Father, through the Son, in the Holy Spirit. The sending of the Son and the Spirit into the world (the divine missions) culminates in the Incarnation, the paschal mystery, and the outpouring of the Spirit at Pentecost. This great movement "from the Father" out to the world through the sending of the Son and Spirit is complemented, in turn, by a "return to the Father." All things come from the Father, and return to the Father, as the summit of their existence. John 16:28: "I came from the Father and have come into the world; again, I am leaving the world and going to the Father." The Spirit awakens in us a sense of the mystery of the Son, who in turn invites us to live as adoptive sons and daughters of God, so as to return to the Father (Gal 4:6). All things are from him and all things are for him (Rom 11:36; Eph 4:6). As the New Testament clearly indicates, the eternal plenitude of the Father, from whom all things are derived, is also that fullness of eternal life toward which we are invited to return in Christ (1 Cor 15:28).

THOMISTIC RELATIONALISM AND
THE DIVINE ECONOMY

Aquinas's relationalist account of the Father, exemplified by his treatment of innascibility as a merely negative term, has extremely important consequences for his theology of the divine economy. As we have noted, in part 2 of this book, Aquinas affirms that the Creator knows and loves all things out of the eternal wellspring of perfect knowledge and love that the Creator has for himself, in which is included the knowledge and love of all that comes forth from him. As a consequence, God does not have to "go out-side of himself" in his eternity in order to be radically present to all that ex-ists in time, nor does he have to change in essence or identity in order to be present to all that exists in flux and development. Realities that devel-op through events in time are the echoes or reflections in finite patterns of what exists in a more perfect and incomprehensible way in divine eternity. If, however, the Father is the principle behind all things and the principle end of all things, and he is also always relative to the Son and to the Spir-it, in generation and spiration respectively, then two consequences follow when we think of the *exitus* and *reditus* of creatures from God.

The first is that all created things that proceed forth from God the Father proceed forth always in his Word and Spirit, to whom he is utterly relative. In this way, just as God, as Father, is present to all things that come forth from him in creation and in time, without going outside of himself, so the Son and Spirit are always also present to all things, since the Father is never Father prior to or without the eternal Word and Spirit. The Trinity is there-fore omnipresent to all that comes forth from the Father even as or *just be-cause* the Father is the eternal primary origin of all things.

Second, just as all things return to the Father, so the Son and the Spir-it must be present to all things insofar as they are able to return to the Fa-ther, in the order of nature or of grace; and just insofar as things do return to God as Father, they will resemble in various ways the Son and the Spir-it. The *reditus* of all things toward God is never exclusively centered on the Father, precisely because he is also always the Father of the Son and Spirit, who are equally God. So too, then, the Son and the Spirit are central to the economy of salvation. For example, we might say that Aquinas's relational account of the primacy of the Father also implies that the creation is itself ultimately pneumatological in orientation. The Spirit is the immanent term of Trinitarian life because the Father and the Son spirate the Spirit as the term of their mutual love. Likewise, the Father and the Son send the Spirit into the world in a temporal mission that echoes the inner life of the Trinity. Accordingly, the Son comes into the world to send the Spirit of his Father upon the creation, and the creation is perfected when all things participate in the life of the Spirit. The Spirit perfects the creation by elevating all things into communion with Christ. (The circle of return thus begins back toward the Father.) This conformity of all things in creation to Christ is Christocen-tric in its own right, since it renders the creation filial, but since the Son is utterly relative to the Father, this "Christocentrism" of the work of the Spirit serves to deliver all things to the Father in Christ. The ultimacy of the Spirit and the ultimacy of the Father are not in contradiction to one another, just as the efficient primacy of the Father as principle in the Trinitarian life and the final primacy of the Spirit as the term of spiration are not in contradiction. Each of these aspects of Trinitarian life is reflected in the creation. The immanent term of the creation is life in the Spirit. The exemplary term is conformity to Christ. The extrinsic term is the return to the Father. Creation is confirmed in Trinitarian life in distinct modes, which correspond to the distinct modes of the divine persons. On a Thomistic rendering, however, this process never transpires in a way that would underscore the ultimacy of one person by excluding the ultimacy of another. The principality of the Father is maintained, but as he is utterly relative, so the ultimacy of the Son and Spirit are also affirmed, in accord with an order of relations, which in turn is reflected in the world of creation.

DISSIMILITUDE TO HUMAN PERSONS

We noted in the previous chapter that Aquinas's theology of persons as subsistent relations allows him to align the natural modes of being of the persons with a clear conception of the distinct personal identity of each. The persons are each fully and equally divine, but, as persons wholly relative to one another in a distinct order, they are also each divine in a unique mode. It follows from this that there are a number of dissimilitudes between the Trinity and any communion or ethical cooperative of human persons, whether supernatural or merely mundane. First, the divine persons subsist only in an immaterial mode, since their incomprehensible divine nature is immaterial. All human communions are expressed in and through material individuation, consisting of personal animals with distinct integral bodies, in quantitative exterior juxtaposition.

Second, the Trinitarian persons enjoy a unity of substance and operation. They are therefore mysteriously wholly interior to one another, in a perfect and pure interiority. The generation of the Word is not outside the Father, even if the Word is wholly distinct from the Father personally. Human persons, however, are distinct in substance from one another, and their operations of knowledge and love, by which they stand in relations of personal communion as rational animals, are mere features of their being, prop-

erties subject to potency and act, not purely actual. Human persons never attain wholly adequate comprehensive knowledge or love of the realities
they know and love. They cannot know and love God or creatures the way
that God alone can know and love himself and creatures.

Third, the divine persons are subsistent relations, having each one his
personal identity only from or unto the others. Created persons (whether
human or angelic) are not subsistent relations, but have relations as properties of their being. This is true in the order of efficient causality, in virtue
of creation. Human beings are caused to be by God in their very act of existence, and therefore truly are wholly relative to God in all they are. However, this profound truth is not to be confused with the *essence* of the human
being, and is "only" a feature of the human being, that is to say, a property
or accident. All created realities are characterized by this relational property
even when they are essentially different kinds of things.[7] In the order of final
causality human beings are also relational only by way of properties. Their
actions and passions, including those in the order of knowledge and love,
develop and evolve in time as expressions of their nature but are not subsistently identical with that nature.[8] Communion in human persons can be or

7. See *ST* I, q. 45, a. 2, ad 2. Also, *ST* I, q. 45, a. 3, corp.: "Creation places something in the
thing created according to relation only; because what is created is not made by movement, or
by change. For what is made by movement or by change is made from something pre-existing.
And this happens, indeed, in the particular productions of some beings, but cannot happen in the
production of all being by the universal cause of all beings, which is God. Hence God by creation
produces things without movement. Now when movement is removed from action and passion,
only relation remains. Hence creation in the creature is only a certain relation to the Creator as to
the principle of its being; even as in passion, which implies movement, is implied a relation to the
principle of motion."

8. I am differing here respectfully with Joseph Ratzinger, in regard to his proposal that the
Thomistic conception of Trinitarian persons as subsistent relations be extended to created persons, something that I think is ontologically impossible, and that, as a way of thinking about human beings, renders unduly obscure the "greater dissimilitude" between the Trinity and creatures
rightly underscored by Aquinas in the wake of the Fourth Lateran Council. See, on this, Joseph
Ratzinger, "Concerning the Notion of Person in Theology," *Communio: International Catholic Review* 17, no. 3 (Fall 1990): 439–54, originally published as *Zum Personverständnis in der Dogmatik*,
in J. Speck, ed., *Das Personverständnis in der Pädagogik und ihren Nachbarwissenschaften* (Münster:
Deutsches Institut für wissenschaftliche Pädagogik, 1966): 157–71. For an analysis of this position
and Aquinas's theory of creation as relation in historical context, see Matthew Dubroy, "Relation
and Person: The Likeness and Unlikeness Between the Human and the Divine" (STD diss., Pontifical Faculty of the Immaculate Conception, 2019); Gilles Emery, "Personne humaine et relation:
La personne se définit-elle par la relation?," *Nova et Vetera* (French edition) 89, no. 1 (2014) 7–29;
"La relation de creation," *Nova et Vetera* (French Edition) 88, no. 1 (2013): 9–43; "Ad Aliquid: Relation in the Thought of St. Thomas Aquinas," in *Theology Needs Philosophy: Acting against Reason Is
Contrary to the Nature of God*, ed. Matthew L. Lamb (Washington, D.C.: The Catholic University
of America Press, 2016), 175–201. For a speculative treatment of the question, see Steven A. Long,

not be, and can come to greater perfection. The Trinitarian communion is substantial, perfect, and eternal. It is proper to the very identity of the persons and essential to the Trinitarian life of God.

Finally, in the divine persons the order of processions and the distinction of natural modes of being imply no inequality. In human beings, meanwhile, orders of derivation typically imply some note of distinction in perfection, amidst the equality of persons. That is to say, human beings are in one sense perfectly equal with one another in virtue of their shared common nature, and the dignity of personhood it implies. However, in their operations of biological life, psychological maturation, and intellectual, ethical, and artistic development, human beings develop in varied ways over time, and acquire perfections in dependency upon the ongoing help of those who precede them either in the temporal or ontological order. The parent is more mature than the child, biologically, psychologically, and spiritually. The teacher typically has more knowledge than the student. The governor has more prudence than many of the citizens. In the human order of communion, therefore, derivation and relational dependency imply inequality of perfection, even as such relationships and the qualities they imply are ever dynamic and developing, so that relationships of equality can emerge, and relations of communication and receptivity often invert in order across time. The child takes care of the elderly parent, the pupil teaches new things to the mentor, and so forth. The equality of the Trinitarian persons helps us retain a nuanced, analogical sense of the equality that all human persons possess. Humans are not only equal in virtue of their unity of essence, but also related by their degrees of perfection. The order of derivation in the Trinitarian persons, and their shared divine perfection, helps us appreciate the fact that derivation in the order of being need not be an obstacle to human flourishing and eventual equality of perfection.[9] In fact, hierarchical

---

"Divine and Creaturely 'Receptivity': The Search for a Middle Term," *Communio: International Catholic Review* 21, no. 1 (Spring 1994): 151–61; and *Analogia Entis*, 1–12.

9. If one follows the Thomistic line of thinking about divine paternity as relational, there is no hierarchy of being in God, due to the perfect equality of the three persons. Created persons, by contrast, are unable to give or receive from others *in totality* the way that the Trinitarian persons can (so as to imply perfect equality). Therefore among created persons, derivation and emergent order between creatures typically presupposes differentiated perfections and hierarchical modes of being in a way it does not in the Trinity. This is not a sign of a moral or ontological defect, but is simply an incumbent trait of finite perfection, which is always ontologically derivative and differentiated. Only a Manichean political ontology that denies the goodness of the finite created order would want to remove all dependency that would entail any trace of hierarchy.

forms of communication in creatures are typically meant to provide conditions for human flourishing in those who receive from these forms. The two ideas (hierarchical derivation, and orientation toward perfection) are complementary and mutually corrective in the human political realm. When the acknowledgement of diverse degrees of excellence is not qualified by a strong sense of basic human equality and the natural potential of each person for perfection, it becomes one-sidedly aristocratic and elitist. It leads to a restriction on the universal imperatives of Christian love and creates societies of division. The acknowledgement of basic equality and of the dispositions in all toward excellence, when it is turned against the acknowledgement of hierarchies of excellence and dependence, becomes demagogic. It can lead to a denial of the universal Christian call to perfection in the order of the intellectual, moral, and artistic virtues. In this latter case, a Christian culture is typically replaced by one espousing a reductive materialistic anthropology (where perfections of spirit are ignored), technological development (available to all), base entertainment, and banal consumerism.

HUMAN BIOLOGICAL PATERNITY AND MATERNITY: METAPHORICAL SIMILITUDES?

Having noted the previous dissimilitudes, we can also ask whether there is a proper analogy in human paternity to the paternity of the Father? Here we should note four considerations. First, the divine nature is immaterial, simple, and incomprehensible. Consequently, as Gregory of Nazianzus noted against Eunomius, we cannot say philosophically that God is a biological father or mother, and indeed we must say that the divine nature transcends all designations of biological paternity or maternity precisely insofar as it is immaterial and transcendent.

Second, the revelation of the God of Israel as Creator entails the use of images of paternity and maternity, but the biblical revelation given to the prophets of Israel does not espouse the view that the Creator is a father per se. Instead, it underscores the transcendence of God vis-à-vis any human anthropological conception of the divine as a progenitor.

Third, then, the specifically Christian revelation of God as Father, communicated by Christ, is first and foremost a revelation about the inner life of God, and by extension a revelation of God's creation of all things in his Word and Spirit, and of his invitation to communion in Trinitarian life. We

call God "Father" insofar as God is the Father of the Lord Jesus Christ, who
sends the Spirit of filial adoption upon the world. This conception of Fatherhood entails, as we have argued, the consistent use of the psychological
analogy, which underscores the immaterial nature of the processions of the
divine persons. Insofar as this is the case, there is not a proper analogy to
biological paternity or maternity in the Christian affirmation of the eternal
Fatherhood of God. Human parenthood inevitably entails material and corporeal conditions of animal life that are not ascribable to the divine nature
per se.[10] Here we should be wary of two errors, each opposed to the other.
The first is that of an all-too-human, univocal conception of the Trinity that
would understand the persons in God after the model of a biological family.
The second is an opposite position that claims that all paternal language for
God is patriarchal and projective. This opposite extreme is typically marked
by an equivocal conception of religious language in which all ascriptions for
God are taken to be merely metaphorical. In this case, when one fails to acknowledge that there are proper analogies for the Trinity, the use of Father
and Son as "mere metaphors" appears arbitrary and therefore contrived by
the conventional consensus of past patriarchal cultures that today can be
dismissed. A Thomistic notion of analogical attribution allows us to avoid
both these theoretically misdirected and mutually reactive extremes.

Finally, we can acknowledge that human parenthood does contains *some*
likenesses to divine generation, ones that allow us to speak of similitudes by
proper analogy even when speaking of the biological generation of persons.
The first such likeness comes from an analogy of substantial generation in a
common nature. Two human parents can conceive and beget a new human
being who is identical with them in nature. They transmit to the child subsistent life in the body (so that the generation is substantial in kind), even
if they do so principally in virtue of the matter of the body, rather than the
spiritual soul, which is created immediately by God. When compared with
Trinitarian generation, this likeness is very imperfect, since human generation is material, not immaterial, and the person who is begotten is substantially distinct from, and not identical with, the parents. Consequently, the
substantial generation that exists among human persons entails material potentiality, not pure actuality.

Second, we can say that in human parenthood, one person is the princi-

---

10. See, on this point, *SCG* IV, c. 11, para. 19.

ple of another in the order of generation, and that one person proceeds from another. This analogy is based on relations of origin. If we place it alongside the first, we can say that human persons are principles of generation to one another, by the transmission of a common nature, one that is substantial in kind.[11]

Third, human persons also can act in knowledge and love, both toward one another in view of the generation of a child, and toward the children they beget. Therefore, like God the Father, they can be principles of life based on spiritual knowledge and love. Unlike God the Father, however, human parents transmit personal life freely rather than by essence, and their acts of knowledge and love are not substantial but utterly accidental. Their personal love can be absent, therefore, from either the sexual act of conceiving or the decision to love the child they conceive. What we can conclude from these comparisons is that human parents are most like God by similitude in two ways, first as principles of generation and second in the teleological term of the generation of children. When parents have begotten a being who is one in nature with them and they actively know and love one another and the child they have begotten, they are most like the uncreated communion of Trinitarian persons.[12] This similitude, while real, merely

11. Aquinas discusses this similitude in *SCG* IV, c. 11: "Hence, the things which belong distinctly to the father or to the mother in fleshly generation, in the generation of the Word are all attributed to the Father by sacred Scripture; for the Father is said not only 'to give life to the Son' (cf. Jn 5:26), but also 'to conceive' and to 'bring forth.'"

12. Do the similitudes of human paternity and maternity differ in this respect? No doubt they do, since the biological mother provides more from the substance of her own body, by nurturing the child in her own womb (a metaphorical similitude for the Word being in the bosom of the Father: Jn 1:18). The biological father is more independent from the child in the process of gestation before birth, which can provide a metaphorical similitude for the distinction of persons in the Trinity, as the Father is an active not passive principle of the Son, wholly distinct personally from the Son by immaterial generation, not in material continuity. These distinctions, while real, should not be pressed, however, since the ascriptions are based on physiological and embodied ways of relating to a child. The fact that the eternal Son became a male human being does not entail that there is human paternity in God, but rather that the Holy Trinity wanted to communicate divine life to us in human form. Similarly, the mystery of the virginal conception and birth of Jesus implies not that God is the biological father of Jesus, but that Jesus Christ fittingly has no human father because he is the eternal Son of the Father. The metaphor of the bridegroom and the bride, for Christ and the Church, does repose upon the fact that Christ is biologically male. The Sonship of Christ is not explained, however, in light of the image of the male bridegroom. Rather, the inverse is the case. Jesus is the bridegroom of the Church because he is the only begotten Son of God. Only God is the true spouse of the human soul, in the order of grace, and so only one who is truly God can truly be the bridegroom of the Church. This eternal Sonship of Jesus is expressed in his humanity, then, as the bridegroom of the Church, without the implication of any materialistic or biological metaphor for eternal generation in God.

obtains imperfectly, however. Were one to develop it without due reference to the analogical notions we considered above—processions, relations, and persons—a conceptually unwarranted form of anthropomorphism would inevitably result.

CONCLUSION

In this chapter, we first saw how the Father is the principle in the Trinity, insofar as he is the fontal origin from whom the Son and the Spirit proceed. In the second place, we saw that "Father" is indeed his personal name, in virtue of his eternal relation to the Son, who proceeds from him. Nevertheless, insofar as creation proceeds from God by a similitude with the generation of the Son, all creatures have a certain participation in the Son's filial relation, and so are truly relative to God as Father according to diverse degrees of likeness. Thus they are patterned after the eternal exemplarity of the Son, who is the Father's consubstantial image and so image *par excellence*. Third, we saw how Aquinas argues, against Bonaventure, that the Father's innascibility is an exclusively negative characteristic: the Father has no principle. What this implies is that the Father cannot be understood prior to and outside of his relation to the persons who proceed from him. His paternity is both fontal and relational. Last, we looked at the analogy to creaturely final causality that exists in the turning of the Son and Spirit back toward the Father from whom they proceed. This turning-toward the Father of the persons who proceed from him is accordingly the transcendent exemplar of the *reditus* movement of creatures, who are teleologically ordered back to their first principle as their last end.

Having looked at the Person of the Father, we may now move on to consideration of the second person of the Trinity, the Father's eternally-begotten Son.

26

God the Son

Having begun with a consideration of God the Father, we must now turn to the mystery of the Son. Aquinas considers this subject especially in *ST* I, qq. 34–35. In consistency with his processional analysis of the immanent life of God, Aquinas approaches the mystery of the eternal generation of the Son by examining two other biblical names: Word and Image, in order to show how they complement and interpret the name Son. Here we will focus especially on Aquinas's explanation of how the biblical name "Word" (Greek: *logos*; Latin: *verbum*), so prominent in the Prologue to St. John's Gospel, clarifies and illumines the spiritual import of the personal name Son as applied to God who "is spirit" (Jn 4:24). This close mutual connection between the terms "Word" and "Son" is already in evidence in Jn 1:14: "*And the Word* became flesh and dwelt among us, full of grace and truth; we have beheld his glory, glory as of *the only-begotten Son* from the Father."[1] In this chapter, my aim, accordingly, will be to show that the name "Word," purified of its creaturely limitations, complements that of "Son"; that the Word is in fact a proper name for the Son; and, moreover, how the name Word, though a proper name in God, also secondarily implies a relation to creatures.

THE SON AS WORD

In discussions of the Son as the Word of the Father, we should begin by making it clear from the outset that we are using the term "word" in the

---

1. Emphases added.

sense of an *interior concept*. In other words, we are talking about the kind of word that proceeds from the mind. The analogy is thus to immaterial procession and not a sensate spoken word. However, the interior concept is also expressed or spoken by an exterior word of speech. This is analogous to the Incarnation: the eternal Logos of the Father is manifest or expressed outwardly through the "speaking forth" of the Word in human nature.

"There are two words in us: that of the heart, and that of the voice. The word of the heart is the very concept of the intellect, *which is hidden to men, except insofar as it is expressed through the voice, or through the word of the voice*. Now, the word of the heart is compared to the eternal Word before the incarnation, *when he was with the Father and hidden to us*; but the word of the voice is compared to the incarnate Word which then appeared to us and was manifest."[2] Aquinas implies here that from the spoken word we come to grasp the inner concept of the speaker, and analogously, from the incarnation of the eternal Word in our human nature, we come to understand that there is an eternal procession of the Logos and Son in God, eternally. The word understood as intellectual concept is, accordingly, that which can be employed to designate the Logos interior to God. As Aquinas puts it tersely in *ST* I, q. 34, a. 1: "word is taken strictly in God, as signifying the concept of the intellect."

To understand this revealed mystery theologically, then, Aquinas employs the similitude of the mental *verbum* or "word" in the human person, where *verbum* denotes an intellectual concept proceeding from the mind, rather than a spoken word proceeding through speech.[3] The ordinary mental concepts in and through which we know things are expressions of our abstracted knowledge, drawn initially from the things themselves through the operation of the agent intellect. As we have already noted above, in chapter 22, for Aquinas our knowledge of a thing depends upon our abstracting its intelligible species or essence from multiple sensible experiences of the thing itself. The intellect, having abstracted the intelligible species, fashions a concept in and through which it proceeds back to the reality, in order that we might think about the experienced reality in overtly conceptual terms. This concept is generated from the mind, through an act of the mind.

---

2. Thomas Aquinas, *Lectura super Matthaeum* (*In Matt.*) I, lec. 4, 112, in *Commentary on the Gospel of Matthew*, trans. J. Holmes and B. Mortensen (Lander, Wyo.: Aquinas Institute, 2013), emphases added. Augustine employs this comparison, as well, in *De Trinitate*, 9.12.
3. See *ST* I, q. 34, a. 1.

What is important to see in this account is the distinction Aquinas makes between our initial abstraction of an essence (intelligible species) received passively into the intellect, and our subsequent use of this knowledge in an active mode through a concept derived from the intelligible species. "The Philosopher [i.e., Aristotle] says that the notion (*ratio*) which a name signifies is a definition. Hence, what is thus expressed, i.e., formed in the soul, is called an interior word. Consequently it is compared to the intellect, not as that by which the intellect understands [i.e., the intelligible species], but as that in which it understands, because it is in what is thus expressed and formed that it sees the nature of the thing understood. Thus we have the meaning of the name 'word.'"[4] Accordingly, we must distinguish the following: (1) a species the mind grasps intelligibly through abstraction; (2) the inner concept or mental word that proceeds from the mind as informed by this abstraction, "in" which the mind thinks; and (3) outer imaginations and vocal sounds (languages and symbols) that accompany the inner mental word. So, for example, the human being who has seen and experienced many trees can abstract from the consideration of them an intelligible kind or essence (the intelligible species), but the same essential content is also then used actively by the mind to think about and signify the tree (the concept or *verbum* as such). This is then signified exteriorly by various conventional linguistic designations used to speak about trees. Aquinas thinks the analogy to the procession of the Word is located in the second of these three instances. This is the case for several reasons: The concept in us is immaterial, not material. It proceeds from the knowing subject by a relation of origin. It remains within the subject in virtue of being an immanent act of the subject.

Aquinas argues, then, that Word or *Verbum* in God is accordingly the proper name for the Son, precisely because it expresses the spiritual generation whereby the Son comes forth from the Father's knowledge of himself as the expression of his own wisdom.[5] The Son, as the expression of the Father's self-knowledge, possesses in himself the plenitude of the divine nature and understanding. He is, for this reason, equal to the Father, but as one who eternally *receives* all that he is from the Father, as his eternal Word, in whom the Father knows all things. The analogy of the Word in this way helps us interpret the analogy of Sonship. Since the Son possesses in him-

4. St. Thomas Aquinas, *In Ioan.* I, lec. 1, 25.
5. See *ST* I, q. 34, a. 2.

self the plenitude of the Father's nature and existence as God, the generation in question need not and does not imply ontological inequality. The Father and Son are not merely one in kind, but are *homoousios*, one in being.[6]

When we have said all this, however, we are not yet finished with the analogy of the mental word. For in order to convey the transcendent perfection
of the Word of God, we must underscore not only the likeness, but also the
much more radical dissimilitude that exists between God the Word and the
created *verbum*. Stated in terms of Dionysius's *triplex via*, it is only by passing through the *via negationis* that can we in turn arrive, by means of the *via
eminentiae*, at the affirmation of the incomprehensibly unique perfection
proper to the Son's generation.[7]

In this vein, Aquinas identifies four principal forms of theological dissimilitude between human thought and the eternal generation of the Word.[8]
The first dissimilitude consists in the difference between the accidental and
substantial mode of the procession of our mental word and God's. We, as
humans, produce intellectual concepts that are merely properties of our being (non-essential characteristics of our person), and that qualify our understanding in some way through our acquired knowledge. In God, however,
the Word is in no way accidental but is "of the very substance" of the Father

6. See the beautiful and exacting analysis of this point in *SCG* IV, c. 11: "Now, since the divine
intellect is not only always in act, but is itself pure act ... the substance of the divine intellect must
be its very act of understanding, and this is the act of the intellect. But the being of the Word
interiorly conceived, or intention understood, is the very act of being understood. Therefore, the
being of the divine Word is identical with that of the divine intellect and, consequently, with that
of God, who is His own intellect. The being of God, of course, is His essence or nature, which is
the same as God Himself. ... The Word of God, therefore, is the divine being and His essence, and
is true God Himself."

7. Aquinas typically employs Dionysius's *triplex via* in speaking about analogical names for
the divine essence. See, for example, *ST* I, q. 13, a. 2, and our discussion, in chapter 12 above, of
St. Thomas's appropriation of the threefold way. However, it seems to be clear that he employs a
similar kind of thinking when speaking of the proper name of the Son as "Word" in *SCG* IV, c. 11,
and in his *In Ioan.*, lec. 1, 1–5.

8. Aquinas's treatment of this subject is most extensive in the *SCG* IV, c. 11, and in the first
lectio of his *In Ioan.* On these four dissimilitudes, see in particular *In Ioan.* I, lec. 1, 26–29. (Although
only three are listed explicitly, the fourth is implied when Aquinas indicates that God's Word, in
differentiation from our word, is *personal*). I am inverting the order of exposition of Aquinas's
arguments, and expressing them in a slightly different form, introducing complementary elements
from *SCG* IV, c. 11.

(Heb 1:3). Note that here we are positing both a negation and an eminent perfection. In his incomprehensible perfection, the Father's generation of the Son communicates to him all that the Father has and is as God.

The second form of dissimilitude has to do with the total self-communication of the divine essence, a communication that results from intellectual procession and production in God. Concepts in the human mind are mere mental *intentiones* (mental intentions, not reality) in and through which we aspire to know reality as it is, while the subjects of our thinking are generally realities distinct from ourselves and from our own thought. By contrast, the Word himself contains the very truth of God's being. The truth in question is not abstract or intentional, but is God's very essence, God's very being.

The third form of dissimilitude consists in the fact that, with God, intellectual procession results in the personal differentiation of God's Word. The concepts that come forth from our thought processes are an aspect of our person, a dimension of our personal thought. We cannot think in conceptual reflection all that we are, or communicate, in our thought, what and who we are substantially. Nor do our thought processes terminate in a person distinct from ourselves. But in the Trinity, the Son, who is God, is truly distinct from the Father hypostatically or personally, even as he proceeds from him eternally as his Word.[9] And in generating the Son, the Father communicates all that he has and is as God, so that the Son is the Word in whom the totality of the divine mystery is expressed.

The fourth form of dissimilitude has to do with the perfect actuality of the Word in question. In us, the generation of thought eventually leads to greater intellectual maturity and perfection, and thus actuates a latent potentiality. In our knowledge we pass from imperfection to greater perfection. In God, however, there is no potency of operation in the generation of the Word. Rather, in his transcendent perfection, the Word *is* the very act of being that the Father is.[10] He is light from light, or act from act, containing in himself the very existence, nature, and operation of the Father, all of which is hidden from our direct gaze. As such, he has no eventual perfec-

---

9. See *In Ioan.* I, lec. 1, 28: "Consequently, the word which our intellect forms is not of the essence of our soul, but is an accident of it. But in God, to understand and to be are the same; and so the Word of the divine intellect is not an accident but belongs to its nature. Thus it must be subsistent, because whatever is in the nature of God is God. Thus Damascene says that God is a substantial Word, and a hypostasis, but our words are concepts in our mind."

10. See *In Ioan.* I, lec. 1, 27. See also *ST* I, q. 34, a. 3; q. 27, a. 1, ad 2; *SCG*, IV, c. 11, para. 11.

tion to acquire, being in himself, as God, the source and summit of all lesser, created perfections, each of which participates in some way in his uncreated Image.[11]

In sum, even as the designation of the Son as "Word" obtains by analogy with the procession of our interior mental word, so too the difference
between God's consubstantial Word and our mental word, in keeping with
the *triplex via*, far outstrips the similarity between the two, because the divine nature sublimely transcends created nature.

"WORD" AS THE PROPER NAME OF THE SON

In *ST* I, q. 34, a. 2, Aquinas asks whether "Word" is the Son's proper name. Is
this a name that is rightly ascribed to the second person of the Trinity alone?
Aquinas's argument is that the notion of Sonship and the name "Word" are
mutually self-interpreting terms. He refers us back to *ST* I, q. 27 a. 2, where
the claim is first made: "'Word,' said of God in its proper sense, is used personally, and is the proper name of the person of the Son. For it signifies an
emanation of the intellect: and the person Who proceeds in God, by way
of emanation of the intellect, is called the Son; and this procession is called
generation, as we have shown above (cf. *ST* I, q. 27, a. 2). Hence it follows
that the Son alone is properly called Word in God." The implication of this
claim is that we cannot rightly understand the name of Son without at the
same time thinking of the other name of Word, and vice versa. In Trinitarian
theology, these are mutually correlated analogical notions.

For its part, Sonship implies begetting and a distinction of persons, who
are yet of the same nature. Word, on the other hand, implies immateriality
and a procession from the Father that is intellectual in nature.

This is why, without the complementary support of the notion "Word,"
Sonship will appear either (1) as materialistic (which historically is one of
the common Islamic accusations, that the Christian doctrine of God implies
a materially begotten son); or (2) as a similitude for a created procession
that is not immanent to the Father, but is instead something created by the
Father (the error of Arianism).

---

11. See *In Ioan.* I, lec. 1, 27: "Since we cannot express all our conceptions in one word, we must
form many imperfect words through which we separately express all that is in our knowledge. But
it is not that way with God. For since he understands both himself and everything else through
his essence, by one act, the single divine Word is expressive of all that is in God, not only of the
Persons but also of creatures; otherwise it would be imperfect."

Moreover, without being referred to the notion of "Sonship," the notion of "Word" will for its part either (1) risk losing a sense of the real distinction of persons (the error of modalism); or else (2) will risk depicting the Word uniquely as a mere property of the God who is speaking, and so lose the notion of an immanent procession in God by which the divine nature is communicated, that is, received by the Word from the Father through eternal generation.

"WORD" INDICATES A RELATION
TO CREATURES

In *ST* I, q. 34, a. 3, Aquinas asks whether the name "Word" also contains a signification of any kind having to do with creatures. On this count, it is important to reaffirm at the outset that God does not formulate his knowledge through a prior encounter with beings other than himself, which he would then come to know for the first time through this encounter, and from which he would learn something. The claim we have made above is that this is not how God's knowledge as Creator works. Rather, God is the First Truth, who creates all things from within the eternal knowledge he has of himself.[12] (All that exists depends upon God's self-knowledge, and not the converse.) Moreover, prior to his knowledge of the creation, the Father knows himself eternally and, in knowing himself eternally, generates his Word.

Accordingly, all that is in the Father is present in the Son as the personal Word that proceeds forth from the Father. And just as the Father creates all things through the knowledge that he has of himself, so too he *also* creates all things through his Word and only-begotten Son, who proceeds forth from him as the eternal expression of his own self-knowledge.[13]

Significantly, however, this priority of God's self-knowledge over knowledge of creatures does not prevent God from knowing creatures. Rather, it simply means that he knows creatures *through* his Word and not apart from him. As Aquinas states in article 3: "Word implies relation to creatures. For God by knowing himself, knows every creature. Now the word conceived in the mind is representative of everything that is actually understood. Hence there are in ourselves different words for the different things which we un-

---

12. *SCG*, IV, c. 11.
13. See *In Ioan.* I, lec. 2, 76.

derstand. But because God by one act understands himself and all things [through himself], his one and only Word is expressive not only of the Father, but of all creatures."

It is in this sense, accordingly, that the name "Word" implies a relation to creatures. The Word whom we confess, from John 1, is not only the eternally begotten Son of God but also the Word through whom all things were made, the exemplar in whom God creates all that he creates. This relation is, of course, entirely secondary and derivative from the intra-divine communication, in which God the Father generates his eternal Word as a constitutive feature of his divine identity.[14] However, it is true to say that God's Word is not only the expression of the Father's self-knowledge but is also the operative, exemplary cause of all creatures.

We can think about this idea in greater depth by considering briefly the *esse* of the Word eternally received from the Father in comparison with the *esse* of creatures received from God the Father through his Word. The analogy of the Word as a "concept" in God implies several likenesses to human understanding. The human concept results from the mind's intellectual apprehension of a certain real object of knowledge (say, human nature) and in doing so contains in an intentional way a content or adequate understanding of the reality known. In God, the "concept" in question, the begotten Word, is adequate in content to all that God the Father is, so that all that the Father possesses as God (the incomprehensible divine nature) is in the Son. Of course this implies that the Word is substantial not intentional, one in being with the Father. Therefore, as his begotten Word or Wisdom, the Son contains in himself all of the *esse* or existence proper to the Father as God, in virtue of his deity. This *esse* is so plenary and perfect in infinite actuality that it is capable of being the principle and cause of a vast multitude of finite things, across an immense scale of perfections, from the smallest material particles, to the highest immaterial angelic persons. We might say that the creation of all finite realities in their *esse* is like a waterfall or cascade poured forth freely from the infinite *esse* of God. If, then, the Son as God eternally receives the infinite plenitude of divine existence from the Father, naturally not freely, as one eternally begotten of the Father not as a creature, then he also eternally receives his being the one who is infinite in *esse*, perfect in actuality, and principle of all creatures. In this sense his uncreated receptiv-

---

14. See too *ST* I, q. 37, a. 2, ad 3: "Thus it is evident that relation to the creatures is implied … in the Word … as it were in a secondary way."

ity of divine existence is always ontologically prior to and is the principle of creatures' created receptivity of finite existence. His eternal generation is the exemplary measure and efficient source of their coming into being.

It follows from this that creatures in their very *esse* bear a resemblance to the Son, by appropriation. They come forth from the Father, Son, and Spirit, but insofar as they receive existence, they are said to be like the Son in an appropriate and distinctive mode. The Son's reception of the plenitude of existence is mirrored in finite existents that are generated or come into existence as a result of the activity of others that precede them. If this Thomistic account is correct, we can note a false dichotomy that one should avoid: it is problematic to oppose the infinite reception of the plenitude of *esse* and the finite reception of the plenitude of *esse*. The universe God creates consists in a vast myriad of diverse kinds of finite beings. By their immense quantitative extension, vast temporal succession, and detailed hierarchical scale of perfections, these realities reflect in a complex way through finite composition something of God's simple and infinite perfection. The eternal procession of the Word from the Father, then, not only causes but in a sense circumscribes or contains eternally this finite procession of creatures from God. The plenitude of divine *esse* in the Word is rich enough to be the source of participated *esse* in creatures, without being constituted by this created procession. Two further ideas follow from this one. First, the Word is in all things, since the creation is a participation in *esse* that comes forth from the Word. It may seem unfathomable to us that the Word is in all things, as the cause of their being, if we consider them in their material exteriority and solidness while thinking of him only in his immateriality, since our conceptual thoughts are external to solid material realities and are mere fragile properties of our understanding. But if we consider the Word in his plenitude of *esse* and communication of *esse*, he is the giver of existence to all material beings and, in virtue of this, is in all things as the ground of their being, and as the author of their inner intelligibility and beauty. Second, it follows that the substantial autonomy of creatures is in no way threatened by the eternal procession of the Word. On the contrary, the plenary reality of creatures in their substantial autonomy is grounded in the ontologically prior eternal procession of the Word, and they are instantiated in being precisely in accord with their likeness to him. They are true causal agents because they receive being from God after the pattern of the Son, and not in spite of this fact. The procession of creatures can unfold then as a genuine history of realities that interact with one another, even so as to cause the substantial generation or corruption of one another. In their history they do truly reflect the receptive procession of the Son, without their history in any way constituting the Son in his eternal procession as God.

CONCLUSION

In this chapter, we saw how the name "Word" as applied to God the Son takes as its point of departure an analogy with the immaterial procession of the mental word in the human mind. Thus, this scriptural designation, "Word," serves well to complement the equally scriptural designation "Son," since it draws out the immanent spiritual nature of the generation of the divine person in question, in this way safeguarding it from crass, materialistic understandings.

However, as every analogical term must be purified from its creaturely shortcomings in its application to God, so the application of the term "Word" to God must also be purified in the four ways specified above by Aquinas. First, as we saw, the intra-divine concept of *this* Word must be conceived of as a substantial and not accidental mode of procession, given that there are no accidents in God (everything in God is substance and relation). Second, this substantial procession results, not in an intentional act, but in a total self-communication of God's substance. Third, this procession, unlike our intellectual procession, accordingly results in *personal* distinction in the divinity, as a new person is set in relation to the person from whom he proceeds by means of this act. A fourth difference is found in the perfect actuality of the Word in question, as God, being pure act, does not pass from potency to act in his act of self-understanding.

Beyond this, we also saw how Word in God secondarily signifies a relation to creatures, not as if God's self-knowledge were in any way dependent on creatures but, on the contrary, insofar as God's Word is their exemplary cause.

Having discussed the persons of the Father and Son, we now turn to the third person in the Trinity, the Holy Spirit.

27

God the Holy Spirit

Eastern and Western Christian traditions alike share from the Nicene era a common commitment to the confession of the procession of the Son from the Father as his eternal Word. By way of contrast, the specifics of the Holy Spirit's procession from the Father, in particular the question of whether he proceeds from the Father *and the Son* (the *"Filioque"*), is a contested point of doctrine that has historically contributed to the split between the Eastern Orthodox and Roman Catholic Churches, a division that continues down to this day. Given not only the theological but also the historic importance of the *Filioque*, we will spend the greater part of this chapter considering the theological bases for its affirmation, as well as the intrinsic intelligibility of the mystery of God designated by this point of Catholic Trinitarian doctrine.

We will proceed in this chapter by first following Aquinas in his consideration of the Holy Spirit as proceeding by way of will, for which reason he is Love in Person. In this connection, we will discuss the Spirit's procession in relation to the paternal principality, and also how the Father and Son are one principle of the Holy Spirit, who accordingly proceeds as their act of mutual love. After this, we will discuss the historical and theological difficulties raised by the *Filioque*, Aquinas's arguments in favor of it, and then close by adverting to modern ecumenical efforts to arrive at a resolution of the historic disagreement on this issue among the Churches.

As we noted in the last chapter, Aquinas identifies a created likeness for the procession of the Son in the notion of the human *verbum* or intelligible concept. The eternal Word proceeds from the Father's understanding as his expressed wisdom or uncreated concept. Extending this same psychological analogy, Aquinas also maintains that the Holy Spirit proceeds from the Father and the Son as the *love* of God. As we saw earlier,[1] however, love can be used either as an essential term or a notional term when referred to God, thus, "God is love in his very essence" as distinct from, "The Holy Spirit is Love in Person." It is the latter idea to which we are referring in speaking of the procession of the Spirit, the act of loving willingly as a relational activity, immaterial in kind, that proceeds from a knowing subject.

This procession of love—here we are speaking of the notional act of *spiration and of being spirated*—has no proper name in scripture, and in this respect is unlike generation or begetting, which are terms we find indicated overtly in the Prologue of John's Gospel when it speaks of the Word as the "only-begotten Son." When we use the word "love" as a proper name for the Holy Spirit, rather than as a common name, we do so in order to designate a relation of origin: the Love that proceeds from the Father and the Son.

To speak about a divine person who is love as the "Holy Spirit" is fitting, for reasons Aquinas gives in *ST* I, q. 36, a. 1. The word "Spirit" denotes immateriality: we are talking about an immaterial procession analogous to the movement of love in the human person by an act of the will, the love that pertains to reason and spiritual action. Spiritual love, simply put, is a movement of the will toward the beloved. The word "Holy," for its part, is attributed to whatever is ordered to God: that which is "holy" is that which makes us tend toward God. But love or charity makes one tend toward God. It is appropriate then to name the person in God who is love by a name, and the name Holy Spirit denotes the holiness of the person who is subsistent love.[2]

---

1. See chapter 23, above.

2. *ST* I, q. 36, a. 1: "The appropriateness of this name may be shown in two ways. Firstly, from the fact that the person who is called 'Holy Spirit' has something in common with the other Persons. For, as Augustine says (*The Trinity* 15.17), 'Because the Holy Spirit is common to both, He Himself is called that properly which both are called in common. For the Father also is a spirit, and the Son is a spirit; and the Father is holy, and the Son is holy.' Secondly, from the proper signification of the name. For the name spirit in things corporeal seems to signify impulse and motion; for we call the breath and the wind by the term spirit. Now it is a property of love to move and impel the will of the lover towards the object loved. Further, holiness is attributed to whatever is ordered

How might we best understand this analogy? Here the analogy to the relational order of wisdom and love in the human person is of importance. Just as a human person may come to know in and through concepts that proceed from the human intellect in its active mode ("generating" such concepts), so the person may come to love in and through the medium of his or her knowledge of the world. What we first come to know actively, we also may come to love, and love inclines us outwardly toward that which we love, and in this sense is also relational. In a human person, love derives from knowledge and proceeds toward the beloved. Consequently, we can understand that if the Spirit proceeds from the Father as his spirated love, he does so as one who proceeds from the Father in and from his begotten Word, according to the analogy of love proceeding from knowledge.

THE FATHER AND SON AS ONE PRINCIPLE
OF THE HOLY SPIRIT

In order to rightly understand the teaching that the Holy Spirit proceeds from both the Father and the Son, we must always begin by placing appropriate stress on the principality of the Father. As the Son has his whole being precisely as Son from the Father, so too all that the Father has, the Son has received—"All that the Father has is mine" (Jn 16:15).[3] This eternal possession includes the reception from the Father of an eternally active role as principle in the spiration of the Spirit. Accordingly, we say, as Aquinas expressly affirms in *ST* I, q. 36, a. 3, that the spiration of the Holy Spirit occurs "*from* the Father *through* the Son [*a patre per filium*],"[4] which is to say, by the Father's power received fully by the Son. Simply stated, the Son truly spirates the Spirit with the Father, but he does so by the same power of spiration that the Father has. The Father, however, imparts this power to the Son precisely in generation. In this way, the Son is truly and completely the principle of the Holy Spirit with the Father, but also only and always *from* the Father. The Father is always and ever the fontal principle of both the Son and the Spirit, even if he gives the Son eternally to be with him the source of the Spirit.

---

to God. Therefore because the divine person proceeds by way of the love whereby God is loved, that person is most properly named 'the Holy Spirit.'" [Trans. slightly modified.]

3. See Aquinas's analysis of Jn 16:14–15 in *ST* I, q. 36, a. 2, ad 1, which conveys the same interpretation of this passage of John's Gospel.

4. Emphases added.

Beyond affirming, however, that the Spirit proceeds from the Father through the Son, we can say in addition that the Father and the Son are jointly *one principle* of the Holy Spirit. In *ST* I, q. 36, a. 4, Aquinas discusses the mystery that there are two who are spirating, but only one spiration, by which the Spirit proceeds equally from the Father and the Son. In the first paragraph of the corpus, St. Thomas gives as the rationale underlying this conclusion the relative opposition of Father and Son: "The Father and the Son are in everything one, wherever there is no distinction between them of opposite relation [which obtains only with regard to generation]. Hence since there is no relative opposition between them as the principle of the Holy Spirit it follows that the Father and the Son are one principle of the Holy Spirit."[5]

Stated more positively, Aquinas's idea is the following: when the Father spirates the Holy Spirit as a person who is love, he does so from all eternity precisely as Father, that is to say, as one who is always already constituted by his paternity. This follows from the Thomistic conception of relativity as constitutive of the persons in the Trinity, which we have discussed above. But since the Father's paternity as such is defined only in relative opposition to sonship, this means that from all eternity, he is always already Father *of the Son*, such that the generation of the Son is always already "there" when the Father spirates the Spirit. Moreover, the Son himself is always already receiving from the Father all that the Father is (save that in which there is relative opposition), and so he has from the Father the power of being one principle of the Holy Spirit together with the Father. As such, the Spirit proceeds not only from the Father, but from the Son, too, who together are one unique principle (the Father with the Son).

Were this not the case, and were the Father and the Son to spirate the Spirit as two distinct principles, then there would be something that would distinguish them in virtue of this spiration. In this case, however, they would

---

5. See also the analysis of the language of spiration in *ST* I, q. 36, a. 4, ad 7: "Some say that although the Father and the Son are one principle of the Holy Spirit, there are two spirators, by reason of the distinction of 'supposita,' as also there are two spirating, because acts refer to subjects. Yet this does not hold good as to the name 'Creator'; because the Holy Spirit proceeds from the Father and the Son as from two distinct persons, as above explained; whereas the creature proceeds from the three persons not as distinct persons, but as united in essence. It seems, however, better to say that because spirating is an adjective, and spirator a substantive, we can say that the Father and the Son are two spirating, by reason of the plurality of the 'supposita' but not two spirators by reason of the one spiration. For adjectival words derive their number from the 'supposita' but substantives from themselves, according to the form signified."

be distinct from one another as God in some way that would not pertain uniquely to the relation of origin between them, of the Father to the Son, as he who eternally begets and communicates divine life to him who eternally is begotten and who receives divine life. This "something else" that would distinguish them would presumably be something pertaining to power or essence and therefore would attenuate the confession of Trinitarian monotheism. If one is to hold to the *Filioque* then, and assert that the Spirit proceeds from the Father and the Son, then it is sensible to hold as well that the Spirit proceeds from them as one principle. This claim is entirely compatible with the former insistence on the paternal principality. It is precisely because the Son receives everything that he has and is as God from the Father that he also receives from him the active power of being the eternal origin of the Spirit, with the Father, as one principle.[6]

THE HOLY SPIRIT AS LOVE

Aquinas discusses the name "Love," as applied to the Holy Spirit, in *ST* I, q. 37, a. 1. What does it mean to claim that the Spirit is the eternal love of the Father and the Son and that he is an eternal person who is subsistent love? We should begin by recalling what we have noted above. Love can be taken as an essential term that refers to God's very nature, "God is love," or as a notional term that refers to the third person, "The Holy Spirit is Love." For this reason, if we think about God's act of will as an act of love, this need not imply a relation per se. For example, when we think of God's activity of loving as such, we might mean to indicate by this an essential term: God knows himself and loves himself from all eternity. As we have noted, in part 2 of this book, it is entirely legitimate to refer to the one God of biblical revelation in this way.

Second, then, this means that if we wish to speak of the relational pro-

---

6. This point is not trivial from an ecumenical point of view. One advantage of the Thomistic way of understanding the person of the Father in utterly relational terms, which we have explored above, is that it allows one to maintain the paternal principality (or "monarchy") in accord with sensitivities in Eastern Christian theology, even while arguing that just because the Father is the eternal Father of the Son, his spiration of the Spirit must implicate the presence of the Son, whom he spirates from or through, and that this is one way of interpreting the idea of the Spirit's proceeding from the Father and the Son as from one principle. In other words, the Thomistic relationalist account of the paternal principality provides a conceptual bridge between the Eastern notion of spiration through the Son and the Western notion of spiration from the Father and the Son as from one principle. I will return to this point below.

cession of the Spirit from the Father and the Son as Love, then we need to identify clearly an analogy from human spiritual love that is *relational*, that is, one that implies a relation of origin, in order to speak by similitude about the Holy Spirit *as a person* who is love. Aquinas identifies such an analogy by speaking of spiritual love in two distinct senses, as *inclinatio* or *affectio* on the one hand and as *impressio* on the other.[7] The notion of love as an *inclinatio* or *affectio* refers to the spiritual tendency toward the beloved that is inherent in love. When one human being perceives intellectually the goodness of another, he or she can begin to love the other person by spiritual inclination or affection. This is an *analogy from efficient causality*, or love's "tendency toward" the object of its love.

St. Thomas also speaks about the characteristic way that love makes an *impressio*, that is to say, an impression or presence of the one who is loved in the heart of the one who loves. Love tends toward the good that is loved, such that the good is in a sense present to or within the one who loves. And the one who loves rests in the beloved as the immanent term of the act or movement of loving. This is the impression that the object loved makes upon the heart of the one who loves, by being present to or in the love of the lover, such that the lover rests spiritually in the beloved. This is accordingly an analogy from final causality or perfection of completed movement.[8]

It is important to note that this relational inclination toward the one loved can be understood by contrasting it with the work of the intellect. The mind is marked by assimilating the truth of the other reality, by being "informed" by this reality, and it generates a concept from its assimilation of the essential truth of the other reality. The relational procession of the concept is immanent to the mind, as something derived from the truth of the external world. The will, however, does not work by assimilation of the truth from the outside in, but by inclination from the inside outward, by an ecstatic motion out from itself toward the other, toward the good that is loved.

---

7. For further consideration of this idea in Aquinas, in its development and conceptual content, see Emery, *The Trinitarian Theology of St. Thomas Aquinas*, 225–33, and Emmanuel Durand, *La périchorèse des personnes divines: Immanence mutuelle, Réciprocité et communion* (Paris: Cerf, 2005).

8. *SCG* IV, c. 19: "Thus, then, what is loved is not only in the intellect of the lover, but in his will as well; but in one way and another. It is in the intellect by reason of the likeness of its species; it is in the will of the lover, however, as the term of a movement is in its proportioned motive principle by reason of the suitability and proportion which the term has for that principle. Just so, in a certain way, there is in fire the upper place by reason of that lightness which gives it proportion and suitability to such a place, but the fire which is generated is in the fire which generates by reason of the likeness of its form."

The *inclinatio* or *affectio* of the will is this turning toward the other that occurs *immanent to the person*, as when we love in the secret of our hearts, in the inner self of our wills, and we are "turned" toward that which we love. The immanent term of the relation is to the person loved, the beloved in his or her own goodness. Notice, of course, that to love, one must first know the reality loved. So, this inclination toward the other who is loved presupposes the "information" of the intellect, the knowledge of that which is loved.

Aquinas will ultimately apply this theological concept to the Trinity using the psychological analogy to speak about the Father's eternal self-knowledge and love. The mystery of the eternal Father may rightly be considered by analogy as a subject who, first, knows himself and in knowing himself generates his Word in whom he knows all things. Second, the Father is one who loves himself and his Word and, in loving himself and the Word, spirates the love that is the inner *inclinatio* or *affectio* of divine love. Just as the Word knows himself and the Father and, in so doing, loves the Father and himself, so too he also spirates love as the *inclinatio* or *affectio* that is common to himself and the Father. This analogy for the Trinity maintains the confession of the distinction of three persons in God, but it merges that confession very closely with the notion of the Father as a personal subject who knows himself and loves himself, in his eternal plenitude of perfection as God. In knowing himself he begets his Wisdom, and in loving himself he spirates his Spirit of Love, through his Word. We should note here also that what was said in the consideration of God's transcendent nature as subsistent knowledge and love is here recapitulated or reduplicated in Trinitarian form. That mystery we denote essentially in the one God as knowledge and love is in fact a mystery of the eternal processions of the Son and the Spirit, as the begotten Word and spirated Love of the Father.

In addition, however, Aquinas also develops the complementary Augustinian analogy of the Spirit as the love shared between the Father and the Son. He does so by considering the Father and the Son in their *act* of mutual love.[9] The Father simply *is* his act of love, and the Son simply *is* his act of love. The Father and the Son in loving one another are mutually present to each other as the beloved is in the one who loves. The Holy Spirit is the eternally spirated term and fruition of this mutual affection or mutual inclination of the love of the Father and the Son for each other. There is, then, a

9. As in *ST* I, q. 37, a. 1, ad 3.

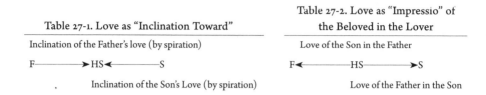

Table 27-1. Love as "Inclination Toward"	Table 27-2. Love as "Impressio" of the Beloved in the Lover
Inclination of the Father's love (by spiration)	Love of the Son in the Father
F————➤HS◄————S	F◄————HS————➤S
Inclination of the Son's Love (by spiration)	Love of the Father in the Son

mutual *impressio*, or presence of the loved one in the will or heart of the lover. The Son is in the Father as the beloved of the Father, and the Father is in the Son as the beloved of the Son. We also can think, then, of the Holy Spirit as this love of mutual impression. The Spirit is the eternal term of the love of the Son within the Father and of the love of the Father within the Son, and accordingly is their shared reciprocal impression of love.[10]

This distinction between love as an "inclination toward" and as "impression" of the beloved in the lover as applied to the Trinity is helpfully illustrated in tables 27.1 and 27.2.

When we say that the Holy Spirit proceeds as the Love of the Father and Son, love is here understood relationally, since the act of love is regarded as an inclination toward the other. However it is understood relationally also because love makes an impression of the beloved in the lover. In both these senses, the Holy Spirit is understood as proceeding from and within the act of the mutual love of Father and Son interior to the divine life.

We should note that our affirmation of this analogical conception of the Spirit as Love requires qualification by the same four kinds of dissimilitudes we considered above in regard to the Word. First, the Love of the Father and the Word is not an accidental feature or property of the godhead. The love in question is personally subsistent. Second, while human love is only a feature of the human being, the Spirit contains in himself all of the godhead, and he is God proceeding from God, just as is the Word. Third, love in any human person is only a characteristic of the singular person in question, but the Spirit who is Love is a person truly distinct from the Father and the Son. Finally, the Spirit is purely actual. He is not a developmental love that becomes more perfect over time or that moves from potency to actuality. He

---

10. This second analogy of mutual love shared between the Father and the Son does not do away with the first but rather completes it. The Father loves himself and his Word by the same love of self, and in doing so eternally spirates the Holy Spirit.

is the eternal fire of divine Love that proceeds from the bosom of the Father and that can never be extinguished or diminish.

One should note that this account of the Holy Spirit as the immanent term of the spirated love of the Father and the Son qualifies and helps perfect the analogical consideration of the divine persons by similitude to a communion of human persons. We noted above several ways that the Trinitarian communion of persons, in virtue of its perfection, is dissimilar to a human communion of persons. Each of the divine persons is wholly God, possessing in himself all that is in the others in virtue of the divine nature, so that each is wholly present to and contains in himself all that is in the others. This idea of perfect co-inherence coincides with that of real personal distinction, so that the persons truly are distinct, even as they contain in themselves all that is in one another as God. Here we see that the psychological analogy is employed by Aquinas to give greater expression to this theological idea. Just as the Son possesses in himself all that is in the Father (the divine *esse* and *essentia* proper to God) in virtue of his generation as the immaterial Word of the Father, so too the Spirit possesses in himself all that is in the Father and the Son (the divine *esse* and *essentia* proper to God) in virtue of his spiration from the Father and the Son as the bond of their mutual love. This understanding of the spiration helps us understand how God is a communion of persons not only in virtue of the shared divine essence, which is transmitted by generation and spiration respectively, but also in virtue of the bond of love shared between the Father and the Son, which is expressed in the person of the Spirit. We might say that because the Father and the Son are in perfect communion, they naturally emit the eternal Spirit of Love as the final term or expression of that communion. The Spirit who proceeds from them, in turn, knows and loves himself as God, and in doing so also knows and loves all that is in the Father and the Son, in an eternal personal communion with them. This also means that when the Father gives existence to creatures, he does so not only through his Word and in light of his Spirit, who is eternal love, but in virtue of the eternal bond of love he possesses with the Son, in their eternal communion. The creation proceeds from the communion of love that is proper to the Trinitarian persons.

The Constantinopolitan Creed, promulgated at the First Council of Constantinople in 381, contains a confession of the divinity of the Holy Spirit, which reads: "We believe in the Holy Spirit, the Lord and Giver of life, *who proceeds from the Father*, who together with the Father and the Son is worshiped and glorified."[11] The Western Church, however, over the course of the first millennium, would progressively come to formulate the Creed with an addition that is still in use in the Western Rite: "We believe in the Holy Spirit, the Lord and Giver of life, *who proceeds from the Father and the Son* [*ex Patre Filioque*]."[12] Is this addition theologically justified? Does the Holy Spirit also proceed from the Son? Traditionally speaking, many in the Western Church have held that this is the case, as have many Eastern Fathers as well.

For an overview of the historical side of the complex question of the *Filioque*, let us first consider the North American Orthodox-Catholic Theological Consultation's helpful summary on this matter:

No clear record exists of the process by which the word *Filioque* was inserted into the Creed of 381 in the Christian West before the sixth century. The idea that the Spirit came forth "from the Father through the Son" is asserted by a number of earlier Latin theologians, as part of their insistence on the ordered unity of all three persons within the single divine Mystery (e.g., Tertullian, *Adversus Praxean* 4 and 5). Tertullian, writing at the beginning of the third century, emphasizes that Father, Son and Holy Spirit all share a single divine substance, quality and power (*ibid.* 2), which he conceives of as flowing forth from the Father and being transmitted by the Son to the Spirit (*ibid.* 8). Hilary of Poitiers, in the mid-fourth century, in the same work speaks of the Spirit as "coming forth from the Father" and being "sent by the Son" (*De Trinitate* 12.55); as being "from the Father through the Son" (*ibid.* 12.56); and as "having the Father and the Son as his source" (*ibid.* 2.29); in another passage, Hilary points to John 16.15 (where Jesus says: "All things that the Father has are mine; therefore I said that [the Spirit] shall take from what is mine and declare it to you"), and wonders aloud whether "to receive from the Son is the same thing as to proceed from the Father" (*ibid.* 8.20). Ambrose of Milan, writing in the 380s, openly asserts that the Spirit "proceeds from (*procedit a*) the Father and the Son," without ever being separated from either (*On the Holy Spirit* 1.11.20). None of these writers, however, makes the Spirit's mode of origin the object of special reflection; all are concerned, rather, to emphasize the equality of status of all three divine persons as God, and all acknowledge that the Father alone is the source of God's eternal being.... The earliest use of *Filioque* language

11. Denzinger, no. 150, emphasis added.
12. Quoted in the Latin version in Denzinger, no. 150, emphasis added.

in a creedal context is in the profession of faith formulated for the Visigoth King Reccared at the local Council of Toledo in 589. This regional council anathematized those who did not accept the decrees of the first four Ecumenical Councils (canon 11), as well as those who did not profess that the Holy Spirit proceeds from the Father and the Son (canon 3). It appears that the Spanish bishops and King Reccared believed at that time that the Greek equivalent of *Filioque* was part of the original creed of Constantinople, and apparently understood that its purpose was to oppose Arianism by affirming the intimate relationship of the Father and Son. On Reccared's orders, the Creed began to be recited during the Eucharist, in imitation of the Eastern practice. From Spain, the use of the Creed with the *Filioque* spread throughout Gaul.... [The text continues at length to discuss the historical spread of the doctrine in the West, and its gradual creedal normalization.] ... A central emphasis of this Creed [as formulated with the *Filioque*] was its strong anti-Arian Christology: speaking of the Spirit as proceeding from the Father *and* the Son implied that the Son was not inferior to the Father in substance, as the Arians held. The influence of this Creed undoubtedly supported the use of the *Filioque* in the Latin version of the Creed of Constantinople in Western Europe, at least from the sixth century onwards.[13]

The *Filioque* has been and remains to this day a source of tension between the Roman Catholic and Eastern Churches. It is a point of contention principally for two reasons. The first controversy has to do with the truth of the statement itself. *Some* Eastern Orthodox think it is heretical in nature, while others think it is merely a theological opinion. Catholics, meanwhile, treat it as an infallible teaching of the magisterial tradition of the Catholic Church. The second point of contention is the question of the juridical normalcy of its proclamation. The Eastern Churches tend to protest that the Western Church made doctrinal alterations to the Creed, ultimately on the pope's authority, without prior consultation of the Christian East, thereby acting independently of the authority of the Eastern sees.

For its part, the Roman Catholic Church does not presently require that Eastern rite churches in communion with Rome pronounce the *Filioque* in the liturgical recitation of the Creed and does not consider the doctrine a Church-dividing issue. The Catholic Church does, of course, rightly insist that the Orthodox sister churches who do not employ the *Filioque* refrain from denouncing it as theologically false.

13. North American Orthodox-Catholic Theological Consultation, *The Filioque: A Church Dividing Issue?: An Agreed Statement*, issued on October 25, 2003; available online at https://www.usccb.org/committees/ecumenical-interreligious-affairs/filioque-church-dividing-issue-agreed-statement.

This all being said, there is a fair amount at stake theologically, Christologically, and soteriologically in the reception of and understanding of the *Filioque*, as suggested first of all by the crisis that gave rise to the elaboration
of this doctrine—the Arian crisis. For the doctrine in the first place makes
it clear that, in keeping with scripture, the Son is truly God, and is also the
Savior from whom the Spirit of salvation and divinization is sent upon the
world, the Spirit by whom believers are adopted into the Father's Spirit of
Sonship.

There are, in the first instance, then, very profound *scriptural* reasons for
affirming the *Filioque*. On this count, three groups of scriptural affirmations
can be mentioned, which we have alluded to already in the first part of this
book. The first grouping consists of texts that refer to the Spirit as the Spirit
of the Son, or *of Jesus*. Thus, Acts 16:7 speaks of "the Spirit of Jesus"; Romans
8:9 of "the Spirit of Christ"; and Galatians 4:6 of "the Spirit of his [the Father's] Son."[14]

The second grouping includes texts that speak of the Son's *sending of the
Spirit*. Examples would include John 15:26, where Jesus speaks of "the Coun-
selor [i.e., the Spirit] ... *whom I shall send to you* from the Father";[15] and
Luke 24:49: "I send the promise of my Father [i.e., the Spirit] upon you."

The third grouping consists especially of Johannine texts that speak
of the Spirit as imparting what he has received from Jesus to the disciples.
For example, in John 16:14 Jesus says that "he [the Spirit] will take what is
mine and declare it to you," a motif that is reiterated again immediately in
John 16:15.

The common denominator in all these texts is that they indicate that the
Spirit is in some way the Spirit of the Son or that the Spirit proceeds from
the Son in the concrete economy of salvation. Moreover, as I will indicate
below, it is profoundly problematic to say that a new relation emerges between the Son and the Spirit in the economy that is not already real from
all eternity. Consequently, if scripture affirms any real relation of origin of
the Spirit's procession from the Son in the economy of salvation, this would
seem to imply in turn an eternal relation in which the Spirit proceeds from
the Son from all eternity.

14. See too Jn 15:26: "the Spirit *of truth*, who proceeds from the Father." Also Rom 8:2 and 8:9.
15. Emphasis added.

Beyond the scriptural foundation just adduced, there is also widespread attestation in the Church Fathers for the doctrine of the Spirit's procession from the Son. The idea is present not only in Western figures, like Tertullian, Hilary, and Augustine.[16] It is also present in various Eastern Fathers. Thus, one finds more or less clear formulations of it in both Athanasius and Cyril of Alexandria.[17] It is defended in a qualified fashion by Maximus the Confessor.[18] Moreover, even the Cappadocians, despite their reticence to speculate about the inner relation of the Son and Spirit, do say in places that the Spirit proceeds from the Father *through* the Son.[19] Thus, there are strong scriptural and patristic bases for affirming the *Filioque* and, as we will see in more detail below, significant theological reasons for affirming it as well, not to mention significant difficulties that arise from its denial.

AQUINAS'S ARGUMENTS FOR THE *FILIOQUE*

For Aquinas, as we have seen, the notion of relation alone can differentiate the persons, and not any other category, analogically applied. He commonly applies this idea to his analysis of the procession of the Spirit. If the Son and Spirit are understood in their distinction as persons in virtue of relations alone (by relations of origin) and both relate in origin *only* to the Father, then there is no distinction between the two that we can clearly identify. In effect they are each defined in precisely the same way. Of course one can simply affirm the distinction of the Son and the Spirit, but if there is no

16. For Tertullian and Hilary on the *Filioque*, see the above quotation from the North American Orthodox-Catholic Theological Consultation. Augustine's affirmations of the Spirit's procession from the Son are numerous and explicit. See chapter 9, above, for discussion.

17. For Athanasius on the Spirit, see his "Epistle to Serapion," 1.19–25, in *Works on the Spirit: Athanasius and Didymus*, trans. M. DelCogliano, A. Radde-Gallwitz, and L. Ayres (Yonkers, N.Y.: St. Vladimir's Seminary Press, 2011), 82–93. For the view that the *Filioque* cannot be derived from the text in question, see A. Edward Siecienski, *The Filioque: History of a Doctrinal Controversy* (Oxford: Oxford University Press, 2010), 38. An excellent critical engagement of Siecienski on this point is provided by Andrew Hofer in his review in *The Thomist* 75, no. 3 (July 2011): 503–7. For Cyril's treatment of the question, see especially Cyril of Alexandria, *Thesaurus de sancta et consubstantiali trinitate*, 34, PG 75, ed. J.-P. Migne (Paris, 1863), 9–656. For the relevant texts and an interpretation that denies that the Spirit also *proceeds* (ἐκπορεύεσθαι) from the Son in Cyril, see Siecienski, *The Filioque*, 47–50.

18. In particular, see Maximus's *Letter to Marinus*. For the relevant text with discussion, see Siecienski, *The Filioque*, 78–86, even if Siecienski somewhat minimizes the import of Maximus's statements.

19. See chapter 8, above, for discussion of Basil's affirmation of the procession of the Spirit from the Father through the Son.

way to articulate what this distinction consists in, then the idea becomes purely formal, devoid of any internal content. Otherwise stated, we may voluntaristically maintain the authoritative teaching of the Church that the Son and Spirit are distinct (by generation and procession respectively), but the distinction of the persons of the Son and Spirit becomes literally "unthinkable" if there is no reference to a relation of origin between the two. For this reason, one of the two must proceed from the other, and both scripture and tradition assign this role not to the Son as proceeding from the Spirit but to the Spirit as proceeding from the Son—or rather, from the Father *through* the Son, and therefore from the Son.

Aquinas's argument on this point is simple but actually quite powerful. It would be a serious mistake to dismiss it as merely a piece of theological rationalism. If we cannot adequately distinguish the persons of the Trinity conceptually, then we ultimately can have no clear concept of the Trinity, even if we adhere to the teaching of the Church and its traditions with solemn respect. And, as there is no way to distinguish the persons of the Son and Spirit other than by relations of origin, so there is no distinction between them from one another simply owing to the fact that both proceed from the Father. As such, a difference in relation of origin must obtain between the proceeding persons if we are to see how the three persons are each truly distinct from one another (by relation of origin) and equal and identical in deity (since the divine life and essence is communicated by way of procession). If Trinitarian monotheism is to be truly intelligible, then there must be a distinction of persons only in this sense, by way of appeal to relations of origin and a shared divine life received from processions of one from another. But the Son and Holy Spirit would not have opposed relations unless they were both really related to one another somehow, either by procession or derivation, since both would otherwise simply be *from the Father*. This claim in no way implies that those who deny the *Filioque* are not Trinitarian. Of course they are and intend to be. But it does raise the question of how intelligible any such Trinitarian theology truly can be without importing features of the economy into the life of the persons of the Son and the Spirit, in order to differentiate them from the Father. The Spirit could be said to be distinct from Son in his procession from the Father because he is sent into the world differently, for example. However, if the persons are really distinguishable as persons only in virtue of the economy, then one is left with a kind of de facto subordinationism of the Son and the

Spirit, in which they are intelligibly distinct from one another only in virtue
of created properties or relationships associated with their missions in the
world, as those sent from the Father into the divine economy.

Here is how Aquinas states his argument in the first paragraph of the
body of *ST* I, q. 36, a. 2:

> It must be said that the Holy Spirit is from the Son. For if He were not from Him,
> He could in no wise be personally distinguished from Him; as appears from what
> has been said above (q.28, a.3; q.30, a.2.). For it cannot be said that the divine Per-
> sons are distinguished from each other in any absolute sense; for it would follow
> that there would not be one essence of the three persons: since everything that is
> spoken of God in an absolute sense, belongs to the unity of essence. Therefore it
> must be said that the divine persons are distinguished from each other only by the
> relations. Now the relations cannot distinguish the persons except forasmuch as
> they are opposite relations; which appears from the fact that the Father has two
> relations, by one of which He is related to the Son, and by the other to the Holy
> Spirit; but these are not opposite relations, and therefore they do not make two
> persons, but belong only to the one person of the Father. If therefore in the Son
> and the Holy Spirit there were two relations only, whereby each of them were re-
> lated to the Father, these relations would not be opposite to each other, as neither
> would be the two relations whereby the Father is related to them. Hence, as the
> person of the Father is one, it would follow that the person of the Son and of the
> Holy Spirit would be one, having two relations opposed to the two relations of the
> Father. But this is heretical since it destroys the Faith in the Trinity. Therefore the
> Son and the Holy Spirit must be related to each other by opposite relations. Now
> there cannot be in God any relations opposed to each other, except relations of
> origin, as proved above (q.28, a.4). And opposite relations of origin are to be un-
> derstood as of a principle, and of what is *from the principle*. Therefore we must con-
> clude that it is necessary to say that either the Son is from the Holy Spirit; which
> no one says; or that the Holy Spirit is from the Son, as we confess.

In other words, the Son and Spirit must be differentiated by a relation of
opposition. After all, they cannot be differentiated by a quantity (or matter), like two "twins" of a human father. Nor can there be a quality that
distinguishes them, since both are equal. Nor can they be distinct in substance, since they are *homoousios*, one in being and essence. Therefore, they
can be distinct and distinguishable only by way of relation, and thus by relative opposition of one to the other. Being relative to the Father as such
does not and cannot distinguish them. In fact, it would make them either
(1) identical in person, or else (2) require that they be distinct in substance.
For this reason, then, there must be a real distinction between the Son and

Spirit as persons, in which one proceeds from the other in relative opposition, or by a relation of origin.

A second argument follows from the idea that the Spirit is understood
by analogy as the Love of the Father. Love's proceeding presupposes a
knowledge that proceeds as word. This idea is fairly self-explanatory. Love
is intelligible for us only as the love of knowledge, as love proceeding from
a word. Accordingly, the Holy Spirit, proceeding as Love in person, proceeds from the Father *through his Word*. As Aquinas puts it in the second
paragraph of the body of *ST* I, q. 36, a. 2: "It was said above ... the Son proceeds by the way of the intellect as the Word, and the Holy Ghost by way of
the will as Love. Now love must proceed from a word. For we do not love
anything unless we apprehend it by a mental conception. Hence also in this
way it is manifest that the Holy Spirit proceeds from the Son." One may of
course object that the Spirit should not be characterized by Love in differentiation from the Son. However, as we have noted above, this would mean
that the spiration of the Spirit would be considered immaterial in nature but
relationally indistinguishable from the generation of the Son as Word, since
there are only two analogies to immaterial procession we can make, one
from knowledge and the other from love. If, then, the Spirit is rightly understood by a similitude to immaterial procession in God, and if in this respect he is intelligible as distinct from the Word, whose procession is clearly
designated in scripture by analogy to understanding, then the Spirit must be
understood by analogy to love. In this case, however, the Love in question is
fittingly understood to proceed from the Word.

Beyond the reasons just given, there is also an important additional argument in favor of the *Filioque*, one that has to do with the relation between
the immanent Trinity and its economic manifestation in the missions of
the Son and the Spirit (their being sent into the world by the Father). The
idea is the following: The missions of the Son and Spirit *ad extra* imply relations between the persons. (The Son and the Spirit are really related to one
another in their temporal missions in the world.) These relations, though
manifested *ad extra*, are nevertheless eternal in themselves, and so are not
derived economically, that is, they are not first produced by the economic
sending of the proceeding persons. Thus, if the Son sends the Spirit upon
the Church—as he is depicted as doing in the scriptures—then the Spirit
proceeds from the Son as a person. This is something true incidental to the
role played by the humanity of Christ in the sending of the Spirit, for the

simple reason that the man Jesus is God the Son *in person*. The relations that divine persons have to one another in time correspond to, and are in fact identical with, the relations that the two have in eternity, precisely because the divine persons are eternal.

Consequently, if we say that Jesus, resurrected, personally sends the Spirit upon the Church, this implies that the person of the Son really relates to the Spirit whom he sends. God the Spirit is related to God the Son as originating from the Son (and the Father) in time. But if God the Spirit were to originate from God the Son in time but not in eternity, then it would follow that God the Spirit would be related to God the Son in a new way interpersonally (in the very Trinitarian relations of God) as a result of the Incarnation and the temporal sending of the Spirit. A new relationship between the persons would emerge in time as a result of the economy of salvation, one that did not exist before in all eternity. If this were the case, then the Trinitarian relations in God would be changed because of the Incarnation and the sending of the Spirit. Or put more succinctly: the economy of salvation would alter the very identity of God, so that the persons would be reconstituted in virtue of their economic history with humanity. This notion is problematic, since it contradicts the Church's reasonable affirmation of the transcendence of the divine nature of God, which we considered in part 2 of this book. Therefore, the relation of the Spirit's coming forth from the Son is something proper to the Son and Spirit not in time only, but also in eternity. In fact, it is the eternal processions of the Son and Spirit that are the unchanging foundation for the temporal missions of the Son and the Spirit, as we will examine further below. The missions make manifest to us in time the real relations that obtain between the persons eternally.

MODERN ECUMENICAL ATTEMPTS AT A COMPREHENSIVE SETTLEMENT

While the arguments I have offered above constitute forthright defenses of the validity and importance of the Catholic Trinitarian tradition, it is of capital importance to note that the Catholic Church does not require consent to the ideas and arguments of any particular theological school and, in this case, does not require that Eastern Churches consent to any of the models of Trinitarian life presented above as a condition for Church unity. Modern ecumenical dialogues have helped clarify the points at issue between East and West in the *Filioque* and have produced nuanced statements that highlight fundamental places of consensus that are sufficient for mutual confession of the Trinitarian faith, and ecclesial inter-communion. Accordingly, more recent statements of the Catholic Church tend to emphasize the paternal principality, on the one hand, and the Spirit's procession *through* the Son as one conjoint principle of the Spirit in and with the Father, on the other.

Consider first the *Catechism of the Catholic Church*'s nuanced formulation of the *Filioque* that specifically highlights the Father's fontal position in the Trinity: "the eternal order of the divine persons in their consubstantial communion implies that the Father, as 'the principle without principle' [Council of Florence; DS 1331] is the first origin of the Spirit, but also that as Father of the only Son, he is, with the Son, the single principle from which the Spirit proceeds [Council of Lyons II; DS 850]."[20] By emphasizing the paternal principality in this way, the *Catechism* is attempting to take careful account of traditional Eastern Christian theological concerns with the *Filioque*. Only the Father is the fontal principle of the life of the Trinity, and both the Son and the Spirit proceed from the Father, who is the origin of all within all.

Is there a possibility for convergence on this issue on the Orthodox side of the confessional divide? Orthodox theologians have traditionally responded to the idea of the *Filioque* in one of three ways.[21] Some simply reject the notion as erroneous, and insist upon the distinction of the generation of the Son from the Father and the procession of the Spirit from the Father (and not the Son). Photius, the ninth-century patriarch of Constantinople, can be seen as a famous representative of this position. The monarchal primacy of the Father is preserved, and out of respect for the mystery of God one does not seek to resolve the question of the eternal relation between the Son and the Spirit. The notion of the Spirit's proceeding through the Son is even to be rejected.

Other Orthodox theologians follow a tradition that shows sympathy for the Augustinian idea of the *Filioque*, understanding there to be a potential convergence of this idea with the classical affirmation that the Spirit pro-

---

20. *Catechism of the Catholic Church*, no. 248.
21. The analysis of Orthodox criticism of the *Filioque* that follows derives in substance from my essay "The Holy Spirit," in the *Oxford Handbook of Catholic Theology*, ed. L. Ayres and M. A. Volpe (Oxford: Oxford University Press, 2019): 183–97.

ceeds from the Father through the Son. A preeminent proponent of this view is Maximus the Confessor (ca. 580–662). This school of thought is less common but has endured historically and is vital to ecumenical conversation.

The most prominent trend, meanwhile, is that promoted by historical figures such as Gregory of Cyprus (1241–90) and Gregory Palamas (1296–1359). It is maintained by influential modern Orthodox theologians such as Vladimir Lossky and Dumitru Stăniloae. This position constitutes a sort of middle way between the former two. It maintains that the doctrine of the *Filioque* as conceived in the Augustinian tradition is problematic. There are said to be two main reasons for this. First, such Orthodox theologians maintain that the Western *Filioque* concept depicts a hypostatic property of the Father as being communicable to the Son with regard to the Spirit. Here, however, they object that what is shared by the persons is the divine nature and life, not personal properties as such. If then the Father gives the power of spiration to the Son, he must do so in virtue of their shared divine essence. In this case, however, it would seem that the divine essence is made the source of the spiration of the Spirit. Second, then, one of two things must follow. Either the Spirit must hold the power to spirate himself, since he also possesses the divine essence (and this is an absurd claim), or the Spirit proceeds from the divine essence of the Father and the Son, in which case he must be a mere creature (which is contrary to the faith of the Church). One can conclude from such arguments that the hypostatic property of the Father whereby he spirates the Spirit is inalienable, and is not transferable to the Son.

Despite these criticisms, this Palamite tradition does assign a positive value to the *Filioque* doctrine insofar as it invites Orthodox theology to consider in greater depth the eternal and temporal relations of the Spirit and the Son. In this sense, Orthodox theologians who follow Palamas are less negatively reactive than those who follow Photius. To think about the Spirit's relation to the Son, they tend to distinguish a twofold mode of this relation: (1) in the eternal mystery of God and (2) in the divine economy. In the eternal life of God, the Spirit proceeds only from the Father but rests upon the Son and is the resplendence of the Son. In this way the Son is the recipient of the Father's eternal love, as one who receives from the Father the glory of the Spirit. In the economy, by analogy, the Spirit is sent by the Father, *through* the Son-made-man, upon the Church. The Son and the Spirit both act together to sanctify human beings, and within the economy the Spirit is the Spirit of the Son. In eternity both persons come forth uniquely from the Father, who breathes the Spirit upon the Son, and sends him into the world as the Spirit of his Son.

The Romanian theologian Dumitru Stăniloae writes:

The Father does not beget the Son, and does not cause the Spirit to proceed as two separate actions, as two Persons who remain separated; but the begetting and the procession, although distinct, are united. Consequently the Person of the Son and the Person of the Spirit also remain united, or interior, to one another.... [T]hough the Spirit's manifestation is by the Son, his coming into existence is not by the Son, even if he is united to the begetting of the Son.... [T]he shining out from the Son marks a progress in the existence which the Spirit receives from the Father, one might say a fulfillment, the achievement of the end for which he came into existence.[22]

One can observe points of convergence here with the Augustinian tradition. At the same time, this position maintains claims about the *Filioque* that are problematic. In fact there is nothing incoherent or contradictory about Augustine's idea that the Son receives a personal characteristic that the Father has (to be a principle of the Spirit). Far from making the Son identical with the Father, this teaching helps us distinguish him personally from both the Father (who alone is the unbegotten source of the Spirit) and the Spirit (who alone proceeds from both the Father and the Son). The Father and the Son do spirate the Spirit in virtue of the divine essence, but it is not the divine essence that spirates. Consequently, the objection that if the *Filioque* is true the Spirit must spirate himself or be a creature does not obtain. In the Western Trinitarian tradition, the persons alone, not their shared essence, are the relational principles of one another. However, this is not a uniquely Western idea, as it is held by the Cappadocian Fathers as forcefully as by Augustine, and is a given of ancient Nicene orthodoxy.

Furthermore, there is an ambiguity to the modern Orthodox notion that new relations may obtain between the persons either (1) at the *term* of the intra-Trinitarian processions, instead of at their origins, or (2) in virtue of the economy, through divine action of God *ad extra*, distinct from the eternal relations in God himself. If, for example, the Spirit comes to rest

22. Dimitru Stăniloae, "The Procession of the Holy Spirit from the Father and His Relation to the Son, as the Basis of Our Deification and Adoption," in *Spirit of God, Spirit of Christ*, ed. L. Vischer (London and Geneva: SPCK and World Council of Churches, 1981): 174–186, at 183–84.

upon the Son eternally, at the term of his spiration, what does he or the Son receive from this, as a new quality, that they did not have in virtue of their relational origin from the Father? If the Father has communicated the plenitude of the nature of God to them and they are equally and identically God, they have nothing to "gain" from the term of the procession, but if they do gain something, then they are initially less than the Father at the origin of their generation and spiration. The equality of the persons seems to be compromised by such an idea. It is best, then, to follow the traditional pattern of distinguishing the persons uniquely by their relational processions of origin, not by an eventual teleological actuation that comes to pass subsequent to eternal generation and spiration. Meanwhile, if the Spirit is sent from the Son in the economy alone, and this relation does not correspond to and presuppose an eternal relation of origin of the Spirit from the Son, then it would seem that there arise in the economy new relations between the eternal Son and the eternal Spirit that have not previously existed in all eternity. In this case, it would seem that these newly developed relations of the Son and Spirit that arise only in the economy either do not reveal to us what God really is in himself, or, what is worse, seem to alter what God is in his inner-relational life, in which case creation alters the identity of the Trinity. In the absence of the affirmation of the *Filioque*, one must be concerned about a potential subordinationism in which the Spirit and Son do not partake fully of the perfection of the Father in virtue of their relations of origin, and must do so subsequently through an intra-divine becoming, or in virtue of their presence in creaturely history.

Recently some Orthodox and Catholic theologians alike have argued, following Maximus the Confessor, that there is a way to think about the *Filioque* in a fashion that converges with traditional Orthodox formulations.[23] One way to do this is to think of the *Filioque* in terms of perichoresis or mutual indwelling. The Son eternally indwells within the Father insofar as the Father *is* Father. Therefore, the Son is eternally present in the Father's spiration of the Spirit, such that perichoresis (the indwelling of the Son in the Father) is the condition for the Father's spiration of the Spirit. For this reason,

23. See in this respect the ecumenically oriented work of Jean Miguel Garrigues, *L'Esprit qui dit 'Père!'*: *L'Esprit-Saint dans la vie trinitaire et le problème du filioque* (Paris: Tequi, 1981); *Le Saint-Esprit, sceau de la Trinité: Le filioque et l'originalité trinitaire de l'Esprit dans sa personne et sa mission* (Paris: Cerf, 2011); *Deux martyrs de l'Église indivise: Saint Maxime le Confesseur et le pape saint Martin* (Paris: Cerf, 2011); *Le Dessein divin d'adoption et le Christ Rédempteur; À la lumière de Maxime le Confesseur et de Thomas d'Aquin* (Paris: Cerf, 2011).

then, the Spirit's spiration can also be reasonably said to be *through the Son*. The idea here is that even when we affirm, for example, that the Spirit proceeds uniquely from the Father as his first source and origin, we also must affirm that the one he proceeds from is the Father who eternally generates the Son. If the Son is eternally in the Father as his only begotten Word, even as the Father spirates the Spirit, then there is an undeniable sense in which the spiration of the Spirit from the Father happens in and through the Word or from the Word, as well.[24]

On all these fronts, the 1995 Vatican Clarification on the *Filioque* is especially helpful. It states:

For the Catholic Church, at the outset the Eastern tradition expresses the Father's character as first origin of the Spirit. By confessing the Spirit as he "who takes his origin from the Father" ("ἐκ τοῦ Πατρὸς ἐκπορευόμενον" cf. Jn 15:26), it affirms that he comes from the Father through the Son. The Western tradition expresses first the consubstantial communion between Father and Son, by saying that the Spirit proceeds from the Father and the Son (*Filioque*).... "This legitimate complementarity, provided it does not become rigid, does not affect the identity of faith in the reality of the same mystery confessed" (*Catechism of the Catholic Church* no. 248). Being aware of this, the Catholic Church has refused the addition of καὶ τοῦ Υἱοῦ to the formula ἐκ τοῦ Πατρὸς ἐκπορευόμενον of the Symbol of Nicaea-Constantinople in the churches, even of Latin rite, which use it in Greek. The liturgical use of this original text remains always legitimate in the Catholic Church.

The Clarification continues:

In the same way, if in the Trinitarian order the Holy Spirit is consecutive to the relation between the Father and the Son, since he takes his origin from the Father as Father of the only Son, it is in the Spirit that this relationship between the Father and the Son itself attains its Trinitarian perfection. Just as the Father is characterized as Father by the Son he generates, so does the Spirit, by taking his origin from the Father, characterize the Father in the manner of the Trinity in relation to the Son and characterizes the Son in the manner of the Trinity in his relation to the Father: in the fullness of the Trinitarian mystery they are Father and Son in the Holy Spirit.[25]

---

24. One could object that the spiration must occur merely in relation to the Word, and in this case either the Spirit proceeds through and from the Word, or the Word is begotten through and from the Spirit. However, there is little historical warrant, in either scripture or tradition, for the latter affirmation, so the former position seems reasonable to entertain.

25. The 1995 Vatican Clarification on the *Filioque*, quoted from *L'Osservatore Romano* (weekly English-language edition) no. 38 (1408), September 20, 1995.

Accordingly, a modern ecumenical *rapprochement* on the matter of the *Filioque* has been attempted, at least, by laying careful stress on (1) the principality of the Father within the Trinitarian processions, and (2) the potential complementarity of the formula expressing the Spirit's procession *through* the Son with that of the *Filioque* (*"and* the Son").

Although Thomism constitutes only one school of theology in the Catholic Church, its way of treating the persons of God as subsistent relations is helpful in this context. If we begin, with the Eastern tradition, by considering the Father as the principle and unique source of the Spirit, and add to this that the Father is relative in all that he is, then we have to think about how the Father, in his spiration of the Spirit, relates to the Son, since the Father's relation to the Son is eternally coexistent with his relation to the Spirit. The Son, however, is in the Father and the Father is in the Son in virtue of the generation, by which the Son receives the divine essence from the Father in its plenitude. Therefore there is no distinct natural quality in the Father that is not in the Son, since the Son has all that the Father has. The only way to distinguish the two is in virtue of their relation of origin, based on the eternal generation of the Son from the Father. If this is the case, then we can maintain that the Father is the source (principle without principle) of the Holy Spirit only if the Father has a relation to the Holy Spirit distinct from the relation the Son has to the Holy Spirit. Otherwise the Son would be the same as the Father in giving rise to the Holy Spirit. The Spirit, however, is also distinguished from the Father and the Son in virtue of relations alone. This in turn implies that the Son has an eternal relation of origin to the Holy Spirit distinct from that of the Father, and such a relation can only function in one of two ways. Either the Spirit is the eternal principle of the Son (which no one claims) or the Son is the eternal principle of the Spirit, not simply in the way the Father is, but in a derivative way, as one who originates from the Father by generation. If the Son is one principle of the Spirit with the Father, this can be only because he receives this spirational activity from the Father, or, as we might otherwise state it, because the Spirit proceeds from the Father through the Son. On this Thomistic relationalist account, one can hold simultaneously to a set of theologically coherent ideas: the principality of the Father, the notion that the Spirit proceeds originally from the Father as from a principle source, and the idea that the Spirit proceeds through the Son and from the Son as one principle with the Father. Far from being incompatible notions, these ideas are mutually complementary and deeply interrelated.

CONCLUSION

As we saw in this chapter, Aquinas extends the psychological analogy, which conceives of the second person in the Trinity as Word, to the Holy Spirit, who is accordingly understood to proceed by way of will as Love in person. The Catholic Church affirms as a point of doctrine that the Father and Son are one principle in this procession of the Spirit. Although the Father is ever regarded as the fontal source in the Trinity, he nevertheless always already imparts all that he has to the Son—except, of course, that in which there is relative opposition—and this includes that he gives to the Son that he spirates the Spirit jointly with him as one principle.

We saw likewise how, in his treatment of the Spirit as Love, Aquinas stresses above all love's relational dimension, both in terms of love as an inclination toward, and as making an impression on, one's beloved. Applied to the Trinity, this means that the Father and Son spirate the Spirit in their mutual act of love for one another, each inclining toward the other and making an impression on the other, the Spirit accordingly forming the bond of love between them.

As to the historically contested question of the *Filioque*, there are, as we saw, many scriptural and traditional bases in favor of its affirmation. In addition, Aquinas affirms it as a necessary component of Trinitarian theology and so of the *intellectus fidei* of this revealed mystery. Simply put, there is no clear way to distinguish the Son and Spirit personally in the immanent life of the Trinity, understood in terms of relation of origin, unless the Son and Spirit have some kind of relational opposition, either by procession or derivation. Moreover, it is also difficult to see how the Son can pour forth the Spirit in salvation history—as he is attested to do in scripture—unless this economic sending is itself the expression of an eternal relation that exists between Son and Spirit.

Last, modern ecumenical *rapprochement* on the issue of the *Filioque* has stressed the principality of the Father, on the one hand, and the potential compatibility of the formulas "proceeds *through* the Son," and "from the Father *and* the Son," on the other, to try to overcome the historical impasse connected with this doctrine.

Having discussed the Father, Son, and Holy Spirit in their distinction from one another, we now turn our attention to their perichoresis, or the mutual indwelling of the persons within one another.

28

Perichoresis and Trinitarian Communion

Having considered the divine persons individually, we must now turn to their mutual inherence in one another in virtue of their one divine essence—what is commonly called in theology *perichoresis*. This shift of emphasis is always necessary in treatments of the three persons so as to underscore the unity of the Trinity as represented in Israel's monotheistic profession of faith, the *Shema*, "Hear O Israel, the Lord our God is one Lord" (Dt 6:4). This chapter will proceed by first looking more closely at the term perichoresis itself. We will then examine the equality and likeness of the persons in God. Last, we will turn again to the question of their mutual indwelling.

PERICHORESIS DEFINED

Perichoresis is a Greek word that was first employed by Gregory of Nazianzus in the fourth century to refer to the mutual inherence of the divinity and humanity in Christ. However, with time, this term—along with its Latin rendering, *circumincessio*—came to be used in theology to refer primarily to the mutual inherence or indwelling of the three persons of the Holy Trinity in one another.[1] The key idea is this: not only do the persons

---

1. For a brief overview of the use of the Greek verb *perichōrein* in theology, see Emery, *The Trinitarian Theology of St. Thomas Aquinas*, 300. For John Damascene's role in importing the term *perichoresis* into Trinitarian theology, see Andrew Louth, *St. John Damascene: Tradition and Originality in Byzantine Theology* (Oxford: Oxford University Press, 2002), 112–13.

proceed from one another; and not only does each of the persons have in himself all that pertains to the divine essence or being; in addition, each person is simultaneously within the others, and in a reciprocity of communion with the others, without ceasing to truly be himself. The Father is in the Son and the Son is in the Father, and yet each is distinct from the other. How can this be?

To draw out the intrinsic intelligibility of this doctrine of the faith on the mutual inherence of the persons and thus their uncreated communion, we will have reference in what follows to Aquinas's treatment of their mutual indwelling, as he presents it in the *Summa theologiae*.[2] In connection with this doctrine, however, we will also have to consider a prior but related question—that of the persons' absolute equality and co-eternity.

Both these questions, on the mutual indwelling and equality of the persons, are important for our understanding of what is unveiled in the biblical revelation of Christ. Christ is the eternal Son of God, made man, one who is both truly Lord and truly human. As such, he is not only subject to the Father as man but also equal to the Father as Lord, something that holds true for his relationship with the Holy Spirit as well. Furthermore, though he is personally distinct from the Father and the Spirit, he is also simultaneously in the Father even as the Father is in him (Jn 14:9–10). Likewise, the Holy Spirit is in him and he is in the Spirit, who proceeds from him. Accordingly, there are great issues at stake for Trinitarian theology when we begin to consider the theandric activity of Jesus as both God and human. When Jesus acts humanly in his teaching, healing, suffering, and so forth, it is also the eternal Son who acts as Lord, in communion with the Father and the Holy Spirit. The Son alone is human, but the Son never acts as God without the Father and the Spirit. He alone reaches out his hand to heal the sick, speaks human words, grieves with a human heart, and suffers physically and psychologically. Yet even while Christ does or suffers these things in a characteristically human way, he also is active as Lord in union with the Father and Spirit, who act with and in him in virtue of their common deity. If the Son of God, then, touches a person who is blind and wills humanly to heal that person, he can effectively perform the miracle principally in virtue of the divine power residual in him, but when he acts in virtue of this divine power he does so only ever with the Father and the Spirit who are in him (Mk 8:22–26; Jn 9:6–7).

2. For more on perichoresis in Aquinas, see Emery, *The Trinitarian Theology of St. Thomas Aquinas*, 298–311.

Consequently, when Christ reveals himself as Lord in his human actions, he also implicitly reveals the hidden presence of the Father and the Spirit.[3]

What is at stake, then, in the doctrine of perichoresis is not only the unity within the Trinity. This doctrine is also important in order to understand how the person of Christ and his salvific deeds, as presented in the gospels, relate to his Father, from whom he comes forth and with whom he acts in his ministry, and to the Spirit who proceeds from him, who likewise is at work in him, through his human sayings and actions.

EQUALITY OF THE TRINITARIAN
PERSONS IN GOD

When speaking of the equality of the three persons in God, Aquinas begins by maintaining that the absolute equality of the persons is ultimately derived from the fact that they are mysteriously *homoousios*, one in being and essence. It is principally on account of the "unity of essence" that "the persons are equal to one another."[4] It is significant that a Thomistic approach to perichoresis as mutual indwelling and communion begins from this characteristically Nicene starting point. One might wonder if such a view is too "essentialist" and "impersonal," since the doctrine of the perichoresis is intended precisely to indicate, however imperfectly and obliquely, the interpersonal communion and mutual presence that must exist in the Holy Trinity. However, as we will argue next, it is precisely this starting point that assures us a deeper understanding of just how unique, profound, and mysterious the interpersonal communion and mutual indwelling of the three persons must be.

In *ST* I, q. 42, a. 2, Aquinas asks whether the proceeding persons are co-eternal with their principle. The principle in question is, of course, the Father, from whom the Son and Spirit proceed. He answers affirmatively and again takes the persons' consubstantiality for his point of departure. The Father communicates the totality of divine life to the Son and the Spirit. Therefore, they possess the divine essence and are co-equal with the Father (a point we have repeatedly underscored above). How is this significant for thinking about perichoresis in particular? The answer unfolds as we begin to contrast eternal processions with temporal processions, and in doing so

---

3. I will explore these themes in greater depth in part 4 of this book, below.
4. *ST* I, q. 42, a. 1, ad 4.

eradicate from our analogical way of thinking about the Trinity any overly anthropomorphic conceptions of the Trinitarian communion, based on
communion in creatures. Toward this end, Aquinas notes that a temporal
succession from a principle can occur for one of three reasons: (1) on the
part of the agent, if he decides to act in time; (2) again on the part of the
agent, if he himself progressively acquires his power to act; or (3) on the
part of the action itself, if the agent freely wills to act successively through
time, bringing an action to progressive accomplishment.[5]

None of these three reasons, however, can or indeed does apply in the
case of the intra-divine processions. For, first of all, the Father does not generate the Son by choice, but naturally, and so the reason given in (1) above
does not apply. Second, however, the Father for his part does not acquire
perfection as Father, but is perfect from all eternity, and so (2) above does
not apply either. Finally, the Father is eternally generating the Son and the
Son is eternally generated, something that is also true for the eternal spiration of the Holy Spirit. For this reason, then, (3) above is not applicable
either. Thus, none of the bases for temporal succession applies or even can
apply when it comes to the intra-divine processions.

What is the significance of this series of negations? First, it allows us
to exclude problematically anthropomorphic notions of the communion
found in God. The communion of persons in God is not one that results
from a free decision on the part of the persons, as if the Father, Son, and
Spirit were to first decide to love one another in a reciprocal love of free
choice, so that only then would their perfect communion result. Rather the
opposite is the case: the Father generates the Son and spirates the Spirit by
nature rather than choice, and just as the persons are eternally constituted
by their processions, so too they eternally know and love one another perfectly in virtue of their shared divine life and essence as God.[6] Second, the

---

5. *ST* I, q. 42, a. 2: "We must say that the Son is co-eternal with the Father. In proof of which
we must consider that for a thing which proceeds from a principle to be posterior to its principle
may be due to two reasons: one on the part of the agent, and the other on the part of the action.
On the part of the agent this happens differently as regards free agents and natural agents. In free
agents, on account of the choice of time; for as a free agent can choose the form it gives to the
effect . . . so it can choose the time in which to produce its effect. In natural agents, however, the
same happens from the agent not having its perfection of natural power from the very first, but ob-
taining it after a certain time; as, for instance, a man is not able to generate from the very first. Considered on the part of action, anything derived from a principle cannot exist simultaneously with
its principle when the action is successive. So, given that an agent, as soon as it exists, begins to act
thus, the effect would not exist in the same instant, but in the instant of the action's termination."

6. An exceptional example of the idea that the Trinity self-constitutes in perichoresis through

personal communion in God does not develop or come to greater perfection through a temporal history, as if the persons in God were obliged to ha-

---

freedom is found in the influential work of John D. Zizioulas, *Being as Communion: Studies in Personhood and the Church* (Crestwood, N.Y.: St. Vladimir's Press, 1995). Zizioulas posits a number of extraordinary theses (pp. 17–49): God owes his Trinitarian existence to the person of the Father, who freely chooses to cause the other two persons to be, through love. The generation of the Son and spiration of the Spirit are acts of freedom of the Father, then, such that God does not exist either by substantial or natural necessity but only as a result of the eternal free decision of the Father that God should exist as Trinity. "The fact that God exists because of the Father shows that His existence, His being is the consequence of a free person; which means, in the last analysis, that not only communion but also *freedom*, the free person, constitutes true being. True being comes only from the free person, from the person who loves freely—that is, who freely affirms his being, his identity, by means of an event of communion with other persons" (Zizioulas, *Being as Communion*, 18). Freedom for love is understood here as the most basic ontological category, one that gives rise to and determines not only nature and substance, but even existence, not only in creation but also in God himself. Here we see another version of the "Franciscan" Trinitarian person of the Father logically pre-constituted in freedom "prior" to generation or spiration. However, in this case, the freedom of the Father has been articulated as the very act of his hypostasis, so that the Trinity comes to be as an eternal act of freedom. Zizioulas sets up a polarity of opposition between a theology that affirms an ontology of Trinitarian substance (the essence of the three persons), which would make freedom an attribute of God, versus an ontology of personhood in which freedom is constitutive of being, choosing the latter against the former. However, in a Thomistic conception of person as subsistent relation, this opposition appears to be unnecessary and even ill-advised. The nature of God only ever subsists in the persons, just as the persons only ever subsist in a nature. To say, as indeed Athanasius and the Cappadocian Fathers did say, that there is a common nature or *ousia* in God, is not to say that the persons are in communion by means of an impersonal essence, but that the person of the Father is wholly in the Son and Spirit because he naturally communicates all that he is as God to them (so as to be *homoousios*). The fact that the generation and spiration are natural, not free, connotes not that God is restrained but that God the Father in knowing and loving himself in the greatest possible love of infinite actuality can and does inevitably communicate all that he is to the Son and to the Spirit. The analogy to freedom in human persons is an analogy to the delight the will takes in the good that is perfectly possessed, so that one is free to love what is best and to love all other goods relative to what is best and perfectly possessed. It is not an analogy to elective freedom by which God the Trinity is said rightly to choose to exist or not exist.

Hans Urs von Balthasar, meanwhile, proposes that the very notion of God as love in Christianity requires that we rethink the way in which we ascribe unity to God, and therefore how we characterize Trinitarianism as a form of monotheism. If God truly is love, then he must be characterized by self-giving in otherness, relationships of reciprocity, and mutual acts of freedom. See Balthasar, *Theo-Drama*, 5:82–83: "The ideal of a mere unity without 'the Other' (Plotinus's *hen*, but also the *Monos Theos* of Judaism and Islam) cannot do justice to the Christian affirmation that God is love. Such a unity would be self-sufficient and could not be communicated; 'otherness' would be a mere declension from it. But where God is defined as love, he must be in essence perfect self-giving, which can only elicit from the Beloved, in return an equally perfect movement of thanksgiving, service and self-giving. Absolute self-giving of this kind cannot exist in the creaturely realm, since man has no control over his existence and, hence, over his 'I,' and 'we cannot give away that over which we have no control' (Brunner, 24). We must try to grasp the fact that where absolute Being is concerned, Being that has possession of itself, 'divine self-possession expresses itself in perfect self-giving and reciprocal surrender; furthermore the creature's own existence, over which it has no control, is drawn into this movement' (Brunner, 25). This self-giving cannot be bitually deliberate, then agree, and finally reach a more perfect moral union. Certain forms of social Trinitarianism that posit God's existing in time and the three persons as three distinct entities with distinct consciousnesses and wills understand the mutual communion in this way.[7] Instead, the communion of the persons is eternal and perfect. Third, based on Aquinas's negation of the analogy of action *ad extra*, the communion of the persons in God is not constituted, qualified, or enriched by the activities of God in the divine economy. There is no temporal or historical condition of possibility for the eventual improvement of the communion that takes place in God, as if the persons of the Trinity should require or make use of the events of the incarnation, passion, and resurrection to complete and perfect their own mutual communion as God.[8] Rather the inverse is the case: the economy is the theatre in which the mystery of the eternal life of perfect personal communion in God is manifested truly to the human race and in which human beings are invited into personal communion with the Holy Trinity.

Second, Aquinas's use of the three negations mentioned above underscores something we already observed in our consideration of the Cappadocian Fathers: even if there is true equality of being among the Father, Son, and Holy Spirit in God, it is equality received according to a certain order of reception or a derived equality, in which the Son is God "from" the Fa-

---

motivated by anything other than itself; hence it is a boundless love where freedom and necessity coincide and where identity and otherness are one: identity, since the Lover gives all that he is and nothing else, and otherness, since otherwise the Lover would love only himself. Yet, even where it is a case of total reciprocal self-giving, this distinction cannot be ultimate: without disappearing, it must transcend itself in a new identity of love given and received, which the lovers themselves are bound to regard as the miracle, ever new, of their mutual love. Thus in God there must be 'an eternal amazement at, and affirmation of, this reciprocal otherness that accompanies the oneness' (Brunner, 42) and 'an eternal newness characterizing perfect, supratemporal constancy' (Brunner, 45)." Balthasar is citing the related study by August Brunner, *Dreifaltigkeit: Personale Zugänge zum Geheimnis* (Einsiedeln: Johannes Verlag, 1976). In fact, Balthasar's claim that God's "unity" is constituted by mutual free actions of self-surrender does not underscore the uniqueness of the unity of the Trinity but accomplishes the opposite of what it intends, since it reduces God's unity to a mere moral union of wills concurring in freedom and in doing so evacuates theology of the traditional (and dogmatic) confession of the unity of God's will. In this way, in virtue of its anthropomorphic bent, Balthasar's thought remythologizes Christian theology and gives unintended stimulus to the traditional Judaic and Islamic criticisms of Christianity as an incipient form of polytheism, and a corruption of prophetic understanding through the reassertion of a neo-pagan mythology that depicts God as a man and man as a God.

7. See, for example, Swinburne, *The Christian God*, pp. 153, 171–73, 187–88.
8. Moltmann provides a good example of this position in *The Trinity and the Kingdom*. He posits that the Trinity is reconstituted in and through the event of the passion (p. 83), and continues to develop in a state of gradually perfecting moral union, in virtue of an ongoing shared life history in the economy of salvation (pp. 94–97).

ther and the Spirit is God "from" the Father and the Son. Aquinas considers this question of the "order of nature" of the divine persons in *ST* I, q. 42, a. 3. He makes the simple point there that, within the co-equal, co-eternal mutual inherence of the persons in the divinity, the relations of origin that constitute the persons still obtain. The three persons are each equally God but also wholly relative to one another within a given order of procession, which Aquinas calls an "order according to origin, without priority." As we will note below, the idea that the persons are related to one another in a given order is key to understanding the personal communion that obtains between them, since it allows us to understand their personal communion with one another, and presence to one another, in terms of relational co-inherence.

What have we concluded up to this stage? First, there is equality among the persons in virtue of the identity of essence they each share as God. Second, the persons are co-eternal. Third, there is also therefore an ordered distinction between the persons, based on eternal relations of origin. These ideas exclude notions of communion in God that would arise through free decision on the part of the persons in God, or that would grow in perfection through mutual decisions of the persons, or that would come to be more perfect because of the divine economy.

This sequence of ideas is what gives rise to Aquinas's next question in *ST* I, q. 42, a. 4, as to "Whether the Son is Equal to the Father in Greatness?" Aquinas's affirmative answer on this point follows quite naturally from what was said in article 1 concerning the equality of the persons. However, it is interesting to next consider carefully what Aquinas says in a. 4, ad 2: although the Father and the Son are equal in greatness, as a result of the identical essence they share, nevertheless the essence in the Father is paternity, while the essence in the Son is filiation.[9] The idea here is that all that the Father has as God is in the Father in a paternal way, or a paternal mode, while all that the Son receives from the Father as God subsists in the Son as filiation, or in a filial mode.[10] Likewise, we should say that all that exists in the Spirit subsists in a spirated mode.

Here then we encounter an idea already presented initially in chapter 24 pertaining to the divine persons. The Thomistic account of the persons as

9. *ST* I, q. 42, a. 4, ad 2: "The same essence, which in the Father is paternity, in the Son is filiation."

10. See also *ST* I, q. 42, a. 6, ad 3.

subsistent relations closely aligns the idea of each of the persons as relational with the notion of the divine nature's subsisting in three distinct modes. The account is neither simply personalistic nor modalistic, but both at once, in a correlated way. Since there is no distinction of substance and accident in God, each person must be considered relational in all that he is. If this is the case, however, all that we attribute to the persons in God in virtue of their divine nature, we must also attribute in such a way that we underscore the identity of the divine nature with the person, and consequently, the personal mode of subsistence of the divine nature. To take a clear example, we rightly should confess that the Father is eternal and all-powerful. The divine attributes of eternity and omnipotence are proper to him as God, just as they are proper also to the Son and the Spirit. Nevertheless, in the Father these divine attributes are also *identical* with his paternity: they are proper to his very subsistence as Father, not mere accidents or properties. But this also means that when we say that the Father is eternal and omnipotent, we also designate that these nature attributes subsist in him only ever in a paternal mode of being. Consequently we can and should speak of three subsistent modes of being of the divine nature. The deity of God (the divine nature) subsists as Father, Son, and Spirit, in three personal modes of being. If we wish we can speak here of a Thomistic modalism, but only if we qualify that statement. The modalism in question is articulated precisely in such a way as to underscore the real distinction and genuine equality of the three persons.

Why is this topic of the subsistent modes of the divine nature in the three persons important for a Thomistic understanding of perichoresis? The idea that the divine nature subsists in three persons according to three distinct modes is closely related conceptually to another principle of Thomistic Trinitarian theology, that of the personal mode of all divine natural action. This second principle is closely related to that which was just considered and is a kind of conceptual mirror image of it. Just as the divine nature only ever subsists in three personal modes, so the three persons who act in a divine way, in virtue of the divine nature that they equally possess as God, also only ever act in accord with their personal mode of being and expression. For example, when the Father creates, he does so through his Word and in his Spirit of Love. When we say this, we mean that the work of the Holy Trinity *ad extra* is only ever the work of all three persons. If God creates by means of the divine wisdom, goodness, and omnipotence, then it is in virtue of these natural attributes present in all three persons that God acts. However, we also mean that each person acts in a distinctive mode. When the Father creates with and in the Son and the Spirit, he acts only in a distinctly paternal way, as the fontal principle of the Word and the Spirit. The Son also acts, in a distinctively filial way, as the Word and Wisdom through whom the Father creates, and the Spirit who is Love acts, in a spirated way, as the source of all creaturely goodness. Just as there are three subsistent modes of being of the divine nature, so there are three distinct personal modes in which God acts naturally.

This is a profound theological idea because it suggests that whenever the persons of the Holy Trinity act together in any operation pertaining to creation or redemption, the action of each one implicates the other two (in virtue of their shared divine nature), but their action is also wholly personal: it has a uniquely personal mode proper to each. The Father who gives being to the created order only ever acts with the Son and the Spirit, in virtue of their shared divine essence and mutual indwelling. When he does so, however, he also always acts personally in a paternal mode, and his activity as God (his deity) is paternal in its mode of being. The works of the Trinity in the economy of creation and grace, then, are marked in various ways by the tri-personal structure of divine activity. For example, the Son communicates grace to us as God, but he does so from the Father, as the Word through whom all things were made, who remakes the creation as its primal exemplar. The Spirit communicates grace to us as God, but he does so from the Father and the Word, as the primal Love in whom all things were made, who wishes to assimilate spiritual creatures to a life of friendship with God and love for God. This idea of Trinitarian modes of personal action is something we will return to below at greater length when we consider the divine economy of salvation in a Trinitarian light.

MUTUAL INDWELLING OF THE PERSONS

We have noted above the perfect equality of the three persons, their order of relation based on the processions of origin, and their unity of action, which implies personal modes of subsistence and personal action. How then can we best understand the communion of the three persons of the Holy Trinity in light of these previous considerations? Obviously it is not to be understood first and foremost after the pattern of a communion between three human persons, as we have already noted. Human beings are distinct in being, not merely distinct persons but also distinct individual substances. They are united in heart and mind by actions that perfect them and bring them to fulfillment, but these actions are not co-extensive with their very substance or essential being. Their unity is moral and political, not substantial. Also, such human agents become perfect in communion gradually or progressively. God's inner life of personal communion must be utterly distinct in all these senses. His communion of persons is one that pertains to three persons who are mysteriously one in being and essence, in virtue of their mysterious and incomprehensible deity. The life of spiritual operations that unites them is not a property of their being but is identical with their very nature as God. The Father's eternal nature as wisdom and love is identical with his very being as God, and this nature is present in the Word by generation and in the Spirit by spiration. The activity by which the communion is "maintained," meanwhile, is eternal and perfect, not temporal, and depends upon the eternal communication of divine life within the Trinity. How then can we better understand the personal communion of the Father, Son, and Spirit, which is eternal and perfect in kind?

If we first understand Trinitarian perichoresis properly, we can in turn make great progress in thinking about the mystery of God's inner communion of persons. In ST I, q. 42, a. 5, Aquinas identifies three foundations for speaking about perichoresis, or the eternal mutual indwelling of the persons, by which there is an eternal communion in God. As is frequently the case, Aquinas begins his reflection from what he takes to be the point of entry that grants the greatest intelligibility of the subject matter. In this case, his first argument stems from an acknowledgement of the unity of essence. Because all that is essentially in the Father is given to the Son, and in turn is given from the Father and the Son to the Spirit, it follows that all that is in the Father is in the Son, and all that is in the Father and the Son is in the Spirit. Not only are they each co-equal, but all that is in one of the persons is present in the other two, without this in any way derogating from the real distinction of persons that arises from the eternal processions and relations of origin. We should note how different this view of perichoresis is from many "social Trinitarian" depictions of God, which see the mutual fellowship of the persons as resulting from a concord of mind and heart, a kind of anthropomorphic projection of human relations upon the mystery of the Holy Trinity. Proponents of this approach sometimes argue that the

Thomistic tradition cannot rightly appreciate the interpersonal communion in God due to its prior commitment to a theology of an impersonal divine essence (a characterization of Aquinas's theology of the divine nature that is misleadingly caricatural) On Aquinas's view, however, one might argue that the personalistic character of the eternal communion of the persons is indicated in incomparably more perfect terms. If the Son and the Spirit possess in themselves all that is in the Father, by way of generation and spiration respectively, then they are personally wholly present to all that the Father is, so that in knowing and loving themselves they know and love all that is in the Father. On this view, there is a perfect natural comprehensiveness of each person to know and love all that he is as God, and all that the other two persons are as God. Precisely due to the distinctive form of interiority that this mutual reciprocity suggests, the persons of the Trinity possess a personal communion that is wholly unique, incomprehensible, and transcendent of creation.

A second foundation for thinking about perichoresis is derived from the relations considered as mutual and as implying reciprocity. Here the ordering of the persons from one another that we noted above comes into play for a deeper understanding of their mutual communion. To bring clarity to this idea we should note first that one person is "in" the other insofar as "toward" the other by eternal "relation of opposition," as the other is "toward" the first.[11] This is a mutual reciprocity implied by the relational character of the divine processions. The Father is Father eternally only in generating the Son, communicating all that he is and has as God to the Son, but by this very measure he is also forever toward and in the Son in all he is. The Son is always only ever in and from the Father as his Word. The Father and the Son are only Father and Son relationally toward the Spirit, and the Spirit likewise is toward the Father and the Son as one who originates from them as their reciprocal love. In the Father and the Son is the Spirit and in the Spirit spirated is the Father and the Son.

This understanding also allows us to posit eternal personal communion in God through the analogy from personal or notional acts in God, that is to say, actions proper to each of the persons, not common to all of them. The Father, who actively generates the Son, is present in that action personally to all that the Son is, and the Son who proceeds as the Word is immanently

11. *ST* I, q. 42, a. 5, corpus: "... each of two relative opposites is in the concept of the other ...";
and ad 3: "one relative opposite is in the other."

present to all that the Father is, even as he, as Son, is distinct from the Father. As the Father and the Son naturally spirate the Spirit as their shared mutual love, they are present personally to each other and to the Spirit in all that he is, just as he is present to them in all that they are because he receives all that he is from them. In this sense, there is a perfect communion of persons in God made possible by the greatest immanent relational reciprocity. Human or creaturely spiritual relationality develops always from the outside, or exists through a distinction of beings, while in God the relation of persons is wholly immanent, so that all that one person is is transparent to the other because it is relationally given or received from the other.

The third foundation for perichoretic communion has to do with origin. The processions are from the Father, but also within the Father, as the Father's generated Word and spiration of Love remain eternally within their principle of origin. So even when the Son is generated as one who is wholly distinct from the Father, he still dwells within the Father, and even when the Holy Spirit is spirated as one who is wholly distinct from the Father and the Son, he still dwells within the Father and the Son. By the same measure, we also can think about who the principle of origin is in the one who originates. The Father who begets the Son by this very measure dwells forever within the Son, and the Father and the Son who spirate the Spirit dwell forever within the Spirit. We saw in the last chapter that this idea has repercussions for how we think about the *Filioque* in an ecumenical perspective. If the Spirit originates from the Father from all eternity (as both Eastern and Western Christians agree upon), then the Son is "already always there" at the point of origin, since the Father from whom the Spirit proceeds is the Father of the Son, and the Son is truly in the Father, not outside of him. We should note that the immanence of one person to another as being "within" the other is in no way material, as if the Son were merely a part of the Father. Nor does this presence within the other occur in a merely intentional mode, as when we say that we understand intellectually and by affective sympathy what is going on in another human person. Material presence is quantitatively juxtapositional: one body is outside or located within a part of another. Spiritual presence is immaterial but accidental: when we know and love another human person we do not truly become that person substantially. However, in the communion of the Trinitarian persons, all that the Father has is given to the Son (the incomprehensible life and nature of God), and so the Son is truly distinct from the Father but also completely "within" the

Father as God from God. The procession of the Son is that of a person eternally distinct from the Father, a person who is in no way naturally alien to, outside of, or juxtaposed in nature and being to the Father. This communion of personal being in God is deeply mysterious, but it is also splendid and perfect in a way that no created personal communion or society can be, no matter how ethically perfect.

In every respect, then, the three persons in the Trinity mutually inhere in one another. In proceeding from the Father, the Son and the Spirit do not "leave" the Father. Rather, even as they are constituted as distinct from the Father by way of the processions and in relations of origin, they are ever likewise "toward" the Father and indwell him in the one divine essence, as he too abides in them.

We can complete this reflection briefly by returning to the notion of Trinitarian agency *ad extra* as action according to personal mode. We said that the Father, Son, and Holy Spirit each act as God in unity and also that each acts in a distinct mode of subsistence, as truly distinct persons who are God. We can now think about this again briefly in light of the three optics we employed above to consider the mutual indwelling and communion of the persons. First, each of the persons is wholly within the other in virtue of their shared common essence. Therefore when one of the persons acts in any way in the economy of creation and redemption, the other two must be active as well, since they are each the one God. When so acting, the persons are also always present to one another in mutual communion with one another, in virtue of their shared nature and natural will.[12] Consequently, all actions of the Holy Trinity *ad extra* in some way reflect or reveal the Holy Trinity, whether in virtue of their shared mutual essence alone or in virtue of their personal modes of activity, by which they act in communion with one another.

---

12. We should say also that the natural will of God subsists in three modes: in the Father in the mode of ungenerated paternity, in the Son as generated, and in the Spirit as spirated. Each of the persons loves and wills only in virtue of this one act of divine willing that they each possess as God, but each also loves and wills in a distinctive personal mode in accord with the order of processions. Consequently when the persons will something in the economy, it is willed by each of them personally and it is willed by all of them corporately in virtue of their shared divine life and unity of will. If the Son eternally loves the Father and naturally wills all that the Father wills, he does so as one who receives all that he is from the Father, one who possesses in himself from the Father his natural love and will. If the Spirit eternally loves the Father and the Son, and naturally wills all that they will, he does so as one who receives all that he is from the Father and the Son, who possesses in himself from them their natural love and will.

Second, we noted that the persons are reciprocally immanent to one another in virtue of the relations, which exist in accord with the order of the processions, so that each person is immanently present to the others personally in all that they are, as principles of personal giving or receiving. In the economy, however, this means that the activity of the persons of the Trinity is always marked by their personal modes of being relative to one another. If the Son, for example, is sent into the world to reveal the Father, he can do so only ever as one who is wholly in relation to the Father in all that he is, and as one related in another order to the Spirit in all he is. Consequently, when the Son becomes human, for example, all his human actions and sufferings, even while pertaining to him as man, will reveal his personal relativity as the Son to the Father and the Spirit. The personal communion, by which the Father, Son, and Spirit are reciprocally related to one another according to an eternal order of mutual inherence, is always revealed to us wherever there is a Trinitarian action of overt self-manifestation. Revelation of the Trinity always entails an unfolding of the relational communion of the three persons, one we are in fact invited to participate in.

Third, we noted that the persons are reciprocally immanent to one another in virtue of their origins, so that nothing that the Son has is alien or extrinsic to the Father, or vice versa. Nothing that the Father and the Son have is alien or extrinsic to what is found in the Spirit. Stated positively, each divine person remains wholly present in those who proceed from him: the Father is in the Son, and the Father and the Son are in the Spirit. In the economy, this means that when one person is sent on mission from another, so as to act in the world, the other two are wholly present and active in that person. When a human person proceeds or is sent forth from another, he brings the presence of that person to a new location imperfectly, only as a mere representative, standing in imperfect union with the sender, not making him immanently present. However, if the Holy Spirit is sent by the Father and the Son into the world, then the Spirit not only reveals the Father and the Son but also acts with them and thereby renders them wholly present in virtue of his own action. Furthermore, we can also say that because of the perfection of their communion, the persons who act "from" another also act only ever in perfect concord with one another, as those who are one in being and divine willing. When the Son acts from the Father, and the Spirit acts from the Father and the Son, the Son acts with the Father, and the Spirit acts with the Father and the Son. When one of them speaks or acts, the other two are intimately present with him in that action and are co-eternal authors of that action. This also implies that if we are granted the grace to know and love one person of the Trinity more particularly (as often is the case), then the other two are wholly present as well (without this implying any reduction of the persons into an impersonal essence). As in the transfiguration, the special presence of the Son in his glory communicates a sense of the presence of the Father who speaks and the Spirit who encompasses the apostles in a cloud. In the grace we receive that facilitates a deeper personal union with one of the divine persons, there is an implicit intensification of communion with the other two persons.

CONCLUSION

The Greek *perichoresis* refers to the mutual inherence or mutual indwelling of the persons of the Trinity within one another. In this chapter, we saw how Aquinas, in *ST* I, q. 42, draws out the intelligibility of this revealed truth by stressing the equality and co-eternity of the persons, based on their consubstantiality with one another, while yet insisting that, though the persons are co-equal and co-eternal with one another, there still exists a certain order of nature within the Trinity based on the relations of origin. The perichoresis or mutual indwelling of the persons, then, refers to the way the three co-equal, co-eternal persons continuously abide within one another, but each according to the mode or manner in which they possess the divine nature, which in turn is based upon their respective relations of origin.

Having discussed the distinction and mutual inherence of the persons in one another, we may now consider the question of how to speak of the persons in distinction from one another in relation to the various divine attributes, and in relation to their unified activity *ad extra* in creation. This is what is called the doctrine of "appropriations."

29

Appropriation, Creation, and
the Unity of Divine Action

DEFINING THE QUESTION: WHAT IS THE PRACTICE OF
TRINITARIAN APPROPRIATION?

The doctrine of appropriation refers to the practice of ascribing essential names or actions of God to particular persons of the Trinity, even though the three persons all possess the essential attributes, and even though all three persons are active in one undivided action. The practice originates with the New Testament and is taken up by patristic authors. Ephesians 1:3, for example, speaks about "the Father ... who has blessed us in Christ with every spiritual blessing," an act that seemingly implies Christ and the Spirit as well. Similarly, Paul claims, in Romans 5:5, that "the love of God has been poured into our hearts through the Holy Spirit," even though this love of God is a grace given to us by the Father as well. The Prologue of John's Gospel states, similarly, that "grace and truth came through Jesus Christ," referring here arguably to the person of the Word as the author of grace, but of course the gospel also insists elsewhere that grace stems from the action of the Father and the Spirit.[1] Such examples are all concerned with a common action of the Holy Trinity, but sacred authors also attribute essential properties to distinct persons. A prominent example is found in 1 Corinthians 1:24: "Christ the power of God and the wisdom of God." Similarly, 2 Corinthians 13:13 speaks of "the grace of the Lord Jesus Christ and the love of

---

1. Jn 1:17; see also Jn 5:19 and 26, on the unity of life and action of the Father and the Son. On the action of the Spirit, see Jn 3:8; 16:13.

God and the fellowship of the Holy Spirit," distinguishing the persons by referring either to their actions or essential properties.

The development of patristic and medieval analysis of this topic has a complex history.[2] Western patristic figures like Hilary of Poitiers and Augustine explored the use of terms such as eternity, species (implying both form and beauty), and use (in Latin, *usus*, in the sense of enjoyment of love) to speak of the three persons respectively.[3] Augustine also spoke of appropriations derived from diverse notions of oneness such as unity, equality, and connective bond, respectively appropriated to the three persons.[4] In medieval reflection, the classic examples of power, wisdom, and goodness were employed by Abelard to speak about the essential properties most fittingly attributed to the respective persons, and this practice gave rise to debate among theologians on the warrant for appropriation.[5] Hugh of St. Victor and Richard of St. Victor, in particular, debated the question whether and in what sense it is appropriate to speak of the Father as all-powerful, the Son as the wisdom of God, and the Spirit as possessing the fullness of divine goodness. Another famous triad of considerations arose from the School of Chartres, in its interpretation of Romans 11:36: "For from him and by him and in him are all things."[6] The statement was taken as applying to the three persons respectively, which raises the question of the order of the persons in their external action, as all things can be said to be "from the Father, by the Son, and in the Spirit." Based on these various *loci classici*, Lombard arranged his analysis of appropriations into four distinct examples:

- that pertaining to eternity, species, and use (from Augustine),
- that pertaining to unity, equality, and connective bond (from Augustine),
- that pertaining to power, wisdom, and goodness (from Abelard),
- that pertaining to the Pauline formula, "from him, by him, and in him."

2. For a helpful overview, see Emery, *The Trinitarian Theology of St. Thomas Aquinas*, 312–37; and the study of Dominique Marie Cabaret, *L'étonnante manifestation des personnes divines: Les appropriations trinitaires chez saint Thomas* (Paris: Parole et Silence, 2015).

3. For Augustine, see *The Trinity*, 6.10.11. In 7.2.4–5, Augustine also argues that the substantive term "wisdom" is generally applied to the Son in revelation based on passages like 1 Cor 1:24. There are precedents for his views in Hilary of Poitiers, *On the Trinity*, 2.1.

4. See Augustine, *On Christian Doctrine*, 1.5.5.

5. As Emery details in *The Trinitarian Theology of St. Thomas Aquinas*, 312–21.

6. See Jean Châtillon, "*Unitas, aequalitas, concordia vel connexio*. Recherches sur les origines de la théorie thomiste des appropriations (*Sum. théol.* I, q.39, art.7–8)," in *St. Thomas Aquinas 1274–1974: Commemorative Studies*, vol. 1, ed. A. Maurer (Toronto: PIMS, 1974), 337–79.

Based on this fourfold instantiation of examples, medieval Doctors such as Bonaventure, Albert, and Aquinas debated whether there is any foundation in Trinitarian ontology for the use of appropriations, and how appropriations rightly function in practice.

In his mature thinking on the topic, Aquinas takes up, in *ST* I, q. 39, aa. 7–8, the question of the appropriation of essential terms and acts to the persons of the Trinity. Beginning with article 7, Aquinas gives various arguments for the appropriation of essential names to the persons.

In the first paragraph of the corpus, Aquinas distinguishes between essential terms—names for God derived from creatures, such as power, wisdom, and goodness—and personal properties, such as the notion of the Father as unbegotten, of the Son as begotten Word, or of the Spirit as the Love and Gift of the Father and the Son. His claim here is simply that the appropriation of various essential terms to the persons allows us to better manifest the inner mystery of the Trinitarian life.

According to Aquinas, eternity, unity, simplicity, and power can be attributed to the Father, not because these attributes do not also pertain to the Son and the Spirit, but because the Father is unbegotten, and, accordingly, is the person who alone is a principle who is not from a principle. As such, all comes from him eternally, and he is the one and simple person from whom the Son and Spirit proceed. He is the one who creates the world in power through the Son in the Spirit and who redeems creation by sending the Son and the Spirit into the world. Wisdom, however, is appropriated to the Son because from all eternity he proceeds as the Father's Word. It is therefore possible to attribute to him the name Truth in particular, since he is the Wisdom proceeding from the Father, who in his characteristic as Light from Light intellectually illumines the whole human race. The Spirit, for his part, is the procession of mutual love and gift from the Father and the Son, and so it is reasonable to attribute to the Spirit goodness, benignity, loving-kindness, and so on.

It is important to stress that, on this view, these "fitting" appropriations are not based only upon our manner of knowing and our subjective spiritual intuitions. The idea, rather, is that they help us to see something real regarding the very mystery of the inner life of God. This is the case because they have an objective basis in the relations existing within the mystery of the Triune God himself.

To the preceding analysis of appropriations, Aquinas adds four additional considerations in *ST* I, q. 39, a. 8. Here he offers an ambitious panorama of various ways that appropriation is typically employed in the Christian tradition, based on essential terms, terms of unity, terms of operation, and terms of God's relation to his effects.

The first of these concerns the diverse ways we signify the possession of the essential attributes of God by the three persons. Aquinas's presupposition seems to be that we come to know better who God is *essentially* precisely by thinking about the appropriations of the essential terms to the Trinitarian persons, just as we also understand better who each of the persons is in and through the same exercise. When we consider, for example, why eternity is appropriated to the Father, we come to a better understanding of the very eternity of God, since it is the Father who is the unoriginated eternal source of all that is. Likewise, we can appropriate species or beauty to the Son, who is the source of all beauty in creation, and use (taken as including the sense of enjoyment) to the Holy Spirit, the goodness and personal joy from whom all things flow.

Aquinas's second consideration proceeds from the consideration of God's unity, which is of course an attribute co-extensive with his being. In this context, Aquinas discusses how Augustine appropriates "*unity* to the Father, *equality* to the Son, [and] *concord* or *union* to the Holy Spirit."[7] Appropriations of this kind point us toward the fundamental unity of the Trinitarian persons, but in different senses. The Father is indicative of divine unity as he who communicates the fullness of the divine life, the divine essence. The Son is indicative of unity as he who receives all from the Father in generation, and who is therefore equal to the Father. The Spirit is indicative of unity as he who is the effect of concord or unifying love between the Father and the Son.

The third consideration proceeds from the point of view of operation or causality. Here, power, wisdom, and goodness are appropriated, respectively, to the Father, Son, and Spirit. These appropriations help us to grasp the unity of operation of the three persons. As noted above, it is all three persons who create and who sanctify, but according to a given order.

7. *ST* I, q. 39, a. 8. As noted, Aquinas is referring back to Augustine's *On Christian Doctrine*, 1.5.

Aquinas's fourth consideration proceeds from a reflection on God's re-lation to his creatures in virtue of his governance. At stake here is the ap-propriation of the expressions "from Whom, by Whom, and in Whom [*ex quo, per quem, et in quo*]."[8] What unfolds in time under the aegis of God's province occurs from the Father, by the Son, and in the Spirit. The ordered appropriation of these expressions helps us to see not only the unity from which the effects of the Trinitarian persons proceed, but also the distinction of the persons who operate simultaneously in the creation and redemption of the world.

Thus, we can in principle attribute to the Father, Son, or Holy Spirit re-spectively (1) essential terms pertaining to the being and essence of God, such as simplicity, perfection, and goodness; (2) terms of unity; (3) terms of operation that denote God's power, wisdom, and goodness; and (4) terms pertaining to God's relation to his effects in the creation and government of the world, as when we say that the Father created all things, the Son gives grace to all men, or the Holy Spirit will consummate all things eschatolog-ically in God. These latter are all appropriations pertaining to the divine economy.

In connection with this last point, we can also see how Aquinas con-siders the Trinitarian persons as principles of effects *ad extra*, and thus ap-propriates to the individual persons effects that are common to the whole Trinity. Accordingly, the Father, who is all-powerful, creates all things, as all things are created by the Son, who is Wisdom, and in the Holy Spirit, who is loving goodness. There is a clear association here between (1) the Father and efficient causality of creatures, insofar as the Father is the princi-ple without a principle in the Trinity; (2) the Son as the exemplary cause of creatures, insofar as he is the Word through whom all things are made; and (3) the Spirit as the final cause or purpose of creation (things are created out of goodness and for goodness), insofar as he is the spirated love of the Father and the Son. This order is manifest also in the economy of grace. The unoriginate Father freely communicates grace to personal creatures so as to elevate them into the life of filial adoption. The Son enlightens members of the Church with truth and grace. The Spirit pours out the gifts of grace and brings human beings into communion with God.

---

8. *ST* I, q. 39, a. 8, emphasis removed.

DOES THE DOCTRINE OF
APPROPRIATIONS RENDER OBSCURE THE
DISTINCTION OF PERSONS?

Some modern Trinitarian theologians have criticized the traditional use of the practice of appropriation, based on the concern that it promotes a theology of an impersonal divine essence, divorced from the consideration of persons in their distinctive relations to creation. Most prominent in this respect is Karl Rahner, whose aim is not to oppose the theory of appropriation itself, but to question its practical utility.[9] Although Rahner accepts the idea underlying appropriations in general, he is critical of the effects of its application in theology.[10] His claim is that it isolates the doctrine of the Trinity from the treatises on creation and grace. "Today's theology hardly ever sees any connection between the Trinity and the doctrine of creation. This isolation is considered legitimate, since the 'outward' divine operations are 'common' to the three divine persons, so that the world as creation cannot tell us anything about the inner life of the Trinity."[11]

The main thrust of this criticism is that when scholastic theology speaks of the Father's omnipotence, the Son's wisdom, or the Spirit's goodness, it is in reality speaking of the divine essence, thereby reducing the activity of the three persons to a modalism of the divine essence. In this way it represents a subtle shift in theology from a real acknowledgement of the persons in God to a "mere" theology of the divine essence. The premises present in the theology of appropriations, its critics say, are inherently depersonalizing. The reasoning behind this criticism seems to be the following. If all works of the Trinity *ad extra* are works of all three persons in virtue of the shared divine essence they have as God, then a common divine essence causes all that is not God. But if this is the case, then all that is not God is attributable not to a person per se, but only to the one God in his essential attributes. It is the all-powerful God who creates, redeems, sanctifies, and so forth. Accordingly, scholastic theology, by insisting on the unity of action of the persons with its doctrine of appropriations, in fact obscures the mystery of the Tripersonal God and the reality of what is distinctly personal in the actions of each of the persons.

---

9. Karl Rahner, *The Trinity*: see, for example, pp. 13–15, where the basic thesis is laid out.
10. For his qualified acceptance of the practice, see Rahner, *The Trinity*, 76–77.
11. Rahner, *The Trinity*, 13–14.

However, this argument has questionable premises. A core problem, for example, is located in the second claim noted above: "all that is not God is attributable not to a person per se, but only to the one God in his essential attributes." In fact, if all that is not God in the order of creation and sanctification is in truth attributable to the incomprehensible essence of God as its transcendent cause (which it is), then it is necessarily also attributable to the three persons of God, who cause all that is, in distinct personal modes. After all, it is always the Father, through his Son and in his Spirit, who creates and sanctifies, and it is precisely this personalist conception of the one God that the doctrine of appropriations is meant to safeguard. In fact, we can say that if any action of God is attributable to the divine essence, it is attributed, at least implicitly, also to the one who is three persons, and that if any action is attributed to one of the three persons, it is attributed implicitly to the divine essence. We might consider, then, the following four propositions, which seek to clarify what the doctrine of appropriations is really about:

1. All actions of the Trinity *ad extra*, that is to say, outside of God, are works of all three persons. As such, they entail the undivided essence of the persons, who are each God and who act as one in virtue of their shared divine life. Such works *ad extra* include creation, the missions of the Son and Holy Spirit (who are present in the world by grace), the work of redemption effected by God, the work of sanctification and divine indwelling.[12]

2. Even if the three persons are one in essence and truly act as one, they also each subsist and act in a distinctive personal mode. This distinctive mode of subsistence of each person is based on the eternal relations of origin. For instance, the Father subsists as God in a paternal mode as the origin of Trinitarian life, the Son in a filial mode, as one begotten, and the Spirit in a spirated mode.

---

12. These examples are distinct, of course, from the Incarnation considered formally as such. Only the Son is human, not the Father or the Holy Spirit. Human characteristics are rightly predicated of the Son in virtue of the created nature assumed and not the divine nature. Consequently, the rationale for proper attribution is different here than in the case of divine action, and so this is not a case of the practice of attribution. However, it remains the case that all actions of the Holy Trinity *ad extra*, even in the case of the Incarnation, are works of the three persons. That the Son alone should become truly human is willed by the Father, Son, and Holy Spirit. In Jesus' historical life and ministry, the Father and the Spirit work divinely with him as God, in and through the Lord's human actions. Nor does the eternal Word undergo an alternation of his personal identity or divine nature in becoming human. Rather, he manifests his divine identity as Son and as God in and through his human nature, in his life among us.

3. Accordingly, the actions of persons can be understood not only in virtue of their common essence or their distinctive personal modes of action, but also in virtue of the divine essence subsisting in them in three ways, in a paternal mode, a filial mode, and a spirated mode.[13] It is this distinction of the mode of subsistence of the divine essence that the doctrine of appropriations seeks to underscore when ascribing the divine essence to a particular person.

4. Furthermore, when the three persons act *ad extra*, they do so in ways that are characteristic of how they possess the divine essence in virtue of their mutual relations. It is this distinction of the personal mode of action that the doctrine of appropriations seeks to underscore indirectly when ascribing a unified divine action to a particular person.

Here we may pause to pose an epistemological question. If creation is the work of all three persons and depends upon their personally distinct activity, why is it that the natural world they have created does not immediately lead us to a proper knowledge of the Trinity? As we noted above, in chapter 20, there are diverse effects of God that are not God, which lead us to diverse but complementary forms of knowledge of God. The effects of natural creation stem from the creative power of God common to the three persons in virtue of their unity of essence, and therefore our philosophical consideration of creatures can facilitate indirect, mediate knowledge of the essence of God, but cannot procure for us any insight into the mystery of the Trinity. Likewise, some effects of God's grace, such as his self-revelation in the Old Testament, only suggest the mystery of the Trinity inchoately, but do not overtly reveal the mystery of the inner communion of persons in God. The revelation of the Holy Trinity in the New Testament, however, permits one to understand, in a recapitulative way, that the properties we ascribe to God as one, in virtue of natural reason and Old Testament revelation, are also rightly ascribed to the mystery of God as Trinity, most notably in regard to the divine essence that is proper to the three persons. Understood in this light, the very existence of the created order, in its vastness and grandeur, can be said to manifest the omnipotence of the Father, while the intelligibility of the created order manifests the wisdom of the Word, and the goodness of the created order manifests the eternal love of the Spirit. The created order is seen retrospectively in light of faith to bear the im-

13. See, on this point, Aquinas, *De pot.*, q. 9, a. 5, ad 23.

press of the mystery of the Trinity. Similarly, the ontology of grace can be understood as a Trinitarian effect. For example, the grace of filial adoption received in baptism manifests the gift of the Father, who has chosen and adopted us from all eternity in his natural Son (Eph 1:3–6). The illumination of faith can be said, by appropriation, to manifest the uncreated light of the Word (Jn 1:9–13), while the charity poured into our hearts by grace manifests the life and activity of the Spirit (Rom 5:5). Ontologically speaking, all works of creation, all illuminations of faith, all graces of love, come forth from all three persons. And yet they can also manifest in various ways what is characteristic of one person in the Trinity more than another. This is why we rightly *appropriate* such works of creation and grace to a particular person, as, for instance, "The Father revealed his Son to the Virgin Mary." "She was illuminated by the Word Incarnate." "The Holy Spirit filled her heart with love and fortitude."

Interpreted in this way, the doctrine of appropriations unfolds logically from an authentic Trinitarian monotheism. The use of the appropriations is monotheistic because all acts *ad extra* are acts of the one God. The use of the appropriations is *Trinitarian* because these acts are truly personal acts, which as such manifest the distinction of persons in God, their eternal processions, distinct modes of subsistence as God, and relational communion. If this latter point is true, then a right practice of appropriation need not lead to a depersonalization of God in the direction of a mere essentialism. In fact it permits us to personalize our understanding of the divine essence, by indicating how the divine essence only ever pertains to a distinct subsistent person, so that even when the persons act as one, they do so as three subjects who are related to one another in mutual communion and common action. At the same time, because it is "essentialist" this form of ascription also helps to safeguard a sense of the unity of nature in God, and thus promotes a robust understanding of Trinitarian faith as intrinsically and inalienably monotheistic.

CHRISTOLOGICAL CONSEQUENCES:
THE HUMANITY OF JESUS REVEALS HIS FILIAL MODE OF
EXERTING THE DIVINE ACTION

The doctrine of appropriations is important not only for Trinitarian theology but also in Christology. The theandric actions that Christ performs as both God and man reveal his unity with the Father and the Spirit, but they also manifest his order of relationality: that he comes forth from the Father, and that with the Father he sends the Spirit. As such, the human words, actions, and gestures of Christ can depict and communicate a sense of his unity with the Father and the Spirit instrumentally, in a distinctively human way, in subordination to his divine nature. When Jesus teaches, heals, or suffers, he does so as one who is from the Father, and who acts in unity with the Father. How is the doctrine of appropriations pertinent in this context?

To answer this question, we should note first that Jesus Christ is one hypostatic subject, the person of the Word made flesh, who is truly God and truly human, possessing two distinct natures. The eternal Word subsists personally in a human nature so that all that he is as human pertains to him in his hypostatic mode of subsistence as the Son of God. It is important to note what results from this: Jesus has one personal mode of being as the eternal Son, which pertains to him in both his natures. He is filial in his way of being God (as God from God, eternally begotten of the Father), and he is filial in his way of being human (as a man who is the eternal Son of God). As God he is personally from the Father and relative to the Father in all that he is, and as man, he is also only ever one who is from the Father and relative to the Father in all that he is. His human actions therefore reveal his personal relation to the Father as God.[14]

It follows from this that all that Christ does as man is truly united with, but also distinct from and subordinate to, what he does as God. It is distinct in nature, as when, in John 11, Christ weeps at the tomb of Lazarus, or cries out in a human voice for Lazarus to come out of the tomb. He does these things, properly speaking, in virtue of his human nature, just as when he miraculously restores Lazarus to bodily life by an act of incomprehensible omnipotence, he does so properly in virtue of his divine nature, with the Father and the Spirit. Nevertheless, when Christ acts instrumentally as man to communicate a divine action (calling Lazarus out of the tomb), he indicates the divine life residual in him as Lord, by manifesting in a human way the divine power residual in him. In addition, however, when he indicates his divine power in a human way, he also indicates the filial mode in which this divine life subsists in him. He acts with the Father in a filial way. In other

14. For further reflections on this idea of the one subsistent personal mode of the two natures of Christ, see my *The Incarnate Lord*, chap. 5.

words, the distinctively *human* way Jesus acts manifests instrumentally the filial way in which he is God.

For example, when Christ addresses the Father in prayer prior to healing Lazarus (Jn 11:41–43), he does so as man, in virtue of his human nature, but this human act of prayer is also an act of the Son. As such, it signifies that the Son is humanly aware that he acts in concord and unity with the Father, as he who is one with the Father (Jn 10:30). It also signifies that when Jesus acts as Lord with the Father, he also acts as one who is from the Father. John 11:42: "I have said this on account of the people standing by, that they may believe that thou didst send me." The human action of Jesus is therefore distinctively human, not divine, but it reveals not only the divine nature and activity he shares with the Father but also the mode in which he shares in this nature and activity, as one who proceeds from the Father, sent by him into the world. If, then, the raising of Lazarus reveals provocatively and obliquely that Jesus is the Lord, one in whom the power of the God of Israel resides, it also reveals that he is the Son, who has all that he has from the Father.

Let us return in this light to our four main medieval formulas for appropriations. How does Jesus in his humanity reveal his distinctively filial way of being God? The first example is that pertaining to eternity, species, and use, from Augustine. We might say that when Christ as man wills to raise Lazarus, his action reveals the eternal power of the Father that he receives from the Father as Lord. It fittingly reveals his own beauty and splendor as the Word, the principle of form and order in creatures, who can truly restore them to their proper form of life. (Christ is the uncreated beauty through whom all things were made, restoring created beauty to human beings, who fell into the ugliness of death.) It fittingly reveals the joy of the Spirit, who is active with the Father and the Son in giving life to the world (cf. Jn 16:7–24).

If we think about this same act in light of Trinitarian unity, Jesus' human action in the raising of Lazarus manifests his hidden unity with the Father, from whom he comes forth eternally and receives all that he is. It shows his equality with the Father as one who is God, and it suggests the hidden connective bond of the Holy Spirit, who comes forth from the Father and the Son in mutual love.

Likewise, we can apply here the classical medieval trifold distinction of divine power, wisdom, and goodness. The theandric action of Christ, as man, in his self-conscious human obedience to the Father, reveals the power of the Father: all that Christ has comes from the Father. His human desire to restore life to the friend he weeps for also reveals Christ as the Wisdom of God, he in whom the order of the universe is being restored by the one who is the transcendent source of its intelligibility. It likewise can be said to point us toward the goodness of the Paraclete, who works in Jesus as man, and whom Jesus intends to send into the world so as to prepare humanity for the resurrection of the dead.

We can say then accordingly that the Pauline formula "through him, by him, and in him" can also be attributed in a Trinitarian fashion to Christ's theandric action, such as in the raising of Lazarus. This act occurs "from the Father," insofar as it reveals the Father as a principle without a principle. It occurs "through the Son," because the Father works through his Son made man, precisely in the theandric action of Christ. The action occurs "in the Spirit," who is active in Jesus as his Spirit, who proceeds from him as Lord and who rests upon him as man, being active in his human soul, inspiring and directing his inner life and intentions.

I have noted above, in chapters 21 and 22, that in the work of most major representatives of post-Kantian Trinitarian theology there is a reticence to employ the psychological analogy as a way to understand the eternal processions in the immanent life of the Trinity. Characteristically, one appeals instead to economic activities of the Son and Spirit as indicative and, indeed, in a sense constitutive of the distinctions that obtain eternally between the persons of the Trinity (as we will illustrate in greater detail in part 4 of this book). It is, for example, Christ's self-emptying obedience, intensive human suffering, and alienation from God in the descent into hell, that reveals to us the inner life of the persons of the Trinity, their personal communion in reciprocal freedom and love. The aspirations of this kind of theology are ambiguous. On the one hand, this strategy seeks to identify ways that Jesus' actions and sufferings in the economy are truly revelatory and indicative of the mystery of the Holy Trinity, which is seen to be the deepest inner ground of the Incarnation and paschal mystery. On the other hand, any theology that makes use of economic and historical features of the humanity of Jesus to determine the inner content of the distinction of persons in God is risk laden. Such a practice can all too readily generate new forms of anthropomorphism, by ascribing features of created existence univocally to God, in problematic fashion. When this occurs, one inevitably obscures the true analogical similitude that obtains between the human and divine natures of Christ, an analogical similitude that is to be kept in mind if we are to show how the human acts of the Lord truly reveal his inner Trinitarian personal communion with the Father and the Spirit, even as we maintain an adequate sense of the transcendence and unity of the three persons in their incomprehensible divine essence as God. If the use of the classical doctrine of appropriations has the Christological resonances that I have claimed here, then the balanced use of this doctrine is essential to a right understanding of the *analogia entis Christi*, the analogy of being in Christ. It is precisely because his human actions resemble but are not identical to his divine actions that they can indicate the latter truly without being confused with the latter by predication and projection. It is precisely because his divine actions and human actions are simultaneously and harmoniously acts of the one person of the Son that they also indicate his filial origination from the Father, and his orientation with the Father toward the spiration of the Spirit. Consequently, as we will note below, the human actions of Jesus, in his obedience, self-emptying, and suffering, can be truly revelatory of the eternal communion and life of mutual love that obtains eternally between the persons in God, without being cast as quasi-formal properties by which that life is characterized essentially. The eternal and incomprehensible mystery of the Trinity is truly revealed in the actions and sufferings of Christ, even particularly in his suffering, death, and resurrection. These latter actions are transparently expressive of the intra-personal communion that exists in God, which is their deepest grounding, but they are not constitutive of the communion that they reveal.

CONCLUSION

We have noted above that the doctrine of appropriations is developed by Aquinas as a way of speaking about the mysterious inner life of the Holy Trinity. Even if the three persons in God are one in nature, they also each possess the divine nature in distinctive ways, which the classical scriptural and patristic practice of appropriations seeks to manifest. If we make use of the doctrine to underscore the distinct personal modes of subsistence of the divine nature, this practice does not render the distinction of persons obscure, in favor of a merely "essentialist" conception of divine life and activity. On the contrary, it helps one understand that even while common names should be ascribed to the three persons equally, they also can be ascribed in ways that denote the distinctively Trinitarian character of Christian belief in God. At the same time, the use of appropriations is entirely fitting, and indeed logically incumbent, if one wishes to underscore the monotheistic character of Christian faith. The claim that one can ascribe essential terms to the distinct persons in distinct ways is consistent with the idea that we know of the Trinity only in light of divine revelation, since this latter knowledge allows us to "re-read" or qualify our knowledge of God's essence acquired either from philosophical reflection or from theological reflection on the Old Testament, in light of a more ultimate form of knowledge. The use of appropriations is also important in Christology since it allows us to explore ways that Christ's distinctively human activity, precisely because it is filial activity, is also indicative instrumentally of his filial way of being God. Therefore a consistent exploration of the theandric acts of Christ as acts that are both divine and human, can and should make use of the theology of Trinitarian appropriations in order to consider in greater depth how the mystery of the Word Incarnate reveals in the economy the inner life of the Trinity, its union of action, and interior communion of persons. We will return to this latter theme in the final section of this book.

30

The Divine Missions

The theology of the missions of the persons of the Holy Trinity has a central significance for the whole of Aquinas's thought. Indeed, this centrality is thoroughly scriptural in origin. New Testament passages speak about the sending of the Son and the Spirit into the world, or of the coming forth or temporal procession of the Son and the Spirit from the Father. For example, in John 12:44–45, Jesus testifies to the reality of his own mission from the Father, saying: "He who believes in me, believes not in me but in him *who sent me*. And he who sees me sees him *who sent me*."[1] Similarly, Jesus testifies to the reality of the mission of the Spirit in John 15:26: "when the Counselor comes, whom *I shall send* to you from the Father...."[2] The missions are a keystone that supports the whole novelty of the revelation of the New Testament and its salvific significance.

The basis for this novelty is found in the new disclosure in time of God's inner identity as Triune and the pouring forth of his own communion of life and charity into the world. Accordingly, the notion of missions implies the idea of a new presence of the Son and the Spirit in time, above and beyond their universal creative presence. This new presence of the persons is also such that it communicates a sense of their eternal identity, and thus their identity in relation to or as proceeding from the Father. If the Son comes into the world by a new presence of filial grace in the lives of men, he does so as one who is eternally from the Father and who reveals to us, via his mission in the economy of grace, who he is eternally. In short, then, the

1. Emphases added.
2. Emphasis added.

missions are the economic manifestations of the persons, in their actions of grace, that reveal to us who the Triune God is immanent to his own eternal life.

Aquinas first takes up the topic of the Trinitarian missions in the *Summa* in *Prima Pars*, question 43, a location in the text that is important for a variety of reasons. First and foremost, at this juncture in the *Summa* Aquinas is in the process of transitioning from his treatment of God to that of the procession of creatures from God via creation. He purposefully locates his treatment of the missions, then, between his reflection on the Trinity and his reflection on creation coming forth from God. This location signals to us that for Aquinas, at base, the mystery of creation is intimately related to the mystery of divinization or sanctification by grace. God created spiritual creatures in order to reveal himself to them, and to dwell in them by grace through the invisible missions of the Son and the Spirit. The angels and human beings who are created in the image of God are such primarily because of the twin spiritual faculties of intellect and will, which are *capax Dei*, capable of God, and which will in fact be divinized or sanctified by being plunged, as it were, into the mystery of the eternal Word, who is the contemplative light of the Father, and into the love of the Holy Spirit, who is the spirated love of the Father and his Word.

It is therefore very significant that Aquinas reflects on the missions as a prelude to the study of the image of God and the life of grace in angels and men. This creation finds its deepest purpose and depth of meaning in the missions.[3] This is also why the missions have ramifications that branch out into the rest of the *Summa*'s structure. Thus, if the *Prima Secundae* begins with the question of the final end of man, which is beatitude, this is because human persons are ultimately made to see God, and therefore to be inhab-

---

3. It should be kept in mind that Aquinas clearly distinguishes the order of nature from the order of grace, and underscores unambiguously that sanctifying grace is distinct from the natural creation, and is given gratuitously to both the angelic and human natures. However, he also argues theologically from scripture and tradition that both angels and human beings were created originally in a state of grace, so as to be ordered from the beginning toward the beatitude of eternal life, in accord with the eternal designs of God. (*ST* I, q. 62, a. 3; q. 95, a. 1) In this qualified sense, then, we should say that spiritual creatures were created for filial adoption by grace, which is received as a free gift, and thus were created "in" the invisible missions of the Son and Spirit. Consequently, while divinization does not pertain to the created order or to human nature by right or by natural inclination (*ST* I-II q. 62, aa. 1–3), it nonetheless is envisaged originally by God as the final purpose of creation, if creation is considered in its concrete dispensation "under grace," as it was inaugurated in the beginning. This supernatural teleological orientation is recapitulated in the economy of the Incarnation, in virtue of the grace of Christ as the New Adam.

ited spiritually by the missions of the Word and the Spirit, so as to be divinized intellectually. Finally, in the *Tertia Pars*, which studies the mystery of the Incarnation and the sacraments, the first question concerns the motives of the Incarnation. There, St. Thomas specifies that God became incarnate as man to visibly manifest the identity of God.[4] The Incarnation of course pertains to the visible mission of the Word, who manifests himself in the flesh so as to lead us into intimacy with God. Here again, then, the missions are fundamental for understanding the order of the *Summa*, and Aquinas's deeper vision of the spiritual life.

In this chapter, we will study various aspects of Aquinas's theology of the divine missions by following his order of analysis in question 43. We will begin by determining what precisely a "divine mission" is. After this, we will look at how these missions affect rational creatures and what they tell us about the formerly hidden inner life of God, which has now been disclosed economically through them.

UNDERSTANDING THE TERM "DIVINE MISSION"

The first article of *ST* I, q. 43, is of central importance, as it specifies Aquinas's understanding of what a divine mission in fact is. The argument offered here can be laid out in a series of steps:

1. A mission in general implies two things: (a) a habitual relation of the sender to the one sent; and (b) a habitual relation of the one sent to the end to which he is sent. For example, the monarch of one nation may send a diplomat as an emissary to the leader of another nation. The diplomat has a habitual relation both to the monarch and to the end he is sent for, the practice of diplomacy. Or we can consider an organic analogy, a tree can send forth a shoot and flowers. The flowers are habitually related to the tree as their source and to the production of seeds as their end.

2. Given our two examples noted above, we can observe that the relation of the sender to the one sent can be structured either: (a) around a request or counsel given to the one sent, as in the case of the monarch and the diplomat, or (b) around something that happens naturally according to origin, as when a tree organically sends forth its flowers.

---

4. *ST* III, q. 1, a. 1, s.c.: "It would seem most fitting that by visible things the invisible things of God should be made known; for to this end was the whole world made."

3. The habitual relation of the one sent to the end to which he is sent implies one of two things: either (a) a new presence to the place where he is sent, because he begins to be there for the first time; or (b) a new way of being present, because he is present in the place in a way he was not present before. For example, the monarch might not yet have established his government in a given land, and might send an emissary to render him present there for the first time, or he might have already established his kingdom, but might now send his son to rule there, and represent him in a new way.

How then should we think about the habitual relation of the Son and Spirit toward the Father and of the Son and Spirit toward the "term" or "place" of their sending?

We might first consider point (1a) above, the habitual relation of the one sent to the one sending: This relation is not derived from the economic missions of the Son and Spirit as if the Son and the Spirit began to relate habitually to the Father *as a consequence* of the economy of salvation. The relations of the persons are constituted by the eternal processions of the persons. Consequently, the Son can be sent into the world only as one "habitually related" to the Father insofar as he proceeds eternally from the Father, by way of originating from him, and likewise the Holy Spirit can be sent from the Father and the Son, insofar as he proceeds from them by way of origin. Positively, it follows from this that if the Son and Spirit are sent into the world, they retain within their temporal missions the very relations that they possess to the Father in virtue of the eternal processions. Their missions manifest to us the very mystery of the inner life of God as Trinitarian. Negatively, it follows from this that the Son and the Spirit cannot be sent into the world by a solitary command of the Father, as if the sending of the Son and the Spirit should arise from a new decision of the Father that the Son and Spirit do not partake of. The Father, Son, and Spirit are one in will and power. Therefore, the Son and the Spirit cannot proceed from the Father by command either in eternity *or in time*. If the Father sends the Son into the world, then, he does so in a unity of will with the Son and the Spirit. Just as the Father wills that the Son come into the created world "visibly," as a human being, so too the Son wills this, in equality with the Father, and the Spirit wills it as well, in concord with the Father and the Son. It is the Holy Trinity that wills the sanctification of creation, by the sending of the Son and the Spirit into the world.

This suggests that the missions occur only by the free elective purpose of God the Holy Trinity (like the monarch sending his diplomat as in 2a), but that the missions are expressive of the eternal processions in God that characterize God in his immanent life (like fruits coming forth from the tree as in 2b). On this view, God freely decides to reveal to us who he is in himself, and so discloses his eternal immanent processional life to us in time.

As regards (3b) above, the relation of a thing to the reality to which it is sent, we should recall here that God as Creator is present to all things that exist, as the cause of their very being. Consequently, the Son and Spirit, who are one in being with the Father, are always, already present to all things in virtue of the divine essence, presence, and power. They are intimately present to and within all things insofar as they cause them to exist. As such, the Son and Spirit cannot begin to be present to creatures for the first time by the divine missions. Rather, they begin to be *present in a new way*: that is to say, by the effects of sanctifying grace in the temporal economy, by which they communicate divine life to spiritual creatures.

In light of these considerations, Aquinas defines a mission in a succinct way in *ST* I, q. 43, a. 2, ad 3: "Mission ... includes the eternal procession, with the addition of a temporal effect." This definition summarizes the reflections offered above in a simple yet profound formula. The missions of the Son and the Spirit just are the eternal processions, insofar as these processions are newly rendered present to spiritual creatures (angels and human beings) by a new economic or temporal effect of grace. The grace in question allows us to grasp who God truly is eternally (granting us knowledge of the processions themselves) and allows us to partake of the very life of the Trinity, by participation in the life of God.

Finally, in addition to the preceding distinctions, we should note another that Aquinas makes, that between the invisible and visible missions, which will appear at least implicitly later in the question. Invisible missions pertain particularly to the sending of the Son and Spirit into the spiritual faculties of angels and human beings, whereby they enjoy friendship with God by grace, particularly through the theological virtues of faith, hope, and charity. Visible missions pertain to the sensible manifestations of the Son and Spirit in visible history, particularly through the incarnation and life, death, and resurrection of the Son, and the visible sending of the Holy Spirit in tongues of fire at Pentecost. The Son and the Spirit are sent both invisibly and visibly, or we could say, they begin to be present in a new way both invisibly and visibly in the divine economy, a point we will return to below.

In *ST* I, q. 43, a. 2, Aquinas clarifies that there are certain terms that relate only to eternal procession, others that relate only to temporal processions and effects, and some that have open significations that can imply either the eternal or temporal, or both simultaneously. In the first place, then, the terms *generation* and *spiration* refer only to the eternal processions of the Son and Spirit in the life of God himself. The terms *mission* or *sending*, on the other hand, have a necessarily temporal signification and therefore imply the relation of the persons to the temporal economy.

Finally, the terms *procession* or *giving* can have a signification that is either eternal or temporal, or both at the same time. For example, when Christ says that he proceeds from the Father, or that the Spirit proceeds from the Father, this can have a twofold significance, referring either to the eternal processions or to their extension in the temporal missions. Again, when he says that the Father gives the Holy Spirit or that the Holy Spirit will be given to the apostles, the giving in question may in fact refer to the temporal mission in which the Spirit is given to the Church. And yet behind this mission there also stands the eternal giving of the Spirit as the mutual gift of the Father and the Son.

THE INVISIBLE MISSIONS AND
SANCTIFYING GRACE

In *ST* I, q. 43, a. 3, Aquinas addresses the question whether the invisible missions of the proceeding persons take place only by way of sanctifying grace. Are the sending of the Son and the Spirit oriented toward the communication of sanctifying grace to human beings? Aquinas answers this question in the affirmative. However, there are two qualifications we should note in this regard.

The first is the rationale for *why* this must be so. God is present everywhere already as the Creator of all that is, as he sustains everything in existence. But there is an additional way he can be present to the rational creature, namely, "as the object known is in the knower, and the beloved in the lover." This additional mode of presence is what makes the rational creature his temple. However, it is sanctifying grace, and it alone, that makes this new mode of presence possible, since it is this created grace, realized especially through the theological virtues, that proportions the rational creature to receive God according to this new mode.

We might conclude from this that the missions terminate in the creation of sanctifying grace. However, this is a misunderstanding that we should correct by the second qualification, which has to do with the relation between this created grace and the missions of the persons in themselves. Granted that sanctifying grace is created as a new quality in the soul, according to Aquinas, it is nevertheless given to the rational creature in order to proportion him or her *for* inhabitation by the divine persons, and therefore *for* the gift of "uncreated grace." By uncreated grace, we mean the gift of the persons themselves, as, in this case, the Holy Spirit, who dwells in believers by the invisible mission of the Spirit. As Aquinas states it in summary fashion in *ST* I, q. 43, a. 3, ad 2: "Sanctifying grace disposes the soul *to possess the divine person*: and this is signified when it is said that the Holy Spirit is given according to the gift of grace."[5]

We should understand, then, that this new presence can be thought about in three ways, according to the efficient, formal, and final causes of sanctifying grace. It pertains to the persons of the Trinity themselves to be present as the origin or efficient cause of the sanctifying. When we receive the grace of friendship with the Holy Trinity, for example, we recognize that the Father is present in a new way within the soul of the person, as one sending the Son and the Spirit. The Son and Spirit also are present as those sent from the Father, and they personally communicate grace to the human being in question. If we consider sanctifying grace formally, that is to say, in itself, it is not identical with the persons of the Trinity or their missions, but

---

5. Emphasis added. We can add to this that the sanctifying grace we receive from the divine missions disposes us toward divine inhabitation (enjoyment of the persons *themselves*) not only or merely by the infusion of the habits of the theological virtues (the principal component of sanctifying grace) but by *the operative effects or gifts* of sanctifying grace (charity and wisdom), cf. *ST* I, q. 43, a. 5, ad 2. In other words, the infused habits are given in view of operative acts, and the perfecting acts facilitate the enjoyment of the uncreated persons themselves. The missions occur in accord with a certain exemplarism, as the effects of charity are ascribed by appropriation to the mission of the Spirit and the effects of wisdom are ascribed by appropriation to the Son. Such appropriations are warranted, because the missions are intended to conform our faculties of mind and heart to the two processions of the Word and the Spirit of Love. I am grateful to Gilles Emery for his helpful clarifications on this point.

is the effect of those missions in the soul, leading the soul into personal intimacy with the Trinity. The creature who enjoys friendship with God by
sanctifying grace is inwardly changed by that grace but is not identical with
God as a result of the divine missions.[6] If we consider the final cause of the
sanctifying grace given to the person, it terminates or is realized perfectly
in friendship with God. In other words, God gives created grace to the soul
precisely so that the person can be inhabited by God and enjoy the uncreated gift of intimacy with the persons of the Holy Trinity themselves. In this
sense the terminological or final end of the missions is true knowledge and
loving possession of God, of the persons in themselves, leading to eventual
beatitude and divinization. Sanctifying grace is created, then, not as an obstacle to perfect union with the divine persons themselves, but rather as the
sign of God's new immanent presence to the person and in view of perfect
communion of the soul with the Father, Son, and Holy Spirit as they are in
themselves.

WHO CAN BE SENT?

In *ST* I, q. 43, a. 4, Aquinas, following Augustine, specifies that the Father
cannot be sent.[7] Why should this be the case? Reflection on this question
goes right to the heart of what is peculiar about the temporal missions in
relation to the immanent Trinity. The reason the Father cannot be sent is
that sending, according to its very idea, implies origination from another
(a "habitual relation" to another, as the diplomat has to the monarch). But
the Father alone among the persons of the Trinity does not originate from
another, and therefore cannot relate back to one from whom he is sent. He
is the principle without a principle both eternally and within the economy. Meanwhile, the other persons *can* be sent temporally precisely because
they proceed from another eternally. The eternal relations by which they
are from another thus are the original foundation for their temporal sending. We see that the logic of this position entails that the missions serve
precisely to render the mystery of the Holy Trinity present in the economy in a new way, God as he is in himself. None of this implies, of course,
that the Father is not present in the temporal missions of the Son and Spir-

---

6. Consider in this respect Aquinas's analysis of the essence of grace in *ST* I-II, q. 110.

7. See Augustine, *The Trinity*, 2.2.8: "The Father alone is nowhere said to have been sent," cited
by Aquinas in the *sed contra*.

it, with whom he is one God. Indeed, as we have just noted, the Father too is present in the rational creature by grace (together with the Son and Spirit), but he is present as one sending, not as one sent. Wherever the Son and the Spirit are present, so too is the Father. His immanence is assured on account of the mutual indwelling of the Father in the Son and Spirit. In fact one can say truly that in a certain respect the main reason for the sending of the Son and the Spirit into the world is precisely so as to make the Father known and manifest to the world. "And this is eternal life, that they know thee the only true God, and Jesus Christ whom thou hast sent" (John 17:3). As noted above, in the communion of persons, all that is in the Father is in the Son and Spirit, so that where the Son and Spirit are present, the Father is wholly present as well. It follows from this that the Father, as the unoriginate principle of all things, is truly present in the missions of the Son and Spirit; he is the one who has sent them, but is not for this reason less present than they are. As such he is given to us to know and to relate to personally. "He who sees me sees the Father" (John 14:9). "If a man loves me, he will keep my word, and my Father will love him, and we will come to him and make our home with him" (John 14:23). In the missions of the Son and Spirit, the true presence of the Father is provided.

VARIOUS SPIRITUAL DIMENSIONS OF THE THEOLOGY OF MISSIONS

Aquinas, in his treatment of the divine missions in *ST* I, q. 43, a. 6, notes that all who participate in grace do so in virtue of the divine missions. His presentation contains a number of noteworthy theological and spiritual claims that help consolidate his coherent account of the missions. The first is that all grace of sanctification in creatures whatsoever throughout history is the result of the divine missions. For this reason, the heart of the divine economy for all human beings of all times and places has been the invisible missions of the Son and Holy Spirit, who work, sometimes more manifestly, sometimes more quietly, to invite human beings in their individual and corporate lives into the life of grace and the theological virtues. "Mission as regards the one to whom it is sent implies two things, the indwelling of grace, and a certain renewal by grace. Thus the invisible mission is sent to all in whom are to be found these two conditions." Moreover, a. 6, ad 1, makes it clear that even before the time of Christ (Aquinas here mentions the Old Testament saints in particular) these invisible missions were always related to the visible missions of the Son and the Spirit. This entails that the grace of life in God given to Jews and gentiles prior to Christ's coming was given in view of the merits of his passion, and in view of the fullness of the sending of the Holy Spirit upon the world through the mission of the Church.[8]

A second point worth noting is found in a. 6, ad 2, where Aquinas speaks of "new missions" of the Son and Holy Spirit that can take place in our individual Christian lives. These new missions occur in connection with our progress in virtue or in connection with our acquisition of proficiency to perform new actions of Christian engagement. They can include the resolve to renounce possessions and enter religious life, or the free acceptance of martyrdom.[9]

The third point is found in a. 6, ad 3, where Aquinas states that the blessed in heaven grow in their knowledge, not of the divine essence per se, but of the mysteries of revelation and of God's work in the divine economy *until the day of judgment*. In what sense is revelation complete and what sense is it ongoing? Aquinas clearly holds that revelation is given in its plenitude to the human race in Christ and in the apostolic age, and that the blessed come to enjoy perfect knowledge of what has already been revealed to us in the economy. Furthermore, this knowledge does not grow in intensity, since each of them has a degree of beatitude corresponding to the intensity of charity they possess upon entering into the state of the blessed. However, their understanding can grow in extension, through the invisible missions of the Trinity, as they understand created things more perfectly in light of

8. *ST* I, q. 43, a. 6, ad 1: "The invisible mission was directed to the Old Testament Fathers, as appears from what Augustine says (*The Trinity*, 4.20), that the invisible mission of the Son 'is in man and with men. This was done in former times with the Fathers and the Prophets.' Thus the words, 'the Spirit was not yet given,' are to be applied to that giving accompanied with a visible sign which took place on the day of Pentecost." On the universality of the grace of Christ offered to all, according to Aquinas, and on Christ as the unique mediator of salvation, see my "The Universal Mediation of Christ and Non-Christian Religions," *Nova et Vetera* (English edition) 14, no. 1 (2016): 177–98.

9. *ST* I, q. 43, a. 6, ad 2: "The invisible mission takes place also as regards progress in virtue or increase of grace. Hence Augustine says (*The Trinity*, 4.20), that 'the Son is sent to each one when He is known and perceived by anyone, so far as He can be known and perceived according to the capacity of the soul, whether journeying towards God, or united perfectly to Him.' Such invisible mission, however, chiefly occurs as regards anyone's proficiency in the performance of a new act, or in the acquisition of a new state of grace; as, for example, the proficiency in reference to the gift of miracles or of prophecy, or in the fervor of charity leading a man to expose himself to the danger of martyrdom, or to renounce his possessions, or to undertake any arduous work."

the Trinity. Their knowledge can extend to new objects in creation because the history of the cosmos continues to unfold, exhibiting the ongoing work of the Son and the Spirit. We see here that Aquinas thinks that the perfect revelation of the Trinity does not change in heaven, but our understanding of it can change, as we see more things unfold in its light.[10]

The fourth point is found in article 6, ad 4, and pertains to how the divine missions relate to the sacraments. The sacraments, Aquinas maintains, are instruments or tools of a divine art.[11] One should note, however, that he does not employ the artistic analogy primarily to speak of the sacraments themselves. Rather, he denotes the sacraments as tools of this art. The art itself is primarily in the human persons God acts upon by and through the sacraments. Certainly the missions of the Son and the Holy Spirit are given *through* the reception of the sacraments, but the giving of the missions is for and to the recipients, whom God wishes to sanctify thereby. It is important to note the presupposition here. The sacraments are instruments designed to convey the missions of the proceeding persons to us, and in doing so they bring about in us the indwelling of the Word breathing forth his Spirit. Although the sacraments are only of use in this earthly life of spiritual pilgrimage, then, they also already give us what endures eternally, namely, the missions of the Son and Holy Spirit, who indwell our minds and hearts by grace.

10. *ST* I, q. 43, a. 6, ad 3: "The invisible mission is directed to the blessed at the very beginning of their beatitude. The invisible mission is made to them subsequently, not by 'intensity' of grace, but by the further revelation of mysteries; which goes on till the day of judgment. Such an increase is by the 'extension' of grace, because it extends to a greater number of objects."

11. *ST* I, q. 43, a. 6, ad 4: "Grace resides instrumentally in the sacraments of the New Law, as the form of a thing designed resides in the instruments of the art designing, according to a process flowing from the agent to the passive object. But mission is only spoken of as directed to its term. Hence the mission of the divine person is not sent to the sacraments, but to those who receive grace through the sacraments."

PART 4

Trinitarian Economy

Creation and Christology

The first part of this book considered the historical foundations for the doctrine of the Trinity and the formulation of Trinitarian doctrine in the early Church. The second and third parts considered the nature of God and the mystery of the immanent Trinity, with reference to the thought of Thomas Aquinas. In the final part of this book we will consider the Trinity in the economy: How is God the Trinity understood by us in God's own self-revelation, in the economy of creation and in the incarnation, life, death and resurrection of Christ? There are two reasons to conclude our study with this subject matter. First, we have sought, in parts 2 and 3, to consider God in himself, as best we can under our limited conditions in this life, knowing God in faith and through the means of creation and divine revelation in Christ. However, once we have thought about the mystery of God's immanent life as Trinity, it makes sense to "return" to the data of revelation and to think anew about how we encounter the Trinity within creation and salvation history. This allows us to see more deeply who God is in his economic activity, understanding him in light of the principles obtained through study of God in himself. Second, this part 4 of our study will allow us to engage briefly with various modern Trinitarian theologians, who typically construe their understanding of God from his activity in the economy. Our approach, following St. Thomas, is to distinguish

God in his immanent life from God's own historical self-expression and self-revelation, not so as to understand God at a "remove" from his creation or from the divine missions of the Son and Spirit but rather to understand who God is who truly reveals himself in creation and is present to us in the economy of salvation. This approach seeks to avoid a projection of historical modes of being into the very life of God. As such, it contrasts in noteworthy ways from various modern trends in Trinitarian theology we can identify in passing. This does not mean that all of the proposals of modern Trinitarian theologians are unworkable or unconstructive. As we shall see, by relying on the previous analysis of St. Thomas, we will be able to preserve and re-articulate in a constructive way many of their key insights, while grounding those ideas in principles of a classical nature, so that they are understood in harmony with the patristic and scholastic tradition.

31

Is There Such a Thing as an Economic Trinity?

On the Trinitarian Activity of Divine Revelation

In this first chapter of our final section we will consider briefly two modern Trinitarian proposals regarding God as he is present in the divine economy. The first is from Karl Barth, who posits the distinction of the persons in God based on God's very activity of revelation. The second is from Karl Rahner, who understands God relationally by reference to the historical economy. The core intuitions of both thinkers contain some ambiguities and give rise to diverse interpretations. After considering the central ideas of each of the two, we will briefly note five key Thomistic principles that help us understand how the eternal mystery of God as Trinity is revealed and rendered present in the unfolding of the economy (through God's self-manifestation in history). We can then consider both the legitimate insights and the problems that arise from the ideas of Barth and Rahner. Most notably, we can take issue with the frequently employed modern distinction of the immanent Trinity and the economic Trinity, and propose instead the central importance of the distinction between the eternal processions and the economic missions, as well as the distinction between the eternal, unchanging divine nature of the Son of God and his historically developing human nature, in and through which he reveals his divine identity.

THEOLOGY UNDER MODERN CONDITIONS

When we speak about the dawn of modern Christian theology, we have to take account of the European Enlightenment, which took place in the seventeenth and eighteenth centuries, and of its effects upon theology. Many Enlightenment thinkers, from Spinoza to Locke to Kant, vigorously opposed the notion of revealed theology as the highest science, and attempted instead to interpret reality primarily by means of the powers of natural human reason.[1] Though many Enlightenment theists sought to prove the existence of God or to discuss divine attributes in some form, they also frequently opposed all theological appeals to the divinity of Christ or to belief in the mystery of the Trinity (mysteries of faith, properly speaking). Reason, including in its conclusions of so-called natural theology, was often set up over and against faith. Arguably the most important influence of the Enlightenment upon modern theology stems from the thought of Immanuel Kant, because Kant both radicalized a number of the aforementioned trends, and also stands as a bridge to the later modern period. He is the beginning of a more modern existentialist predicament of the human subject seeking meaning across a spectrum of diverse cultures, constructs, and worldviews, unable to identify pure and enduring knowledge of the transcendent God. We can consider briefly in this respect four elements of Kant's thinking.

First, Kant in effect overturned the previously widespread Enlightenment conviction that one can demonstrate the existence of God by natural reason, and his philosophy is axiomatically agnostic in this respect.[2] We can, for Kant, neither demonstrate reasonably nor disprove effectively that God exists. We cannot in fact demonstrate the existence of anything immaterial, since our ordinary way of knowing is constrained to a range of applications only within the field of sense phenomena.[3] Consequently, all the divine names of God from a treatise like the *De Deo Uno* of Aquinas's *Summa* cannot be considered as a dimension of authentic knowledge, nor can such

---

1. See the helpful historical background provided by Jonathan Israel, *Radical Enlightenment*.

2. See in particular, Immanuel Kant, *Critique of Pure Reason*, I, II/II, bk. II, chap. 3 (A 568/B 596–A 704/B 732), pp. 485–570.

3. Immanuel Kant, *Prolegomena to Any Future Metaphysics*, trans. P. Carus and J. Ellington (Indianapolis, Ind.: Hackett Publishing, 1977), no. 56: "As the psychological, cosmological, and theological ideas are nothing but pure concepts of reason, which cannot be given in any experience, the questions which reason asks us about them are put to us, not by the objects, but by mere maxims of our reason for the sake of its own satisfaction." See also no. 36, and no. 40.

a be employed constructively in a decidedly post-Kantian theology. Nor can one "speculate" about the immanent life of Trinitarian processions of Word and Spirit, using the psychological analogy from immaterial acts of knowledge and love as found in the human person, since knowledge of the immaterial as such is rendered problematic.

Second, Kant sees the human person as a transcendental subject immersed in historical experience. That is to say, the bodily senses present the human subject with a given set of empirical experiences (phenomena), which the mind then places into basic categories of understanding. The sensible world we experience is interpreted, then, in "categorical" terms. However, the categorical terms of our understanding pertain not to how things are in themselves (the *noumena*: things in the world which we cannot know per se), but to the way we, as subjects, organize and interpret our experience of the world. In addition, behind or beneath the categorical modes of our understanding, there is the subject, which transcends, or which undergirds, all else, and which we cannot perceive or intuit directly, but which we can analyze obliquely through its manifestation in the processes of thinking and acting.[4] This is the transcendental subject, the hidden ground of the self: not a spiritual soul per se. Kant is agnostic theoretically about whether human beings have an immaterial soul-principle as the source of their acts of knowledge and love, and he believes this idea cannot be either demonstrated or disproved by critical reason.[5] But the inner ground of thinking and action that underlies all of the complex multiplicity of internal and external behavior is what we might call a personal subject.

Third, there is the emergence in Kant's thought of a historicizing anthropology. Given his philosophical restrictions on human knowledge, we cannot get at the sense of what things are in themselves, nor directly at what a human person is in him- or herself. What we can observe and study are the processes of history: the history of empirical phenomena outside ourselves, and the history of cultural constructions within ourselves. Human beings and human cultures construct meaning for themselves categorically in and

---

4. See Kant, *Critique of Pure Reason*, I, II/II, bk. II, chap. I (A 341–A 361), pp. 328–41.

5. Kant, *Critique of Pure Reason*, A 684/B 712, p. 558: "The psychological idea [of a soul] can signify nothing but the schema of a regulative concept. For were I to enquire whether *the soul in itself* is of a spiritual nature, the question would have no meaning. In employing such a concept I not only abstract from corporeal nature, but from nature in general, that is, from all predicates of any possible experience, and therefore from all conditions requisite for thinking an object for such a concept; yet only as related to an object can the concept be said to have a meaning."

through history and culture, in various spatio-temporal settings. What results from this anthropological philosophy is a kind of historicism. The human being is only ever intelligible to himself within history and is revealed to himself gradually in new ways, as an unfolding process in and through history.[6] There is no facile appeal to anything transcendent in the classical sense of the term, then, as ontologically prior to and beyond history. Consequently, if we are to find God under the constraints of a post-Kantian philosophy, we can find God only within history, and even in a sense as historical, not as something outside of or transcendent of the world and of historical processes. In fact, this will be the way Hegel depicts the idea of God after Kant: God is the deepest ground of history: the historical process of the world, especially the historical development of spirit, of the human spirit, in and through human culture.[7]

Fourth, however, these Kantian positions give rise to a central problem in modern thought. Is there any objective meaning prior to our attempts to understand reality, or is everything subjectively constructed and arbitrarily imposed? Does each culture through time simply reinvent meaning for itself, based upon arbitrary premises? Is there anything discernably stable and perpetually true down through time? Kant affords a privileged place to the modern observational sciences, which are based upon detailed study of the physical phenomena of the world. These may give us objective and universal knowledge. But what meaning should we assign to human existence and to human freedom beyond the mere truths of the physical sciences? What about human dignity, or human exceptionalism? Are we simply of the same value as other animals? Can we find any transcendent basis in human beings, in culture, or beyond human beings in God, to ground a reasonable concept of respect of human rights and of human freedom? Kant attempts to resolve the problem in large part by an appeal to practical reason: the human being must live practically as if he or she is free and responsible, and show respect for the freedom and responsibility of others, constructing a liberal society around this premise.

Modern theologians generally presuppose that this predicament of hu-

---

6. Hegel develops this idea thematically in *The Phenomenology of Mind*, in part in reaction against what he takes to be Kant's excessively static account of reason, in which, in Hegel's view, Kant fails to draw out the innermost conclusions of his own principles.

7. See, for example, *The Phenomenology of Mind*, 757–85, where Hegel develops his initial understanding of God as a kenotic and historical process. The idea is developed thematically in *Lectures on the Philosophy of Religion* (1827).

man meaning and moral orientation that Kant's philosophy underscores is related intimately to a deeper human crisis of truth, and to a collective absence of confidence in any kind of stable metaphysical explanation of reality across time and cultures, be it religious or non-religious.[8] This metaphysical problem of explanations is related, of course, to the problem of universal moral truth, and the question of whether there is a unique ontological dignity to the human person, and, if so, why? Accordingly, modern theologians ask how one might address the widespread crisis of meaning in the modern world. Trinitarian theologians in the modern period have at times depicted the revelation of God the Trinity in history as *the key* means by which human beings may rightly perceive genuine meaning and gain ultimate perspective in the midst of an otherwise perplexing and disorienting array of heterogeneous cultures and competing ideas.

In one sense, Hegel's reflection on God as Trinity is developed in direct counter-reaction to Kant, since Hegel seeks to break with Kant's prohibition on philosophical thinking about God in himself, or the Trinity, or Christology, in a post-Enlightenment context. In his own unique way, Hegel places Trinitarian thought at the center of his whole philosophy and interpretation of human historical culture. At the same time, Hegel assimilates aspects of Kant's critical philosophy up into his own dialectical philosophy. Yes, it is true that we now realize that we cannot find the absolute spirit of God outside of history, but we do have the possibility of finding it precisely within history. Yes, it is true that the older ideas of Christian dogma and supernatural revelation seem to conflict with post-Enlightenment rationalism, but we can in fact reinterpret these dogmas positively as imperfect symbolic suggestions of philosophical truths. Philosophy thus acts as a solvent on classical religious forms, reinterpreting them appreciatively in what one might call a de-mythologized mode. Hegel thus takes the classical dogma of the Trinity to be an outward representation of the most important of all philosophical ideas, one that corresponds to the truth about God as the absolute ground of all world historical processes.[9] The Christian representa-

---

8. The idea is articulated with wonderful poignancy by Karl Rahner in his book *Hearer of the Word: Laying the Foundation for a Philosophy of Religion*, trans. J. Donceel (New York: Continuum, 1994). See the very different but parallel depiction of the modern conundrum in Hans Urs von Balthasar, *Love Alone Is Credible*, trans. D. C. Schindler (San Francisco: Ignatius, 2004).

9. Hegel, *Lectures on the Philosophy of Religion*, vol. 3, *The Consummate Religion*, 417–37. See especially pp. 417–18: "... we consider God in his eternal idea, as he is in and for himself, prior to or apart from the creation of the world, so to speak.... But God is the creator of the world; it belongs

tion of the Father corresponds to the first principle and ground of reality as
infinite and transcendent of the unfolding of all finite being, including all
material things, living beings, or human agents who express themselves in
historical culture.[10] The Son represents this same absolute principle (God)
insofar as it is freely subject to diremption, a process of self-emptying by
which the infinite becomes finite and the eternal becomes temporal.[11] Ontologically, the Son denotes God's self-identification with human existence
in particular, in the limitations of historical reason, finitude, suffering, and
death.[12] It is within these very processes in history that absolute spirit is unfolding. The Holy Spirit, then, represents the synthesis of the infinite and
the finite accomplished in and through world history (the reconciliation of
the "Father" and the "Son"). This occurs especially through the movement
from pre-modern religious culture to modern secular political culture (conducted through the Enlightenment, the French Revolution, and by means
of Hegel's philosophy itself), with the latter secular culture constituting the
apotheosis or spiritual purification of the former religious culture.[13] Human
spirit seeks its own unity with the infinite through the modern emergence of
the international order of secular democracies, as a perfect expression of absolute reason and absolute freedom in history. Modern Protestantism is the
most perfect antecedent form of religion because it has ushered in the free-

---

to his being, his essence, to be the creator.... His creative role is not an *actus* that 'happened' once;
[rather,] what takes place in the idea is an *eternal* moment, an eternal determination of the idea....
Specifically, the eternal idea is expressed in terms of the holy *Trinity*: it is God himself, eternally
triune. Spirit is this process, movement, life. This life is self-differentiation, self-determination, and
the first differentiation is that spirit *is* as this universal idea itself." I take it that Hegel is saying that
God is always already related both to himself (in self-differentiation) and to his creation, by a dynamic of life and movement, and that the Trinitarian idea is at base the expression of this reality.

10. Hegel, *Lectures on the Philosophy of Religion*, vol. 3, *The Consummate Religion*, 426–27:
"When we say, 'God in his eternal universality, posits an other to himself, and likewise sublates the
distinction, thereby remaining present to himself, and is spirit only through this process of being
brought forth,' then the understanding enters in and counts one, two, three." See also pp. 421–22.

11. "Diremption" here refers to the process of self-differentiation by which the absolute (God)
self-distinguishes in diverse modes, as infinite and finite, eternal and temporal. This takes place in
view of an ultimate divine coherence, through the reconciliation of finite and infinite within one
process.

12. Hegel, *Lectures on the Philosophy of Religion*, vol. 3, *The Consummate Religion*, 433–34: "Eternal being-in-and-for-itself is what discloses itself, determines itself, divides itself, posits itself as
what is differentiated from itself.... only in this way is it spirit.... The act of differentiation is only a
movement, a play of love with itself.... the other is to this extent defined as 'Son'; in terms of sensibility, what-has-being-in-and-for-itself is defined as love, while in a higher mode of determinacy,
it is defined as spirit that is present to itself and free."

13. See Hegel, *Lectures on the Philosophy of Religion*, vol. 3, *The Consummate Religion*, 470–90.

dom and reason of the democratic state, which is the ultimate realization of the so-called age of the Holy Spirit, once it is understood in philosophical terms demythologized of its medieval trappings.[14]

Hegel's philosophy can be seen merely as a form of modern philosophical rationalism, devoid of real theological content. In this sense it is sometimes contrasted with the Trinitarian thinking of many key modern figures (Barth, Bulgakov, Rahner, Balthasar, Moltmann, Pannenberg), insofar as the latter seek to revive and restate classical Nicene and Chalcedonian dogmas and refuse the radical philosophical re-interpretations of these councils that Hegel introduces. The historical reality, however, is much more complex, and still largely understudied. It is true that the modern Trinitarian revival does entail a reaction against key premises of Hegel's depiction of the Trinity. However, there are also central points of continuity that exist between Hegel and the main protagonists of modern Trinitarian theology. Here I will seek to note only two of these. One concerns Hegel's kenotic Christology, and the other the influence of his concept of divine freedom-for-diremption. The two ideas, as we will note, are deeply interconnected.

Hegel's philosophy is often thought of as a form of rationalism assimilating Christology to itself, but in some ways it can be thought of in the inverse sense. Hegel's Christology is key to understanding his thought as a whole and, paradoxically, it has immediate roots in his Lutheran theological formation. Hegel was aware, from his theological training, of the seventeenth-century debate between the Giessen and Tübingen schools of Lutheran thought regarding the communication of idioms, the predication of divine and human attributes to the one person of Christ. The former school held that the Son of God made man simply concealed his divine prerogatives during the course of his earthly life, while the other held that he in some sense suspended their use by way of a kenotic self-abandonment of divine properties.[15] This latter position suggests that the persons of the

---

14. See the analysis of Jon Stewart, *Hegel's Interpretation of the Religions of the World: The Logic of the Gods* (Oxford: Oxford University Press, 2018).

15. See the helpful analysis of these two schools of thought in Wolfhart Pannenberg, *Jesus God and Man*, 307–23. Neither of these positions corresponds to the historical, orthodox position, in which the attributes of each nature are attributed to the one person of Christ but not to each respective nature. We can say for example that God the Son personally suffered in virtue of his humanity but not that his divinity suffered or that the divine nature was subject to alteration. These two Lutheran schools, however, presuppose that there is some attribution of the *divine attributes* to the *human nature* of Christ, and accordingly have to try to work out how he is humanly omnipresent while also located in a particular time and place. The solution of the Giessen school

Trinity might share in the same essential nature and divine properties only accidentally and sporadically depending on a particular moment or phase of the divine economy. When the Son is human, his divinity is kenotically disavowed, at least in certain respects, which in turn affects the ground of union of the three persons of the Trinity and in effect redefines the historical unity of the Trinity by reference to and in relational dependence upon the history of salvation. The immanent Trinity becomes an economic historicized process and the unity of the Trinity is subject to development, perhaps open to an as-yet-unrealized future.

Hegel does not simply adopt this Tübingen perspective but instead comes up with his own original approach. The two schools of Christology mentioned above both presupposed some version of what some theologians call the *genus majestaticum*: the idea that it is the properties of the divine nature that are communicated to the human nature of Christ in virtue of the Incarnation.[16] In the 1827 *Lectures on the Philosophy of Religion*, Hegel inverts the perspective of the Tübingen school regarding the *genus majestaticum*. Whereas they speculated on how or in what way the attributes of the deity might be communicated to the humanity (omnipresence, omnipotence), Hegel speculates on how the attributes of the humanity might be communicated to the divinity. Theologians will later call this idea the *genus tapeinoticum*. In virtue of the Incarnation, God is able to take attributes of human finitude, such as temporality, suffering, and death, into his own divine essence. The foundation for this capacity of the deity is located in God's freedom, his capacity to self-identify even with his ontological contrary by way of self-exploratory diremption.

The most famous and illustrative case in Hegel's work pertains to the human death of Christ. Hegel considers the death of the Son to be an ontologi-

---

would tend conceptually toward monophysitism, eclipsing in effect the reality of the humanity of Jesus. Calvin rightly anticipates this problem with Luther's Christology in his *Institutes of the Christian Religion*, 4, chap. 17, 17, in *Institutes of the Christian Religion*, 2 vols., trans. F. Battles (Philadelphia: Westminster Press, 1960). The latter position of Tübingen tends toward monophysitism in a divinity-denying way. It does so in its articulation of a kenoticist and historicized depiction of the eternal God. God can acquire his humanity only by voiding or foregoing divine prerogatives and suspending the activity of his divine attributes, at least in his personal mode of being as the Son of God. Barth rightly notes this problem in his critical appraisal in *CD*, 4:1, 179–83.

16. As I have noted in the footnote above, I take it that this very idea is itself problematic and contrary to the mainstream use of the communication of idioms in patristic representatives such as Gregory of Nazianzus, Cyril of Alexandria, Leo the Great, and John Damascene. They attribute natural properties of each nature not to the alternative nature but only to the person of the Son, who genuinely subsists in each nature, such that the natures are united but not confused.

cal reality that pertains to the very being of God as spirit. In Christ's human death, God in his very being and nature is subject to death and non-being. This occurs within a process of dialectical reconciliation within the very life of God, wherein God passes into non-being and back to being again, which is accomplished in what we call the resurrection, wherein God as spirit is revealed to be and reaches self-actualization as love.[17]

As I have already suggested, this first idea is logically interconnected with a second, that pertaining to divine freedom. In effect, God is able to exist simultaneously across a spectrum of ontologically contrasting states (as eternal and temporal, infinite and finite, impassible and suffering, living and subject to death). Behind this process there is a vibrant ontology of freedom which is connected to reason and dialectic. The ultimate principle in history, divine spirit, develops across contrary states through a process of alienation (in which God identifies with his contrary) and reconciliation (in which the diremption is brought back into an ever-greater unity or synthesis). We might say in this respect that divine freedom is elevated by Hegel above any logic of identity or of essence, and in a sense then, freedom replaces nature as a more fundamental category of ontology. God is free to exist across contrary states, and this is the process he is exploring through incarnation, finite human life, death, and resurrection.

As Bruce Marshall has rightly noted, there is some substantial continuity between Hegel's theory and the teachings of many modern Trinitarian theologians on both these points. In his analysis, modern Trinitarian theologians tend to retain from Hegel, first, the notion of a process of alienation and reconciliation that takes place between the eternal persons of God, one that is in some way constitutive of their divine nature. The history of God with us, including in his human finitude, suffering, and death, becomes either constitutive of or at least expressive of the eternal mystery of God the

---

17. See Hegel, *Lectures on the Philosophy of Religion*, vol. 3, *The Consummate Religion*, 452–69, esp. pp. 468–69: "'God himself is dead,' it says in a Lutheran hymn, expressing an awareness that the human, the finite, the fragile, the weak, the negative are themselves a moment of the divine, that they are within God himself, that finitude, negativity, otherness are not outside of God and do not, as otherness, hinder unity with God. Otherness, the negative, is known to be a moment of the divine nature itself. This involves the highest idea of spirit.... this is the explication of reconciliation: that God is reconciled with the world, that even the human is not something alien to him, but rather that this otherness, this self-distinguishing [of the divine nature through diremption], finitude as it is expressed, is a moment in God himself...." On historical aspects of the communication of idioms in the Tübingen school, see also Kasper, *The Absolute in History*, 459–65.

Trinity in itself.[18] Second, the notion of divine freedom displaces the traditional discussions of the divine nature or essence of the three persons. Hegel's critical disdain for classical ontological questions about unity, identity, and distinction enters into modern theology and leads to a dismissal, or evacuation, of classical forms of analysis of the unity of the divine essence and the distinction of the three persons, by which one seeks to understand how each of the three persons is truly God even while being truly distinct. Instead, the three persons are now commonly distinguished by their free role in the economy, wherein their distinctions manifest themselves by and through their historical engagements with human beings and creation.[19]

In fact, we might seek to advance the analysis in a modest way by suggesting that twentieth-century Trinitarian theologians like Barth and Rahner have typically played the ideas of Kant and Hegel off one another critically in distinct and coherent ways. On the one hand, these thinkers have sided with Kant against pre-modern philosophy and against Hegel, by

18. See Bruce Marshall, "The Absolute and the Trinity," *Pro Ecclesia* 13, no. 2 (2014): 147–64, at 151: "Spirit's reconciliation with its own finitude really takes place in history, at just the moment when alienation has reached its outermost limit and death has entered into the divine—or, more precisely, when the most extreme negativity and otherness 'is known to be a moment of the divine nature itself.' This reconciliation of spirit with itself, exhibited in the Christian narrative of the death and Resurrection of Christ, is at the same time the full realization of spirit's own absolute and unbreakable unity. Up to this point spirit's supreme unity had been, like the reconciliation that accomplishes it, only implicit. By embracing, as it were, its own most extreme antithesis, by showing that 'it can endure this contradiction,' spirit overcomes the contradiction and 'attains [its own] unity through the negation of the antithesis.'" Marshall is quoting Hegel from *Lectures on the Philosophy of Religion*, vol. 3, *The Consummate Religion*, 468.

19. See Marshall's contrasting position, "The Absolute and the Trinity," 163: "In particular, the contingency of creation and reconciliation entails that neither the distinctions among the divine three, nor their unity as the one God, can be a mere abstract starting point or background for their temporal acts. Since all such actions are contingent, neither the distinctions among the three Persons nor their unity as God can depend, in even the slightest degree, on any such action, nor be its term or outcome. (Unless, of course, the identity of God is itself contingent. But even at their most Hegelian Christian theologians have been understandably reluctant to go that far.) No action or event in creation or the economy of salvation, in other words, can be at all constitutive either of the personal uniqueness of Father, Son, and Spirit or of their essential unity. Both the individuating characteristics unique to each Person, what the Scholastic tradition called their *propria*, and the numerical identity of the essence and existence of the three must, on the contrary, constitute the unalterable presupposition of all that comes to pass in creation and reconciliation. We may come to know that the one God is a Trinity of Persons from the revealed economy of salvation, and perhaps even from creation itself, but nothing in the contingent history of creation or salvation realizes, perfects, intensifies, or otherwise alters the divine Persons in either their distinction or their unity. Post-Hegelian theology had made it seem as though the unity of the three Persons somehow depends on what comes to pass in creation or the saving economy, but if the temporal acts of the Triune God are genuinely contingent, the opposite is the case: what happens in creation and reconciliation wholly depends on the unity of the divine Persons."

underscoring the radical transcendence and incomprehensibility of the divine nature, which defies any access by way of "natural theology" or metaphysical consideration of the attributes of the divine nature. The Trinity as God remains inaccessible and unknowable, defying the rationalistic speculations of Hegel. As I have noted, in chapter 21, above, this facet of modern theology seems to entail a restatement, in more radical terms, of the nominal minimalism of Ockham. By our natural powers we can know little or nothing of the divine essence, or for that matter of the immaterial soul in its spiritual faculties of knowledge and love, which would bear a similitude to the two processions of the Word and the Spirit. Classical ways to understand God and the Trinity either in philosophical or theological modes of thinking are now blocked by a form of radical apophaticism.

On the other hand, however, key ideas of Hegel are employed by these thinkers against Kant. We cannot find God "above" history but we can locate God now "within" history. God's own being can be understood precisely insofar as God freely chooses to self-identify with us in a human life of obedience, suffering, death, and resurrection. In fact, it is these very facets of *human nature* that God the Son takes on freely by his incarnation that allow us to understand what God is in his being. The persons of the Trinity in their free interaction in history with us reveal to us what they are in virtue of the relationships they exert among us and with us. Here the Kantian prohibition on thinking about God is transgressed by a theology that is inspired by the Hegelian notion of divine becoming in freedom. We can come to know God precisely because God is free to be diremptive and dipolar, through his self-identification with the finite.

As we noted above, in chapter 21, we can find in this facet of modern Trinitarian theology a strange mirror image of the medieval Franciscan tendency toward "univocity" in Trinitarian theology. There we observed that Bonaventure and Scotus each consider ways that distinct natural forms of action (in the divine nature) track onto or correspond to distinct personal properties, those notions by which we distinguish the persons. Here there is something similar that will emerge. However, after Hegel it is the human nature of Jesus that reveals what is proper to the Son, so as to distinguish the persons in the inner life of the Trinity. The Son's free act of self-revelation to us in becoming human is what distinguishes him from the Father and the Spirit (an idea expressed by both Barth and Rahner). The Father's free act of creation is indicative of what he is as one who must empty himself of his divine prerogatives (facets of his divine nature) as a condition for creation (as is affirmed by Bulgakov and Moltmann). The Son's kenosis in the Incarnation is indicative of his personal property as the Word, who is eternally distinct from the Father in virtue of his natural state of self-emptying even in the eternal life of God, before the foundation of the world (according to Pannenberg). The Son's human obedience is indicative of the eternal obedience of the Son, a natural act by which he is distinguished from the Father (so Barth claims). The Son's temporal human suffering is indicative of his eternal love of self-surrender, a natural act of love proper to him as Son by which he is distinguished from the Father and the Spirit (in the view of Moltmann and Balthasar).

The chapters below will briefly explore the contours of these various ideas. At this juncture the main point we need to underscore is the novelty of the modern continental "tradition" of Trinitarian theology. It foregoes any proper consideration of the divine essence common to the three persons, and replaces this with a central commitment to the notion of divine freedom. By his self-determination in Christ, God reveals himself to us through the states of being he freely undertakes in the economy. This motif takes precedence over the classical consideration of the divine attributes, the use of the psychological analogy to distinguish the persons in God, and the distinction of the persons by use of the category of relations. Meanwhile, other issues arise with regard to Christology. This modern Trinitarian form of theology may commit in principle to a Chalcedonian doctrine of two natures in Christ. In practice, however, as we shall see, the human nature of Christ becomes the indicative expression of the divine nature of the Son, by a form of thinking I will term "inverted monophysitism." The persons in God are thereby distinguished by the natural acts of Jesus as man. What I will propose below is a notion of analogical resemblance of the human nature of Christ to his divine nature. The latter (the divine nature of Christ) cannot be fully understood without the kind of investigation into the divine nature that we undertook in part 2 of this book. It is because we have sought to understand that-in-virtue-of-which the three persons are each the one God (i.e., the divine essence) and have accordingly undertaken a distinctively theological, analogical consideration of the persons in God (in part 3) that we can think coherently about the mystery of Christ as a divine person subsisting in two natures. This, in turn, allows us to understand how the visible mission of the Son as man is truly revelatory of his divine nature and of the personal relations in God. The activity of the Trinity in the economy does truly reveal the Trinity, most especially in virtue of the incarnation, life, obedience, suffering, death, and resurrection of Christ. How can we affirm this central truth of modern theology while taking account of the unity of the three persons in one divine nature and the distinction of the two natures of Christ in one divine person? This question stands at the heart of our discussions below, in the final section of this book.

"GOD WITH US": THE TRINITY CONCEIVED AS A DIVINE ACTIVITY OF SELF-REVELATION

While modern theologians are not concerned to restate and defend all the presuppositions either of Kantian critical philosophy or German idealism, it is the case that several influential theological projects have arisen in response to this modern intellectual tradition. Such Trinitarian theologies sometimes express ideas that contrast with the classical heritage (for reasons we will discuss), but they also present us with new challenges, opportunities, and potential insights. It is often possible to correlate their views with those of the classical tradition in constructive ways, while also confronting with sound criticism the challenges they provide.

Arguably the foundational text of revival of twentieth-century Trinitarian theology is found in the first volume of the *Church Dogmatics* of Karl Barth. In that work Barth, himself a Reformed theologian, takes issue with the abandonment of Trinitarian dogmatics in liberal Protestantism and seeks to retrieve in his own way the scholastic idea of the Trinity as the central object of study in Christian theology. Nevertheless, Barth does this in keeping with his own neo-Kantian philosophical formation, and presupposes that the pre-modern classical metaphysical heritage has largely been evacuated of foundation. Likewise, he famously denies the possibility of any form of demonstrable philosophical knowledge of God or natural theology, taking issue with the dogmatic teaching of the First Vatican Council on this score, which he expressly contests.[20] It follows from this that Barth discounts the possibility in a modern context of constructing anything like the *de Deo ut uno* treatise of the *Summa theologiae*, which we have examined above, insofar as it

---

20. See, for example, Barth, CD 1:1, xiii, 10–12, 41, and CD 2:1, 82–85. On Barth's neo-Kantian philosophical presuppositions, see Bruce McCormack, *Karl Barth's Critically Realistic Dialectical Theology: Its Genesis and Development, 1909–1936* (Oxford: Clarendon Press, 1995).

makes extensive use of philosophical and ontological reflection about the nature and mystery of God. Nor can Barth appeal to the classical (biblical and patristic) notion of the psychological analogy of the procession of the Son as Logos and of the Holy Spirit as Love, since he follows Kant in treating with skepticism the Augustinian claim regarding immaterial capacities of human thought and willing.[21] How then to speak about the Trinity?

Barth seeks to recharacterize the life of God as Trinity in two ways. First, he understands the mystery of the Trinity as a transcendental subject freely acting in history, not as one who is human, but in accord with God's own unique transcendent freedom.[22] We do not have to find God "above" history through metaphysical investigation but instead God comes to us in our history, and makes it his own. In other words, Barth employs a "psychological analogy" from the post-Kantian world of modern German philosophy, rather than the patristic or medieval world of scholastic metaphysics. God is freely conveying his divine life to us through the historical revelation of himself in his Word, Jesus Christ.[23]

Second, then, the persons of the Trinity are distinguished, for Barth, principally by their activity in the economic history of revelation. The Father, Son and Spirit are characterized not as distinct personal subjects, but as modes of being by which God expresses himself in his act of self-revelation. God is he who reveals: the Father who expresses himself to us in his Word.

21. On the background and historical development of Barth's approach to Trinitarian theology leading up to and including the first volume of the *Church Dogmatics*, see Bruce L. McCormack, "The Trinity," in *The Oxford Handbook of Karl Barth*, ed. P. D. Jones and P. T. Nimmo (Oxford: Oxford University Press, 2020), 227–45.

22. Barth, CD 1:1, 307: "Godhead in the Bible means freedom, ontic and noetic autonomy.... It is thus, as One who is free, as the only One who is free, that God has lordship in the Bible.... The self-sufficiency or immediacy so characteristic of the biblical revelation is the very thing that characterizes it as God's revelation...."

23. Barth, CD 1:1, 306: "According to Scripture God's revelation is God's own direct speech which is not to be distinguished from the act of speaking and therefore is not to be distinguished from God Himself.... in God's revelation God's Word [in which God actively reveals himself] is identical with God Himself." On p. 333 Barth follows up on this idea of God in his act of revelation by articulating an idea that prefigures (and no doubt influenced) Rahner's *Grundaxiom*: "Our concepts of unimpaired unity and unimpaired distinction, modes of being to be distinguished in this essence, and finally the polemical assertion ... that God's triunity is to be found not merely in His revelation but, because in His revelation, in God Himself, and in Himself too, so that the Trinity is to be understood as 'immanent' and not just 'economic' ... none of this is ... explicitly stated in the Bible.... [But] the doctrine of the Trinity is concerned with a problem that is really and very centrally posed by the biblical witness to revelation." Barth's central argument here is that the activity of God's revealing himself in the biblical revelation is the ground for the elaboration of the doctrine of the immanent Trinity, as the very God who freely reveals himself in the economy.

God is he who is revealed: the Son and Word of God who becomes human. And God is the one who makes possible the act of revelation in us, by awakening us inwardly to the reality of Jesus Christ: God in his mode of being as Holy Spirit.[24]

This second idea is ambiguous. On the one hand it invites us to reflect on who God is prior to and transcendent of his self-revelation in Christ, as Holy Trinity. God, after all, exists prior to and independently of his creation and freely chooses to reveal himself.[25] On the other hand, Barth's revelatory account of the distinction of persons risks depriving us of any way to speak about God apart from or transcendent of his historical set of relationships with creatures, since we only know God precisely as related to creatures, as he who reveals, is revealed, and is the act of revelation. In other words, God's act of self-manifestation to us implies that he freely makes himself ontologically relative to creation, and that this act of self-revelation by God defines who God is. Barth speaks in this respect of an *analogia relationis* between God and creation, determined from the side of God in his freedom.[26] Taken to an extreme, this would suggest that God just *is* the activity

24. Barth, *CD* 1:1, 332: "If we have been right to emphasize in the biblical witness to revelation the three elements of unveiling, veiling and impartation, or form, freedom and historicity, or Easter, Good Friday and Pentecost, or Son, Father and Spirit.... if our threefold conclusion that God reveals Himself as the Lord is not, then, an illicit move but a genuine finding, then we may now conclude that revelation must indeed be understood as the root or ground of the doctrine of the Trinity." See likewise p. 296. Barth is skeptical about the use of the term "person" to describe the distinct modes of being in God, because he believes the idea of three persons who are one in being is largely incomprehensible in a post-Cartesian world, where "person" is conceived of most readily as an embodied consciousness. It is an error to see this form of thinking as "modalist" in the classical sense. Barth clearly affirms the real distinction of Father, Son, and Holy Spirit as characterizing God in himself in his pre-existent eternity. It is precisely this mystery of who God truly is in himself that is revealed to us in the economy.

25. See, for example, *CD* 1:2, 135: "God acts with inward freedom and not in fulfillment of a law to which He is supposedly subject. His Word will still be His Word apart from this becoming, just as Father, Son and Holy Spirit would be none the less eternal God, if no world had been created." In *CD* 4:2, 346 Barth writes: "In the triune God there is no stillness in which He desires and must seek movement, or movement in which He desires and must seek stillness. This God has no need of us. This God is self-sufficient. This God knows perfect beatitude in Himself. He is not under any need or constraint. It takes place in an inconceivably free overflowing of His goodness if He determines to co-exist with a reality distinct from Himself, with the world of creatures, ourselves; and if He determines that we should co-exist with Him ... God does not have to will and do all this. But He does will and do it." I am grateful to Paul Molnar for pointing these texts out to me.

26. See, for example, *CD* 3:3, 103–5. Speaking of the *analogia relationis et operationis* between God and creatures, Barth states on p. 103: "The divine *causa*, as distinct from the creaturely, is self-grounded, self-positing, self-conditioning and self-causing. It causes itself ... in the triune life which God enjoys as Father, Son and Holy Spirit, and in which He has His divine basis from eternity to eternity. This is how God is a subject. And this is how he is a *causa*."

of self-revelation he undertakes by choosing eternally to relate to creatures. In subsequent texts, Barth does sometimes speak in ways that suggest that this more "radical" reading is permissible. God the Trinity is not only he who elects the human race to eternal life but is also one who elects as an expression of who he is. The inner life of God is therefore constituted by the decision to become incarnate to save the human race.[27] One may interpret this idea as meaning that in his election of us we come to know who God truly is eternally as Trinity prior to and transcendent of his activity of election. But some theologians also draw the conclusion that God is an economic life of election, undergoing historical development in himself based on his relation to creation.[28] In his later Christological work, Barth also speaks of the temporal obedience of Jesus Christ as indicative of a pre-existent eternal obedience that exists in God from all eternity, wherein God in his mode of being as Son who obeys is eternally subordinate to the Father who commands. He maintains that the historical economy of the Son, in his human lowliness and obedience, is characteristic of who God is in himself, but thereby suggests again the possibility that God is in fact determined eternally in view of his relationship with creation, which God then explores within the economy of election, incarnation, and redemption.[29]

A basic ambiguity in Barth's Trinitarian thought stems from his concept of divine freedom. He consistently emphasizes God's sovereign freedom as

27. CD 4:2 contains strong formulations that tend in a Hegelian direction at times, as does CD 2:2. Consider CD 4:2, 84–85, 108–15. Speaking of the Incarnation as God's self-communication to humanity in CD 4:2, 84, Barth writes: "We must begin with the fact that what takes place in this address is also and primarily a determination of divine essence: not an alteration, but a determination. God does not first elect and determine man but Himself. In His eternal counsel, and then in its execution in time He determines to address Himself to man, and to do so in such a way that He Himself becomes man. God elects and determines Himself to be the God of man. And this undoubtedly means . . . that He elects and determines Himself for humiliation."

28. One finds this interpretation of the Trinity as constituted by free election for Barth, for example, in Walter Kasper, *Jesus the Christ*, 172; Wolfhart Pannenberg, *Systematic Theology*, 2:368; and in Bruce McCormack, "Grace and Being: The Role of God's Gracious Election in Karl Barth's Theological Ontology," in *The Cambridge Companion to Karl Barth*, ed. J. Webster (Cambridge: Cambridge University Press, 2000), 92–110. The latter viewpoint may or may not constitute a misreading of Barth, but Barth's writing has given rise to a widespread historicized view of the Holy Trinity, often developed by persons who appeal in some way to Barth's influence.

29. See CD 4:1, 177: "Who the true God is, and what He is, i.e., what is His being as God. . . his divine nature . . . all this we have to discover from the fact that as such he is very man and a partaker of human nature, from His becoming man. . . . For, to put it more pointedly, the mirror in which it can be known (and is known) that He is God, and of the divine nature, is His becoming flesh and His existence in the flesh. . . . From the point of view of the obedience of Jesus Christ as such, fulfilled in that astonishing form, It is a matter of the mystery of the inner being of God as the being of the Son in relation to the Father."

a constitutive element of divine identity, but freedom can be interpreted in a variety of ways. Interpreters of Barth who read him in continuity with the classical theological tradition emphasize active power, the transcendent freedom of the Creator to act in light of his own wisdom and love in creation and redemption. The emphasis is on freedom as capacity for efficient causation. Other interpreters read Barth on freedom as denoting final causality: what God acts *for* in creation and redemption is seen to constitute or characterize who God is eternally. Thus, God is identified as one who *eternally* elects humanity by grace, who freely intends to become incarnate as the expression of his own being, who freely intends just in virtue of his eternal Sonship to obey the Father, eventually expressing this as man, in Christ. For these latter interpreters, the terminus of the freedom by which God relates himself to creation in the Son (Barth's *analogia relationis*) determines God's very identity from all eternity.

For Aquinas, by contrast, God's relationship to creatures does not determine his eternal existence. Rather, the analogy to "final causality" in God is that of God's eternal freedom to love God's own eternal goodness. There is no analogy of being as Barth understands it, an *analogia relationis* of freedom, whereby God can be somehow identified with his relational activities of election, creation, and incarnation. These actions do of course truly manifest God's transcendent identity as Trinity and are revelatory of his eternal wisdom and love, but they do not constitute the distinction of persons in God as such, nor do they alter his divine nature. Barth has his own analogy of being, then, based on freedom, and derived more or less from modern philosophical depictions of the freedom of human subjectivity in history.[30] The question remains, however, whether this depiction of freedom is sufficiently refined in light of the advances of classical Christian philosophy so as to adequately convey the sense of divine transcendence. The classical approach arguably provides superior analogies for the divine essence, especially when speaking of final causality in God with regard to intellect and will, and speaks in this light of God's eternal contemplation of his own essence and love of his own goodness.

30. There is an analogy of being in Barth that is not in Aquinas; it is built on Barth's peculiar and innovative idea of the analogy of relation, and I am suggesting that it leads to projection of human modes of being onto God, precisely the kind of thing Barth wished to avoid and accused Catholic theology of cultivating, and which he might have avoided or rethought in more responsible ways had he made a more disciplined and judicious use of traditional reflection on analogy and relation in the Trinitarian tradition.

THE IMMANENT TRINITY AS
AN ECONOMIC TRINITY

Karl Rahner articulated the foundations for a Trinitarian theology similar to that of Barth, taking self-conscious inspiration from the first volume of the *Church Dogmatics*. His most influential work in this regard is his 1967 book *The Trinity*.[31] However, even while taking inspiration from Barth, Rahner developed his own original perspectives.

While Barth was opposed to the use of philosophical theology in principle, Rahner distances himself from it for a practical reason. He claims that the classical treatise *de Deo ut uno* as elaborated by a thinker like Thomas Aquinas was emphasized by mainstream Catholic theology in such a way as to deemphasize consideration of the Trinity as such.[32] The pastoral consequence of this theoretical imbalance was such that modern Catholics have become mere monotheists in practice who fail to see the centrality of the Trinity, the core feature of their faith.[33] Consequently, to recover a sense of the mystery of God as Trinity, contemporary theology should focus on how God is manifest and active in the economy, in the life history and experience of human beings as modern historical subjects. If we approach things this way, the Trinity can be seen primarily as a mystery of salvation, rather than primarily as a theoretical idea.[34] Trinitarian theology can then be restored to a central place in Christian theology as the answer to a human problem, rather than by appeal primarily to ontological analysis of reality. By becoming human God renders himself present and communicates his

31. The influence of Barth is most evident in the decision to refer to the three persons as distinct modes of being by which God manifests himself in the economy. See Karl Rahner, *The Trinity*, 44, 74, and 110. See also the earlier developments in this regard in Rahner's essay "Remarks on the Dogmatic Treatise 'De Trinitate,'" in *Theological Investigations*, vol. 4, *More Recent Writings*, trans. K. Smyth (London: Darton, Longman, & Todd, 1967), originally published in German in 1960.

32. Rahner, *The Trinity*, 10–21.

33. Rahner, *The Trinity*, 10: " . . . despite their orthodox confession of the Trinity, Christians are, in their practical life, almost mere 'monotheists.'"

34. Rahner, *The Trinity*, 21: "The Trinity is a mystery of *salvation*, otherwise it would never have been revealed. . . . We must point out in *every* dogmatic treatise that what it says about salvation does not make sense without referring to this primordial mystery of Christianity." Taken in itself this statement is obviously true. The question is whether this truth requires the abandonment of the ontological study of God as one, and the use of the psychological analogy to consider the immanent processions of the Word and the Spirit in God eternally. Rahner claims as much explicitly.

life to human subjects within history, there where we as modern free subjects are seeking to uncover the meaning of existence.[35]

This set of considerations forms the backdrop for Rahner's *Grundaxiom*,
his famous statement that "The 'economic' Trinity is the 'immanent' Trinity and the 'immanent' Trinity is the 'economic' Trinity."[36] In one sense,
this statement rests upon traditional foundations: in the temporal missions
of the Son and the Spirit who are sent into the world by the Father, we encounter the two eternal processions of the Word and the Spirit that characterize God's own eternal life. Consequently, we learn who God is in his immanent life from his economic manifestation among us. In another sense,
the statement may be taken to mean something more novel: that God in his
imminent life as Trinity "just is" an economic and historical activity of "God
being with us," so that God only ever has his life among us, as One being in
relation to us.

Whether Rahner intended his axiom to be taken in this latter sense is
unclear, since his *depictions* of the *Grundaxiom* are ambiguous. Nevertheless, some of Rahner's bold claims in his Trinitarian theology suggest this
latter, more idealist approach as the determinate one.[37]

Among these are his novel claim—novel from the point of view of classical Catholic theology—that only the Son of God can become incarnate,
and not the Father or the Spirit. Rahner takes issue with medieval figures
like Aquinas who asked, as a standard theological question of the thirteenth
century, whether the Father or the Holy Spirit could have become incarnate.[38] The original purpose of this question was not to indulge in a hypo-

35. However distinct the two thinkers may be, Rahner resembles Luther in his emphasis on
the primacy of soteriological-anthropological and historical-Christological thinking, and in his
appeal to this anthropological turn as a reason for the break with scholasticism. The Trinitarian
God revealed in Christ concretely in the economy grants us perspective concerning the absolute
meaning of human existence in history. We should notice how Rahner's position acknowledges
Kantian postulates regarding classical metaphysics for reasons different from Barth's, but finishes
in a similar intellectual vicinity.

36. Rahner, *The Trinity*, 22.

37. Rahner's ambiguity was sometimes intentional, as he often sought to present perspectives
that suggested (but did not overtly posit) the reconciliation of classical theological perspectives
with modern ontological views of God and history. This precarious balance of position can always
suggest either the reformulation of positions derived from nineteenth-century German idealism
in more classical terms or the inverse. This is why "Rahnerianism" inevitably lends itself to both
"classical" and "idealist" renderings, depending on the aspirations of the interpreter.

38. See Aquinas, *ST* III, q. 3, aa. 5 and 8. Rahner considers this topic in *The Trinity*, 28–30, and
reaches a point of view opposed to that of Aquinas. His conclusion is based on the idea that there

thetical, counterfactual theology regarding an alternative salvation economy that never was. ("What would the world have looked like if the Father
had become incarnate?") The purpose was to identify three simultaneously
true principles: first, that God willed the Incarnation freely and not as a result of any internal natural necessity, second, that each of the three persons
is wholly and truly God, and consequently, it is possible from the consideration of God's absolute power to conclude by logical necessity that any of
the three persons could have become incarnate, but third, it is *most fitting*
and in accord with God's wisdom that the Son alone became incarnate. The
Son is the principle through whom all things were made; all things in their
intelligibility are patterned after him as the Word of God, who is from the
Father; and all spiritual creatures are called in him to filial adoption by grace.
Consequently, by becoming human, he in particular is the person through
whom all things are to be remade, who illumines human beings as to the
true nature of God as Trinity, and who leads them to the Father as their first
unoriginated principle of origin.[39] In sum, the Incarnation is understood by
Aquinas and other medievals as a fitting manifestation of the Son, precisely because the economy is meant to reveal the Trinity. It is the Word made
flesh who reveals the origin of all things from the Father, as well as the creation and filial adoption of human beings in the Son, and the sending of the
Spirit of life from the Father and the Son.

　　Rahner, however, reads this same tradition of medieval reflection as
an unintentional betrayal of the New Testament and of Trinitarian realism
more generally. He claims that the medieval tradition lost intellectual focus

---

must obtain an ontological relativity (a real relation) of the Son's person as eternal Word to the
creation in virtue of the hypostatic union (see esp. Rahner, *The Trinity*, pp. 26–28).

　　39. *ST* III, q. 3, a. 8: "It was most fitting that the Person of the Son should become incarnate.
First, on the part of the union.... the Word of God, who is [the] eternal concept [of the Father],
is the exemplar likeness of all creatures. And therefore as creatures are established in their proper species, though movably, by the participation of this likeness, so by the non-participated and
personal union of the Word with a creature, it was fitting that the creature should be restored in
order to its eternal and unchangeable perfection.... Moreover, He has a particular agreement with
human nature, since the Word is a concept of the eternal Wisdom, from whom all man's wisdom
is derived.... And hence for the consummate perfection of man it was fitting that the very Word of
God should be personally united to human nature. Secondly ... it was fitting that by him who is the
natural Son, men should share this likeness of sonship by adoption, as the Apostle says in the same
chapter (Romans 8:29): 'For whom He foreknew, He also predestinated to be made conformable
to the image of His Son.' Thirdly, the reason for this fitness may be taken from the sin of our first
parent, for which Incarnation supplied the remedy. For the first man sinned by seeking knowledge,
as is plain from the words of the serpent, promising to man the knowledge of good and evil. Hence
it was fitting that by the Word of true knowledge man might be led back to God..."

on the existential primacy of the Son's incarnation by focusing on the shared divine nature in virtue of which any of the three persons could become incarnate. In fact, he argues, the economy of salvation is centered on the Son made human, and this tells us something about the Trinity itself. To render this idea more tangible, Rahner makes three bold assertions. The first is that God does not have to create but that, if he does create, it is only in view of incarnation in a human nature, such that creation entails incarnation, and incarnation requires human nature. Consequently, the human being just is what happens when God expresses himself outside of himself. To communicate himself to what is other than himself, God must create human beings and communicate himself most maximally by becoming human.[40] Second, if God becomes human, he must do so by expressing himself in his Word, and consequently, for God to self-communicate to and in his creatures, God must become incarnate in his Word, or Son. Neither the Father nor the Spirit can become incarnate, even considered from the point of view of God's absolute power.[41] Third, in this process of self-communication to creatures, the persons of the Trinity acquire real individual relations to human subjects. That is to say, the Father relates ontologically to human beings in one way, the Son in another way, and the Holy Spirit in a third way. Only if this is the case can human beings really relate to the three persons individually and know them as three distinct modes of being found primordially in God himself, the immanent Trinity.[42] God has to become really relative to us in order for us to become really relative to him, and each of the persons

40. Rahner, *The Trinity*, 32–33: "Human nature in general is a possible object of the creative knowledge and power of God, because and insofar as the Logos is by nature the one who is 'utterable' (even into that which is not God); because he is the Father's Word, in which the Father can express himself, and, freely, empty himself into the non-divine; because, when this happens, that precisely is born which we call human nature. . . . Man is possible because the exteriorization of the Logos is possible." Notice here already the Son is distinct specifically or "by nature" from the Father and the Spirit because he is defined (eternally) by his unique capacity to be incarnate as human.

41. Rahner, *The Trinity*, 29: "A revelation of the Father without the Logos and his incarnation would be like speaking without words." Ibid., 33: ". . . what Jesus is and does as man reveals the Logos himself; it is the reality of the Logos as our salvation amidst us. Then we can assert, in the full meaning of the words: here the Logos with God and the Logos with us, the immanent and the economic Logos, are strictly the same." We should acknowledge the radicality of Rahner's claim, since it is made so explicitly against the backdrop of the traditional scholastic "solution." In becoming human, the Logos really relates ontologically to what is human in creation and this capacity or act of relating to creatures constitutes something particular to the Logos immanently in God. Consequently, the Logos's economic relation to creatures is constitutive of his very relation to the Father and the Spirit as well.

42. Rahner, *The Trinity*, 34–38.

of the Trinity must do so in a unique way so that we can relate to each in a unique way.

Two interesting consequences follow from this manner of depicting the mystery of the Trinity. The first is that, as Rahner notes, Catholic theology can now safely abandon its appeal to the psychological analogy as a way of depicting the inner life of God (the immanent Trinity) as the eternal immaterial generation of the Logos and the eternal immaterial spiration of the Spirit who is Love.[43] Instead it is the historical and economic manifestation of God as the ground of history that allows us to determine the distinction of persons. The Word who has become human is the principle of God's self-communication to human beings, the one through whom we are configured to the divine life. Consequently, in the Word's manifestation of God we discover the Father, and in the Word's operation upon human nature by grace we discover the Holy Spirit. There is a historical dimension to this mystery. The Father is the backdrop or the original horizon of human history, the absolute mystery of human existence, who remains unknown to us unless he is revealed in Jesus Christ. The Word is the immanent principle within history who reveals to us the inner meaning of human existence as "filial": we see in Jesus Christ that we can relate to the unknown absolute as "Father," and that the mystery of God is disclosed to us concretely in history in the Son, Jesus, who is the Word of God through whom God speaks to us or discloses himself. The Holy Spirit then emerges as the principle through whom the future of humanity is open to God, who is at work in the human race, always already preparing human nature for the absolute encounter with God, for the immediate intuitive knowledge of God that Christ makes possible. The gift of the Spirit then discloses God the Trinity as the eschatological future of the world, and the final purpose or essence of history.[44]

43. See Rahner, *The Trinity*, 19, 46–48, 115–20. Rahner states his view succinctly in *Foundations of Christian Faith*, 135–6: "... psychological speculation about the Trinity has in any case the disadvantage that in the doctrine of the Trinity it does not really give enough weight to a starting point in the history of revelation and dogma which is within the *historical and salvific* experience of the Son and of the Spirit as the reality of the divine self-communication to us, so that we can understand from this historical experience what the doctrine of the divine Trinity really means. The psychological theory of the Trinity neglects the experience of the Trinity in favor of a seemingly almost Gnostic speculation about what goes on in the inner life of God. In the process it really forgets that the countenance of God which turns towards us in this self-communication is, in the trinitarian nature of this encounter, the very being of God as he is in himself, and must be if indeed the divine self-communication in grace and in glory really is the communication of God in his own self to us."

44. Rahner, *The Trinity*, 58–68, 94–98.

Second, Rahner, like Barth, is concerned that the notion of three divine "persons" in God is too hopelessly anthropomorphic or mythological for modern human beings to accept.[45] Consequently, he too wishes to speak of the Trinitarian persons primarily as "modes of subsistence" or modes of being.[46] However, because of his insistence on the economic modality of God's revelation to us, and the consequent fact that we grasp the distinction of persons only in the economy, it follows that Rahner's Trinitarian modes of subsistence are distinguished primarily by their economic functions. For example, the notion of Christ as God's "Word" is inherently ambiguous. Does the term denote here only a relation of God to his creatures (God in his mode of being as self-manifesting and addressing creatures), or also a relation in God that pre-exists independently of the economy of salvation? For Aquinas, as we have seen, the notion implies both an eternal relation of generation that exists independently of creation and a relation to creatures, since all things are created in the Word. The former procession is the ground or foundation for the latter relationship, since all things are created by the Father through the Word. In Rahner's presentation, however, the state of affairs is less clear.[47] Do we call Jesus Christ the "Word" of God precisely because God is communicating himself to us in the life, death, and resurrection of Jesus of Nazareth? If so, does this term "Word" connote something that pre-exists in God prior to the Incarnation? If it does, mustn't we have recourse to the classical theology of the tradition to determine what the eternal procession of the Word is? In this case we would need to make use of the psychological analogy and the study of the divine names (*de Deo ut uno*) in order to speak about the Word as the immanent procession of the Father. If the attribution of "Word" to Jesus does not have this classical sense, then either the term is nominalistic and is only an expression we use, in our given religious tradition, to talk about Jesus of Nazareth as a disclosure of the absolute truth about God "for us" : "The Koran is a Word of God for some, while Jesus is a Word of God for others" (in which case we are in the line of

45. Rahner, *The Trinity*, 73–76, 103–15.

46. Rahner, *The Trinity*, 113–14: "—the one God subsists in three distinct manners of subsisting . . .—the Father, Son, and Spirit are the one God each in a different manner of subsisting and in this sense we may count 'three' in God."

47. See, for example, Rahner, *The Trinity*, 64 and 102: The Word "just is" the self-expression of the Father, which is always, already *both* immanent in God (communication of what the Father is to us in his Word) *and* his self-expression in what is not God (in creation and the human nature of Christ). God *freely* chooses to self-communicate, but he also seems somehow to determine himself eternally in his identity as Father, Word, and Spirit for and in relation to creation.

thinking of the Christological relativism of Ernst Troeltsch).[48] Or Christ is the Word only in the economy, because God himself as Trinity is ever only "for" or "toward" historical manifestation. That is to say, God can only ever be God in view of his economic self-communication to us. In this case, the economic Trinity is all there is. God incarnates and self-communicates precisely as the unfolding historical expression of God's own being.[49]

Rahner does not resolve the question for us, and leaves room for any of these three interpretations, one more classical, one typical of liberal Protestantism, and one more Hegelian. Nevertheless, there are good reasons to read him as privileging the last option. Namely, if God the Son and Word alone can become incarnate, and not the Father or the Holy Spirit, then there is a sense in which God the Word pre-exists in distinction from the Father and the Spirit *as God* precisely in view of a relationship to creation and self-communication through incarnation. Otherwise, the three persons, being truly equal and identically God, would each have the absolute power to become human. If this capacity is proper to the Son alone, then it is due to something that defines him relationally with respect to the Father and the Spirit, but this can only be something in the economy, in virtue of incarnation. Consequently, there is a way that the Incarnation is precisely that which distinguishes the Word and Son *in his eternal identity*, at least as an eternal predisposition to the self-communication of divine life to creatures through incarnation. In short, the economy has become in some way constitutive of the distinction of persons in God, and in that sense it is a necessary part of God's eternal identity. God only ever exists in view of his historicization.

This viewpoint acquires greater consistency if one considers Rahner's stridently novel claim, in the face of precedent theology, that each of the persons of the Trinity must have an individual relation to creatures. This would be uncontroversial if Rahner were merely saying that by the grace of God, human beings truly come to experience mystically, know by faith, and relate personally to the Father, the Son, and the Holy Spirit in their distinctness. But he is saying something far more (or other), since he posits that the

---

48. See, for example, the liberal Protestant Christology of Jesus as an exemplary human religious figure who is taken as a "word of God" for Christians, according to Ernst Troeltsch, *The Absoluteness of Christianity and the History of Religions*, trans. D. Reid (London: John Knox, 1971), and similarly in Jacques Dupuis, *Toward a Christian Theology of Religious Pluralism* (Maryknoll, N.Y.: Orbis, 1997).

49. See Hegel, *Lectures on the Philosophy of Religion* (1827), 432–70, on God's self-distinction as Son in virtue of God's historical existence as human.

Father, Son, and Holy Spirit each really relate to creatures, and therefore are each individually defined ontologically at least in part by their distinctive modes of relativity to creatures. If taken to its logical consequence, this idea would imply that the three divine persons or modes of subsistence in God have distinctive properties that are determined in the economy by their individual relations to creatures. The obvious conclusion of such a position would be that the three persons have distinctive *natural properties* that derive from creation and history, rather than a shared divine nature that they each possess in absolute equality. Having dismissed the use of the classical *de Deo ut uno* treatise within Trinitarian theology, Rahner finishes by conceiving of the nature of the Trinitarian persons in a new way, one based not on the unity of the transcendent divine nature of God, but on the relational functions of the persons in salvation history. If interpreted in a radically consistent way, this would suggest that God just is in himself a series of historical events. Rahner did not himself adopt this view, but many who have taken inspiration from him subsequently have in fact done so. Once we see this tendency of his thought, Rahner's pastoral modernization of Trinitarian theology now begins to look less successful in its apologetic or pastoral relevance, and less innocent in its consequences. It also appears potentially naïve in its dismissal of core elements from the traditions of patristic and scholastic theology.[50]

50. We should note also a curious paradox of Rahner's theology. On the one hand, by jettisoning the classical notion of divine "persons" and by presenting his theology in terms of the communication of God in "his Word," he presents us with God the Trinity as a "monological subject," something analogically akin to a Kantian transcendental subject in history who communicates his life through unfolding processes, not wholly unlike the Hegelian concept of God as spirit. Consequently, he has "translated" the classical psychological analogy of the Word and Spirit into a modern post-Kantian idiom, in which God is understood not by analogies from immateriality but by analogies from freedom of expression in history. So at the end of this process we have less to do with a Trinity and more to do with God as a monopersonal subject, precisely the point of departure that Rahner set out to criticize. Second, for Rahner the personal modes of subsistence in God have to be differentiated at least in part by economic functions, but this compromises a true and deep sense of the divine unity of nature, as we have noted. Consequently, the persons are in fact accorded differentiation or distinction principally by way of a distinction of natural actions and properties. In other words, Rahner's position not by its intention but by the logical outcome of some of its principles, tends to the affirmation not of three persons acting in virtue of one divine nature, but of one transcendental subject acting in three "natures," or in three operational modes of being. This is virtually the opposite of the Nicene formulation, which of course Rahner intentionally affirmed and sought in his own way to uphold. It is not clear in the end, however, that his project holds together well. We have good reason, then, to question the normativity of the Rahnerian paradigm in modern Catholic Trinitarian theology. Sometimes progress means letting go of the past.

THOMISTIC QUALIFICATIONS

Despite potential criticisms that may be leveled against the approach of either of these two thinkers, there are reasons to acknowledge some of their fundamental aspirations and contributions. Barth sought in the face of liberal Protestantism to return to the Trinitarian mystery as the center of Christian theology and dogmatic reflection. Both he and Rahner understandably emphasized the centrality of the concrete encounter with God in history, even if they did so in part through the filter of philosophical presuppositions (both inherited from Kant and Hegel and developed in reaction to them) that are contestable. Likewise, they can be seen, each in his own way, as attempting to restate the classical truth that the divine missions of the Son and the Spirit reveal the immanent life of God, the eternal processions that characterize the very life of God. By focusing on divine self-communication, Rahner sought to underscore the purpose of the Trinitarian revelation in existential and practical terms: this is a mystery that saves the human person in concrete history even as it unveils the deepest ground of reality and the ultimate explanatory principle of human existence.

At the same time, there are obstacles to a plenary reception of the views of these two seminal thinkers. Before we consider these, let us first recall some core principle or insights from the third part of our study above.

1. We encounter the mystery of God's internal processions of Word and Spirit only ever in the economy in virtue of the missions, and the missions are the processions with the addition of an added effect. For example, we come to know the eternal Word of the Father only because the Father has first elected to send the Son into the world and because "the Word became flesh ... full of grace and truth" (Jn 1:14). "He who has seen me has seen the Father" (Jn 14:9). Nevertheless, in encountering the Son in his visible mission, we discern that the Son is truly God, one with the Father, and by this same measure we also come by necessity to distinguish his deity—and thus his pre-existent eternal personhood as Son—from his humanity, that is to say, from the human nature he took upon himself in order to reveal himself to us. We can and must say both that the Word is with God "from the beginning," (Jn 1:1–2), that is to say, before all things, and is he "through whom all things were made" (Jn 1:3), and that we have come to know the Word in

and through his human life among us (Jn 1:14), as well as his passion, death, and resurrection.

2. Therefore we can understand the economic activity of the Trinity only in light of the eternal communion of persons in the Trinity in their transcendence and unity of action. If the Son is truly God, then he acts with the Father and the Spirit *as the primary principle* in every divine initiative. But God the Holy Trinity is God the Creator, the one true God who is simple in nature (not composite in the way of creatures). He is perfect in actuality (not actuated to perfection by his creation), eternal (not temporal), all knowing (not ignorant), omnipotent (not powerless). Consequently, the Son as God, with the Father and the Spirit, must be characterized by all that properly pertains to God the Creator, to the Father in his transcendent deity as the primary author of all reality. This means also then that all that pertains to the nature of God as studied in the *de Deo ut uno* treatise (the study of the divine attributes) is attributed to the Son as God. Accordingly, the study of the divine attributes is essential if we are to understand that in virtue of which the Trinitarian persons are one and are transcendent of creation (i.e., in their simplicity, divine perfection, eternity, and so forth) and how they act as one in all they do in the economy, in virtue of their shared divine life, wisdom, love, and power.

3. Furthermore, the three persons of God act as one in virtue of their shared nature and life as God but also act as persons, and we need not posit any opposition of these two ideas. There is a modal action of the persons, as efficient causes or origins, even when they act together in the divine action in creation and redemption. For example, the Father, as the unoriginated source of all things, creates (in a distinctively paternal mode), and he does so through the Son as the Wisdom he eternally begets, and in the Spirit, who is the Love of the Father and the Son. Such personal modes of action are rightly predicated of the persons in all actions *ad extra* of creation and salvation. This is why, *pace* Rahner, it is always only all three persons who act together as one, but, in accord with Rahner's concern regarding the revelation of the persons, we can say that this unified action in fact manifests the distinct mode of personal action of each person, and so is deeply revelatory of the distinction of the three persons. In addition, in their final causality or purpose, such actions take place in view of distinct effects of grace that can create in the human subject a privileged communion with one person or another. For example, the Holy Spirit, sent by the Father and the Son into the

world, always acts with the Father and the Son as source of grace, even if he does so *as* the Spirit, in a spirated mode. And in doing so, the Spirit may illumine a human person so as to awaken him to the distinctive personal presence of the Son of God in particular, allowing the person to recognize and have a personal relationship to the Son in his resurrection. "And because you are sons, God has sent the Spirit of his Son into our hearts, crying, 'Abba! Father!' So through God you are no longer a slave but a son, and if a son then an heir" (Gal 4:6–7).

4. Therefore we can say that all activity of the three persons reflects Trinitarian action in both a personal, communal way, and in a natural way as divine action. If God elects, it is the Father, through the Son, in the Spirit, who does so. But it is also only the omnipotent, eternally wise and loving Trinitarian God and Creator who elects, and action of this kind is characterized by the inalienable attributes of divine transcendence.

5. Finally, if Christ acts, he does so only ever as both God and man, by two natures, operations, and wills: divine and human. Consequently, his human decisions and actions in concrete history manifest and express his divine will but are not identical per se with his natural will as God. When, for example, the Lord Jesus Christ heals a blind person, it is only the Son as man who wills humanly to stretch out his hand, touch the blind man, and say, "I will it." It is the Son as true God, however, with the Father and the Holy Spirit, who acts divinely to heal in and through his concrete act of human touch, and he does so in virtue of the divine power residing in him as Lord. Furthermore, the human action of the Son made man is the human action of God the Son, and so it reflects as *personal* action the relation of origin of the Son from Father and of the Spirit from the Father and the Son. The Son works as one from the Father, and in the Spirit of his Father. The concrete action of Christ's healing within history, as a human being with divine power, thus manifests that he is the Lord, one who truly comes from the Father, not only in his temporal mission, but also in his procession as Son, from all eternity. This healing action of the Father takes place by the Son, who reveals the Father in so doing. But it also occurs in the Spirit, who is active in and through the human action of Jesus, as the Spirit of the Lord, the Spirit of the Son. The Spirit thus reveals Jesus as the Son, and in doing so manifests the Father. The order of the Trinitarian persons in their eternal relations is present in the concrete historical action of Jesus.

In light of these principles we can offer some preliminary critical evaluations of the economic depiction of the Holy Trinity.

Barth distinguishes the persons of the Trinity in virtue of God's act of self-revelation. It is the Father who is the revealer, the Son who is revealed, and the Holy Spirit who is the agent of revelation within human beings. How might we evaluate this idea from a Thomistic perspective? First, we may recall the principle that all acts of the Holy Trinity *ad extra* are acts of all three persons, conducted in virtue of the shared divine nature they each possess. Furthermore, Trinitarian revelation terminates in true knowledge of and intimacy with all three persons. Such revelation is meant to result in the genuine Trinitarian indwelling of God in the human subject by grace. Consequently, the Father, Son, and Holy Spirit are *together* the origin of divine revelation (the revealer), the subject of revelation (the revealed), and the indwelling principle of agency by which we come to know God (the agent of the revealing). Revelation is Trinitarian and pertains to the one God.

However, there is a foundation for the Barthian idea if it is understood in another sense. Revelation as an action of God is conducted by all three persons, but it is also always conducted according to Trinitarian modes of personal distinction proper to each person.[51] We must say, for example, that while the Father acts always only in unity with the Son and the Spirit, the Father also acts always only *as Father*, in a paternal mode as the principle and fontal origin of Trinitarian life, while the Son acts only in a filial mode, as the spoken Word who communicates the life of the Father to us, who points us back to the Father.[52] The Spirit acts only as the one sent forth from

51. See on this notion the important study of Gilles Emery, "The Personal Mode of Trinitarian Action in Saint Thomas Aquinas," *The Thomist* 69, no. 1 (2005): 31–77.

52. This idea is particularly evident in the always-relational dynamic present in John's Christological vision, in which the works of Jesus not only attest to his deity but also always indicate paternal origin and turn all things "back" to the Father. "Jesus said to [Philip], 'Have I been with you so long, and yet you do not know me, Philip? He who has seen me has seen the Father; how can you say, 'Show us the Father'? Do you not believe that I am in the Father and the Father in me? The words that I say to you I do not speak on my own authority; but the Father who dwells in me does his works. Believe me that I am in the Father and the Father in me; or else believe me for the sake of the works themselves. Truly, truly, I say to you, he who believes in me will also do the works that I do; and greater works than these will he do, because I go to the Father'" (Jn 14:9–13).

the Father and the Word, as their mutual Love. This Trinitarian imprint is essential to the activity of revelation. The Father manifests his paternity of the Son precisely by sending and revealing the Son, who comes from him, and communicates his own life to us in his Word made flesh, so that we may become adopted sons by grace. The Son manifests the Father to us in a distinctively filial mode through his human conception, life, and death, showing us that the Father is the origin and final end of all things. In doing so, he also reveals himself as the exemplary principle of creation, the eternally begotten Wisdom through whom all things were made. The Holy Spirit sent forth from the Father and the Son manifests Jesus to the world. He does so precisely as the eternally uncreated Gift of the Father and the Son, who moves us inwardly so as to lead us back to the Father, in the Son.[53]

Furthermore, by appealing to the classical doctrine of appropriations, we can *appropriate* the act of revelation to the three persons in accord with the modal distinctions of persons just alluded to. We can speak, for example, of the Father as the primal "Revealer" of the Son because the Son comes forth eternally from him as his spoken Word, and is sent by him into the world.[54] We can speak of the Son as the "Revealed" by appropriation precisely because the Word made flesh makes the unoriginated Father known.[55] The Spirit can be called the "Protagonist of Revelation" by appropriation because he is sent from the Father and the Son precisely to illumine the human race, and the Father and the Son in turn act upon us in and through the Spirit's mission.[56] Barth speculates in a defensible man-

53. Jn 15:26: "But when the Counselor comes, whom I shall send to you from the Father, even the Spirit of truth, who proceeds from the Father, he will bear witness to me."

54. Mt 16:17: "... Jesus answered him, 'Blessed are you, Simon Bar-Jona! For flesh and blood has not revealed this to you, but my Father who is in heaven.'" See, likewise, in a Johannine key, Jn 1:14; 3:34; 17:8–17; 18:37. Meanwhile, Paul tells us (Gal 1:16) that the Father "was pleased to reveal his Son to me, in order that I might preach him among the Gentiles ..."

55. For Matthew, as for John and Paul, the paternal origin of the Son stands at the foreground of revelation and is that which the Son manifests by his life, death, and resurrection. Only the Father knows the Son, and, at the same time, it is only the Son who can "reveal" the Father: Mt 11:27: "All things have been delivered to me by my Father; and no one knows the Son except the Father, and no one knows the Father except the Son and any one to whom the Son chooses to reveal him."

56. We have only to think here of Luke's attribution of revelatory activity to the Holy Spirit acting within and upon human persons, before, during, and after the human life of Jesus, so as to manifest him as the Son of God: Lk 1:35, 41, 67; 2:26; 3:16, 22; 4:1, 18; 12:12; Acts 1:5, 8; 2:4, 38; 4:8; 5:32. See likewise Jn 16:7–11: the Counselor will convict the world of the truth of Christ through the preaching of the apostles. So too for Paul in Gal 3:2–5; 5:17, and especially Gal 4:6: the Spirit of filial adoption makes us sons of the Father in Christ, and frees us from both our moral futility and condemnation under Mosaic law, and the law of the flesh, manifest in the inimical persistence of sin and death (cf. Rom 7–8).

ner, then, when he argues that the event of Jesus' crucifixion and death on Good Friday teaches that the Father remains transcendent and hidden, even in the midst of the revelation of the Incarnation and the atonement. Easter, by contrast, manifests the Son as the eternal Word that God speaks to us in human flesh. Pentecost unveils to us the gift of the Spirit, who enlivens the Church from within so that she can respond to the mystery of Christ.

Nevertheless, in depicting the Holy Trinity in this way, we are *distinguishing* the free act of self-revelation on the part of God from the eternal processions that constitute the immanent life of God as such. The free act of revelation in God *does* reveal to us who God is as Trinity and manifests the distinct persons who relate to us, so that we may in turn relate to them interpersonally by grace.[57] However, the persons are not eternally distinguished or constituted by their relation to us or their decision from all eternity to communicate the mystery of God to humanity. To distinguish adequately between God in himself, as one who is eternally free to reveal himself, and God's economic activity of self-revelation, we in fact need to appeal to the simplicity and perfection of the divine nature, in virtue of which God remains transcendent of and distinct from creation as its source and origin, even in the historical act of self-revelation. Even in self-disclosure, God remains simple and perfect, and therefore is in no way ontologically dependent upon or relative to creation. Without a right understanding of the simplicity and perfection of the Trinity, we risk characterizing God by his history of relationship to creation. In this case, the economy inevitably becomes in some way constitutive of God's self-definition.

It is no accident that the abandonment of the classical *de Deo ut uno* treatise as an integral part of the study of Trinitarian theology leads to conundrums of this kind. In modern theology after Barth an important number of Trinitarian theologians understand God as a historical process and in doing so in fact undermine the confession of the Trinity as the transcendent Creator of all things and the unilateral giver of being to all creation. Without a way of thinking constructively of the biblical notion of the Creator in his divine aseity by means of the analogy of being, theology runs the perpetual risk of fashioning a god of history after the image of the free historical

57. So, Jesus speaks of divine inhabitation in Jn 14:23: "Jesus answered him, 'If a man loves me, he will keep my word, and my Father will love him, and we will come to him and make our home with him.'" This is related to the reception of the Spirit in Jn 14:26.

human subject, constituted progressively over time through its relationship to the world. Barth was correct in his assessment of modern liberal theology when he claimed polemically that "fear of scholasticism is the mark of a false prophet."[58] However, he was naïve to associate (following Kant in the first *Critique*) the use of the analogy of being in theology with mere immanentism as a collation of projections and conjectures of human reason. It is precisely the biblical confession of the transcendence of God as Creator that is at stake in the retention of the classical notion of God as simple, perfect, eternal, and omnipotent, a notion safeguarded by the study of the divine attributes; and this study is made possible (in part) by the Christian philosophy of God elaborated over time in the patristic and scholastic tradition. To be faithful to Barth's best impulses in underscoring the transcendent reality and mystery of God as Trinity, one has need of Aquinas's study of the divine nature in the treatise *de Deo ut uno*. In some real respect, then, it is the contemporary Thomists who are the true inheritors of Barth's best aspirations in Trinitarian theology.

THE "ECONOMIC TRINITY": WHY WE SHOULD BID FAREWELL TO THE NOTION

We arrive at a more difficult case when we consider the subject of Rahner's *Grundaxiom* claim that "the economic Trinity is the immanent Trinity and the immanent Trinity is the economic Trinity." It seems that the statement can be taken in one of three ways. First, one can understand it to mean that God reveals in Christ and through the historical economy who he is immanently in his eternal life as Trinity. In this case, the revelation conveys adequate knowledge to us of who God is in his unchangingly perfect identity. Colossians 1:17 speaks in this sense of God the Son being "before all things," and as manifesting his identity as God to us in time. He has his "pre-existence" independently of history, and he would be God even had he never created the world, but he has come among us precisely to manifest to us who he truly is from all eternity.

Second, however, as we have noted, Rahner's famous axiom can also be taken to mean that God in his immanent life is constituted by his economic

---

58. Barth, *CD* 1:1, 279.

relation with creatures. There are reasons to take this interpretation seriously, based on the internal logic of Rahner's positions. As noted, for example,
he argues that the Son is the only person of the Holy Trinity who can become incarnate, and that the creation of the human race and the Incarnation just are what happens when God desires to communicate himself, his
own divine life, in what is other than himself. This means however, if we follow through on the logic of personal differentiation of the three persons of
the Holy Trinity, that the Son is distinct from the Father and the Holy Spirit personally as Word not only because of his relation to the Father in eternal generation but also because of his relation to creatures as the expression
of the Father in the Father's divine "othering" of speaking himself outside
of himself, in creation. Furthermore, Rahner is categorical about the three
persons' having distinctive relations to creatures, by which each seemingly
acquires notes or properties that the others do not have. Such positions suggest, in their logical consequences, that Trinitarian identity is constituted,
at least in part, through a series of God's relationships to what is other than
God, so that the Trinity necessarily unfolds economically and historically,
through relationships with creation. Distinct natural actions pertaining to
each person unfold as constitutive elements of their distinctive modes of
being.

    A third possibility constitutes a kind of middle position: there is an "an-
alogical interval" between the economic Trinity and the immanent Trinity. Hans Urs von Balthasar, for example, interprets the *Grundaxiom* in this
sense, in his own theology.[59] The idea begins from the warranted assertion that we come to know God in himself through his economic revelation. However, it allies this assertion with a second claim, which is that God,
who is transcendent and eternal, must adapt himself to our circumstances
in order to render himself immanent in temporal history. Our understanding of God in the economy, then, is based not only on our epistemological
vantage point as learners immersed in history, but also on God's mode of

---

59. See Hans Urs von Balthasar, *Theo-Drama*, 4:319–28. Balthasar follows Bulgakov in affirming an analogy of kenosis, in which the eternal kenotic generation of the Son in the immanent
Trinity is the transcendent foundation for the temporal kenosis of the Son in the economy. See
Theo-Drama, 4:333: "If Jesus can be forsaken by the Father, the conditions for this 'forsaking' must
lie within the Trinity, in the absolute distance/distinction between the Hypostasis who surrenders
the Godhead and the Hypostasis who receives it." The notion of an "analogical interval" between
the economic Trinity and the immanent Trinity is also proposed by David Bentley Hart in *The
Beauty of the Infinite*, 165–66.

self-adaptation, in making himself present to us in the world. God's mode of being among us *as economic* (i.e., the "economic Trinity") is distinct from his mode of being in himself eternally (the immanent Trinity). The distinction of modes is ontological and not merely a matter of our epistemological vantage-point or degree of imperfect knowledge. In other words, the persons of the Trinity exist among us according to a different set of relationships than they do in themselves eternally.

What Rahner himself originally intended, and whether he was purposefully vague, are questions of secondary importance. The final reality is that each of the readings enunciated above have become commonplace in modern theology, and obviously arrive at different, incompatible results. Our argument here will simply be that *all three* of these ways of speaking are in some sense problematic, for different reasons, and that therefore we should simply abandon Rahner's *Grundaxiom* and all discourse related to the notion of an "economic Trinity," something that does not exist and is not an idea truly pertinent to Trinitarian theology. To make the case, let us briefly consider these three interpretations of the *Grundaxiom* in inverse order of presentation.

The third idea—that the economic Trinity pertains to God's existing in an economic mode analogous to God's immanent mode of being—has as its inevitable consequence that it posits a real ontological distinction between the life of the Trinity in itself and the ontological modes of being of the three persons in their economic self-manifestation. Stated somewhat brutally, the claim gives rise to two Trinities, or at least to two "modal identity configurations" of the three persons: one in themselves prescinding from creation, and one among themselves in the economy. There are many distinct versions of this idea. Balthasar, for example posits a Trinitarian inversion in the economy wherein the Son of God kenotically foregoes being the origin of the Spirit for the duration of his temporal human life among us, and instead makes himself subject to the Spirit, "inverting" the order of the processions of the person only in the economic Trinity, in view of the realization of the mission of the Son and the temporal sending of the Spirit.[60] After the res-

---

60. See Balthasar, *Theo-Drama*, 3:183–91 and 521–23, on the notion of an economic "Trinitarian inversion." The processions of the Son and the Spirit are supposedly inverted in the economy, as a result of this kenosis of the Son, so that during the time of his incarnation and prior to the resurrection, the Son proceeds from the Spirit and is utterly relative to him not merely in his human instincts of mind and heart (i.e., in virtue of Christ's capital grace), but rather in his very person and being as Son.

urrection, which the Son cannot effectuate of himself in his kenotic mode of being human, the order of the processions is re-established.[61] This kind of theology aspires to argue that the economic life of the Son made man reveals the mystery of the Trinity to us, God as he is in himself. However, such constructions inevitably run the risk of effectively reconstituting God according to his historical life in *parallelism* with God in his immanent life. We come very close here to two simultaneous errors over-laid upon each other. One error is to see God as constituted by his history among us (the relations between the divine persons themselves actually change as a result of history). The other is to see the immanent life of the Trinity as hidden or rendered hopelessly obscure by the economy, since the economic Trinity is in some real sense utterly distinct from the immanent Trinity.[62] In either case, the actual eternal life of the immanent Trinity is not really made present to us in history, in Christ.

The problem with the second interpretation is that the identification of God with the economic history of divine actions he lives out among us inevitably makes the historical economy in some way constitutive of the very life of God and therefore makes God a part of the world. After all, if the relations of the persons in God depend for their very constitution on the distinctive relation that the person of the Son has (even in mere potency) to the creation, and if the persons acquire natural characteristics that differentiate them as God by relations they each have to the creation, then the persons in some way depend upon creation for their identity as divine persons. God and the creation, then, simultaneously co-exist in mutual dependency interior to one unfolding story of ontology, a problematic view that Erich Przywara helpfully termed "Theopanism."[63] God and the world are distinct but can exist alongside one another only within a larger interdependent process. A good, if extreme, example of this view is found in the Trinitarian theology of Jürgen Moltmann, who affirms that in the crucifixion of Jesus of Nazareth, the Son is subject to death and non-being, not only in

---

61. See, for example, *Theo-Drama*, 4:335–37: the Son who is crucified and dies is utterly powerless in his very person, touching upon the very constitution of the Trinitarian persons, and therefore cannot be in any way the agent of resurrection.

62. If the economic Trinity is only analogous to the immanent Trinity, the problem arises as to whether we really know the latter at all, and whether it exists.

63. See, for example, Erich Przywara, "The Scope of Analogy as a Fundamental Catholic Form," in *Analogia Entis Metaphysics: Original Structure and Universal Rhythm*, trans. J. Betz and D. B. Hart (Grand Rapids, Mich.: Eerdmans, 2014), 388–89.

his humanity but also in his very person as Son.[64] Consequently, suffering, death, and non-being are not only predicated of the human nature of God the Son but are said to enter into the very life of the Trinity in the economy. The Son dies, the Father grieves, the Spirit acts as the agent of resurrection.[65] The relations between the three persons are radically reconstituted in changing and ongoing ways through the economy of the Son's suffering, death, and bodily resurrection. In a case like this, there is no longer any real possibility of an immanent Trinity, and classical monotheism is abandoned. Moltmann is not only aware of this consequence, but wishes quite intentionally to do away with the divine attributes from classical theology, traditional notions of the Creator, and the Chalcedonian insistence on the two natures of Christ. A Creator and giver of being who cannot suffer or change in his divine nature is a conceptual idol that must be swept away.[66] What Moltmann leaves us with, however, is a God of modern German idealism who is in some real sense identical with our world process, himself subject to suffering, and who is not transcendent of history. Because he is no longer the biblical Creator, as rightly understood in the classical tradition by the Fathers and scholastics, he is also incapable of truly delivering us from suffering. On the contrary, suffering is now constitutive of the historical identity of God, so that even if he should overcome suffering eschatologically, we should accept that this overcoming may only be temporary, as the historical process in God continues. After all, a God who has been constituted by agony, death, and non-being once, by definition can suffer such difficulties again. Perhaps he may even do so cyclically, as in some versions of ancient pre-Christian mythology. To be united to him perennially, then, is to be united to one who is always in some sense defined by suffering, even in his eternal divine nature, and who therefore is always capable of joining us to suffering, whether he would wish to be so united or not.[67]

64. See Moltmann, *The Trinity and the Kingdom*, 81–88.

65. Moltmann, *The Trinity and the Kingdom*, 89–90.

66. See the thematic argument of Moltmann in *The Crucified God*.

67. This formulation of Moltmann's position is no doubt caricatural in some regard, but it is also based on a logical characterization of the inward tendency of many of his statements about God, if such a God exists. See Moltmann, *The Trinity and the Kingdom*, 81: "The Son suffers death in this forsakenness. The Father suffers the death of the Son. So the pain of the Father corresponds to the death of the Son. And when in this descent into hell the Son loses the Father, then in this judgment the Father also loses the Son. Here the innermost life of the Trinity is at stake. Here the communicating love of the Father *turns into infinite pain* over the sacrifice of the Son. Here the responding love of the Son *becomes infinite suffering* over his repulsion and rejection by the Father. What happens on Golgotha *reaches into the innermost depths of the Godhead, putting its impress*

The first interpretation of the axiom noted above is of course in greater accord with the classical tradition. However, I would argue that even interpreted in this way, the language of the *Grundaxiom* is intrinsically unhelpful. If there is no economic Trinity, which follows necessarily from our exclusion of the second and third interpretations, then there is only ever eternally an immanent Trinity that in no way differs from the Trinity revealed in the economy and that is in no way constituted by the economic life of self-revelation. In this case, it is inevitably misleading even to refer to an "economic Trinity" as a subject of history who can be distinguished in any way from the eternal Trinity, and it makes little sense even to raise the question of how this Trinity differs from *or is identical with* the immanent Trinity.[68]

Instead of making use of any terminology of the economic Trinity, then, we would do well to return to the classical way of designating the mystery by speaking of the eternal processions of the persons, and their temporal missions.[69] As we noted above, Aquinas says that the temporal missions of the Son and Spirit just are the eternal processions with the addition of a new

---

on the trinitarian life in eternity." [Emphasis mine.] We should note how the classical divine attributes of infinity and eternity become interesting to Moltmann when they help him emphasize his case for divine suffering. However, in this (and apart from the clear question of theoretical self-contradiction) the suffering of God is now subject to eternal hypostasization and enters implicitly into the very identity of God. Moltmann wants to posit a God who can suffer, in order to respond theologically to the great political evils of the twentieth century. Unintentionally, however, he transforms God after the Shoah into a God of "infinite pain," an unending Shoah.

68. There is only one God who is eternal and unchanging, the Holy Trinity. If there is no such thing as the economic Trinity, then the affirmation of the identity of the two (economic and immanent) has no real meaning, other than to state simply that "the eternal Trinity is the eternal Trinity." It would be more helpful to state that "the inner mystery of the Trinity is genuinely revealed in the economy" or that "the God who is present in the economy, and who reveals himself, is God in himself, the immanent Trinity." Rahner's formulation is based in fact on the premise that history in some way *changes* who God is (i.e., the economic Trinity), which is precisely what we are contesting here. God's revelation of himself in the economy does occur through the medium of the divine missions, and the knowledge it gives rise to in faith is imperfect (1 Cor 13:9). However, this revelation is genuine and effective all the same, so that by the sending of the Son and the Spirit into the world, we come to know *who God truly is in himself*, from all eternity, in eternal processions of the Son and the Spirit. Consequently, to ask how we come to know the immanent Trinity in the economic Trinity is simply to mis-formulate the question, and it is one that never appeared in the Church until the 1960s. For the same reason it is a question that can also go out of existence any time theologians rightly decide to abandon it and ask instead: how in virtue of the divine missions do we come to know truly the eternal processions of the Trinity?

69. In arguing thus I am building on the previous arguments of Bruce D. Marshall, "The Unity of the Triune God: Reviving an Ancient Question," *The Thomist* 74, no. 1 (2010): 1–32, and Gilles Emery, "*Theologia* and *Dispensatio*: The Centrality of the Divine Missions in St. Thomas's Trinitarian Theology," *The Thomist* 74, no. 4 (2010): 515–61.

presence.[70] The advantage of this approach over the Rahnerian formulation is threefold. First, it provides all the historical realism we need in order to maintain that in the concrete historical economy it is the very life of God that is revealed and communicated, without suggesting that the processions are in any way constituted by the missions. The Son sent into the world by the Father truly reveals *and renders present* the eternal procession of the Son from the Father, and the Father in the Son. The Spirit sent into the world at Pentecost from the Father and the Son as the "Spirit of sonship" (Gal 4:6) reveals *and renders present* the eternal procession of the Spirit, and so also the Father and the Son as the font of the Spirit. However, these sendings are not novel occasions for the ontological development of the inner Trinitarian relationships. The processions-missions distinction maintains the economic realism of God's real presence in history without the confusions or illusions that derive from the mistaken substantive denotation of an economic Trinity.

Second, this appeal to the language of processions and missions makes implicit use of the theology of the divine nature that unites the three persons as God eternally, and thus allows us adequately to distinguish God, in his transcendence and incomprehensibility, from his creation. Rahner seems to have cautiously formulated the *Grundaxiom* as an experimental alternative to scholastic notions of Trinitarian theology, and in the wake of his skepticism regarding the viability of a *de Deo ut uno* treatise in particular. He argued that the scholastic preference for the *De Deo Uno* treatise had led to the eclipse of Trinitarian theology in popular Christian consciousness (as if most Christians are practical monotheists not Trinitarians). However warranted his pastoral concern, any balanced response requires that one still maintain the consideration of the unity and nature of God as an essential dimension of Trinitarian theology. In jettisoning the treatise on the oneness of the divine nature and the immaterial processions of the persons, Rahner needed another way to articulate the distinction of persons in God and the ground of their unity. He sought to rediscover these in the personal and soteriological actions of God within history. God is the inner meaning of the economic unfolding of the creation even if he is also distinct from that creation. However, the classical approach of the Fathers and scholastics that reflects on the divine nature shared by the three persons is an essential

70. *ST* I, q. 43, a. 1.

component of our reflection on the transcendence and incomprehensibility of God. One can believe either in the classical Nicene affirmation of the *homoousios* (the ineffable singular divine essence of the three persons) or in an "economic Trinity" but arguably not in both. The latter notion makes sense only if God is in some way constituted in his distinction of modes of being by his ontological relativity to history.

Third, the classical use of the notion of a divine mission alludes to the reality of an eternal procession now "present in a new mode" in virtue of an effect or addendum to the procession per se, even while affirming that the procession is truly manifest in the mission. For example, the Son who is sent from the Father into the world, by becoming human in his incarnation, renders himself present and manifest in concrete history as the One who proceeds eternally from the Father. This idea of mission allows us to maintain a twofold sense of the "created effect" in the economy as a medium of the revelation of the person: true conveyance of divine identity (which implies the effective transparence of the created medium), and imperfect or analogical knowledge of the uncreated procession in virtue of the medium. Christ's human nature provides the most important illustration of this idea. The human life of the Word made flesh, his teaching, miracles, suffering, death, and bodily glorification, all reveal him as One who is eternally from the Father. However, it is also the case that the Son's human nature is distinct from his divine nature and life. Consequently, there is an analogical similitude of the human nature of Christ to his divine nature. When we contemplate the human life of the Son, we come to know who God is, living a human life among us, but in seeing the human actions and sufferings of the Son as such, we do not perceive immediately the actions or sufferings of God in his deity. There is truly therefore an "analogical interval" or ontological similitude that exists between the human nature and the divine nature (and not between the economic Trinity and the immanent Trinity). It is here above all in the concept of the two natures of Christ that we should look to understand how the missions of the persons both reveal and conceal the processions, and it is here that we should speak of an analogical interval. Jesus reveals his own identity as the Son of God in and through his human actions, but his human life is also a venue in which God is truly present in a hidden way. The manifestation is genuine but also imperfect or veiled. The same can be said of the Spirit's work in the life of the Church, in the fire and tongues of Pentecost, in the constitution of the Church in the work and preaching of the apostolic college, in the unfolding of the sacramental life of the Church, in her development as a unified subject through time, in the radiant charity and teaching of her saints and martyrs, and in her eschatological orientation through history. All of this truly manifests the Spirit, who is present in his visible mission in history as the uncreated soul of the Church. Yet it also conceals the Spirit, who remains transcendent of his effects and mysteriously numinous. "The wind blows where it wills … you do not know whence it comes or whither it goes; so it is with everyone who is born of the Spirit" (Jn 3:8). The created effects of the Spirit are adequate to reveal genuinely his eternal procession from the Father and the Son, but they do not yield to us yet in this life any immediate plenary perception of the mystery that is unveiled in faith.

CONCLUSION

In this chapter we considered some of the common challenges that Trinitarian theology faces in a modern context and considered briefly two prominent modern Trinitarian theologies, those of Karl Barth in the early part of his *Church Dogmatics* and Karl Rahner in his thematic work *The Trinity*. Next, we discussed five principles derived from the Thomistic tradition in order to offer constructive analysis of a central modern Trinitarian "tradition." In light of these principles we criticized the notion that the Trinitarian persons are in some way constituted or ontologically qualified in their common nature or their shared relations by their relationship with history or by their common activity in the economy of salvation. We noted, however, that Barth's idea of a distinction of Trinitarian persons based on the activity of divine revelation (God as the paternal Revealer of the Word, the Word Revealed, and the Spirit who Reveals) can be grounded in classical Trinitarian theology in two ways. One is by referring to the mode in which each person acts even when they act together as one, so that the Father, Son, and Holy Spirit reveal the truth of God in Christ, with each acting in a distinct personal way, as Paternal in sending the Son and Spirit, as Filial in the mystery of the Incarnation, and as Spirated, as the one sent by the Father and the Son to manifest the Son to the Church. Second, the distinction of persons in the act of revelation is underscored by appropriation of the common action of the Trinity to the particular persons, in accordance with the order of the processions. The act is from the Father, through the Son,

and in the Spirit. Finally, we considered Rahner's notion of the economic Trinity, which he identifies with the immanent Trinity. We noted that
there are at least three ways of interpreting this axiom, one of which suggests an ontological distinction of the two Trinities, despite the continuity
of revelatory content shared between the two. A second interpretation suggests that God is immanently qualified by his economic life among us. The
third interpretation underscores that it is precisely what God is eternally
and immanently as Trinity that is revealed in truth in the economy. We noted problems with all three of these interpretations, even the last, insofar as
the very notion of an economic Trinity that must be explained in relation
to the immanent Trinity (or vice versa), frames the explanation of the revelation of God in problematic terms. Rahner's novel approach should not
be taken for granted as an advance of theological thinking simply because it
has recently and often been cited in theological literature. The classical distinction between the eternal processions and the divine missions provides
a better framework, in fact, for addressing even the most contemporary of
concerns regarding the way God can make himself known to us, as he is in
himself, precisely in and through a shared history with us in the economy.
Having considered these more general points of Trinitarian theology in the
economy, we can now turn to three core domains pertaining to the economy: the creation, the incarnation and life of Jesus, and the passion, death,
and resurrection of Christ, to consider briefly some ways that each of these
"moments" in the economy reveals the mystery of the Trinity.

32

The Trinity and Creation

INTRODUCTION

Theologians in the twentieth century were concerned to retrieve the idea of the Trinity as the principle of creation in Christian theology, and to rethink the economy of creation and salvation as Trinitarian activities. In this chapter we will consider briefly theories of creation based on a concept of intra-Trinitarian kenosis. We will then offer some critical reflections on these theories in light of the ideas explored in part 3 of this book, before proceeding to consider ways in which the mystery of the creation derives from ongoing Trinitarian activity and how the mystery of the Trinity is reflected in material creation, living things, and human beings.

KENOTIC TRINITARIAN CREATION IN MODERN THEOLOGY

As we noted at the end of part 3 of this book, medieval theologians such as Aquinas understood the activities of creation and redemption as Trinitarian activities, in a way that stands in fundamental continuity with major patristic figures such as the Cappadocians and Augustine. All works of the Trinity *ad extra* are works of all three persons, but even when the three persons act as one, each acts in a particular way, or in accord with his personal mode of being as God. The Father creates as Father, in and through his begotten Wisdom, and in and through the Spirit, who is the Spirit of the Father and the Son.

Influential twentieth-century theological figures sought to rethink the classical notion of creation in a Trinitarian light. They did so in various ways by reconceiving the divine attributes in light of post-Kantian ontology derived, in the German idealist tradition, from Hegel, Fichte, and Schelling, as well as in light of the "post-metaphysical" critical theories of Heidegger. The exploration of this modern trend in German philosophical ontology exceeds the scope of our study, but it is important simply to note that many of the novelties that arise in modern Trinitarian theology of creation derive especially from the philosophical influences that stand behind them, where these philosophies are employed instrumentally and creatively by the modern theologians in question. Here we can illustrate clear and helpful examples by considering briefly the creation theology of two influential thinkers, Sergius Bulgakov and Jürgen Moltmann. Despite the significant differences between the two, they have in common the fact that they treat the act of Trinitarian creation as an act of divine self-limitation (which deeply affects their interpretation of the attributes of the divine essence), and as an intra-Trinitarian act of mutual self-limitation (which affects their interpretation of the divine persons). Understanding their respective views allows us to see clearly how, for each of them, the act of creation in fact gives rise to an alteration in the nature of God and, in a sense, also in the relationships of the persons. It is interesting in turn to compare and contrast this view with that of patristic and scholastic authors, in light of our previous considerations.

THE KENOSIS OF THE TRINITY AS A CONDITION OF CREATION (SERGIUS BULGAKOV)

Bulgakov's understanding of Trinitarian creation occurs within the context of his multifaceted theory of "wisdom" as a pre-existent reality in both God and creation. As is clearly denoted in scripture, God is wise and expresses himself in the intelligible wisdom of his creation. For Bulgakov, however, there is not only a relationship but also a kind of ontological continuity between the wisdom of God and the wisdom of his creation. He articulates this theory under the title of "sophianicity" (for *sophia* or "wisdom" in Greek).[1] An analysis of Bulgakov's broader theory of wisdom exceeds the purpose of this study and defies succinct summary. For our purposes, there

---

1. See the extended treatments in Sergius Bulgakov, *The Bride of the Lamb*, 3–124, and in *The Lamb of God*, trans. B. Jakim (Grand Rapids, Mich.: Eerdmans, 2008), 89–212.

are three aspects of key importance that touch upon his understanding of the Trinity.

First, for Bulgakov, the act of creation, the giving of being to all things, is one in which God self-determines from all eternity to be in relation and therefore to become ontologically relative to creation. The uncreated *sophia* common to all three persons, the wisdom of the divine nature, is always already from all eternity relative to and "for" the created wisdom that characterizes the creation (the intelligible order of creation that precedes and also informs concretely all particular creaturely realities). The dipolar understanding of this event is significant: God is not inevitably relative to creation but only because he wishes to be, through a free decision, but in choosing to be so, God is really "newly" characterized in his very essence by the self-determination to create.[2]

Second, this act is kenotic, because it requires divine wisdom to be always already self-emptying, so as to give rise from itself to created wisdom. That is to say, the underlying ontological essence of created wisdom is the divinity itself in a kenotic mode of being. This means that the eternal divine life is present in temporal creation and in a certain sense as the very wisdom of that creation, in a self-emptying mode, and it implies that temporal creation is always already eternal since it relates back to and is contained within a kenotic process that characterizes the life of God himself.[3]

---

2. Bulgakov, *The Bride of the Lamb*, 60: "The world as the creaturely Sophia lives by the Divine Sophia, by the fullness and glory of God's world. The Divine Sophia is present in God's world as the intelligent heaven, as eternal power and divinity. The creaturely Sophia is not another Sophia expressly created with and for the world. She is only a special *mode* of the being of the Divine Sophia, the revelation of the Divine Sophia in the creaturely Sophia. Having its foundation in the Divine Sophia, the world is not created but eternal, by this eternity of its foundation. But the world is also created and belongs to temporal being, for, in it, as the creaturely Sophia, the Divine Sophia acquires the mode of her being—not only in the eternal life of God in God and for God in His triune hypostases, but also by herself, in her becoming. In relation to essential fullness, this becoming is, like temporality in relation to eternity, a diminished, kenotic state. The creaturely Sophia is, in this sense, the kenosis of the Divine Sophia. God's creation of the world is a kenotic act in divinity, first in the general sense that God, by placing alongside His absoluteness the relative being of creation, kenotically places Himself into a correlation with the latter by the voluntary sacrifice of love for it. Insofar as he is the Creator and Provider, He becomes correlative to the world, and receives this correlativeness into the depths of His self-determination. This is a hypostatic kenosis."

3. Bulgakov, *The Bride of the Lamb*, 60–61: "Posting alongside His divine world the becoming world, of the creaturely Sophia alongside the Divine Sophia, God realizes kenosis in His own life, whereby Sophia becomes in 'nothing' or is created out of 'nothing'.... The Divine Sophia and the creaturely Sophia are not two but one, although in two modes of being: as ideal reality belonging to eternity and as the entelechic character of creation in the autonomous being of the created world. As a result of the unity of Sophia in her two modes, the world is both created and not created, belongs to temporality in its being and to eternity in its foundation."

Third, this act of self-emptying proper to the divine essence is also one that has repercussions for the Trinitarian persons. Bulgakov ascribes a kenosis to the Son particularly in the Incarnation. The Son surrenders divine attributes of power and omnipresence precisely so as to become human, and in the interim period of his human life, ceases to possess these divine characteristics.[4] However, this kenosis of the Son that is present in the Incarnation has its primary basis in the antecedent kenosis of divine Sophia that takes place in creation.[5] When God the Trinity creates, God surrenders his divine wisdom's sovereignty to give being to created wisdom, and in doing so creates a kind of space for creaturely being and freedom, by which creatures can relate personally to the Father.[6] This self-emptying of God that permits creation its "space" is also reflected in the kenosis of the Incarnation, where the Son surrenders characteristics of his divine nature precisely so as to become human. Furthermore, behind the paternal act of creation there is an even more primal kenosis of the Father in begetting the Son, as the Father empties himself to give a place to the Son to be, in relation to him. The Son in turn empties himself in the act of receiving all from the Father.[7] Therefore, the Father's kenosis of loving generation of the Son and the Son's loving kenosis of giving himself back to the Father in self-emptying are the ontological "background" to the Trinitarian self-emptying that occurs in the

4. See Bulgakov, *The Lamb of God*, 233–36; 264–65, esp. 234: "The Father sent and the Son went: the Son extinguished His proper divine life in Himself and thus His divine consciousness. He laid it at the Father's feet. He 'gave Himself' to the Father in the same way that He commended His spirit into the hands of the Father when He was dying on the cross ..."

5. See, for example, Bulgakov, *The Lamb of God*, 111 and 174–75, where the Son in his eternal generation is said to exist kenotically, such that in his divine nature he embodies or realizes the kenotic mode of God's nature as created Sophia. That is to say, something in the eternal generation of the Son as kenosis is the prototype of God's kenotic act of creation.

6. See, for example, Bulgakov, *The Bride of the Lamb*, 63, 126–28, 133–34.

7. Bulgakov, *The Lamb of God*, 98–99: "For the Father, begetting is self-emptying, the giving of Himself and of His own to the Other; it is the sacrificial ecstasy of all-consuming jealous love for the Other.... The Son, as the Son, has Himself and His own not as Himself and His own but as the Father's, in the image of the Father. Spiritual sonhood consists precisely in the Son's depleting Himself in the name of the Father. Sonhood is already *eternal kenosis*.... The sacrifice of the Father's love consists in self-renunciation and in self-emptying in the begetting of the Son. The sacrifice of the Son's love consists in self-depletion in the begottenness from the Father, in the acceptance of birth as begottenness. These are not only pre-eternal facts but also acts for both the one and the other. The *sacrifice* of love, in its reality is pre-eternal suffering.... This suffering of sacrifice not only does not contradict the Divine all-blessedness but, on the contrary, is its foundation, for this all-blessedness would be empty and unreal if it were not based on authentic sacrifice, on the reality of suffering. If God is love, He is also sacrifice, which manifests the victorious power of love and its joy only through suffering."

creation, where the divine essence practices a kind of kenoticism, rendering itself relative ontologically, to allow the creation to come to be and to exist autonomously.

Bulgakov's Trinitarian speculations are best understood as apologetic responses to characterizations of human freedom in modern German idealism, as in the thought of either Hegel or Schelling. In the face of a modern ontology that would characterize both God and the human person as historical becoming of spirit (Hegel) or that would see the person as a quasi-substantial process of freedom (Schelling), Bulgakov is seeking to restate the distinction and analogy between uncreated freedom in the Trinity as freedom for sacrificial love, and created freedom in human beings as redeemed and divinized in Christ. The primal kenosis is that of intra-Trinitarian love, a love that is, in its own way, characterized by "sacrificial" giving to the Other. This is the basis of every other expression of freedom: God's free act of giving being to creation, the free decision of the Son to become human, the freedom of the Son as human to offer himself for the human race's divinization in the sacrifice of the Cross. Trinitarian creation therefore is one moment or instance within a larger economy of sacrificial love.[8]

CREATION AS AN ACT OF TRINITARIAN SELF-LIMITATION (JÜRGEN MOLTMANN)

One finds a position analogous to that of Bulgakov in the work of the twentieth-century Reformed theologian Jürgen Moltmann. Moltmann begins his analysis of creation by distinguishing his position from that of classical theism, in which God chooses to create freely by his own elective decision. In contradiction to this position, Moltmann affirms that God is inclined by nature to create, and although his act of communicating being to things is free, it is an expression of God's own internal self-determination in love. That is to say, for Moltmann, as for Bulgakov, God is eternally related to creation, always, already, in virtue of a free decision made in love that constitutes God's own identity. Consequently, God is not identical with creation (Moltmann distances himself from pantheism as such) nor is he utterly transcendent of creation, as in classical monotheism, but is instead

---

8. These ideas from Bulgakov are also thematic in Balthasar's Trinitarian theology. See, for instance, *Theo-Drama* 4:317–426, esp. 328–32 on Trinitarian creation.

always related to and in the process of realizing creation, in view of his own glory and the glorification of his creation.[9] In this sense God is developing in himself in relation to creation.

This process can occur only if God determines freely to limit himself, from all eternity, in such a way as to create space for the creation. Here Moltmann repeatedly draws in his work on the medieval Jewish kabbalistic notion of *zimzum*, the idea that God must delimit himself as a condition of possibility for the creation to come into being.[10] This means concretely that God must choose to delimit his infinite nature in order to permit the finite creation to coexist alongside himself. He must give up his omnipresence to allow for the real presence of creaturely autonomy, and must suspend characteristics of his eternity to allow for creation's temporality.[11] We should note, then, that for Moltmann the classical divine attributes of the Christian tradition that we have considered in this book stand in ontological opposition to the possibility of an integral autonomous creation, rather than being seen (as Aquinas sees them) as foundations for the existence of the creation in its real autonomy, because the creation participates in being communicated to it from the fullness of the Trinity.

It is clear that, for Moltmann, freedom becomes the category of being that is utterly fundamental in God, such that other attributes (infinity, omnipresence, eternity) are subject to freedom and can be suspended. The deity is subject by divine freedom to a dipolar state in which God can elect to become his seeming contrary, through the motivations of love.[12] In this line of thinking, Moltmann even specifies that God freely accepts nothingness into God's own self in order to create, since self-negation is a part of creative

---

9. Moltmann, *The Trinity and the Kingdom*, 80–83.

10. Jürgen Moltmann, *God in Creation: A New Theology of Creation and the Spirit of God*, trans. M. Kohl (Minneapolis, Minn.: Fortress, 1993), 86–88.

11. Moltmann, *The Trinity and the Kingdom*, 109: "And if . . . we have to say that there is a 'within' and a 'without' for God—and that he therefore goes creatively 'out of himself', communicating himself creatively [to] the one who is Other than himself—then we must after all assume a *self-limitation* of the infinite, omnipresent God, preceding his creation. In order to create something 'outside' himself, the infinite God must have made room for this finitude beforehand, 'in himself'. . . . The trinitarian relationship of the Father, the Son and the Holy Spirit is so wide that the whole creation can find space, time and freedom in it." See likewise Moltmann, *God in Creation*, 87: both omnipresence and infinity must be subject to a negation in God as a condition for creation. The infinite must withdraw so that the finite can exist (implying a quasi-spatial notion of the positive infinite as spatial extension).

12. This order of reflection resembles ideas one finds in Hegel, concerning divine diremption, and in Schelling, regarding divine freedom and God's suspension, in revelation, of his act of being.

love.[13] This capacity to embrace or be subject to nothingness in God's own nature is the condition of possibility also for God's divine suffering in the crucifixion, where the very being of the Son is subject to non-being. The resurrection of Christ also shows God's capacity in freedom not only to be subject to nothingness but also to reinvent the terms of his ontological relationship to creation, in resurrection.[14] Not only is the resurrection concerned with the redemption and eschatological glorification of creation, it is also something that affects and changes the inner life of God in himself.

As in Bulgakov, we find in Moltmann that the divine self-limitation is construed not only in terms of the divine nature but also in terms of the Trinitarian persons. This is evident first and foremost with regard to the notion of God's free act of creation. God the Father is always eternally a freedom of love that tends toward free creation in the Son, even in the generation of the Son. This means that the creation flows organically from the generation of the Son as a quasi-immediate ontological consequence.[15] This act of creation "already present" in the generation of the Son occurs through the aforementioned self-limitation of God's infinite and omnipresent being, but it also occurs through the mutual self-limitation of the persons who relate to each other, so that creation is "in" or "between" the persons in their complementarity.[16] In a certain sense, then, creation literally unfolds in the ontological space between the persons of the Trinity, who subject themselves freely to finite form in view of creation.

If we think about this external state of affairs, transferring it by a process of reflection to the inner relationship of the Trinity, then it means that the Father, through an alteration of his love for the Son (that is to say through a contraction of the Spirit), and the Son, through an alteration in his response to the Father's love (that is, through an inversion of the Spirit) have opened up the space, the time and the freedom for that "outwards" into which the Father utters himself creatively through the Son. For God himself this utterance means an emptying of himself—a

---

13. Moltmann, *God in Creation*, 87–88, esp. 88: "Nothingness contradicts, not merely creation but God too, since he is creation's Creator. Its negations lead into that primordial space which God freed within himself before creation. As a self-limitation that makes creation possible, the *nihil* does not yet have this annihilating character; for it was conceded in order to make an independent creation 'outside' God possible. But this implies the possibility of the annihilating Nothingness. It emerges from this that in a doctrine of Nothingness, a distinction has to be made between the non-being of a creature, the non-being of creation, and the non-being of the Creator. It is only in connection with the last of these that we can talk about Nothingness."

14. Moltmann, *The Trinity and the Kingdom*, 88–96.

15. The idea is clearly articulated in Moltmann, *The Trinity and the Kingdom*, 106–8.

16. Moltmann, *The Trinity and the Kingdom*, 108–11.

self-determination for the purpose of a self-limitation. Time is an interval in eternity, finitude is a space in infinity, and freedom is a concession of the eternal love. God withdraws himself in order to go out of himself.[17]

Furthermore, in another provocative break with tradition, Moltmann affirms that the activities that transpire in creation are not common to the persons of the Trinity but are differentiated in the three persons. Only the Father creates. Only the Son is the immanent archetype through and for whom the Father creates, acting effectively as the immanent term and measure of creation. Only the Spirit communicates to the creation itself, from within, the inner grace and energy to respond to the Father.[18] Moltmann underscores clearly that this kind of ascription of activities is not reducible to appropriation. Evidently, then, the real relations of the three persons to the creation are distinct in kind, so that the persons in God are each constituted not only by the eternal processions that distinguish them, but also by the distinct temporal relations each person subjects himself to and upholds historically through distinct kinds of interaction with creation. The identity of each person is constituted individually through the economy, then.[19] Such a perspective effectively abandons the traditional idea of the one being and nature of God shared by three persons in equality and identity, and instead places us firmly on the pathway toward a radical historicization of God's identity and, indeed, also toward tri-theism. Each of the persons evolves

17. Moltmann, *The Trinity and the Kingdom*, 111. While some readers may find such prose entirely implausible, it is important to see that Moltmann is in some respect simply drawing out the logical inferences from Rahner's own positions articulated more tentatively in the form of the *Grundaxiom*, concerning the relation of the Son alone toward incarnation. On this view, the natural state of the Son in the economy must in some way affect the inner determination of the identity of the Trinitarian persons and their mutual relations. After all, as Aristotle and Aquinas note, relations are typically founded upon action or passion and upon quantitative juxtaposition. If the Trinitarian persons are distinguished in *their* mutual relations *by* relations to the finite, temporal world, then they must be determined in action and passion or in temporal and spatial quantity (or both) as they each relate to the created world and so to one another. It might be argued, then, that Moltmann's program of economic re-specification of the Trinitarian persons employs elements of relational ontology coherently and consistently, once one adopts the premises of the *Grundaxiom*. If the Son's eternal identity is construed by reference to the real relations he adopts in the economy, then it is affected by human relations of action and passion, as well as quantity (time and place). In this case one may legitimately re-envisage the Trinitarian relations based on reciprocal relations of both these kinds. There is a real question in this respect as to whether a Rahnerian who is not a Moltmannian is really a very thorough-going and coherent Rahnerian.

18. Moltmann, *The Trinity and the Kingdom*, 112–13.

19. It bears keeping in mind that this idea of a historicized economic Trinity is in turn quite consistent with Moltmann's views of the inner Trinitarian effects of the crucifixion, as laid out in *The Crucified God*.

differently in his distinctive natural properties through his historical engagement with creation.

There are common traits present in the thought of Bulgakov and Moltmann, despite their significant differences. We find in each a restatement of biblical themes and an emphasis on the centrality of the Trinity in creation. However, each also breaks with classical notions of the transcendence of God in his aseity and each re-thinks in radical ways the distinction of the Trinitarian persons, in light of the economy, such that the act of creation is in a sense constitutive of the life of God from all eternity. Core features of the account of each rest upon their notion of freedom, as dipolar and able to self-identify with contrary features of existence. Each sees kenotic love as a precondition of God's identity and his act of creation, also further evidenced in mysteries of the Incarnation and crucifixion.

What might we say about these two thinkers by way of analysis? First, each sees God's real relationality to creation as constitutive of God's inner life but also as constitutive of the real relations between the three persons of the Trinity. In other words, God in his personal life as Trinity is really relative to the creation, and this ontological relativity is a dimension of the way in which the persons themselves are distinguished in God's own life. God therefore has, as a dimension of his being, a history with creation, and the Trinity is in a sense defined by this history.

Second, freedom for love becomes the primary foundation of all other attributes of God, a decision we might characterize critically as a distinctively modern form of anthropomorphism, constructed for apologetic purposes. There is no immanent Trinity or transcendent divine aseity. God is only ever an "economic Trinity" existing in and through historical relationships with creatures.

Ironically, such revisionist concepts of the Trinity undermine the very thing they are meant to emphasize: divine freedom as love and its exemplary realization in creation and in the mysteries of salvation. Any authentic understanding of the divine freedom for love needs to acknowledge in sufficient ways that God the Creator transcends all created being, and communicates being to it, without entering into any kind of competition with creation, or panentheistic composition with it. Only the transcendent, eternal Creator is free to give being to creatures out of his pre-existent wisdom, love, and freedom, so that they participate in the dignity of being in ways that assure their proper reality, autonomy, and teleological realization. Acknowledgement of this transcendent freedom for love that is present in God as Creator (in virtue of his nature) is also essential to any right understanding of the true grounds of unity of persons in God, as one in being, so that it is truly the Trinity (Father, Son, and Spirit) who give being to all things, and not only one of the persons (while the other two exist in kenotic realization).

Bulgakov and Moltmann each wish to react creatively against a nominalist doctrine of divine sovereignty and a Divine voluntarism that would make the act of creation arbitrary and depict it only as a brute act of the divine essence, rather than the communion of persons in the Trinity. But by jettisoning the *de Deo ut uno* dimension of Trinitarian theology, they break with the patristic tradition in radical ways. They also therefore fall into the other extreme of nominalism by placing God and creation in competition and ontological mutual exclusion, as if God and his creation could exist in rivalry, by the mathematics of a zero-sum game.[20] God then has to delimit or self-empty as God in his nature so that creatures may come into being and thrive. What is lacking in Bulgakov's and Moltmann's schemas, then, is a notion of participated *esse*, in which the perfection of the Creator is the very condition for the genuine communication of the gift of being to the creation. For Aquinas, God is understood as the incomprehensible, transcendent foundation of creaturely dignity and autonomy, and therefore in no way as their rival. Finite, temporal realities exist only because of divine perfection, infinity, and eternity, shared by the Father, Son, and Holy Spirit, and not in exclusion of these divine qualities. Nor can divine freedom-for-love rightly be conceived of in opposition to human freedom, as if it must delimit itself so that creaturely freedom-for-love might exist. Rather, precisely because God's freedom stems from God's pure actuality, it is a freedom mysteriously able to communicate being to creatures gratuitously, a freedom that stems from God's eternal divine goodness and that expresses his wisdom

---

20. Moltmann refers to infinite space and finite space and the possible mutual competition between the two, suggesting that the divine infinity must self-reduce in order to provide a place for finite being to exist alongside it. The spatial imagination of infinity here seems inadvertently all too quantitative.

and love. This activity is the foundation of human freedom, not its antithesis. Accordingly, spiritual creatures exist in such a way as to have their own natural integrity as true "secondary causes." They are able to pursue freely knowledge of truth, within a life of deliberative willing and loving, one that unfolds through its own genuine history. As such, rational creatures participate mysteriously in their own histories in the spiritual freedom of God in history, without ever being identical with the very being of the Creator as such.

Nevertheless, we should wish to safeguard the aspiration of these thinkers to recover a properly Trinitarian doctrine of creation. How may we do so?

TRINITARIAN MODES OF EXPRESSION IN CREATION

We noted in the previous section of this book that while the act of creation by God *ad extra* ("outside of God") is a work of each of the three persons acting in virtue of their divine unity as God, it is also a work of each person in a distinctive mode. The Father creates as the progenitor of being, so to speak, creating all things through the Son, after the model of the Word, and in the Spirit, who is the expression of his goodness and love. The diverse modes of appropriation of creation to the distinct persons, then, signify something more than arbitrary denotations. This way of thinking can be extended in turn by considering how the mystery of the Trinity is imprinted upon created being. How are created things, in virtue of their Trinitarian derivation, similar to the mystery of the diverse persons of the Trinity? Evidently, in what follows we are not contradicting our previous argument that the mystery of the Trinity cannot be discovered from the consideration of creation by mere natural reason. This remains true: the Trinity is a mystery made known by revelation alone. However, in light of the revelation, a Trinitarian similitude in creatures is discernable, and it is this similitude that we may now seek to identify.

Scripture itself distinguishes a unique similitude of the Trinity that is found in spiritual creatures that are made in the image of God, notably human beings and angels, who are personal creatures. In virtue of their two spiritual faculties of intellect and will these realities are said to be like the Trinity in a special way, since in each of them we find immaterial knowledge and immaterial willing love. The operations of knowledge proceed forth from the knower, and the operations of love proceed forth from the lover through his knowledge, since one can love only what one has first come to know. In this respect, there is a distinctly spiritual analogy of being that is found in spiritually personal creatures made in the image of God, an analogy by which the procession of the Word and the procession of the Spirit as love are discernable in such creatures, under a similitude, albeit in a very different form.[21]

What should we say, however, more generally about the Trinitarian imprint in other creatures? Is there a Trinitarian similitude found in material beings, for example? And what about in living things, both vegetative and animal? Here the Christian tradition typically employs the notion of "vestiges" of the Holy Trinity, basing itself on a classical Augustinian reading of Wisdom 9:21. In that text the sacred author speaks of the "number," "weight," and "measure" of every created reality. The terms from the book of Wisdom are quantitative in kind but are taken by Augustine to be metaphorical denotations of a broader metaphysical vision of reality.[22] "Measure," he argues, refers to the derivation of a given creature such that it has a distinct and limited mode of being, apportioned by the Creator. "Number" refers to the species of a given thing, as reflecting intelligibility and form derived from the Wisdom of God. "Weight" denotes the orientation and tendencies in things, and therefore implies that each thing exists in view of a given end, in accord with its intrinsic goodness. Understood in this way, each reality contains a trace of the Trinity: it is from the Father, from whom it has an apportioned participation in being. It contains a distinctive formal intelligibility in accord with its nature, derived from the uncreated Logos "through whom all things were made" (Jn 1:3). Every finite creature tends toward some limited realization of goodness, through a likeness to the Spir-

---

21. After all, in God the Holy Trinity the processions of the Word and the Spirit are persons distinct from the Father, not merely personal activities of a personal subject, and the generation and spiration communicate the very substance of divine life, while human acts of knowledge and love are mere "accidents" or properties of a given substance who is a human person.

22. See, for example, Augustine, *On the Nature of the Good*, c. 3, in *Nicene and Post-Nicene Fathers*, vol. 4, trans. A. H. Newman, ed. P. Schaff (Buffalo, N.Y.: Christian Literature Publishing, 1887). In one of the texts that forms a *locus classicus* for treatment of Trinitarian vestiges, *The Trinity*, 6.10, Augustine comments on a passage from Hilary (*On the Trinity*, 2.1) where the latter distinguishes the three persons as eternity, form, and use or enjoyment (*usus*) of the gift. Augustine goes on to distinguish the Trinitarian imprint in creatures in accord with their relative "unity and form and order," each reflecting a respective uncreated person.

it, and in this respect is expressive of the uncreated Love who proceeds from
the Father and the Son.[23]

Given this suggested line of analysis, we can see how a Trinitarian light
is cast on all material realities, and upon all living things, in light of the eternal procession of the Son, and in light of the spiration of the Spirit. Physical
realities may seem in one respect to be entirely dissimilar to the generation
of the Word, because that generation is immaterial in kind and eternal, while
physical generation takes place only in a world of changing corruptible realities. Nevertheless, however modest the similitude, there is an ontological
likeness, and it is a significant one. It is precisely because there is a material world at all that there can exist within creatures some form of successive
begetting, which is reflective, despite all of its fragility, of the eternal generation of the Son. That infinite mystery of communication of being and life
is simple and eternal, but it is expressed outwardly in material creation in finite realities, through an immense and complex web of finite material generations. Only matter permits this form of ontological "imitation" of God. Angels, which are purely spiritual creatures, can in no way beget or engender,
even though their natures are more like the divine nature than those of any
other creature precisely in virtue of being purely spiritual, and being characterized by angelic intellect and will.

This material begetting present in physical realities that come into being
and go out of being, always in dependence upon others, is an ontological
sign of their derivation from the Father. They each participate in being in a
limited, temporary, and passing way. The vastness of the physical cosmos,
in its sheer magnitude and intelligible history of order and change, is an ex-

---

23. See on this Aquinas, *ST* I, q. 45, a. 7: "... in all creatures there is found the trace of the Trinity, inasmuch as in every creature are found some things which are necessarily reduced to the divine Persons as to their cause. For every creature subsists in its own being, and has a form, whereby it is determined to a species, and has relation to something else. Therefore as it is a created
substance, it represents the cause and principle; and so in that manner it shows the person of the
Father, who is the 'principle from no principle.' According as it has a form and species, it represents
the Word as the form of the thing made by art is from the conception of the craftsman. According
as it has relation of order, it represents the Holy Spirit, inasmuch as He is love, because the order of
the effect to something else is from the will of the Creator. And therefore Augustine says that the
trace of the Trinity is found in every creature, according 'as it is one individual,' and according 'as
it is formed by a species,' and according as it 'has a certain relation of order.' And to these also are
reduced those three, 'number,' 'weight,' and 'measure,' mentioned in the Book of Wisdom (9:21).
For 'measure' refers to the substance of the thing limited by its principles, 'number' refers to the
species, 'weight' refers to the order. And to these three are reduced the other three mentioned by
Augustine (*On the Nature of the Good*, c. 3), 'mode,' 'species,' and 'order' ..."

pression of the Father's creative power, a visible iconostasis that simultaneously reveals and conceals his goodness and paternity.

Material creatures imitate the Son due to their inner intelligibility, or form. Each is a species of the truth. In non-living material beings this "form" is quite limited ontologically. It always coexists with material potency in each body. Consequently, no material body in this world is ever utterly determined in form, ontologically enduring, or historically stable. The physical world is a world of flux, despite being marked in each thing by the Logos. Often in physical bodies like a star or a lake, the physical *qualities* are more pronounced and more stable than the particular quantity, and these qualities are in perpetual interaction with those of other substances, such that each is continuously renegotiating its range of presence and activity. This alterability is a sign of the imperfection of the vestige of the Son in material things, but their persistence in their identity (substantial, elemental, chemical, atomic) represents by a shadowy imitation the Son as enduring Logos.

The goodness of each material being derives first from its mere subsistence, the given-ness of its brute existence, but also is expressed in the natural forms and expressive qualities of each thing. Every material being, no matter how microscopic, tends to assert its own nature and properties in interaction with others, and this is a vestige of that transcendent goodness that is eternal, found in the Holy Spirit. He has given a kind of permanent goodness to the world, that is expressed in the myriad activities of the diverse created things themselves, and in their mutual interaction. This goodness is finite and limited, expressed through the flux and change of the cosmos, but it has an uncreated ground in the exemplary goodness of the eternal Spirit, who is Love and who communicates being to all things.

Living things imitate the Holy Trinity differently and more perfectly than non-living things in key respects. The first and most important pertains to the generation of offspring, both in plants and in animals, whereby one individual communicates its nature to another, in and through embodied material existence. This is something found in plants, animals, and human beings alone that resembles the eternal generation of the Son in a unique way. In the Son, the divine nature is generated substantially in one who is other than the Father, so that all that is in the Father is in the Son. In plant, animal, and human life also, the generation is substantial and communicates an identical nature or essential kind from one to another. By dissimilitude the generation is material, and results in a distinct substance, not an entity that is consubstantial. It is communicated in a finite, temporal, and transitory way, not as something eternal. However, precisely because these material creatures can perpetually transmit their species from one generation to another, they "image" the eternal begetting of the Son, and the Logos who is eternal, by maintaining the various created "natures" that reflect him, through a succession of generations. Evidently in this process of generation, there is a kind of paternity present insofar as creatures beget creatures, and a filiation, as creatures are each begotten of others. The Spirit is represented in his goodness by the goodness of offspring and by the fruitfulness of life. Just as God's eternal transmission of life by generation and spiration is infinite and eternal in kind, unchanging in its perfection, so the world of living things, like a mirror of this simple perfection of God, consists in a superabundance of finite, limited realities. The fact that the creation is teeming with life, in a great diversity of plant and animal forms, speaks to the eternal plenitude of life that is in God's generation of the Word and the goodness of the eternal gift of love, who is the Spirit. This plenitude is communicated *ad extra* as only it can be, through a myriad of finite forms that reflect the eternal splendor and vitality of God.

A second way that living things reflect the mystery of the Trinity is in virtue of their immanent operative activity. Non-living physical beings are not characterized by immanent activities, like nutrition or sensation, thinking or willing. Angelic creatures do have immanent spiritual, immaterial activities of knowledge and love, in virtue of which they resemble the Trinity in especial ways. Only living material beings, however, have immanent vital operations that are grounded in their organic interiority. For example, plants and animals have the capacity to nourish themselves from material sources and digest food, with a view to substantial growth of the body, repair from injuries, and eventual activities of reproduction. They produce offspring or gestate offspring from within themselves, by reproductive bodily processes. These are features of interiority that are rooted in matter, typically expressed in "specialized" bodily organs. This kind of vegetative organic interiority that allows such beings to nourish and reproduce materially is faintly similar to the Logos in a distinctive way, in his procession from the Father, since the material beings in question operate through inner organs as expressions or species of their own substantial life. This organic inner life is not immaterial, nor is it purely substantial (organs are mere properties of the body even if we often cannot live without them). But their operations are inner expressions of life that stem from within their living being.

Animals are characterized by sensation, and therefore possess a form of interiority or immanent activity distinct from that of plants. Animal knowledge and appetite are intentional in form, meaning that when an animal rightly senses something outside itself by sight or hearing, it does not become that thing nor does that thing become it. Nor is such knowledge equivalent to a generation of life, as when a living being begets a substance distinct from itself. Sensate knowledge and appetite in animals, however imperfect, is interior life present within the animal by which the animal can assimilate real knowledge of others outside itself. This form of interiority is higher in perfection than what we find in plants, which evidence no capacity to assimilate within themselves sensate knowledge of others. The capacity of animals for assimilation of alterity (knowledge of what is other than themselves) is more like the Trinitarian persons under an aspect than is the life we find in plants. The Father eternally knows the Son, and the Son, the Father. The Trinitarian persons are eternally "other" to one another in person, even as they are one in essence and wholly "interior" to one another as God. Animals also have knowledge of alterity, but can know and desire what is other than themselves only in very imperfect ways. They interpret this knowledge instinctually in view of their natural ends of nutrition, self-protection, self-sustenance, and reproduction. Theirs is the lowest form of knowledge, but it does exist with its own dignity and beauty, and it is open to spiritual life, as we see in human animals and in human rational engagement with and cultivation of the animal world.

Human beings recapitulate these Trinitarian vestiges within themselves in unique ways, as personal beings made in the image of God, in virtue especially of their spiritual souls and interior operations of immaterial knowledge and love. The human being can know and love God spiritually, and by grace can even participate in the uncreated wisdom of the Son and the goodness and love of the Spirit. The spiritual faculties of the human person are thus radiated by the persons of the Trinity. This means that human beings are called ultimately to contemplation and worship of the Trinitarian God, in this life and in the life to come. But in responding to this calling, they also contemplate and love the Trinity through and in their bodies, animated by vegetative and sensate activities, so that all of human existence, visible and invisible, individual and collective, is capable of acquiring a Trinitarian form. In this way the whole cosmos can return to God in the human person, as the image of God and the highest reality of the visible creation.

Human beings can image God not only by returning to God directly in their bodies but also by begetting human persons through interpersonal love. The transmission of human life is distinct from that of all other animals insofar as the parents freely decide to reproduce, and that reproduction typically happens within a human friendship, one marked by justice, temperance, and love. The child's body is conceived by the parents, but its human soul is created immediately by God, as Creator, who cooperates with the parents in the creation of a new human person. The child in turn is not only raised by the parents "biologically" but also above all spiritually and interpersonally, in a communion of persons. This natural image of Trinitarian begetting and interpersonal love has evident similitudes to the Trinitarian communion.

Finally, human persons living in the body echo the mystery of the Trinity as knowledge and love by communicating properties of knowledge and love through and beyond themselves in the material world, by activities of the human body. The various distinctively human activities of education through language and culture; of work, art, and manual labor; of liturgical worship of the Trinity, these are all ways that the human being can sanctify the world intellectually and deliberately in accord with Trinitarian knowledge and love. The sacraments, instituted by Christ and the apostolic college, act within this sphere to elevate it and give it an orientation toward God, in the midst of all the concrete complexity of human physical and historical existence in the cosmos. In this sense, the Trinitarian imprint of being in the physical world, emergent in various modes and degrees of perfection in non-living things, plants, animals, and human persons, is the ontological foundation of the mystery of the Church.

CONCLUSION

In this chapter we considered two modern theologies of the Trinitarian economy of creation, one from Sergius Bulgakov and the other from Jürgen Moltmann. As we noted, Bulgakov grounds the economy of creation in a mystery of eternal self-emptying or kenosis, which characterizes both the divine essence of God as *Sophia* and the three persons of the Trinity in their mutual relations. God undergoes an inward dipolar alteration as a condition of possibility for the creation of the world and for the subsequent events of incarnation and crucifixion. Moltmann, in a similar way, appeals to the

idea of a pre-creational act of self-limitation on the part of God so as to create space within the Trinity and between the persons as the ground for the
finite space, time, and human freedom that are found in creation. Both of
these thinkers laudably wish to re-accentuate the centrality of the mystery
of the Trinity and that of creation, and wish to identify an inextricable link
between the two. However, precisely because each of them distances himself in pronounced ways from the patristic and scholastic heritage of thinking about the one God, each also generates significant problems at least as
great as any he wishes to address or overcome. Each in his own way understands the divine nature to depend essentially upon the creation for its eventual evolution or alteration. Each in his own way also permits the distinction
of persons in God to take shape only in inevitable dependence upon relations of the persons to creation and its unfolding history.

In contrast with this viewpoint, we have noted how the traditional understanding of Trinitarian appropriation, far from obscuring any sense of
the Trinitarian imprint in creatures, allows us to identify in an unmistakable
way how the creation, precisely as the offspring of all three persons acting
as one, bears the trace of the three persons in distinguishable ways, in all
that exists. Furthermore, by admitting the spiritual analogy of the human
person to God, and the consequent classical psychological analogy of the
processions of the Word and Spirit, we are able to denote clearly a hierarchy
of being in creation in which there are resemblances to the Trinity across a
spectrum of perfections. Non-living physical beings truly reflect the Trinity,
though not as living things do; and non-sentient living things reflect God
differently from sentient animals. Human beings, who have spiritual faculties, meanwhile, are truly in the image of God in a distinctive way among
visible material creatures, and they recapitulate the Trinitarian vestiges of
"lower" creatures within themselves in a uniquely personal way, based on
their corporeality, living reproductive capacities, and sensate knowledge,
which in humans are made subject to the agency of spiritual knowledge and
love. This hierarchy of being is distinguishable only if we also have a theology of natures, one that takes the natural forms of reality to be expressions
of the uncreated nature of the Holy Trinity. In order to explore an integral
Trinitarian theology of creation, then, we have need of an integral use of the
classical patristic and scholastic tradition that considers both the threefold
distinction of persons in God and the shared divine nature, a study of the
mystery of God simultaneously *de Deo ut uno et ut trino*.

33

The Trinity in the Incarnation
and Life of Christ

INTRODUCTION

How is the Trinity revealed in the economy of the Incarnation and in the human life of Jesus? What does it mean to say that the life of Jesus is Trinitarian in form, that it reveals the Father, Son, and Spirit in virtue of the visible mission of the Son? In this chapter we will note three features of a typical post-Hegelian theological answer to this question. I will characterize this view as a form of "inverted monophysitism" and consider critically some of its limitations or problems. Most notably I will argue that this position eclipses or acknowledges insufficiently the classical dogmatic teaching of the Catholic Church that there are two wills and operations in Christ: divine and human (dyothelitism). Having done so, I will then consider Thomistic principles that help one think constructively about the Son's visible mission of incarnation and about his human life and actions in the gospel as indicative of his divine unity with the Father and the Spirit. The basic argument of this chapter is that classical principles of both dyothelitism and the divine unity of will (the idea of there being one shared nature and will of the three persons in God) are essential to any constructive understanding of the way that the Son's incarnation and human life among us reveal the inner Trinitarian wisdom and love of God, as well as the missions of the Son and Spirit, respectively.

INVERTED MONOPHYSITISM

We noted above that modern theology confronts the limitation, placed by Immanuel Kant and others, on human thinking of God as one who is transcendent of history. Consequently, the typical tendency in post-Kantian theological paradigms since Hegel is to seek to find God above all or exclusively in history, rather than as one who is understood metaphysically as transcendent of it. This idea is typically applied Christologically: it is principally or exclusively in virtue of God's human existence among us that we may come to know him.[1] What God is immanently as Trinity, then, is manifest above all in the economic life of God among us. In the unfolding event of God's human life among us, however, it is also often thought to be the case that God realizes or explores something new in his own inner immanent life as Trinity. The human form of Christ (his life, suffering, and death) manifests and in a sense enacts what is present ontologically in the Trinitarian relations themselves. God is potentially identical with and in part defined by or enriched by his historical act of self-giving love, which is expressed in the Incarnation and the suffering of the crucifixion. Therefore, the human actions and sufferings of God (what the Son experiences as human) indicate the relations of action and receptivity that exist among the persons of the Trinity. The mutual self-giving of the persons in God is the eternal precondition for God's actions of incarnation and suffering, even as the latter events themselves may give rise to new states within God. How, then, does this manner of thinking approach the specific mystery of the Incarnation, and that of Christ's human life among us?

We might speak of the dominant paradigm for thinking about the Incarnation in this regard as one of "inverted monophysitism." Here the term monophysitism is used in an analogous sense to the way it is employed in the study of patristic theology. Classically, the title of monophysitism is given to those forms of thought that insisted on "one nature after the union" of God and man, such that there subsists in the Incarnate Word only one nature, which is divine.[2] According to this ancient theory, the divine na-

1. Epitomal examples of this tendency are to be found, I take it, in the Christologies of thinkers like Wolfhart Pannenberg and Hans Urs von Balthasar, who radicalized ideas of Barth in the service of Rahner's *Grundaxiom*, as I shall note below.
2. On the history and definition of monophysitism, see Aloys Grillmeier, *Christ in Christian Tradition*, vol. 1, *From the Apostolic Age to Chalcedon (451)*, as well as Grillmeier, *Christ in Christian Tradition*, vol. 2, part 1, *From Chalcedon to Justinian I*, trans P. Allen and J. Cawte (Philadelphia:

ture assimilates the human in virtue of the hypostatic union, the superior assimilating the inferior. However, the idea was condemned as heretical by the Council of Chalcedon in 451, wherein the Church affirmed clearly that Christ is one person, the eternal Son, subsisting in two natures, so that he is truly God and truly human.[3] More nuanced forms of monophysitism resurfaced in subsequent centuries with the affirmation that Christ has only one natural operation and only one natural will. The Church correspondingly stipulated at the Third Council of Constantinople (680–81) that Christ has two natural operations and two natural wills, those pertaining to his divine nature and human nature respectively. In the former, he is one with the Father and the Spirit, while in the latter he is one in kind with the human race.[4]

Modern monophysitism is inverted because it does not assimilate the human nature, operations, and will to the divine (so as to seemingly evaporate what is human) but rather the contrary: the divinity of the Son is manifest in and is in a sense *constituted by* the kenotic act of being human.[5] Ac-

---

Westminster, 1987), which considers in detail various strands of anti-Chalcedonian monophysitism in the period following the council. It should be noted that in the era of Cyril of Alexandria, the *mia physis* formula (one nature in Christ after the union) was wrongly attributed to Athanasius, whereas it is now commonly thought to derive from Apollinarius, who denied that there was an integral humanity in Christ, the Word made flesh. Consequently, Cyril in his own nuanced way defended the phrase, and others after him radicalized the interpretation, insisting on the assimilation of the human nature to the divine nature.

3. The Council of Chalcedon states: "... we all with one voice teach the confession of one and the same Son, our Lord Jesus Christ: the same perfect in divinity and perfect in humanity, the same truly God and truly man, of a rational soul and a body; consubstantial with the Father as regards his divinity, and the same consubstantial with us as regards his humanity; like us in all respects except for sin.... one and the same Christ, Son, Lord, only-begotten, acknowledged in two natures which undergo no confusion, no change, no division, no separation; at no point was the difference between the natures taken away through the union, but rather the property of both natures is preserved and comes together into a single person and single subsistent being" (*Decrees*, ed. Tanner, 1:86).

4. The letter of Pope Agatho that is contained in the documents of the Third Council of Constantinople thus affirms: "... [the Church] confesses and preaches two natural wills and two natural operations in [Christ] for if anyone understood will as personal, since three Persons are spoken of in the Holy Trinity, it would be necessary to say that there are three personal wills and three personal operations (which is absurd and exceedingly profane). But since the truth of the Christian faith maintains that the will is natural, where this one nature is predicated of the holy and inseparable Trinity, it follows that one natural will and one natural operation are to be understood. Where, however, in the one Person of our Lord Jesus Christ, Mediator between God and man, we confess two natures, namely, divine and human, in which after the wondrous union he exists as one and the same in two natures, so we also confess two natural wills and two natural operations" (Denzinger, 545).

5. This idea seems to have its origins in part in Hegel's innovative interpretation of

cordingly the Son is commonly distinguished from the Father even in his intra-Trinitarian personal distinctness primarily or exclusively in virtue of the operations and willing he manifests as man. Here we can note three features of this dominant paradigm in modern Trinitarian Christology.

First, the Son's obedience and free self-emptying (kenotic love) are understood to be what constitute him in his personal relationality to the Father from all eternity. Consequently, this obedience and self-emptying love are both eternal and temporal. We might say that the visible mission of the Son not only manifests the Son's eternal self-emptying, but is in a sense its perfect expression and actualization. The kenosis of the Son from all eternity occurs in view of the economy so that the hominization (the becoming human) gives realization to what God is in his filial mode of being as Son.[6]

Second, the temporal expression of this filial identity in God is manifest precisely in the *human* activity of Christ. In its most extreme form, the idea is this: the Son of God made man does not have two wills and operations, one divine, one human. Rather, he empties himself in time and history precisely by acting as human exclusively, in obedience and subordination to the Father and in docility to the Spirit. Pannenberg, for example, simply takes issue with the dyothelitism of the Third Council of Constantinople, which he fears falsifies any true perspective on the mystery of Christ. The Son in his kenotic mode of being among us acts only as man.[7] Moltmann

the communication of idioms, which I discussed in chapter 31. God in his kenotic act of self-identification with the finite takes on human forms of being, such that the human attributes of the God-human are rightly attributed to the divine nature.

6. As we have seen, Bulgakov presents us with one early twentieth-century view of this idea. Barth offers an alternative version with his theory of divine obedience in the Trinity, in *CD* 4:1, 157–357. Barth argues that the human obedience of Christ in time reveals a pre-existent eternal obedience that characterizes the eternal Son as God, by which he is eternally differentiated from the Father: see especially Barth, *CD* 4:1, 200–201: "We have not only not to deny but actually to affirm and understand as essential to the being of God the offensive fact that there is in God Himself an above and a below, a *prius* and a *posterius*, a superiority and a subordination. And our present concern is with what is apparently the most offensive fact of all, that there is a below, a *posterius*, a subordination, that it belongs to the inner life of God that there should take place within it obedience." Wolfhart Pannenberg is deeply influenced by this theological idea in his *Jesus—God and Man*, 307–23, and later in his *Systematic Theology*, 2:375–79, as we shall return to below. For Jürgen Moltmann's dependence upon this text, see *The Crucified God*, 200–278, especially 202–4, which leads off Moltmann's core reflection in the book. Balthasar's work is deeply influenced by Barth's theology of divine obedience. See especially Balthasar, *The Glory of the Lord: A Theological Aesthetics*, vol. 1, *Seeing the Form*, trans. E. Leiva-Merikakis (San Francisco: Ignatius, 1982), 478–80; and *Theo-Drama*, 3:183–91 and 521–23; *Theo-Drama* 5:236–39.

7. See Pannenberg, *Jesus—God and Man*, 307–23. He objects to the two wills doctrine in the following way on p. 319: "If God's self-humiliation to unity with a man is conceived only as man-

holds a similar view, in sharp distinction from the councils of the Catholic Church.[8] Balthasar, meanwhile, maintains that the divine will of the Son is present in the Son made man but is practically quiescent. In virtue of the self-emptying love that constitutes the Incarnation, the Son made man, for the duration of his time among us, acts only as man, in subordination to the divine will of the Father and the Spirit, so as to forsake the prerogatives of his divine will and omnipotence.[9] Bulgakov has a similar perspective.[10]

ifestation of the divine glory and not as sacrifice of essential elements of the divine being, this expression does not help make the full humanity of Jesus in the Incarnation intelligible; for then Jesus would remain an almighty, omniscient, omnipresent man, even though he humbly hides his glory. Or he remains a dual being with two faces in which divine majesty and human lowliness live and work parallel to one another, but without living unity with one another." As an alternative, Pannenberg posits that the eternal distinction of the Son from the Father is actuated and realized precisely in his human mode of being and willing as man. See, for example, *Systematic Theology*, 2:377: "By distinguishing the Father from himself as the one God, the Son certainly moved out of the unity of the deity and became man. But in so doing he actively expressed his divine essence as the Son. The self-emptying of the Preexistent is not a surrender or negation of his deity as the Son. It is its activation. Hence the end of his earthly path in obedience to the Father is the revelation of his deity." Pannenberg here cites Barth, *CD* 4:1, 129; 177; 179.

·8. See Moltmann, *The Crucified God*, 227–35.

9. See, in this regard, the important notion of a Trinitarian inversion in Balthasar, *Theo-Drama* 3:183–91 and 521–23, and especially 186–87: "We know no other economic form of the Trinity but that which entered into history, and of its essence it also has a soteriological meaning: the Son, who is eternally subject to the Father, as man had to 'learn obedience through what he suffered' (Heb. 5:8).... But it is the Spirit in him and over him who makes this obedience possible, by the way in which, in his economic form, he mediates the Father's will to the Son.... this absolute, free consent between [the Son made man] and the Father is the economic form of their common spiration of the Spirit. For reasons of salvation history, however, this spiration has to go into hiding.... [In the economy] the Spirit takes over the function of presenting the obedient Son with the Father's will ..." Balthasar argues that the processions of the Son and the Spirit are inverted in the economy, due to this kenosis of the Son, such that during the time of his incarnation and prior to the resurrection, he proceeds from the Spirit and is utterly relative to him not merely in his human heart and mind, moved inwardly by the grace of the Holy Spirit, as is traditionally affirmed, but also in his very person and being as Son. Balthasar appeals to the notion of the divine mission of the Son, a classical teaching of scripture and tradition, as we have seen. However, he differs from a thinker like Aquinas on Trinitarian mission in at least three respects. First, he has no concept of the invisible mission of the Son and Word that precedes the visible mission, so that, for Balthasar, the mission is identical with the incarnation and human life of Christ. Second, he identifies the person of the Son with his mission (the Son as one always related to his Father is constituted by his mission), which means that it becomes difficult to distinguish in principle the eternal procession of the Son from his mission. Therefore, the humanity of Christ and his dereliction become a cypher whereby we see directly into the eternal distinction of the persons in procession. Third, Balthasar emphasizes the self-consciousness of Christ as man as a distinctive locus of the mission, so that it is precisely in Jesus' human awareness, obedience, and suffering that we acquire a vision into the eternal life of the Son. Such decisions lead to a form of inverted monophysitism, whereby the Son is virtually identified in his very person with his human modes of being.

10. See the thematic argument of Bulgakov, *The Lamb of God*, 247–63, 305–20, who interprets the Third Council of Constantinople in a kenotic way, so that the human consciousness of Christ

Barth, by contrast, argues that all that the Son does as man under obedience corresponds to an already existing eternal obedience in the divine will of the Son, so that the human activity of Christ always mirrors (quasi-univocally) a divine obedience that exists from all eternity and that constitutes the Son as distinct from the Father.[11]

One can observe in all these models what I take to be the absence or eclipse of authentic dyothelitism. The traditional dyothelite teaching maintains the reality and distinction of the two natures, as well as the analogy or similitude between them, and the subordination of the human to the divine. On this view, the human obedience and self-emptying of Christ as man are truly indicative of the divine will but not identical with it or co-extensive with it in practical signification. Christ's human acts of love and obedience resemble and express the divine love that he shares with the Father and the Spirit in virtue of their incomprehensible deity. These acts are instrumentally subordinate to the divine will, and operate in perfect concord with it, so that all the actions and sufferings of Jesus as man manifest authentically the nature and mystery of the divine love of the Trinity. This is a point we will return to below.

Third, then, inverted monophysitism tends to hold that Jesus' human operations are directly indicative of the natural constitution of his divine person. In other words, what Jesus does as man, the properties that accrue to him due to his human activity, accrue also to him as God the Son in his

---

in his historical life, suffering, and dereliction are *commensurate* with his divine self-emptying love. The distinction of natures is reinterpreted as a diremption of the divine nature into a human form. "In the Incarnation, the Son removes from Himself his divine glory, empties Himself of his Divinity, extinguishes it in Himself, as it were. Therefore, the hierarchical place that is pre-eternally proper to Him in the Holy Trinity and, in particular, His relation to the Father, takes on externally 'subordinationist' traits. This relation becomes one of voluntary and absolute obedience. By His will the Father takes the place in the Son of the Son's own Divinity, so to speak, which the Son, as it were, has abandoned" (Bulgakov, *The Lamb of God*, 305–6).

11. Barth, *CD* 4:1, 209: "The One who in this obedience is the perfect image of the ruling God is Himself—as distinct from every human and creaturely kind—God by nature, God in His relationship to Himself, that is, God in His mode of being as the Son in relation to God in His mode of being as the Father, One with the Father and of one essence. In His mode of being as the Son He fulfils the divine subordination, just as the Father in His mode of being as the Father fulfils the divine superiority. In humility as the Son who complies, He is the same as is the Father in majesty as the Father who disposes. He is the same in consequence (and obedience) as the Son as is the Father in origin. He is the same as the Son, that is, as the self-posited God ... as is the Father as the self-positing God.... The Father as the origin is never apart from Him as the consequence, the obedient One. The self-positing of God is never apart from Him as the One who is posited as God by God. The One who eternally begets is never apart from the One who is eternally begotten."

constitution as a divine person and in doing so they indicate natural properties that he alone has as God that are not directly attributable to the Father or the Spirit. So if Jesus obeys as man, then we must say not only that it
is God the Son who obeys, which is true, but also that God the Son is eternally constituted in his relational distinction from the Father by his obedience, and the natural properties of divine obedience must in some way be
in the Son, in a way that differentiates him from the Father or the Spirit. Besides obedience, what other qualities can we attribute to God the Son so
as to distinguish him from God the Father from all eternity? Theologians
differ, but one can speak of a broad family resemblance. So, for example,
Balthasar does not hesitate to speak of something analogous to a divine suffering in God the Son in his infinite distance from the Father, an eternally
self-sacrificial love that constitutes him in his distinction from the Father
from all eternity.[12] Bulgakov similarly speaks of a self-emptying love in God
the Son that is before the incarnation but that constitutes the inner ground
of the incarnation.[13] Moltmann no doubt goes the furthest, with Hegel, in
claiming that the Son's identification with us in death and non-being invites
these realities into God's own being and life, so that God in the person of
the Son experiences death and non-being in his very deity. This mode of being differentiates the Son from the Father in the economy.[14] Pannenberg
remains more reserved: the human obedience of the Son in time is expressive of an eternal subordination or act of surrender to the Father, one that
constitutes the Son in his mode of being from all eternity.[15]

12. See, for example, Balthasar, *Theo-Drama*, 4:317–32, especially 325: "This Son is infinitely
Other, but he is also the infinitely Other *of the Father*. Thus he both grounds and surpasses all we
mean by separation, pain and alienation in the world and all we can envisage in terms of loving
self-giving, personal relationship and blessedness. He is not the direct identity of the two but their
presupposition, sovereignly surpassing them. Hence, too, he is not the mere foundation of a potential 'history of God,' a God who would achieve unity through the pain involved in 'bifurcation'
(within himself and/or in the world): he is the concrete, complete presupposition ('prepositing')
of this bifurcation." We see here how Balthasar's anti-Hegelian speculation is similar in some respects to that of Hegel. God does not become in history, but his diremption in eternity is the
transcendent condition of possibility for his kenotic activity in time.
13. Bulgakov, *The Lamb of God*, 216–17.
14. See Moltmann, *The Crucified God*, 200–290, esp. 235–48.
15. Pannenberg, *Systematic Theology*, 2:375: "This obedience [of Christ] led him into the situation of extreme separation from God and his immortality, in the dereliction of the cross. The
remoteness from God on the cross was the climax of his self-distinction from the Father."

PROBLEMS ARISING FROM
INVERTED MONOPHYSITISM

In all these various formulations of Christology we can observe four endur-ing problems that continue to have a legacy within contemporary theolo-gy. The first problem has to do with the simplicity and perfection of divine love. This issue arises from the final point mentioned above: the attribution of obedience to the Son as a natural property that distinguishes him eternal-ly from the Father. Seemingly, if the Son and the Father are truly one in be-ing and essence (*homoousios*) then the obedience of the Son is not a natural property that distinguishes him essentially from the Father: after all, they are each the one God. In this case, the distinct natural characteristic that the Son alone possesses in his obedience to the Father is divinely *non-essential* (by the logic of the *homoousios* formula), and thus by analogy something like a proper accident. However, this idea seems to be necessarily anthro-pomorphic in an important sense, since it attributes an operative act to the Son that is merely accidental in nature, and properties of nature, as we have argued in part 2 of this book, cannot be present in God except in a subsis-tent mode. A human person may exist and continue to have the same na-ture whether he or she is obedient or not, loving or not, knowledgeable or not. Obedience in a human being is a property of the person, albeit one that is important, but not one that is identical with the nature of the person as such. In God, however, due to divine simplicity and perfection, nature and operation are mysteriously identical. God is his natural act of willing and loving, or what we denote analogically as God's incomprehensible natural love is numinously identical with his very essence and being.

However, a love that is perfect possesses the good in a perfect fashion, and so, correspondingly, if the divine nature is perfect in love, that love must possess all that pertains to God, his goodness, power, and so on. In this case, the natural divine will of God cannot obey itself, as the divine nature cannot be subject (by diremptive bifurcation) to diverse modes of command and obedience. Were this the case, each agent would possess the good in imper-fect fashion, as one commanding (asking for something good from the oth-er) or as one obeying (conforming to the good required by the other), but not as persons each having a divine will naturally in perfect possession of the good. Consequently the nature of God would not be simple, and there would be differentiating features of perfection whereby the Father would be or become perfect in one way and the Son in another. Neither would be perfect in love, and so in a certain sense neither would fully possess the deity. Or perhaps, if the Father were to possess the perfection of the divine essence, and if the essence of God is purely actual and perfect (such that God cannot naturally obey himself), then the Father would be perfect in love. If, then, the Son were to possess obedience as a property found in him but not in the Father, then the Son would not share in the very same perfection of divine love as the Father. God the Father would become something other or more perfect than the Son in the order of love, or the Son would be somehow naturally other or less than the Father. Such ideas are difficult to reconcile with the confession of the unity of God and with Nicene Trinitarian orthodoxy. In fact, in the face of these conundrums it is reasonable to retain the well-tested teaching of the tradition on this point. God is naturally love, a love of perfect possession of the divine goodness, and the Father and Son are one in nature and thus one in love. The Father loves, the Son loves, and the Spirit loves, each in a distinct personal way or mode, but each also loves in virtue of the simple and perfect natural love that each possesses as God. If we wish to say that the Son is perfect in divine love, it seems that we should avoid saying that the Son is eternally obedient to the Father.

A second problem with this paradigm is related. Obedience and free submission or self-offering to the will of another cannot be differentiating principles of Trinitarian persons, because such ideas inevitably imply a distinction of wills in God. If the Son is *constituted* personally by the eternal free act of obedience to the Father, then he must have a will distinct from that of the Father, by which he submits himself to the Father's command, or surrenders himself to the Father in some form of self-emptying. Otherwise, precisely because the Son is identified by means of this free surrender and obedience, there is no way (based on the principles of the view we are criticizing) to distinguish him sufficiently from the Father. But to obey simply is to submit one's will to the command of another, formally speaking, so if the Son is constituted by obedience, and so distinguished from the Father in this respect, he must submit his will to the will of the Father. However, what inevitably results from this vision is a duality of wills in the Trinity properly speaking. Here our appeals to analogy and apophaticism cannot be called readily into service, precisely because the idea of a real distinction of wills carries over quasi-univocally into the way we signify divine persons, based on the essential definition of a divine person. A divine person just is one who commands or obeys (and so freely surrenders in love to) the will of another. In this case, the Son must possess not only a distinct will but also a will characterized eternally by different natural properties than that of the Father (because the will of the Son must lovingly submit to the command of the Father and so be characterized differently). This idea inevitably introduces both a real distinction of wills and a real distinction of natural qualities of willing into the unity of essence of the Trinity, and, as we have seen, such an idea is excluded by the Third Council of Constantinople as theologically problematic. According to the Church's dogmatic tradition, which appeals in reasonable ways to the unity of God revealed in scripture, the persons of the Trinity are truly one in being and essence, and therefore must have one eternal natural act of knowledge and will, possessed in three personal modes. It follows from this that one divine person cannot obey the other or be constituted by a freedom to respond or not to respond to another divine person. The persons of the Trinity know and love one another perfectly and comprehensively, and do so in virtue of their shared divine life of knowledge and love.

A third issue pertains to an unresolved tension in modern Trinitarian thought, a tension inherited from Hegel. Hegel attributes to God diverse naturally contradictory or simultaneously incompatible states by assigning them to distinct persons, in accord with God's own historical becoming. The Father possesses modes of being in his transcendence as God that are distinct from those of the Son in his historical mode of being as God. As we noted in chapter 31, the most famous case is that pertaining to the human death of Christ, which Hegel posits as an ontological reality pertaining to the very being of God as spirit, who is subject to "death" in the divine nature. This occurs internal to a process of dialectical reconciliation, which is accomplished in the resurrection, wherein God as spirit is revealed to be and reaches self-actualization as love. But Hegel is not concerned with the canons of classical Catholic orthodoxy, and in fact seeks to assimilate them into something greater that stems from his own philosophical originality. Theologians who wish to preserve contact with Nicaea and Chalcedon, therefore, are hard pressed to put this Hegelian historical model into service in their Trinitarian thought, no matter how many qualifications they may make, since the very idea of a modal distinction of persons identified from natural properties of the Son in the historical economy brings with it the idea of a historical diversification of the divine persons. Or at least, such an approach suggests that the eternal distinction of the persons occurs only

ever in view of the historical incarnation of the Son, so that the Son must incarnate and obey in time, precisely so as to realize from within history God's
own eternal pre-disposition to personal distinction.

A final problem that arises from either the rejection or the eclipse of
dyothelitism in post-Hegelian Trinitarian theology is related to the analogical similitude of the human nature of Jesus and his divine nature. Modern
theologians like Pannenberg typically reject the classical idea of dyothelitism (two operations and wills in Christ) precisely because they believe it
will lead to a falsifying artificial vision. Jesus will no longer be taken seriously as one who is truly human, a subject in historical time like us, but will be
seen instead as "merely" a divine person acting out a pre-scripted drama in
an instrumentalized human nature, so that the psychology and freedom of
Christ as man are likened to a human puppet being manipulated by a divine
actor above the stage of history.[16] Behind this suspicion stands the linger-
ing influence of nominalism, which posits an incompatibility of simultaneous divine and human causality. The objection posits an ontological rivalry
of the two natures: If God the Son is truly human, he must not have a divine will that is active and present in his human nature. If he is truly God,
he cannot become truly human, unless he first surrenders something essential to his godhead in order to do so or consents to change into something
else. However, the language of classical dyothelitism was developed by the
Church Fathers precisely so as to underscore the soteriological realism of
the Incarnation. God himself can truly become human and be Immanuel,
"God with us" (Is 7:14), without in any way ceasing to be God. And God
can be authentically and fully human in such a way as to be the most human
of us all. The two natures are truly united in Christ, but each remains distinct, and each operates in coordination with the other, such that the human
nature is always subordinate to the divine nature, even while also being fully
itself. God's most maximal and perfect presence among us does not initiate
a rivalry with our human nature, then, but is the condition for its greatest
flourishing. The deity of Christ and human nature are not identical but they
also are not opposed. In fact, God can express himself in our world personally best of all precisely in a human nature.

16. See the criticism in Pannenberg, *Jesus—God and Man*, 307–64, and similarly Karl Rahner,
"Current Problems in Christology," *Theological Investigations*, vol. 1, trans. C. Ernst (Baltimore,
Md.: Helicon Press, 1963), 149–200. I have proposed more developed responses to this objection
in *The Incarnate Lord*, chap. 1.

This perspective, of conciliar Christology, presupposes that human action is analogical to divine action, not identical with it or indicative of it in a quasi-univocal fashion.[17] God the Son can express himself as man, in his human nature, actions, and sufferings, so that we really come to know who he is as Son, and come to know the will and intentions of the Father, Son, and Holy Spirit. This occurs, however, without any confusion of the human operation of Jesus with his divine operation as such. In virtue of his human nature, Christ can reach out to touch a blind man and can knowingly intend in his heart to heal him. In virtue of his divine nature, in which he acts with the Father and in the Spirit, he can heal the blind man, by the power of God and in virtue of the perfect love of God. Consequently, the human activity of Jesus is instrumental and indicative of his divine activity, not identical with it. Both operations, divine and human, concur to bring about one concrete *theandric* act. That is to say, the Son expresses himself as God and as man, simultaneously, in two natures, so that the divine activity and human activity of Christ always coincide and are harmonious, but are never identical.[18] The human agency of the Son is instrumental, though it is not an external tool: the Word made flesh acts divinely as God through his human agency.[19]

17. The teaching of the Fourth Lateran Council, in 1215, regarding analogy and similitude between God and creatures should be read in continuity with the Christological councils mentioned above. The dissimilitude between Trinitarian persons and human persons is greater than the similitude, because God the Holy Trinity is one in being in a way that human persons are not. Modern theologians after Barth often treat the topic of analogy in Lateran IV as if its teaching is concerned with natural theology, but in doing so they look back in an anachronistic way. The Council is in fact concerned primarily with the Trinitarian confession of faith and its ontological presuppositions and implications. Without the Trinitarian analogy of being in theology, what results is anthropomorphism, a problematic form of conceptual projection of human traits onto God. (The council was concerned with this danger emerging from the thought of Joachim of Fiore.) The analogy of being in Trinitarian theology then, far from being a source of idolatry, is a remedy for it, and the rejection of this analogy, far from freeing the person from problematic conceptual projections, can readily lead to it.

18. The rejection of this analogy of the two natures leads to equivocal language about the divine nature (where we cannot say anything about God's divine nature in our human language) and univocal identification of the human nature with the mystery of the Trinity, so that what is said of the human nature of Jesus is ascribed anthropomorphically directly to his deity.

19. *ST* III, q. 19, a. 1, ad 1: "Dionysius places in Christ a theandric, i.e., a God-manlike or Divino-human, operation not by any confusion of the operations or powers of both natures, but inasmuch as His Divine operation employs the human, and His human operation shares in the power of the Divine. Hence, as he says in a certain epistle (*Ad Caium* iv), 'what is of man He works beyond man; and this is shown by the Virgin conceiving supernaturally and by the unstable waters bearing up the weight of bodily feet.' Now it is clear that to be begotten belongs to human nature, and likewise to walk; yet both were in Christ supernaturally. So, too, He wrought Divine things

THE OUTPOURING LOVE OF THE
TRINITARIAN PERSONS

Despite these criticisms, one can see that the modern trend we are analyzing seeks to depict the action of the Trinity in the historical economy
as an expression of intra-Trinitarian life and love. The kenosis of God in
the incarnation, life of Christ, and crucifixion, has its deepest grounding
in the eternal self-emptying of intra-Trinitarian love. How might we understand this latter idea in accord with the classical tradition represented in
this book?

We should first note that each person of the Trinity is characterized by
what Aquinas calls "active potency." This is not the potency to evolve, develop in perfection, or become something more, as we find in imperfect human
persons, who are still merely capable of knowing or loving. Nor is it a capacity for self-emptying in the proper sense of the term, since self-diminishment
is not possible for the persons of the Trinity, given God's perfection and pure
actuality. Instead, active potency denotes the already existing capacity for active self-communication that is present precisely in virtue of God's incomprehensible plenitude of perfection.[20] This active potency can be thought
about in two ways, *ad intra*, in the relations between the persons of the Trinity, and *ad extra*, in their relation to that which they create or redeem. *Ad intra*, the Father has the personal active power to communicate all that he has
and is as God to the Son and the Spirit, in virtue of his paternity and his common spiration, through the medium of eternal generation and spiration. He
does so not in virtue of any passive potency for development or capacity for
self-emptying, but only as one who is pure actuality. Or we might say that the
Father just is an eternal act of self-communication, since he only ever has his
nature as God in a paternal way, as he who is the fontal origin of Trinitarian
life, and as one who is also the Father of creation, in the Word and the Spirit.[21] The Son meanwhile eternally receives all he has from the Father, includ-

---

humanly, as when He healed the leper with a touch. Hence in the same epistle he adds: 'He performed Divine works not as God does, and human works not as man does, but, God having been
made man, by a new operation of God and man.' ... Hence it is clear that the human operation, in
which the Father and the Holy Ghost do not share, except by Their merciful consent, is distinct
from His operation, as the Word of God, wherein the Father and the Holy Ghost share."

20. See on this Aquinas, *De pot.*, q. 1, a. 1; q. 2, aa. 1–6; *ST* I, q. 40, a. 4; q. 41, aa. 2–6, and the
study by Emmanuel Perrier, *La fécondité en Dieu: La puissance notionnelle dans la Trinité selon Saint
Thomas d'Aquin* (Paris: Parole et Silence, 2009).

21. See, in this respect, *ST* I, q. 27, a. 5, ad 3: "God understands all things by one simple act;

ing the active potency of the Father to spirate the Spirit. Receiving all from
the Father, the Son eternally loves the Father in an inevitable reciprocity of
love, and in doing so spirates the Spirit with the Father as their shared mutual
love. Consequently, the Son also has no passive potency but is pure actuality
from pure actuality, God from God, light from light.

If we wish to speak about this mystery of the *ad intra* communication
of divine life between the persons, which is manifest in the economy of the
incarnation and the passion, it seems disadvantageous to do so by appeal
to the metaphor of self-emptying, since this notion inevitably brings with
it the idea of ontological self-diminishment or progressive development
and, in this sense, tends to militate against a proper understanding and acceptance of the incomprehensible perfection of God. However, we might
suggest in its place an alternative metaphor for the active potency of the
persons, one that originates in the early Christian tradition: that of divine
outpouring.

We see this metaphor used of the Father, as eternal fountain source of
the originate Son, already in the anti-Arian writings of Athanasius. He employs it to underscore the unity and equality of the Father and the Son. He
appeals in his writings to Baruch 3:12 ("You have forsaken the fountain of
wisdom") and correlates this to Jeremiah 2:13 ("they have forsaken me, the
fountain of living waters"). The fountain is interpreted here as the Father,
while the Son is the eternal Wisdom that pours forth from the Father, in
whom all things are made.[22] In fact, in his use of the metaphor, Athanasius
argues that the Fountain of outpouring is never diminished, always undiminishable, and thus just as the Father ever is the source of his own Wisdom, so too the Son is eternally present, as one who is from the Father.
"What is generated from the Father is His Word, and Wisdom, and Radiance; what is to be said but that, in maintaining, 'Once the Son was not'
they [the Arians] rob God of His Word ... and openly predicated of Him
that He was once without His proper Word and Wisdom, and that the Light
was once without radiance, and the Fountain was once barren and dry?"[23]
He continues:

---

and by one act also He wills all things. Hence there cannot exist in Him a procession of Word from
Word, nor of Love from Love: for there is in Him only one perfect Word, and one perfect Love;
thereby being manifested His perfect fecundity," and *ST* I, q. 33, a. 4, ad 1: "... source and authority
signify in God nothing but the principle of origin."

22. See Athanasius, *Defence of the Nicene Definition*, 3.12 and 4.15.

23. Athanasius, *Against the Arians*, 1.5.

If God be, and be called, the Fountain of wisdom and life (Jer. 2:13; Bar. 3:12)—
this implies that life and wisdom are not foreign to the Essence of the Fountain,
but are proper to It, nor were at any time without existence, but were always. Now
the Son is all this, who says, "I am the Life," (John 14:6) and, "I Wisdom dwell
with prudence" (Prov. 8:12). Is it not then irreligious to say, "Once the Son was
not?" for it is all one with saying, "Once the Fountain was dry, destitute of Life and
Wisdom." But a fountain it would then cease to be; for what begets not from itself,
is not a fountain. What a load of extravagance! For God promises that those who
do His will shall be as a fountain which the water fails not, saying by Isaiah ... "And
the Lord shall satisfy your soul in drought, and make your bones fat; and you shall
be like a watered garden, and like a spring of water, whose waters fail not." (Isa.
58:11).... God is the eternal Fountain of His proper Wisdom; and, if the Fountain
be eternal, the Wisdom also must needs be eternal. For in It were all things made,
as David says in the Psalm, "In Wisdom have You made them all"; and Solomon
says, "The Lord by Wisdom has formed the earth, by understanding has He established the heavens" (Prov. 3:19).[24]

Here Athanasius is underscoring three things. First, that there is a shared
life and wisdom in God that is communicated from the Father to the Son,
second, that this communication or divine outpouring (as it is depicted
metaphorically) is eternal and everlasting, and, third, that the creation is
given being and grace in virtue of this divine outpouring. The eternal procession of the Son *ad intra* is the foundation for the *ad extra* emanation of
creation from God.

   This traditional image of divine outpouring is, evidently, coarsely material in kind, but it conveys adequately, in metaphorical fashion, the notion
of a substantial communication of divine life. Just as a stream of living water
is a substance that flows forth from a fountainhead as its source, so the Son
pours forth eternally in his substance from the Father, possessing in himself
all that is in the Father.

   If we conjoin this Athanasian metaphor of outpouring with the Thomistic notion of active potency, we can ascribe personal agency to the outpouring and say, for example, that the Father by his active power is able to communicate all that he is and has as God to the Son, by an eternal outpouring
of his whole substance to the Son, one in which he knows no diminishment
of any kind. In virtue of his personal active potency, the Son can be said
metaphorically by a quantitative image to pour out all that he is and has as
God to the Spirit just insofar as he communicates with the Father the total-

---

24. Athanasius, *Against the Arians*, 1.6.

ity of divine life to the Holy Spirit. In addition, we may speak of this out-pouring in God as one that implies interpersonal love. The notional acts of generation and spiration do not occur by choice (the Trinitarian persons do not choose to become Trinitarian) but the notional acts of the persons do imply natural love. The Father has the active potency to communicate all that he has to the Son by generation, in a divine outpouring of his being, and in doing so loves his begotten Son, just as the Son who receives all that he has from the Father loves the Father. From their mutual love they spirate the Spirit as a common principle, to whom they communicate all that they are as God. The Spirit loves those from whom he receives all that he has. Only the persons of the Trinity, precisely because they share a common sin-gular being and essence, are capable of giving all that they have to one an-other, as a perfect expression of love, or are capable of receiving all that they are from another in that same perfection of love. In the eternal outpouring of love that is proper to the Trinitarian persons alone, they give all that they are to one another, the very substance of the godhead, in a communion of reciprocal love. They do so only ever in their pure actuality that is eternally undiminishable.[25]

Ad extra, this eternal activity of Trinitarian self-giving is reflected *imper-fectly and in a participated fashion* in the activities of creation and redemp-tion. In creation, God the Holy Trinity emanates or "pours out" being, from within the ontologically prior eternal emanation of the Word and spiration of the Spirit. All that comes into being from the Father comes to be as a gift of being, modeled after the pattern of the Son and Word. All created beings are in a sense the offspring of the Father, intelligible kinds, in whom he free-ly expresses his eternal wisdom. All created beings are made in the Spirit, as fruitful expressions of the Father's love, carried in the bosom of the Father, "nourished" and "nurtured" in being, as a gift of God's goodness. All of this is an expression of God's active potency, his eternal plenitude of power to create, by which he freely communicates the gift of being to that which is outside of himself. In this sense all things can be said to emanate or pour forth from God as a river emanates from its source or fontal origin.

In the Incarnation, however, God gives himself to humanity, or renders himself present, in the highest mode. He has the active power to do so in-

---

25. This is why the notion of eternal outpouring of divine life can be employed only meta-phorically of the inner life of the Trinity, not by proper attribution: material outpouring always implies some diminishment of the fontal source.

sofar as he can communicate all that he has as God to a rational nature that is created, in a mode proper to that created nature. The eternal processions of the Son and the Spirit are communicated to humanity, then, in the most perfect way possible, ontologically speaking, in the mystery of the Incarnation. God communicates the divine nature to us by taking on the lowliness of our human nature, so as to reveal to us, through his human life among us as man, the inner personal relations of the Trinity. The Father, for example, manifests the eternal generation of the Son to us in the hypostatic union, in which the Son becomes human in such a way that he is personally relative to the Father in all that he is as man.[26] This mystery is indicated already by Christ's miraculous conception in the womb of the Virgin Mary. He who has no paternal progenitor is, in his person, the transcendent Son, who proceeds eternally from the Father and is born in time of a human mother. This temporal generation, his human birth, is a created expression of his eternal immaterial generation from the Father.[27] As man, Jesus obeys the Father in all his human activities of knowledge and love, and so expresses his personal relation to the Father, a relation that characterizes him in his personal identity as Son. Thus, his actions and sufferings only ever reflect his derivation from the Father. Consequently, when he gives himself humanly to the Father's will in his human actions of obedience and love, he pours himself out humanly in his life, suffering, and death, so as to express, in a distinctively human mode, his eternal relativity to the Father and his shared will with the Father as God. Likewise, the Spirit is sent into the world by the Father upon and through his Word made flesh. The Spirit, who comes forth from the Word, reposes upon the human nature of Christ, fills him with grace, inspires his human actions of knowledge and love, and moves him from within to embrace the mystery of the Cross.[28] The Spirit is sent forth from the wounded side of Christ crucified at Golgotha, and from Christ resurrected on Easter night, and is poured out upon the Church and the world, as an expression of the inner love of the Father and the Son, who eternally spirate the Spirit, in a mutual act of self-giving love.

How can we better understand these mysteries, just alluded to? In the final sections of this chapter, I will focus briefly on two main mysteries, those of the Incarnation and the theandric activity of Christ, considering each as

26. See on this point, Aquinas, *ST* III, q. 2, a. 7.
27. *ST* III, q. 35, a. 5.
28. *ST* III, q 7, aa 1, 5, 6, 11, 13; q. 46, aa. 1 2.

expressions of the Trinitarian mystery of God. As we will see, the key contribution of the Thomistic tradition to the consideration of these mysteries
is found in the notion of the mutual compatibility and non-rivalry of causes
with regard to the divine nature and the human nature of Christ. The transcendence and immanence of the deity of Christ are such that his godhead
never stands in ontological opposition to his perfect humanity. Rather, the
two natures are coordinated hierarchically within one hypostatic subject,
and are symphonic in operation and mutual expression.

THE INCARNATION AS AN EXPRESSION
OF TRINITARIAN LIFE

In what way should we see the Incarnation as an expression of Trinitarian
life? Much can be said on this topic.[29] Here we will limit ourselves to a few
core observations. We should begin with one based on our considerations,
in part 2 of this book, regarding the divine nature. God is the transcendent
author of all that exists, and precisely on account of the fact that he is the
total cause of all that exists, he is also intimately present to all that exists.
As Augustine notes, God is more interior to us than our innermost being.[30]
God is not his creation, but his creation is utterly transparent to him in all
that it is, so that we can say that, in a sense, all things are within God and
God is within all things.[31] This unique kind of divine immanence, which
is not to be confused with pantheism, is applicable to God exclusively because of his unique form of transcendence and causality as Creator.

It follows from this idea of divine immanence, however, that God can
become human and exist as God in a human nature, without in any way going outside of himself and without being altered or reduced in his divine
nature (i.e., without expansion or retraction). This is the case first of all because he is already omnipresent to all that is, and can give of himself to creation without this implying any form of self-perfection or enrichment. Likewise, God can become human without altering or diminishing the formal
integrity of what it is to be human. Just as God sustains in being all that is

29. See the important study by Dominic Legge, *The Trinitarian Christology of St. Thomas Aquinas* (Oxford: Oxford University Press, 2017).

30. Augustine, *The Confessions*, 3.6.11. Aquinas develops his own reflection on this theme in
ST I, q. 8, aa. 3 and 4.

31. Or likewise as Dionysius claims in *The Divine Names*, c. 5, and as Aquinas notes approving-
ly in *ST* I, q. 4, a. 2, God is all things just insofar as he is the cause of all things.

human in us, as our Creator, so God can become one of us and be entirely
human, and even perfectly so, as our Redeemer.

The Incarnation takes place by means of that mystery that the Church
refers to as the hypostatic union. The hypostasis, or personal subject, of
the Son takes on a human nature, so that the divine and human natures of
Christ are united in his divine person, without any confusion of the two natures.[32] As a consequence of this mystery, the human nature, actions, words,
gestures, and sufferings of the man Jesus are those of the second person of
the Trinity. Jesus is God the Son. His actions as a man therefore manifest
and express his personal identity to us in a typically human way. Due to the
divine simplicity, all that is in the Son in virtue of his deity is present in the
Father and in the Spirit. This means that whatever Jesus does as God, he
necessarily does only ever with the Father and the Holy Spirit. This unity of
natural action takes place in a personal way, according the order of the Trinitarian processions of persons. That is to say, any action that the Son performs not only as man but also as God, he performs as the one who comes
forth from the Father, who acts in the Spirit, and who sends the Spirit. Consequently, the Incarnation by its very "structure" presupposes ontologically
and manifests externally the personal relationships Jesus has with the other
two persons of the Trinity.

In light of this claim, how might we understand the relation of the two
natures of Christ? For the purposes of our discussion here, the main thing
we should note is that all that the human nature of Jesus is, is the "instrument" of his divinity. It is an instrument, first, because it is ontologically dependent upon and inferior to his deity, and thus subordinate to it. However,
as Aquinas notes, the instrumentality in question is entirely unique, because
the person of the Word subsists in human nature and so the human nature
is conjoined to the Word personally. (It is not "something else" external to
the Word, as an instrumental tool is external to a human person).[33] Furthermore, the instrument in question is spiritual in nature, so that God express-

---

32. It is in this sense that we can speak of Christ as a composite person, subsisting in two
natures. See Aquinas, *ST* III, q. 2, a. 4: "The Person or hypostasis of Christ may be viewed in two
ways. First as it is in itself, and thus it is altogether simple, even as the Nature of the Word. Secondly, in the aspect of person or hypostasis to which it belongs to subsist in a nature; and thus the
Person of Christ subsists in two natures. Hence though there is one subsisting being in Him, yet
there are different aspects of subsistence, and hence He is said to be a composite person, insomuch
as one being subsists in two."

33. *ST* III, q. 19, a. 1, corp. and ad 2

es *himself* to us precisely in what is most genuinely human *in us*, human actions of knowledge and love.[34] As a consequence, God the Son expresses himself personally and acts divinely through the medium of his humanity. When the Son acts as man, he expresses his filial identity as God.[35] He does so by acting simultaneously as one who is truly God and truly human. This does not mean that his humanity is unreal, artificial, or that it functions like a marionette. On the contrary, the Incarnate Word is utterly humane in his way of being personal toward us, expressing himself in integral historical actions of knowledge and love. When Jesus learns, reflects, makes decisions, communicates, or initiates acts of compassion, it is the Son who acts. The filial mode in which he is human manifests the filial mode in which he is God, since all he does and suffers as a subject of history indicates that he is one who is always "from" the Father, and "for" him. However, while being among us as one who is truly human, he is also the most human. As man, he is filled with the grace of the Holy Spirit, so that precisely in his unique perfection *as man* he might manifest his identity and perfection as God.

It follows from this that the action of Jesus in his historical life is Trinitarian in form. In his preaching, physical gestures (like walking or sleeping), in his prayer, and in his free acceptance of suffering and death, he reveals himself as one who is from the Father, sent into the world to redeem us. The paternity of the Father therefore overshadows all that Jesus is and does as man. All that Jesus does, he does for the Father. Likewise, in his authoritative teaching and miracles he manifests that he is Lord, who is one with the Father from before the foundation of the world. Even when Christ is crucified, it is the Lord who is crucified: "[they] crucified the Lord of glory" (1 Cor 2:8); "When you have lifted up the Son of Man, then you will know that I Am" (Jn 8:28). Jesus also possesses in himself the plenitude of the Spirit, which can be considered in two ways, according to his divine person and according to his human nature. As the Son and Word, Jesus possesses the Spirit from the Father and is the source of the Spirit, in both his eternal procession and temporal mission. As man, Jesus is filled with the Spirit, who reposes upon him, and who anoints him as messiah (Is 61:1; Lk 4:18). This means that Jesus receives in his human nature and consciousness a plenitude of grace, given to him by the Spirit, and is led by the Spirit throughout

---

34. *ST* III, q. 19, a. 1, ad 1.
35. I have explored this theme at greater length in *The Incarnate Lord*, chaps. 1 and 5.

his human life.[36] It also means that he can send the Spirit upon the Church, not only in virtue of his deity, as the Son from whom the Spirit proceeds, but also in virtue of his humanity, instrumentally, since he wills as man, in his human mind and heart, to send the Spirit upon his disciples (Jn 16:7).

THE HUMAN KNOWLEDGE AND ACTION OF CHRIST AS REVELATION OF THE TRINITY

Based on apostolic teaching, the Catholic Church confesses not only that Jesus Christ is true God and true man (having in himself two distinct and united natures) but also that he has two wills and operative activities, that of his deity and that of his humanity. When Jesus performs miracles, for example, he does so by the power of God that resides in him, a power he possesses from the Father and with the Father, and that he communicates to the Holy Spirit. However, he also performs miracles as one who is human, intending them in his human mind and heart, expressing is desire in his physical gestures and sensate words, as when he touches a blind man, speaks to him, and so heals him.

It is important to understand the non-competitive nature of these two "forms" of operation in Christ, the divine and the human. Jesus of Nazareth is a genuinely free human being, and as such is subject to ordinary activities of reflection, psychological maturation, progressive learning, thinking and speaking in the language and symbols of a given culture, making new decisions and choices.[37] His divine nature and its activity do not in any way suppress or destroy any of these natural human activities. On the contrary, they elevate and ennoble such activities so that they are perfectly human. God is the most human of us all, in all his developmental stages of life and death. This perfection of Jesus' human acts is made possible especially due to the created grace that inundates his human soul. As the Son of God, Jesus possesses a plenitude of grace in his soul, which is fitting for several reasons.[38] First, it is fitting due to the proximity of his human nature to the divine source of grace: his is the humanity of God. Second, he possesses this

---

36. See on this point, Legge, *The Trinitarian Christology of St. Thomas Aquinas*, 187–210.
37. See the more developed argument in White, "The Infused Science of Christ."
38. See Aquinas, *ST* I, q. 7, a. 1, and q. 8, a. 1. I have changed slightly the order of Aquinas's presentation in my own, to emphasize the universal and ecclesial dimension of the act of self-offering on the part of Christ.

plenitude on behalf of others: Christ is the New Adam, the exemplar of our "re-creation" in grace, from whom we receive all grace. "From his fullness have we all received, grace upon grace" (Jn 1:16). "Now you are the body of Christ and individually members of it" (1 Cor 12:27). Third, the human spiritual faculties of intellect and will in Christ must be enlightened and elevated so that the Son of God as man may understand and desire the will of the Father, in an especial way, as a constitutive feature of his visible mission among us. His human activities of understanding and willing are inspired from within by the divine wisdom and will, subordinate to them, and expressive of them. In this way Jesus as man can understand the saving design of God and act in accord with it. In doing so he reveals to us who God is, in a genuinely human way, by his human actions and sufferings, in and through his life, death, and resurrection. He can do all this only because his human soul is filled with grace, his intellect is illumined with a fullness of wisdom, and his human heart is enlivened by a plenitude of charity.

We can develop this idea briefly by considering, in turn, how Jesus' human knowledge, his human action, and his emotional and bodily endurance are each expressive of, or affected by, his filial identity and the mystery of the Trinity.

The Human Knowledge of Christ

Jesus' human knowledge is naturally developmental, as we have said, and is exerted and expressed in a given cultural setting, language, time, and place. Jesus' self-awareness developed from infancy to childhood, from adolescence to adulthood, and throughout the course of his adult life. At the same time, by grace, Jesus was humanly conscious of the Father, aware of his presence, and aware of his profound union with the Father, from whom he was sent into the world.[39] He would come to articulate this in inspired and

---

39. See, in this respect, the 1985 document of the International Theological Commission, *The Consciousness of Christ Concerning Himself and His Mission* (available online at https://www.vatican.va/roman_curia/congregations/cfaith/cti_documents/rc_cti_1985_coscienzagesu_en.html), which maintains as normative for Catholic theology four propositions concerning Christ's human consciousness: (1) "The life of Jesus testifies to his consciousness of a filial relationship with the Father." (2) "Jesus was aware of the purpose of his mission: to announce the Kingdom of God and make it present in his own Person, in his actions, and in his words, so that the world would become reconciled with God and renewed. He freely accepted the Father's will: to give his own life for the salvation of all mankind. He knew the Father had sent him to serve and to give his life 'for many' (Mk 14:24)." (3) "To realize his salvific mission, Jesus wanted to unite men with the coming Kingdom and to gather them around himself. With this end before him, he did

successively profound ways in the course of his ministry and would enact this union with the Father in his teaching, parables, and miracles as well as in his embrace of death at the hands of men, for the sake of the Father, and moved by his love for the human race. Jesus was also conscious, therefore, of his unique filial identity as the Son of God, and of his own pre-existence and divine status as Lord. He could express in a human way that he had come into the world to reveal the mystery of the Father and, in doing so, simultaneously make manifest his own authority and Lordship, as the Son sent from the Father. Jesus is also conscious of the Holy Spirit, who is present in his public ministry and whom Christ speaks of repeatedly as a person and in an interpersonal sense. He is aware as man that he is filled with the Spirit, who rests upon him and anoints him with grace. Jesus is conscious of being moved from within by the Spirit, and also knows that he will send the Spirit upon the world.[40] Indeed, he shows us that he has come into the world first and foremost precisely in order to send the Spirit upon the world, who will in turn make of human beings adopted children of the Father, in the Son.[41]

The Human Action of Christ

Jesus Christ also reveals the Trinity through his free actions as a man. This is the case first and foremost because of his obedience to the Father. The obedience of Jesus pertains to him uniquely in virtue of his human nature, not his divine nature.[42] This must be the case if there is in the Holy Trinity only one nature and one will, which is proper to the Father, Son, and Holy

---

certain definite acts that, if taken altogether, can only be explained as a preparation for the Church, which will be definitively constituted at the time of the Easter and Pentecost events. It is therefore to be affirmed of necessity that Jesus willed the foundation of the Church." (4) "The consciousness that Christ had of being the Father's emissary to save the world and to bring all mankind together in God's people involves, in a mysterious way, a love for all mankind so much so that we may all say: 'The Son of God loved me and gave himself up for me' (Gal 2:20)." This fourth proposition seemingly underscores the universality of Christ's soteriological intention.

40. On the consciousness of Christ, see Bernard Lonergan, *The Ontological and Psychological Constitution of Christ*, vol. 7 of *Collected Works* (Toronto: University of Toronto Press, 2002); Thomas Joseph White, "Dyotheletism and the Instrumental Human Consciousness of Jesus," *Pro Ecclesia* 17, no. 4 (2008): 396–422.

41. This interpretation of Aquinas is based on the idea that the essence of the New Law is the gift of the Holy Spirit. See *ST* I-II, q. 106, a. 1, which in turn refers to Rom 8 and Augustine's interpretation of Paul in *On the Spirit and the Letter*, c. 24.

42. See the helpful analysis of this issue by Guy Mansini, "Can Humility and Obedience be Trinitarian Realities?," in *Thomas Aquinas and Karl Barth, An Unofficial Catholic-Protestant Ecumenical Dialogue*, ed. B. L. McCormack and T. J. White (Grand Rapids, Mich.: Eerdmans, 2013), 71–98.

Spirit. Obedience implies a subordination of one will to another, and therefore a duality of wills and a distinction of voluntary properties. Such a distinction cannot exist between persons of the Holy Trinity, simply because the divine persons share identically and equally in the one nature and will of God. It is true to say, then, that all that the eternal Son wills as Lord, he wills from the Father, and with the Father, and so in a distinctly filial mode, but that he also does so as one who is truly God, and thus one in being and will with the Father.[43] Consequently, when Jesus wills to obey the Father, he does so not in his divine nature, but specifically as man, in his human voluntary capacity, which is subordinate to the will of God. This being said, the human acts of obedience of the Son do reveal to us something about the mystery of the persons of the Holy Trinity. By his human actions of deference to the Father's commands, the Son manifests in a human way that he is one sent by the Father, and this sending, as we have seen, has its deepest foundation in the eternal processions of the persons.[44] Just because the Son is eternally from the Father, he can be sent by the Father into the world, to manifest the Father. He does this in his visible mission as man by carrying out his mission in obedience to the Father. He does so freely, as one like us in all things but sin.

By extension, we also can and must say that Jesus obeys himself as God, in the sense that he subordinates his human action to the divine will that is present within, which he is humanly conscious of as his own divine will that he shares with the Father. He also obeys the Holy Spirit, who is present in him, and who moves him as man to surrender joyfully to the will of God. In a mysterious way then, the human activity of the Lord manifests to us that

---

43. See Aquinas, *SCG* IV, c. 8: "The saying also, then, 'the Son cannot do anything of Himself,' (Jn 5:19) does not point to any weakness of action in the Son. But, because for God to act is not other than to be, and His action is not other than His essence, as was proved above, so one says that the Son cannot act from Himself but only from the Father, just as He is not able to be from Himself but only from the Father. For, if He were from Himself, He would no longer be the Son. Therefore, just as the Son cannot not be the Son, so neither can He act of Himself. However, because the Son receives the same nature as the Father and, consequently, the same power, although the Son neither is of Himself nor operates of Himself, He nevertheless is through Himself and operates through Himself, since just as He is through His own nature received from the Father, so He operates through His own nature received from the Father. Hence, after our Lord had said: 'the Son cannot do anything of Himself,' to show that, although the Son does not operate of Himself, He does operate through Himself, He adds: 'Whatever He does'—namely, the Father—'these the Son does likewise.'" *Summa Contra Gentiles* IV, trans. C. O'Neil (Garden City, N.Y.: Doubleday, 1955).

44. I have explored this idea in greater detail in *The Incarnate Lord*, chap. 6.

he is truly the Son, one who is from the Father in all that he is, and one who has come into the world to send us the Spirit that he shares with the Father. Christ's human activities of love for the Father inform all that he does in his visible mission: his preaching of the kingdom of God, forgiveness of sins and inclusion of sinners, his poor and itinerant way of life, his teaching and miracles, his formation of the apostles and institution of the sacraments: all of these manifest his fundamental desire to reveal the Father, to send the Spirit, and to save the human race.

Emotional and Bodily Endurance

Jesus' emotional and bodily endurance in carrying out his divine mission also manifests his filial identity and therefore the mystery of the Trinity. This occurs in a variety of ways. The first is by way of simple ontological presence. The Lord's being among us as a human being instantiates a new and perpetual presence of God in history, in holiness and mysterious hiddenness. The Son of God is present in the universe as one who is human, and where he is present, so too the Father and the Spirit are also rendered present, in a distinctive, new way. "He who has seen me has seen the Father" (Jn 14:9). Those who come into his presence, both then and now, grasp this: "Depart from me, for I am a sinful man, O Lord" (Lk 5:8). It is in this sense that his body is a new and greater temple, the Holy of Holies: wherever Jesus Christ is, God is manifest (Jn 2:19–21; Heb 10:19–20). Therefore, even if Jesus sleeps in a boat, or walks on the shores of Galilee, in these most ordinary instances of human life, he renders God present among us in a most extraordinary fashion.

Likewise, if Jesus freely acts in a bodily way, for example, through physical gestures, this also reveals his action as the Son of God, and, by consequence, it indirectly signals the commandment of the Father and the activity of the Holy Spirit moving him from within. For example, we are told by Luke that Jesus, foreseeing his eventual rejection and execution by the authorities of Israel, "set his face to go to Jerusalem" (Lk 9:51). Mark recounts that he walked ahead of his apostles on the road to the city, because they were afraid (Mk 10:32). These events manifest, however discreetly and indirectly, Christ's filial consciousness, his awareness of his mission, and the courage and resolve of his inner life of charity, in which he seeks placidly to accomplish the Father's will. The plenitude of the Father's life has been communicated to the Son, and the Son wishes to communicate to us a share in this divine life, a reality instantiated even in his physical gestures and bodily actions.

Jesus' suffering and emotional vulnerability are also indicative of his filial identity insofar as freely, out of love, he makes himself subject to suffering and even in suffering makes use of the vulnerability he incurs to manifest more perfectly his love for the Father. Already Jesus' simplicity of life and itinerant poverty demonstrate that he is utterly for the Father, and centered on his mission, even in his body and passions.[45] However, in accepting the betrayal of a trusted friend, and the abandonment of his fearful disciples, rejection by many of his own his people, civic injustice, public humiliation and ridicule, physical torment, and bodily execution, Christ manifests in all this his patient, profound love for the human race, grounded in a yet deeper love for the Father, and a desire to fulfill the designs of God and accomplish the redemption of the world.[46] Because the intensity of his suffering is so great, and because it is borne out of filial love, Christ's suffering also manifests the intensity of his love and the truth of his identity as the Lord, present among us, who remains one with the Father, even in his passion. All of this suggests that the Trinity can be revealed in a particularly profound way in and through the passion, death, and resurrection of Christ. This is a topic we will turn to in the final chapter of this book.

CONCLUSION

In this chapter I have noted that there exists in modern theology a prevalent trend that sees the human actions of obedience or loving self-surrender in Jesus Christ as indicative of his personal relation to the Father. However, it does so while deemphasizing those elements of the Church's teaching tradition that pertain to the two wills and activities of Christ, along with those that pertain to his divine nature and human nature respectively. The claim some theologians make is that this conciliar tradition forms an impasse,

---

45. See the analysis of Aquinas, ST III, q. 40, as associated with qq. 43 and 45.

46. The Johannine affirmation of this paternal origin of Christ's self-offering is clear. Jn 10:17–18: "For this reason the Father loves me, because I lay down my life, that I may take it again. No one takes it from me, but I lay it down of my own accord. I have power to lay it down, and I have power to take it again; this charge I have received from my Father." Jn 6:40: "For this is the will of my Father, that everyone who sees the Son and believes in him should have eternal life; and I will raise him up at the last day."

since it suggests either that the divine will of Jesus overwhelms his human will (making it unreal) or that his human will conceals his divine will from us (so that Christ's human action has nothing to do with the Father's will and therefore obscures his divinity problematically). As our alternative account suggests, however, both of these objections rest upon questionable assumptions. In fact, the divine will of Christ respects and ennobles his human will, just as his divine nature respects and ennobles his human nature. Indeed, we can go further and say that there is a need for a doctrine of the unicity of the divine nature and will of Christ as God precisely so as to preserve an authentic sense of the divine love manifest in his human activities as man. For only if Jesus is one in nature and will with the Father and the Spirit as God can he possess in himself the perfection of divine love. Likewise, it is only in this case that his human activity becomes decipherable as manifesting truly the perfect love of God present within him. By contrast, if he is eternally subordinate to the Father in virtue of some kind of divine obedience, then his nature and qualities as Son must be in some real sense distinct from those of the Father and the Spirit. In such a case it would be not the divine love of the Father and the Spirit that we possess in Christ, as truly manifest in his human activity, but a surrogate or external second-order love other than that of the Father. If we affirm instead, with the patristic tradition, that the human obedience of Christ is proper to him as man, not as God, we should still affirm that it manifests to us his filial identity. Christ's obedience to the Father stems from his human love for the Father, and is therefore distinct from the divine will he possesses as God, with the Father and from the Father. Precisely because they are distinctly human, however, this love and obedience of Christ are subordinate to the divine will within him, which he receives from the Father. Therefore, they can reveal to us in a genuinely human way what the Son truly wills with the Father, in virtue of their shared divine life. Otherwise said, only because the Son is God can we discover in him that which the Father wills, since he has this same divine will in him from the Father. And only because the Son is man can his human actions of willing communicate and manifest this divine will to us, in a specifically human way. It is especially in this sense that Jesus is the human icon of the Father, and his "exegete" or interpreter: because he can make clear to us who the Father is, and he does so in his very action, decision making, and freely undertaken suffering as man.

34

The Revelation of the Trinity in the Crucifixion and Resurrection of Christ

INTRODUCTION

We can conclude our study of the revelation of the Trinity in the economy with a consideration of the mysteries of the passion, death, and resurrection of Christ, as well as his sending of the Holy Spirit upon the Church and the world. How do these mysteries unveil to us the inner life of God as Father, Son, and Holy Spirit? In this final chapter we will sketch out suggestive responses to this question by considering in turn various mysteries, or distinct "dimensions" of the one paschal mystery. Beginning with Christ's agony in the Garden of Gethsemane, we will then consider his suffering and crucifixion, his death and descent into hell, his bodily resurrection and exaltation to "the right hand of God" (Heb 10:12; Acts 7:55), and his sending of the Holy Spirit. In each of these moments we can perceive the manifestation of the relationship of the Father, Son, and Holy Spirit, evinced in the human nature of the Son, through his human action, free acceptance of suffering, subjection to death, and filial mode of glorification.

THE GARDEN OF GETHSEMANE: THE SON'S REVELATION OF THE TRINITY IN HIS HUMAN ACCEPTANCE OF THE PASSION

In the synoptic gospels, the events of the Garden of Gethsemane are a kind of advent story for the passion narrative. Jesus, expecting and awaiting his forthcoming suffering, experiences natural repulsion in the face of torture

and death, and prays to the Father, accepting his redemptive mission with
obedience, lowliness of heart, and love. The account of Mark's Gospel underscores Christ's internal agony. Mark 14:32–36:

And they went to a place which was called Gethsem'ane; and he said to his disciples, "Sit here, while I pray." And he took with him Peter and James and John, and
began to be greatly distressed and troubled. And he said to them, "My soul is very
sorrowful, even to death; remain here, and watch." And going a little farther, he fell
on the ground and prayed that, if it were possible, the hour might pass from him.
And he said, "Abba, Father, all things are possible to thee; remove this cup from
me; yet not what I will, but what thou wilt."

Jesus is left alone as his closest disciples fall asleep. "'Simon, are you asleep?
Could you not watch one hour? Watch and pray that you may not enter
into temptation; the spirit indeed is willing, but the flesh is weak'" (Mk
14:37–38).

Matthew and Luke provide similar accounts (Mt 26:36–46; Lk 22:40–
46), though some manuscript traditions of Luke depict an angel of consolation appearing to Christ as he prays, while he sweats blood in agony
(Lk 22:43–44). This passage is traditionally taken to indicate a supernatural
mystery of spiritual agony that takes place in the heart and mind of Jesus as
he knowingly confronts the mystery of iniquity, and prepares for the crucifixion. John's Gospel contains no account of Christ's agony in the garden,
but provides a parallel passage in John 12:27–28, where Jesus enters into his
"hour" of suffering:[1] "'Now is my soul troubled. And what shall I say? 'Father, save me from this hour'? No, for this purpose I have come to this hour.
Father, glorify thy name.' Then a voice came from heaven, 'I have glorified
it, and I will glorify it again.'" John acknowledges that the soul of Jesus is
troubled in the face of death, but he depicts the agony in a less developmental way. Jesus does not first experience the natural revulsion at death (as is
seemingly the case in Matthew or Mark) or supernatural agony in the face of
evil (as in Luke) and then subsequently resolve these experiences through
an act of human resolution. Rather, the troubling of his soul is genuine but
also always already assimilated into a deeper intention that structures his life
and mission. He has come into the world to manifest the Father's love for
the world, by laying down his life (Jn 3:16; 10:17) despite the agony, and the
Father already bears witness to him.[2]

---

1. Cf. Jn 12:23: "The hour has come that the Son of man should be glorified."
2. For an extensive analysis of the synoptic accounts of the prayer of Christ in the garden of

We can discern commonalities amid the diverse depictions of Mark, Luke, and John. Jesus suffers from a natural revulsion in the face of death, but is also able humanly, without sin, to assimilate this revulsion into a deeper, more encompassing act of resolution. Aquinas follows Maximus the Confessor and John Damascene in distinguishing here the "will as natural" and the "will as reasonable."[3] In the face of a human trial, such as impending battle or submission to surgery, a person will typically feel a natural inclination to turn away, due to the moral or natural evil that one is likely to encounter in the ensuing trial. However, the notion of the "will as reasonable" indicates one's moral capacity to surmount natural repulsion in order to choose freely the rational good. The soldier may decide freely to go into battle or the patient may decide freely to submit to a reasonable medical procedure, despite its seriousness. The natural inclination to avoid death exists not only in our reason, but also in our animal sensibility. Therefore, Aquinas further distinguishes the natural repulsions of sensibility from the natural disinclinations of reason.[4] In effect, it is one thing for Christ to suffer sensible fear or dread in his emotional life, and another for him to undergo the natural revulsion of his will in the face of death.

We can further qualify this account of Christ's sinless natural revulsion if we take to heart the idea from Luke that there is a supernatural "color" to Christ's human suffering in Gethsemane. This occurs in virtue of his heightened human awareness of the gravity of what he is about to undergo. Not only is he aware by prophetic foreknowledge of the mystery of the crucifixion, and the mode of his torture and execution, he is also aware of the gravity of the act, since he is himself the innocent author of life (Acts 3:15), who is falling into the hands of sinners who will put him to death. Privileged knowledge of the objective reality of what is transpiring places Christ in a deep human solitude, alone with the Father and the Holy Spirit, in the face of his forthcoming betrayal, abandonment, rejection, revilement, and death. Aquinas notes that Christ suffers spiritually in the passion in the heights of

---

Gethsemane, see Raymond E. Brown, *The Death of the Messiah from Gethsemane to the Grave*, vol. 1, *A Commentary on the Passion Narratives in the Four Gospels* (New York: Doubleday, 1993), 110–234.

3. See *ST* III, q. 18, a. 3, where Aquinas references John Damascene's *Exposition on the Orthodox Faith* 2, c. 22. Damascene in turn seems influenced here by Maximus, *Dial. cum Pyrrh.* and *Epist. 1 ad Marin.* For a helpful study of Aquinas on the Garden of Gethsemane, see Paul Gondreau, "St. Thomas Aquinas, the Communication of Idioms, and the Suffering of Christ in the Garden of Gethsemane," in Keating and White, *Divine Impassibility and the Mystery of Human Suffering*, 214–45.

4. *ST* III, q. 19, a. 2.

his intellect and will, since he has a uniquely intensive and extensive knowledge of human sinfulness, and since he grieves for human sin with a charity of contrition which is the most intense that has ever been.[5] Since Christ enters into his "hour" of trial at Gethsemane in prayer to the Father, it is reasonable to conclude that he also enters here into a new stage of deliberate confrontation with human sinfulness and with the gravity of spiritual evil. His road to victory passes through the agony of obedience unto death, and in the face of this task, he sweats blood.

How is this initial moment of the passion indicative of the mystery of the Holy Trinity? The key to an orthodox answer depends upon the acknowledgement of the revealed deposit of faith under the heading of two signature teachings of the Third Council of Constantinople: the affirmation of the unity of the divine will of the Trinitarian persons, and the affirmation of the distinction of two wills in Christ, divine and human. We should recall in light of these teachings that Jesus Christ as man suffers in his human mind and heart in ways we have just indicated. However, as Lord, as Son and Word of the Father, he also possesses in himself the plenitude of the divine nature. Consequently, he also has, as Lord, the divine will and power of God residing in him, even as he eternally receives all that he has and is from the Father.

From this we can draw three conclusions. First, Jesus' human will is fully subordinate to the divine will, so that his eventual free embrace of human suffering, even in the face of agony, is humanly indicative of the divine will. In embracing the crucifixion, he carries out the will of God.

Second, this will of God is not impersonal but only ever intra-Trinitarian. It is the Father who "so loved the world that he gave his only Son" (Jn 3:16), and it is due to the Father's word and will that Jesus chooses in Gethsemane to suffer the foreseen passion. "Father ... remove this cup from me; yet not what I will, but what thou wilt" (Mk 14:36). Consequently, all that Christ embraces here manifests the Father, from whom he proceeds, and who has sent him into the world. As Son and Lord, Jesus also possesses this same divine activity of willing. What the Father wills from all eternity, the Son wills from all eternity. This means that in some real sense, Jesus also "obeys himself." He chooses freely as man to do that which is in accord with his own

---

5. *ST* III, q. 46, a. 7. I have given more extensive consideration to this aspect of the passion in *The Incarnate Lord*, chap. 7.

divine wisdom and intent, for the redemption of the human race.[6] This human activity is also interpersonal: the Son wills all that God wills, but only ever as one who receives all that he is from the Father, as one who has come into the world both to receive and to communicate the Spirit. Therefore, his human obedience takes on a filial mode of expression. Because this obedience is human, it pertains to Jesus' created human nature, not to his divine nature as such, but because it is the human obedience of one who is the Son of God, it is expressive of his person. When Jesus obeys as man, his action is indicative of his Sonship, his personal origin in the Father, and of the divine will he possesses from the Father. In this sense, as personal activity, all his human activity manifests the eternal relations of the persons and the order of the processions. The Son even in his distinctively human form of life is always "from" the Father and "for" the Spirit, in all he says, does, and suffers as man. In accepting suffering freely out of charity on behalf of the human race, Jesus manifests that he is sent by the Father, and that he is intending to send the Spirit upon humanity.

Third, then, Jesus' human obedience is indicative of his relation to the Holy Spirit, which also must be considered in light of the two natures of Christ. As Son and Lord, Jesus is the principle of the Spirit, who proceeds eternally from both him and the Father, and whom they together send on mission into the world. As man, however, Jesus possesses a created human nature that is subject to the Spirit. The Spirit inundates him with the grace of holiness and moves him in accord with the divine will. Therefore, his human will is subordinate to the will of the Holy Spirit.[7] In Gethsemane and

---

6. See the analysis of Aquinas in *ST* III, q. 20, a. 2: "... to be master or servant is attributed to a person or hypostasis according to a nature. Hence when it is said that Christ is the master or servant of Himself, or that the Word of God is the Master of the Man Christ, this may be understood in two ways. First, so that this is understood to be said by reason of another hypostasis or person, as if there was the person of the Word of God ruling and the person of the man serving; and this is the heresy of Nestorius.... Secondly, it may be understood of the diversity of natures in the one person or hypostasis. And thus we may say that in one of them, in which He agrees with the Father, He presides and rules together with the Father; and in the other nature, in which He agrees with us, He is subject and serves.... Yet it must be borne in mind that since this name 'Christ' is the name of a Person, even as the name 'Son,' those things can be predicated essentially and absolutely of Christ which belong to Him by reason of the Person, Which is eternal; and especially those relations which seem more properly to pertain to the Person or the hypostasis. But whatever pertains to Him in His human nature is rather to be attributed to Him with a qualification; so that we say that Christ is simply greatest, Lord, Ruler, whereas to be subject or servant or less is to be attributed to Him with the qualification, in [virtue of] His human nature."

7. *ST* III, q. 7, aa. 1 and 5; q. 32, aa. 1–3.

in the passion and crucifixion, Jesus is also obeying the interior movements of the Holy Spirit and is receiving and manifesting his gifts.[8] When the Son obeys as man, he does so as a human being acting under the movement of the Holy Spirit, as one who is filled with the grace of the Spirit in his human soul.[9] And he carries out his mission in view of the communication of the Spirit, whose mission reflects the order of the processions. Just as the Father and the Son eternally communicate the godhead to the Spirit, so the Father and the Son send forth the Holy Spirit into the world as one who proceeds from each of them. The Spirit's visible mission, in which he comes forth from the Cross of the Son, as the expression of the love and mutual gift of the Father and the Son, is a temporal manifestation of the eternal origin of processions. Gethsemane is the gate of entry that Jesus goes through, in an agony of love, whereby he initiates meritoriously this new communication of Trinitarian life to the world.

SUFFERING AND CRUCIFIXION

Atonement as Trinitarian Revelation

The atonement is that process by which Christ merits for the human race the forgiveness of sins, filial adoption, and participation in divine life. He does this in virtue of his earthly obedience as man, in all that he does and suffers, culminating in the free acceptance of his death.[10] This obedience is impetrative or intercessory. The Letter to the Hebrews tells us that Christ acted as our "high priest" and interceded with "loud cries and tears" for our salvation (Heb 5:5–7). In Mark 10:45 Christ self-identifies as the "Son of

8. When we say that Jesus receives his grace from the Holy Spirit, we do so by way of appropriation. The three persons of the Trinity are the origin of the created grace of the human soul of the Son. But it is appropriate to attribute this authorship of grace to the Spirit, as the scriptures frequently do, precisely because the Spirit is the "uncreated gift" of the Father and Son, the spirated person of their eternal love, who is behind the "created gift" of grace that comes from the Father and the Son "in" their Spirit. See, on this point, *ST* I, q. 37, a. 1, and *ST* III, q. 32, a. 1.

9. See the helpful analysis of Legge, *The Trinitarian Christology of St. Thomas Aquinas*, 201–10.

10. Aquinas argues in multiple texts that all of the actions and sufferings of Christ's life are redemptive of the human race, even though it is also fitting that the passion should be especially intensively meritorious in this respect, as a kind of summit or apex of the mystery of the redemption. See, in this respect, *ST* III, q. 48, a. 6 where he states that "all Christ's actions and sufferings operate instrumentally in virtue of His Godhead for the salvation of men," and *ST* III, q. 46, aa. 1–4, where he argues that God willed that Christ fittingly suffer the mystery of the passion for our sake. See, on these matters, Richard Schenk, "*Omnis Christi actio nostra est instructio.* The Deeds and Sayings of Jesus as Revelation in the View of Aquinas," in *La doctrine de la révélation divine de saint Thomas d'Aquin, Studi Tomistici* 37 (Vatican City: Libreria Editrice Vaticana, 1990), 104–31.

Man" who "give[s] his life as a ransom for many," arguably a reference both
to Daniel 7, where the messianic Son of Man is exalted and served by the
gentile nations, and Isaiah 53, where the Suffering Servant gives his life as a
ransom for many. The theology here is paradoxical. The Son of Man did not
come to be served in fact, but to serve. It is the Suffering Servant in the crucifixion who is to be the exalted Christ and Lord, a theology we also find in
Paul in Philippians 2:6–9: "… who though he was in the form of God, did
not count equality with God a thing to be grasped, but emptied himself,
taking the form of a servant, being born in the likeness of men. And being found in human form he humbled himself and became obedient unto
death, even death on a cross. Therefore, God has highly exalted him …."

If we seek to understand the merit of Christ in his passion and death, we
can account for it in three distinct ways, by speaking, respectively, of that
which is *foundational, formal,* and *intensive*.[11] The foundation of the merit of
Christ crucified is hypostatic or personal. Who is subject to suffering and
crucifixion? Who is it that freely offers his life to the Father in charity, as
reparation for the sins of the human race? The person in question is divine,
the one who is Lord, eternal Son and Word of the Father. Because of the
hypostatic union, by which a human nature is united to the divine nature
(without confusion) in the person of the Son, there accrues to the human
nature of Jesus an infinite dignity. His is the human body and soul of God.
Consequently, when he is crucified it is God who is crucified, and when he
offers his human life to the Father, it is God the Son who offers his human
life to the Father. The infinite dignity of the self-offering of Christ in his passion and death stems from this foundation, which undergirds or colors all
that he does and suffers as man.

The formal principle of the merit of Christ, that which is essential to
the atonement per se, is his human charity, the free offering he makes of
himself to the Father as a human being, for the sake of others, which stems
from love. Here Aquinas notes that the love and obedience in question are
substitutionary, not in the sense that Christ is deemed guilty so as to bear
the punishments of the human race, but in the sense that he substitutes his
righteousness for the unrighteousness of the human race, his love and obedience for their lack thereof.[12] This is not something that remains purely ex-

11. This formulation stems from my own interpretation of *ST* III, q. 48, a. 2.

12. *ST* III, q. 48, a. 2: "He properly atones for an offense who offers something which the
offended one loves equally, or even more than he detested the offense. But by suffering out of love

trinsic to the human race, because Christ merits grace for others and shares it with them in the economy of the resurrection, the sending of the Holy Spirit, and the sacramental life of the Church. In this sense, his grace and merit are "capital": he is, as Paul notes, the head of the members of his body, who communicates to them and shares with them his own life of transformative grace.[13] Christ in fact possesses a fullness of grace, and from him all others receive (Jn 1:14, 16), so that we can say that his action as man is the efficient cause of the justification and sanctification of all others. Because his action is human, sinless, and full of grace, it is humanly meritorious on behalf of other fellow members of the human race. Because his action is that of one who is God (the fundamental principle noted above), it is of an infinite value, and his impetration for human beings is of such a depth as to be unfathomable, able to atone for the sins of all human persons, for all time.[14]

The intensive principle of Christ's merit stems from the intensity of his freely embraced suffering. He not only gave his life out of love for the Father and the human race, but he gave it in such a way as to manifest both the gravity of human sin and the intensity of divine love. Christ's death entailed intense spiritual, emotional, and bodily suffering, and was incurred by one

---

and obedience, Christ gave more to God than was required to compensate for the offense of the whole human race. First of all, because of the exceeding charity from which He suffered; secondly, on account of the dignity of His life which He laid down in atonement, for it was the life of one who was God and man; thirdly, on account of the extent of the Passion, and the greatness of the grief endured (cf. *ST* III, q. 46, a. 6). And therefore Christ's Passion was not only a sufficient but a superabundant atonement for the sins of the human race; according to 1 Jn 2:2: 'He is the propitiation for our sins: and not for ours only, but also for those of the whole world.'"

13. *ST* III, q. 48, a. 2, ad 1: "The head and members are as one mystic person; and therefore Christ's satisfaction belongs to all the faithful as being His members." See also *ST* III, q. 8, aa. 1–2.

14. We should note that this does not mean that God "needs" the atonement of Christ to propitiate his justice, as if he would otherwise be unable to forgive sins. Aquinas argues, on the contrary, that God could have forgiven sins only from a wellspring of mercy without a just redeemer acting as a principle of reconciliation. However, he also argues that the latter reality is not only more just, but also more merciful, because it allows God to communicate the very righteousness of Christ to human beings so as to transform them inwardly (in history and eschatologically) in accord with the justification of Christ. The argument for this mode of salvation, then, is one of fittingness, or wisdom, goodness, and beauty, not strict necessity. See *ST* III, q. 46, aa. 1–3, esp. a. 1, ad 3: "That man should be delivered by Christ's Passion was in keeping with both His mercy and His justice. With His justice, because by His Passion Christ made satisfaction for the sin of the human race; and so man was set free by Christ's justice: and with His mercy, for since man of himself could not atone for the sin of all human nature, God gave him His Son to atone for him, according to Rom. 3:24–25: 'Being justified freely by His grace, through the redemption that is in Christ Jesus, whom God hath proposed to be a propitiation, through faith in His blood.' And this came of more copious mercy than if He had forgiven sins without satisfaction. Hence it is said (Eph. 2:4): 'God, who is rich in mercy, for His exceeding charity wherewith He loved us, even when we were dead in sins, hath quickened us together in Christ.'" (Trans slightly altered.)

who was not only innocent and holy, humanly speaking, but of infinite dignity, and all holy, as God. It was God who innocently suffered religious rejection, political injustice, human torture, social exclusion, and crucifixion. Consequently, Jesus' love is all the more intense and all the more meritorious in virtue of the realities to which he submitted himself and in which he exemplified love, in the forgiveness of sins, and in the offering of his life for the many. In this he effectuated the communion of eschatological divine life to the world. Accordingly, we see in the resurrection that God "fittingly" raised Jesus up, and exalted him in glory, as a proportionate "reward" or just response to what he suffered.[15]

How is this threefold principle of the merit of Christ, which is on display in the atonement, revelatory of the mystery of the Trinity? We can speak here of the paternal origins of the redemption, the Lordship of Christ crucified, and the derivation of the Spirit from the Cross.

The paternal origins of the crucifixion event should be clear. "For God so loved the world that he gave his only Son, that whoever believes in him should not perish but have eternal life" (Jn 3:16). The Father should not be said to will in any way (whether directly or indirectly) the sins of the human race, including those that led to the execution of Jesus. The Father does will, however, in light of human sin, to send the eternal Son into the world to bring about the reconciliation of the human race with God, through the merit of the passion and death of Christ. This divine dynamic activity of willing on the Father's part is indicative of the wisdom, goodness, love, justice, mercy, and other attributes of the Father's nature as God. Christ as man freely consents to this intention, bringing himself into accord with it, to offer his life for the world, and in doing so he loves the Father in a plenitude of charity even from the Cross. His human activity of meritorious love therefore manifests the Father's wisdom and love for the world and also manifests the Son's eternally shared wisdom and love for the world, which he always has from the Father.

It follows from this that even on the Cross the Son is the Word of the Father, the one who "speaks" the identity of God out into the world from within his passion: "I Am." "When you have lifted up the Son of man, then you will know that I Am" (Jn 8:28). The "I am He who is" of Exodus 3:14, therefore, is reiterated from the Cross in a yet more perfect form of expression.

---

15. See Aquinas, *ST* III, q. 53, a. 1, on the justice of God manifest in the resurrection, where the logic of his argument resembles that of Paul in Phil 2:10–11.

The very nature and being of God, who is almighty, is manifest to the human race now not from Mount Sinai, but in the crucifixion of the Son. God, who is utterly transcendent, the Creator and origin of all things, is he who alone can save the human race (Is 45), but God has done this precisely by entering into the deepest form of human suffering, identifying with human beings in their most vulnerable state. It is from within this most profound depth of vulnerability and surrender that God has acted as one who is human, meritoriously, to reconcile the world to himself. Therefore, the merits of Christ in his atonement are revelatory of his Lordship, his goodness, mercy, and justice. Indeed, it is the crucified God who is Lord. From the Cross, Jesus acts as both God and man to redeem the human race, to forgive sins, communicate divine grace, establish the Church, and initiate the eschaton. This Lordship is sovereign, but it is also filial. The crucified Lord is the Son of God. Therefore, all that Christ does from the Cross with divine authority mirrors or echoes the Father, from whom he receives all that he is. Even as he is dying the Son loves the Father and lives out his commandments. It is in acting "from" the Father that he is able effectively to impetrate for the human race, to forgive others (Lk 23:34, 43), and give grace to the world (1 Cor 1:18).

John's Gospel makes it clear that the merits of Christ are also a kind of principle of the sending of the Spirit: ". . . it is to your advantage that I go away, for if I do not go away, the Counselor will not come to you; but if I go, I will send him to you. And when he comes, he will convince the world concerning sin and righteousness and judgment . . ." (John 16:7–8). The Holy Spirit is, of course, the second counselor or advocate. The first is Jesus (1 Jn 2:1). The metaphor of an advocate or counselor is legal in nature. The human race stands in a court of justice, accused before God, but the first advocate has come to be an "expiation for our sins, and not for ours only but also for the sins of the whole world" (1 Jn 2:2). The second advocate can be sent only once the reconciliation is effectuated by Christ, and the Spirit's role is to bring the effects of that reconciliation to perfection by communicating it inwardly to the world. His convicting of the world is interior, as he communicates to human beings the grace of faith, by which they are awakened to a realistic sense of sin and are simultaneously initiated into the mystery of Christ's righteousness, which is a mystery of love (Jn 14:23).

How, then, do the merits of Christ's passion relate to and reveal the Holy Spirit? On the one hand, as we have noted, in the section above, these same merits derive from the Holy Spirit, who is the origin of the grace of Christ. Jesus as man is filled with the grace of the Holy Spirit, who moves him to embrace the passion and suffer it out of love, meritoriously. Therefore, in his longsuffering, patience, humility, peacefulness, and mercy, we see the fruits of the Spirit.[16] "But the fruit of the Spirit is love, joy, peace, patience, kindness, goodness, faithfulness, gentleness, self-control; against such there is no law" (Gal. 22–23). Christ crucified is inundated with the Spirit. He is a visible icon of his grace, a messianic king anointed in the Spirit, reigning on his Cross. On the other hand, the Spirit can be sent, fittingly, in a new way upon the world, only once the hour of Jesus is passed. It is the accomplishment of the atonement that serves as the condition for the sending of the Spirit upon the Church and the world. This relationship of the Son to the Spirit pertains, of course, to the temporal aspect of the visible mission, but we see mirrored in it the eternal relation of the Son to the Spirit, as the Spirit is he who proceeds eternally from the begotten Son and Word of the Father. The relationships of temporal sending manifest the relationships of eternal proceeding, since the missions of the persons simply are the processions with an additional effect *ad extra* in the world. The Son's human self-offering to the Father is a most fitting temporal manifestation of the eternal relation of the Son to Father. This act of self-offering culminates at the Cross. So, too, the fact that the Spirit's sending forth into the world from the Father and the Son is conditioned upon the Son's temporal act of self-offering as man is also fittingly indicative of the ordering of the persons in eternal Trinitarian life. The Son, who is one with the Father, sends the Spirit from the Cross. The Father, Son, and Holy Spirit eternally will that it should be so, that the event of the atonement conducted in Christ's human suffering and death should manifest their shared Trinitarian life, in accord with the very order of life and love they have with one another, from all eternity. In the mystery of the crucifixion, then, we come to know who God the Trinity really is in himself, and he truly communicates to us by grace a knowledge of his mystery and a participation in his very life as God.

The Suffering Love of the Son

In a previous chapter we noted that there is a way in which, by making use of the traditional notion of active potency, we can speak metaphorically of

---

16. *ST* III, q. 7, a. 5.

an eternal outpouring of love in the life of the Trinity. The Father eternally has the active power pertaining to him personally to generate the Son and to spirate the Spirit with the Son. This potency implies no ontological potentiality but rather is indicative of God's pure actuality. The Father is able in his perfect actuality to communicate all that he has and is as God to the Son, and the Son is able to do this with the Father for the Spirit. Therefore, only a Trinitarian person can communicate all that he has and is to the other, and in this sense, we can speak poetically and metaphorically of an outpouring love of the Trinitarian persons. This metaphor is viable because the Father, in begetting, pours out all that he has as God to the Son, but we have to acknowledge simultaneously that this begetting implies no diminution of the pure act of the Father. The Father eternally communicates all that he has and is as God to the Son, who emanates forth from him, but the Father is also always unfathomably perfect in doing so. The Son too is undiminishable in perfection and actuality, God from God and light from light, even as he spirates with the Father the eternal love of the Spirit, who is wholly and infinitely actual, an eternally perfect fire of divine love.

Can this mystery be mirrored or revealed in the human suffering of the Son in his passion? Is there present in the crucifixion a kind of analogy to divine self-communication in love, in virtue of Christ's human activities of longsuffering and self-offering? To explore this question briefly, we can note first that Jesus' suffering is varied, and pertains to his spiritual faculties, his emotions or passions, and to his physical body.[17] He is subject to agony in his intellect and will as he confronts the gravity of human sin and grieves for it. He suffers emotionally from the experience of betrayal and abandonment, from the sad injustice and misguided religious zeal of those around him, and from the suffering of his mother and other followers who witness these events. He suffers bodily from physical torture, the acute pain of crucifixion, and the weight of encroaching asphyxiation. In all these senses, the suffering—which is typically human—entails passivity and therefore ontological potentiality. As a human being, Christ is in potency to suffer physically, emotionally, and spiritually, as one subject to the action of other human beings. This kind of actuation of a human potency to suffer obviously should not be attributed directly to the divine nature, which is purely actual and impassible. Christ in his divine nature transcends human suffering, even if his

17. I have given more developed consideration to the forms of Christ's suffering in *The Incarnate Lord*, chap. 7.

deity is present "in and through" his human suffering. Nor can the potentiality of suffering be ascribed in any way to the interpersonal processions, as if this suffering of the Son were indicative of something in the life of the Trinity per se, such as the historical constitution of the divine relations (Moltmann), a kenotic pre-history in God (Bulgakov), or an eternal distance in the freedom of love that obtains between the Father and the Son (Balthasar). On my view such approaches are theologically unwarranted and ultimately unviable.

However, there is a likeness, in the passion, between Christ's human nature and his divine nature in at least one significant respect, and it pertains to charity as the actuating principle of the *human* potency of the Son. To understand this argument, we should begin from a consideration of the human love of Christ in his passion and death. Motivated by the perfection of charity in his human heart, Jesus *as man* freely loves both God and the human race, in and through his threefold suffering (spiritual, emotional, and physical). This activity of loving constitutes a form of perfection or actuation, that takes place in and through the suffering, where the latter is freely accepted and endured out of love. In this case, the bodily and psychological potentiality of the sufferer is now a potency for alteration not only by external persons (by those who inflict suffering upon Christ and put the body to death), but also from within, by he who exhibits the virtue of love even in and through suffering and death. That is to say, when Christ endures suffering patiently, he both actuates and manifests charity more perfectly. "Greater love has no man than this, that a man lay down his life for his friends" (Jn 15:13). This progressive and perfect actuation pertains to the human nature of Christ, not his divine nature, since the divine nature is purely actual. In the passion, it is the passive potency of human nature that is perfected, not the active potency of the divine person of the Son. But the Son's love for the world, exhibited in his human endurance of suffering, does manifest, by analogy or similitude, the eternal love of self-communication that is present in the Father, Son, and Spirit, which we have mentioned above. It is like it, participates in it, and is expressive of it, in a human form. How is this the case?

First, in the passivity of his free suffering unto death out of love, Jesus manifests that he has received all that he has from the Father, and that the Father loves him in all that he is: "... the Father loves the Son, and has given all things into his hand" (Jn 3:35, cf. Jn 13:3).[18] This means that even in

---

18. Commenting on John 3:35 ("... the Father loves the Son, and has given all things into his hand"), Aquinas notes that the statement can refer either to the Son as divine or the Son as

Christ suffering and crucified, the plenitude of the divine life is present: "For in him the whole fullness of deity dwells bodily ..." (Col 2:9). This is true at the Cross, where Christ loves the world, as man, in light of the love that the Father has for the world, a love that is eternally perfect, and that he communicates from all eternity to the Son, so that the Son is radiant even in his crucifixion with this divine love for the world.

Second, then, the Son as man gives all that he is and has back to the Father. Jesus "returns" to the Father on the Cross, by bringing his human life among us to fulfillment. This "return to the Father" that Jesus accomplishes in virtue of his human nature corresponds in the divine life to the love that the Son has for the Father, in his common spiration of the Holy Spirit.[19] In their reciprocal love they, as one principle, co-spirate the Holy Spirit. In his human life of charity, Jesus expresses this giving of himself "back to the Father" through the offering to God of all he has as man. The giving of himself even unto death is the human, temporal expression of perfect charity that participates in, corresponds to, and manifests that eternal act of filial love whereby he is entirely from the Father and for the Father, as Son and Word, in the spiration of the Spirit.

Third, then, the Son who suffers and dies as man, is also the Lord, who is always giving all that he is to the Spirit, with the Father, as the expression of the eternal love that he has for the Father. The way this is manifest in the human suffering of Christ is that he gives of himself to the Father, in human obedience and love for the human race even unto death, in order to "pour out" the Holy Spirit upon the Church and the world. In giving his life in order to send the Spirit, the Son manifests in human form, through the humility of self-emptying death, the self-giving love he has eternally for the Father, which finds its perfect expression in the breathing forth of the Spirit of love.

In his own suffering then, Jesus freely offers everything out of love, even

human. If it refers to the former, and therefore to the intra-Trinitarian life, it cannot mean that the Father generates the Son because he loves him, since this would imply that the Father generates the Son by an act of the will, which is the heresy of Arianism. Furthermore, the love with which the Father loves the Son is his Holy Spirit, and the Spirit is not the source of the generation of the Son. Therefore, we should not state that the Father generates the Son by love but that the Father eternally loves the eternally begotten Word, which love is the spiration of the Spirit. This love is the sign that the Father has communicated the divine life to the Son and loves him, not the cause of that communication. See *In Ioan.* III, lec. 6, 545.

19. On the analogy of the "return" to the Father in the Son's human life, see the study of Emmanuel Durand, *Le Père, Alpha et Oméga de la vie trinitaire* (Paris: Cerf, 2008).

in the midst of the passion and expiration. He drinks the cup to the last drop, expires in agony and peace, and blood and water issue from the side of his dead body, as a miraculous sign of his total self-offering (Jn 19:34).[20] All of this actuates all the potency of his human self-offering, so that his created human nature is an icon of divine communication. This "icon" of Jesus' human nature both manifests and conceals his divine nature, because it is only analogous to the divine nature.[21]

In all of this, Jesus crucified is also the eternal Word of the Father, not only because he bespeaks who God is as Lord, but also because he gives the Spirit. As Aquinas notes, Christ crucified is a *verbum spirans amorem*, a "Word spirating Love."[22] Aquinas is referring to the eternal spiration of the Spirit, but we can also introduce here a note of reflection on the human activity of Christ that is subjacent to this mystery of the eternal procession. At the Cross, Jesus is manifestly the Word of the Father, who speaks or expresses the love he has for the Father in the very distinctively human act of freedom by which he accepts death. Understood in this light, Jesus' acceptance of physical mortality is a sign of the freedom of love, a human act of

---

20. The exsanguination is a moment of consummation, the last sign of the offering of everything.

21. One can agree readily with Balthasar when he suggests that the death of Christ constitutes a concrete manifestation of the eternal love of the Son who comes forth from the Father, being united to him by a principle of Love. This love is manifest even in the Son's human death, and in the cadaver on the Cross. Nevertheless, the states we associate with surrender, suffering, and death cannot realistically be attributed to God's nature or personal relations, even by a loose analogy. To claim that this could be the case seems to me at some basic level incompatible with the conciliar claims of the Catholic Church, which underscore the unicity of the divine persons and simplicity of their divine nature. I am suggesting, as a kind of counter alternative, that it is only in virtue of the distinction of the divine nature and human nature of Christ that can we understand how God in his sovereign freedom of love is able in wisdom to assimilate and assume the state of human agony and death (that which originally is "not God") so as to manifest, in and through these typically human features, the presence, reality, and even hidden triumph of God's radiantly omnipotent love and immortal life. Moltmann seems right to say, following Hegel, that God can take death up into himself; and indeed, we must say that truly God died on the Cross. God, the Lord and Son, takes up death into himself hypostatically as something he experiences personally and humanly, yet not as something that affects inwardly or reconstitutes his identity as God. Nor does Christ's death alter the interpersonal processions and relational life of the Trinity. Were this the case, then moral and physical evil would seem to constitute God in some way, in his ontological identity, despite his overcoming of it in a developmental history. It is best to say, then, not only that such attributions of intra-divine sundering are impossible, but that even in the face of human anguish and suffering, and indeed especially in the face of it, God in his nature and personal communion enjoys happiness that is infinitely perfect and eternally undiminishable. It is precisely to unite us to this eternal life of beatitude that God suffered and died humanly, and not so as to redefine himself in dependence upon our human suffering.

22. See *ST* I, q. 43, a. 5, ad 2.

charity, and behind this human activity stands the eternal love he has for the Father. His passion, then, is a definitive statement of the reality, primacy, transcendence, and victory of eternal love, even in the midst of the worst human suffering. Likewise, as one who has received all that he has from the Father, Jesus as man gives all that he has to the Father, signifying in this temporal "return" or handing of all things over to the Father that he exists as Son unto or for the Father, to spirate the Spirit of love with the Father. So, too, from the Cross the Son will breath or expirate the Spirit of love upon the Church and the world. The Holy Spirit, then, is indicated to us as the uncreated gift of eternal love, in a distinctive way, because he is given from the Cross. He is the fruit of the crucified, dead Christ. The "grain of wheat that falls into the earth and dies ... bears much fruit" (Jn 12:24–25). The Spirit is sent forth from the Cross of the Son, in a temporal and visible mission that reflects the eternal procession of the Spirit, whereby the Son communicates all that he has and is as God to the Spirit, in his mutual love with the Father. This eternal self-communication in God, which is total (of the Father to the Son, of the Father and the Son in mutual love to the Spirit), is recapitulated at the Cross. This does not mean that the Holy Trinity is ontologically enriched, altered in identity, or changed in its divine life by the Cross, but rather the contrary is indicated. It means that the unchanging God of love manifests his eternal mystery of interpersonal communion even here, at Golgotha, as a mystery of re-creative love. The very relations of the divine persons, in which there transpires the eternal communication of divine life, are manifest even in, or especially in, the Son's human gift of himself to the Father out of love, in obedient suffering even unto death, so as to send the Spirit upon the world.

SEPARATION OF BODY AND SOUL, AND DESCENT INTO HELL

Jesus' acceptance in his person of the consequences of death demonstrates his solidarity with the human race. It also manifests his Lordship, and his capacity even in death on Holy Saturday to address the universal effects of human death. We can consider these features of the paschal mystery briefly as implicit manifestations of the mystery of the Trinity.

     Human death is the separation of the organic physical body and the immaterial spiritual soul, which acts as the form of the body. As such, death constitutes a substantial rupture, because the soul and the body united constitute one concrete substance, not two.[23] I am the subsisting compound of my body and soul, one being who is a spiritual animal, a corporeal living person. Death undermines or destroys this unity of the person as body and soul, but the soul of the person, which includes the personal faculties of the intellect and will, subsists after death and is perpetually subsistent and incorruptible, or "immortal."[24] Jesus experiences genuine human death, and therefore is submitted to the separation of body and soul that is common to all human beings who die. However, he is a divine person subsisting in a human nature, and his person, therefore, is not subject either to alteration or corruption in death. Nor does it cease to subsist in either his body or his soul. Rather, the Word made flesh, after the death of Christ, subsists both in his cadaver and in his separated soul. The dead body on the Cross, a body that is no longer animated by a soul, is the dead body of the Lord. The Word subsists and is present in this body, so that those who touch the cadaver of Christ, taking it down from the Cross, touch the dead body of God.[25] They hold the eternal Word in their arms and place his body in the tomb.

We can perceive two profound Trinitarian truths in this mystery of the cadaver of the Word. The first pertains to the solidarity of love. The second pertains to divine power. The Lord, the Son and Word of God, has so identified with the human condition as to show a solidarity with us even in physical death, taking up the cadaveric state into his own person as Son, so as to manifest his love for us. "He loved them to the end" (Jn 13:1). However, there is also a hidden aspect to this mystery of solidarity. Concealed within

23. See on this point, Aquinas, *In Aristotelis librum De anima commentarium* (*In De anima*) II, lec. 3; *ST* I, q. 75, a. 4; q. 76, a. 1. See on Aquinas's doctrine of the hylomorphic character of the person, Gilles Emery, "The Unity of Man, Body and Soul, in St. Thomas Aquinas," in *Trinity, Church, and the Human Person*, 209–35.

24. See *ST* I, q. 75, aa. 2, 3, 6. The teaching that the soul of the human person is immaterial and that it subsists after death is considered a dogmatic teaching of the Catholic Church, revealed by God in the New Testament and confirmed by sacred tradition and the Church's magisterium. See on this point the 1979 letter of the Congregation of the Doctrine of the Faith, "On Certain Questions Concerning Eschatology," which states, "The Church affirms that a spiritual element survives and subsists after death, an element endowed with consciousness and will, so that the 'human self' subsists. To designate this element, the Church uses the word 'soul,' the accepted term in the usage of Scripture and Tradition. Although not unaware that this term has various meanings in the Bible, the Church thinks that there is no valid reason for rejecting it; moreover, she considers that the use of some word as a vehicle is absolutely indispensable in order to support the faith of Christians." (Available online at http://www.vatican.va/roman_curia/congregations/cfaith/documents/rc_con_cfaith_doc_19790517_escatologia_en.html)

25. Aquinas, *ST* III, q. 50, a. 3.

the cadaver of the Lord is also the power of the Lord. The power of the Creator is present latently even in the cadaver of the Word, which lies silently in the tomb on Holy Saturday. This power is Trinitarian. It is the power that has created the world and that sustains all things in being, and consequently it is also an infinite power, able to raise the dead. This Trinitarian omnipotence of eternal love is present now even in our death, our being dead and consigned to dust (Gn 3:19), and is able to "make all things new" (Rv 21:5).

Meanwhile, the soul of Christ separated from the body "descends into hell." This is an affirmation of the Apostles' Creed, and a dimension of the confession of the Church's faith. But what does it mean? Can we understand this idea constructively as something other than a historically antiquated symbol, or an eccentric private mythology?[26] Do other options exist?

Aquinas is helpful on this score, because he points out that the soul of Christ is an instrumental principle of illumination of the souls of the "just," those who died before the time of Christ and who await the fullness of redemption.[27] What is meant by this claim? First, Aquinas presupposes that all those who came before Christ were offered the grace of redemption either in more overt or more hidden ways, and that many of them cooperated effectively with this grace.[28] This is the case whether we are speaking of the faithful in Israel who came before Christ, or the much more vast and significant number of pre-Christian "gentiles," symbolized archetypally in the bible by the figure of Noah, the righteous man of God and "holy pagan."[29] Nevertheless, even if many before Christ died in a state of grace, in friendship with God, they also were still taking part implicitly in a collective economic process of salvation, one that reaches its apex and culmination in the paschal mystery. They too, then, were to be saved by the Cross, in collective unity with the whole human race, with all those who are offered grace and who cooperate with it effectively. They are part of the Church, broadly

26. For my critical reflections on Balthasar's constructive attempts to face the challenge of a modern theology of Holy Saturday, see *The Incarnate Lord*, chap. 9.

27. See the treatment of the whole *quaestio* in *ST* III, q. 52.

28. On the universal offer of salvation to all see Aquinas, *Super I Epistolam ad Timotheum* (*In I Tim.*) II, lec. 1; *Super Epistolam ad Hebraeos* (*In Heb.*) XII, lec. 3; and *SCG* III, c. 159, among other texts. This teaching coheres with St. Thomas's explicit avowal that Christ died for all human beings and that the merits of the passion are sufficient to procure effectively the salvation of any and all. See *ST* III, q. 48, a. 2. See also *ST* III, q. 46, a. 6, ad 4. On implicit faith among pre-Christian persons, see *ST* II-II, q. 2, aa. 7–8.

29. See on this idea, Aquinas, *In Heb.* XI, lec. 2; from *Commentary on the Epistle to the Hebrews*, trans. C. Baer (South Bend, Ind.: St. Augustine's Press, 2006), esp. nos. 575–79. Jean Danielou, *Holy Pagans of the Old Testament*, trans. P. Faber (London: Longmans & Green, 1957).

speaking.[30] For this reason, then, they received grace prior to the time of Christ by anticipation of his mystery, in view of the merits of his passion, and his passion was itself the ontological principle of their salvation and its accomplishment. The final fulfillment, then, of their beatification, their union with God, took place in light of the passion, as they were illuminated fully by God and entered into the joy of the beatific vision, once the mystery of redemption had been fully accomplished. Otherwise stated, the Cross also illuminates hell, as it speaks to the souls of all who have died (1 Pt 3:19). On Holy Saturday, those who are already friends with God are called into the fullness of eternal beatitude. Those who are still being purified by God are consoled and confirmed in the expectation of their desires. Those in hell eternally are those who have culpably rejected true knowledge of God and his mystery, his initiatives of grace, or the manifest teachings and inner inclinations of the natural law, without final repentance.[31] They too are illuminated, in a qualified sense, by the greater knowledge of the truth about God and themselves that they have willingly chosen to avoid and refuse.[32]

On Holy Saturday, the eternal Word himself illumines the souls of all those who came before him, and in doing so he reveals to all the light of the Father and the love of the Spirit. Fundamentally, then, it is as God and Lord that Jesus, the Word, enlightens humanity. However, the instrumental principle through which he illumines the souls of the dead is his separated soul. The Word's separated soul is a principle "in and through which" the souls of all others are illumined. This is the case first because he now exists in a state of ontological solidarity with all those who died before him, and who are now saved by God's descent into the same state as theirs. This is the case secondly and relatedly, because their illumination is effectuated by the light of grace that inhabits the human soul of the Son. The created grace of the soul of Christ is therefore the instrumental efficient cause of the grace that they possess. In other words, he communicates his grace of headship to

---

30. *ST* III, q. 8, a. 3; see also *Lumen Gentium*, chap. 2, para. 16, which refers to this passage in Aquinas when it teaches about ways that various non-Christian groups may be related to the Church as the universal sign and instrument of salvation.

31. The Catholic tradition has regularly reaffirmed the scriptural teaching, of divine origin, that the state of damnation in hell exists as a consequence of human sin, and that it is a permanent state. The *Catechism of the Catholic Church* states in para. 1035: "The teaching of the Church affirms the existence of hell and its eternity. Immediately after death the souls of those who die in a state of mortal sin descend into hell, where they suffer the punishments of hell, 'eternal fire.' The chief punishment of hell is eternal separation from God, in whom alone man can possess the life and happiness for which he was created and for which he longs."

32. See, on this point, Aquinas, *ST* III, q. 52, aa. 1 and 6.

them, not only as God but also as man, and he does so precisely from within the state of ontological solidarity that he shares with them as one who has died. His is a light that shines in their darkness, and that brings them into the ambit of the Trinitarian mystery. The Word as God illumines them, but he does so as the Word who is human, who in his human soul is "full of truth and grace" (Jn 1:14). Finally, the perfection of the grace of the soul of Christ is a kind of exemplary cause of the perfection of the souls of the human race. As they enter into the plenary grace of beatitude, they become like him, as they know the mystery of God intimately, in their spiritual activities of intellect and will.

Understood in this sense, Holy Saturday is not primarily a "day" in human time, though the event does have a correlation with Jesus' one day period of being dead, and with the real separation of his body and soul. Rather, it is primarily a "state of being" that Christ was subject to in solidarity with the human race, in virtue of his death, and that he acted through upon the whole human race. Precisely because he was subject to this state as an instrumental medium of our salvation, so even now in the resurrection, when he is no longer dead or able to die, he is able to communicate to all the grace of Holy Saturday, that which pertains to his solidarity with the dying and the dead. So, too, he can illumine after death the souls of all those who die in a state of friendship with God, so as to communicate to them the plenitude of divine life that he possesses in virtue of his deity as the Word of God. Holy Saturday, then, as a Trinitarian event, continues to unfold *in its effects*, even after the resurrection and exaltation of Christ.

BODILY RESURRECTION AND EXALTATION: THE ECONOMIC REVELATION OF JESUS AS SON AND LORD

The exaltation of Jesus on Easter day is a revelation of the Trinity. Paul's letters clearly suggest that there is a distinctive manifestation of Jesus as both Son and Lord that takes place in virtue of his resurrection.

Romans 1:1–4: "Paul, a servant of Jesus Christ, called to be an apostle, set apart for the gospel of God which he promised beforehand through his prophets in the holy scriptures, the gospel concerning his Son, who was descended from David according to the flesh and designated Son of God in power according to the Spirit of holiness by his resurrection from the dead, Jesus Christ our Lord ..."

Philippians 2:9–11: "Therefore God has highly exalted him and bestowed on him the name which is above every name, that at the name of Jesus every knee should bow, in heaven and on earth and under the earth, and every tongue confess that Jesus Christ is Lord, to the glory of God the Father."

Because Paul affirms the pre-existence of Jesus as Lord and eternal Son, these texts are generally interpreted to mean that Jesus has always been Lord and Son, prior to Easter, but that only in his resurrection is his identity made fully manifest. How, then, do the resurrection and exaltation of Christ reveal the mystery of the Son and, in doing so, reveal the mystery of the Trinity? Here we can briefly consider an answer in two stages. In the first, we can consider how the glorification of the body and soul of Christ in the resurrection reveals his origin as the Son, eternally begotten of the Father. In the second we can consider how his exaltation in the ascension (metaphorically, "to the right hand of God") reveals his Lordship.

Resurrection as Revelation of the Eternally Begotten Son

The first consideration invites us to identify briefly what the resurrection is, insofar as it signifies the glorification of the body and soul of the human nature of Christ. Evidently, here the Christian faith confesses something different than a mere miraculous resuscitation or return to ordinary human life.[33] Instead, the bodily resurrection of Jesus entails a radical transformation of his whole human subject, a glorification of both the body and the soul of Christ, in an eschatological state that inaugurates the end times of the cosmos. It is in this sense that Christ is a New Adam and a new creation (Rom 5:12–21; 1 Cor 15:45; 2 Cor 5:17). In him a second "cosmological Big Bang" has occurred, so that he is an eschatological principle, which will eventually affect all created things. He is an exemplary cause, after the pattern of which all other things are to be reconfigured.[34]

Classical Catholic theology identifies several features of the glorified humanity of Jesus. In his resurrected body, on Easter night, he enjoys a new

---

33. *Catechism of the Catholic Church*, para. 646: "Christ's Resurrection was not a return to earthly life, as was the case with the raisings from the dead that he had performed before Easter: Jairus' daughter, the young man of Naim, Lazarus. These actions were miraculous events, but the persons miraculously raised returned by Jesus' power to ordinary earthly life. At some particular moment they would die again. Christ's Resurrection is essentially different. In his risen body he passes from the state of death to another life beyond time and space. At Jesus' Resurrection his body is filled with the power of the Holy Spirit: he shares the divine life in his glorious state, so that St. Paul can say that Christ is 'the man of heaven' (1 Cor 15:35–50)."

34. See, on this point, Aquinas, *ST* III, q. 56, a. 1.

form of impassibility, subtlety, agility, and clarity.[35] To speak of his bodily impassibility is to denote that the resurrected Christ can no longer die or suffer, and cannot lose his psychosomatic unity. His resurrected body is now perennially incorruptible, sustained in being forever by the power of God, and qualified mysteriously by an intrinsic bodily perfection. Subtlety refers to the numinous spiritual transformation of the glorified body. In the resurrection, the flesh of Christ is subject to a kind of spiritualization not because it ceases to be a material body, but because it enters a higher plane, where the glorified material body is perfectly subject to the soul and indicative of its inner spiritual states. Agility follows from this, which is a note of the resurrected body that refers to unique abilities and actions of which the glorified body is now capable. Christ can appear to the disciples behind closed doors, and be present where he wishes. In doing so, he manifests himself in his whole person as Son, under the circumstances and for the duration of the time that he wishes. Some apparitions are humble in form and almost hidden (Jn 20:11–18), others overwhelming (Rv 1:12–18). The clarity or splendor of the body refers to its beauty, which has instrumental power to communicate the spiritual presence of Christ. In the gospels, his apparitions are discreet and surprising, but also splendid and spiritually luminous. Those who come into contact with the risen Lord are amazed and transformed by his splendor.

The human soul of Christ is also altered in the glorification of Easter night. His knowledge and love of God *prior to the resurrection* are perfect in their genre, as a result of the plenitude of grace he possesses in his human soul for the duration of his early life.[36] In all four gospels, Jesus of Nazareth is depicted as being clearly aware of his unique status and authority.[37] He knows that the God of Israel is his unique Father and that he is the unique Son, destined to send the Holy Spirit. He also possesses in all of his earthly ministry a moral beauty and a virtuous, conquering love, which stem from

---

35. Aquinas refers to this subject matter in *SCG* IV, c. 86, para. 5, and in *ST* III, q. 54, aa. 1 and 2. See the studies of Marilyn McCord Adams, "The Resurrection of the Body According to Three Medieval Aristotelians: Thomas Aquinas, John Duns Scotus, William Ockham," *Philosophical Topics* 20, no. 2, (1992): 1–33; and Bryan Kromholtz, *On the Last Day: The Time of the Resurrection of the Dead according to Thomas Aquinas* (Fribourg: Academic Press Fribourg, 2010).

36. I have argued to this effect in greater detail in other places, including *The Incarnate Lord*, chap. 5, and "Dyotheletism and the Instrumental Human Consciousness of Jesus." See also the important treatment of the question by Simon Gaine, *Did the Saviour See the Father? Christ, Salvation, and the Vision of God* (London: T&T Clarke, 2015).

37. I have underscored this theme, in part 1 of this book.

the perfection of his charity and authentic human freedom. Therefore, we should not affirm that Christ's perfect understanding of his own identity or the perfect intensity of his charity come about only as a result of the resurrection. Rather, he enjoys the grace of perfect knowledge and love in the higher reaches of his soul even during his earthly life.[38] This all being duly noted, the effects of his spiritual grace upon his sense faculties and his body are of limited scope during the course of his earthly life, in a way that they are not in the resurrection.[39] In the course of his earthly life Jesus knows the Father and is capable of love in a way that is unique, but he is also the "man of sorrows" (Is 53:3) subject to suffering, the enduring of evils, and the hardships of the passion. In the resurrection however, the perfect knowledge and love that Christ possesses as human, in virtue of his capital grace, extends to all the powers of his soul, in all its modalities, in both the spiritual faculties and the sense faculties.[40] Christ is now beatified in all of his human and psychological subjectivity, irradiated by extended effects of his beatific vision and by his plenitude of charity, in all that he is and experiences as man. Consequently, there is nothing now that Christ knows as man that can diminish his beatitude or cause him disruptive harm or pain. If one were to posit the hypothesis of a spiritual sorrow in the heart of Christ in glory (in the face of ongoing human sin, for example), this might occur only interior to love, and as the expression of a yet-deeper peace that he enjoys inviolably in virtue of his human beatitude.[41]

How, then, does the glorification of Christ's body and soul just alluded to reveal his Sonship as such? It does so first and foremost because the resurrection is a work of the Father, who raises Jesus in order to reveal his Sonship.

"I do not cease to give thanks for you, remembering you in my prayers, that the God of our Lord Jesus Christ, the Father of glory, may give you a spirit of wis-

38. See on this point, Aquinas, *ST* III, q. 7, aa. 2, 9, 10 and q. 9, a. 1.

39. Aquinas speaks in this regard of a *dispensatio* whereby the effects of the grace of Christ in the spiritual faculties of his soul do not occlude the possibility of profound spiritual, emotional, and corporeal suffering. See *ST* III, q. 14, a. 1, ad 2; q. 15, a. 5, ad 3; q. 45, a. 2; q. 46, a. 8.

40. *ST* III, q. 54, a. 2.

41. Pascal, for instance, writes that "Jesus will be in agony until the end of the world." [*Pensées*, no. 919, trans. A. J. Krailsheimer (New York: Penguin, 1995).] The idea is taken by some to suggest that Christ in glory suffers on account of the ongoing reality of human sin and suffering in the world. I am suggesting that if there is any spiritual sorrow in the mind and heart of Christ in glory, it only ever occurs within the sublime beatitude he experiences in the whole of his human subjectivity. It could in no way taint or corrupt that perfect beatitude.

dom and of revelation in the knowledge of him.... according to the working of his
great might which he accomplished in Christ when he raised him from the dead
and made him sit at his right hand in the heavenly places ..." (Eph 1:16–17, 19–20)

How might we understand this claim about the Father, and why does his
action reveal the Sonship of Jesus? The resurrection is a work of God *ad extra*, and in all such works of God it is always all three persons who act together. We rightly should say, then, that the Father raises Jesus, and that the
Son raises himself by the power of his deity (Jn 10:18) and that the Holy
Spirit raises Jesus.[42] The resurrection is a work of the Trinity. Nevertheless,
this activity is fittingly attributed to the Father for several reasons. The Father is the principle of Trinitarian life, from whom the Son and Spirit eternally receive all that they are. The Father creates and sustains the world in
being through his eternally begotten Wisdom and in the goodness of his
Spirit, so that all of creation comes from the Father. The Father redeems
the world by sending the Son and Spirit into the world in their invisible
and visible missions. So, too, the Father recreates the world by raising up
the Son in glory, and by manifesting him to the nations as Lord (Phil 2:6–
11). The attribution of the resurrection to the Father underscores his principality in all of these domains. He is the font of Trinitarian communion
in God, the paternal origin of the creation, and he who reveals to us in the
redemption both his eternal Fatherhood and our adoptive sonship. This
apocalypse of God's paternity making itself known in our world is exemplified in the meta-historical event of the resurrection.

By this same measure, however, the resurrection also fittingly manifests
the Son as the only-begotten of the Father. Just as the Father is the Father of
the creation and the re-creation through his Son and Word, so the Son is the
only-begotten, through whom God has made all things, and is the final prin-

---

42. *ST* III, q. 53, a. 4: "Our Lord says (John 10:18) 'No one taketh My soul from Me, but I lay it
down, and I take it up again.' But to rise is nothing else than to take the soul up again. Consequently, it appears that Christ rose again of His own power. [For] ... in consequence of death Christ's
Godhead was not separated from His soul, nor from His flesh. Consequently, both the soul and
the flesh of the dead Christ can be considered in two respects: first, in respect of His Godhead;
secondly, in respect of His created nature. Therefore, according to the virtue of the Godhead united to it, the body took back again the soul which it had laid aside, and the soul took back again the
body which it had abandoned: and thus Christ rose by His own power. And this is precisely what
is written (2 Cor 13:4): 'For although He was crucified through our weakness, yet He lives by the
power of God.' But if we consider the body and soul of the dead Christ according to the power of
created nature, they could not thus be reunited, but it was necessary for Christ to be raised up by
God."

ciple in whom the re-creation of all things is inaugurated. This parallelism is underscored vividly by Paul in Colossians 1:15–16, 18: "He is the image of the invisible God, the first-born of all creation [the pre-existent source and origin of all things]; for in him all things were created, in heaven and on earth, visible and invisible. . . . He is [also] the head of the body, the church; he is the beginning [of the new creation], the first-born from the dead, that in everything he might be pre-eminent." All things come forth from Christ in the beginning, and Christ is the recapitulation of all things in the resurrection. Here we see a kind of alpha and omega of Sonship. The creation comes to be through the Son, and it is guided in view of re-creation and filial adoption by grace in the Son. Both these elements are revealed in the resurrection. The eternal generation of the Son (who is from the beginning) is rendered present in a new mode in the economy in virtue of the glorification of his humanity. The resurrection of Jesus instantiates in a new way, within the economy, that which was before the foundation of the world: that Jesus is the eternally begotten Son of God. So Colossians 1:26 goes on to speak of "the mystery hidden for ages and generations but now made manifest to his saints," and 1 John 1:1–2 states: "That which was from the beginning, which we have heard, which we have seen with our eyes, which we have looked upon and touched with our hands, concerning the word of life—the life was made manifest, and we saw it, and testify to it, and proclaim to you the eternal life which was with the Father and was made manifest to us." Likewise, the resurrection reveals the Son as the principle of filial adoption. Creation is now entering into a new age of the children of God. (Rom. 8:19) All things are being re-created, and Christ is the omega point of creation. It is fitting, then, that the apostles fully understand only in light of his resurrection that Jesus is the eternally begotten Son.[43] They can become adopted children of God only in the Son, who is risen from the dead. Just as the Father originally made all things in the Son, so too he is now making all things new in the Son's resurrection (Rv 21:5). Jesus is in this sense "the alpha and the omega" of all things (Rv 22:13).

We have noted above that the material potency of Christ's body that is subject to suffering can be actuated by love in his passion and that the gift of

---

43. As depicted in John 20:27–28 by Thomas's confession of the divinity of Christ only once he sees and touches the resurrected flesh of Christ, and in Acts 9, where Paul discovers the reality of Jesus on the way to Damascus, and subsequently begins to preach "in the synagogues . . . 'he is the Son of God'" (Acts 9:20).

himself that he makes to the Father even unto death in his human body (his "return" to the Father in his human nature) corresponds to the eternal love that he has for the Father as the begotten Son, in the spiration of the Spirit. The actuation of his human nature by love is analogically similar to and indirectly revelatory of the pure actuality of the eternal love that he has for the Father as Son. Something similar exists also in the mystery of the resurrection of the humanity of Christ. The eternal life that is in the eternally begotten Son is purely actual, as the Son receives from the Father all that he is as perfect God. The human nature of the Son is not capable of pure actuality, of course, since this pertains only to his divine nature as God. This being said, the glorification of the human nature of the Son in his resurrection does confer upon it a more intensive perfection and actualization of being than it possessed prior to the eschatological state. The spiritual and psychosomatic components of the humanity of Jesus now subsist in an eschatological mode, so that he is most perfectly human, in a numinous way that is indicative of the final state of humanity in the world to come. The glory of his human body actuates the matter of his flesh most perfectly, even if his glorified body still retains all the potentiality that is indicative of a real material body, however transformed. All the powers of his human soul are affected and transformed interiorly by the grace of his glorified mind and will. It follows from all this that the Son's pure actuality as God from God and light from light, which he possesses from the Father, is also communicated to his human nature in a limited and participated way, so that his human nature is resplendent with divine glory, and most perfectly actuated according to its particular mode, insofar as a human nature can be. There is an analogy, then, between the pure actuality of the Son's deity and the relatively perfect actuation of his resurrected humanity. Consequently, we can rightly say that in the resurrection God reveals to us the perfect man, the last eschatological Adam, and the principle of the new creation. In doing so, he also reveals to us the glory of divine life, the life of the Son as God, resplendent in his human nature.

Finally, we may mention why the filiation of the Son is rightly revealed to the world after the mystery of the Cross. Jesus' pre-existent Sonship is appropriately unveiled to the human race fully only in light of the resurrection, not only because the resurrection is a temporal recapitulation of the Son's role in creation (all things were made through him and all things will be likened to him eschatologically), but also because his redemptive suffering and death have now transpired. The passion, and not the resurrection, is the principle of merit for the gift of grace to all human beings. Thus only once Christ has atoned fittingly for human sins is the gift of eternal life made fully manifest and communicated. In this sense, the resurrection reveals the infinite mercy of God that was at work in the atonement. Likewise, it is fitting for reasons of divine "righteousness" or justice that God should reveal the Sonship of the Lord not only during the time of his lowliness and humiliation but also and especially after the time of his exaltation and vindication. The Son in his human nature receives the fitting reward for his act of obedient self-offering even unto death. The resurrection therefore manifests in its own sublime way the justice of God and the righteousness of Christ. Consequently, his divine identity as Son is fittingly revealed once he has been vindicated justly by God, so that the lowliness of the crucifixion is contextualized by God's final word, and is now understood more profoundly in light of his exaltation (Phil 2:10–11).

Jesus as Lord in His Exaltation

Let us also consider finally how the resurrection reveals Jesus' Lordship, the mystery of his identification with the God of Israel as "He who is." If the Sonship is revealed because Jesus is raised by the Father, the Lordship is revealed by Christ's exaltation in his human nature. "... that at the name of Jesus every knee should bow ... and every tongue confess that Jesus Christ is Lord, to the glory of God the Father" (Phil 2:10–11). As the Lord Jesus Christ, he is invested with authority and power. "All authority in heaven and on earth has been given to me" (Mt 28:18). He sits at the right hand of the Father, whence he reigns and whence he will come to judge the living and the dead. "He reflects the glory of God and bears the very stamp of his nature, upholding the universe by his word of power. When he had made purification for sins, he sat down at the right hand of the Majesty on high ..." (Heb 1:3). How might we interpret these various affirmations?[44]

I have noted above that the actual perfection of Christ's resurrected flesh and glorified soul reflect and are similar to the perfection of his eternally begotten Sonship, in which he possesses the pure actuality of divine life eternally from the Father. It follows from this line of thinking that his human

---

44. On the interpretation and theology of the Ascension as such, see the seminal essay by Pierre Benoit, "The Ascension," *Jesus and the Gospel*, vol. 1, trans. B. Weatherhead (New York: Herder & Herder, 1973), 209–53.

nature now participates regally in the authority that he possesses as Son and Lord. When Jesus is made the eschatological judge and regent of the world in his exaltation or Ascension, his human nature in both soul and body is given to participate in the authority that he already has from all eternity as Lord. We have noted above that the I Am of Jesus, his divine identity and power, are present even in his suffering and crucifixion and, indeed, even in his dead cadaver, but they are present in a discreet or even very hidden way. This presence of his divine authority and power are made manifest economically, however, in his resurrection. In virtue of its exaltation, his humanity participates and operates in the glory and authority of the eternal Lord. Therefore, when Jesus judges us, it is not only as God, nor merely as man, but only ever as both God and man. The judgment of God is a theandric act. It is he who has suffered, died, and been buried, who also will judge each member of the human race in light of his own eschatological criteria. The principle of final judgment is entirely Christocentric. In the eschaton, everything that rises toward God will converge upon Christ.[45]

THE SENDING OF THE SPIRIT

The risen Christ sends the Spirit upon the apostles and, through the medium of their ministry, upon the Church and the world. I take it that there are three "moments" of the sending of the Spirit denoted in scripture, the first of which is from the Cross. There we are told in the Johannine literature that blood and water flowed from his side (Jn 19:34), an overt reference to the institution of the sacraments of Eucharist and baptism. However, we also are told in John 3:5 that we must be "born of water and the Spirit," which suggests that the Spirit is given in view of baptismal life. Likewise in 1 John 5:8, it says that "There are three witnesses, the Spirit, the wa-

---

45. The Johannine character of this theological affirmation is quite clear. See John 5:22–29: "The Father judges no one, but has given all judgment to the Son, that all may honor the Son, even as they honor the Father. He who does not honor the Son does not honor the Father who sent him. Truly, truly, I say to you, he who hears my word and believes him who sent me, has eternal life; he does not come into judgment, but has passed from death to life. Truly, truly, I say to you, the hour is coming, and now is, when the dead will hear the voice of the Son of God, and those who hear will live. For as the Father has life in himself, so he has granted the Son also to have life in himself, and has given him authority to execute judgment, because he is the Son of man. Do not marvel at this; for the hour is coming when all who are in the tombs will hear his voice and come forth, those who have done good, to the resurrection of life, and those who have done evil, to the resurrection of judgment." See, likewise, Acts 10:42; 2 Cor 5:10; Mt 19:28; Rv 19:11.

ter, and the blood; and these three agree." The three that are mentioned are witnesses of the redemptive death of Jesus, all of them stemming from the Cross. So, too, Jesus tells the disciples that he can send the Spirit only once he has died (Jn 16:7), as previously noted, which suggests that once he has died, he does send the Spirit. From these passages one may make a reasonable argument from scripture that the Spirit of redemption is sent first and foremost from the Cross, once the act of atonement is consummated, in the hidden power of Christ even in his cadaveric state, who already is inaugurating the mystery of the Church, by the Spirit working in water and in blood.

The second sending is overtly noted in John 20:21–23, where the risen Lord speaks to his apostles on the evening of the first day of his resurrection. "'Peace be with you. As the Father has sent me, even so I send you.' And when he had said this, he breathed on them, and said to them, 'Receive the Holy Spirit. If you forgive the sins of any, they are forgiven; if you retain the sins of any, they are retained.'" Here, the promises of John 14–16 are already being effectuated. Jesus is giving the apostles the Counselor, who will be with them, to recall to them the fullness of his teaching, to enlighten their understanding, and to convey to them the sacramental power to communicate the life of grace, including in the forgiveness of sins. The physical gesture of breathing is important. The one who spirates the Spirit eternally with the Father now sends the Spirit upon the Church in the economy, in virtue of his visible mission. The embodied gesture of breathing evokes the human instrumental activity: it is as both God and man that Jesus sends the Spirit, a point to which we will return below.

The third sending denoted in scripture occurs at Pentecost, fifty days after the resurrection (Acts 2:1–4). The Spirit descends upon the twelve, who are gathered in the upper room with the Mother of the Lord. The ecclesial symbolism is significant. The Spirit is the uncreated soul of the apostolic Church, given to the twelve in view of their universal mission of preaching, an idea that is illustrated thematically by Luke in his presentation of the Church in Acts, as represented by Spirit-inspired leaders like Peter, Stephen, and Paul, who are being configured to Christ. If the Spirit appears in flames of fire and the miraculous speaking of many languages, it is to signify the flame of love and courage that alights in the hearts of the apostles, giving them the loving zeal and fortitude to preach the gospel publicly, even under threat of death. The many languages brought into unity represent the

Church as a new universal font of truth, a reversal to the curse of Babel in Genesis 11:1–9, which signifies the many divisions of human culture that stem from the sins and illusory pretensions of the human race.

As we have noted in earlier chapters, both John and Paul tell us that it is the Lord who sends the Spirit (Jn 16:7), and that he is "the Spirit of Christ," (Rom 8:9), the Spirit of the Son (Gal 4:6). Consequently, the first thing we must say about the sending of the Spirit is that it is the ultimate moment in the economy of the revelation of the Trinitarian life of God.[46] In sending the Spirit, the Son makes manifest in his visible mission in time what is true from all eternity, that he and the Father co-spirate the Spirit eternally as their shared mutual love. The Spirit is the eternal uncreated gift of the Father to the Son and of the Son to the Father, the mutual impression of spirated love. This same gift is now given to the Church temporally in the visible mission of the Spirit. Just as the Son came into the world to reveal the Father, so too he came into the world to prepare for the sending of the Spirit, who in turn reveals the Son and the Father. The order of illumination is inverted when compared with the order of procession and sending. The Spirit who is sent last comes upon us first, to illumine us and draw us into the ambit of the Son. In discovering the reality of Jesus Christ we, in turn, are led toward the Father. The Spirit adopts us as sons and daughters in the Son, so that we may return by grace to the Father.

The second thing we can note is that the Son sends the Spirit not only as God but also as man.[47] We have mentioned above that the Son is the eternal origin of the Spirit as Lord, but that the Spirit rests upon him as man, and fills him with grace, so that Christ in his apostolic life, and in his suffering and death, exemplifies what it means to speak of life in the Spirit. This idea emphasizes that Christ as man is subordinate to the Spirit, obedient and docile to the Spirit's inner movements and promptings. However, it is also true to say that the Son in his human mind and will wishes to give his life as a ransom for the many (Mk 10:45) in order to send the Spirit upon the world. Jesus not only "listens" to the Spirit (Jn 3:8); he also desires in his human heart to send the Spirit upon the Church—from the Cross, and

46. Aquinas makes this argument, in effect, in his treatment of the "new law" of the gospel as pertaining to the gift and the age of the Spirit. ST I-II, q. 106, aa. 1, 3, and 4. See the study of this subject by Charles Journet in L'Église du Verbe Incarné, vol. 6, Essai de théologie de l'histoire du salut (Paris: Saint Augustin, 2004).

47. See on this Aquinas, De ver., q. 29, a. 5; Super Epistolam ad Titus (In Titus), III, lect. 1, 93, and the analysis of Legge, The Trinitarian Christology of St. Thomas Aquinas, 213–23.

on the night of Easter, and again, from within his glory, on the day of Pentecost. Of course, the human nature of Jesus does not ontologically reconstitute the eternal processions as such, or alter their identity. The Son as man does, however, receive the grace in his human mind and heart to participate instrumentally in the processions and in the sending. Jesus wills as man in virtue of his human nature and his plenitude of grace what he wills as God in virtue of his divine nature: to send the Spirit. The Holy Spirit himself as God wills in accord with the Father and the Son to give the human nature of the Son the inward desire to spirate the Spirit upon the world. Why is this significant? It introduces into the economy of salvation the note of Christological exemplarity, in which the Spirit we receive from Christ personally is given to us to conform us inwardly to him, in his human nature and in his life of grace. Christ in his headship shares this life with us by willingly sending us his Spirit, who wishes in turn to communicate to us a participation in the perfection of Christ's capital grace as human. By the work of the Spirit we become living members of the mystical body of Christ, participants in his grace, conformed progressively to his perfection. Therefore, the mystery of the resurrection of Jesus, his sending the Spirit upon the Church as both God and man, and our conformity to the life of Christ in the Spirit, are all related ontologically by an analogy of faith, a coherence of similitude that obtains among the various mysteries of the faith.

Finally, then, how does the Spirit in his own visible mission reveal to us the Father and the Son? What is the significance of his dwelling among us and of his acting upon us, as the Spirit of the Father and the Son?

The Spirit reveals the Father first and foremost because of his primary origin: he is sent most originally from the Father into the world and is the Spirit of the Father. Even when the Son sends the Spirit with the Father, there is still a paternal principality that remains, as we have noted in previous chapters. The Son has the capacity to spirate the Spirit only ever as something he receives eternally from the Father, and enjoys with him, in mutual love. So, we can say truly, then, that the Father spirates the Spirit "through" the Son, and that in the temporal economy of the missions, it is the Father who sends the Spirit upon the world "through" the Son.[48] This paternal origin of the Spirit is also manifest in the Spirit's effects. He acts upon the human race to initiate us by faith and baptism into filial adop-

---

48. *ST* I, q. 36, a. 3.

tion, so that we become sons and daughters of God by grace. In this sense, the Spirit's mission is to make us aware of the mystery of the Father, and to lead us to the Father. Even when the Spirit enlightens us so that we come to know Jesus as the genuine Son of God, now raised from the dead, this discovery of the Son itself invites us to turn "in Jesus" toward the gaze of the Father. Conformed inwardly to Christ by the grace of the Spirit, we are able to say, "*Abba*, Father" (Rom 8:15). The Father, then, remains the origin and end of Trinitarian life.

That the Spirit manifests the Son has been made sufficiently clear. We also have noted that the Spirit conveys the grace of Christ to the human race and conforms members of Christ's body to the mystery of the Lord, freeing them inwardly for participation in his life. "For freedom Christ has set us free; stand fast therefore, and do not submit again to a yoke of slavery" (Gal 5:1). This means, however, that the gifts of the Holy Spirit manifest in the life, suffering, and death of Christ, and poured out upon him in virtue of his plenitude of capital grace, are now communicated in turn to his members by the visible mission of the Spirit. Where Jesus as man was filled with wisdom, understanding, knowledge, counsel, piety, meekness, fortitude, and holy fear, in his life and in his passion, so now his members are given a participation in these gifts as a result of the outpouring of the Spirit. These gifts represent an intensification of the theological virtues of faith, hope, and love, whereby human beings know, hope in, and love God more intensively, and are thus conformed inwardly and more intensively to the processions of the Holy Trinity. By faith, Christians may participate in the eternal light of the Word, and by hope and charity, they may participate in the eternal Love of the Spirit. In both these ways, they are united to the Father, who is known in his Word and in his Spirit. The mission of the Spirit, then, prepares human beings in the economy by faith, hope, and love, for more perfect union with God in the beatific vision.

Finally, we can note that the Spirit sent into the world by the Father and the Son not only manifests the two who sent him, but also reveals himself directly to us. He is the Spirit of love, a person who is the eternally subsistent love of the Father and Son, a living flame of love, who wishes to transform the hearts of all human beings. The Holy Spirit delights in the souls of the faithful and grants them joy and friendship with himself by alighting upon them. He dwells within them, and reveals to them inwardly the mystery and hidden presence of the Holy Trinity. As Jesus says in John 14:23, "If a man loves me, he will keep my word, and my Father will love him, and we will come to him and make our home with him." The principle of our love for God is the Holy Spirit, who discreetly initiates our hearts into the mystery of Trinitarian indwelling.

The Holy Spirit is also fittingly referred to by appropriation as the author and safe-guardian of the communion of the Church. He is said to be so inasmuch as he is the source of the infused grace of charity in the souls of all the faithful, the supernatural love that binds and unites human beings to one another in the common life of the Church. He is the exemplar of ecclesial communion above all, however, because he is a principle of communion in God himself. The Father and the Son in their mutual love spirate the Spirit as the living bond of their mutual communion. The Spirit is an uncreated eternal love that unites the Father and the Son in this bond, and the Spirit himself in turn enjoys and loves the Father and the Son, as the source of his origin, from whom he receives the eternal plenitude of his deity. So too the Spirit is given to the Church to fashion a created communion of created persons in the image of the uncreated communion of the Trinitarian persons. The Spirit who is sent into the world continually acts with the Father and the Son to form a communion of human persons by grace, so that the Church is a participation in the communion of love that they enjoy from all eternity. Christian life accordingly is a life in the Spirit (Rom 8:2). Christians who walk by the Spirit (Gal 5:16–17) enter into a Trinitarian communion of divine life, living corporately in the light of Christ, in the love of the Spirit, in view of the paternal homeland of the Father. The Spirit is given to the Church so that the collective life of human beings may be conformed to that of the Holy Trinity itself.

CONCLUSION

In this final chapter of our work we have offered a succinct presentation of ways that the paschal mystery of Jesus Christ reveals the inner life of the Trinity within the economy of the visible missions of the Son and the Spirit. The mystery of Christ's agony in the Garden of Gethsemane and his free acceptance of the passion is made theologically intelligible if we consult conciliar teaching regarding the two wills of Christ and the unity of the divine will present in the life of the Holy Trinity. This understanding sets the stage for a right interpretation of the atoning merit of Christ's passion, as a manifestation of Trinitarian wisdom and love. The suffering of the Son in his human body and soul, precisely because it is a suffering accepted and endured in the fullness of charity, is revelatory of the Son's eternal love for the Father as God, and of his desire to give the Spirit to the world, a gift won as the fruit of the redemption. The death of Christ and his descent into hell manifest the solidarity of the Son with the human race in our precarious state, and the divine intent of the Father, Son, and Holy Spirit to offer grace to all human persons, to all those who came before Christ and to all those who come after. The resurrection of the Son of God constitutes a new revelation of his eternal generation from the Father, and so also manifests the fatherhood of God to the world. His exaltation is a manifestation of his Lordship, since Jesus in his human nature participates in the divine judgment and regency of the world. The sending of the Holy Spirit in the wake of the passion and resurrection reveals the Father, as the paternal font of the Trinitarian life, and inducts us by grace into the life of the Son. We are given access in the Spirit to the mystery of Trinitarian communion, as the Spirit is himself the eternal bond of mutual love shared by the Father and the Son. In all this we are given to perceive the deepest ground and reason for the temporal missions of the Son and the Spirit. The Holy Trinity desires from all eternity to communicate to rational creatures a participation by grace in the uncreated life of God.

Conclusion

On Being Trinitarian

———:———

At the term of our study we can draw four main conclusions, each one developed primarily out of one of the four main parts of this book, but illustrated and magnified by reference to the other parts.

On the Organic Development of Trinitarian Notions

The first conclusion pertains to the first part of the book. It is the idea that one can interpret the New Testament in light of patristic tradition in such a way as to derive a credible basis for Trinitarian theology from historical study of the Church's early tradition. This early matrix of Christian notions of the Trinity can and should in turn serve as the basis for coherent thinking about the Trinity.

To illustrate this thesis, let us briefly summarize the first part of the book. There we considered the seeds of Trinitarian doctrine as they are provided in revelation itself. God is unveiled to us, in the Old and New Testaments, as one God, who is Father, Son, and Holy Spirit. The Son in his human life among us makes overt reference to the Father and the Spirit as interpersonal subjects distinct from himself and manifests his divine identity and authority in implicit and explicit ways. In light of Jesus' resurrection and exaltation, the early Christian community confessed him as Lord, worshiped him, and articulated a notion of his pre-existence, incarnation, divine identity, and unity with the Father. The apostolic doctrine of Paul, John, and the letter to the Hebrews, which contains this teaching, provides sure ground for the Church's eventual dogmatic expression of faith in the one God as Father, Son, and Holy Spirit.

In the early Church, prior to the council of Nicaea, diverse conceptual models and traditions arose for thinking about God theologically. I denoted one of these as the "monological model" of the early Christian apologists, who taught that Christ is the Logos of the Father, thus depicting God as a transcendent subject who creates all things in his Reason and his Spirit. I distinguished this model from that of "economic Trinitarianism" represented by Irenaeus, who spoke of the Father, Son, and Spirit as distinct personal subjects manifested by their activity in the economy of creation and redemption. Although these models are compatible, and were often employed by the same Church Fathers simultaneously, they remain of themselves something incomplete, still in need of integration into a more developed and collectively unified vision. The catalyst for this development came about as a result of the twin challenges of Sabellianism and Arianism, which galvanized the Church to treat overtly topics such as the divinity and eternal hypostatic distinction of the Son and Spirit, the unity of essence in the Trinity, and the question of Trinitarian monotheism (how there can exist three distinct personal subjects in God who are each the one God). Here, several motifs emerged that were to become central to the Church's Trinitarian doctrine and theological self-understanding. The first is the notion of *three distinct hypostases*, or personal subjects, in God—the Father, the Son, and the Holy Spirit—who are *consubstantial*, that is to say, one in being and essence. The second is the notion that a distinction of persons in God arises chiefly from *relations of origin*, such that the Son is truly God (having all that pertains to the divine nature) but has this only ever from the Father, as one eternally begotten of the Father. The Spirit likewise is truly God, but as one who is eternally spirated by the Father through and with the Son. Third, this depiction of the inner life of the Trinity makes overt use of an analogy from human acts of the mind, those pertaining to knowledge and love, whereby the eternal procession of the Son from the Father as his Word is understood by a similitude drawn from the procession of human conceptual knowledge from the knower, while the eternal procession of the Spirit from the Father and the Son is understood by a similitude drawn from the procession of human love toward the beloved. I have argued that this psychological analogy has its roots in scripture and pre-Nicene patristic traditions, going all the way back to John 1:1–3, and is rightly understood as an essential element of the early Church's confession of the Trinitarian faith. Finally, we can add the notion of a distinction between the eternal processions of the persons in God and the temporal missions of the Son and the Spirit, who come into the world to reveal the Trinity.

The first, second, and third of the notions just mentioned allowed post-Nicene Catholic Christians to harmonize the two predominant models from the pre-Nicene period. The model of the apologists is understood in light of the psychological analogy: God is characterized by an eternal immanent life of Logos and Spirit that transcends, precedes, and gives being to creation (God creates by his Reason and Spirit). However, there is also a real distinction of divine persons in God. Even though the Son and Spirit are personally distinct from the Father, from all eternity, they are also truly God, and equal to the Father, because each of them possesses from the Father the fullness of the deity. The fourth notion mentioned above (Augustine's distinction of processions and missions) permitted pro-Nicene theologians to acknowledge the distinction of the persons manifest in the economy (rightly underscored by the economic Trinitarianism of the pre-Nicene period), without casting into doubt the pre-existing distinction of the persons. In fact, the pre-existent distinction of the persons in their eternal processions is the basis for the temporal missions, since the persons sent proceed from the Father, and the missions do genuinely reveal the eternal persons in their immanent relations. The Trinity, however, does not arise as a result of the economy and is not constituted developmentally by the economic missions of the persons.

Based on these fundamental notions of Trinitarian doctrine, the patristic authors in turn developed the idea of proper names given only to one person (such as Father, Word, and Spirit) and common names attributed to the divine nature, common to all three persons (such as simplicity, power, wisdom, and goodness). The first set of names is essential to Trinitarian theology in order to develop an understanding of the real distinction of hypostatic persons in God, while the second is essential in order to acknowledge the unicity of being and nature that is characteristic of the Trinity as the one God. The early Church began to develop sophisticated theological reflection on both of these types of divine names, as various theories emerged regarding the proper way to make attribution of terms to God. Of particular importance in this regard was the theory of Dionysius the Areopagite, who posited a threefold qualification for our language of God, based on causal resemblance, apophatic negation, and pre-eminent excellence. His emphasis on the incomprehensibility and transcendence of the divine nature was to inspire Western medieval thought, especially that of Thomas Aquinas. Meanwhile, Augustine sowed the seeds of later medieval discourse about the persons (proper names for persons) with his claim that relations in the Trinity are not accidental, as they are in created substances. Augustine realized that if the relations that distinguish the persons are mere properties of the persons, then there are distinguishing properties held by each person singularly that are not held by all of them collectively, in which case it is difficult to see how they are truly one in being and essence. Consequently, Augustine posited that relations in God mysteriously characterize the persons in all that they are, since the persons of the Son and Spirit receive all that they are as God by way of generation and spiration. This insight opened a pathway toward the later medieval idea (expressed at the Fourth Lateran Council) that the persons of the Trinity are both one in essence and personally relative to one another in ways that are utterly dissimilar to human creaturely persons. Because they are truly one in being and consubstantial, their unity and their relationality must be characterized in a highly qualified fashion when comparing their communion with our created communion of persons, even when human persons resemble the Trinity, by grace, in the common life of the Church.

We now can return to our conclusion from this first part of the book, regarding the organic development of Christian theological teaching, and it can be stated in a threefold way. First, the arguments of this book are meant to suggest that one can identify and represent credibly an intelligible line of development of doctrine in regard to the mystery of the Trinity.[1] It is one that stems from the prophetic and apostolic relation of the Old and New Testaments and that unfolds in pre- and post-Nicene Christian authors, giving rise eventually to articulated notions that are enunciated in conciliar definitions (such as those of Nicaea, Chalcedon, and Lateran IV) and that in turn give rise to speculative theological reflection on the mystery of God. The post-Nicene traditions of speculative theology from the patristic era in turn deeply affect and inform the medieval theological and spiritual writing that is done on the Trinity.

Second, the arguments of the first part of this book clearly suggest that within this larger setting of a developmental patrimony of Trinitarian ideas

---

1. Here, by doctrine I mean to indicate *sacra doctrina* in an extended sense. Taken in this way the term indicates divine revelation itself, as received and interpreted in the authoritative ecclesial tradition, which includes dogmatic formulas, but also in the successive mainstream traditions of theological reception and articulation to which scripture and tradition give rise, and which typically collate into schools of theology and traditions of theological reflection.

transmitted creatively through successive eras, we can locate the Trinitarian thought of Thomas Aquinas as one deeply informed by patristic ideas. He receives and interprets each of the central notions mentioned above: hypostatic personal distinction, unity of essence (consubstantiality), relations of origin, the use of the psychological analogy to understand the eternal processions, the distinction of processions and missions, the notion that the persons are relational in a non-accidental way, the fundamental distinction and use of proper names and common names, and the use of analogy, in the service of a moderate apophaticism, to signal the transcendence and incomprehensible mystery of God. Of course, Aquinas does much more than this, and his own reflection on the Trinity is living and creative, not slavishly traditionalistic. But he clearly is a theologian informed profoundly by patristic insights and sensibilities, such that it is intellectually misleading to think of him as conducting a form of theology somehow opposite to or juxtaposed against the patristic way of thinking about the Trinity, or even more crassly, as a rationalist philosopher of the divine essence whose thought inevitably militates against any real encounter with and reflection on the Trinitarian persons. To say that Aquinas is an authentic student of and inheritor of patristic traditions, both East and West, is not to say that he is the only such inheritor, or that those in the Thomistic tradition have a uniquely privileged vantage point from which to judge the patristic patrimony. Trinitarian theology in the Thomistic tradition does tend to emphasize certain central interpretive tenets (such as the notion of the persons in God as subsistent relations), and does tend to evaluate the antecedent and subsequent tradition in light of such notions. Every school of theology creates hermeneutical points of emphasis of this kind, as does every theologian, however latently, who reflects on such matters. Nevertheless, one can present what one takes to be a conceptually advantageous principle of interpretation of patristic Trinitarian traditions, such as the notion of subsistent relations derived from Thomism, while also acknowledging that in principle notions from this same early tradition can be received and interpreted in alternative ways. Augustine, for example, is in "obediential potency" to both Thomism and Bonaventurianism, as he is to many other subsequent schools of theological interpretation and understanding. Our point, then, is not the idea that only Thomism is truly patristic, but that Aquinas is truly patristic. And, indeed, one should also expand the claim more generally: the Western scholastic enterprise of the High Middle Ages typically is deeply affected by patristic principles when it comes to the elaboration and articulation of Trinitarian doctrine. Strong oppositions of medieval versus patristic, or Thomistic versus patristic, Trinitarian theology are thus ill advised.

The third and final conclusion of this first part is more suggestive than instantiated. It is the claim that the patristic principles, as interpreted by Aquinas, remain highly relevant for Trinitarian theology today, as expressed in a modern and contemporary mode. Precisely because theology cannot forego a grounding in the perennial principles of the past, it must creatively retrieve them in the context of new intellectual questions, spiritual experiences, and cultural challenges. Complex debates arise about how this is best accomplished, and whether and how Thomistic thought can play a constructive role within modern Trinitarian theology. What the first part of this book suggests, however, is that even antecedent to the question of whether and how Thomism might make a contribution to modern Trinitarian theology there is the question of what Trinitarian notions from the classical patristic era are to be preserved in the modern one, and in what fashion. In the subsequent parts of this book, I have argued that there is, within Trinitarian theology, a normative role to be played by a theology of the divine nature (as expressed by Aquinas in the *de Deo ut uno* treatise), and my argument is coupled with an appeal to the patristic concept of relations of origin and the use of the psychological analogy to understand the immanent life of the Trinity. These are not fashionable views. So theologians should reflect upon such strong claims, because if I am correct, then modern Trinitarian theology is typically somewhat off-kilter. In related fashion, following Gilles Emery and Bruce Marshall, I have emphasized the capital importance of the distinction of eternal processions and temporal missions as a key to the discussion of the economy. These are essential elements of the ancient pro-Nicene doctrinal synthesis, ones that can and should be preserved in a contemporary theological context. In appealing to the Thomistic Trinitarian tradition in order to retrieve these patristic principles, and by interpreting them in a Thomistic way in the process, I am suggesting one particular way that the liveliness of the Nicene Trinitarian tradition can be received and extended into present theological discourse. (I will return to this point below, in my fourth conclusion.) Of course what I have presented in this book is only one proposal of a Thomistic pathway forward in modern theology, not an attempt to provide a normative declaration of dogmatic definitions. (Theologians who want to live in the Church with others need to

learn to distinguish ecclesial dogma from schools of theology.) Nevertheless, everyone must seek to think about what he or she believes about God
in our modern context, and, in this regard, I am arguing that Thomism is a
helpful guide for thinking about the contemporary relevance of Athanasius,
Gregory of Nazianzus, Augustine, and Dionysius, as expositors of Nicene
Trinitarianism.

On the Essential Importance of a Trinitarian Theology
of the Divine Nature

A second main thesis derives from the second part of the book and pertains
to the divine nature. Trinitarian theology always includes the question of
what God is. Precisely because the Father, Son, and Holy Spirit are truly
one in being and essence, and thus consubstantial, it is essential to consider that in virtue of which they are one, namely, the divine nature. Likewise,
Christianity implies a plenary reception of Old Testament prophetic revelation, and thus it is truly monotheistic. Accordingly, the notions of the
simplicity of the divine nature and the transcendent unity of God are not
accidental to Trinitarian thinking. Without such ideas, the doctrine of the
Trinity itself makes no sense, and so reflection on such notions is essential
to any coherent and profound understanding of the Trinity.

As we noted in the first part of this book, the Cappadocians and Augustine were, all of them, concerned to reflect on the mystery of the divine nature precisely so as to respond to the challenge of Arianism as well as to a
nascent rationalism of theologians like Eunomius, who refused the mystery
of the Trinity in the name of a theology of divine unity. Thus, they sought
to articulate a theology of the divine nature, in its incomprehensible transcendence, precisely so as to name that in virtue of which the three persons
are one. This allowed them to underscore the mystery of the Son's and the
Spirit's plenary possession of the fullness of the divine nature and life, which
they receive from the Father.

Aquinas's treatise on the names or attributes of God as one (*de Deo ut
uno*) forms an essential constituent of his Trinitarian theology that cannot
be ignored if a retrieval of his thinking about God is to be conducted in
an integral fashion. Every one of the divine attributes that he considers has
consequences for our way of thinking about the Trinity, consequences that
are of the utmost significance. In studying the simplicity of the Trinity, we
are better able to acknowledge the incomprehensible transcendence of God,

who is not physically composite, and whose nature is unique (only the one God is God). His being is utterly other than beings that have created existence, as his existence is underivative, unparticipated, and thus unfathomable. He does not actuate his perfections accidentally through time and history but contains all time and history within his transcendent plenitude of perfection. Likewise, the persons of the Father, Son, and Spirit, if they are truly one in essence, and if that essence is simple, must each possess all that pertains to God wholly and truly, so that each person is wholly within the other, and has in himself all that pertains to the others, as God from God, light from light, and true God from true God.

If the divine nature is infinitely perfect and good, then we must underscore that there is neither developmental history nor ontological evil in the life of the Trinity. The life of God, being infinite, cannot be characterized by a series of developmental stages of perfection or by moral evolution through his engagement with the economy. We cannot rightly project onto God the ontological limitations and defects of the finite cosmos nor the failures of spiritual persons manifest in angelic and human history. This perfection does not somehow remove God from us, however. Quite the contrary is the case. If the Trinity is infinite, then the Trinity is also able to be present within and unto all that is, omnipresent to the history of creation. As author of our being, the Trinity is closer to us than we are to ourselves, and as the author of grace, the Trinity is present personally within our souls, illumining our minds and inflaming our hearts so that we might know and possess God by faith, hope, and love in this life, and by vision in the next. No natural defect and no moral failure is so great that it could create an abyss or rupture that God could not cross, precisely because God is always already present to us, as the heart of our being, awaiting us and stirring us up from within to consent freely to the re-creative activity of divine wisdom and love.

The Trinity is immutable and impassible, not because God is indifferent to creatures, incapable of knowing and loving them, or incapable of relating to them personally. Rather, the contrary is the case: God is so perfectly present and personal, as only God can be in his infinite perfection, that God is able to give without receiving, to know intimately all that we are without learning from us, and to love in his infinite goodness without self-amelioration. Even when one of the Trinity suffers and dies as a human being, in agony, and thus really suffers personally, the divine nature of that person remains impassible, transcendent in its splendor and perfection. This is important for metaphysical reasons, related to the confession of the one God and the transcendence of the Trinity as the Creator who gives all things being, without receiving its being from them (thus excluding alterations of the divine nature incurred through passible suffering). However, it is also important for soteriological reasons. God expresses God's identification and solidarity with us by suffering in agony as one who is truly human. But, because of his eternal and unchanging power of love, God can also act even from within his suffering to effectively redeem the world and overcome our suffering. If Jesus is not God in his crucifixion, then he cannot save us, and it is only by a genuine theology of the divine nature that we can have some understanding of what it means to say that Jesus is God. Consequently, a genuine theology of the divine nature is essential to any authentic theology of the Cross, one that confesses not only that Jesus is the only savior of all human beings, but that also confesses that he is so precisely because he is truly God and truly human.

The Trinity is eternal and is one in knowledge and in love. As we have noted, Aquinas follows Boethius in understanding eternity not only as perennial being, but as the plenary possession of perfect life. God is life, and his life is eternal. It consists in a transcendent and incomprehensible plenitude of knowledge and love. God knows himself and, in knowing himself, knows all things that he creates. God loves himself in his own infinite goodness and, in doing so, freely communicates being to all creatures, as a finite (but for us immeasurable) expression outside himself of his own goodness. Understood in this way, there can be no competition or confusion between the eternal life of the Trinity, on the one hand, and the historical and ontological unfolding of the economy on the other. God's eternity is neither external to our temporal creation nor identical with it. We can say, rather, in a true sense, that creation unfolds within the eternity of God, and God's eternal Triune life is present within all of history. God's life of knowledge and love is shared by all three persons in God. They each know and love all of creation, all that has been, all that is, and all that will come to be and exist in time. They know and love created persons in particular, each of whom is created in the image of the Trinity and is intended for union with God by grace and divine inhabitation by the persons of God. Their eternal knowledge and love thus encompass and accompany the unfolding history of human persons, in their collectivity and individuality. The trinity is the uncreated communion of persons that eternally precedes the created communion of persons that is the Church. At the same time, the Trinitarian persons are not constituted or created by their knowledge and love of creation, nor is their communion in any way dependent upon the life of the Church, the decisions of created persons, or the unfolding features of creation, with its complex and multilayered cosmic history.

The persons of the Trinity are one in nature, and omnipotent in their shared active power. There is only one God, and God can do all things. It is due to their natural unicity and omnipotence that the persons of the Trinity act only ever as one, from all eternity, when they create and redeem. All action of God *ad extra* is the action of all three persons of the Holy Trinity. It is the Father, Son, and Holy Spirit who create and redeem together as distinct hypostatic subjects, who are truly one in virtue of their shared nature, wisdom, will, and power. Some worry that this traditional theological notion, derived from Cappadocian theology, will interfere with the right acceptance of the distinctive action and communication of grace proper to each Trinitarian person. However, the contrary is in fact the case, as we have noted in this book. The monotheistic acknowledgement of the unity of the divine action and willing of the three persons is a necessary theological prelude to a consideration of the personal mode of action of the Father, Son, and Holy Spirit. If the divine persons truly act together as one God, and are truly distinct personally, then they must be distinguished by relations of origin, not by degrees of possession of the divine attributes. But if each person is truly God only ever "relatively," as one who is from another or toward another, then each one is truly God only ever in a unique personal mode, be it paternal, filial, or spirated. Thus, each one is all-powerful and active in a personal way, as only the Father is, or as only the Son is, or as only the Holy Spirit is. While the persons eternally only ever act together, in their shared divine willing, they also eternally only ever act in three distinctive ways, as the Father does, as the Son does, and as the Spirit does. Their personal mystery can be reflected in their common activity and common effects, therefore, as all creatures bear, in some way, a manifest trace of the Trinity, and this Trinitarian reflection of God's effects is evidenced particularly in the works of grace and redemption, which reveal the three persons.

We can summarize these remarks by noting key ways that the theology of the divine nature plays an essential role in any classically originated theology of the Holy Trinity. First, such a theology marks out the transcendence of the Trinity, as the one God and Creator, utterly distinct from creatures in his incomprehensible mystery, even if also omnipresent to all creation. Without a theology of the divine nature, it ultimately becomes difficult to distinguish the persons of the Trinity from the economy in which they manifest themselves.

Second, this theology of the divine nature is essential in order to understand the unity and equality of the three persons. If we wish to say that they are each truly God, then the notion of God must have a meaningful content that pertains to each of them, and this requires that there must be a theology of the divine nature, of what God is.

Third, however, we also must have recourse to a theology of the divine nature to understand the real distinction of the three persons, and how it can be conceived rightly. If the three persons are each the one God and, therefore, entirely equal in essence and one in being, and if the divine nature of God is simple, then the persons are distinguished by their relations of origin, as the common Greek and Latin traditions of the Church maintain. In this case, however, as Augustine understood, their relationality is not accidental. Instead, the mystery of the divine persons can be thought of principally under the auspices of relationality. They are truly relative to one another in all they are, as subsisting relations. Without a theology of the divine nature, and a corresponding reflection on the simplicity of the one God, this relational understanding of the three persons is not fully accessible to us intellectually. Without such an understanding, our grasp of Trinitarian monotheism becomes tenuous.

Fourth, if we employ the psychological analogy to understand the immanent life of the Holy Trinity, it is important to have a theology of the divine nature, precisely so that we can understand how this analogy applies to the persons of the Trinity, in accordance with the doctrine of relations of origin. The act of the human mind that produces a concept does bear a similitude to the procession of the Son from the Father as the Word of God, and the act of the will by which a person loves another does bear a similitude to the procession of the Spirit from the Father and the Word, as their mutually spirated Love. Nevertheless, such similitudes are highly qualified, since the Son and Spirit each possess the plenitude of knowledge and love that the Father possesses in virtue of the divine nature and life within him, which he communicates to the Son in generation and to the Spirit with the Son in spiration. Only if one has a theology of the divine nature, so as to reflect on what is common to the Son and Spirit, can one appropriate a theology of the psychological analogy coherently in a qualified way, so as to maintain a monotheistic understanding of the unity of the persons, while still acknowledging the proper value of the analogy as a way of designating the inner life of the Trinitarian processions.

Fifth, the doctrine of the divine nature is essential to a coherent theology of Trinitarian perichoresis, since it is especially when we acknowledge that the Father, Son, and Holy Spirit are one in divine essence that we come to understand rightly how they are present in one another personally. Because the Son possesses in himself the plenitude of the divine life and nature from the Father by generation, so he has all that is in the Father within himself, and all that is in himself is within the Father. This is true in turn of the Spirit in virtue of spiration.

Sixth and finally, it is nearly impossible to understand rightly the distinction of the eternal processions and the temporal missions if we do not have an adequate sense of the divine nature in its distinction from creation and the economy of grace. This is nowhere truer than in the case of the visible mission of the Word, in which he takes on a human nature in the Incarnation. In virtue of the hypostatic union, the second person of the Trinity subsists in two natures, without confusion or separation. In virtue of one of these natures, which is mysterious and incomprehensible, he is one with the Father and the Spirit. He is true God and Lord. In virtue of the other he is truly human, and possesses a humanity mysteriously perfected by a plenitude of grace. Christ's hypostatic person, which subsists in both divine and human natures, is the locus par excellence of the revelation of the Trinity. We cannot approach this mystery rightly, however, in its almost unfathomable depths, if we do not also acknowledge a theology of the divine nature of Christ, the nature in virtue of which he is truly one with the Father and the Spirit, and in which he is naturally distinct from us, insofar as, unlike all other human beings, he is truly God.

The Psychological Analogy and a Relationalist
Account of the Trinity

Our third conclusion originates principally from the arguments of the third part of this book. As we noted there, the appeal to an analogy from acts of the mind (acts of knowledge and love) forms the basis for a traditional Western theological understanding of the immanent processions of the Son and Spirit from the Father. This appeal to the so-called psychological analogy is typically Augustinian, but I have argued that it has roots in scrip-ture and takes on various expressions prior to Augustine, in the work of the pre-Nicene apologists and Athanasius. In my presentation of Aquinas, as a receiver and interpreter of the patristic heritage, I have argued that this no-tion is of capital importance for the articulation of a properly analogical (as opposed to merely metaphorical) presentation of the immanent life of the Holy Trinity.

The argument as I have stated it could be summarized somewhat in these terms.[2] Christians can know the mystery of God's intra-Trinitarian life based on God's manifestation of it to us in the economy, as we see there dis-tinct personal processions: the Son and the Spirit who proceed from the Fa-ther, as God from God. Such processions are either immanent or transitive, that is to say, they take place in God himself as constituting God's own eter-nal life ontologically prior to creation and without necessary reference to it, or they take place in view of the external action of creation and thus in nec-essary relation to it. In the latter case, the processions of the Son and Spirit can take place only in view of an economic activity, and thus are only ever "eternally" related to created realities distinct from God. God's eternal pro-cessional life would thus be constituted eternally by a self-determination for creation and in view of the economy. However, if God is truly the Creator of all that is, who gives to creation all that it is, without receiving his eternal identity from creation, such transitive economic processions are not possi-ble. Therefore, the eternal processions of Trinitarian life should be under-stood as immanent, not transitive.

However, there are only two created immanent immaterial activities known to us, that of knowing and that of loving. We cannot have any under-standing of the mystery of the intra-Trinitarian life except by analogy with these two activities. Accordingly, we need to make use of the psychological analogy if we wish to achieve some theological insight into the mystery of the immanent life of the Trinity, and thus base our Christian contempla-tion of the Trinity on something intellectual and not merely voluntarist (by mere obedient submission to Church dictate) or pietistic (through religious emotivism).

This thesis can be illustrated negatively by considering various options

---

2. In the following paragraphs I am greatly indebted to Guy Mansini, who helped me restate the argument of the book in this way.

in modern theology. If we wish to understand the mystery of the immanent Trinitarian life of distinct persons, but not by way of immanent activities and processions, then we must appeal to transitive activity to account for distinct persons. Transitive divine activity can be conceived of as (a) creative, (b) as terminating in an effect upon creation, for example through the economy of salvation, or (c) as something accidental to the Trinitarian persons that arises strictly between them but that newly qualifies them. In the first case, the processions are acts of creation: the Father creates the Son and the Spirit. In the patristic era this idea took shape in Arianism, and was rejected by the Church. In a modern context it takes on a new form in what Barth called "modernist Protestantism," where the notion of a divine procession is seen merely as a conceptual super-structure projected by the early Church onto a merely human Jesus, who was himself a religious genius and major spiritual figure, but not the second person of the Trinity. The second idea is typical of continental Trinitarian theology in the twentieth century: the processions of the Son and Spirit are intelligible to us precisely as transitive acts terminating in the incarnation, passion, and resurrection of the Son, and the sending of the Spirit. According to this second way, the persons are really related, from all eternity, to created realities. In some real sense, then, God's life is not in fact wholly immanent in itself, independent of, and eternally transcendent of the created order. His Trinitarian life is constituted by his free decision to create, incarnate, and redeem, or at least it has no other intelligibility to us than under these auspices. In the third notion of processions as transitive acts, the relations of the persons are accidental. They arise only from free decisions of the persons, subsequent to their constitution. Here the Trinitarian persons are depicted as pre-existing individual subjects who "agree" to work together and forge a moral union of transitive activity, based on a common consensus of distinct minds and wills. Their life of "procession" amounts to the relational order of their common decision making and initiation of shared action. This third way, which is suggested by ideas one finds in some analytic philosophers, is excessively tritheistic. Effectively, it abandons the idea of immanent processions in God, for we end up with three gods transitively related to one another, each one of whose inner life is opaque to us. In neither the second nor the third way, therefore, do we attain to an immanent Trinitarian life such as is disclosed to us in scripture.

In defending the normative value of the psychological analogy, I am not, of course, arguing in favor of something distinctively Thomistic, since this analogy is employed in various ways, so I have argued, by persons as diverse as Justin Martyr, Irenaeus, Athanasius, Gregory of Nazianzus, Augustine, Bonaventure, Aquinas, Scotus, and (in a highly attenuated sense) Ockham, and a host of more contemporary theologians, Eastern and Western, Catholic, Orthodox, and Protestant. The ways in which the analogy can be interpreted, then, are many. Not all of them depend upon explicit appeal to the Augustinian notion of voluntary love as a similitude for the procession of the Spirit, but all of them do make some appeal to a similitude to the Trinity taken from acts of the human mind.

However, some aspects of Aquinas's vision of this analogy are seminal and of perennial value. In differentiation from Richard of St. Victor, Bonaventure, and Scotus, Aquinas does not think that one can demonstrate argumentatively that there is a distinction of persons in God based upon the premise that God is knowledge and love. Nor does he hold that knowledge and love are formally distinct in God's nature. He does note, however, that if there are two processions in God, as is revealed in scripture, then we can understand these immanent acts of God in his eternal life only by appeal to similitudes of knowledge and love *as relational terms.* Here he appeals to the traditional notion of relations of origin to understand the processions of knowledge and love in God, but qualifies these by his teaching on divine simplicity. Since there are no ontological accidents in God, the relations in God cannot be mere properties, or accidents of the divine persons. Rather, the persons must be defined mysteriously as "subsistent relations." Each divine person is wholly relational, being always only from another or for another in procession, and yet simultaneously each person is wholly divine, truly God in all that he is.

This idea has many consequences. First, it allows us to understand the immanent life of the Trinity as one in which the three persons are truly distinct, wholly equal, and consubstantial. They are truly distinct because each one is related to the others as the fontal source of the others (the Father), or as proceeding from one and as fontal source of the other (the Son), or as proceeding from the other two as from one principle (the Spirit). They are truly equal because each one possesses the totality and plenitude of the divine nature. They are consubstantial because each possesses the singular godhead, being the one God in three distinct ways, paternal Source, generated Word, or spirated Spirit.

Second, this idea allows one to construe an analogy of personhood that is applicable to the Trinitarian persons. If a human person is an individual of a rational nature, a divine person is a subsistent mode of being of the divine nature. The Father subsists eternally as God in a paternal mode, the Son in a filial mode, and the Spirit in a spirated mode. The mode of subsistence of each person depends upon his relational order of being, as one who generates and spirates, or as one who is generated and spirates, or as one who is spirated. Each of them is a person who subsists in a unique way as God.

Third, as we have seen in part 3 of this book, Aquinas's notion of subsistent relations has consequences for one's understanding of the procession of the Spirit and the dogmatic expression of the *Filioque*, interpreted in an ecumenical light. On a Thomistic understanding of relational personhood, if the Father is the eternal origin of the Spirit, he can be so only as one who is also always related to the Son, who also proceeds from him (precisely as Father). Therefore, the Son is always present in the Father who spirates the Spirit, and therefore as one through whom he spirates. Furthermore, if the Son is distinguishable from the Spirit according to a relation of origin (which is the only way to distinguish intelligibly two persons who are each wholly God), and if the Spirit comes forth through the Son (and not the inverse), then it becomes incumbent upon us to take seriously the notion that the Spirit originates eternally from the Father and the Son. To be distinguished from the Son as one who comes "through" the Son is to be distinguished also as one who is "from" the Son. Even here, however, one must underscore that the Son has all that he has from the Father, by a relation of origin, so that even if the Spirit proceeds from the Father and the Son as from one principle (as Western theology typically asserts), he must still proceed from the Father principally and from the Son derivatively, insofar as the Son receives all that he has from the Father, including the power of spiration of the Spirit.

Fourth, Aquinas's relationalist account of persons in the Trinity allows us to understand perichoresis in an especially poignant way, as we have noted. This approach underscores that the Son has all that pertains to divine life from the Father, while the Spirit has it from the Father and the Son. Consequently, all that is in the Father is in the Son, and all that is in the Father and the Son is in the Spirit. Furthermore, in virtue of the doctrine of subsistent relations, we can say that each person is present to all that is in another person in virtue of eternal generation and spiration, since the activity of procession in one person terminates immanently in all that the other person is, who receives all that he is from the other. Intra-divine actions result not only in a distinction of persons but also in an immanent mutual reciprocity. The persons are utterly present to and within one another eternally in virtue of their reciprocal relations.

Fifth, this notion of subsistent relations allows us to make coherent sense of the patristic practice of "appropriation" as something other than mere conjecture or subjective projection. The persons possess in equality the essential divine attributes considered in the second part of the book, but they are rightly said to enjoy them according to a relational mode of subsistence. The Father is powerful like the Son and Spirit, but as the paternal origin of all things, while the Son is wise like the Spirit and the Father, but as the Word through whom all things are made, and the Spirit is good from and with the Father and the Son, but as their eternally spirated Love, the source of all goodness in creation.

Sixth, Aquinas's concept allows one to understand the unity and personal mode of Trinitarian action. The three persons act outside themselves only ever as one, in virtue of their shared divine nature, understanding, and will, and yet they also only ever act as three persons, each one operating in a personal mode, as paternal Source, filial Word, and spirated Love. No opposition should be posited between God's unity of action in the economy, on the one hand, and the manifestation of the three persons, on the other. The former, unity of action, is the condition of possibility for the manifestation of the three persons, and always presupposes the eternal communion of the three in their personal activity.

Seventh and finally, Aquinas's relationalist account affects the way one conceives of the divine missions of the Son and the Spirit. The Son and the Spirit can be sent into the world because they proceed eternally from the Father, but when they are sent, they are also always consubstantial with the Father. Consequently, as divine persons, they also will their own sending with the Father and from the Father. He does not do anything that he does without them. The divine missions therefore bear the imprint of the common will of the Trinity, as God wills to render the inner processional life of God present in the world by grace. When the Son acts in the world in his visible mission he acts with the Father and in the Spirit, as one who is from the Father and who is the source of the Spirit. When the Spirit acts in the world he acts as the Spirit of the Father and the Son, sent by them into the world to manifest himself as the Love who proceeds, and in so doing to manifest the Father and the Son from whom he proceeds. The mission activity of the Son and the Spirit reveals, then, both the unity of the Trinity and the real distinction of persons in their inner life of processions of origin. The work of the missions arises from the eternal communion that the persons possess prior to all action in the economy, but it also renders that life present within the economy. It is meant to lead us by grace beyond the created order into an intimate encounter with divine persons in their eternal communion. The immanent Trinity is thus the alpha and omega of the whole economy of creation, redemption, and divinization.

On the Distinction of Processions and Missions, and the Two Natures of Christ

A fourth conclusion stems from the fourth part of this book. It is the claim that the distinction of eternal processions and temporal missions is the key to a theology of the divine economy, one that helps us understand the promise of Thomistic theology within a post-Hegelian setting. The temporal missions of the Son and the Spirit manifest the eternal processions of Trinitarian life. As such they truly invite us into communion with God as he is in himself. However, the missions do not constitute the eternal processions, nor do they enrich or transform them. Consequently, all that pertains to the divine economy—election, creation, revelation, incarnation, the paschal mystery, Pentecost—occurs as subsequent to the mystery of God, who is "pre-constituted" as Trinitarian from all eternity and unto all eternity, and whose life can encompass all events in time.

It follows from this line of thinking that there really is no such thing as an economic Trinity, that is to say, a Trinity that undergoes development through a history of shared life with creatures. God is eternally identical with himself, not imperfectly static but incomprehensibly alive, and perfectly actual in life. The Trinity in its perfection therefore transcends the creation ontologically, but is also immanently present to it, as God in his perfection continually communicates existence to all creatures and grace to created persons. The whole economy comes forth from the undiminishable bountifulness of the Trinity, which is not restricted by creaturely finitude, or diminished by suffering or evil. Far from rendering God uncompassionate, this perfection of the Trinity is the *sine qua non* for God's perfectly rendering himself present to all things, an activity that includes his presence to and in our human suffering. Only the One who is infinite in perfection can be omnipresent to all things as Creator and can act by grace in all times and places. God the Father does this particularly through the missions of the Son and Spirit, in a process that reaches its pinnacle in the life, death, and resurrection of Jesus Christ, and in the outpouring of the Spirit at Pentecost.

We can qualify this first idea of the distinction of processions and missions by a second one, mentioned above: that pertaining to the personal modes of action of the three persons of the Trinity. As previously noted, the Father, Son, and Holy Spirit act *ad extra* only ever as one, in virtue of their shared nature, life, and will, but they also act only in three distinct personal modes, so that their action always bears the imprint of their personal relations and internal order of procession. This idea applies to the missions themselves. They are simultaneously the work of the Father, Son, and Spirit. However, they also reveal the modal distinctions of the three persons. When the Son is sent into the world, he always works with the Father and in doing so reveals the Father, from whom he originates, as well as the Spirit, whom he spirates and sends with the Father. His revelation of himself is filial, even as it is conducted with the Father and the Spirit. In the Spirit's mission, the Spirit acts only with the Father and the Son as their common Spirit, who reveals them even as he also manifests himself as their uncreated Gift and Love. Understood in this light, the economic revelation of the Trinity always bears the imprint of the immanent Trinity, manifesting both the real distinction and the real unity of the three persons.

We should note how, on this view, the second, third, and fourth parts of this book interlock. There is only one God (part 2), and in virtue of the one nature of God that is simple, we can understand that the processions of God are based on relations of origin (part 3). The relations are not accidents in God but are substantial, such that each person is a subsistent relation. In virtue of eternal generation and spiration, all that is in one person is in another. There are three truly distinct persons in God, but there is only one God subsisting in three really distinct personal modes. Consequently, when the Trinitarian persons act outside of themselves in creation, they act as one in being and nature and they act as three persons (part 4). Their work of self-revelation in the divine missions therefore reveals who they truly are in their personal distinctions, based on the eternal processions, and it truly reveals that they are each the one God.

What, then, does it mean to say that the original creation itself is Trinitarian, or that the creation bears the imprint of the Trinity? According to our line of analysis, the original gift of creation does not stem from an antecedent kenosis that takes place in the life of God. Only one who has an infinitely perfect power, wisdom, and goodness can create. These attributes are inalienable in God. They are present in all three persons eternally and are not subject to alteration or diminishment. Creation is Trinitarian not because the Father freely empties himself so as to make space for the Son to exist freely apart from himself, and then creates all things in the distance between himself and the Son (as Bulgakov and Balthasar evocatively suggest). Creation is Trinitarian because the Father freely gives all things being from his eternal plenitude of divine goodness, in his Son and in his Spirit. From all eternity, the Son and the Spirit, because they possess the Father's divine fullness perfectly, share fully in this free action of communicating existence to all things. The Son can create with the Father in the freedom of divine love just because, being from the Father, he has in himself all that the Father has, including the Father's goodness and active power of creation, just as the Spirit can create with them because, being of the Father and the Son, he too possesses this same plenitude of goodness, power, and creative freedom. The interior communion of Trinitarian life, wherein the Father eternally gives all that he is to the Son, and the Father and the Son eternally give all that they are to the Spirit, precedes and is the primal measure of all creational giving, all participated existence. The uncreated communion of personhood is the ontological premise of the created communion of persons.

Creatures resemble the Trinity, then, in a threefold way. They bear the ontological insignia of the Father insofar as each one of them is substantial and enduring. However they also refer back to him as each originates from another, and is given being. Their derived existence is itself a testimony to the gift of being, which stems ultimately from the divine paternity. Insofar as creatures are intelligible, they bear the imprint of the generated Word, through whom God made all things, and who is the source of order and intelligibility in creation. Insofar as they are good in themselves and tend toward perfection, they resemble the goodness of the Spirit, the Love in whom God has made all that is good. Human beings, who are made in the image of God, resemble the Trinity in a particularly privileged way, as persons, with immaterial faculties of intellect and will. They are able to image the Trinity both individually and collectively, by spiritual communion in truth and in love. This occurs especially by grace, when human understanding is enlightened by the Word and understands all things in light of Jesus

Christ, and when the human will is enkindled with charity by the Holy Spirit, and conformed inwardly in freedom to the uncreated love of God.

The Incarnation is the visible mission par excellence. We have noted, in part 3 of this book, that a mission is the procession of God with the addition of a temporal effect, rendering the procession manifest in the economy. The Incarnation is the "effect" wherein the second person of the Trinity is manifest to us outwardly in a human nature, by his conception, birth, childhood, adult life, ministry, suffering, death, and bodily glorification. In the fourth part of this book we insisted on the importance of the Chalcedonian dogmatic distinction of the two natures in Christ. He is fully God and fully human. The actions and sufferings of God the Son in his human nature are not fully commensurate with the actions (or supposed sufferings) of God the Son in his divine nature. There are, however, similitudes between the human nature of Jesus and his divine nature. His human actions are indicative of the divine will, as are his human sufferings, which he accepts freely out of love, and his personal actions as man are revelatory of his personal relation to the Father and the Spirit. The Son's human nature, action, and suffering therefore reveal the Trinity to us. When we see the man Jesus, in his nature, actions, and sufferings, we see the Son of the Father and the sender of the Spirit. This idea can be explored without appeal to any kenotic theory that would project traits of human nature upon the divine nature. It can be explored also without making any univocal projection of human attributes onto the persons of the Trinity, so that the persons would be distinguished as God in virtue of these distinct natural attributes (what I have called inverted monophysitism).

What I am suggesting, then, is that modern Trinitarian theology has all too often drifted toward an obsession with the analogy or likeness between the immanent Trinity and the supposed economic Trinity (which I have argued is an ontological fiction), and in doing so has either projected human attributes onto the divinity of Christ, or has used distinctly human traits to distinguish the Trinitarian persons (such as command and obedience, or mutual and free self-surrender, suffering, and detachment). A Trinitarian theology that takes the economy seriously might more profitably consider the analogy or likeness between the human nature of Jesus and the divine nature of Jesus. How does the human nature of God reveal his divine nature (without any confusion of the two)? How are the human actions and sufferings of Jesus, the Son of God made man, truly indicative of the personal relations of the eternal Son to his Father and his Spirit, and of the cooperative divine life in which they share? To answer these questions in a reasonable way, one that does justice to the mystery of God in its transcendence, one must be in possession of a moderately apophatic theology of the divine nature, so as to distinguish it from the human nature of Christ. One must also be in possession of a genuine theology of divine persons as distinguished by relations of origin and not by attributions of nature (what the medieval theologians called common names), since the three persons are truly one and identical in nature. If the three persons are truly consubstantial (as designated by the *homoousios* formula), and if there are truly two natures in Christ, then the dogmatic expressions of Nicaea and Chalcedon are not optional components of Trinitarian Christology. They present us with notions that are essential to a theology of mystery, and to any rightly balanced understanding of the Trinity and the Incarnation. A Trinitarian theology of the economy can and should avert to them in a systematic way, so as to respect the numinous character of God's inner life revealed in Christ.

God does not become someone other than himself in the Incarnation. From the first moment of his conception in the womb of the Virgin Mary, the Son of God is himself God from God, light from light, true God from true God. There is not a time when the man Jesus is not the Son of God. In fact, he is the eternal Word who comes to exist among us as human, and his human nature is that of the existent Word. Anyone who physically touches the Word of life in his human body, touches God (1 John 1:1–2). Nor does God need to alter his eternal perfection or go outside of himself by augmentation or diminishment, in order to become human, since all that is in creation is already "within God," who communicates being to all things, just as the Creator is most immanent within his creation (by the causal communication of existence). Accordingly, God can begin newly to exist personally as human without altering his identity in any way and so can manifest his identity among us as one who is authentically human, just as he can create the world without altering his identity and so manifest his Trinitarian mystery in creation without being constituted by the act of creation.

In his suffering, death, and resurrection, the Son as man returns to his Father. He pours out his human life for the salvation of the world. The charity he exhibits is human. His suffering is human. His death, burial, and descent into hell are human, and his physical glorification in the resurrection is human. All of these events, however, are also events predicated of the Son of God. God suffers, dies, is buried, and rises on the third day. In all of these human experiences his divine identity is manifest to the world, and so too, then, is his relation to the Father and the Spirit, as well as the ground of unity they share as God. When Jesus acts or suffers as man, he does so as Lord, and as he who is one with the Father and the Spirit. Before the Son freely obeys and suffers as man, there is the uncreated love of God. The Father, Son, and Holy Spirit have willed the Incarnation and the redemption of the world in their transcendent, utterly mysterious unity of love. The human obedience and love of Christ in his passion and death manifests, then, this interpersonal Trinitarian love to the world. For example, the Son's human self-offering to the Father is indicative of his personal origin. It reveals what he knows humanly: that he receives all that he is from the Father, and that he is one with the Father. It reveals also that he wills, with the Father, to send the Spirit upon the world, a temporal and economic echo of an uncreated relation: the Father and the Son spirate the Spirit eternally as their mutually shared Love. It is this Trinitarian communion of uncreated love that is unveiled on the Cross. Understood in this way, the paschal mystery is a temporal iteration of the eternal processions, a visible manifestation of the eternal persons, in the flesh of Christ crucified.

The life that the Father and the Son wish to share with us is the life of the Spirit. We should think of this life in both its origin and its final end. The Spirit originates from the Father and the Son eternally as their uncreated Gift, as mutual Love, present in both the Father and the Son in the immanent reciprocity of their mutual self-giving. It is precisely this eternal Spirit that is given to us. We are invited to share by grace in the uncreated Gift of the Father and the Son, and to be transformed by that gift, to be sanctified in the Spirit, a person who is Love. As a term of human orientation, or final end, the Spirit leads us toward our common homeland, the city of God. This is a place consisting in the perfect possession of God. In this life we tend toward it by faith, and in the life to come we possess it perfectly by vision. The Spirit, who comes forth from the Father and the Son, gives us knowledge and love of the Father, in the Son, and in himself. He divinizes us above all by conforming our minds and hearts to the mystery of the Trinity. The heart of Christian life in the Spirit, then, is a mystical life of transformation by knowledge and by love.

We began this book by speaking of the role of *sacra doctrina* within the Christian life, as one with its own integrity, irreducible to that of philosophy or mystical life, but as complementary to both. We can now return to that starting point. The study of the Trinity is a distinctively theological enterprise, one that is not philosophical as such, nor identical with the mystical life of participation in the Trinity. However, it presupposes and makes use of a philosophy of the divine nature, within itself and without becoming alienated from itself. It also assists the mystical life, without pretending to constitute it or substitute for it. Theological reflection on the Trinity helps members of Christ's body live truthfully in the Spirit, so that they might contemplate the Son and serve him, and in doing so return to the Father. Trinitarian theology helps them think rightly about their own ecclesial communion of shared life in God.

It was said of St. Dominic that he spent his life either speaking to God or speaking of God. St. Thomas Aquinas was a genuine disciple of his spiritual mentor, St. Dominic, and his theology serves as a resource for the Church in her quest to speak truthfully to God and about God. To contemplate God and to preach to others from the fruits of one's contemplation: this two-fold process is essential to the mission of the Church. To serve the Trinity in this great mission of preaching, the Church today can and should still have recourse to the theology of Thomas Aquinas, and to the living Thomistic tradition, as a privileged means of interpreting and advancing her own understanding of the mystery of God.

Selected Bibliography

―――――:―――――

WORKS BY THOMAS AQUINAS

Collationes super Credo in Deum. Paris: Nouvelles Editions Latines, 1969.

De ente et essentia. In *Opuscula philosophica,* vol. 1, edited by R. Spiazzi. Turin and Rome: Marietti, 1950.

De malo. In *Sancti Thomae de Aquino opera omnia,* vol. 23. Leonine Edition. Rome: Editori di San Tommaso, 1982.

De potentia Dei. Edited by P. M. Pession. In *Quaestiones disputatae,* vol. 2, edited by R. Spiazzi. Turin and Rome: Marietti, 1965.

De rationibus fidei contra Saracenos, Graecos et Armenos ad Cantorem Antiochenum. In *Opuscula Theologica,* vol. 1, edited by R. Spiazzi and R. Verardo. Turin and Rome: Marietti, 1954.

De substantiis separatis. In *Sancti Thomae de Aquino opera omnia,* vol. 40. Leonine Edition. Rome: Editori di San Tommaso, 1968.

De veritate. In *Sancti Thomae de Aquino opera omnia,* vol. 22. Leonine Edition. Rome: Editori di San Tommaso, 1975–76.

Expositio libri Peryermenias. In *Sancti Thomae de Aquino opera omnia,* vol. 1. Leonine Edition. Rome: Editori di San Tommaso, 1882.

Expositio libri Posteriorum. In *Sancti Thomae de Aquino opera omnia,* vol. 1. Leonine Edition. Rome: Editori di San Tommaso, 1882.

Expositio super librum Boethii de Trinitate. In *Sancti Thomae de Aquino opera omnia,* vol. 50. Leonine Edition. Rome: Editori di San Tommaso, 1992.

In Aristotelis librum De anima commentarium. Edited by A. Pirotta. Edited by R. Cai. Turin and Rome: Marietti, 1959.

In duodecim libros Metaphysicorum Aristotelis expositio. Edited by M. R. Cathala and R. M. Spiazzi. Turin and Rome: Marietti, 1964.

In librum beati Dionysii de divinis nominibus expositio. Edited by C. Pera. Turin and Rome: Marietti, 1950.

In librum de causis expositio. In *Opuscula Omnia,* vol. 1, edited by P. Mandonnet. Paris: P. Lethielleux, 1927.

In octo libros Physicorum Aristotelis expositio. Edited by P. M. Maggiòlo. Turin and Rome: Marietti, 1965.

Scriptum super libros Sententiarum magistri Petri Lombardi episcopi Parisiensis. Vols. 1–2, edited by P. Mandonnet. Paris: P. Lethielleux, 1929. Vols. 3–4, edited by M. Moos. Paris: P. Lethielleux, 1933–47.

Summa contra Gentiles. Vols. 13–15 of *Sancti Thomae Aquinatis opera omnia.* Leonine Edition. Rome: R. Garroni, 1918–30.

Super Epistolas S. Pauli. Edited by R. Cai. Turin and Rome: Marietti, 1953.

Super Evangelium S. Joannis Lectura. Edited by R. Cai. Turin and Rome: Marietti, 1952.

Super Evangelium S. Matthaei Lectura. Edited by R. Cai. Turin and Rome: Marietti, 1951.

Summa theologiae. Vols. 4–12 of *Sancti Thomae Aquinatis opera omnia.* Leonine Edition. Rome: 1888–1906.

TRANSLATIONS OF WORKS BY THOMAS AQUINAS

Aristotle: On Interpretation. Commentary by St. Thomas and Cajetan. Translated by J. Oesterle. Milwaukee, Wis.: Marquette University Press, 1962.

Commentary on Aristotle's De Anima. Translated by K. Foster and S. Humphries. Notre Dame, Ind.: Dumb Ox Books, 1994.

Commentary on Aristotle's Metaphysics. Translated by J. P. Rowan. Notre Dame, Ind.: Dumb Ox Books, 1995.

Commentary on the Book of Causes. Translated by V. Guagliardo, C. Hess, and R. Taylor. Washington, D.C.: The Catholic University of America Press, 1996.

Commentary on Ephesians. Translated by M. Lamb. Albany, N.Y.: Magi, 1966.

Commentary on the Epistle to the Hebrews. Translated by C. Baer. South Bend, Ind.: St. Augustine's Press, 2006.

Commentary on the Gospel of St. John. Translated by J. Weisheipl. Vol. 1. Albany, N.Y.: Magi Press, 1980. Vol. 2. Petersham, Mass.: St. Bede's Publications, 2000.

Commentary on the Gospel of Matthew. Translated by J. Holmes and B. Mortensen. Lander, Wyo.: Aquinas Institute, 2013.

Concerning Being and Essence. Translated by G. G. Leckie. New York and London: D. Appleton-Century, 1937.

The Division and Methods of the Sciences: Questions V and VI of his Commentary on the De Trinitate of Boethius. Translated by A. Maurer. Toronto: PIMS, 1986.

Faith, Reason and Theology. Translated by A. Maurer. Toronto: PIMS, 1987.

The Power of God. Translated by R. J. Regan. Oxford: Oxford University Press, 2012.

Summa contra Gentiles I. Translated by A. C. Pegis. Garden City, N.Y.: Doubleday, 1955.

Summa contra Gentiles II. Translated by J. Anderson. Garden City, N.Y.: Doubleday, 1956.

Summa contra Gentiles III. 2 vols. Translated by V. J. Burke. Garden City, N.Y.: Doubleday, 1956.

Summa contra Gentiles IV. Translated by C. J. O'Neil. Garden City, N.Y.: Doubleday, 1956.

Summa Theologica. Translated by the English Dominican Province. New York: Benziger Brothers, 1947.

Thomas Aquinas: Selected Writings. Translated by R. McInerny. London: Penguin Books, 1998.

Thomas Aquinas's Quodlibetal Questions. Translated by T. Nevitt and B. Davies. Oxford: Oxford University Press, 2020.

The Three Greatest Prayers: Commentaries on the Lord's Prayer, the Hail Mary, and the Apostles' Creed. Manchester, N.H.: Sophia Institute Press, 1990.

Truth. 3 vols. Translated by J. V. McGlenn, R. W. Mulligan, and R. W. Schmidt. Indianapolis, Ind.: Hackett, 1994.

CLASSICAL, PATRISTIC, AND MEDIEVAL WORKS

Albert the Great. *Opera omnia.* Paris: Vivès, 1843.

The Analytical Lexicon to the Greek New Testament. Edited by W. D. Mounce. Grand Rapids, Mich.: Zondervan, 1993.

Anselm. *Anselm of Canterbury: The Major Works.* Edited by Brian Davies and G. R. Evans. Oxford: Oxford University Press 2008.

The Apostolic Fathers, with Justin Martyr and Irenaeus. Vol. 1 of *Ante-Nicene Fathers.* Edited by A. Roberts, J. Donaldson, and A. Ċ. Coxe. Buffalo, N.Y.: Christian Literature Publishing, 1885.

Aristotle. *The Complete Works of Aristotle.* Edited by J. Barnes. Translated by W. D. Ross. 2 vols. Princeton: Princeton University Press, 1984.

———. *Physics.* Translated by R. Waterfield. Oxford: Oxford University Press, 2008.

Athanasius. "Epistle to Serapion." In *Works on the Spirit: Athanasius and Didymus,* translated by M. DelCogliano, A. Radde-Gallwitz, and L. Ayres. Yonkers, N.Y.: St. Vladimir's Seminary Press, 2011.

———. "Four Discourses Against the Arians." In *Select Works and Letters,* vol 4 of *Nicene and Post-Nicene Fathers, Second Series.* Edited by P. Schaff and H. Wace. Peabody, Mass.: Hendrickson Publishers, 2004.

———. *De synodis.* Translated by E. R. Hardy in *The Christology of the Later Fathers,* Library of Christian Classics 3. Philadelphia: Westminster, 1954.

Augustine. *The Confessions.* Translated by M. Boulding. New York: Vintage Spiritual Classics, 1998.

———. *On the Nature of the Good.* In *Nicene and Post-Nicene Fathers,* vol. 4, edited by P. Schaff, translated by A. H. Newman. Buffalo, N.Y.: Christian Literature Publishing, 1887.

———. *The Trinity.* Edited by J. E. Rotelle. Translated by E. Hill. Hyde Park, N.Y.: New City Press, 1991.

Avicenna. *Avicenna Latinus, Liber de Philosophia Prima sive Scientia Divina.* Edited by S. Van Riet. Leiden: Brill, 1977.

Basil. *Basil: Letters and Select Works,* vol 8 of *Nicene and Post-Nicene Fathers, Second Series.* Edited by P. Schaff and H. Wace. Buffalo, N.Y.: Christian Literature Publishing, 1895.

Biblia sacra: Iuxta vulgatam versionem. 5th ed. Edited by B. Fischer, I. Gribomont, et al. Stuttgart: Deutsche Bibelgesellschaft, 2007.

Boethius. *The Consolation of Philosophy.* Translated by V. E. Watts. London: Penguin Books, 1969.

Bonaventure. *Breviloquium.* Translated by D. V. Monti. St. Bonaventure, N.Y.: Franciscan Institute Publications, 2005.

———. *Commentaria in quatuor libros Sententiarum.* 4 vols. Ad Claras Aquas, Quaracchi: Prope Florentiam Ex Typographia Collegii S. Bonaventurae, 1882–89.

———. *Commentary on the Sentences: Philosophy of God.* Translated by R. E. Houser and T. B. Noone. St. Bonaventure, N.Y.: Franciscan Institute Publications, 2013.

Calvin, John. *Institutes of the Christian Religion.* 2 vols. Translated by F. Battles. Philadelphia: Westminster Press, 1960.

Dionysius. *Pseudo-Dionysius: The Complete Works.* Translated by C. Luibheid and P. Rorem. Mahwah, N.J.: Paulist Press, 1987.

Duns Scotus, John. *Opera omnia.* Edited by C. Balić and others. Rome: Typis Polyglottis Vaticanis, 1950–2013.

Gilbert of Poitiers. *The Commentaries on Boethius by Gilbert of Poitiers.* Edited by N. Häring. Toronto: PIMS, 1966.

The Greek New Testament: SBL Edition. Edited by M. W. Holmes. Atlanta, Ga., and Bellingham, Wa.: Society of Biblical Literature and Logos Bible Software, 2010.

Gregory of Nazianzus. *Orations 28–31.* In *On God and Christ: The Five Theological Orations and Two Letters to Cledonius,* translated by F. Williams and L. Wickham. Crestwood, N.Y.: St. Vladimir's Seminary Press, 2002.

——. *Oration 31.* Translated by C. G. Browne and J. E. Swallow. In *Nicene and Post-Nicene Fathers, Second Series,* vol. 7, edited by P. Schaff and H. Wace. Buffalo, N.Y.: Christian Literature Publishing, 1894.

Gregory of Nyssa. *Life of Moses.* Translated by A. Malherbe and E. Ferguson. New York: Paulist Press: 1978.

——. *On "Not Three Gods": To Ablabius.* In *Letters and Select Works,* vol. 5 of *Nicene and Post-Nicene Fathers, Second Series,* edited by P. Schaff and H. Wace. Peabody, Mass.: Hendrickson Publishers, 2004.

Hippolytus. *Against Noetus,* in *Ante-Nicene Fathers,* vol. 5, edited by A. Roberts, J. Donaldson, and A. C. Coxe, translated by J. H. MacMahon. Buffalo, N.Y.: Christian Literature Publishing, 1886.

Irenaeus. *Demonstration of the Apostolic Preaching.* Translated by J. A. Robinson. London: SPCK, 1920.

John Damascene. *Exposition of the Orthodox Faith.* In *Nicene and Post-Nicene Fathers, Second Series,* vol. 9, edited by P. Schaff and H. Wace, translated by E. W. Watson and L. Pullan. Buffalo, N.Y.: Christian Literature Publishing, 1899.

Luther, Martin. *Heidelberg Disputation.* Translated by Aaron T. Fenker. Holt, Mo.: Higher Things, 2018.

Maimonides. *The Guide of the Perplexed.* Translated by S. Pines. Chicago: University of Chicago Press, 1963.

Maximus the Confessor. *Maximus Confessor: Selected Writings.* Translated by G. C. Berthold. Mahwah, N.J.: Paulist Press, 1985.

Origen. *Commentary on the Gospel of John,* in *Ante-Nicene Fathers,* vol. 9, edited and translated by A. Menzies. Buffalo, N.Y.: Christian Literature Publishing, 1896.

——. *Contra Celsus,* in *Ante-Nicene Fathers,* vol. 9, edited and translated by A. Menzies. Buffalo, N.Y.: Christian Literature Publishing, 1896.

——. *On First Principles.* 2 vols. Edited and translated by J. Behr. Oxford: Oxford University Press, 2017.

Plato. *Complete Works.* Edited by J. M. Cooper. Translated by G. M. A. Grube. Indianapolis, Ind.: Hackett, 1997.

Plotinus. *The Enneads.* Translated by S. MacKenna. Burdett, N.Y.: Larson Publications, 1992.

The Presocratic Philosophers. Edited and translated by G. S. Kirk and J. E. Raven. Cambridge: Cambridge University Press, 1957.

Proclus. *Elements of Theology.* Translated by E. R. Dodds. Oxford: Clarendon, 1963.

Richard of St. Victor. *On the Trinity*. Translated by C. P. Evans. In Coolman and Coulter, *Trinity and Creation*. Victorine Texts in Translation 1. Turnhout, Belgium: Brepols, 2010.

The Septuagint with Apocrypha: Greek and English. Translated by Sir Lancelot C. L. Brenton. Peabody, Mass.: Hendrickson Publishers, 1992.

Tertullian. *Writings*. Vol. 3 of *Ante-Nicene Fathers*. Edited by A. Roberts, J. Donaldson, and A. C. Coxe. Translated by P. Holmes. Buffalo, N.Y.: Christian Literature Publishing, 1885.

William of Ockham. *Opera theologica*. Vols. 1–10. St. Bonaventure, N.Y.: Franciscan Institute Publications, 1967–86.

CONCILIAR, MAGISTERIAL, AND PAPAL WORKS

Catechism of the Catholic Church. 2nd ed. Vatican City: Libreria Editrice Vaticana, 1997.

Conciliorum œcumenicorum generaliumque decreta. Editio critica. Edited by G. Alberigo et alii. Vol. 1, *The Œcumenical Councils: From Nicaea I to Nicaea II (325–787)*. Corpus Christianorum Texts and Studies (CC-TS). Turnhout: Brepols, 2006. Vol. II-1, *The General Councils of Latin Christendom: From Constantinople IV to Pavia-Siena (869–1424)*. CC-TS. Turnhout: Brepols, 2013. Vol. II-2, *The General Councils of Latin Christendom: From Basel to Lateran V (1431–1517)*. CC-TS. Turnhout: Brepols, 2013. Vol. III: *The Œcumenical Councils of the Roman Catholic Church: From Trent to Vatican II (1545–1965)*. CC-TS. Turnhout: Brepols, 2010.

Decrees of the Ecumenical Councils. Edited by N. P. Tanner. Washington, D.C.: Georgetown University Press, 1990.

Denzinger, Heinrich. *Compendium of Creeds, Definitions, and Declarations on Matters of Faith and Morals*. 43rd ed. Edited by P. Hünermann, edited for English by R. Fastiggi and A. E. Nash. San Francisco: Ignatius Press, 2012.

John Paul II. *Centesimus Annus*. AAS 83, 1991: 763–867. Available online at vatican.va

———. *Veritatis Splendor*. Washington, D.C.: USCCB Publishing, 1993.

———. *Fides et Ratio*. Washington, D.C.: USCCB Publishing, 1998.

MODERN WORKS

Adams, Marilyn McCord. *William Ockham*. 2 vols. Notre Dame, Ind.: University of Notre Dame, 1989.

———. "The Resurrection of the Body According to Three Medieval Aristotelians: Thomas Aquinas, John Duns Scotus, William Ockham." *Philosophical Topics* 20, no. 2 (1992): 1–33.

Aertsen, Jan. *Medieval Philosophy as Transcendental Thought: From Philip the Chancellor (ca. 1225) to Francisco Suárez*. Leiden: Brill, 2012.

Allison, Dale C. *Constructing Jesus: Memory, Imagination, and History*. Ada, Mich.: Baker Academic, 2010.

Anatolios, Khaled. "Faith, Reason, and Incarnation in Irenaeus of Lyons." *Nova et Vetera* (English Edition) 16, no. 2 (2018): 543–60.

———. *Retrieving Nicaea: The Development and Meaning of Trinitarian Doctrine*. Grand Rapids, Mich.: Baker Academic, 2018.

Anderson, Bernhard W. *Understanding the Old Testament*. 5th ed. New York: Pearson, 2006.

Attridge, Harold W. "Trinitarian Theology and the Fourth Gospel." In *The Bible and Early Trinitarian Theology*, edited by C. A. Beeley and M. E. Weedman, 71–83. Washington, D.C.: The Catholic University of America Press, 2018.

Ayres, Lewis. *Nicaea and Its Legacy: An Approach to Fourth-Century Trinitarian Theology*. Oxford: Oxford University Press, 2004.

———. *Augustine and the Trinity*. Cambridge: Cambridge University Press, 2010.

Balthasar, Hans Urs von. *The Glory of the Lord: A Theological Aesthetics*. Vol. 1, *Seeing the Form*. Translated by E. Leiva-Merikakis. San Francisco: Ignatius, 1982.

———. *Theo-Drama: Theological Dramatic Theory*. Vol. 3, *The Dramatis Personae: Persons in Christ*. Translated by G. Harrison. San Francisco: Ignatius, 1993.

———. *Theo-Drama: Theological Dramatic Theory*. Vol. 4, *The Action*. Translated by G. Harrison. San Francisco: Ignatius Press, 1994.

———. *Theo-Drama: Theological Dramatic Theory*. Vol. 5, *The Last Act*. Translated by G. Harrison. San Francisco: Ignatius Press, 1998.

———. *Epilogue*. Translated by E. Oakes. San Francisco: Ignatius Press, 2004.

———. *Love Alone Is Credible*. Translated by D. C. Schindler. San Francisco: Ignatius, 2004.

———. *Theo-Logic: Theological Logical Theory*. Vol. 2, *The Truth of God*. Translated by A. Walker. San Francisco: Ignatius Press, 2004.

Barnes, Michel René. "De Régnon Reconsidered." *Augustinian Studies* 26, no. 2 (1995): 51–79.

———. "Irenaeus' Trinitarian Theology." *Nova et Vetera* (English Edition) 7, no. 1 (2009): 67–106.

Barth, Karl. *Church Dogmatics*. 4 vols. Edited and translated by G. W. Bromiley and T. F. Torrance. Edinburgh: T&T Clark, 1936–75.

Bauckham, Richard. *The Climax of Prophecy: Studies on the Book of Revelation*. Edinburgh: T&T Clark, 2000.

———. *Jesus and the God of Israel: God Crucified and Other Studies on the New Testament's Christology of Divine Identity*. Grand Rapids, Mich.: Eerdmans, 2008.

Bauerschmidt, Frederick Christian. *Thomas Aquinas: Faith, Reasoning, and Following Christ*. Oxford: Oxford University Press, 2015.

Beeley, Christopher A. *Gregory of Nazianzus on the Trinity and the Knowledge of God: In Your Light We Shall See Light*. Oxford: Oxford University Press, 2008.

Benoit, Pierre. *Aspects of Biblical Inspiration*. Translated by J. Murphy-O'Connor and K. Ashe. Chicago: Priory Press, 1965.

———. "The Ascension." In *Jesus and the Gospel*, vol. 1, translated by B. Weatherhead, 209–53.

Benoit, Pierre, and P. Synave. *Prophecy and Inspiration: A Commentary on the "Summa Theologica II-II," Questions 171–178*. Translated by A. Dulles and T. Sheridan. New York: Desclée, 1961.

Blankenhorn, Bernhard. "God Speaks: Divine Authorship of Scripture in Karl Rahner and Pierre Benoit." *Angelicum* 93, no. 3 (2016): 445–62.

———. *The Mystery of Union with God: Dionysian Mysticism in Albert the Great and Thomas Aquinas*. Washington, D.C.: The Catholic University of America Press, 2015.

Bockmuehl, Marcus. "*Creatio ex nihilo* in Palestinian Judaism and Early Christianity." *Scottish Journal of Theology* 65, no. 3 (2012): 253–70.

Bonino, Serge-Thomas. *Angels and Demons: A Catholic Introduction*. Translated by M. J. Miller. Washington, D.C.: The Catholic University of America Press, 2016.

———. *Dieu, "Celui Qui Est"; De Deo ut Uno*. Paris: Parole et Silence, 2016.

Boulnois, Olivier. "Duns Scot et la déduction *a priori* de la Trinité." *Les Études philosophiques* 2020/2, no. 202: 67–90.

Braine, David. *The Reality of Time and the Existence of God: The Project of Proving God's Existence*. Oxford: Clarendon Press, 1988.

Brower, Jeffrey. "Making Sense of Divine Simplicity." *Faith and Philosophy* 25, no. 1 (2008): 3–30.

Brown, Raymond E. *The Death of the Messiah from Gethsemane to the Grave*. Vol. 1, *A Commentary on the Passion Narratives in the Four Gospels*. New York: Doubleday, 1993.

———. *An Introduction to New Testament Christology*. New York: Paulist Press, 1994.

Brueggemann, Walter. *Theology of the Old Testament: Testimony, Dispute, Advocacy*. Minneapolis, Minn.: Fortress, 2012.

Brunner, August. *Dreifaltigkeit: Personale Zugänge zum Geheimnis*. Einsiedeln: Johannes Verlag, 1976.

Bulgakov, Sergius. *The Bride of the Lamb*. Translated by B. Jakim. Grand Rapids, Mich.: Eerdmans, 2002.

———. *The Lamb of God*. Translated by B. Jakim. Grand Rapids, Mich.: Eerdmans, 2008.

Burrell, David B. *Aquinas: God and Action*. London: Routledge & Kegan Paul, 1979.

Cabaret, Dominique-Marie. *L'étonnante manifestation des personnes divines: Les appropriations trinitaires chez saint Thomas*. Paris: Parole et Silence, 2015.

Châtillon, Jean. "*Unitas, aequalitas, concordia vel connexio*. Recherches sur les origines de la théorie thomiste des appropriations (*Sum. théol.* I, q. 39, art. 7–8)." In *St. Thomas Aquinas 1274–1974: Commemorative Studies*, vol. 1, edited by A. Maurer, 337–79. Toronto: PIMS, 1974.

Childs, Brevard. *Old Testament Theology in a Canonical Context*. Philadelphia: Fortress Press, 1985.

———. *Biblical Theology of the Old and New Testaments: Theological Reflection on the Christian Bible*. Minneapolis, Minn.: Fortress, 1992.

Clavier, Paul. *Ex nihilo*. 2 vols. Paris: Hermann, 2011.

Congar, Yves. *Tradition and Traditions: An Historical and a Theological Essay*. Translated by M. Naseby and T. Rainborough. London: Burns & Oates, 1966.

Coolman, B. T., and D. M. Coulter, eds. *Trinity and Creation*. Victorine Texts in Translation 1. Turnhout, Belgium: Brepols, 2010.

Craig, William Lane. *The Kalām Cosmological Argument*. Eugene, Ore.: Wipf & Stock, 2000.

Cross, F. M. "Yahweh and the God of the Patriarchs." *Harvard Theological Review* 55, no. 4 (1962): 225–59.

Cross, Richard. *Duns Scotus*. Oxford: Oxford University Press, 1999.

———. *Duns Scotus on God*. Aldershot: Ashgate, 2005.

Daley, Brian. "Apokatastasis and 'the Honorable Silence' in the Eschatology of Maximus the Confessor." In *Maximus Confessor*, edited by F. Heinzer and C. Schönborn, 309–39. Fribourg: Fribourg University Press, 1982.

———. *God Visible: Patristic Christology Reconsidered*. Oxford: Oxford University Press, 2018.

Daniélou, Jean. *Holy Pagans of the Old Testament*. Translated by F. Faber. London: Longmans & Green, 1957.

———. *The Origins of Latin Christianity*. Translated by D. Smith and J. A. Baker. Philadelphia: Westminster Press, 1977.

Davies, Brian. "Simplicity." In *The Cambridge Companion to Christian Philosophical Theology*, edited by C. Taliaferro and C. Meister, 31–45. Cambridge: Cambridge University Press, 2010.

de Lubac, Henri. *The Drama of Atheist Humanism*. Translated by M. Sebanc. San Francisco: Ignatius, 1995.

Descartes, René. *Meditations on First Philosophy: With Selections from the Objections and Replies*. Edited and translated by J. Cottingham. Cambridge: Cambridge University Press, 2013.

de Vaux, Roland. *The Early History of Israel*. 2 vols. Translated by D. Smith. London: Darton, 1978.

Dewan, Lawrence. "Saint Thomas, Alvin Plantinga, and the Divine Simplicity." *Modern Schoolman* 66, no. 2 (1989): 141–51.

———. "The Existence of God: Can It Be *Demonstrated*?" *Nova et Vetera* (English edition) 10, no. 3 (2012): 731–56.

———. *Form and Being: Studies in Thomistic Metaphysics*. Washington, D.C.: The Catholic University of America Press, 2014.

Dodd, C. H. *The Interpretation of the Fourth Gospel*. Cambridge: Cambridge University Press, 1968.

Dubroy, Matthew. "Relation and Person: The Likeness and Unlikeness Between the Human and the Divine." STD diss., Pontifical Faculty of the Immaculate Conception, 2019.

Duby, Steven J. *Divine Simplicity: A Dogmatic Account*. Edinburgh: T&T Clark, 2015.

Dupuis, Jacques. *Toward a Christian Theology of Religious Pluralism*. Maryknoll, N.Y.: Orbis, 1997.

Durand, Emmanuel. *La périchorèse des personnes divines: Immanence mutuelle, Réciprocité et communion*. Paris: Cerf, 2005.

———. *Le Père, Alpha et Oméga de la vie trinitaire*. Paris: Cerf, 2008.

Eichrodt, Walther. *Theology of the Old Testament*. 2 vols. Philadelphia: Westminster, 1961.

Eire, Carlos. *Reformations: The Early Modern World, 1450–1650*. New Haven, Conn.: Yale University Press, 2016.

Emery, Gilles. "Essentialism or Personalism in the Treatise on God in St. Thomas Aquinas?" *The Thomist* 64, no. 4 (2000): 521–63.

———. "La relation dans la théologie de saint Albert le Grand." In *Albertus Magnus: zum Gedenken nach 800 Jahren: Neue Zugänge, Aspekte, und Perspektiven*, edited by W. Senner, 455–65. Berlin: Akademie Verlag, 2001.

———. "The Personal Mode of Trinitarian Action in Saint Thomas Aquinas." *The Thomist* 69, no. 1 (2005): 31–77.

———. *Trinity in Aquinas*. Naples, Fla.: Sapientia Press, 2005.

———. *Trinity, Church, and the Human Person*. Naples, Fla.: Sapientia Press, 2007.

———. "*Theologia* and *Dispensatio*: The Centrality of the Divine Missions in St. Thomas's Trinitarian Theology." *The Thomist* 74, no. 4 (2010): 515–61.

———. *The Trinitarian Theology of St. Thomas Aquinas*. Translated by F. Murphy. Oxford: Oxford University Press, 2010.

———. "La relation de creation." *Nova et Vetera* (French edition) 88, no. 1 (2013) 9–43.

———. "Personne humaine et relation: La personne se définit-elle par la relation?" *Nova et Vetera* (French edition) 89, no. 1 (2014): 7–29.

———. "*Ad Aliquid*: Relation in the Thought of St. Thomas Aquinas." In *Theology Needs Philosophy: Acting against Reason Is Contrary to the Nature of God*, edited by Matthew L. Lamb, 175–201. Washington, D.C.: The Catholic University of America Press, 2016.

Emery, G., and M. Levering, M., eds. *The Oxford Handbook of the Trinity*. Oxford: Oxford University Press, 2011.

Evans, G. R. *Bernard of Clairvaux*. Oxford: Oxford University Press, 2000.

Fabro, Cornelius. *God in Exile: Modern Atheism*. New York: Newman Press, 1968.

Feser, Edward. *Aquinas*. Oxford: Oneworld, 2009.

Feuerbach, Ludwig. *The Essence of Christianity*. Translated by G. Elliot. New York: Prometheus, 1989.

Flores, Juan Carlos. *Henry of Ghent: Metaphysics and the Trinity; with a Critical Edition of Question Six of Article Fifty-Five of the "Summa Quaestionum Ordinariarum."* Leuven: Leuven University Press, 2006.

Freud, Sigmund. *Civilization and Its Discontents*. Translated by D. McLintock. London: Penguin, 2002.

Friedman, Russell L. *Intellectual Traditions at the Medieval University: The Use of Philosophical Psychology in Trinitarian Theology among the Franciscans and Dominicans, 1250–1350*. 2 vols. Leiden: Brill, 2012.

———. *Medieval Trinitarian Theology from Aquinas to Ockham*. Cambridge: Cambridge University Press, 2013.

Frye, Northrop. *The Great Code: The Bible and Literature*. London: Routledge & Kegan Paul, 1982.

Gaine, Simon. *Did the Saviour See the Father? Christ, Salvation, and the Vision of God*. London: T&T Clark, 2015.

Garrigou-Lagrange, Réginald. *Predestination: The Meaning of Predestination in Scripture and the Church*. Translated by B. Rose. Charlotte, N.C.: TAN, 1998.

Garrigues, Jean Miguel. *L'Esprit qui dit 'Père!': L'Esprit-Saint dans la vie trinitaire et le problème du filioque*. Paris: Tequi, 1981.

———. *Le Dessein divin d'adoption et le Christ Rédempteur: À la lumière de Maxime le Confesseur et de Thomas d'Aquin*. Paris: Cerf, 2011.

———. *Deux martyrs de l'Église indivise: Saint Maxime le Confesseur et le pape saint Martin*. Paris: Cerf, 2011.

———. *Le Saint-Esprit, sceau de la Trinité: Le filioque et l'originalité trinitaire de l'Esprit dans sa personne et sa mission*. Paris: Cerf, 2011.

Gathercole, Simon. *The Pre-existent Son: Recovering the Christologies of Matthew, Mark and Luke*. Grand Rapids, Mich.: Eerdmans, 2006.

Geiger, L.-B. "Les rédactions successives de *Contra Gentiles* I, 53, d'après l'autographe." In *St. Thomas d'Aquin aujourd'hui*, edited by J. Y. Jolif et al., 221–40. Paris: Desclée de Brouwer, 1963.

Gilson, Étienne. *Being and Some Philosophers*. Toronto: PIMS, 1949.

———. *L'athéisme difficile*. Paris: Vrin, 2014.

Goldingay, John. *Old Testament Theology*. 3 vols. Downers Grove, Ill.: IVP Academic, 2003–9.

Gondreau, Paul. "St. Thomas Aquinas, the Communication of Idioms, and the Suffering of

Christ in the Garden of Gethsemane." In Keating and White, *Divine Impassibility and the Mystery of Human Suffering*, 214–45.

Goris, Harm J. M. J. *Free Creatures of an Eternal God: Thomas Aquinas on God's Infallible Foreknowledge and Irresistible Will*. Utrecht: Peeters, 1996.

———. "Theology and Theory of the Word in Aquinas." In *Aquinas the Augustinian*, edited by M. Dauphinais, B. David, and M. Levering, 62–78. Washington, D.C.: The Catholic University of America Press, 2007.

Gregory, Brad S. *The Unintended Reformation: How a Religious Revolution Secularized Society*. Cambridge, Mass.: Belknap, 2015.

Grillmeier, Aloys. *Christ in Christian Tradition*. Vol. 2, part 1, *From Chalcedon to Justinian I*. Translated by P. Allen and J. Cawte. Philadelphia: Westminster, 1987.

———. *Christ in Christian Tradition*. Vol. 1, *From the Apostolic Age to Chalcedon (451)*. 2nd ed. Translated by J. Bowden. Philadelphia: Westminster, 1988.

Hart, David Bentley. "No Shadow of Turning: On Divine Impassibility." *Pro Ecclesia* 11, no. 2 (2002): 184–206.

———. *The Beauty of the Infinite*. Grand Rapids, Mich.: Eerdmans, 2003.

Hasker, William. *God, Time, and Knowledge*. Ithaca, N.Y.: Cornell University Press, 1989.

———. *Metaphysics and the Tri-Personal God*. Oxford: Oxford University Press, 2013.

Hayes, Zachary. "Bonaventure's Trinitarian Theology." In *A Companion to Bonaventure*, edited by J. M. Hammon, J. A. W. Hellmann, and J. Goff, 189–246. Leiden: Brill, 2014.

Hegel, Georg W. F. *Lectures on the Philosophy of Religion, The Lectures of 1827*. 3 vols. Edited by P. C. Hodgson. Translated by R. F. Brown, P. C. Hodgson, J. M. Stewart. Berkeley: University of California Press, 2006.

———. *The Phenomenology of Spirit (The Phenomenology of Mind)*. Translated by J. B. Baillie. Overland Park, Kans.: Digireads.com Publishing, 2009.

Heidegger, Martin. *Identity and Difference*. Translated by J. Staumbaugh. New York: Harper & Row, 1969.

Hengel, Martin. *The Son of God: The Origin of Christology and the History of Jewish-Hellenistic Religion*. Translated by J. Bowden. Philadelphia: Fortress, 1976.

———. *Studies in Early Christology*. Edinburgh: T&T Clark, 1995.

———. *Judaism and Hellenism: Studies in their Encounter in Palestine during the Early Hellenistic Period*. London: SCM Press, 2012.

Hengel, Martin, with Schwemer, A. M. *Jesus und das Judentum, Geschichte des frühen Christentums*. Tübingen: Mohr Siebeck, 2007.

Herrara, Juan José. *La simplicidad divina según santo Tomás de Aquino*. Salta, Argentina: Ediciones de la Universidad del Norte Santo Tomás de Aquino, 2011.

Hochschild, Joshua P. *The Semantics of Analogy: Rereading Cajetan's "De Nominum Analogia."* Notre Dame, Ind.: University of Notre Dame Press, 2010.

Hofer, Andrew. Review of *The Filioque: History of a Doctrinal Controversy*, by A. Edward Siecienski, *The Thomist* 75, no. 3 (July 2011): 503–7.

Hughes, Christopher. *On a Complex Theory of a Simple God: An Investigation in Aquinas' Philosophical Theology*. Ithaca: Cornell University Press, 1987.

Humbrecht, Thierry-Dominique. *Théologie négative et noms divins chez Saint Thomas d'Aquin*. Paris: J. Vrin, 2005.

———. *Trinité et création au prisme de la voie négative chez saint Thomas d'Aquin*. Paris: Parole et Silence, 2011.

Hume, David. *Enquiries concerning Human Understanding and concerning the Principles of Morals.* 3rd ed. Oxford: Oxford University Press, 1975.

Hurtado, Larry. *Lord Jesus Christ: Devotion to Jesus in Earliest Christianity.* Grand Rapids, Mich.: Eerdmans, 2003.

———. *How on Earth Did Jesus Become a God? Historical Questions about Earliest Devotion to Jesus.* Grand Rapids, Mich.: Eerdmans, 2005.

Iribarren, *Isabel. Durandus of St. Pourcain: A Dominican Theologian in the Shadow of Aquinas.* Oxford: Oxford University Press, 2005.

Isayeva, Natalia. *Shankara and Indian Philosophy.* Albany, N.Y.: SUNY Press, 1993.

Israel, Jonathan. *Radical Enlightenment: Philosophy in the Making of Modernity 1650–1750.* Oxford: Oxford University Press, 2001.

Ivanovic, Filip. *Desiring the Beautiful: The Erotic-Aesthetic Dimension of Deification in Dionysius the Areopagite and Maximus the Confessor.* Washington, D.C.: The Catholic University of America Press, 2016.

Jenson, Robert. *Systematic Theology.* Vol. 1, *The Triune God.* Oxford: Oxford University Press, 2001.

Johnson, Luke Timothy. *The Real Jesus: The Misguided Quest for the Historical Jesus and the Truth of the Traditional Gospels.* San Francisco: Harper, 1996.

Journet, Charles. *The Meaning of Evil.* Translated by M. Barry. New York: P. J. Kenedy, 1963.

———. *L'Église du Verbe Incarné.* Vol. 6, *Essai de théologie de l'histoire du salut.* Paris: Saint Augustin, 2004.

Jüngel, Eberhard. *God as the Mystery of the World: On the Foundation of the Theology of the Crucified One in the Dispute between Theism and Atheism.* Translated by D. L. Gouder. Grand Rapids, Mich.: Eerdmans, 1983.

Kant, Immanuel. *Critique of Pure Reason.* Translated N. K. Smith. New York: St. Martin's, 1965.

———. *Prolegomena to Any Future Metaphysics.* Translated by P. Carus and J. Ellington. Indianapolis, Ind.: Hackett, 1977.

———. *Religion within the Boundaries of Mere Reason.* Edited and translated by A. Wood and G. di Giovanni. Cambridge: Cambridge University Press, 1998.

Kasper, Walter. *Jesus the Christ.* Translated by V. Green. London: Burns & Oates, 1976.

———. *The Absolute in History: The Philosophy and Theology of History in Schelling's Late Philosophy.* Translated by K. Wolff. New York: Paulist Press, 2018.

Keating, J. F., and T. J. White, eds. *Divine Impassibility and the Mystery of Human Suffering.* Grand Rapids, Mich.: Eerdmans, 2009.

Kelly, J. N. D. *Early Christian Doctrines.* 5th ed. London: A&C Black, 1977.

Koons, Robert C., and Timothy H. Pickavance. *Metaphysics: The Fundamentals.* Oxford: Wiley Blackwell, 2015.

Kretzmann, Norman. *The Metaphysics of Theism: Aquinas's Natural Theology in "Summa Contra Gentiles I".* Oxford: Oxford University Press, 1997.

Kromholtz, Bryan. *On the Last Day: The Time of the Resurrection of the Dead according to Thomas Aquinas.* Fribourg: Academic Press Fribourg, 2010.

Lagrange, Marie-Joseph. *L'Evangile selon Saint Marc.* Paris: J. Gabalda, 1921.

Lantigua, David M. *Infidels and Empires in a New World Order: Early Modern Spanish Contributions to International Legal Thought.* Cambridge: Cambridge University Press, 2020.

Laurentin, René. *The Truth of Christmas: Beyond the Myths; The Gospels of the Infancy of Christ.* Translated by M. J. Wrenn. Petersham, Mass.: St. Bede's Press, 1986.

Leftow, Brian. *Time and Eternity.* Ithaca, N.Y.: Cornell University Press, 1991.

Legaspi, Michael C. *Wisdom in Classical and Biblical Tradition.* Oxford: Oxford University Press, 2018.

Legge, Dominic. *The Trinitarian Christology of St. Thomas Aquinas.* Oxford: Oxford University Press, 2017.

Lehner, Ulrich L. *The Catholic Enlightenment: The Forgotten History of a Global Movement.* Oxford: Oxford University Press, 2018.

Leinsle, Ulrich G. *Introduction to Scholastic Theology.* Translated by M. Miller. Washington, D.C.: The Catholic University of America Press, 2010.

Levering, Matthew. *Engaging the Doctrine of the Holy Spirit: Love and Gift in the Trinity and the Church.* Grand Rapids, Mich.: Baker Academic, 2016.

Lindbeck, George. *The Nature of Doctrine: Religion and Theology in a Postliberal Age.* 2nd ed. Philadelphia: Westminster, 2009.

Lohfink, Gerard. *Jesus of Nazareth: What He Wanted, Who He Was.* Translated by L. H. Maloney. Collegeville, Minn.: Michael Glazier, 2012.

Lonergan, Bernard. *Grace and Freedom* and *Gratia Operans.* Vol. 1 of *The Collected Works of Bernard Lonergan.* Toronto: University of Toronto Press, 2000.

––––––. *The Ontological and Psychological Constitution of Christ.* Vol. 7 of *Collected Works.* Toronto: University of Toronto Press, 2002.

Long, D. Stephen. *Speaking of God: Theology, Language and Truth.* Grand Rapids, Mich.: Eerdmans, 2009.

Long, Steven A. "Divine and Creaturely 'Receptivity': The Search for a Middle Term." *Communio: International Catholic Review* 21, no. 1 (Spring 1994): 151–61.

––––––. *Analogia Entis: On the Analogy of Being, Metaphysics, and the Act of Faith.* Notre Dame, Ind.: University of Notre Dame Press, 2011.

Louth, Andrew. *St. John Damascene: Tradition and Originality in Byzantine Theology.* Oxford: Oxford University Press, 2002.

Lynch, Reginald. *The Cleansing of the Heart: The Sacraments as Instrumental Causes in the Thomistic Tradition.* Washington, D.C.: The Catholic University of America Press, 2017.

McCormack, Bruce L. *Karl Barth's Critically Realistic Dialectical Theology: Its Genesis and Development, 1909–1936.* Oxford: Clarendon Press, 1995.

––––––. "Grace and Being: The Role of God's Gracious Election in Karl Barth's Theological Ontology." In *The Cambridge Companion to Karl Barth*, edited by J. Webster, 92–110. Cambridge: Cambridge University Press, 2000.

––––––. "The Trinity." In *The Oxford Handbook of Karl Barth*, edited by P. D. Jones and P. T. Nimmo, 227–45. Oxford: Oxford University Press, 2020.

McGinn, Bernard. *The Harvest of Mysticism in Medieval Germany (1300–1500).* Vol. 4 of *The Presence of God: A History of Western Christian Mysticism.* New York: Crossroad, 2005.

MacIntyre, Alasdair. *After Virtue.* South Bend, Ind.: Notre Dame University Press, 1981.

Madden, James. *Mind, Matter & Nature: A Thomistic Proposal for the Philosophy of Mind.* Washington, D.C.: The Catholic University of America Press, 2013.

Mansini, Guy. "Can Humility and Obedience Be Trinitarian Realities?" In *Thomas Aquinas and Karl Barth: An Unofficial Catholic-Protestant Ecumenical Dialogue*, edited by B. L. McCormack and T. J. White, 71–98. Grand Rapids, Mich.: Eerdmans, 2013.

Marcus, Joel. *Mark 1–8: A New Translation with Introduction and Commentary*. Anchor Bible. New York: Doubleday, 2000.

Marion, Jean-Luc. "De 'la mort de Dieu' au noms divines: L'itinéraire théologique de la métaphysique." In *L'Être et Dieu*, edited by D. Bourg. Paris: Cerf, 1986.

———. *God without Being*. Translated by T. A. Carlson. Chicago: University of Chicago Press, 1991.

———. "Saint Thomas d'Aquin et l'onto-théo-logie." *Revue Thomiste* 95, no. 1 (1995): 31–66.

———. *The Idol and the Distance*. Translated by T. A. Carlson. New York: Fordham University Press, 2001.

———. *Being Given: Toward a Phenomenology of Givenness*. Translated by J. L. Kosky. Stanford, Calif.: Stanford University Press, 2002.

———. *Givenness & Revelation*. Translated by S. E. Lewis. Oxford: Oxford University Press, 2016.

Marshall, Bruce D. "*Utrum Essentia Generet*: Semantics and Metaphysics in Later Medieval Trinitarian Theology." In *Trinitarian Theology in the Medieval West*, edited by P. Kärkkäinen, 88–123. Helsinki: Luther-Agricola Society, 2008.

———. "The Unity of the Triune God: Reviving an Ancient Question." *The Thomist* 74, no. 1 (2010): 1–32.

———. "The Absolute and the Trinity." *Pro Ecclesia* 13, no. 2 (2014): 147–64.

Marx, Karl. *Karl Marx: Early Writings*. New York: Penguin, 1992.

Mascall, Eric. *The Triune God: An Ecumenical Study*. London: Pickwick Publications, 1986.

Matthieu, Luc. *La Trinité créatrice d'après Saint Bonaventure*. Paris: Institut Catholique, 1968.

Maurer, Armand A. *The Philosophy of William of Ockham in the Light of Its Principles*. Toronto: Pontifical Institute of Mediaeval Studies, 1999.

Meier, John P. *A Marginal Jew: Rethinking the Historical Jesus*. 5 vols. Anchor Bible Reference Library Series. New Haven, Conn.: Yale University Press, 1991–2016.

Milbank, John. *Theology and Social Theory: Beyond Secular Reason*. Oxford: Blackwell, 1990.

———. *The Suspended Middle: Henri de Lubac and the Debate concerning the Supernatural*. Grand Rapids, Mich.: Eerdmans, 2005.

Moberly, R. W. L. *Old Testament Theology: Reading the Hebrew Bible as Christian Scripture*. Grand Rapids, Mich.: Baker Academic, 2013.

Moltmann, Jürgen. *The Crucified God: The Cross of Christ as the Foundation and Criticism of Christian Theology*. Translated by R. A. Wilson. San Francisco: Harper & Row, 1974.

———. *The Trinity and the Kingdom: The Doctrine of God*. Translated by M. Kohl. San Francisco: Harper & Row, 1981.

———. *God in Creation: A New Theology of Creation and the Spirit of God*. Translated by M. Kohl. Minneapolis, Minn.: Fortress, 1993.

Montagnes, Bernard. *La doctrine de l'analogie de l'être d'après saint Thomas d'Aquin*. Louvain: Éditions Peeters, 1963.

Moreland, Anna Bonta. *Known by Nature: Thomas Aquinas on Natural Knowledge of God*. New York: Crossroad, 2010.

Mullaney, Thomas U. "Created Personality: The Unity of the Thomistic Tradition." *The New Scholasticism* 29, no. 4 (1955): 369–402.

Newman, John Henry. *The Arians of the Fourth Century*. 3rd ed. London: Longmans, Green & Co., 1908.

Nicolas, Jean-Hervé. *Synthèse dogmatique: Complément, de l'univers à la Trinité.* Fribourg: Éditions Universitaires Fribourg, 1993.

Nietzsche, Friedrich. *"On the Genealogy of Morals" and Other Writings.* Translated by C. Diethe. Cambridge: Cambridge University Press, 2018.

Oderberg, David S. *Real Essentialism.* London: Routledge, 2007.

O'Rourke, Fran. *Pseudo-Dionysius and the Metaphysics of Aquinas.* Notre Dame, Ind.: University of Notre Dame Press, 2015.

Osborn, Eric. *Justin Martyr.* Tübingen: Mohr Siebeck, 1973.

Paasch, J. T. *Divine Production in Late Medieval Trinitarian Theology: Henry of Ghent, Duns Scotus, and William of Ockham.* Oxford: Oxford University Press, 2012.

Paissac, Henri. *Théologie du Verbe: St. Augustin et St. Thomas.* Paris: Cerf, 1951.

Paley, William. *Natural Theology: Or, Evidences of the Existence and Attributes of the Deity Collected from the Appearances of Nature.* Boston: Gould & Lincoln, 1869.

Pannenberg, Wolfhart. *Jesus—God and Man.* 2nd ed. Translated by L. L. Wilkins and D. A. Priebe. Philadelphia: Westminster, 1968.

———. *Systematic Theology.* Vol. 2. Translated by G. W. Bromiley. Grand Rapids, Mich.: Eerdmans, 1994.

Pascal, Blaise. *Pensées.* Translated by A. J. Krailsheimer. New York: Penguin, 1995.

Pelletier, Jenny E. *William Ockham on Metaphysics: The Science of Being and God.* Leiden: Brill, 2013.

Perl, Eric D. *Theophany: The Neoplatonic Philosophy of Dionysius the Areopagite.* New York: SUNY Press, 2012.

Perrier, Emmanuel. *La fécondité en Dieu: La puissance notionnelle dans la Trinité selon Saint Thomas d'Aquin.* Paris: Parole et Silence, 2009.

Petry, Sven. *Die Entgrenzung JHWHs: Monolatrie, Bilderverbot und Monotheismus im Deuteronomium, in Deuterojesaja und im Ezechielbuch.* Tübingen: Mohr Siebeck, 2007.

Pfau, Thomas. *Minding the Modern: Human Agency, Intellectual Traditions and Responsible Knowledge.* South Bend, Ind.: Notre Dame University Press, 2015.

Pinckaers, Servais. *Sources of Christian Ethics.* Translated by M. Noble. Washington, D.C.: The Catholic University of America Press, 1995.

Plantinga, Alvin. *Does God Have a Nature?* Milwaukee, Wisc.: Marquette University Press, 1980.

Porro, Pasquale. *Thomas Aquinas: A Historical and Philosophical Profile.* Translated by J. Trabbic and R. Nutt. Washington, D.C.: The Catholic University of America Press, 2016.

Powell, Samuel M. *The Trinity in German Thought.* Cambridge: Cambridge University Press, 2001.

Preller, Victor. *Divine Science and the Science of God: A Reformulation of Thomas Aquinas.* Princeton, N.J.: Princeton University Press, 1967.

Przywara, Erich. *Analogia Entis Metaphysics: Original Structure and Universal Rhythm.* Translated by J. Betz and D. B. Hart. Grand Rapids, Mich.: Eerdmans, 2014.

Rahner, Karl. *Theological Investigations.* Vol. 1. Translated by C. Ernst. Baltimore, Md.: Helicon Press, 1963.

———. *Theological Investigations.* Vol. 4, *More Recent Writings.* Translated by K. Smyth. London: Darton, Longman, & Todd, 1967.

———. *Foundations of Christian Faith: An Introduction to the Idea of Christianity.* Translated by W. V. Dych. New York: Seabury, 1978.

———. *Hearer of the Word: Laying the Foundation for a Philosophy of Religion*. Translated by J. Donceel. New York: Continuum, 1994.

———. *The Trinity*. Translated by J. Donceel. London: Continuum, 2001.

Ratzinger, Joseph. *Biblical Interpretation in Crisis: On the Question of the Foundations and Approaches of Exegesis Today*. New York: Rockford, 1988.

———. "Concerning the Notion of Person in Theology." *Communio: International Catholic Review* 17, no. 3 (Fall 1990): 439–54.

———. *Truth and Tolerance: Christian Belief and World Religions*. Translated by H. Taylor. San Francisco: Ignatius Press, 2003.

———. *Jesus of Nazareth*. 3 vols. New York: Image, 2007–12.

Rocca, Gregory. *Speaking the Incomprehensible God: Thomas Aquinas on the Interplay of Positive and Negative Theology*. Washington, D.C.: The Catholic University of America Press, 2004.

Rogers, Eugene F. *Thomas Aquinas and Karl Barth: Sacred Doctrine and the Natural Knowledge of God*. South Bend, Ind.: Notre Dame University Press, 1999.

Rowe, C. Kavin. "Romans 10:13: What Is the Name of the Lord?" *Horizons in Biblical Theology* 22, no. 1 (2000): 135–73.

Ruello, F. "Une source probable de la théologie trinitaire de St Thomas." *Recherches de science religieuse* 43, no. 1 (1955): 104–28.

———. "Le commentaire inédit de saint Albert le Grand sur les *Noms divins*. Présentation et aperçus de théologie trinitaire," *Traditio* 12 (1956): 231–314.

Scheeben, Matthias Joseph. *The Mysteries of Christianity*. Translated by C. Vollert. St. Louis, Mo.: Herder, 1954.

———. *Nature and Grace*. Translated by C. Vollert. Eugene, Ore.: Wipf & Stock, 2009.

———. *Handbook of Catholic Dogmatics*. Bk. 1, *Theological Epistemology*, part 1, *The Objective Principles of Theological Knowledge*. Translated by M. Miller. Steubenville, Ohio: Emmaus Academic, 2019.

Schenk, Richard. "*Omnis Christi actio nostra est instructio*. The Deeds and Sayings of Jesus as Revelation in the View of Aquinas." In *La doctrine de la révélation divine de saint Thomas d'Aquin*, Studi Tomistici 37, pp. 104–31. Vatican City: Libreria Editrice Vaticana, 1990.

Schmaus, Michael. *Der liber Propugnatorius des Thomas Angelicus und die Lehrunterschiede zwischen Thomas von Aquin und Duns Scotus*. 2 vols. Munster: Aschendorff, 1930.

Schmid, Hans Heinrich. "Creation, Righteousness, and Salvation: "Creation Theology" as the Broad Horizon of Biblical Theology." In *Creation in the Old Testament*, edited by B. W. Anderson, 102–17. Philadelphia: Fortress, 1984.

Schnackenburg, Rudolf. *Jesus in the Gospels: A Biblical Christology*. Translated by O. C. Dean. Louisville, Ky.: Westminster John Knox, 1995.

Shanley, Brian J. "Eternity and Duration in Aquinas." *The Thomist* 61, no. 4 (1997): 525–48.

Siecienski, A. Edward. *The Filioque: History of a Doctrinal Controversy*. Oxford: Oxford University Press, 2010.

Simonin, H.-D. "Autour de la solution thomiste du problème de l'amour." AHDLMA 6 (1931): 174–276.

Smith, James K. A. *Introducing Radical Orthodoxy: Mapping a Post-secular Theology*. Grand Rapids, Mich.: Baker Academic, 2004.

Stăniloae, Dimitru. "The Procession of the Holy Spirit from the Father and His Relation to the Son, as the Basis of Our Deification and Adoption." In *Spirit of God, Spirit of*

Christ, edited by L. Vischer, 174–86. London and Geneva: SPCK and World Council of Churches, 1981.

Stewart, Jon. *Hegel's Interpretation of the Religions of the World: The Logic of the Gods*. Oxford: Oxford University Press, 2018.

Studer, Basil. *Augustins "De Trinitate". Eine Einführung*. Paderborn: Schöningh, 2005.

Stump, Eleonore. *Aquinas*. London: Routledge, 2006.

———. *The God of the Bible and the God of the Philosophers*. Milwaukee, Wisc.: Marquette University Press, 2016.

———. "Simplicity and Aquinas's Quantum Metaphysics." In *Die Metaphysik des Aristoteles im Mittelalter: Rezeption und Transformation*, edited by G. Krieger, 191–210. Berlin: De Gruyter, 2016.

Stump, Eleonore, and Norman Kretzmann. "Eternity." *The Journal of Philosophy* 78, no. 8 (1981): 429–58.

Swinburne, Richard. *Revelation*. Oxford: Clarendon Press, 1992.

———. *The Christian God*. Oxford: Clarendon Press, 1994.

———. *The Coherence of Theism*. Rev. ed. Oxford: Clarendon Press, 2010.

Taylor, Charles. *Hegel*. Cambridge: Cambridge University Press, 1975.

———. *Sources of the Self: The Making of the Modern Identity*. Cambridge, Mass.: Harvard University Press, 1990.

———. *A Secular Age*. Cambridge, Mass.: Belknap Press, 2007.

Te Velde, Rudi. *Aquinas on God: The "Divine Science" of the "Summa Theologiae"*. Aldershot: Ashgate, 2006.

Torre, Michael D. *Do Not Resist the Spirit's Call: Francisco Marín-Sola on Sufficient Grace*. Washington, D.C.: The Catholic University of America Press, 2013.

Troeltsch, Ernst. *The Absoluteness of Christianity and the History of Religions*. Translated by D. Reid. London: John Knox, 1971.

von Harnack, Adolf. *What Is Christianity?* Translated by T. Saunders. Philadelphia: Fortress Press, 1957.

von Rad, Gerhard. *Old Testament Theology*. 2 vols. New York: Harper & Row, 1962.

———. *Wisdom in Israel*. Translated by J. D. Martin. Nashville, Tenn.: Abingdon Press, 1972.

Webster, John. *Confessing God: Essays in Christian Dogmatics II*. London: T&T Clark, 2005.

———. *God without Measure: Working Papers in Christian Theology*. Vol. 1, *God and the Works of God*. London: T&T Clark, 2016.

Weisheipl, James. "The Meaning of Sacra Doctrina in *Summa theologiae* I, q. 1." *The Thomist* 38, no. 1 (1974): 49–80.

White, Thomas Joseph. "Dyotheletism and the Instrumental Human Consciousness of Jesus." *Pro Ecclesia* 17, no. 4 (2008): 396–422.

———. "Imperfect Happiness and the Final End of Man: Thomas *Aquinas* and the Paradigm of Nature-Grace Orthodoxy." *The Thomist* 78, no. 2 (2014): 247–89.

———. *The Incarnate Lord: A Thomistic Study in Christology*. Washington, D.C.: The Catholic University of America Press, 2015.

———. "Catholic Predestination: The Omnipotence and Innocence of Divine Love." In *Thomism and Predestination: Principles and Disputations*, edited by S. A. Long, R. W. Nutt, and T. J. White, 94–126. Ave Maria, Fla.: Sapientia Press, 2016.

———. "Divine Simplicity and the Holy Trinity." *International Journal of Systematic Theology* 18, no. 1 (2016): 66–93.

———. *Exodus*. Grand Rapids, Mich.: Brazos, 2016.

———. "Nicene Orthodoxy and Trinitarian Simplicity." *American Catholic Philosophical Quarterly* 90, no. 4 (2016): 727–50.

———. "The Universal Mediation of Christ and Non-Christian Religions." *Nova et Vetera* (English edition) 14, no. 1 (2016): 177–98

———. *Wisdom in the Face of Modernity: A Thomistic Study in Natural Theology*. 2nd ed. Naples, Fla.: Sapientia, 2016.

———. "Beauty, Transcendence, and the Inclusive Hierarchy of Creation." *Nova et Vetera* (English edition) 16, no. 4 (2018): 1215–26.

———. "The Infused Science of Christ." *Nova et Vetera* (English edition) 16, no. 2 (2018): 617–41.

———. "The Holy Spirit." In *Oxford Handbook of Catholic Theology*, edited by L. Ayres and M. A. Volpe, 183–97. Oxford: Oxford University Press, 2019.

Whitehead, Albert North. *Process and Reality: An Essay in Cosmology*. Edited by D. R. Griffin and D. W. Sherburne. New York: The Free Press, 1978.

Wilken, Robert Louis. *Liberty in the Things of God: The Christian Origins of Religious Freedom*. New Haven, Conn.: Yale University Press, 2019.

Williams, Rowan. *Arius: Heresy and Tradition*. London: DLT, 1987.

Wippel, John. *The Metaphysical Thought of Thomas Aquinas*. Washington, D.C.: The Catholic University of America Press, 2000.

Witherington III, Ben. *The Christology of Jesus*. Minneapolis, Minn.: Fortress, 1990.

———. *The Many Faces of the Christ: The Christologies of the New Testament and Beyond*. New York: Crossroad, 1998.

Wright, N. T. *The Climax of the Covenant: Christ and the Law in Pauline Theology*. Minneapolis, Minn.: Fortress, 1993.

———. *Jesus and the Victory of God: Christian Origins and the Question of God*. Minneapolis, Minn.: Augsburg Fortress, 1996.

———. *The Resurrection of the Son of God: Christian Origins and the Question of God*. Minneapolis, Minn.: Augsburg Fortress, 2003.

———. *Paul and the Faithfulness of God*. 2 vols. Minneapolis, Minn.: Fortress Press, 2013.

Young, Frances M. *From Nicaea to Chalcedon: A Guide to the Literature and Its Background*. London: SCM, 1983.

Zimmermann, Albert. *Ontologie oder Metaphysik?* Louvain: Peeters, 1998.

Zizioulas, John D. *Being as Communion: Studies in Personhood and the Church*. Crestwood, N.Y.: St. Vladimir's Press, 1995.

Index

———— : ————

Psychological analogy, 13–17, 97–98, 117–21,
133–35, 377–80, 384–85, 388–89, 392–93,
397–404, 407, 409–429, 439–41, 451–52,
468, 482, 487, 489, 504, 531, 549, 558, 560,
564n34, 568–69, 571n50, 605, 668–72,
677–81

Rahner, Karl, 16, 17, 53n5, 67n1, 114n6, 396n39,
400–401, 402n46, 403–4, 452, 454, 525, 547,
551n8, 553, 556–57, 560n23, 564–73, 578–80,
583n68, 584, 586–87, 595n17, 607n1, 616n16
Ratzinger, Joseph, 33n3, 53n4, 67n1, 79n46,
424n25, 465n8
Real distinction of *esse* and *essentia*, 206–7,
249–53, 318–20
Real relations, 426–31
Reccared, 491
Relations of origin, 10, 13, 106–7, 144–46,
165n26, 180, 241, 258–59, 382, 384–85, 391–
94, 399, 409–10, 425–441, 446n5, 448, 453,
469, 493–95, 501, 511, 514, 517, 519, 526, 668,
671–72, 676–77, 681, 685, 688
Religious traditions, 25–28
Resurrection, 76, 78–81, 86, 88–89, 91, 274n5,
290, 294–95, 302, 345, 347, 348, 404–8, 453–
54, 532, 538, 545, 555–57, 569, 572–74, 576n55,
633, 641, 652–660, 666–67, 680, 685, 688–89
Revelation, in Old Testament, 50–64; and philosophy, 28–30; in the life of Christ, 65–84;
in the passion and resurrection of Christ,
633–66
Richard of St. Victor, 355–60, 361n23, 362–65,
375, 378, 380, 381n13, 383, 385, 393, 442n1,
521, 681
Rocca, Gregory, 218n1
Rogers, Eugene F., 189n4
Rousseau, Jean-Jacques, 36
Rowe, C. Kavin, 93n7
Ruello, F., 433n15

Sabellius, 120, 126, 127, 142
Sabellianism, 120, 392, 412, 415, 428, 668
Scheeben, Matthias Joseph, 192n13, 349n11,
424n25
Schelling, Friedrich Wilhelm, 36, 293, 406n54,
589, 592, 593n12
Schenk, Richard, 638n10
Schmaus, Michael, 374n2
Schmid, Hans Heinrich, 59n9
Schnackenburg, Rudolf, 67n1
Scholasticism, 34–35, 40, 43, 406n54, 565n35,
578

Schweitzer, Albert, 68n4
Second Vatican Council, 44n28, 48n33, 48n44
Secularism, 32, 34–35, 38, 44, 48–49
Shankara, Adi, 289n17
Shanley, Brian J., 308n1
Siecienski, A. Edward, 493n17, 493n18
Smith, James K.A., 192n12
Spinoza, Baruch, 36, 347, 548
Stăniloae, Dumitru, 499–500
Stein, Edith, 43, 46n30
Stewart, Jon, 553n14
Studer, Basil, 154n1
Stump, Eleonore, 242n9, 256n20, 308n1, 313n9
Subordinationism, 120, 122–27, 132, 145, 155,
158, 494, 501
Subsistent relations, 13, 15, 146, 165n26, 375,
378–79, 381n18, 384–86, 389, 392–93,
400n43, 407, 410, 426, 431, 433–34, 441,
446n5, 448–51, 460, 464–65, 503, 509n6,
512, 671, 681–83, 685
Substance and accidents, 226–28, 243, 254–55,
328, 428, 448, 512
Swinburne, Richard, 234–35, 256n20, 308n1,
312n7, 422n22, 510n7

Taylor, Charles, 32n1, 35n10, 37n12, 191n11
Te Velde, Rudi, 201n27, 218n1, 242n9
Teleology, 34, 36, 195, 196n19, 213–15, 268–69,
277, 311, 336, 462, 469, 470, 501, 535n3, 597
Teresa of Àvila, 46n30
Tertullian, 116n11, 120, 121n22, 122, 156n3, 490,
493
Theology, as *sacra doctrina*, 1–5, 7, 114n5, 187–
89, 215, 279, 299, 670n1, 689–90, as Thomistic, 5–9
Thérèsè of Lisieux, 6
Thijssen, Hans, 33n4
Thomas Aquinas, 1, 2, 5–8, 10–16, 18, on
pre-philosophical knowledge of God,
22–25, 27, 30–31, 32n1, 44, 54n8, 75n38, 108,
109n27, 111, 135–36, 146, 154, 165n26, 167n32,
170–72, 176, 180–82, 185–90, 192–206, 208–
22, 224–26, 228–35, 237–38, 240, 242–57,
260–61, 263–68, 270–79, 281–82, 284–92,
296–301, 308–309, 311–13, 314n14, 316–22,
333n14, 324–27, 329–30, 332–34, 336, 338–
40, 342–44, 346, 352–56, 358–66, 368–69,
373–78, 379n14, 381, 383–85, 387–89, 391–96,
400n43, 401, 403, 406, 409–15, 417, 419–21,
422n21, 424n25, 425–28, 429n11, 430n12,
431–35, 437n21, 438–43, 445n4, 447–448,
449n8, 451–54, 456–57, 458n3, 459–60, 462–

Series Editors: Matthew Levering
Thomas Joseph White, OP

Catholic Dogmatic Theology, A Synthesis
Book I, On the Trinitarian Mystery of God
Jean-Hervé Nicolas, OP
Translated by Matthew K. Minerd

A Thomistic Christocentrism
Recovering the Carmelites of Salamanca on the Logic
of the Incarnation
Dylan Schrader

Habits and Holiness
Ethics, Theology, and Biopsychology
Ezra Sullivan, OP

Reading Job with St. Thomas Aquinas
Edited by Matthew Levering, Piotr Roszak, and Jörgen Vijgen

To Stir a Restless Heart
Thomas Aquinas and Henri de Lubac on Nature, Grace,
and the Desire for God
Jacob W. Wood

Aquinas on Transubstantiation
The Real Presence of Christ in the Eucharist
Reinhard Hütter

Bound for Beatitude
A Thomistic Study in Eschatology and Ethics
Reinhard Hütter